Residential Repair & Remodeling Costs

Contractor's Pricing Guide 2002

Senior Editor
Robert W. Mewis, CCC

Contributing Editors
Barbara Balboni
Robert A. Bastoni
Howard M. Chandler
John H. Chiang, PE
Jennifer L. Curran
Stephen E. Donnelly
J. Robert Lang
Robert C. McNichols
Melville J. Mossman, PE
John J. Moylan
Jeannene D. Murphy
Peter T. Nightingale
Stephen C. Plotner
Michael J. Regan
Marshall J. Stetson
Phillip R. Waier, PE

*Senior Engineering
Operations Manager*
John H. Ferguson, PE

*Vice President &
General Manager*
Roger J. Grant

Senior Vice President
Charles Spahr

*Vice President,
Sales & Marketing*
John M. Shea

Production Manager
Michael Kokernak

Production Coordinator
Marion E. Schofield

Technical Support
Thomas J. Dion
Jonathan Forgit
Mary Lou Geary
Gary L. Hoitt
Paula Reale-Camelio
Robin Richardson
Kathryn S. Rodriguez
Sheryl A. Rose
Elizabeth Testa

Book & Cover Design
Norman R. Forgit

RSMeans
CMD Understanding your craft.
Advancing your business.

Contractor's Pricing Guide 2002

Residential Repair & Remodeling Costs

- Quick Costs to Help You Estimate
- New, Easy-to-Use Format . . . Organized the Way You Build
- Hundreds of Work Items with Material, Labor & Equipment

Published by the R.S. Means Company, Inc.

$36.95 per copy. (In United States).
Price subject to change without prior notice.

Copyright 2001

R.S. Means Company, Inc.

Construction Publishers & Consultants

Construction Plaza

63 Smiths Lane

Kingston, MA 02364-0800

(781) 585-7880

Printed in the United States of America

ISSN Pending
ISBN 0-87629-655-5
First Printing

Foreword

R.S. Means Co., Inc. is a subsidiary of CMD (Construction Market Data), a leading provider of construction information, products, and services in North America and globally. CMD's project information products include more than 100 regional editions, national construction data, sales leads, and over 70 local plan rooms in major business centers. CMD PlansDirect provides surveys, plans and specifications. The First Source suite of products consists of *First Source for Products*, SPEC-DATA™, MANU-SPEC™, CADBlocks, Manufacturer Catalogs and First Source Exchange (www.firstsourceexchange.com) for the selection of nationally available building products. CMD also publishes ProFile, a database of more then 20,000 U.S. architectural firms. R.S. Means provides construction cost data, training, and consulting services in print, CD-ROM and online. CMD is headquartered in Atlanta and has 1,400 employees worldwide. CMD is owned by Cahners Business Information (www.cahners.com), a leading provider of critical information and marketing solutions to business professionals in the media, manufacturing, electronics, construction and retail industries. Its market-leading properties include more than 135 business-to-business publications, over 125 Webzines and Web portals, as well as online services, custom publishing, directories, research and direct-marketing lists. Cahners is a member of the Reed Elsevier plc group (NYSE: RUK and ENL)—world-leading publisher and information provider operating in the science and medical, legal, education and business-to-business industry sectors.

Our Mission

Since 1942, R.S. Means Company, Inc. has been actively engaged in construction cost publishing and consulting throughout North America.

Today, over 50 years after the company began, our primary objective remains the same: to provide you, the construction and facilities professional, with the most current and comprehensive construction cost data possible.

Whether you are a contractor, an owner, an architect, an engineer, a facilities manager, or anyone else who needs a fast and reliable construction cost estimate, you'll find this publication to be a highly useful and necessary tool.

Today, with the constant flow of new construction methods and materials, it's difficult to find the time to look at and evaluate all the different construction cost possibilities. In addition, because labor and material costs keep changing, last year's cost information is not a reliable basis for today's estimate or budget.

That's why so many construction professionals turn to R.S. Means. We keep track of the costs for you, along with a wide range of other key information, from city cost indexes . . . to productivity rates . . . to crew composition . . . to contractor's overhead and profit rates.

R.S. Means performs these functions by collecting data from all facets of the industry, and organizing it in a format that is instantly accessible to you. From the preliminary budget to the detailed unit price estimate, you'll find the data in this book useful for all phases of construction cost determination.

The Staff, the Organization, and Our Services

When you purchase one of R.S. Means' publications, you are in effect hiring the services of a full-time staff of construction and engineering professionals.

Our thoroughly experienced and highly qualified staff works daily at collecting, analyzing, and disseminating comprehensive cost information for your needs. These staff members have years of practical construction experience and engineering training prior to joining the firm. As a result, you can count on them not only for the cost figures, but also for additional background reference information that will help you create a realistic estimate.

The Means organization is always prepared to help you solve construction problems through its five major divisions: Construction and Cost Data Publishing, Electronic Products and Services, Consulting Services, Insurance Services, and Educational Services.

Besides a full array of construction cost estimating books, Means also publishes a number of other reference works for the construction industry. Subjects include construction estimating and project and business management; special topics such as HVAC, roofing, plumbing, and hazardous waste remediation; and a library of facility management references.

In addition, you can access all of our construction cost data through your computer with Means CostWorks 2002 CD-ROM, an electronic tool that offers over 50,000 lines of Means detailed construction cost data, along with assembly and whole building cost data. You can also access Means cost information from our Web site at www.rsmeans.com

What's more, you can increase your knowledge and improve your construction estimating and management performance with a Means Construction Seminar or In-House Training Program. These two-day seminar programs offer unparalleled opportunities for everyone in your organization to get updated on a wide variety of construction-related issues.

Means also is a worldwide provider of construction cost management and analysis services for commercial and government owners and of claims and valuation services for insurers.

In short, R.S. Means can provide you with the tools and expertise for constructing accurate and dependable construction estimates and budgets in a variety of ways.

Robert Snow Means Established a Tradition of Quality That Continues Today

Robert Snow Means spent years building his company, making certain he always delivered a quality product.

Today, at R.S. Means, we do more than talk about the quality of our data and the usefulness of our books. We stand behind all of our data, from historical cost indexes... to construction materials and techniques... to current costs.

If you have any questions about our products or services, please call us toll-free at 1-800-334-3509. Our customer service representatives will be happy to assist you or visit our Web site at www.rsmeans.com

Table of Contents

How the Book is Built: An Overview

A Powerful Construction Tool

You have in your hands one of the most powerful construction tools available today. A successful project is built on the foundation of an accurate and dependable estimate. This book will enable you to construct just such an estimate.

For the casual user the book is designed to be:

- quickly and easily understood so you can get right to your estimate
- filled with valuable information so you can understand the necessary factors that go into the cost estimate

For the regular user, the book is designed to be:

- a handy desk reference that can be quickly referred to for key costs
- a comprehensive, fully reliable source of current construction costs, so you'll be prepared to estimate any project
- a source book for project cost, product selections, and alternate materials and methods

To meet all of these requirements we have organized the book into the following clearly defined sections.

Unit Price Section

The cost data has been divided into 23 sections representing the order of construction. Within each section is a listing of components and variations to those components applicable to that section. Costs are shown for the various actions that must be done to that component.

Reference Section

This section includes information on Location Factors, and a listing of Abbreviations.

Location Factors: Costs vary depending upon regional economy. You can adjust the "national average" costs in this book to over 930 major cities throughout the U.S. and Canada by using the data in this section.

Abbreviations: A listing of the abbreviations used throughout this book, along with the terms they represent, is included.

Index

A comprehensive listing of all terms and subjects in this book to help you find what you need quickly when you are not sure where it falls in the order of construction.

The Scope of This Book

This book is designed to be as comprehensive and as easy to use as possible. To that end we have made certain assumptions and limited its scope in three key ways:

1. We have established material prices based on a "national average."
2. We have computed labor costs based on a 7 major region average of open shop wage rates.
3. We have targeted the data for projects of a certain size range.

Project Size

This book is intended for use by those involved primarily in Residential Repair and Remodeling construction costing between $10,000-$100,000.

With reasonable exercise of judgment the figures can be used for any building work. For other types of projects, such as new home construction or commercial buildings, consult the appropriate Means publication for more information.

How to Use the Book: The Details

What's Behind the Numbers? The Development of Cost Data

The staff at R.S. Means continuously monitors developments in the construction industry in order to ensure reliable, thorough and up-to-date cost information.

While *overall* construction costs may vary relative to general economic conditions, price fluctuations within the industry are dependent upon many factors. Individual price variations may, in fact, be opposite to overall economic trends. Therefore, costs are continually monitored and complete updates are published yearly. Also, new items are frequently added in response to changes in materials and methods.

Costs–$ (U.S.)

All costs represent U.S. national averages and are given in U.S. dollars. The Means Location Factors can be used to adjust costs to a particular location. The Location Factors for Canada can be used to adjust U.S. national averages to local costs in Canadian dollars.

Material Costs

The R.S. Means staff contacts manufacturers, dealers, distributors, and contractors all across the U.S. and Canada to determine national average material costs. If you have access to current material costs for your specific location, you may wish to make adjustments to reflect differences from the national average.

Included within material costs are fasteners for a normal installation. R.S. Means engineers use manufacturers' recommendations, written specifications and/or standard construction practice for size and spacing of fasteners. Adjustments to material costs may be required for your specific application or location. Material costs do not include sales tax.

Labor Costs

Labor costs are based on the average of open shop wages from across the U.S. for the current year. Rates along with overhead and profit markups are listed on the inside back cover of this book.

- If wage rates in your area vary from those used in this book, or if rate increases are expected within a given year, labor costs should be adjusted accordingly.

Labor costs reflect productivity based on actual working conditions. These figures include time spent during a normal workday on tasks other than actual installation, such as material receiving and handling, mobilization at site, site movement, breaks, and cleanup.

Productivity data is developed over an extended period so as not to be influenced by abnormal variations and reflects a typical average.

Equipment Costs

Equipment costs include not only rental costs, but also operating costs such as fuel, oil, and routine maintenance. Equipment and rental rates are obtained from industry sources throughout North America—contractors, suppliers, dealers, manufacturers, and distributors.

Factors Affecting Costs

Costs can vary depending upon a number of variables. Here's how we have handled the main factors affecting costs.

Quality—The prices for materials and the workmanship upon which productivity is based represent sound construction work. They are also in line with U.S. government specifications.

Overtime—We have made no allowance for overtime. If you anticipate premium time or work beyond normal working hours, be sure to make an appropriate adjustment to your labor costs.

Productivity—The labor costs for each line item are based on working an eight-hour day in daylight hours in moderate temperatures. For work that extends beyond normal work hours or is performed under adverse conditions, productivity may decrease.

Size of Project—The size, scope of work, and type of construction project will have a significant impact on cost. Economies of scale can reduce costs for large projects. Unit costs can often run higher for small projects. Costs in this book are intended for the size and type of project as previously described in "How the Book Is Built: An Overview." Costs for projects of a significantly different size or type should be adjusted accordingly.

Location—Material prices in this book are for metropolitan areas. However, in dense urban areas, traffic and site storage limitations may increase costs. Beyond a 20-mile radius of large cities, extra trucking or transportation charges may also increase the material costs slightly. On the other hand, lower wage rates may be in effect. Be sure to consider both these factors when preparing an estimate, particularly if the job site is located in a central city or remote rural location.

In addition, highly specialized subcontract items may require travel and per diem expenses for mechanics.

Other factors –
- season of year
- contractor management
- weather conditions
- building code requirements
- availability of:
  - adequate energy
  - skilled labor
  - building materials
- owner's special requirements/restrictions
- safety requirements
- environmental considerations

General Conditions—The extreme right-hand column of each chart gives the "Totals." These figures contain the installing contractor's O&P (in other words, the contractor doing the work). Therefore, it is necessary for a general contractor to add a percentage of all subcontracted items. For a detailed breakdown of O&P see the inside back cover of this book.

Unpredictable Factors—General business conditions influence "in-place" costs of all items. Substitute materials and construction methods may have to be employed. These may affect the installed cost and/or life cycle costs. Such factors may be difficult to evaluate and cannot necessarily be predicted on the basis of the job's location in a particular section of the country. Thus, where these factors apply, you may find significant, but unavoidable cost variations for which you will have to apply a measure of judgment to your estimate.

Final Checklist

Estimating can be a straightforward process provided you remember the basics. Here's a checklist of some of the items you should remember to do before completing your estimate.

Did you remember to . . .

- factor in the Location Factor for your locale
- take into consideration which items have been marked up and by how much
- mark up the entire estimate sufficiently for your purposes
- include all components of your project in the final estimate
- double check your figures to be sure of your accuracy
- call R.S. Means if you have any questions about your estimate or the data you've found in our publications

Remember, R.S. Means stands behind its publications. If you have any questions about your estimate . . . about the costs you've used from our books . . . or even about the technical aspects of the job that may affect your estimate, feel free to call the R.S. Means editors at 1-800-334-3509.

Unit Price Section

Table of Contents

Unit Price Section

Table of Contents

How to Use the Unit Price Pages

The prices in this publication include all overhead and profit mark-ups for the installing contractor. If a general contractor is involved, an additional 10% should be added to the cost shown in the "Total" column.

The costs for material, labor and any equipment are shown here. Material costs include delivery, and a 10% mark-up. No sales taxes are included. Labor costs include all mark-ups as shown on the inside back cover of this book. Equipment costs also include a 10% mark-up.

The cost in the total column should be multiplied by the quantity of each item to determine the total cost for that item. The sum of all item's total costs becomes the project's total cost.

The book is arranged into 23 categories that follow the order of construction for residential projects. The category is shown as white letters on a black background at the top of each page.

A brief specification of the cost item is shown here.

Graphics representing some of the cost items are found at the beginning of each category.

The cost data is arranged in a tree structure format. Major cost sections are left justified and are shown as bold headings within a grey background. Cost items and sub-cost items are found under the bold headings. The complete description should read as "bold heading, cost item, sub-cost item."
For example, the identified item's description is "Beam/Girder, Solid Wood Beam, 2″ x 8″."

Each action performed to the cost item is conveniently listed to the right of the description. See the explanation below for the scope of work included as part of the action.

The unit of measure upon which all the costs are based is shown here. An abbreviations list is included within the reference section found at the back of this book.

Rough Frame / Structure

Rough Framing

Beam / Girder	Unit	Material	Labor	Equip.	Total	Specification
Solid Wood Beam						
2″ x 8″						
Demolish	L.F.		.56		.56	Cost includes material and labor to
Install	L.F.	.96	.88		1.84	install 2″ x 8″ beam.
Demolish and Install	L.F.	.96	1.44		2.40	
Clean	L.F.	.09	.18		.27	
Paint	L.F.	.12	1.38		1.50	
Minimum Charge	Job		142		142	
2″ x 10″						
Demolish	L.F.		.69		.69	Cost includes material and labor to
Install	L.F.	1.36	.95		2.31	install 2″ x 10″ beam.
Demolish and Install	L.F.	1.36	1.64		3	
Clean	L.F.	.11	.22		.33	
Paint	L.F.	.15	.85		1	
Minimum Charge	Job		142		142	
2″ x 12″						
Demolish	L.F.		.84		.84	Cost includes material and labor to
Install	L.F.	1.87	1.04		2.91	install 2″ x 12″ beam.
Demolish and Install	L.F.	1.87	1.88		3.75	
Clean	L.F.	.13	.26		.39	
Paint	L.F.	.18	2.04		2.22	
Minimum Charge	Job		142		142	
4″ x 8″						
Demolish	L.F.		2.85		2.85	Cost includes material and labor to
Install	L.F.	3.75	1.29	.67	5.71	install 4″ x 8″ beam.
Demolish and Install	L.F.	3.75	4.14	.67	8.56	
Clean	L.F.	.11	.22		.33	
Paint	L.F.	.15	.85		1	
Minimum Charge	Job		142		142	
4″ x 10″						
Demolish	L.F.		3.57		3.57	Cost includes material and labor to
Install	L.F.	4.70	1.36	.70	6.76	install 4″ x 10″ beam.
Demolish and Install	L.F.	4.70	4.93	.70	10.33	
Clean	L.F.	.13	.26		.39	
Paint	L.F.	.18	.99		1.17	
Minimum Charge	Job		142		142	
4″ x 12″						
Demolish	L.F.		4.29		4.29	Cost includes material and labor to
Install	L.F.	5.60	1.43	.74	7.77	install 4″ x 12″ beam.
Demolish and Install	L.F.	5.60	5.72	.74	12.06	
Clean	L.F.	.14	.30		.44	
Paint	L.F.	.18	2.04		2.22	
Minimum Charge	Job		142		142	

Action	Scope
Demolish	Includes removal of the item and hauling the debris to a truck, dumpster, or storage area.
Install	Includes the installation of the item with normal placement and spacing of fasteners.
Demolish and Install	Includes the demolish action and the install action.
Reinstall	Includes the reinstallation of a removed item.
Clean	Includes cleaning of the item.
Paint	Includes up to two coats of finish on the item (unless otherwise indicated).
Minimum Charge	Includes the minimum labor or the minimum labor and equipment cost. Use this charge for small quantities of material.

Job Costs

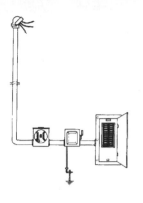

Scaffolding	Temporary Electrical Service	Air Compressor

Construction Fees		Unit	Material	Labor	Equip.	Total	Specification
Asbestos Test	Minimum Charge	Job		170		170	Minimum charge for testing.
Architectural	Minimum Charge	Day	480			480	Minimum labor charge for architect.
Engineering	Minimum Charge	Day	250			250	Minimum labor charge for field engineer.

Construction Permits		Unit	Material	Labor	Equip.	Total	Specification
Job (less than 5K)	Minimum Charge	Job	110			110	Permit fees, job less than 5K.
Job (5K to 10K)	Minimum Charge	Job	220			220	Permit fees, job more than 5K, but less than 10 K.
Job (10K to 25K)	Minimum Charge	Job	550			550	Permit fees, job more than 10K, but less than 25K.
Job (25K to 50K)	Minimum Charge	Job	1100			1100	Permit fees, job more than 25K, but less than 50K.
Job (50K to 100K)	Minimum Charge	Job	2200			2200	Permit fees, job more than 50K, but less than 100K.
Job (100K to 250K)	Minimum Charge	Job	5500			5500	Permit fees, job more than 100K, but less than 250K.
Job (250K to 500K)	Minimum Charge	Job	11000			11000	Permit fees, job more than 250K, but less than 500K.
Job (500K to 1M)	Minimum Charge	Job	22000			22000	Permit fees, job more than 500K, but less than 1 million.

Job Costs

Trade Labor		Unit	Material	Labor	Equip.	Total	Specification
Carpenter							
Daily (8 hours)							
	Install	Day		285		285	Daily labor rate for one carpenter.
	Minimum Charge	Job		142		142	
Weekly (40 hours)							
	Install	Week		1425		1425	Weekly labor rate for one carpenter.
	Minimum Charge	Job		142		142	
Drywaller							
Daily (8 hours)							
	Install	Day		285		285	Daily labor rate for one carpenter.
	Minimum Charge	Job		142		142	
Weekly (40 hours)							
	Install	Week		1425		1425	Weekly labor rate for one carpenter.
	Minimum Charge	Job		142		142	
Roofer							
Daily (8 hours)							
	Install	Day		270		270	Daily labor rate for one skilled roofer.
	Minimum Charge	Job		135		135	
Weekly (40 hours)							
	Install	Week		1350		1350	Weekly labor rate for one skilled
	Minimum Charge	Job		135		135	roofer.
Painter							
Daily (8 hours)							
	Install	Day		255		255	Daily labor rate for one painter.
	Minimum Charge	Job		128		128	
Weekly (40 hours)							
	Install	Week		1275		1275	Weekly labor rate for one painter.
	Minimum Charge	Job		128		128	
Mason							
Daily (8 hours)							
	Install	Day		286		286	Daily labor rate for one skilled mason.
	Minimum Charge	Job		143		143	
Weekly (40 hours)							
	Install	Week		1425		1425	Weekly labor rate for one skilled
	Minimum Charge	Job		143		143	mason.
Electrician							
Daily (8 hours)							
	Install	Day		310		310	Daily labor rate for an electrician.
	Minimum Charge	Job		155		155	
Weekly (40 hours)							
	Install	Week		1550		1550	Weekly labor rate for an electrician.
	Minimum Charge	Job		155		155	
Plumber							
Daily (8 hours)							
	Install	Day		315		315	Daily labor rate for a plumber.
	Minimum Charge	Job		157		157	
Weekly (40 hours)							
	Install	Week		1575		1575	Weekly labor rate for a plumber.
	Minimum Charge	Job		157		157	
Common Laborer							
Daily (8 hours)							
	Install	Day		207		207	Daily labor rate for a common laborer.
	Minimum Charge	Job		103		103	

Job Costs

Trade Labor

Trade Labor		Unit	Material	Labor	Equip.	Total	Specification
Weekly (40 hours)							
	Install	Week		1025		1025	Weekly labor rate for a common
	Minimum Charge	Job		103		103	laborer.

Temporary Utilities

Temporary Utilities		Unit	Material	Labor	Equip.	Total	Specification
Power Pole							
Job Site Electricity							
	Install	Month	29.50			29.50	Includes average cost of electricity per
	Minimum Charge	Job		155		155	month.
Water Service							
Job Site Water							
	Install	Month	62.50			62.50	Includes average costs for water for
	Minimum Charge	Month	62.50			62.50	one month.
Telephone							
	Install	Month	224			224	Includes average cost for local and
	Minimum Charge	Month	224			224	long distance telephone service for one month.
Chemical Toilet							
	Install	Month			238	238	Monthly rental of portable toilet.
	Minimum Charge	Day			11.90	11.90	
Office Trailer							
Place and Remove							
	Install	Job	206			206	Includes cost to a contractor to deliver,
	Minimum Charge	Job		118		118	place and level an office trailer and remove at end of job.
Storage Container							
	Install	Job	144			144	Includes cost to a contractor to deliver
	Minimum Charge	Job		118		118	and place a storage container and remove at end of job.
Fencing							
	Install	L.F.	1.80			1.80	Includes material costs for temporary
	Minimum Charge	L.F.	275			275	fencing.
Railing							
	Install	L.F.	6.75	8.30	.55	15.60	Includes material and labor to install
	Minimum Charge	L.F.	275			275	primed steel pipe.

Equipment Rental

Equipment Rental		Unit	Material	Labor	Equip.	Total	Specification
Flatbed Truck							
Daily Rental							
	Install	Day			171	171	Daily rental of flatbed truck.
	Minimum Charge	Job			171	171	
Weekly Rental							
	Install	Week			855	855	Weekly rental of flatbed truck.
	Minimum Charge	Job			171	171	
Monthly Rental							
	Install	Month			3425	3425	Monthly rental of flatbed truck.
	Minimum Charge	Job			171	171	

Job Costs

Equipment Rental		Unit	Material	Labor	Equip.	Total	Specification
Dump Truck							
Daily Rental							
	Install	Day			390	390	Daily rental of dump truck.
	Minimum Charge	Day			390	390	
Weekly Rental							
	Install	Week			1950	1950	Weekly rental of dump truck.
	Minimum Charge	Day			390	390	
Monthly Rental							
	Install	Month			7775	7775	Monthly rental of dump truck.
	Minimum Charge	Day			390	390	
Forklift							
Daily Rental							
	Install	Day			231	231	Daily rental of forklift.
	Minimum Charge	Day			231	231	
Weekly Rental							
	Install	Week			1150	1150	Weekly rental of forklift.
	Minimum Charge	Day			231	231	
Monthly Rental							
	Install	Month			4625	4625	Monthly rental of forklift.
	Minimum Charge	Day			231	231	
Bobcat							
Daily Rental							
	Install	Day			144	144	Daily rental of wheeled, skid steer loader.
	Minimum Charge	Day			144	144	
Weekly Rental							
	Install	Week			720	720	Weekly rental of wheeled, skid steer loader.
	Minimum Charge	Day			144	144	
Monthly Rental							
	Install	Month			2875	2875	Monthly rental of wheeled, skid steer loader.
	Minimum Charge	Day			144	144	
Air Compressor							
Daily Rental							
	Install	Day			70	70	Daily rental of air compressor.
	Minimum Charge	Day			70	70	
Weekly Rental							
	Install	Week			350	350	Weekly rental of air compressor.
	Minimum Charge	Day			70	70	
Monthly Rental							
	Install	Month			1400	1400	Monthly rental of air compressor.
	Minimum Charge	Day			70	70	
Jackhammer							
Daily Rental							
	Install	Day			18.25	18.25	Daily rental of air tool, jackhammer.
	Minimum Charge	Day			18.25	18.25	
Weekly Rental							
	Install	Week			91	91	Weekly rental of air tool, jackhammer.
	Minimum Charge	Day			18.25	18.25	
Monthly Rental							
	Install	Month			365	365	Monthly rental of air tool, jackhammer.
	Minimum Charge	Day			18.25	18.25	
Concrete Mixer							
Daily Rental							
	Install	Day			78.50	78.50	Daily rental of concrete mixer.
	Minimum Charge	Day			78.50	78.50	

Job Costs

Equipment Rental		Unit	Material	Labor	Equip.	Total	Specification
Weekly Rental							
	Install	Week			395	395	Weekly rental of concrete mixer.
	Minimum Charge	Day			78.50	78.50	
Monthly Rental							
	Install	Month			1575	1575	Monthly rental of concrete mixer.
	Minimum Charge	Day			78.50	78.50	
Concrete Bucket							
Daily Rental							
	Install	Day			17.60	17.60	Daily rental of concrete bucket.
	Minimum Charge	Day			17.60	17.60	
Weekly Rental							
	Install	Week			88	88	Weekly rental of concrete bucket.
	Minimum Charge	Day			17.60	17.60	
Monthly Rental							
	Install	Month			350	350	Monthly rental of concrete bucket.
	Minimum Charge	Day			17.60	17.60	
Concrete Pump							
Daily Rental							
	Install	Day			750	750	Daily rental of concrete pump.
	Minimum Charge	Day			750	750	
Weekly Rental							
	Install	Week			3750	3750	Weekly rental of concrete pump.
	Minimum Charge	Day			750	750	
Monthly Rental							
	Install	Month			15000	15000	Monthly rental of concrete pump.
	Minimum Charge	Day			750	750	
Generator							
Daily Rental							
	Install	Day			33.50	33.50	Daily rental of generator.
	Minimum Charge	Day			33.50	33.50	
Weekly Rental							
	Install	Week			167	167	Weekly rental of generator.
	Minimum Charge	Day			33.50	33.50	
Monthly Rental							
	Install	Month			670	670	Monthly rental of generator.
	Minimum Charge	Day			33.50	33.50	
Welder							
Daily Rental							
	Install	Day			66	66	Daily rental of welder.
	Minimum Charge	Day			66	66	
Weekly Rental							
	Install	Week			330	330	Weekly rental of welder.
	Minimum Charge	Day			66	66	
Monthly Rental							
	Install	Month			1325	1325	Monthly rental of welder.
	Minimum Charge	Day			66	66	
Sandblaster							
Daily Rental							
	Install	Day			29.50	29.50	Daily rental of sandblaster.
	Minimum Charge	Day			29.50	29.50	
Weekly Rental							
	Install	Week			148	148	Weekly rental of sandblaster.
	Minimum Charge	Day			29.50	29.50	

Job Costs

Equipment Rental

Equipment Rental		Unit	Material	Labor	Equip.	Total	Specification
Monthly Rental							
	Install	Month			590	590	Monthly rental of sandblaster.
	Minimum Charge	Day			29.50	29.50	
Space Heater							
Daily Rental							
	Install	Day			23	23	Daily rental of space heater.
	Minimum Charge	Day			19.60	19.60	
Weekly Rental							
	Install	Day			115	115	Weekly rental of space heater.
	Minimum Charge	Day			19.60	19.60	
Monthly Rental							
	Install	Day			460	460	Monthly rental of space heater.
	Minimum Charge	Day			19.60	19.60	

Move / Reset Contents

Move / Reset Contents		Unit	Material	Labor	Equip.	Total	Specification
Small Room							
	Install	Room		25		25	Includes cost to remove and reset the
	Minimum Charge	Job		103		103	contents of a small room.
Average Room							
	Install	Room		30.50		30.50	Includes cost to remove and reset the
	Minimum Charge	Job		103		103	contents of an average room.
Large Room							
	Install	Room		42		42	Includes cost to remove and reset the
	Minimum Charge	Job		103		103	contents of a large room.
Extra Large Room							
	Install	Room		66.50		66.50	Includes cost to remove and reset the
	Minimum Charge	Job		103		103	contents of a extra large room.
Store Contents							
Weekly							
	Install	Week	152			152	Storage fee, per week.
Monthly							
	Install	Month	455			455	Storage fee, per month.

Cover and Protect

Cover and Protect		Unit	Material	Labor	Equip.	Total	Specification
Cover / Protect Walls							
	Install	SF Wall		.08		.08	Includes labor costs to cover and
	Minimum Charge	Job		103		103	protect walls.
Cover / Protect Floors							
	Install	SF Flr.		.08		.08	Includes labor costs to cover and
	Minimum Charge	Job		103		103	protect floors.

Temporary Bracing

Temporary Bracing		Unit	Material	Labor	Equip.	Total	Specification
Shim Support Piers							
	Install	Ea.	3.11	83		86.11	Includes labor and material to install
	Minimum Charge	Job		249		249	shims support for piers.

Job Costs

Jack and Relevel

		Unit	Material	Labor	Equip.	Total	Specification
Single Story							
	Install	Ea.	1.17	1		2.17	Includes labor and equipment to jack
	Minimum Charge	Job		249		249	and relevel single-story building.
Two-story							
	Install	Ea.	1.17	1.66		2.83	Includes labor and equipment to jack
	Minimum Charge	Job		249		249	and relevel two-story building.

Dumpster Rental

		Unit	Material	Labor	Equip.	Total	Specification
Small Load							
	Install	Week			450	450	Dumpster, weekly rental, 2 dumps, 5
	Minimum Charge	Week			450	450	yard container.
Medium Load							
	Install	Week			560	560	Dumpster, weekly rental, 2 dumps, 10
	Minimum Charge	Week			560	560	yard container.
Large Load							
	Install	Week			950	950	Dumpster, weekly rental, 2 dumps, 30
	Minimum Charge	Week			950	950	yard container.

Debris Hauling

		Unit	Material	Labor	Equip.	Total	Specification
Per Ton							
	Install	Ton		65.50	38.50	104	Includes hauling of debris by trailer or
	Minimum Charge	Ton		490	288	778	dump truck.
Per Cubic Yard							
	Install	C.Y.		22	12.80	34.80	Includes hauling of debris by trailer or
	Minimum Charge	Job		490	288	778	dump truck.
Per Pick-up Truck Load							
	Install	Ea.		115		115	Includes hauling of debris by pick-up
	Minimum Charge	Job		490	288	778	truck.

Dump Fees

		Unit	Material	Labor	Equip.	Total	Specification
Per Cubic Yard							
	Install	C.Y.	6.95			6.95	Dump charges, building materials.
	Minimum Charge	C.Y.	6.95			6.95	
Per Ton							
	Install	Ton	55.50			55.50	Dump charges, building materials.
	Minimum Charge	Ton	55.50			55.50	

Scaffolding

		Unit	Material	Labor	Equip.	Total	Specification
4' to 6' High							
	Install	Month	51.50			51.50	Includes monthly rental of scaffolding,
	Minimum Charge	Month	51.50			51.50	steel tubular, 30" wide, 7' long, 5' high.
7' to 11' High							
	Install	Month	61.50			61.50	Includes monthly rental of scaffolding,
	Minimum Charge	Month	61.50			61.50	steel tubular, 30" wide, 7' long, 10' high.

Job Costs

Scaffolding

Scaffolding		Unit	Material	Labor	Equip.	Total	Specification
12' to 16' High							
	Install	Month	71			71	Includes monthly rental of scaffolding,
	Minimum Charge	Month	71			71	steel tubular, 30" wide, 7' long, 15' high.
17' to 21' High							
	Install	Month	95			95	Includes monthly rental of scaffolding,
	Minimum Charge	Month	95			95	steel tubular, 30" wide, 7' long, 20' high.
22' to 26' High							
	Install	Month	105			105	Includes monthly rental of scaffolding,
	Minimum Charge	Month	105			105	steel tubular, 30" wide, 7' long, 25' high.
27' to 30' High							
	Install	Month	114			114	Includes monthly rental of scaffolding,
	Minimum Charge	Month	114			114	steel tubular, 30" wide, 7' long, 30' high.

Construction Clean-up

Construction Clean-up		Unit	Material	Labor	Equip.	Total	Specification
Initial							
	Clean	S.F.		.26		.26	Includes labor for general clean-up.
	Minimum Charge	Job		103		103	
Progressive							
	Clean	S.F.		.13		.13	Includes labor for progressive site/job
	Minimum Charge	Job		103		103	clean-up on a weekly basis.

Building Demolition	Unit	Material	Labor	Equip.	Total	Specification
Wood-framed Building						
1 Story Demolition						
Demolish	S.F.		.99	1.26	2.25	Includes demolition of 1 floor only light
Minimum Charge	Job		1550	2000	3550	wood-framed building, including hauling of debris. Dump fees not included.
2nd Story Demolition						
Demolish	S.F.		1	1.28	2.28	Includes demolition of 2nd floor only
Minimum Charge	Job		1550	2000	3550	light wood-framed building, including hauling of debris. Dump fees not included.
3rd Story Demolition						
Demolish	S.F.		1.31	1.67	2.98	Includes demolition of 3rd floor only
Minimum Charge	Job		1550	2000	3550	light wood-framed building, including hauling of debris. Dump fees not included.
Masonry Building						
Demolish	S.F.		1.41	1.80	3.21	Includes demolition of one story
Minimum Charge	Job		1550	2000	3550	masonry building, including hauling of debris. Dump fees not included.
Concrete Building						
Unreinforced						
Demolish	S.F.		2.86	1.05	3.91	Includes demolition of a one story
Minimum Charge	Job		1550	2000	3550	non-reinforced concrete building, including hauling of debris. Dump fees not included.
Reinforced						
Demolish	S.F.		3.28	1.20	4.48	Includes demolition of a one story
Minimum Charge	Job		1550	2000	3550	reinforced concrete building, including hauling of debris. Dump fees not included.
Steel Building						
Demolish	S.F.		1.87	2.39	4.26	Includes demolition of a metal
Minimum Charge	Job		1550	2000	3550	building, including hauling of debris. Dump fees not included. No salvage value assumed for scrap metal.

Job Preparation

General Clean-up

General Clean-up		Unit	Material	Labor	Equip.	Total	Specification
Remove Debris							
	Clean	S.F.		.64	.17	.81	Includes removal of debris caused by the loss including contents items and loose debris.
	Minimum Charge	Job		320	85.50	405.50	
Muck-out							
	Clean	S.F.		.40		.40	Includes labor to remove 2″ of muck and mud after a flood loss.
	Minimum Charge	Job		103		103	
Deodorize / Disinfect							
	Clean	SF Flr.		.14		.14	Includes deodorizing building with application of mildicide and disinfectant to floors and walls - will vary depending on the extent of deodorization required.
	Minimum Charge	Job		103		103	
Clean Walls							
Heavy							
	Clean	S.F.		.10		.10	Includes labor and material for heavy cleaning (multiple applications) with detergent and solvent.
	Minimum Charge	Job		103		103	
Clean Ceiling							
Light							
	Clean	S.F.		.17		.17	Includes labor and material to clean light to moderate smoke and soot.
	Minimum Charge	Job		103		103	
Heavy							
	Clean	S.F.		.26		.26	Includes labor and material to clean heavy smoke and soot.
	Minimum Charge	Job		103		103	

Flood Clean-up

Flood Clean-up		Unit	Material	Labor	Equip.	Total	Specification
Emergency Service Call							
After Hours / Weekend							
	Minimum Charge	Job		138		138	Includes minimum charges for deflooding clean-up after hours or on weekends.
Grey Water / Sewage							
	Minimum Charge	Job		103		103	Includes minimum charges for deflooding clean-up.
Water Extraction							
Clean (non-grey)							
	Clean	SF Flr.	.02	.41		.43	Includes labor to remove clean uncontaminated water from the loss.
	Minimum Charge	Job		103		103	
Grey (non-solids)							
	Clean	SF Flr.	.02	.83		.85	Includes labor to remove non-solid grey water from the loss.
	Minimum Charge	Job		103		103	
Sewage / Solids							
	Clean	SF Flr.	.03	1.03		1.06	Includes labor to remove water from the loss that may contain sewage or solids.
	Minimum Charge	Job		103		103	

Job Preparation

Flood Clean-up		Unit	Material	Labor	Equip.	Total	Specification
Mildicide Walls							
Topographical							
	Clean	SF Wall		.19		.19	Clean-up of deflooding including
	Minimum Charge	Job		103		103	topographical mildicide application.
Injection Treatments							
	Clean	SF Flr.	25	3.18		28.18	Clean-up of deflooding including
	Minimum Charge	Job		103		103	mildicide injection.
Carpet Cleaning							
Uncontaminated							
	Clean	SF Flr		.13		.13	Includes labor to clean carpet.
	Minimum Charge	Job		103		103	
Contaminated							
	Clean	SF Flr.		.21		.21	Includes labor to clean contaminated
	Minimum Charge	Job		103		103	carpet.
Stairway							
	Clean	Ea.	.10	2.43		2.53	Includes labor to clean contaminated
	Minimum Charge	Job		103		103	carpet on a stairway.
Carpet Treatment							
Disinfect / Deodorize							
	Clean	SF Flr.		.13		.13	Includes disinfecting and deodorizing
	Minimum Charge	Job		103		103	of carpet.
Disinfect For Sewage							
	Clean	SF Flr.		.33		.33	Includes labor to disinfect and
	Minimum Charge	Job		103		103	deodorize carpet exposed to sewage.
Mildicide							
	Clean	SF Flr.	.01	.13		.14	Includes labor and materials to apply
	Minimum Charge	Job		103		103	mildicide to carpet.
Thermal Fog Area							
	Clean	SF Flr.	.03	.32		.35	Includes labor and materials to
	Minimum Charge	Job		103		103	perform thermal fogging during
							deflooding clean-up.
Wet Fog / ULV Area							
	Clean	SF Flr.	.02	.18		.20	Includes labor and materials to
	Minimum Charge	Job		103		103	perform wet fogging / ULV during
							deflooding clean-up.
Steam Clean Fixtures							
	Clean	Ea.	.01	20.50		20.51	Includes labor and materials to steam
	Minimum Charge	Job		103		103	clean fixtures during deflooding
							clean-up.
Pressure Wash Sewage							
	Clean	SF Flr.		1.88		1.88	Includes labor to pressure wash
	Minimum Charge	Job		103		103	sewage contamination.
Airmover							
	Minimum Charge	Day			19.60	19.60	Daily rental of air mover.

Job Preparation

Flood Clean-up

Flood Clean-up		Unit	Material	Labor	Equip.	Total	Specification
Dehumidifier							
Medium Size							
	Minimum Charge	Day			32.50	32.50	Daily rental of dehumidifier, medium.
Large Size							
	Minimum Charge	Day			65	65	Daily rental of dehumidifier, large.
Air Purifier							
HEPA Filter-Bacteria							
	Minimum Charge	Ea.	195			195	HEPA filter for air purifier.

Asbestos Removal

Asbestos Removal		Unit	Material	Labor	Equip.	Total	Specification
Asbestos Analysis							
	Minimum Charge	Job		170		170	Minimum charge for testing.
Asbestos Pipe Insulation							
1/2″ to 3/4″ Diameter							
	Demolish	L.F.	.34	4.39		4.73	Minimum charge to remove asbestos. Includes full Tyvek suits for workers changed four times per eight-hour shift with respirators, air monitoring and supervision by qualified professionals.
	Minimum Charge	Job		2725		2725	
1″ to 3″ Diameter							
	Demolish	L.F.	1.06	13.60		14.66	Minimum charge to remove asbestos. Includes full Tyvek suits for workers changed four times per eight-hour shift with respirators, air monitoring and supervision by qualified professionals.
	Minimum Charge	Job		2725		2725	
Asbestos-based Siding							
	Demolish	S.F.	2.34	30		32.34	Minimum charge to remove asbestos. Includes full Tyvek suits for workers changed four times per eight-hour shift with respirators, air monitoring and supervision by qualified professionals.
	Minimum Charge	Job		2725		2725	
Asbestos-based Plaster							
	Demolish	S.F.	1.80	23.50		25.30	Minimum charge to remove asbestos. Includes full Tyvek suits for workers changed four times per eight-hour shift with respirators, air monitoring and supervision by qualified professionals.
	Minimum Charge	Job		2725		2725	
Encapsulate Asbestos Ceiling							
	Install	S.F.	.29	.13		.42	Includes encapsulation with penetrating sealant sprayed onto ceiling and walls with airless sprayer.
	Minimum Charge	Job		2725		2725	
Scrape Acoustical Ceiling							
	Demolish	S.F.	.07	.77		.84	Minimum charge to remove asbestos. Includes full Tyvek suits for workers changed four times per eight-hour shift with respirators, air monitoring and supervision by qualified professionals.
	Minimum Charge	Job		2725		2725	

Job Preparation

Asbestos Removal

Asbestos Removal		Unit	Material	Labor	Equip.	Total	Specification
Seal Ceiling Asbestos							
	Install	S.F.	1.10	2.56		3.66	Includes attaching plastic cover to
	Minimum Charge	Job		2725		2725	ceiling area and sealing where asbestos exists, taping all seams, caulk or foam insulation in cracks and negative air system.
Seal Wall Asbestos							
	Install	S.F.	1.10	2.28		3.38	Includes attaching plastic cover to wall
	Minimum Charge	Job		2725		2725	area and sealing where asbestos exists, taping all seams, caulk or foam insulation in cracks and negative air system.
Seal Floor Asbestos							
	Install	S.F.	1.76	4.56		6.32	Includes attaching plastic cover to floor
	Minimum Charge	Job		2725		2725	area and sealing where asbestos exists, taping all seams, caulk or foam insulation in cracks and negative air system.
Negative Air Vent System							
	Install	Day			43.50	43.50	Daily rental of negative air vent
	Minimum Charge	Week			218	218	system.
HEPA Vacuum Cleaner							
	Install	Day			31	31	Daily rental of HEPA vacuum, 16
	Minimum Charge	Week			155	155	gallon.
Airless Sprayer							
	Install	Day			34.50	34.50	Daily rental of airless sprayer.
	Minimum Charge	Week			172	172	
Decontamination Unit							
	Install	Day			133	133	Daily rental of decontamination unit.
	Minimum Charge	Week			665	665	
Light Stand							
	Install	Day			15.70	15.70	Daily rental of floodlight w/tripod.
	Minimum Charge	Week			78.50	78.50	

Room Demolition

Room Demolition		Unit	Material	Labor	Equip.	Total	Specification
Strip Typical Room							
	Demolish	S.F.		2.07		2.07	Includes 4 labor hours for general
	Minimum Charge	Job		115		115	demolition.
Strip Typical Bathroom							
	Demolish	S.F.		2.76		2.76	Includes 4 labor hours for general
	Minimum Charge	Job		115		115	demolition.
Strip Typical Kitchen							
	Demolish	S.F.		2.65		2.65	Includes 4 labor hours for general
	Minimum Charge	Job		115		115	demolition.
Strip Typical Laundry							
	Demolish	S.F.		2.36		2.36	Includes 4 labor hours for general
	Minimum Charge	Job		115		115	demolition.

Selective Demolition		Unit	Material	Labor	Equip.	Total	Specification
Concrete Slab							
4" Unreinforced							
	Demolish	S.F.		1.39	.26	1.65	Includes labor and equipment to remove unreinforced concrete slab and haul debris to truck or dumpster.
	Minimum Charge	Job		590	108	698	
6" Unreinforced							
	Demolish	S.F.		1.97	.36	2.33	Includes labor and equipment to remove unreinforced concrete slab and haul debris to truck or dumpster.
	Minimum Charge	Job		590	108	698	
8" Unreinforced							
	Demolish	S.F.		3.23	.59	3.82	Includes labor and equipment to remove unreinforced concrete slab and haul debris to truck or dumpster.
	Minimum Charge	Job		590	108	698	
4" Reinforced							
	Demolish	S.F.		1.75	.32	2.07	Includes labor and equipment to remove reinforced concrete slab and haul debris to truck or dumpster.
	Minimum Charge	Job		590	108	698	
6" Reinforced							
	Demolish	S.F.		2.62	.48	3.10	Includes labor and equipment to remove reinforced concrete slab and haul debris to truck or dumpster.
	Minimum Charge	Job		590	108	698	
8" Reinforced							
	Demolish	S.F.		4.29	.79	5.08	Includes labor and equipment to remove reinforced concrete slab and haul debris to truck or dumpster.
	Minimum Charge	Job		590	108	698	
Brick Wall							
4" Thick							
	Demolish	S.F.		1.93	.35	2.28	Includes labor and equipment to remove brick wall and haul debris to a central location for disposal.
	Minimum Charge	Job		590	108	698	
8" Thick							
	Demolish	S.F.		2.65	.49	3.14	Includes labor and equipment to remove brick wall and haul debris to a central location for disposal.
	Minimum Charge	Job		590	108	698	
12" Thick							
	Demolish	S.F.		3.54	.65	4.19	Includes labor and equipment to remove brick wall and haul debris to a central location for disposal.
	Minimum Charge	Job		590	108	698	
Concrete Masonry Wall							
4" Thick							
	Demolish	S.F.		2.14	.39	2.53	Includes minimum labor and equipment to remove 4" block wall and haul debris to a central location for disposal.
	Minimum Charge	Job		590	108	698	
6" Thick							
	Demolish	S.F.		2.65	.49	3.14	Includes minimum labor and equipment to remove 6" block wall and haul debris to a central location for disposal.
	Minimum Charge	Job		590	108	698	

Job Preparation

Selective Demolition		Unit	Material	Labor	Equip.	Total	Specification
8″ Thick							
	Demolish	S.F.		3.27	.60	3.87	Includes minimum labor and
	Minimum Charge	Job		590	108	698	equipment to remove 8″ block wall
							and haul debris to a central location
							for disposal.
12″ Thick							
	Demolish	S.F.		4.72	.87	5.59	Includes minimum labor and
	Minimum Charge	Job		590	108	698	equipment to remove 12″ block wall
							and haul debris to a central location
							for disposal.
Tree Removal							
Small, 4″ - 8″							
	Demolish	Ea.		75	58	133	Minimum charge, tree removal.
	Minimum Charge	Job		103		103	
Medium, 9″ - 12″							
	Demolish	Ea.		112	87.50	199.50	Minimum charge, tree removal.
	Minimum Charge	Job		103		103	
Large, 13″ - 18″							
	Demolish	Ea.		135	105	240	Minimum charge, tree removal.
	Minimum Charge	Job		345	105	450	
Very Large, 19″ - 24″							
	Demolish	Ea.		168	131	299	Minimum charge, tree removal.
	Minimum Charge	Job		345	105	450	
Stump Removal							
	Demolish	Ea.		47.50	113	160.50	Includes minimum charges for a site
	Minimum Charge	Job		190	54.50	244.50	demolition crew and backhoe /
							loader.

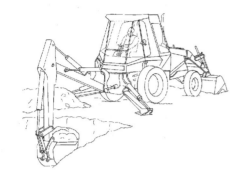

Backhoe/Loader - Wheel Type	Tractor Loader - Wheel Type	Backhoe - Crawler Type

Excavation		Unit	Material	Labor	Equip.	Total	Specification
Footings							
Hand Trenching							
	Install	L.F.		1.29		1.29	Includes hand excavation for footing or
	Minimum Charge	Job		51.50		51.50	trench up to 10" deep and 12" wide.
Machine Trenching							
	Install	L.F.		.49	.20	.69	Includes machine excavation for
	Minimum Charge	Job		246	98	344	footing or trench up to 10" deep and 12" wide.
Trenching w / Backfill							
Hand							
	Install	L.F.		2.07		2.07	Includes hand excavation, backfill and
	Minimum Charge	Job		51.50		51.50	compaction.
Machine							
	Install	L.F.		2.46	4.67	7.13	Includes machine excavation, backfill
	Minimum Charge	Job		103	47.50	150.50	and compaction.

Backfill		Unit	Material	Labor	Equip.	Total	Specification
Hand (no compaction)							
	Install	C.Y.		12.15		12.15	Includes backfill by hand in average
	Minimum Charge	Job		103		103	soil without compaction.
Hand (w / compaction)							
	Install	C.Y.		24.50		24.50	Includes backfill by hand in average
	Minimum Charge	Job		103		103	soil with compaction.
Machine (no compaction)							
	Install	C.Y.		2.46	.98	3.44	Includes backfill, by 55 HP wheel
	Minimum Charge	Job		246	98	344	loader, of trenches from loose material piled adjacent without compaction.
Machine (w / compaction)							
	Install	C.Y.		6.55	2.62	9.17	Includes backfill, by 55 HP wheel
	Minimum Charge	Job		246	98	344	loader, of trenches from loose material piled adjacent with compaction by vibrating tampers.

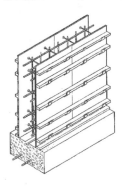

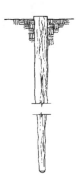

Concrete Footing and Formwork

Wood Pile

Piles	Unit	Material	Labor	Equip.	Total	Specification
Treated Wood, 12″ Butt						
To 30′						
Demolish	L.F.		3.31	.95	4.26	Includes material, labor and equipment
Install	V.L.F.	9.80	3.27	3.32	16.39	to install up to 30′ long treated wood
Demolish and Install	V.L.F.	9.80	6.58	4.27	20.65	piling.
Paint	L.F.	.37	1.46		1.83	
Minimum Charge	Job		2050	2075	4125	
30′ to 40′						
Demolish	L.F.		3.31	.95	4.26	Includes material, labor and equipment
Install	V.L.F.	10	2.92	2.96	15.88	to install 30′ to 40′ long treated wood
Demolish and Install	V.L.F.	10	6.23	3.91	20.14	piling.
Paint	L.F.	.37	1.46		1.83	
Minimum Charge	Job		2050	2075	4125	
40′ to 50′						
Demolish	L.F.		3.31	.95	4.26	Includes material, labor and equipment
Install	V.L.F.	9.95	2.84	2.88	15.67	to install 40′ to 50′ long treated wood
Demolish and Install	V.L.F.	9.95	6.15	3.83	19.93	piling.
Paint	L.F.	.37	1.46		1.83	
Minimum Charge	Job		2050	2075	4125	
50′ to 60′						
Demolish	L.F.		3.31	.95	4.26	Includes material, labor and equipment
Install	V.L.F.	10.85	2.55	2.59	15.99	to install 50′ to 60′ long treated wood
Demolish and Install	V.L.F.	10.85	5.86	3.54	20.25	piling.
Paint	L.F.	.37	1.46		1.83	
Minimum Charge	Job		2050	2075	4125	
60′ to 80′						
Demolish	L.F.		3.31	.95	4.26	Includes material, labor and equipment
Install	V.L.F.	18.55	2.83	2.88	24.26	to install 60′ to 80′ long treated wood
Demolish and Install	V.L.F.	18.55	6.14	3.83	28.52	piling.
Paint	L.F.	.37	1.46		1.83	
Minimum Charge	Job		2050	2075	4125	
Untreated Wood, 12″ Butt						
To 30′						
Demolish	L.F.		3.31	.95	4.26	Includes material, labor and equipment
Install	V.L.F.	6.25	3.27	3.32	12.84	to install up to 30′ long untreated
Demolish and Install	V.L.F.	6.25	6.58	4.27	17.10	wood piling.
Paint	L.F.	.37	1.46		1.83	
Minimum Charge	Job		2050	2075	4125	

Foundation

Piles

	Unit	Material	Labor	Equip.	Total	Specification
30' to 40'						
Demolish	L.F.		3.31	.95	4.26	Includes material, labor and equipment
Install	V.L.F.	6.25	2.92	2.96	12.13	to install 30' to 40' long untreated
Demolish and Install	V.L.F.	6.25	6.23	3.91	16.39	wood piling.
Paint	L.F.	.37	1.46		1.83	
Minimum Charge	Job		2050	2075	4125	
40' to 50'						
Demolish	L.F.		3.31	.95	4.26	Includes material, labor and equipment
Install	V.L.F.	6.25	2.84	2.88	11.97	to install 40' to 50' long untreated
Demolish and Install	V.L.F.	6.25	6.15	3.83	16.23	wood piling.
Paint	L.F.	.37	1.46		1.83	
Minimum Charge	Job		2050	2075	4125	
50' to 60'						
Demolish	L.F.		3.31	.95	4.26	Includes material, labor and equipment
Install	V.L.F.	6.40	2.55	2.59	11.54	to install 50' to 60' long untreated
Demolish and Install	V.L.F.	6.40	5.86	3.54	15.80	wood piling.
Paint	L.F.	.37	1.46		1.83	
Minimum Charge	Job		2050	2075	4125	
60' to 80'						
Demolish	L.F.		3.31	.95	4.26	Includes material, labor and equipment
Install	V.L.F.	8	2.43	2.47	12.90	to install 60' to 80' long untreated
Demolish and Install	V.L.F.	8	5.74	3.42	17.16	wood piling.
Paint	L.F.	.37	1.46		1.83	
Minimum Charge	Job		2050	2075	4125	

Precast Concrete

	Unit	Material	Labor	Equip.	Total	Specification
10" Square						
Demolish	L.F.		3.38	.97	4.35	Includes material, labor and equipment
Install	V.L.F.	7.70	2.92	2.96	13.58	to install a precast, prestressed, 40'
Demolish and Install	V.L.F.	7.70	6.30	3.93	17.93	long, 10" square concrete pile.
Paint	L.F.	.37	1.46		1.83	
Minimum Charge	Job		2050	2075	4125	
12" Square						
Demolish	L.F.		3.63	1.04	4.67	Includes material, labor and equipment
Install	V.L.F.	9.75	3	3.05	15.80	to install a precast, prestressed, 40'
Demolish and Install	V.L.F.	9.75	6.63	4.09	20.47	long, 12" square concrete pile.
Paint	L.F.	.37	1.46		1.83	
Minimum Charge	Job		2050	2075	4125	
14" Square						
Demolish	L.F.		3.71	1.07	4.78	Includes material, labor and equipment
Install	V.L.F.	11.55	3.40	3.46	18.41	to install a precast, prestressed, 40'
Demolish and Install	V.L.F.	11.55	7.11	4.53	23.19	long, 14" square concrete pile.
Paint	L.F.	.37	1.46		1.83	
Minimum Charge	Job		2050	2075	4125	
16" Square						
Demolish	L.F.		3.90	1.12	5.02	Includes material, labor and equipment
Install	V.L.F.	18.35	3.65	3.70	25.70	to install a precast, prestressed, 40'
Demolish and Install	V.L.F.	18.35	7.55	4.82	30.72	long, 16" square concrete pile.
Paint	L.F.	.37	1.46		1.83	
Minimum Charge	Job		2050	2075	4125	
18" Square						
Demolish	L.F.		4.23	1.21	5.44	Includes material, labor and equipment
Install	V.L.F.	22	4.56	4.65	31.21	to install a precast, prestressed, 40'
Demolish and Install	V.L.F.	22	8.79	5.86	36.65	long, 18" square concrete pile.
Paint	L.F.	.37	1.46		1.83	
Minimum Charge	Job		2050	2075	4125	

Piles

		Unit	Material	Labor	Equip.	Total	Specification
Cross Bracing							
Treated 2″ x 6″							
	Demolish	L.F.		.68		.68	Cost includes material and labor to
	Install	L.F.	1.23	4.01		5.24	install 2″ x 6″ lumber for cross-bracing
	Demolish and Install	L.F.	1.23	4.69		5.92	of foundation piling or posts.
	Reinstall	L.F.		3.21		3.21	
	Clean	S.F.		.26		.26	
	Paint	L.F.	.15	.98		1.13	
	Minimum Charge	Job		500		500	
Treated 2″ x 8″							
	Demolish	L.F.		.68		.68	Cost includes material and labor to
	Install	L.F.	1.60	4.15		5.75	install 2″ x 8″ lumber for cross-bracing
	Demolish and Install	L.F.	1.60	4.83		6.43	of foundation piling or posts.
	Reinstall	L.F.		3.32		3.32	
	Clean	S.F.		.26		.26	
	Paint	L.F.	.21	1.02		1.23	
	Minimum Charge	Job		500		500	
Treated 2″ x 10″							
	Demolish	L.F.		.70		.70	Cost includes material and labor to
	Install	L.F.	2.04	4.29		6.33	install 2″ x 10″ lumber for
	Demolish and Install	L.F.	2.04	4.99		7.03	cross-bracing of foundation piling or
	Reinstall	L.F.		3.43		3.43	posts.
	Clean	S.F.		.26		.26	
	Paint	L.F.	.25	1.04		1.29	
	Minimum Charge	Job		500		500	
Treated 2″ x 12″							
	Demolish	L.F.		.84		.84	Cost includes material and labor to
	Install	L.F.	2.33	4.44		6.77	install 2″ x 12″ lumber for
	Demolish and Install	L.F.	2.33	5.28		7.61	cross-bracing of foundation piling or
	Reinstall	L.F.		3.55		3.55	posts.
	Clean	S.F.		.26		.26	
	Paint	L.F.	.30	1.06		1.36	
	Minimum Charge	Job		500		500	
Metal Pipe							
6″ Concrete Filled							
	Demolish	L.F.		4.70	1.35	6.05	Includes material, labor and equipment
	Install	V.L.F.	11.65	4.26	4.32	20.23	to install concrete filled steel pipe pile.
	Demolish and Install	V.L.F.	11.65	8.96	5.67	26.28	
	Paint	L.F.	.29	1.46		1.75	
	Minimum Charge	Job		2050	2075	4125	
6″ Unfilled							
	Demolish	L.F.		4.70	1.35	6.05	Includes material, labor and equipment
	Install	V.L.F.	9.90	3.89	3.95	17.74	to install unfilled steel pipe pile.
	Demolish and Install	V.L.F.	9.90	8.59	5.30	23.79	
	Paint	L.F.	.29	1.46		1.75	
	Minimum Charge	Job		2050	2075	4125	
8″ Concrete Filled							
	Demolish	L.F.		4.70	1.35	6.05	Includes material, labor and equipment
	Install	V.L.F.	11.30	4.44	4.51	20.25	to install concrete filled steel pipe pile.
	Demolish and Install	V.L.F.	11.30	9.14	5.86	26.30	
	Paint	L.F.	.29	1.46		1.75	
	Minimum Charge	Job		2050	2075	4125	
8″ Unfilled							
	Demolish	L.F.		4.70	1.35	6.05	Includes material, labor and equipment
	Install	V.L.F.	10.50	4.08	4.15	18.73	to install unfilled steel pipe pile.
	Demolish and Install	V.L.F.	10.50	8.78	5.50	24.78	
	Paint	L.F.	.29	1.46		1.75	
	Minimum Charge	Job		2050	2075	4125	

Foundation

Piles		Unit	Material	Labor	Equip.	Total	Specification
10" Concrete Filled							
	Demolish	L.F.		4.85	1.39	6.24	Includes material, labor and equipment
	Install	V.L.F.	14.65	4.54	4.61	23.80	to install concrete filled steel pipe pile.
	Demolish and Install	V.L.F.	14.65	9.39	6	30.04	
	Paint	L.F.	.29	1.46		1.75	
	Minimum Charge	Job		2050	2075	4125	
10" Unfilled							
	Demolish	L.F.		4.85	1.39	6.24	Includes material, labor and equipment
	Install	V.L.F.	13.10	4.08	4.15	21.33	to install unfilled steel pipe pile.
	Demolish and Install	V.L.F.	13.10	8.93	5.54	27.57	
	Paint	L.F.	.29	1.46		1.75	
	Minimum Charge	Job		2050	2075	4125	
12" Concrete Filled							
	Demolish	L.F.		4.85	1.39	6.24	Includes material, labor and equipment
	Install	V.L.F.	17.10	4.92	5	27.02	to install concrete filled steel pipe pile.
	Demolish and Install	V.L.F.	17.10	9.77	6.39	33.26	
	Paint	L.F.	.29	1.46		1.75	
	Minimum Charge	Job		2050	2075	4125	
12" Unfilled							
	Demolish	L.F.		4.85	1.39	6.24	Includes material, labor and equipment
	Install	V.L.F.	16.25	4.30	4.36	24.91	to install unfilled steel pipe pile.
	Demolish and Install	V.L.F.	16.25	9.15	5.75	31.15	
	Paint	L.F.	.29	1.46		1.75	
	Minimum Charge	Job		2050	2075	4125	
Steel H Section							
H Section 8 x 8 x 36#							
	Demolish	L.F.		3.28	.94	4.22	Includes material, labor and equipment
	Install	V.L.F.	9.65	3.19	3.24	16.08	to install steel H section pile.
	Demolish and Install	V.L.F.	9.65	6.47	4.18	20.30	
	Paint	L.F.	.29	1.46		1.75	
	Minimum Charge	Job		2050	2075	4125	
H Section 10 x 10 x 57#							
	Demolish	L.F.		3.59	1.03	4.62	Includes material, labor and equipment
	Install	V.L.F.	15.25	3.35	3.40	22	to install steel H section pile.
	Demolish and Install	V.L.F.	15.25	6.94	4.43	26.62	
	Paint	L.F.	.29	1.46		1.75	
	Minimum Charge	Job		2050	2075	4125	
H Section 12 x 12 x 74#							
	Demolish	L.F.		3.71	1.07	4.78	Includes material, labor and equipment
	Install	V.L.F.	19.80	4.02	4.09	27.91	to install steel H section pile.
	Demolish and Install	V.L.F.	19.80	7.73	5.16	32.69	
	Paint	L.F.	.29	1.46		1.75	
	Minimum Charge	Job		2050	2075	4125	
H Section 14 x 14 x 89#							
	Demolish	L.F.		3.90	1.12	5.02	Includes material, labor and equipment
	Install	V.L.F.	23.50	4.39	4.47	32.36	to install steel H section pile.
	Demolish and Install	V.L.F.	23.50	8.29	5.59	37.38	
	Paint	L.F.	.29	1.46		1.75	
	Minimum Charge	Job		2050	2075	4125	

Foundation Post		Unit	Material	Labor	Equip.	Total	Specification
Wood Foundation Post							
4" x 4"							
	Demolish	L.F.		.53	.15	.68	Cost includes material and labor to
	Install	L.F.	.88	3.45		4.33	install 4" x 4" treated wood post by
	Demolish and Install	L.F.	.88	3.98	.15	5.01	hand in normal soil conditions.
	Reinstall	L.F.		2.76		2.76	
	Minimum Charge	Job		500		500	

Foundation

Foundation Post		Unit	Material	Labor	Equip.	Total	Specification
4" x 6"							Cost includes material and labor to
	Demolish	L.F.		.53	.15	.68	install 4" x 6" treated wood post by
	Install	L.F.	1.34	3.45		4.79	hand in normal soil conditions.
	Demolish and Install	L.F.	1.34	3.98	.15	5.47	
	Reinstall	L.F.		2.76		2.76	
	Minimum Charge	Job		500		500	
6" x 6"							Cost includes material and labor to
	Demolish	L.F.		.53	.15	.68	install 6" x 6" treated wood post by
	Install	L.F.	1.98	3.45		5.43	hand in normal soil conditions.
	Demolish and Install	L.F.	1.98	3.98	.15	6.11	
	Reinstall	L.F.		2.76		2.76	
	Minimum Charge	Job		500		500	
Water Jet							Includes material, labor and equipment
	Demolish	Ea.		61.50		61.50	to water jet a 6" x 6" wood post under
	Install	Ea.	52.50	475		527.50	an existing building. Cost may vary
	Demolish and Install	Ea.	52.50	536.50		589	depending upon location and access.
	Reinstall	Ea.		472.69		472.69	
	Minimum Charge	Job		415		415	
Shim							Includes labor and material to trim or
	Install	Ea.	2.92	50		52.92	readjust existing foundation posts
	Minimum Charge	Job		500		500	under an existing building. Access of 2 - 4 foot assumed.
Cross-bracing							
Treated 2" x 6"							Cost includes material and labor to
	Demolish	L.F.		.68		.68	install 2" x 6" lumber for cross-bracing
	Install	L.F.	1.23	4.01		5.24	of foundation piling or posts.
	Demolish and Install	L.F.	1.23	4.69		5.92	
	Reinstall	L.F.		3.21		3.21	
	Clean	S.F.		.26		.26	
	Paint	L.F.	.15	.98		1.13	
	Minimum Charge	Job		500		500	
Treated 2" x 8"							Cost includes material and labor to
	Demolish	L.F.		.68		.68	install 2" x 8" lumber for cross-bracing
	Install	L.F.	1.60	4.15		5.75	of foundation piling or posts.
	Demolish and Install	L.F.	1.60	4.83		6.43	
	Reinstall	L.F.		3.32		3.32	
	Clean	S.F.		.26		.26	
	Paint	L.F.	.21	1.02		1.23	
	Minimum Charge	Job		500		500	
Treated 2" x 10"							Cost includes material and labor to
	Demolish	L.F.		.70		.70	install 2" x 10" lumber for
	Install	L.F.	2.04	4.29		6.33	cross-bracing of foundation piling or
	Demolish and Install	L.F.	2.04	4.99		7.03	posts.
	Reinstall	L.F.		3.43		3.43	
	Clean	S.F.		.26		.26	
	Paint	L.F.	.25	1.04		1.29	
	Minimum Charge	Job		500		500	
Treated 2" x 12"							Cost includes material and labor to
	Demolish	L.F.		.84		.84	install 2" x 12" lumber for
	Install	L.F.	2.33	4.44		6.77	cross-bracing of foundation piling or
	Demolish and Install	L.F.	2.33	5.28		7.61	posts.
	Reinstall	L.F.		3.55		3.55	
	Clean	S.F.		.26		.26	
	Paint	L.F.	.30	1.06		1.36	
	Minimum Charge	Job		500		500	

Foundation

Concrete Footing

Concrete Footing		Unit	Material	Labor	Equip.	Total	Specification
Continuous							
12″ w x 6″ d							
	Demolish	L.F.		1.01	.85	1.86	Includes material and labor to install
	Install	L.F.	3.10	2.36	.02	5.48	continuous reinforced concrete footing
	Demolish and Install	L.F.	3.10	3.37	.87	7.34	poured by chute cast against earth
	Minimum Charge	Job		570		570	including reinforcing, forming and finishing.
12″ w x 12″ d							
	Demolish	L.F.		1.95	1.63	3.58	Includes material and labor to install
	Install	L.F.	7.75	4.73	.05	12.53	continuous reinforced concrete footing
	Demolish and Install	L.F.	7.75	6.68	1.68	16.11	poured by chute cast against earth
	Minimum Charge	Job		570		570	including reinforcing, forming and finishing.
18″ w x 10″ d							
	Demolish	L.F.		2.53	2.12	4.65	Includes material and labor to install
	Install	L.F.	7.05	5.80	.06	12.91	continuous reinforced concrete footing
	Demolish and Install	L.F.	7.05	8.33	2.18	17.56	poured by chute cast against earth
	Minimum Charge	Job		570		570	including reinforcing, forming and finishing.
24″ w x 24″ d							
	Demolish	L.F.		4.22	3.54	7.76	Includes material and labor to install
	Install	L.F.	20.50	18.90	.20	39.60	continuous reinforced concrete footing
	Demolish and Install	L.F.	20.50	23.12	3.74	47.36	poured by chute cast against earth
	Minimum Charge	Job		570		570	including reinforcing, forming and finishing.
Stem Wall							
Single Story							
	Demolish	L.F.		9.40	7.85	17.25	Includes material and labor to install
	Install	L.F.	9.45	49.50	41.50	100.45	stem wall 24″ above and 18″ below
	Demolish and Install	L.F.	9.45	58.90	49.35	117.70	grade for a single story structure.
	Minimum Charge	Job		570		570	Includes 12″ wide and 8″ deep footing.
Two Story							
	Demolish	L.F.		9.40	7.85	17.25	Includes material and labor to install
	Install	L.F.	11.70	71	59.50	142.20	stem wall 24″ above and 18″ below
	Demolish and Install	L.F.	11.70	80.40	67.35	159.45	grade typical for a two story structure,
	Minimum Charge	Job		570		570	includes 18″ wide and 10″ deep footing.

Concrete Slab

Concrete Slab		Unit	Material	Labor	Equip.	Total	Specification
Reinforced							
4″							
	Demolish	S.F.		1.75	.32	2.07	Cost includes material and labor to
	Install	S.F.	1.62	.37		1.99	install 4″ reinforced concrete
	Demolish and Install	S.F.	1.62	2.12	.32	4.06	slab-on-grade poured by chute
	Clean	S.F.	.03	.23		.26	including forms, vapor barrier, wire
	Paint	S.F.	.11	.55		.66	mesh, 3000 PSI concrete, float finish,
	Minimum Charge	Job		130		130	and curing.

Foundation

Concrete Slab

Concrete Slab		Unit	Material	Labor	Equip.	Total	Specification
6"							
	Demolish	S.F.		2.62	.48	3.10	Cost includes material and labor to
	Install	S.F.	2.23	.56	.01	2.80	install 6" reinforced concrete
	Demolish and Install	S.F.	2.23	3.18	.49	5.90	slab-on-grade poured by chute
	Clean	S.F.	.03	.23		.26	including forms, vapor barrier, wire
	Paint	S.F.	.11	.55		.66	mesh, 3000 PSI concrete, float finish,
	Minimum Charge	Job		130		130	and curing.
8"							
	Demolish	S.F.		4.29	.79	5.08	Cost includes material and labor to
	Install	S.F.	2.88	.74	.01	3.63	install 8" reinforced concrete
	Demolish and Install	S.F.	2.88	5.03	.80	8.71	slab-on-grade poured by chute
	Clean	S.F.	.03	.23		.26	including forms, vapor barrier, wire
	Paint	S.F.	.11	.55		.66	mesh, 3000 PSI concrete, float finish,
	Minimum Charge	Job		130		130	and curing.
Unreinforced							
4"							
	Demolish	S.F.		1.39	.26	1.65	Cost includes material and labor to
	Install	S.F.	1.01	.65	.01	1.67	install 4" concrete slab-on-grade
	Demolish and Install	S.F.	1.01	2.04	.27	3.32	poured by chute, including forms,
	Clean	S.F.	.03	.23		.26	vapor barrier, 3000 PSI concrete, float
	Paint	S.F.	.11	.55		.66	finish, and curing.
	Minimum Charge	Job		130		130	
6"							
	Demolish	S.F.		1.97	.36	2.33	Cost includes material and labor to
	Install	S.F.	1.49	.66	.01	2.16	install 6" concrete slab-on-grade
	Demolish and Install	S.F.	1.49	2.63	.37	4.49	poured by chute, including forms,
	Clean	S.F.	.03	.23		.26	vapor barrier, 3000 PSI concrete, float
	Paint	S.F.	.11	.55		.66	finish, and curing.
	Minimum Charge	Job		130		130	
8"							
	Demolish	S.F.		3.23	.59	3.82	Cost includes material and labor to
	Install	S.F.	2.04	.69	.01	2.74	install 8" concrete slab-on-grade
	Demolish and Install	S.F.	2.04	3.92	.60	6.56	poured by chute, including forms,
	Clean	S.F.	.03	.23		.26	vapor barrier, 3000 PSI concrete, float
	Paint	S.F.	.11	.55		.66	finish, and curing.
	Minimum Charge	Job		130		130	
Lightweight							
	Demolish	S.F.		.61	.20	.81	Includes material and labor to install
	Install	S.F.	1.36	1.94		3.30	lightweight concrete, 3" - 4" thick.
	Demolish and Install	S.F.	1.36	2.55	.20	4.11	
	Clean	S.F.	.03	.23		.26	
	Paint	S.F.	.11	.55		.66	
	Minimum Charge	Job		130		130	
Gunite							
	Demolish	S.F.		.76	.22	.98	Includes material and labor to install
	Install	S.F.	1.06	.83	.37	2.26	gunite on flat plane per inch of
	Demolish and Install	S.F.	1.06	1.59	.59	3.24	thickness using 1" as base price. No
	Clean	S.F.	.03	.23		.26	forms or reinforcing are included.
	Paint	S.F.	.11	.55		.66	
	Minimum Charge	Job		730		730	
Epoxy Inject							
	Install	L.F.	1.68	2.61		4.29	Includes labor and material to inject
	Minimum Charge	Job		130		130	epoxy into cracks.

Foundation

Concrete Slab		Unit	Material	Labor	Equip.	Total	Specification
Pressure Grout							
	Install	S.F.	2.23	1.93		4.16	Includes labor, material and equipment to install pressure grout under an existing building.
	Minimum Charge	Job		130		130	
Scrape and Paint							
	Paint	S.F.	.17	.64		.81	Includes labor and materials to scrape and paint a concrete floor.
	Minimum Charge	Job		128		128	
Vapor Barrier							
	Install	S.F.	.02	.08		.10	Cost includes material and labor to install 4 mil polyethylene vapor barrier 10' wide sheets with 6" overlaps.
	Minimum Charge	Job		142		142	

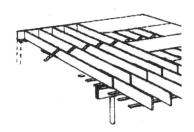

Rough Framing

Beam / Girder	Unit	Material	Labor	Equip.	Total	Specification
Solid Wood Beam						
2" x 8"						
Demolish	L.F.		.56		.56	Cost includes material and labor to
Install	L.F.	.96	.88		1.84	install 2" x 8" beam.
Demolish and Install	L.F.	.96	1.44		2.40	
Clean	L.F.	.09	.18		.27	
Paint	L.F.	.12	1.38		1.50	
Minimum Charge	Job		142		142	
2" x 10"						
Demolish	L.F.		.69		.69	Cost includes material and labor to
Install	L.F.	1.36	.95		2.31	install 2" x 10" beam.
Demolish and Install	L.F.	1.36	1.64		3	
Clean	L.F.	.11	.22		.33	
Paint	L.F.	.15	.85		1	
Minimum Charge	Job		142		142	
2" x 12"						
Demolish	L.F.		.84		.84	Cost includes material and labor to
Install	L.F.	1.87	1.04		2.91	install 2" x 12" beam.
Demolish and Install	L.F.	1.87	1.88		3.75	
Clean	L.F.	.13	.26		.39	
Paint	L.F.	.18	2.04		2.22	
Minimum Charge	Job		142		142	
4" x 8"						
Demolish	L.F.		2.85		2.85	Cost includes material and labor to
Install	L.F.	3.75	1.29	.67	5.71	install 4" x 8" beam.
Demolish and Install	L.F.	3.75	4.14	.67	8.56	
Clean	L.F.	.11	.22		.33	
Paint	L.F.	.15	.85		1	
Minimum Charge	Job		142		142	
4" x 10"						
Demolish	L.F.		3.57		3.57	Cost includes material and labor to
Install	L.F.	4.70	1.36	.70	6.76	install 4" x 10" beam.
Demolish and Install	L.F.	4.70	4.93	.70	10.33	
Clean	L.F.	.13	.26		.39	
Paint	L.F.	.18	.99		1.17	
Minimum Charge	Job		142		142	
4" x 12"						
Demolish	L.F.		4.29		4.29	Cost includes material and labor to
Install	L.F.	5.60	1.43	.74	7.77	install 4" x 12" beam.
Demolish and Install	L.F.	5.60	5.72	.74	12.06	
Clean	L.F.	.14	.30		.44	
Paint	L.F.	.18	2.04		2.22	
Minimum Charge	Job		142		142	

Beam / Girder		Unit	Material	Labor	Equip.	Total	Specification
6" x 8"							
	Demolish	L.F.		4.29		4.29	Cost includes material and labor to
	Install	L.F.	10.10	2.46	1.27	13.83	install 6" x 8" beam.
	Demolish and Install	L.F.	10.10	6.75	1.27	18.12	
	Clean	L.F.	.13	.26		.39	
	Paint	L.F.	.18	.99		1.17	
	Minimum Charge	Job		142		142	
6" x 10"							
	Demolish	L.F.		5.35		5.35	Cost includes material and labor to
	Install	L.F.	4.10	1.14		5.24	install 6" x 10" triple beam.
	Demolish and Install	L.F.	4.10	6.49		10.59	
	Clean	L.F.	.14	.30		.44	
	Paint	L.F.	.20	1.13		1.33	
	Minimum Charge	Job		142		142	
6" x 12"							
	Demolish	L.F.		6.35		6.35	Cost includes material and labor to
	Install	L.F.	5.60	1.20		6.80	install 6" x 12" triple beam.
	Demolish and Install	L.F.	5.60	7.55		13.15	
	Clean	L.F.	.17	.33		.50	
	Paint	L.F.	.22	1.28		1.50	
	Minimum Charge	Job		142		142	
Steel I-type							
W8 x 31							
	Demolish	L.F.		6	3.54	9.54	Includes material and labor to install
	Install	L.F.	23	1.95	1.45	26.40	W shaped steel beam / girder.
	Demolish and Install	L.F.	23	7.95	4.99	35.94	
	Minimum Charge	Job		355		355	
W8 x 48							
	Demolish	L.F.		6	3.54	9.54	Includes material and labor to install
	Install	L.F.	36	2.04	1.51	39.55	W shaped steel beam / girder.
	Demolish and Install	L.F.	36	8.04	5.05	49.09	
	Minimum Charge	Job		355		355	
W8 x 67							
	Demolish	L.F.		6	3.54	9.54	Includes material and labor to install
	Install	L.F.	49.50	2.14	1.59	53.23	W shaped steel beam / girder.
	Demolish and Install	L.F.	49.50	8.14	5.13	62.77	
	Minimum Charge	Job		355		355	
W10 x 45							
	Demolish	L.F.		6	3.54	9.54	Includes material and labor to install
	Install	L.F.	33.50	2.04	1.51	37.05	W shaped steel beam / girder.
	Demolish and Install	L.F.	33.50	8.04	5.05	46.59	
	Minimum Charge	Job		355		355	
W10 x 68							
	Demolish	L.F.		6	3.54	9.54	Includes material and labor to install
	Install	L.F.	50.50	2.14	1.59	54.23	W shaped steel beam / girder.
	Demolish and Install	L.F.	50.50	8.14	5.13	63.77	
	Minimum Charge	Job		355		355	
W12 x 50							
	Demolish	L.F.		6	3.54	9.54	Includes material and labor to install
	Install	L.F.	37	2.04	1.51	40.55	W shaped steel beam / girder.
	Demolish and Install	L.F.	37	8.04	5.05	50.09	
	Minimum Charge	Job		355		355	
W12 x 87							
	Demolish	L.F.		8.85	5.20	14.05	Includes material and labor to install
	Install	L.F.	64.50	2.14	1.59	68.23	W shaped steel beam / girder.
	Demolish and Install	L.F.	64.50	10.99	6.79	82.28	
	Minimum Charge	Job		355		355	

Rough Frame / Structure

Beam / Girder

Beam / Girder		Unit	Material	Labor	Equip.	Total	Specification
W12 x 120							
	Demolish	L.F.		8.85	5.20	14.05	Includes material and labor to install
	Install	L.F.	89	2.20	1.63	92.83	W shaped steel beam / girder.
	Demolish and Install	L.F.	89	11.05	6.83	106.88	
	Minimum Charge	Job		355		355	
W14 x 74							
	Demolish	L.F.		8.85	5.20	14.05	Includes material and labor to install
	Install	L.F.	55	2.14	1.59	58.73	W shaped steel beam / girder.
	Demolish and Install	L.F.	55	10.99	6.79	72.78	
	Minimum Charge	Job		355		355	
W14 x 120							
	Demolish	L.F.		8.85	5.20	14.05	Includes material and labor to install
	Install	L.F.	89	2.20	1.63	92.83	W shaped steel beam / girder.
	Demolish and Install	L.F.	89	11.05	6.83	106.88	
	Minimum Charge	Job		355		355	

Column

Column		Unit	Material	Labor	Equip.	Total	Specification
Concrete							
Small Diameter							
	Demolish	L.F.		9.85	1.81	11.66	Includes material and labor to install
	Install	L.F.	62	8.90	2.26	73.16	small diameter concrete column.
	Demolish and Install	L.F.	62	18.75	4.07	84.82	
	Minimum Charge	Job		445	113	558	
Large Diameter							
	Demolish	L.F.		29.50	5.40	34.90	Includes material and labor to install
	Install	L.F.	182	10.50	2.66	195.16	large diameter concrete column.
	Demolish and Install	L.F.	182	40	8.06	230.06	
	Minimum Charge	Job		445	113	558	

Floor Framing System

Floor Framing System		Unit	Material	Labor	Equip.	Total	Specification
12" O.C.							
2" x 6" Joists							
	Demolish	S.F.		.47		.47	Cost includes material and labor to
	Install	S.F.	.73	.23		.96	install 2" x 6" joists, 12" O.C.
	Demolish and Install	S.F.	.73	.70		1.43	including box or band joist. Blocking
	Reinstall	S.F.		.18		.18	or bridging not included.
	Minimum Charge	Job		142		142	
2" x 8" Joists							
	Demolish	S.F.		.49		.49	Cost includes material and labor to
	Install	S.F.	1.12	.26		1.38	install 2" x 8" joists, 12" O.C.
	Demolish and Install	S.F.	1.12	.75		1.87	including box or band joist. Blocking
	Reinstall	S.F.		.21		.21	or bridging not included.
	Minimum Charge	Job		142		142	
2" x 10" Joists							
	Demolish	S.F.		.50		.50	Cost includes material and labor to
	Install	S.F.	1.60	.32		1.92	install 2" x 10" joists, 12" O.C.
	Demolish and Install	S.F.	1.60	.82		2.42	including box or band joist. Blocking
	Reinstall	S.F.		.25		.25	or bridging not included.
	Minimum Charge	Job		142		142	

Floor Framing System		Unit	Material	Labor	Equip.	Total	Specification
2" x 12" Joists							
	Demolish	S.F.		.52		.52	Cost includes material and labor to
	Install	S.F.	2.18	.33		2.51	install 2" x 12" joists, 12" O.C.
	Demolish and Install	S.F.	2.18	.85		3.03	including box or band joist. Blocking
	Reinstall	S.F.		.26		.26	or bridging not included.
	Minimum Charge	Job		142		142	
Block / Bridge							
	Demolish	Ea.		.72		.72	Includes material and labor to install
	Install	Ea.	1.83	1.60		3.43	set of cross bridging or per block of
	Demolish and Install	Ea.	1.83	2.32		4.15	solid bridging for 2" x 10" joists cut to
	Minimum Charge	Job		142		142	size on site.

16" O.C.

Floor Framing System		Unit	Material	Labor	Equip.	Total	Specification
2" x 6" Joists							
	Demolish	S.F.		.35		.35	Cost includes material and labor to
	Install	S.F.	.56	.34		.90	install 2" x 6" joists including box or
	Demolish and Install	S.F.	.56	.69		1.25	band joist installed 16" O.C. Does not
	Reinstall	S.F.		.27		.27	include beams, blocking or bridging.
	Minimum Charge	Job		142		142	
2" x 8" Joists							
	Demolish	S.F.		.37		.37	Cost includes material and labor to
	Install	S.F.	.86	.39		1.25	install 2" x 8" joists including box or
	Demolish and Install	S.F.	.86	.76		1.62	band joist installed 16" O.C. Does not
	Reinstall	S.F.		.31		.31	include beams, blocking or bridging.
	Minimum Charge	Job		142		142	
2" x 10" Joists							
	Demolish	S.F.		.38		.38	Cost includes material and labor to
	Install	S.F.	1.23	.47		1.70	install 2" x 10" joists including box or
	Demolish and Install	S.F.	1.23	.85		2.08	band joist 16" O.C. Does not include
	Reinstall	S.F.		.38		.38	beams, blocking or bridging.
	Minimum Charge	Job		142		142	
2" x 12" Joists							
	Demolish	S.F.		.39		.39	Cost includes material and labor to
	Install	S.F.	1.68	.49		2.17	install 2" x 12" joists including box or
	Demolish and Install	S.F.	1.68	.88		2.56	band joist installed 16" O.C. Does not
	Reinstall	S.F.		.39		.39	include beams, blocking or bridging.
	Minimum Charge	Job		142		142	
Block / Bridge							
	Demolish	Ea.		.72		.72	Includes material and labor to install
	Install	Ea.	1.83	1.60		3.43	set of cross bridging or per block of
	Demolish and Install	Ea.	1.83	2.32		4.15	solid bridging for 2" x 10" joists cut to
	Minimum Charge	Job		142		142	size on site.

24" O.C.

Floor Framing System		Unit	Material	Labor	Equip.	Total	Specification
2" x 6" Joists							
	Demolish	S.F.		.24		.24	Cost includes material and labor to
	Install	S.F.	.40	.11		.51	install 2" x 6" joists including box or
	Demolish and Install	S.F.	.40	.35		.75	band joist installed 24" O.C. Does not
	Reinstall	S.F.		.09		.09	include beams, blocking or bridging.
	Minimum Charge	Job		142		142	
2" x 8" Joists							
	Demolish	S.F.		.25		.25	Cost includes material and labor to
	Install	S.F.	.62	.13		.75	install 2" x 8" joists including box or
	Demolish and Install	S.F.	.62	.38		1	band joist installed 24" O.C. Does not
	Reinstall	S.F.		.10		.10	include beams, blocking or bridging.
	Minimum Charge	Job		142		142	
2" x 10" Joists							
	Demolish	S.F.		.25		.25	Cost includes material and labor to
	Install	S.F.	.87	.16		1.03	install 2" x 10" joists including box or
	Demolish and Install	S.F.	.87	.41		1.28	band joist installed 24" O.C. Does not
	Reinstall	S.F.		.13		.13	include beams, blocking or bridging.
	Minimum Charge	Job		142		142	

Floor Framing System

Floor Framing System		Unit	Material	Labor	Equip.	Total	Specification
2" x 12" Joists							Cost includes material and labor to
	Demolish	S.F.		.26		.26	install 2" x 12" joists including box or
	Install	S.F.	1.20	.16		1.36	band joist installed 24" O.C. Does not
	Demolish and Install	S.F.	1.20	.42		1.62	include beams, blocking or bridging.
	Reinstall	S.F.		.13		.13	
	Minimum Charge	Job		142		142	
Block / Bridge							Includes material and labor to install
	Demolish	Ea.		.72		.72	set of cross bridging or per block of
	Install	Ea.	1.83	1.60		3.43	solid bridging for 2" x 10" joists cut to
	Demolish and Install	Ea.	1.83	2.32		4.15	size on site.
	Minimum Charge	Job		142		142	
Engineered Lumber, Joist							
9-1/2"							Includes material and labor to install
	Demolish	S.F.		.38		.38	engineered lumber truss / joists per
	Install	S.F.	1.40	.28		1.68	S.F. of floor area based on joists 16"
	Demolish and Install	S.F.	1.40	.66		2.06	O.C. Beams, supports and bridging
	Reinstall	S.F.		.23		.23	are not included.
	Minimum Charge	Job		142		142	
11-7/8"							Includes material and labor to install
	Demolish	S.F.		.39		.39	engineered lumber truss / joists per
	Install	S.F.	1.51	.29		1.80	S.F. of floor area based on joists 16"
	Demolish and Install	S.F.	1.51	.68		2.19	O.C. Beams, supports and bridging
	Reinstall	S.F.		.23		.23	are not included.
	Minimum Charge	Job		142		142	
14"							Includes material and labor to install
	Demolish	S.F.		.40		.40	engineered lumber truss / joists per
	Install	S.F.	1.65	.31		1.96	S.F. of floor area based on joists 16"
	Demolish and Install	S.F.	1.65	.71		2.36	O.C. Beams, supports and bridging
	Reinstall	S.F.		.25		.25	are not included.
	Minimum Charge	Job		142		142	
16"							Includes material and labor to install
	Demolish	S.F.		.42		.42	engineered lumber truss / joists per
	Install	S.F.	2.06	.33		2.39	S.F. of floor area based on joists 16"
	Demolish and Install	S.F.	2.06	.75		2.81	O.C. Beams, supports and bridging
	Reinstall	S.F.		.26		.26	are not included.
	Minimum Charge	Job		142		142	
Block / Bridge							Includes material and labor to install
	Demolish	Pr.		.72		.72	set of steel, one-nail type cross
	Install	Pr.	1.49	2.11		3.60	bridging for trusses placed 16" O.C.
	Demolish and Install	Pr.	1.49	2.83		4.32	
	Minimum Charge	Job		142		142	
Block / Bridge							
2" x 6"							Includes material and labor to install
	Demolish	Ea.		.72		.72	set of cross bridging or per block of
	Install	Ea.	.84	1.28		2.12	solid bridging for 2" x 6" joists cut to
	Demolish and Install	Ea.	.84	2		2.84	size on site.
	Minimum Charge	Job		142		142	
2" x 8"							Includes material and labor to install
	Demolish	Ea.		.72		.72	set of cross bridging or per block of
	Install	Ea.	1.28	1.42		2.70	solid bridging for 2" x 8" joists cut to
	Demolish and Install	Ea.	1.28	2.14		3.42	size on site.
	Minimum Charge	Job		142		142	

Rough Frame / Structure

Floor Framing System	Unit	Material	Labor	Equip.	Total	Specification
2″ x 10″						
Demolish	Ea.		.72		.72	Includes material and labor to install
Install	Ea.	1.83	1.60		3.43	set of cross bridging or per block of
Demolish and Install	Ea.	1.83	2.32		4.15	solid bridging for 2″ x 10″ joists cut to
Minimum Charge	Job		142		142	size on site.
2″ x 12″						
Demolish	Ea.		.72		.72	Includes material and labor to install
Install	Ea.	2.50	1.89		4.39	set of cross bridging or per block of
Demolish and Install	Ea.	2.50	2.61		5.11	solid bridging for 2″ x 12″ joists cut to
Minimum Charge	Job		142		142	size on site.
Ledger Strips						
1″ x 2″						
Demolish	L.F.		.19		.19	Cost includes material and labor to
Install	L.F.	.23	.83		1.06	install 1″ x 2″ ledger strip nailed to the
Demolish and Install	L.F.	.23	1.02		1.25	face of studs, beams or joist.
Minimum Charge	Job		142		142	
1″ x 3″						
Demolish	L.F.		.19		.19	Includes material and labor to install
Install	L.F.	.66	.95		1.61	up to 1″ x 4″ ledger strip nailed to the
Demolish and Install	L.F.	.66	1.14		1.80	face of studs, beams or joist.
Minimum Charge	Job		142		142	
1″ x 4″						
Demolish	L.F.		.19		.19	Includes material and labor to install
Install	L.F.	.66	.95		1.61	up to 1″ x 4″ ledger strip nailed to the
Demolish and Install	L.F.	.66	1.14		1.80	face of studs, beams or joist.
Minimum Charge	Job		142		142	
2″ x 2″						
Demolish	L.F.		.21		.21	Cost includes material and labor to
Install	L.F.	.28	.86		1.14	install 2″ x 2″ ledger strip nailed to the
Demolish and Install	L.F.	.28	1.07		1.35	face of studs, beams or joist.
Minimum Charge	Job		142		142	
2″ x 4″						
Demolish	L.F.		.23		.23	Cost includes material and labor to
Install	L.F.	.40	1.14		1.54	install 2″ x 4″ ledger strip nailed to the
Demolish and Install	L.F.	.40	1.37		1.77	face of studs, beams or joist.
Reinstall	L.F.		.91		.91	
Minimum Charge	Job		142		142	
Ledger Boards						
2″ x 6″						
Demolish	L.F.		.23		.23	Cost includes material and labor to
Install	L.F.	1.66	1.78		3.44	install 2″ x 6″ ledger board fastened to
Demolish and Install	L.F.	1.66	2.01		3.67	a wall, joists or studs.
Reinstall	L.F.		1.42		1.42	
Minimum Charge	Job		142		142	
4″ x 6″						
Demolish	L.F.		.38		.38	Cost includes material and labor to
Install	L.F.	4.07	1.78		5.85	install 4″ x 6″ ledger board fastened to
Demolish and Install	L.F.	4.07	2.16		6.23	a wall, joists or studs.
Reinstall	L.F.		1.42		1.42	
Minimum Charge	Job		142		142	
4″ x 8″						
Demolish	L.F.		.51		.51	Cost includes material and labor to
Install	L.F.	5	1.78		6.78	install 4″ x 8″ ledger board fastened to
Demolish and Install	L.F.	5	2.29		7.29	a wall, joists or studs.
Reinstall	L.F.		1.42		1.42	
Minimum Charge	Job		142		142	

Rough Frame / Structure

Floor Framing System

Floor Framing System		Unit	Material	Labor	Equip.	Total	Specification
Sill Plate Per L.F.							
2" x 4"							
	Demolish	L.F.		.25		.25	Cost includes material and labor to
	Install	L.F.	.55	1.04		1.59	install 2" x 4" pressure treated lumber,
	Demolish and Install	L.F.	.55	1.29		1.84	drilled and installed on foundation
	Reinstall	L.F.		.83		.83	bolts 48" O.C. Bolts, nuts and washers
	Minimum Charge	Job		142		142	are not included.
2" x 6"							
	Demolish	L.F.		.25		.25	Cost includes material and labor to
	Install	L.F.	1.23	1.14		2.37	install 2" x 6" pressure treated lumber,
	Demolish and Install	L.F.	1.23	1.39		2.62	drilled and installed on foundation
	Reinstall	L.F.		.91		.91	bolts 48" O.C. Bolts, nuts and washers
	Minimum Charge	Job		142		142	not included.
2" x 8"							
	Demolish	L.F.		.25		.25	Cost includes material and labor to
	Install	L.F.	1.60	1.27		2.87	install 2" x 8" pressure treated lumber,
	Demolish and Install	L.F.	1.60	1.52		3.12	drilled and installed on foundation
	Reinstall	L.F.		1.01		1.01	bolts 48" O.C. Bolts, nuts and washers
	Minimum Charge	Job		142		142	not included.
Earthquake Strapping							
	Install	Ea.	1.57	1.78		3.35	Includes labor and material to replace
	Minimum Charge	Job		142		142	an earthquake strap.

Subflooring

Subflooring		Unit	Material	Labor	Equip.	Total	Specification
Plywood							
1/4"							
	Demolish	S.F.		.30		.30	Cost includes material and labor to
	Install	S.F.	.53	.38		.91	install 1/4" lauan subfloor, standard
	Demolish and Install	S.F.	.53	.68		1.21	interior grade, nailed every 6".
	Minimum Charge	Job		142		142	
1/2"							
	Demolish	S.F.		.30		.30	Cost includes material and labor to
	Install	SF Flr.	.41	.31		.72	install 1/2" plywood subfloor, CD
	Demolish and Install	SF Flr.	.41	.61		1.02	standard interior grade, plugged and
	Minimum Charge	Job		142		142	touch sanded.
5/8"							
	Demolish	S.F.		.30		.30	Cost includes material and labor to
	Install	SF Flr.	.48	.34		.82	install 5/8" plywood subfloor, CD
	Demolish and Install	SF Flr.	.48	.64		1.12	standard interior grade, plugged and
	Reinstall	SF Flr.		.27		.27	touch sanded.
	Minimum Charge	Job		142		142	
3/4"							
	Demolish	S.F.		.31		.31	Cost includes material and labor to
	Install	SF Flr.	.55	.37		.92	install 3/4" plywood subfloor, CD
	Demolish and Install	SF Flr.	.55	.68		1.23	standard interior grade, plugged and
	Reinstall	SF Flr.		.29		.29	touch sanded.
	Minimum Charge	Job		142		142	
Particle Board							
3/8"							
	Demolish	S.F.		.29		.29	Cost includes material and labor to
	Install	S.F.	.42	.18		.60	install 3/8" particle board subfloor.
	Demolish and Install	S.F.	.42	.47		.89	
	Minimum Charge	Job		142		142	

Rough Frame / Structure

Subflooring

Subflooring		Unit	Material	Labor	Equip.	Total	Specification
1/2"							
	Demolish	S.F.		.30		.30	Cost includes material and labor to
	Install	SF Flr.	.52	.38		.90	install 1/2" particle board subfloor.
	Demolish and Install	SF Flr.	.52	.68		1.20	
	Minimum Charge	Job		142		142	
5/8"							
	Demolish	S.F.		.30		.30	Cost includes material and labor to
	Install	S.F.	.59	.21		.80	install 5/8" particle board subfloor.
	Demolish and Install	S.F.	.59	.51		1.10	
	Minimum Charge	Job		142		142	
3/4"							
	Demolish	S.F.		.31		.31	Cost includes material and labor to
	Install	SF Flr.	.66	.46		1.12	install 3/4" particle board subfloor.
	Demolish and Install	SF Flr.	.66	.77		1.43	
	Minimum Charge	Job		142		142	
Plank Board							
	Demolish	S.F.		.97		.97	Cost includes material and labor to
	Install	S.F.	1.43	.32		1.75	install 1" x 6" standard grade plank
	Demolish and Install	S.F.	1.43	1.29		2.72	flooring.
	Reinstall	S.F.		.32		.32	
	Minimum Charge	Job		142		142	
Felt Underlay							
	Demolish	S.F.		.05		.05	Includes material and labor to install
	Install	S.F.	.02	.08		.10	#15 felt building paper.
	Demolish and Install	S.F.	.02	.13		.15	
	Minimum Charge	Job		142		142	
Prep (for flooring)							
	Install	S.F.		.25		.25	Preparation of subflooring for
	Minimum Charge	Job		132		132	installation of new finished flooring. Cost reflects average time to prep area.

Wall Framing System

Wall Framing System		Unit	Material	Labor	Equip.	Total	Specification
2" x 4"							
8' High							
	Demolish	L.F.		3.06		3.06	Cost includes material and labor to
	Install	L.F.	2.89	3.35		6.24	install 2" x 4" x 8' high wall system,
	Demolish and Install	L.F.	2.89	6.41		9.30	including studs, treated bottom plate,
	Reinstall	L.F.		2.68		2.68	double top plate and one row of fire
	Minimum Charge	Job		142		142	blocking.
9' High							
	Demolish	L.F.		3.43		3.43	Cost includes material and labor to
	Install	L.F.	3.19	3.35		6.54	install 2" x 4" x 9' wall system
	Demolish and Install	L.F.	3.19	6.78		9.97	including studs, treated bottom plate,
	Reinstall	L.F.		2.68		2.68	double top plate and one row of fire
	Minimum Charge	Job		142		142	blocking.
10' High							
	Demolish	L.F.		3.83		3.83	Cost includes material and labor to
	Install	L.F.	3.49	3.35		6.84	install 2" x 4" x 10' wall system
	Demolish and Install	L.F.	3.49	7.18		10.67	including studs, treated bottom plate,
	Reinstall	L.F.		2.68		2.68	double top plate and one row of fire
	Minimum Charge	Job		142		142	blocking.

Wall Framing System	Unit	Material	Labor	Equip.	Total	Specification
12' High						
Demolish	L.F.		4.60		4.60	Cost includes material and labor to
Install	L.F.	4.07	4.07		8.14	install 2″ x 4″ x 12′ wall system
Demolish and Install	L.F.	4.07	8.67		12.74	including studs, treated bottom plate,
Reinstall	L.F.		3.25		3.25	double top plate and one row of fire
Minimum Charge	Job		142		142	blocking.
2″ x 6″						
8' High						
Demolish	L.F.		2.87		2.87	Cost includes material and labor to
Install	L.F.	4.96	6.20		11.16	install 2″ x 6″ x 8′ wall system
Demolish and Install	L.F.	4.96	9.07		14.03	including studs, treated bottom plate,
Reinstall	L.F.		4.98		4.98	double top plate and one row of fire
Minimum Charge	Job		142		142	blocking.
9' High						
Demolish	L.F.		3.24		3.24	Cost includes material and labor to
Install	L.F.	5.40	6.20		11.60	install 2″ x 6″ x 9′ wall system
Demolish and Install	L.F.	5.40	9.44		14.84	including studs, treated bottom plate,
Reinstall	L.F.		4.98		4.98	double top plate and one row of fire
Minimum Charge	Job		142		142	blocking.
10' High						
Demolish	L.F.		3.53		3.53	Cost includes material and labor to
Install	L.F.	5.90	6.20		12.10	install 2″ x 6″ x 10′ wall system
Demolish and Install	L.F.	5.90	9.73		15.63	including studs, treated bottom plate,
Reinstall	L.F.		4.98		4.98	double top plate and one row of fire
Minimum Charge	Job		142		142	blocking.
12' High						
Demolish	L.F.		4.18		4.18	Cost includes material and labor to
Install	L.F.	6.80	7.65		14.45	install 2″ x 6″ x 12′ wall system
Demolish and Install	L.F.	6.80	11.83		18.63	including studs, treated bottom plate,
Reinstall	L.F.		6.12		6.12	double top plate and one row of fire
Minimum Charge	Job		142		142	blocking.
Fireblock						
2″ x 4″, 16″ O.C. System						
Demolish	L.F.		.29		.29	Cost includes material and labor to
Install	L.F.	.40	.95		1.35	install 2″ x 4″ fireblocks in wood frame
Demolish and Install	L.F.	.40	1.24		1.64	walls per L.F. of wall to be blocked.
Reinstall	L.F.		.76		.76	
Minimum Charge	Job		142		142	
2″ x 4″, 24″ O.C. System						
Demolish	L.F.		.29		.29	Cost includes material and labor to
Install	L.F.	.40	.95		1.35	install 2″ x 4″ fireblocks in wood frame
Demolish and Install	L.F.	.40	1.24		1.64	walls per L.F. of wall to be blocked.
Reinstall	L.F.		.76		.76	
Minimum Charge	Job		142		142	
2″ x 6″, 16″ O.C. System						
Demolish	L.F.		.29		.29	Cost includes material and labor to
Install	L.F.	.63	.95		1.58	install 2″ x 6″ fireblocks in wood frame
Demolish and Install	L.F.	.63	1.24		1.87	walls per L.F. of wall to be blocked.
Reinstall	L.F.		.76		.76	
Minimum Charge	Job		142		142	
2″ x 6″, 24″ O.C. System						
Demolish	L.F.		.29		.29	Cost includes material and labor to
Install	L.F.	.63	.95		1.58	install 2″ x 6″ fireblocks in wood frame
Demolish and Install	L.F.	.63	1.24		1.87	walls per L.F. of wall to be blocked.
Reinstall	L.F.		.76		.76	
Minimum Charge	Job		142		142	

Rough Frame / Structure

Wall Framing System		Unit	Material	Labor	Equip.	Total	Specification
Bracing							
1″ x 3″							
	Demolish	L.F.		.22		.22	Cost includes material and labor to
	Install	L.F.	.21	1.78		1.99	install 1″ x 3″ let-in bracing.
	Demolish and Install	L.F.	.21	2		2.21	
	Minimum Charge	Job		142		142	
1″ x 4″							
	Demolish	L.F.		.22		.22	Cost includes material and labor to
	Install	L.F.	.40	1.78		2.18	install 1″ x 4″ let-in bracing.
	Demolish and Install	L.F.	.40	2		2.40	
	Minimum Charge	Job		142		142	
1″ x 6″							
	Demolish	L.F.		.22		.22	Cost includes material and labor to
	Install	L.F.	.56	1.90		2.46	install 1″ x 6″ let-in bracing.
	Demolish and Install	L.F.	.56	2.12		2.68	
	Minimum Charge	Job		142		142	
2″ x 3″							
	Demolish	L.F.		.29		.29	Cost includes material and labor to
	Install	L.F.	.28	1.90		2.18	install 2″ x 3″ let-in bracing.
	Demolish and Install	L.F.	.28	2.19		2.47	
	Reinstall	L.F.		1.52		1.52	
	Minimum Charge	Job		142		142	
2″ x 4″							
	Demolish	L.F.		.29		.29	Cost includes material and labor to
	Install	L.F.	.40	1.90		2.30	install 2″ x 4″ let-in bracing.
	Demolish and Install	L.F.	.40	2.19		2.59	
	Reinstall	L.F.		1.52		1.52	
	Minimum Charge	Job		142		142	
2″ x 6″							
	Demolish	L.F.		.29		.29	Cost includes material and labor to
	Install	L.F.	.63	2.03		2.66	install 2″ x 6″ let-in bracing.
	Demolish and Install	L.F.	.63	2.32		2.95	
	Reinstall	L.F.		1.63		1.63	
	Minimum Charge	Job		142		142	
2″ x 8″							
	Demolish	L.F.		.29		.29	Cost includes material and labor to
	Install	L.F.	.96	2.03		2.99	install 2″ x 8″ let-in bracing.
	Demolish and Install	L.F.	.96	2.32		3.28	
	Reinstall	L.F.		1.63		1.63	
	Minimum Charge	Job		142		142	
Earthquake Strapping							
	Install	Ea.	1.57	1.78		3.35	Includes labor and material to replace
	Minimum Charge	Job		142		142	an earthquake strap.
Hurricane Clips							
	Install	Ea.	1.39	1.96		3.35	Includes labor and material to install a
	Minimum Charge	Job		142		142	hurricane clip.
Stud							
2″ x 4″							
	Demolish	L.F.		.23		.23	Cost includes material and labor to
	Install	L.F.	.40	.52		.92	install 2″ x 4″ wall stud per L.F. of stud.
	Demolish and Install	L.F.	.40	.75		1.15	
	Reinstall	L.F.		.41		.41	
	Minimum Charge	Job		142		142	

Wall Framing System		Unit	Material	Labor	Equip.	Total	Specification
2″ x 6″							
	Demolish	L.F.		.29		.29	Cost includes material and labor to
	Install	L.F.	.63	.57		1.20	install 2″ x 6″ stud per L.F. of stud.
	Demolish and Install	L.F.	.63	.86		1.49	
	Reinstall	L.F.		.46		.46	
	Minimum Charge	Job		142		142	
Plates							
2″ x 4″							
	Demolish	L.F.		.21		.21	Cost includes material and labor to
	Install	L.F.	.40	.71		1.11	install 2″ x 4″ plate per L.F. of plate.
	Demolish and Install	L.F.	.40	.92		1.32	
	Reinstall	L.F.		.57		.57	
	Minimum Charge	Job		142		142	
2″ x 6″							
	Demolish	L.F.		.22		.22	Cost includes material and labor to
	Install	L.F.	.63	.76		1.39	install 2″ x 6″ plate per L.F. of plate.
	Demolish and Install	L.F.	.63	.98		1.61	
	Reinstall	L.F.		.61		.61	
	Minimum Charge	Job		142		142	
Headers							
2″ x 6″							
	Demolish	L.F.		.20		.20	Includes material and labor to install
	Install	L.F.	.63	1.58		2.21	header over wall openings and around
	Demolish and Install	L.F.	.63	1.78		2.41	floor, ceiling and roof openings or
	Clean	L.F.	.01	.26		.27	flush beam.
	Paint	L.F.	.09	1.02		1.11	
	Minimum Charge	Job		142		142	
2″ x 8″							
	Demolish	L.F.		.22		.22	Includes material and labor to install
	Install	L.F.	.96	1.68		2.64	header over wall openings and around
	Demolish and Install	L.F.	.96	1.90		2.86	floor, ceiling and roof openings or
	Clean	L.F.	.02	.26		.28	flush beam.
	Paint	L.F.	.12	1.38		1.50	
	Minimum Charge	Job		142		142	
2″ x 10″							
	Demolish	L.F.		.22		.22	Includes material and labor to install
	Install	L.F.	1.36	1.78		3.14	header over wall openings and around
	Demolish and Install	L.F.	1.36	2		3.36	floor, ceiling and roof openings or
	Clean	L.F.	.02	.26		.28	flush beam.
	Paint	L.F.	.14	1.70		1.84	
	Minimum Charge	Job		142		142	
2″ x 12″							
	Demolish	L.F.		.23		.23	Includes material and labor to install
	Install	L.F.	1.87	1.90		3.77	header over wall openings and around
	Demolish and Install	L.F.	1.87	2.13		4	floor, ceiling and roof openings or
	Clean	L.F.	.03	.27		.30	flush beam.
	Paint	L.F.	.18	2.04		2.22	
	Minimum Charge	Job		142		142	
4″ x 8″							
	Demolish	L.F.		.41		.41	Includes material and labor to install
	Install	L.F.	3.75	2.19		5.94	header over wall openings and around
	Demolish and Install	L.F.	3.75	2.60		6.35	floor, ceiling and roof openings or
	Clean	L.F.	.02	.26		.28	flush beam.
	Paint	L.F.	.12	1.38		1.50	
	Minimum Charge	Job		142		142	

Rough Frame / Structure

Wall Framing System

Wall Framing System	Unit	Material	Labor	Equip.	Total	Specification
4" x 10"						
Demolish	L.F.		.44		.44	Includes material and labor to install
Install	L.F.	4.70	2.37		7.07	header over wall openings and around
Demolish and Install	L.F.	4.70	2.81		7.51	floor, ceiling and roof openings or
Clean	L.F.	.02	.26		.28	flush beam.
Paint	L.F.	.14	1.70		1.84	
Minimum Charge	Job		142		142	
4" x 12"						
Demolish	L.F.		.46		.46	Includes material and labor to install
Install	L.F.	5.60	3		8.60	header over wall openings and around
Demolish and Install	L.F.	5.60	3.46		9.06	floor, ceiling and roof openings or
Clean	L.F.	.03	.27		.30	flush beam.
Paint	L.F.	.18	2.04		2.22	
Minimum Charge	Job		142		142	
6" x 8"						
Demolish	L.F.		.41		.41	Includes material and labor to install
Install	L.F.	10.10	1.58		11.68	header over wall openings and around
Demolish and Install	L.F.	10.10	1.99		12.09	floor, ceiling and roof openings or
Clean	L.F.	.02	.26		.28	flush beam.
Paint	L.F.	.12	1.38		1.50	
Minimum Charge	Job		142		142	
6" x 10"						
Demolish	L.F.		.44		.44	Includes material and labor to install
Install	L.F.	10.10	3.45		13.55	header over wall openings and around
Demolish and Install	L.F.	10.10	3.89		13.99	floor, ceiling and roof openings or
Clean	L.F.	.02	.26		.28	flush beam.
Paint	L.F.	.14	1.70		1.84	
Minimum Charge	Job		142		142	
6" x 12"						
Demolish	L.F.		.46		.46	Includes material and labor to install
Install	L.F.	13.95	4.07		18.02	header over wall openings and around
Demolish and Install	L.F.	13.95	4.53		18.48	floor, ceiling and roof openings or
Clean	L.F.	.03	.27		.30	flush beam.
Paint	L.F.	.18	.71		.89	
Minimum Charge	Job		142		142	

Rough-in Opening

Rough-in Opening	Unit	Material	Labor	Equip.	Total	Specification
Door w / 2" x 4" Lumber						
3' Wide						
Demolish	Ea.		7.20		7.20	Includes material and labor to install
Install	Ea.	16.55	8.90		25.45	header, double studs each side,
Demolish and Install	Ea.	16.55	16.10		32.65	cripples, blocking and nails, up to 3'
Reinstall	Ea.		7.12		7.12	opening in 2" x 4" stud wall 8' high.
Minimum Charge	Job		142		142	
4' Wide						
Demolish	Ea.		7.20		7.20	Includes material and labor to install
Install	Ea.	17.80	8.90		26.70	header, double studs each side,
Demolish and Install	Ea.	17.80	16.10		33.90	cripples, blocking and nails, up to 4'
Reinstall	Ea.		7.12		7.12	opening in 2" x 4" stud wall 8' high.
Minimum Charge	Job		142		142	
5' Wide						
Demolish	Ea.		7.20		7.20	Includes material and labor to install
Install	Ea.	22.50	8.90		31.40	header, double studs each side,
Demolish and Install	Ea.	22.50	16.10		38.60	cripples, blocking and nails, up to 5'
Reinstall	Ea.		7.12		7.12	opening in 2" x 4" stud wall 8' high.
Minimum Charge	Job		142		142	

Rough Frame / Structure

Rough-in Opening		Unit	Material	Labor	Equip.	Total	Specification
6' Wide							
	Demolish	Ea.		7.20		7.20	Includes material and labor to install
	Install	Ea.	24	8.90		32.90	header, double studs each side,
	Demolish and Install	Ea.	24	16.10		40.10	cripples, blocking and nails, up to 6'
	Reinstall	Ea.		7.12		7.12	opening in 2" x 4" stud wall 8' high.
	Minimum Charge	Job		142		142	
8' Wide							
	Demolish	Ea.		7.65		7.65	Includes material and labor to install
	Install	Ea.	35	9.50		44.50	header, double studs each side,
	Demolish and Install	Ea.	35	17.15		52.15	cripples, blocking and nails, up to 8'
	Reinstall	Ea.		7.59		7.59	opening in 2" x 4" stud wall 8' high.
	Minimum Charge	Job		142		142	
10' Wide							
	Demolish	Ea.		7.65		7.65	Includes material and labor to install
	Install	Ea.	50.50	9.50		60	header, double studs each side,
	Demolish and Install	Ea.	50.50	17.15		67.65	cripples, blocking and nails, up to 10'
	Reinstall	Ea.		7.59		7.59	opening in 2" x 4" stud wall 8' high.
	Minimum Charge	Job		142		142	
12' Wide							
	Demolish	Ea.		7.65		7.65	Includes material and labor to install
	Install	Ea.	64.50	9.50		74	header, double studs each side,
	Demolish and Install	Ea.	64.50	17.15		81.65	cripples, blocking and nails, up to 12'
	Reinstall	Ea.		7.59		7.59	opening in 2" x 4" stud wall 8' high
	Minimum Charge	Job		142		142	

Door w / 2" x 6" Lumber

		Unit	Material	Labor	Equip.	Total	Specification
3' Wide							
	Demolish	Ea.		7.20		7.20	Includes material and labor to install
	Install	Ea.	24	8.90		32.90	header, double studs each side,
	Demolish and Install	Ea.	24	16.10		40.10	cripples, blocking and nails, up to 3'
	Reinstall	Ea.		7.12		7.12	opening in 2" x 6" stud wall 8' high.
	Minimum Charge	Job		142		142	
4' Wide							
	Demolish	Ea.		7.20		7.20	Includes material and labor to install
	Install	Ea.	25.50	8.90		34.40	header, double studs each side,
	Demolish and Install	Ea.	25.50	16.10		41.60	cripples, blocking and nails, up to 4'
	Reinstall	Ea.		7.12		7.12	opening in 2" x 6" stud wall 8' high.
	Minimum Charge	Job		142		142	
5' Wide							
	Demolish	Ea.		7.20		7.20	Includes material and labor to install
	Install	Ea.	29.50	8.90		38.40	header, double studs each side,
	Demolish and Install	Ea.	29.50	16.10		45.60	cripples, blocking and nails up to 5'
	Reinstall	Ea.		7.12		7.12	opening in 2" x 6" stud wall 8' high.
	Minimum Charge	Job		142		142	
6' Wide							
	Demolish	Ea.		7.20		7.20	Includes material and labor to install
	Install	Ea.	32	8.90		40.90	header, double studs each side,
	Demolish and Install	Ea.	32	16.10		48.10	cripples, blocking and nails up to 6'
	Reinstall	Ea.		7.12		7.12	opening in 2" x 6" stud wall 8' high.
	Minimum Charge	Job		142		142	
8' Wide							
	Demolish	Ea.		7.65		7.65	Includes material and labor to install
	Install	Ea.	42.50	9.50		52	header, double studs each side,
	Demolish and Install	Ea.	42.50	17.15		59.65	cripples, blocking and nails up to 8'
	Reinstall	Ea.		7.59		7.59	opening in 2" x 6" stud wall 8' high.
	Minimum Charge	Job		142		142	
10' Wide							
	Demolish	Ea.		7.65		7.65	Includes material and labor to install
	Install	Ea.	58.50	9.50		68	header, double studs each side,
	Demolish and Install	Ea.	58.50	17.15		75.65	cripples, blocking and nails up to 10'
	Reinstall	Ea.		7.59		7.59	opening in 2" x 6" stud wall 8' high.
	Minimum Charge	Job		142		142	

Rough Frame / Structure

Rough-in Opening

Rough-in Opening	Unit	Material	Labor	Equip.	Total	Specification
12' Wide						
Demolish	Ea.		7.65		7.65	Includes material and labor to install
Install	Ea.	71.50	9.50		81	header, double studs each side,
Demolish and Install	Ea.	71.50	17.15		88.65	cripples, blocking and nails, up to 12'
Reinstall	Ea.		7.59		7.59	opening in 2" x 6" stud wall 8' high.
Minimum Charge	Job		142		142	

Rough-in Opening

Rough-in Opening	Unit	Material	Labor	Equip.	Total	Specification
Window w / 2" x 4" Lumber						
2' Wide						
Demolish	Ea.		9.55		9.55	Includes material and labor to install
Install	Ea.	17.45	11.85		29.30	header, double studs each side of
Demolish and Install	Ea.	17.45	21.40		38.85	opening, cripples, blocking, nails and
Reinstall	Ea.		9.49		9.49	sub-sills for opening up to 2' in a 2" x
Minimum Charge	Job		142		142	4" stud wall 8' high.
3' Wide						
Demolish	Ea.		9.55		9.55	Includes material and labor to install
Install	Ea.	20.50	11.85		32.35	header, double studs each side of
Demolish and Install	Ea.	20.50	21.40		41.90	opening, cripples, blocking, nails and
Reinstall	Ea.		9.49		9.49	sub-sills for opening up to 3' in a 2" x
Minimum Charge	Job		142		142	4" stud wall 8' high.
4' Wide						
Demolish	Ea.		9.55		9.55	Includes material and labor to install
Install	Ea.	22.50	11.85		34.35	header, double studs each side of
Demolish and Install	Ea.	22.50	21.40		43.90	opening, cripples, blocking, nails and
Reinstall	Ea.		9.49		9.49	sub-sills for opening up to 4' in a 2" x
Minimum Charge	Job		142		142	4" stud wall 8' high.
5' Wide						
Demolish	Ea.		9.55		9.55	Includes material and labor to install
Install	Ea.	27.50	11.85		39.35	header, double studs each side of
Demolish and Install	Ea.	27.50	21.40		48.90	opening, cripples, blocking, nails and
Reinstall	Ea.		9.49		9.49	sub-sills for opening up to 5' in a 2" x
Minimum Charge	Job		142		142	4" stud wall 8' high.
6' Wide						
Demolish	Ea.		9.55		9.55	Includes material and labor to install
Install	Ea.	30.50	11.85		42.35	header, double studs each side of
Demolish and Install	Ea.	30.50	21.40		51.90	opening, cripples, blocking, nails and
Reinstall	Ea.		9.49		9.49	sub-sills for opening up to 6' in a 2" x
Minimum Charge	Job		142		142	4" stud wall 8' high.
7' Wide						
Demolish	Ea.		9.55		9.55	Includes material and labor to install
Install	Ea.	39.50	11.85		51.35	header, double studs each side of
Demolish and Install	Ea.	39.50	21.40		60.90	opening, cripples, blocking, nails and
Reinstall	Ea.		9.49		9.49	sub-sills for opening up to 7' in a 2" x
Minimum Charge	Job		142		142	4" stud wall 8' high.
8' Wide						
Demolish	Ea.		10.45		10.45	Includes material and labor to install
Install	Ea.	43.50	12.95		56.45	header, double studs each side of
Demolish and Install	Ea.	43.50	23.40		66.90	opening, cripples, blocking, nails and
Reinstall	Ea.		10.36		10.36	sub-sills for opening up to 8' in a 2" x
Minimum Charge	Job		142		142	4" stud wall 8' high.

Rough-in Opening

Rough-in Opening	Unit	Material	Labor	Equip.	Total	Specification
10' Wide						
Demolish	Ea.		10.45		10.45	Includes material and labor to install
Install	Ea.	60	12.95		72.95	header, double studs each side of
Demolish and Install	Ea.	60	23.40		83.40	opening, cripples, blocking, nails and
Reinstall	Ea.		10.36		10.36	sub-sills for opening up to 10' in a 2" x
Minimum Charge	Job		142		142	4" stud wall 8' high.
12' Wide						
Demolish	Ea.		10.45		10.45	Includes material and labor to install
Install	Ea.	76	12.95		88.95	header, double studs each side of
Demolish and Install	Ea.	76	23.40		99.40	opening, cripples, blocking, nails and
Reinstall	Ea.		10.36		10.36	sub-sills for opening up to 12' in a 2" x
Minimum Charge	Job		142		142	4" stud wall 8' high.

Window w / 2" x 6" Lumber

	Unit	Material	Labor	Equip.	Total	Specification
2' Wide						
Demolish	Ea.		9.55		9.55	Includes material and labor to install
Install	Ea.	26.50	11.85		38.35	header, double studs each side of
Demolish and Install	Ea.	26.50	21.40		47.90	opening, cripples, blocking, nails and
Reinstall	Ea.		9.49		9.49	sub-sills for opening up to 2' in a 2" x
Minimum Charge	Job		142		142	6" stud wall 8' high.
3' Wide						
Demolish	Ea.		9.55		9.55	Includes material and labor to install
Install	Ea.	30.50	11.85		42.35	header, double studs each side of
Demolish and Install	Ea.	30.50	21.40		51.90	opening, cripples, blocking, nails and
Reinstall	Ea.		9.49		9.49	sub-sills for opening up to 3' in a 2" x
Minimum Charge	Job		142		142	6" stud wall 8' high.
4' Wide						
Demolish	Ea.		9.55		9.55	Includes material and labor to install
Install	Ea.	5.30	11.85		17.15	header, double studs each side of
Demolish and Install	Ea.	5.30	21.40		26.70	opening, cripples, blocking, nails and
Reinstall	Ea.		9.49		9.49	sub-sills for opening up to 4' in a 2" x
Minimum Charge	Job		142		142	6" stud wall 8' high.
5' Wide						
Demolish	Ea.		9.55		9.55	Includes material and labor to install
Install	Ea.	37.50	11.85		49.35	header, double studs each side of
Demolish and Install	Ea.	37.50	21.40		58.90	opening, cripples, blocking, nails and
Reinstall	Ea.		9.49		9.49	sub-sills for opening up to 5' in a 2" x
Minimum Charge	Job		142		142	6" stud wall 8' high.
6' Wide						
Demolish	Ea.		9.55		9.55	Includes material and labor to install
Install	Ea.	41.50	11.85		53.35	header, double studs each side of
Demolish and Install	Ea.	41.50	21.40		62.90	opening, cripples, blocking, nails and
Reinstall	Ea.		9.49		9.49	sub-sills for opening up to 6' in a 2" x
Minimum Charge	Job		142		142	6" stud wall 8' high.
7' Wide						
Demolish	Ea.		9.55		9.55	Includes material and labor to install
Install	Ea.	51	11.85		62.85	header, double studs each side of
Demolish and Install	Ea.	51	21.40		72.40	opening, cripples, blocking, nails and
Reinstall	Ea.		9.49		9.49	sub-sills for opening up to 7' in a 2" x
Minimum Charge	Job		142		142	6" stud wall 8' high.

Rough Frame / Structure

Rough-in Opening

Rough-in Opening	Unit	Material	Labor	Equip.	Total	Specification
8' Wide						
Demolish	Ea.		10.45		10.45	Includes material and labor to install
Install	Ea.	55.50	12.95		68.45	header, double studs each side of
Demolish and Install	Ea.	55.50	23.40		78.90	opening, cripples, blocking, nails and
Reinstall	Ea.		10.36		10.36	sub-sills for opening up to 8' in a 2" x
Minimum Charge	Job		142		142	6" stud wall 8' high.
10' Wide						
Demolish	Ea.		10.45		10.45	Includes material and labor to install
Install	Ea.	73	12.95		85.95	header, double studs each side of
Demolish and Install	Ea.	73	23.40		96.40	opening, cripples, blocking, nails and
Reinstall	Ea.		10.36		10.36	sub-sills for opening up to 10' in a 2" x
Minimum Charge	Job		142		142	6" stud wall 8' high.
12' Wide						
Demolish	Ea.		10.45		10.45	Includes material and labor to install
Install	Ea.	90	12.95		102.95	header, double studs each side of
Demolish and Install	Ea.	90	23.40		113.40	opening, cripples, blocking, nails and
Reinstall	Ea.		10.36		10.36	sub-sills for opening up to 12' in a 2" x
Minimum Charge	Job		142		142	6" stud wall 8' high.

Glue-Laminated Beams

Glue-Laminated Beams	Unit	Material	Labor	Equip.	Total	Specification
3-1/2" x 6"						
Demolish	L.F.		2.85		2.85	Includes material and labor to install
Install	L.F.	4.88	2.15	1.11	8.14	glue-laminated wood beam.
Demolish and Install	L.F.	4.88	5	1.11	10.99	
Reinstall	L.F.		1.72	.89	2.61	
Clean	L.F.	.09	.26		.35	
Paint	L.F.	.28	.75		1.03	
Minimum Charge	Job		142		142	
3-1/2" x 9"						
Demolish	L.F.		2.85		2.85	Includes material and labor to install
Install	L.F.	4.88	2.15	1.11	8.14	glue-laminated wood beam.
Demolish and Install	L.F.	4.88	5	1.11	10.99	
Reinstall	L.F.		1.72	.89	2.61	
Clean	L.F.	.12	.27		.39	
Paint	L.F.	.35	.97		1.32	
Minimum Charge	Job		142		142	
3-1/2" x 12"						
Demolish	L.F.		4.29		4.29	Includes material and labor to install
Install	L.F.	6.05	2.15	1.11	9.31	glue-laminated wood beam.
Demolish and Install	L.F.	6.05	6.44	1.11	13.60	
Reinstall	L.F.		1.72	.89	2.61	
Clean	L.F.	.15	.28		.43	
Paint	L.F.	.43	1.22		1.65	
Minimum Charge	Job		142		142	
3-1/2" x 15"						
Demolish	L.F.		4.29		4.29	Includes material and labor to install
Install	L.F.	8.20	2.22	1.15	11.57	glue-laminated wood beam.
Demolish and Install	L.F.	8.20	6.51	1.15	15.86	
Reinstall	L.F.		1.78	.92	2.70	
Clean	L.F.	.18	.29		.47	
Paint	L.F.	.51	1.42		1.93	
Minimum Charge	Job		142		142	

Rough Frame / Structure

Glue-Laminated Beams		Unit	Material	Labor	Equip.	Total	Specification
3-1/2" x 18"							
	Demolish	L.F.		5.35		5.35	Includes material and labor to install
	Install	L.F.	9.80	2.22	1.15	13.17	glue-laminated wood beam.
	Demolish and Install	L.F.	9.80	7.57	1.15	18.52	
	Reinstall	L.F.		1.78	.92	2.70	
	Clean	L.F.	.21	.30		.51	
	Paint	L.F.	.59	1.65		2.24	
	Minimum Charge	Job		142		142	
5-1/8" x 6"							
	Demolish	L.F.		4.29		4.29	Includes material and labor to install
	Install	L.F.	9.45	2.15	1.11	12.71	glue-laminated wood beam.
	Demolish and Install	L.F.	9.45	6.44	1.11	17	
	Reinstall	L.F.		1.72	.89	2.61	
	Clean	L.F.	.10	.26		.36	
	Paint	L.F.	.29	.82		1.11	
	Minimum Charge	Job		142		142	
5-1/8" x 9"							
	Demolish	L.F.		5.35		5.35	Includes material and labor to install
	Install	L.F.	9.45	2.15	1.11	12.71	glue-laminated wood beam.
	Demolish and Install	L.F.	9.45	7.50	1.11	18.06	
	Reinstall	L.F.		1.72	.89	2.61	
	Clean	L.F.	.13	.27		.40	
	Paint	L.F.	.37	1.05		1.42	
	Minimum Charge	Job		142		142	
5-1/8" x 12"							
	Demolish	L.F.		6.35		6.35	Includes material and labor to install
	Install	L.F.	10.80	2.15	1.11	14.06	glue-laminated wood beam.
	Demolish and Install	L.F.	10.80	8.50	1.11	20.41	
	Reinstall	L.F.		1.72	.89	2.61	
	Clean	L.F.	.15	.28		.43	
	Paint	L.F.	.46	1.28		1.74	
	Minimum Charge	Job		142		142	
5-1/8" x 18"							
	Demolish	L.F.		10.70		10.70	Includes material and labor to install
	Install	L.F.	16.05	2.22	1.15	19.42	glue-laminated wood beam.
	Demolish and Install	L.F.	16.05	12.92	1.15	30.12	
	Reinstall	L.F.		1.78	.92	2.70	
	Clean	L.F.	.22	.30		.52	
	Paint	L.F.	.54	1.72		2.26	
	Minimum Charge	Job		142		142	
6-3/4" x 12"							
	Demolish	L.F.		6.35		6.35	Includes material and labor to install
	Install	L.F.	14.10	2.22	1.15	17.47	glue-laminated wood beam.
	Demolish and Install	L.F.	14.10	8.57	1.15	23.82	
	Reinstall	L.F.		1.78	.92	2.70	
	Clean	L.F.	.18	.29		.47	
	Paint	L.F.	.51	1.42		1.93	
	Minimum Charge	Job		142		142	
6-3/4" x 15"							
	Demolish	L.F.		10.70		10.70	Includes material and labor to install
	Install	L.F.	17.60	2.22	1.15	20.97	glue-laminated wood beam.
	Demolish and Install	L.F.	17.60	12.92	1.15	31.67	
	Reinstall	L.F.		1.78	.92	2.70	
	Clean	L.F.	.21	.30		.51	
	Paint	L.F.	.59	1.65		2.24	
	Minimum Charge	Job		142		142	

Rough Frame / Structure

Glue-Laminated Beams

Glue-Laminated Beams	Unit	Material	Labor	Equip.	Total	Specification
6-3/4″ x 18″						
Demolish	L.F.		10.70		10.70	Includes material and labor to install
Install	L.F.	21	2.30	1.19	24.49	glue-laminated wood beam.
Demolish and Install	L.F.	21	13	1.19	35.19	
Reinstall	L.F.		1.84	.95	2.79	
Clean	L.F.	.23	.31		.54	
Paint	L.F.	.68	1.88		2.56	
Minimum Charge	Job		142		142	

Hardware

	Unit	Material	Labor	Equip.	Total	Specification
5-1/4″ Glue-Lam Seat						
Install	Ea.	45.50	1.58		47.08	Includes labor and material to install
Minimum Charge	Job		142		142	beam hangers.
6-3/4″ Glue-Lam Seat						
Install	Ea.	47.50	1.58		49.08	Includes labor and material to install
Minimum Charge	Job		142		142	beam hangers.
8-3/4″ Glue-Lam Seat						
Install	Ea.	54	1.58		55.58	Includes labor and material to install
Minimum Charge	Job		142		142	beam hangers.
Earthquake Strapping						
Install	Ea.	1.57	1.78		3.35	Includes labor and material to replace
Minimum Charge	Job		142		142	an earthquake strap.
Hurricane Clips						
Install	Ea.	1.39	1.96		3.35	Includes labor and material to install a
Minimum Charge	Job		142		142	hurricane clip.

Metal Stud Framing

Metal Stud Framing	Unit	Material	Labor	Equip.	Total	Specification
16″ O.C. System						
4″, 16 Ga.						
Demolish	S.F.		.86		.86	Includes material and labor to install
Install	S.F.	.73	.88		1.61	load bearing cold rolled metal stud
Demolish and Install	S.F.	.73	1.74		2.47	walls, to 10′ high, including studs, top
Reinstall	S.F.		.70		.70	and bottom track and screws.
Minimum Charge	Job		142		142	
6″, 16 Ga.						
Demolish	S.F.		.86		.86	Includes material and labor to install
Install	S.F.	.91	.89		1.80	load bearing cold rolled metal stud
Demolish and Install	S.F.	.91	1.75		2.66	walls, to 10′ high, including studs, top
Reinstall	S.F.		.71		.71	and bottom track and screws.
Minimum Charge	Job		142		142	
4″, 25 Ga.						
Demolish	S.F.		.59		.59	Includes material and labor to install
Install	S.F.	.23	.60		.83	cold rolled metal stud walls, to 10′
Demolish and Install	S.F.	.23	1.19		1.42	high, including studs, top and bottom
Reinstall	S.F.		.48		.48	track and screws.
Minimum Charge	Job		142		142	
6″, 25 Ga.						
Demolish	S.F.		.59		.59	Includes material and labor to install
Install	S.F.	.34	.61		.95	cold rolled metal stud walls, to 10′
Demolish and Install	S.F.	.34	1.20		1.54	high, including studs, top and bottom
Reinstall	S.F.		.48		.48	track and screws.
Minimum Charge	Job		142		142	

Rough Frame / Structure

Metal Stud Framing

	Unit	Material	Labor	Equip.	Total	Specification
24″ O.C. System						
4″, 25 Ga.						
Demolish	S.F.		.50		.50	Includes material and labor to install
Install	S.F.	.18	.38		.56	cold rolled metal stud walls, to 10′
Demolish and Install	S.F.	.18	.88		1.06	high, including studs, top and bottom
Reinstall	S.F.		.31		.31	track and screws.
Minimum Charge	Job		142		142	
6″, 25 Ga.						
Demolish	S.F.		.50		.50	Includes material and labor to install
Install	S.F.	.25	.39		.64	cold rolled metal stud walls, to 10′
Demolish and Install	S.F.	.25	.89		1.14	high, including studs, top and bottom
Reinstall	S.F.		.31		.31	track and screws.
Minimum Charge	Job		142		142	
4″, 16 Ga.						
Demolish	L.F.		5.75		5.75	Includes material and labor to install
Install	S.F.	.53	.63		1.16	load bearing cold rolled metal stud
Demolish and Install	S.F.	.53	6.38		6.91	walls, to 10′ high, including studs, top
Reinstall	S.F.		.51		.51	and bottom track and screws.
Minimum Charge	Job		142		142	
6″, 16 Ga.						
Demolish	L.F.		5.75		5.75	Includes material and labor to install
Install	S.F.	.66	.65		1.31	load bearing cold rolled metal stud
Demolish and Install	S.F.	.66	6.40		7.06	walls, to 10′ high, including studs, top
Reinstall	S.F.		.52		.52	and bottom track and screws.
Minimum Charge	Job		142		142	

Metal Joist

	Unit	Material	Labor	Equip.	Total	Specification
Bar Joist						
18K9						
Demolish	L.F.		.68	.40	1.08	Includes material, labor and equipment
Install	L.F.	5.15	1.59	.88	7.62	to install open web joist.
Demolish and Install	L.F.	5.15	2.27	1.28	8.70	
Reinstall	L.F.		1.27	.70	1.97	
Minimum Charge	Job		1275	670	1945	
16K6						
Demolish	L.F.		.68	.40	1.08	Includes material, labor and equipment
Install	L.F.	2.83	1.08	.07	3.98	to install open web joist.
Demolish and Install	L.F.	2.83	1.76	.47	5.06	
Reinstall	L.F.		.86	.06	.92	
Minimum Charge	Job		178		178	

Exterior Sheathing

	Unit	Material	Labor	Equip.	Total	Specification
CDX Plywood						
5/16″						
Demolish	S.F.		.20		.20	Cost includes material and labor to
Install	S.F.	.47	.36		.83	install 5/16″ CDX plywood sheathing.
Demolish and Install	S.F.	.47	.56		1.03	
Minimum Charge	Job		142		142	
3/8″						
Demolish	S.F.		.20		.20	Cost includes material and labor to
Install	S.F.	.48	.47		.95	install 3/8″ CDX plywood sheathing.
Demolish and Install	S.F.	.48	.67		1.15	
Minimum Charge	Job		142		142	

Rough Frame / Structure

Exterior Sheathing

		Unit	Material	Labor	Equip.	Total	Specification
1/2"							
	Demolish	S.F.		.20		.20	Cost includes material and labor to
	Install	S.F.	.54	.51		1.05	install 1/2" CDX plywood sheathing.
	Demolish and Install	S.F.	.54	.71		1.25	
	Minimum Charge	Job		142		142	
5/8"							
	Demolish	S.F.		.21		.21	Cost includes material and labor to
	Install	S.F.	.63	.54		1.17	install 5/8" CDX plywood sheathing.
	Demolish and Install	S.F.	.63	.75		1.38	
	Minimum Charge	Job		142		142	
3/4"							
	Demolish	S.F.		.21		.21	Cost includes material and labor to
	Install	S.F.	.73	.58		1.31	install 3/4" CDX plywood sheathing.
	Demolish and Install	S.F.	.73	.79		1.52	
	Minimum Charge	Job		142		142	
OSB							
1/2"							
	Demolish	S.F.		.20		.20	Cost includes material and labor to
	Install	S.F.	.39	.22		.61	install 4' x 8' x 1/2" OSB sheathing.
	Demolish and Install	S.F.	.39	.42		.81	
	Minimum Charge	Job		142		142	
5/8"							
	Demolish	S.F.		.21		.21	Cost includes material and labor to
	Install	S.F.	.54	.23		.77	install 4' x 8' x 5/8" OSB sheathing.
	Demolish and Install	S.F.	.54	.44		.98	
	Minimum Charge	Job		142		142	
Vapor Barrier							
Black Paper							
	Install	S.F.	.02	.08		.10	Includes material and labor to install
	Minimum Charge	Job		142		142	#15 felt building paper.

Plywood Sheathing

		Unit	Material	Labor	Equip.	Total	Specification
Finish Plywood							
5/16"							
	Demolish	S.F.		.20		.20	Includes material and labor to install
	Install	S.F.	.58	.18		.76	exterior 5/16" AC plywood on walls.
	Demolish and Install	S.F.	.58	.38		.96	
	Minimum Charge	Job		142		142	
3/8"							
	Demolish	S.F.		.20		.20	Includes material and labor to install
	Install	S.F.	.58	.24		.82	exterior 3/8" AC plywood on walls.
	Demolish and Install	S.F.	.58	.44		1.02	
	Minimum Charge	Job		142		142	
1/2"							
	Demolish	S.F.		.20		.20	Includes material and labor to install
	Install	S.F.	.70	.25		.95	exterior 1/2" AC plywood on walls.
	Demolish and Install	S.F.	.70	.45		1.15	
	Minimum Charge	Job		142		142	
5/8"							
	Demolish	S.F.		.21		.21	Includes material and labor to install
	Install	S.F.	.77	.25		1.02	exterior 5/8" AC plywood on walls.
	Demolish and Install	S.F.	.77	.46		1.23	
	Reinstall	S.F.		.25		.25	
	Minimum Charge	Job		142		142	

Rough Frame / Structure

Plywood Sheathing

	Unit	Material	Labor	Equip.	Total	Specification
3/4"						
Demolish	S.F.		.21		.21	Includes material and labor to install
Install	S.F.	.94	.25		1.19	exterior 3/4" AC plywood on walls.
Demolish and Install	S.F.	.94	.46		1.40	
Reinstall	S.F.		.25		.25	
Minimum Charge	Job		142		142	

Stairs

	Unit	Material	Labor	Equip.	Total	Specification
Job-Built						
Treads and Risers						
Demolish	Ea.		28.50		28.50	Includes material and labor to install
Install	Ea.	420	35.50		455.50	three 2" x 12" stringers, treads and
Demolish and Install	Ea.	420	64		484	risers of 3/4" CDX plywood, installed
Clean	Flight	2.81	18.10		20.91	in a straight or "L" shaped run
Paint	Ea.	.08	51		51.08	including carpet.
Minimum Charge	Job		142		142	
Landing						
Demolish	S.F.		.23		.23	Includes material and labor to install
Install	S.F.	45	1.98		46.98	landing framing, 3/4" CDX plywood
Demolish and Install	S.F.	45	2.21		47.21	surface and carpet.
Clean	S.F.		.26		.26	
Paint	S.F.	.25	.63		.88	
Minimum Charge	Job		142		142	

Ceiling Framing

	Unit	Material	Labor	Equip.	Total	Specification
16" O.C. System						
2" x 6" Joists						
Demolish	S.F.		.35		.35	Cost includes material and labor to
Install	S.F.	.47	.47		.94	install 2" x 6" joists including end and
Demolish and Install	S.F.	.47	.82		1.29	header joist installed 16" O.C. Does
Reinstall	S.F.		.37		.37	not include beams, ledger strips,
Minimum Charge	Job		142		142	blocking or bridging.
2" x 8" Joists						
Demolish	S.F.		.37		.37	Cost includes material and labor to
Install	S.F.	.73	.58		1.31	install 2" x 8" joists including end and
Demolish and Install	S.F.	.73	.95		1.68	header joist installed 16" O.C. Does
Reinstall	S.F.		.46		.46	not include beams, ledger strips,
Minimum Charge	Job		142		142	blocking or bridging.
2" x 10" Joists						
Demolish	S.F.		.38		.38	Cost includes material and labor to
Install	S.F.	1.03	.68		1.71	install 2" x 10" joists including end and
Demolish and Install	S.F.	1.03	1.06		2.09	header joist installed 16" O.C. Does
Reinstall	S.F.		.55		.55	not include beams, ledger strips,
Minimum Charge	Job		142		142	blocking or bridging.
2" x 12" Joists						
Demolish	S.F.		.39		.39	Cost includes material and labor to
Install	S.F.	1.42	.83		2.25	install 2" x 12" joists including end and
Demolish and Install	S.F.	1.42	1.22		2.64	header joist installed 16" O.C. Does
Reinstall	S.F.		.67		.67	not include beams, ledger strips,
Minimum Charge	Job		142		142	blocking or bridging.

Rough Frame / Structure

Ceiling Framing		Unit	Material	Labor	Equip.	Total	Specification
Block / Bridge							Includes material and labor to install
	Demolish	Ea.		.72		.72	set of cross bridging or per block of
	Install	Ea.	1.83	1.60		3.43	solid bridging for 2" x 10" joists cut to
	Demolish and Install	Ea.	1.83	2.32		4.15	size on site.
	Minimum Charge	Job		142		142	
24" O.C. System							
2" x 6" Joists							Cost includes material and labor to
	Demolish	S.F.		.24		.24	install 2" x 6" joists including end and
	Install	S.F.	.32	.31		.63	header joist installed 24" O.C. Does
	Demolish and Install	S.F.	.32	.55		.87	not include beams, ledger strips,
	Reinstall	S.F.		.25		.25	blocking or bridging.
	Minimum Charge	Job		142		142	
2" x 8" Joists							Cost includes material and labor to
	Demolish	S.F.		.25		.25	install 2" x 8" joists including end and
	Install	S.F.	.48	.38		.86	header joist installed 24" O.C. Does
	Demolish and Install	S.F.	.48	.63		1.11	not include beams, ledger strips,
	Reinstall	S.F.		.31		.31	blocking or bridging.
	Minimum Charge	Job		142		142	
2" x 10" Joists							Cost includes material and labor to
	Demolish	S.F.		.25		.25	install 2" x 10" joists including end and
	Install	S.F.	.69	.45		1.14	header joist installed 24" O.C. Does
	Demolish and Install	S.F.	.69	.70		1.39	not include beams, ledger strips,
	Reinstall	S.F.		.36		.36	blocking or bridging.
	Minimum Charge	Job		142		142	
2" x 12" Joists							Cost includes material and labor to
	Demolish	S.F.		.26		.26	install 2" x 12" joists including end and
	Install	S.F.	.95	.56		1.51	header joist installed 24" O.C. Does
	Demolish and Install	S.F.	.95	.82		1.77	not include beams, ledger strips,
	Reinstall	S.F.		.44		.44	blocking or bridging.
	Minimum Charge	Job		142		142	
Block / Bridge							Includes material and labor to install
	Demolish	Ea.		.72		.72	set of cross bridging or per block of
	Install	Ea.	1.83	1.60		3.43	solid bridging for 2" x 10" joists cut to
	Demolish and Install	Ea.	1.83	2.32		4.15	size on site.
	Minimum Charge	Job		142		142	
Ledger Strips							
1" x 2"							Cost includes material and labor to
	Demolish	L.F.		.19		.19	install 1" x 2" ledger strip nailed to the
	Install	L.F.	.23	.83		1.06	face of studs, beams or joist.
	Demolish and Install	L.F.	.23	1.02		1.25	
	Minimum Charge	Job		142		142	
1" x 3"							Includes material and labor to install
	Demolish	L.F.		.19		.19	up to 1" x 4" ledger strip nailed to the
	Install	L.F.	.66	.95		1.61	face of studs, beams or joist.
	Demolish and Install	L.F.	.66	1.14		1.80	
	Minimum Charge	Job		142		142	
1" x 4"							Includes material and labor to install
	Demolish	L.F.		.19		.19	up to 1" x 4" ledger strip nailed to the
	Install	L.F.	.66	.95		1.61	face of studs, beams or joist.
	Demolish and Install	L.F.	.66	1.14		1.80	
	Minimum Charge	Job		142		142	
2" x 2"							Cost includes material and labor to
	Demolish	L.F.		.21		.21	install 2" x 2" ledger strip nailed to the
	Install	L.F.	.28	.86		1.14	face of studs, beams or joist.
	Demolish and Install	L.F.	.28	1.07		1.35	
	Minimum Charge	Job		142		142	

Rough Frame / Structure

Ceiling Framing

Ceiling Framing	Unit	Material	Labor	Equip.	Total	Specification
2" x 4"						
Demolish	L.F.		.23		.23	Cost includes material and labor to
Install	L.F.	.40	1.14		1.54	install 2" x 4" ledger strip nailed to the
Demolish and Install	L.F.	.40	1.37		1.77	face of studs, beams or joist.
Reinstall	L.F.		.91		.91	
Minimum Charge	Job		142		142	
Ledger Boards						
2" x 4"						
Demolish	L.F.		.23		.23	Cost includes material and labor to
Install	L.F.	1.63	1.58		3.21	install 2" x 4" ledger board fastened to
Demolish and Install	L.F.	1.63	1.81		3.44	a wall, joists or studs.
Reinstall	L.F.		1.27		1.27	
Minimum Charge	Job		142		142	
4" x 6"						
Demolish	L.F.		.38		.38	Cost includes material and labor to
Install	L.F.	4.07	1.78		5.85	install 4" x 6" ledger board fastened to
Demolish and Install	L.F.	4.07	2.16		6.23	a wall, joists or studs.
Reinstall	L.F.		1.42		1.42	
Minimum Charge	Job		142		142	
4" x 8"						
Demolish	L.F.		.51		.51	Cost includes material and labor to
Install	L.F.	5	1.78		6.78	install 4" x 8" ledger board fastened to
Demolish and Install	L.F.	5	2.29		7.29	a wall, joists or studs.
Reinstall	L.F.		1.42		1.42	
Minimum Charge	Job		142		142	
Earthquake Strapping						
Install	Ea.	1.57	1.78		3.35	Includes labor and material to replace
Minimum Charge	Job		142		142	an earthquake strap.
Hurricane Clips						
Install	Ea.	1.39	1.96		3.35	Includes labor and material to install a
Minimum Charge	Job		142		142	hurricane clip.

Roof Framing

Roof Framing	Unit	Material	Labor	Equip.	Total	Specification
16" O.C. System						
2" x 4" Rafters						
Demolish	S.F.		.52		.52	Cost includes material and labor to
Install	S.F.	.30	.25		.55	install 2" x 4", 16" O.C. rafter framing
Demolish and Install	S.F.	.30	.77		1.07	for flat, shed or gable roofs, 25' span,
Reinstall	S.F.		.20		.20	up to 5/12 slope, per S.F. of roof.
Minimum Charge	Job		142		142	
2" x 6" Rafters						
Demolish	S.F.		.55		.55	Cost includes material and labor to
Install	S.F.	.46	.27		.73	install 2" x 6", 16" O.C. rafter framing
Demolish and Install	S.F.	.46	.82		1.28	for flat, shed or gable roofs, 25' span,
Reinstall	S.F.		.21		.21	up to 5/12 slope, per S.F. of roof.
Minimum Charge	Job		142		142	
2" x 8" Rafters						
Demolish	S.F.		.56		.56	Cost includes material and labor to
Install	S.F.	.72	.28		1	install 2" x 8", 16" O.C. rafter framing
Demolish and Install	S.F.	.72	.84		1.56	for flat, shed or gable roofs, 25' span,
Reinstall	S.F.		.23		.23	up to 5/12 slope, per S.F. of roof.
Minimum Charge	Job		142		142	

Rough Frame / Structure

Roof Framing		Unit	Material	Labor	Equip.	Total	Specification
2" x 10" Rafters							Cost includes material and labor to
	Demolish	S.F.		.56		.56	install 2" x 10", 16" O.C. rafter
	Install	S.F.	1.02	.43		1.45	framing for flat, shed or gable roofs,
	Demolish and Install	S.F.	1.02	.99		2.01	25' span, up to 5/12 slope, per S.F.
	Reinstall	S.F.		.35		.35	of roof.
	Minimum Charge	Job		142		142	
2" x 12" Rafters							Cost includes material and labor to
	Demolish	S.F.		.57		.57	install 2" x 12", 16" O.C. rafter
	Install	S.F.	1.40	.47		1.87	framing for flat, shed or gable roofs,
	Demolish and Install	S.F.	1.40	1.04		2.44	25' span, up to 5/12 slope, per S.F.
	Reinstall	S.F.		.38		.38	of roof.
	Minimum Charge	Job		142		142	
24" O.C. System							
2" x 4" Rafters							Cost includes material and labor to
	Demolish	S.F.		.39		.39	install 2" x 4", 24" O.C. rafter framing
	Install	S.F.	.20	.19		.39	for flat, shed or gable roofs, 25' span,
	Demolish and Install	S.F.	.20	.58		.78	up to 5/12 slope, per S.F. of roof.
	Reinstall	S.F.		.15		.15	
	Minimum Charge	Job		142		142	
2" x 6" Rafters							Cost includes material and labor to
	Demolish	S.F.		.41		.41	install 2" x 6", 24" O.C. rafter framing
	Install	S.F.	.31	.20		.51	for flat, shed or gable roofs, 25' span,
	Demolish and Install	S.F.	.31	.61		.92	up to 5/12 slope, per S.F. of roof.
	Reinstall	S.F.		.16		.16	
	Minimum Charge	Job		142		142	
2" x 8" Rafters							Cost includes material and labor to
	Demolish	S.F.		.42		.42	install 2" x 8", 24" O.C. rafter framing
	Install	S.F.	.47	.21		.68	for flat, shed or gable roofs, 25' span,
	Demolish and Install	S.F.	.47	.63		1.10	up to 5/12 slope, per S.F. of roof.
	Reinstall	S.F.		.17		.17	
	Minimum Charge	Job		142		142	
2" x 10" Rafters							Cost includes material and labor to
	Demolish	S.F.		.42		.42	install 2" x 10", 24" O.C. rafter
	Install	S.F.	.68	.32		1	framing for flat, shed or gable roofs,
	Demolish and Install	S.F.	.68	.74		1.42	25' span, up to 5/12 slope, per S.F.
	Reinstall	S.F.		.26		.26	of roof.
	Minimum Charge	Job		142		142	
2" x 12" Rafters							Cost includes material and labor to
	Demolish	S.F.		.43		.43	install 2" x 12", 24" O.C. rafter
	Install	S.F.	.94	.35		1.29	framing for flat, shed or gable roofs,
	Demolish and Install	S.F.	.94	.78		1.72	25' span, up to 5/12 slope, per S.F.
	Reinstall	S.F.		.28		.28	of roof.
	Minimum Charge	Job		142		142	
Rafter							
2" x 4"							Cost includes material and labor to
	Demolish	L.F.		.53		.53	install 2" x 4" rafters for flat, shed or
	Install	L.F.	.40	.83		1.23	gable roofs, up to 5/12 slope, 25'
	Demolish and Install	L.F.	.40	1.36		1.76	span, per L.F.
	Reinstall	L.F.		.66		.66	
	Minimum Charge	Job		142		142	
2" x 6"							Cost includes material and labor to
	Demolish	L.F.		.54		.54	install 2" x 6" rafters for flat, shed or
	Install	L.F.	.63	.71		1.34	gable roofs, up to 5/12 slope, 25'
	Demolish and Install	L.F.	.63	1.25		1.88	span, per L.F.
	Reinstall	L.F.		.57		.57	
	Minimum Charge	Job		142		142	

Rough Frame / Structure

Roof Framing

Roof Framing		Unit	Material	Labor	Equip.	Total	Specification
2" x 8"							
	Demolish	L.F.		.55		.55	Cost includes material and labor to
	Install	L.F.	.96	.76		1.72	install 2" x 8" rafters for flat, shed or
	Demolish and Install	L.F.	.96	1.31		2.27	gable roofs, up to 5/12 slope, 25'
	Reinstall	L.F.		.61		.61	span, per L.F.
	Minimum Charge	Job		142		142	
2" x 10"							
	Demolish	L.F.		.56		.56	Cost includes material and labor to
	Install	L.F.	1.36	1.15		2.51	install 2" x 10" rafters for flat, shed or
	Demolish and Install	L.F.	1.36	1.71		3.07	gable roofs, up to 5/12 slope, 25'
	Reinstall	L.F.		.92		.92	span, per L.F.
	Minimum Charge	Job		142		142	
2" x 12"							
	Demolish	L.F.		.57		.57	Cost includes material and labor to
	Install	L.F.	1.87	1.25		3.12	install 2" x 12" rafters for flat, shed or
	Demolish and Install	L.F.	1.87	1.82		3.69	gable roofs, up to 5/12 slope, 25'
	Reinstall	L.F.		1		1	span, per L.F.
	Minimum Charge	Job		142		142	
2"x 4" Valley / Jack							
	Demolish	L.F.		.53		.53	Includes material and labor to install
	Install	L.F.	.63	1.20		1.83	up to 2" x 6" valley/jack rafters for
	Demolish and Install	L.F.	.63	1.73		2.36	flat, shed or gable roofs, up to 5/12
	Reinstall	L.F.		.96		.96	slope, 25' span, per L.F.
	Minimum Charge	Job		142		142	
2"x 6" Valley / Jack							
	Demolish	L.F.		.54		.54	Includes material and labor to install
	Install	L.F.	.63	1.20		1.83	up to·2" x 6" valley/jack rafters for
	Demolish and Install	L.F.	.63	1.74		2.37	flat, shed or gable roofs, up to 5/12
	Reinstall	L.F.		.96		.96	slope, 25' span, per L.F.
	Minimum Charge	Job		142		142	
Ridgeboard							
2" x 4"							
	Demolish	L.F.		.51		.51	Cost includes material and labor to
	Install	L.F.	.40	.52		.92	install 2" x 4" ridgeboard for flat, shed
	Demolish and Install	L.F.	.40	1.03		1.43	or gable roofs, up to 5/12 slope, 25'
	Reinstall	L.F.		.41		.41	span, per L.F.
	Minimum Charge	Job		142		142	
2" x 6"							
	Demolish	L.F.		.53		.53	Cost includes material and labor to
	Install	L.F.	.63	1.14		1.77	install 2" x 6" ridgeboard for flat, shed
	Demolish and Install	L.F.	.63	1.67		2.30	or gable roofs, up to 5/12 slope, 25'
	Reinstall	L.F.		.91		.91	span, per L.F.
	Minimum Charge	Job		142		142	
2" x 8"							
	Demolish	L.F.		.54		.54	Cost includes material and labor to
	Install	L.F.	.96	1.27		2.23	install 2" x 8" ridgeboard for flat, shed
	Demolish and Install	L.F.	.96	1.81		2.77	or gable roofs, up to 5/12 slope, 25'
	Reinstall	L.F.		1.01		1.01	span, per L.F.
	Minimum Charge	Job		142		142	
2" x 10"							
	Demolish	L.F.		.56		.56	Cost includes material and labor to
	Install	L.F.	1.36	1.42		2.78	install 2" x 10" ridgeboard for flat,
	Demolish and Install	L.F.	1.36	1.98		3.34	shed or gable roofs, up to 5/12 slope,
	Reinstall	L.F.		1.14		1.14	25' span, per L.F.
	Minimum Charge	Job		142		142	

Rough Frame / Structure

Roof Framing		Unit	Material	Labor	Equip.	Total	Specification
2" x 12"							
	Demolish	L.F.		.57		.57	Cost includes material and labor to
	Install	L.F.	1.87	.81		2.68	install 2" x 12" ridgeboard for flat,
	Demolish and Install	L.F.	1.87	1.38		3.25	shed or gable roofs, up to 5/12 slope,
	Reinstall	L.F.		.65		.65	25' span, per L.F.
	Minimum Charge	Job		142		142	
Collar Beam							
1" x 6"							
	Demolish	L.F.		.40		.40	Cost includes material and labor to
	Install	L.F.	.56	.36		.92	install 1" x 6" collar beam or tie for
	Demolish and Install	L.F.	.56	.76		1.32	roof framing.
	Reinstall	L.F.		.28		.28	
	Minimum Charge	Job		142		142	
2" x 6"							
	Demolish	L.F.		.47		.47	Cost includes material and labor to
	Install	L.F.	.63	.36		.99	install 2" x 6" collar beam or tie for
	Demolish and Install	L.F.	.63	.83		1.46	roof framing.
	Reinstall	L.F.		.28		.28	
	Minimum Charge	Job		142		142	
Purlins							
2" x 6"							
	Demolish	L.F.		.46		.46	Cost includes material and labor to
	Install	L.F.	.63	.32		.95	install 2" x 6" purlins below roof
	Demolish and Install	L.F.	.63	.78		1.41	rafters.
	Reinstall	L.F.		.25		.25	
	Minimum Charge	Job		142		142	
2" x 8"							
	Demolish	L.F.		.46		.46	Cost includes material and labor to
	Install	L.F.	.96	.32		1.28	install 2" x 8" purlins below roof
	Demolish and Install	L.F.	.96	.78		1.74	rafters.
	Reinstall	L.F.		.26		.26	
	Minimum Charge	Job		142		142	
2" x 10"							
	Demolish	L.F.		.47		.47	Cost includes material and labor to
	Install	L.F.	1.36	.32		1.68	install 2" x 10" purlins below roof
	Demolish and Install	L.F.	1.36	.79		2.15	rafters.
	Reinstall	L.F.		.26		.26	
	Minimum Charge	Job		142		142	
2" x 12"							
	Demolish	L.F.		.47		.47	Cost includes material and labor to
	Install	L.F.	1.87	.33		2.20	install 2" x 12" purlins below roof
	Demolish and Install	L.F.	1.87	.80		2.67	rafters.
	Reinstall	L.F.		.26		.26	
	Minimum Charge	Job		142		142	
4" x 6"							
	Demolish	L.F.		.47		.47	Cost includes material and labor to
	Install	L.F.	2.82	.33		3.15	install 4" x 6" purlins below roof
	Demolish and Install	L.F.	2.82	.80		3.62	rafters.
	Reinstall	L.F.		.26		.26	
	Minimum Charge	Job		142		142	
4" x 8"							
	Demolish	L.F.		.48		.48	Cost includes material and labor to
	Install	L.F.	3.75	.34		4.09	install 4" x 8" purlins below roof
	Demolish and Install	L.F.	3.75	.82		4.57	rafters.
	Reinstall	L.F.		.27		.27	
	Minimum Charge	Job		142		142	

Roof Framing		Unit	Material	Labor	Equip.	Total	Specification
Ledger Board							
2" x 6"							
	Demolish	L.F.		.23		.23	Cost includes material and labor to
	Install	L.F.	.63	1.28		1.91	install 2" x 6" ledger board nailed to
	Demolish and Install	L.F.	.63	1.51		2.14	the face of a rafter.
	Reinstall	L.F.		1.03		1.03	
	Minimum Charge	Job		142		142	
4" x 6"							
	Demolish	L.F.		.38		.38	Cost includes material and labor to
	Install	L.F.	2.82	1.89		4.71	install 4" x 6" ledger board nailed to
	Demolish and Install	L.F.	2.82	2.27		5.09	the face of a rafter.
	Reinstall	L.F.		1.51		1.51	
	Minimum Charge	Job		142		142	
4" x 8"							
	Demolish	L.F.		.51		.51	Cost includes material and labor to
	Install	L.F.	3.75	2.17		5.92	install 4" x 8" ledger board nailed to
	Demolish and Install	L.F.	3.75	2.68		6.43	the face of a rafter.
	Reinstall	L.F.		1.74		1.74	
	Minimum Charge	Job		142		142	
Outriggers							
2" x 4"							
	Demolish	L.F.		.16		.16	Cost includes material and labor to
	Install	L.F.	.40	1.14		1.54	install 2" x 4" outrigger rafters for flat,
	Demolish and Install	L.F.	.40	1.30		1.70	shed or gabled roofs, up to 5/12
	Reinstall	L.F.		.91		.91	slope, per L.F.
	Minimum Charge	Job		142		142	
2" x 6"							
	Demolish	L.F.		.24		.24	Cost includes material and labor to
	Install	L.F.	.63	1.14		1.77	install 2" x 6" outrigger rafters for flat,
	Demolish and Install	L.F.	.63	1.38		2.01	shed or gabled roofs, up to 5/12
	Reinstall	L.F.		.91		.91	slope, per L.F.
	Minimum Charge	Job		142		142	
Lookout Rafter							
2" x 4"							
	Demolish	L.F.		.53		.53	Cost includes material and labor to
	Install	L.F.	.40	.47		.87	install 2" x 4" lookout rafters for flat,
	Demolish and Install	L.F.	.40	1		1.40	shed or gabled roofs, up to 5/12
	Reinstall	L.F.		.38		.38	slope, per L.F.
	Minimum Charge	Job		142		142	
2" x 6"							
	Demolish	L.F.		.54		.54	Cost includes material and labor to
	Install	L.F.	.63	.48		1.11	install 2" x 6" lookout rafters for flat,
	Demolish and Install	L.F.	.63	1.02		1.65	shed or gabled roofs, up to 5/12
	Reinstall	L.F.		.39		.39	slope, per L.F.
	Minimum Charge	Job		142		142	
Fly Rafter							
2" x 4"							
	Demolish	L.F.		.53		.53	Cost includes material and labor to
	Install	L.F.	.40	.47		.87	install 2" x 4" fly rafters for flat, shed or
	Demolish and Install	L.F.	.40	1		1.40	gabled roofs, up to 5/12 slope, per
	Reinstall	L.F.		.38		.38	L.F.
	Minimum Charge	Job		142		142	

Rough Frame / Structure

Roof Framing

	Unit	Material	Labor	Equip.	Total	Specification
2" x 6"						
Demolish	L.F.		.54		.54	Cost includes material and labor to
Install	L.F.	.63	.48		1.11	install 2" x 6" fly rafters for flat, shed or
Demolish and Install	L.F.	.63	1.02		1.65	gabled roofs, up to 5/12 slope, per
Reinstall	L.F.		.39		.39	L.F.
Minimum Charge	Job		142		142	

Residential Trusses

	Unit	Material	Labor	Equip.	Total	Specification
W or Fink Truss						
24' Span						
Demolish	Ea.		6.95		6.95	Includes material, labor and equipment
Install	Ea.	48.50	21.50	11.15	81.15	to install wood gang-nailed residential
Demolish and Install	Ea.	48.50	28.45	11.15	88.10	truss, up to 24' span.
Reinstall	Ea.		21.29	11.14	32.43	
Minimum Charge	Job		142		142	
28' Span						
Demolish	Ea.		7.40		7.40	Includes material, labor and equipment
Install	Ea.	59	24	12.60	95.60	to install wood gang-nailed residential
Demolish and Install	Ea.	59	31.40	12.60	103	truss, up to 28' span.
Reinstall	Ea.		24.11	12.61	36.72	
Minimum Charge	Job		142		142	
32' Span						
Demolish	Ea.		8.20		8.20	Includes material, labor and equipment
Install	Ea.	83	25.50	13.35	121.85	to install wood gang-nailed residential
Demolish and Install	Ea.	83	33.70	13.35	130.05	truss, up to 32' span.
Reinstall	Ea.		25.55	13.37	38.92	
Minimum Charge	Job		142		142	
36' Span						
Demolish	Ea.		8.85		8.85	Includes material, labor and equipment
Install	Ea.	104	28	14.55	146.55	to install wood gang-nailed residential
Demolish and Install	Ea.	104	36.85	14.55	155.40	truss, up to 36' span.
Reinstall	Ea.		27.77	14.53	42.30	
Minimum Charge	Job		142		142	
40' Span						
Demolish	Ea.		9.55		9.55	Includes material, labor and equipment
Install	Ea.	153	29.50	15.55	198.05	to install wood gang-nailed residential
Demolish and Install	Ea.	153	39.05	15.55	207.60	truss, up to 40' span.
Reinstall	Ea.		29.71	15.54	45.25	
Minimum Charge	Job		142		142	
Gable End						
24' Span						
Demolish	Ea.		6.95		6.95	Includes material, labor and equipment
Install	Ea.	69	23	11.95	103.95	to install wood gang-nailed residential
Demolish and Install	Ea.	69	29.95	11.95	110.90	gable end truss, up to 24' span.
Reinstall	Ea.		22.81	11.94	34.75	
Clean	Ea.	1.17	27.50		28.67	
Paint	Ea.	3.40	34		37.40	
Minimum Charge	Job		142		142	
28' Span						
Demolish	Ea.		7.40		7.40	Includes material, labor and equipment
Install	Ea.	83.50	27	14.20	124.70	to install wood gang-nailed residential
Demolish and Install	Ea.	83.50	34.40	14.20	132.10	gable end truss, up to 30' span.
Reinstall	Ea.		27.18	14.22	41.40	
Clean	Ea.	1.22	37.50		38.72	
Paint	Ea.	3.54	46.50		50.04	
Minimum Charge	Job		142		142	

Rough Frame / Structure

Residential Trusses

Residential Trusses	Unit	Material	Labor	Equip.	Total	Specification
32' Span						
Demolish	Ea.		8.20		8.20	Includes material, labor and equipment
Install	Ea.	93.50	28	14.55	136.05	to install wood gang-nailed residential
Demolish and Install	Ea.	93.50	36.20	14.55	144.25	gable end truss, up to 32' span.
Reinstall	Ea.		27.77	14.53	42.30	
Clean	Ea.	1.28	49		50.28	
Paint	Ea.	3.71	61		64.71	
Minimum Charge	Job		142		142	
36' Span						
Demolish	Ea.		8.85		8.85	Includes material, labor and equipment
Install	Ea.	111	32	16.70	159.70	to install wood gang-nailed residential
Demolish and Install	Ea.	111	40.85	16.70	168.55	gable end truss, up to 36' span.
Reinstall	Ea.		31.94	16.71	48.65	
Clean	Ea.	1.33	62		63.33	
Paint	Ea.	3.88	76.50		80.38	
Minimum Charge	Job		142		142	
40' Span						
Demolish	Ea.		9.55		9.55	Includes material, labor and equipment
Install	Ea.	123	33.50	17.60	174.10	to install wood gang-nailed residential
Demolish and Install	Ea.	123	43.05	17.60	183.65	gable end truss, up to 40' span.
Reinstall	Ea.		33.62	17.59	51.21	
Clean	Ea.	4.07	76.50		80.57	
Paint	Ea.	4.07	94.50		98.57	
Minimum Charge	Job		142		142	
Truss Hardware						
5-1/4" Glue-Lam Seat						
Install	Ea.	45.50	1.58		47.08	Includes labor and material to install
Minimum Charge	Job		142		142	beam hangers.
6-3/4" Glue-Lam Seat						
Install	Ea.	47.50	1.58		49.08	Includes labor and material to install
Minimum Charge	Job		142		142	beam hangers.
8-3/4" Glue-Lam Seat						
Install	Ea.	54	1.58		55.58	Includes labor and material to install
Minimum Charge	Job		142		142	beam hangers.
2" x 4" Joist Hanger						
Install	Ea.	.56	1.63		2.19	Includes labor and material to install
Minimum Charge	Job		142		142	joist and beam hangers.
2" x 12" Joist Hanger						
Install	Ea.	.47	1.73		2.20	Cost includes labor and material to
Minimum Charge	Job		142		142	install 2" x 12" joist hanger.

Commercial Trusses

Commercial Trusses	Unit	Material	Labor	Equip.	Total	Specification
Engineered Lumber, Truss / Joist						
9-1/2"						
Demolish	S.F.		.38		.38	Includes material and labor to install
Install	S.F.	1.40	.28		1.68	engineered lumber truss / joists per
Demolish and Install	S.F.	1.40	.66		2.06	S.F. of floor area based on joists 16"
Reinstall	S.F.		.23		.23	O.C. Beams, supports and bridging
Minimum Charge	Job		142		142	are not included.
11-7/8"						
Demolish	S.F.		.39		.39	Includes material and labor to install
Install	S.F.	1.51	.29		1.80	engineered lumber truss / joists per
Demolish and Install	S.F.	1.51	.68		2.19	S.F. of floor area based on joists 16"
Reinstall	S.F.		.23		.23	O.C. Beams, supports and bridging
Minimum Charge	Job		142		142	are not included.

Rough Frame / Structure

Commercial Trusses

		Unit	Material	Labor	Equip.	Total	Specification
14"							
	Demolish	S.F.		.40		.40	Includes material and labor to install
	Install	S.F.	1.65	.31		1.96	engineered lumber truss / joists per
	Demolish and Install	S.F.	1.65	.71		2.36	S.F. of floor area based on joists 16"
	Reinstall	S.F.		.25		.25	O.C. Beams, supports and bridging
	Minimum Charge	Job		142		142	are not included.
16"							
	Demolish	S.F.		.42		.42	Includes material and labor to install
	Install	S.F.	2.06	.33		2.39	engineered lumber truss / joists per
	Demolish and Install	S.F.	2.06	.75		2.81	S.F. of floor area based on joists 16"
	Reinstall	S.F.		.26		.26	O.C. Beams, supports and bridging
	Minimum Charge	Job		142		142	are not included.
Bowstring Truss							
100' Clear Span							
	Demolish	SF Flr.		.39	.41	.80	Includes material, labor and equipment
	Install	SF Flr.	5.45	.32	.27	6.04	to install bow string truss system up to
	Demolish and Install	SF Flr.	5.45	.71	.68	6.84	100' clear span per S.F. of floor area.
	Minimum Charge	Job		142		142	
120' Clear Span							
	Demolish	SF Flr.		.43	.46	.89	Includes material, labor and equipment
	Install	SF Flr.	5.85	.36	.30	6.51	to install bow string truss system up to
	Demolish and Install	SF Flr.	5.85	.79	.76	7.40	120' clear span per S.F. of floor area.
	Minimum Charge	Job		142		142	

Roof Sheathing

		Unit	Material	Labor	Equip.	Total	Specification
Plywood							
3/8"							
	Demolish	S.F.		.30		.30	Cost includes material and labor to
	Install	S.F.	.48	.37		.85	install 3/8" CDX plywood roof
	Demolish and Install	S.F.	.48	.67		1.15	sheathing.
	Reinstall	S.F.		.37		.37	
	Minimum Charge	Job		142		142	
1/2"							
	Demolish	S.F.		.30		.30	Cost includes material and labor to
	Install	S.F.	.54	.41		.95	install 1/2" CDX plywood roof
	Demolish and Install	S.F.	.54	.71		1.25	sheathing.
	Minimum Charge	Job		142		142	
5/8"							
	Demolish	S.F.		.30		.30	Cost includes material and labor to
	Install	S.F.	.63	.44		1.07	install 5/8" CDX plywood roof
	Demolish and Install	S.F.	.63	.74		1.37	sheathing.
	Minimum Charge	Job		142		142	
3/4"							
	Demolish	S.F.		.30		.30	Cost includes material and labor to
	Install	S.F.	.73	.47		1.20	install 3/4" CDX plywood roof
	Demolish and Install	S.F.	.73	.77		1.50	sheathing.
	Minimum Charge	Job		142		142	
OSB							
1/2"							
	Demolish	S.F.		.30		.30	Cost includes material and labor to
	Install	S.F.	.39	.22		.61	install 4' x 8' x 1/2" OSB sheathing.
	Demolish and Install	S.F.	.39	.52		.91	
	Minimum Charge	Job		142		142	

Rough Frame / Structure

Roof Sheathing

Roof Sheathing		Unit	Material	Labor	Equip.	Total	Specification
5/8"							Cost includes material and labor to install 4' x 8' x 5/8" OSB sheathing.
	Demolish	S.F.		.30		.30	
	Install	S.F.	.54	.23		.77	
	Demolish and Install	S.F.	.54	.53		1.07	
	Minimum Charge	Job		142		142	
Plank							Cost includes material and labor to install 1" x 6" or 1" x 8" utility T&G board sheathing laid diagonal.
	Demolish	S.F.		.30		.30	
	Install	S.F.	1.43	.79		2.22	
	Demolish and Install	S.F.	1.43	1.09		2.52	
	Reinstall	S.F.		.79		.79	
	Minimum Charge	Job		142		142	
Skip-type							
1" x 4"							Includes material and labor to install sheathing board material 1" x 4", 7" O.C.
	Demolish	S.F.		.46		.46	
	Install	S.F.	.50	.24		.74	
	Demolish and Install	S.F.	.50	.70		1.20	
	Minimum Charge	Job		142		142	
1" x 6"							Includes material and labor to install sheathing board material 1" x 6", 7" or 9" O.C.
	Demolish	S.F.		.46		.46	
	Install	S.F.	.56	.20		.76	
	Demolish and Install	S.F.	.56	.66		1.22	
	Minimum Charge	Job		142		142	

Wood Deck

Wood Deck		Unit	Material	Labor	Equip.	Total	Specification
Treated							Includes material and labor to install unfinished deck using 2" x 4" treated decking, with 2" x 6" double beams 24" O.C., 4" x 4" posts 5' O.C. set in concrete.
	Demolish	S.F.		.96		.96	
	Install	S.F.	5.10	7.10		12.20	
	Demolish and Install	S.F.	5.10	8.06		13.16	
	Reinstall	S.F.		5.70		5.70	
	Clean	S.F.	.06	.21		.27	
	Paint	S.F.	.06	.20		.26	
	Minimum Charge	Job		142		142	
Redwood							Includes material and labor to install unfinished deck using 2" x 4" select redwood decking, with 2" x 6" double beams 24" O.C., 4" x 4" posts 5' O.C. set in concrete.
	Demolish	S.F.		.96		.96	
	Install	S.F.	15.75	7.10		22.85	
	Demolish and Install	S.F.	15.75	8.06		23.81	
	Reinstall	S.F.		5.70		5.70	
	Clean	S.F.	.06	.21		.27	
	Paint	S.F.	.06	.20		.26	
	Minimum Charge	Job		142		142	
Cedar							Includes material and labor to install unfinished deck using 2" x 4" select cedar decking, with 2" x 6" double beams 24" O.C., 4" x 4" posts 5' O.C. set in concrete.
	Demolish	S.F.		.96		.96	
	Install	S.F.	7.55	7.10		14.65	
	Demolish and Install	S.F.	7.55	8.06		15.61	
	Reinstall	S.F.		5.70		5.70	
	Clean	S.F.	.06	.21		.27	
	Paint	S.F.	.06	.20		.26	
	Minimum Charge	Job		142		142	
Stairs							Includes material and labor to install wood steps.
	Demolish	Ea.		276		276	
	Install	Ea.	32	495		527	
	Demolish and Install	Ea.	32	771		803	
	Reinstall	Ea.		395.65		395.65	
	Clean	Flight	2.81	18.10		20.91	
	Paint	Flight	9.95	34		43.95	
	Minimum Charge	Job		142		142	

Rough Frame / Structure

Wood Deck

	Unit	Material	Labor	Equip.	Total	Specification
Railing						
Demolish	L.F.		3.53		3.53	Includes material and labor to install
Install	L.F.	9.90	12.95		22.85	porch rail with balusters.
Demolish and Install	L.F.	9.90	16.48		26.38	
Clean	L.F.	.56	1.29		1.85	
Paint	L.F.	.47	2.13		2.60	
Minimum Charge	Job		142		142	
Bench Seating						
Demolish	L.F.		3.83		3.83	Includes material and labor to install
Install	L.F.	3.01	14.25		17.26	pressure treated bench seating.
Demolish and Install	L.F.	3.01	18.08		21.09	
Reinstall	L.F.		11.39		11.39	
Clean	L.F.	.11	1.03		1.14	
Paint	L.F.	.48	2.04		2.52	
Minimum Charge	Job		142		142	
Privacy Wall						
Demolish	SF Flr.		.92		.92	Includes material, labor and equipment
Install	SF Flr.	.42	.49		.91	to install privacy wall.
Demolish and Install	SF Flr.	.42	1.41		1.83	
Reinstall	SF Flr.		.39		.39	
Clean	SF Flr.	.06	.21		.27	
Paint	S.F.	.06	.20		.26	
Minimum Charge	Job		142		142	

Porch

	Unit	Material	Labor	Equip.	Total	Specification
Treated						
Demolish	S.F.		1.91		1.91	Includes material and labor to install
Install	S.F.	6	14.25		20.25	floor and roof frame and decking
Demolish and Install	S.F.	6	16.16		22.16	using 2" x 4" treated decking, with 2"
Reinstall	S.F.		11.39		11.39	x 6" double beams 24" O.C., 4" x 4"
Clean	S.F.	.11	.43		.54	posts 5' O.C. set in concrete.
Paint	S.F.	.17	.51		.68	
Minimum Charge	Job		142		142	
Redwood						
Demolish	S.F.		1.91		1.91	Includes material and labor to install
Install	S.F.	16.90	14.25		31.15	floor and roof frame and decking
Demolish and Install	S.F.	16.90	16.16		33.06	using 2" x 4" redwood decking, with
Reinstall	S.F.		11.39		11.39	2" x 6" double beams 24" O.C., 4" x
Clean	S.F.	.11	.43		.54	4" posts 5' O.C. set in concrete.
Paint	S.F.	.17	.51		.68	
Minimum Charge	Job		142		142	
Cedar						
Demolish	S.F.		1.91		1.91	Includes material and labor to install
Install	S.F.	8.70	14.25		22.95	floor and roof frame and cedar
Demolish and Install	S.F.	8.70	16.16		24.86	decking using 2" x 4" select cedar,
Reinstall	S.F.		11.39		11.39	with 2" x 6" double beams 24" O.C.,
Clean	S.F.	.11	.43		.54	4" x 4" posts 5' O.C. set in concrete.
Paint	S.F.	.17	.51		.68	
Minimum Charge	Job		142		142	
Stairs						
Demolish	Ea.		276		276	Includes material and labor to install
Install	Ea.	32	495		527	wood steps.
Demolish and Install	Ea.	32	771		803	
Reinstall	Ea.		395.65		395.65	
Clean	Flight	2.81	18.10		20.91	
Paint	Flight	9.95	34		43.95	
Minimum Charge	Job		142		142	

Porch		Unit	Material	Labor	Equip.	Total	Specification
Railing							
	Demolish	L.F.		3.53		3.53	Includes material and labor to install
	Install	L.F.	9.90	12.95		22.85	porch rail with balusters.
	Demolish and Install	L.F.	9.90	16.48		26.38	
	Clean	L.F.	.56	1.62		2.18	
	Paint	L.F.	.47	2.13		2.60	
	Minimum Charge	Job		142		142	
Bench Seating							
	Demolish	L.F.		3.83		3.83	Includes material and labor to install
	Install	L.F.	3.01	14.25		17.26	pressure treated bench seating.
	Demolish and Install	L.F.	3.01	18.08		21.09	
	Reinstall	L.F.		11.39		11.39	
	Clean	L.F.	.11	1.03		1.14	
	Paint	L.F.	.48	2.04		2.52	
	Minimum Charge	Job		142		142	
Privacy Wall							
	Demolish	SF Flr.		.92		.92	Includes material, labor and equipment
	Install	SF Flr.	.42	.49		.91	to install privacy wall.
	Demolish and Install	SF Flr.	.42	1.41		1.83	
	Reinstall	SF Flr.		.39		.39	
	Clean	SF Flr.	.06	.21		.27	
	Paint	S.F.	.06	.20		.26	
	Minimum Charge	Job		142		142	
Wood Board Ceiling							
	Demolish	S.F.		.38		.38	Includes material and labor to install
	Install	S.F.	1.77	1.27		3.04	wood board on ceiling.
	Demolish and Install	S.F.	1.77	1.65		3.42	
	Clean	S.F.	.02	.12		.14	
	Paint	S.F.	.15	.32		.47	
	Minimum Charge	Job		142		142	
Re-screen							
	Install	S.F.	.51	1.14		1.65	Includes labor and material to
	Minimum Charge	Job		142		142	re-screen wood frame.

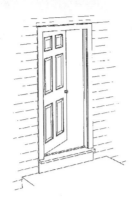

Exterior Trim

Exterior Trim	Unit	Material	Labor	Equip.	Total	Specification
Stock Lumber						
1″ x 2″						
Demolish	L.F.		.19		.19	Cost includes material and labor to
Install	L.F.	.28	.86		1.14	install 1″ x 2″ pine trim.
Demolish and Install	L.F.	.28	1.05		1.33	
Clean	L.F.	.01	.14		.15	
Paint	L.F.	.02	.40		.42	
Minimum Charge	Job		142		142	
1″ x 3″						
Demolish	L.F.		.19		.19	Cost includes material and labor to
Install	L.F.	.21	.95		1.16	install 1″ x 3″ pine trim.
Demolish and Install	L.F.	.21	1.14		1.35	
Clean	L.F.	.01	.14		.15	
Paint	L.F.	.02	.40		.42	
Minimum Charge	Job		142		142	
1″ x 4″						
Demolish	L.F.		.19		.19	Cost includes material and labor to
Install	L.F.	.64	1.14		1.78	install 1″ x 4″ pine trim.
Demolish and Install	L.F.	.64	1.33		1.97	
Clean	L.F.	.01	.14		.15	
Paint	L.F.	.02	.40		.42	
Minimum Charge	Job		142		142	
1″ x 6″						
Demolish	L.F.		.19		.19	Cost includes material and labor to
Install	L.F.	1.22	1.14		2.36	install 1″ x 6″ pine trim.
Demolish and Install	L.F.	1.22	1.33		2.55	
Clean	L.F.	.01	.14		.15	
Paint	L.F.	.07	.40		.47	
Minimum Charge	Job		142		142	
1″ x 8″						
Demolish	L.F.		.21		.21	Cost includes material and labor to
Install	L.F.	1.41	1.42		2.83	install 1″ x 8″ pine trim.
Demolish and Install	L.F.	1.41	1.63		3.04	
Reinstall	L.F.		1.14		1.14	
Clean	L.F.	.02	.15		.17	
Paint	L.F.	.07	.40		.47	
Minimum Charge	Job		142		142	

Exterior Trim

Exterior Trim		Unit	Material	Labor	Equip.	Total	Specification
1" x 10"							
	Demolish	L.F.		.32		.32	Cost includes material and labor to
	Install	L.F.	1.58	1.58		3.16	install 1" x 10" pine trim.
	Demolish and Install	L.F.	1.58	1.90		3.48	
	Minimum Charge	Job		142		142	
1" x 12"							
	Demolish	L.F.		.32		.32	Cost includes material and labor to
	Install	L.F.	1.49	1.58		3.07	install 1" x 12" pine trim.
	Demolish and Install	L.F.	1.49	1.90		3.39	
	Minimum Charge	Job		142		142	

Fascia		Unit	Material	Labor	Equip.	Total	Specification
Aluminum							
	Demolish	L.F.		.40		.40	Includes material and labor to install
	Install	S.F.	1.09	1.36		2.45	aluminum fascia.
	Demolish and Install	S.F.	1.09	1.76		2.85	
	Reinstall	S.F.		1.08		1.08	
	Clean	L.F.		.26		.26	
	Minimum Charge	Job		142		142	
Vinyl							
	Demolish	L.F.		.40		.40	Cost includes material and labor to
	Install	L.F.	2.34	1.63		3.97	install 6" vinyl fascia with 12" vinyl
	Demolish and Install	L.F.	2.34	2.03		4.37	soffit and J-channel.
	Reinstall	L.F.		1.30		1.30	
	Clean	L.F.		.26		.26	
	Minimum Charge	Job		142		142	
Plywood							
	Demolish	L.F.		.40		.40	Cost includes material and labor to
	Install	L.F.	1	.63		1.63	install 12" wide plywood fascia.
	Demolish and Install	L.F.	1	1.03		2.03	
	Reinstall	L.F.		.51		.51	
	Clean	L.F.	.03	.17		.20	
	Paint	L.F.	.14	.64		.78	
	Minimum Charge	Job		142		142	
Cedar							
	Demolish	L.F.		.40		.40	Cost includes material and labor to
	Install	L.F.	1.54	.63		2.17	install 12" wide cedar fascia.
	Demolish and Install	L.F.	1.54	1.03		2.57	
	Reinstall	L.F.		.51		.51	
	Clean	L.F.	.03	.17		.20	
	Paint	L.F.	.14	.64		.78	
	Minimum Charge	Job		142		142	
Redwood							
1" x 6"							
	Demolish	L.F.		.31		.31	Cost includes material and labor to
	Install	L.F.	2.10	1.14		3.24	install 1" x 6" redwood fascia board.
	Demolish and Install	L.F.	2.10	1.45		3.55	
	Reinstall	L.F.		.91		.91	
	Minimum Charge	Job		142		142	
1" x 8"							
	Demolish	L.F.		.35		.35	Cost includes material and labor to
	Install	L.F.	2.88	1.27		4.15	install 1" x 8" redwood fascia board.
	Demolish and Install	L.F.	2.88	1.62		4.50	
	Reinstall	L.F.		1.01		1.01	
	Minimum Charge	Job		142		142	

Exterior Trim

Fascia

		Unit	Material	Labor	Equip.	Total	Specification
2" x 6"							
	Demolish	L.F.		.31		.31	Cost includes material and labor to
	Install	L.F.	2.04	1.27		3.31	install 2" x 6" redwood fascia board.
	Demolish and Install	L.F.	2.04	1.58		3.62	
	Reinstall	L.F.		1.01		1.01	
	Minimum Charge	Job		142		142	
2" x 8"							
	Demolish	L.F.		.35		.35	Cost includes material and labor to
	Install	L.F.	2.75	1.42		4.17	install 2" x 8" redwood fascia board.
	Demolish and Install	L.F.	2.75	1.77		4.52	
	Reinstall	L.F.		1.14		1.14	
	Minimum Charge	Job		142		142	

Hem-fir Std & Better

		Unit	Material	Labor	Equip.	Total	Specification
2" x 6"							
	Demolish	L.F.		.31		.31	Cost includes material and labor to
	Install	L.F.	.63	2.28		2.91	install 2" x 6" hem-fir exterior trim
	Demolish and Install	L.F.	.63	2.59		3.22	board.
	Reinstall	L.F.		1.82		1.82	
	Clean	L.F.	.01	.17		.18	
	Paint	L.F.	.14	.64		.78	
	Minimum Charge	Job		142		142	
2" x 8"							
	Demolish	L.F.		.35		.35	Cost includes material and labor to
	Install	L.F.	.96	2.53		3.49	install 2" x 8" hem-fir exterior trim
	Demolish and Install	L.F.	.96	2.88		3.84	board.
	Reinstall	L.F.		2.03		2.03	
	Clean	L.F.	.02	.17		.19	
	Paint	L.F.	.14	.64		.78	
	Minimum Charge	Job		142		142	
2" x 10"							
	Demolish	L.F.		.40		.40	Cost includes material and labor to
	Install	L.F.	1.36	3.16		4.52	install 2" x 10" hem-fir exterior trim
	Demolish and Install	L.F.	1.36	3.56		4.92	board.
	Reinstall	L.F.		2.53		2.53	
	Clean	L.F.	.03	.19		.22	
	Paint	L.F.	.14	.64		.78	
	Minimum Charge	Job		142		142	

Barge Rafter

		Unit	Material	Labor	Equip.	Total	Specification
2" x 6"							
	Demolish	L.F.		.61		.61	Cost includes material and labor to
	Install	L.F.	.63	.32		.95	install 2" x 6" barge rafters.
	Demolish and Install	L.F.	.63	.93		1.56	
	Reinstall	L.F.		.25		.25	
	Clean	L.F.	.01	.17		.18	
	Paint	L.F.	.14	.64		.78	
	Minimum Charge	Job		142		142	
2" x 8"							
	Demolish	L.F.		.62		.62	Cost includes material and labor to
	Install	L.F.	.96	.34		1.30	install 2" x 8" barge rafters.
	Demolish and Install	L.F.	.96	.96		1.92	
	Reinstall	L.F.		.27		.27	
	Clean	L.F.	.02	.17		.19	
	Paint	L.F.	.14	.64		.78	
	Minimum Charge	Job		142		142	

Exterior Trim

Fascia

	Unit	Material	Labor	Equip.	Total	Specification
2″ x 10″						
Demolish	L.F.		.63		.63	Cost includes material and labor to
Install	L.F.	1.36	.35		1.71	install 2″ x 10″ barge rafters.
Demolish and Install	L.F.	1.36	.98		2.34	
Reinstall	L.F.		.28		.28	
Clean	L.F.	.03	.19		.22	
Paint	L.F.	.14	.64		.78	
Minimum Charge	Job		142		142	

Soffit

	Unit	Material	Labor	Equip.	Total	Specification
Aluminum						
12″ w / Fascia						
Demolish	L.F.		.40		.40	Cost includes material and labor to
Install	L.F.	2.70	1.63		4.33	install 12″ aluminum soffit with 6″
Demolish and Install	L.F.	2.70	2.03		4.73	fascia and J-channel.
Reinstall	L.F.		1.30		1.30	
Clean	L.F.		.26		.26	
Paint	L.F.	.18	.64		.82	
Minimum Charge	Job		142		142	
18″ w / Fascia						
Demolish	L.F.		.40		.40	Cost includes material and labor to
Install	L.F.	3.21	1.90		5.11	install 18″ aluminum soffit with 6″
Demolish and Install	L.F.	3.21	2.30		5.51	fascia and J-channel.
Reinstall	L.F.		1.52		1.52	
Clean	L.F.		.26		.26	
Paint	L.F.	.18	.64		.82	
Minimum Charge	Job		142		142	
24″ w / Fascia						
Demolish	L.F.		.40		.40	Cost includes material and labor to
Install	L.F.	3.76	2.11		5.87	install 24″ aluminum soffit with 6″
Demolish and Install	L.F.	3.76	2.51		6.27	fascia and J-channel.
Reinstall	L.F.		1.69		1.69	
Clean	L.F.		.38		.38	
Paint	L.F.	.18	.64		.82	
Minimum Charge	Job		142		142	
Vinyl						
Demolish	L.F.		.40		.40	Cost includes material and labor to
Install	L.F.	2.34	1.63		3.97	install 6″ vinyl fascia with 12″ vinyl
Demolish and Install	L.F.	2.34	2.03		4.37	soffit and J-channel.
Reinstall	L.F.		1.30		1.30	
Clean	L.F.		.26		.26	
Paint	L.F.	.18	.64		.82	
Minimum Charge	Job		142		142	
Plywood						
Demolish	L.F.		.44		.44	Cost includes material and labor to
Install	L.F.	1	.81		1.81	install 12″ wide plywood soffit
Demolish and Install	L.F.	1	1.25		2.25	including 6″ fascia.
Reinstall	L.F.		.65		.65	
Clean	L.F.	.03	.17		.20	
Paint	L.F.	.14	.64		.78	
Minimum Charge	Job		142		142	

Exterior Trim

Soffit		Unit	Material	Labor	Equip.	Total	Specification
Redwood							
	Demolish	L.F.		.44		.44	Cost includes material and labor to
	Install	L.F.	4.20	.81		5.01	install 12" wide redwood soffit
	Demolish and Install	L.F.	4.20	1.25		5.45	including 6" fascia.
	Reinstall	L.F.		.65		.65	
	Clean	L.F.	.03	.17		.20	
	Paint	L.F.	.14	.64		.78	
	Minimum Charge	Job		142		142	
Cedar							
	Demolish	L.F.		.44		.44	Cost includes material and labor to
	Install	L.F.	1.54	.81		2.35	install 12" wide cedar soffit including
	Demolish and Install	L.F.	1.54	1.25		2.79	6" fascia.
	Reinstall	L.F.		.65		.65	
	Clean	L.F.	.03	.17		.20	
	Paint	L.F.	.14	.64		.78	
	Minimum Charge	Job		142		142	
Douglas Fir							
	Demolish	L.F.		.44		.44	Cost includes material and labor to
	Install	L.F.	1.49	.81		2.30	install 12" wide Douglas fir soffit
	Demolish and Install	L.F.	1.49	1.25		2.74	including 6" fascia.
	Reinstall	L.F.		.65		.65	
	Clean	L.F.	.03	.17		.20	
	Paint	L.F.	.14	.64		.78	
	Minimum Charge	Job		142		142	

Roofing and Flashing

Tile Roofing

Metal Flashing	Unit	Material	Labor	Equip.	Total	Specification
Galvanized						
6"						
Demolish	L.F.		.15		.15	Includes material and labor to install
Install	L.F.	.41	.68		1.09	flat galvanized steel flashing, 6" wide.
Demolish and Install	L.F.	.41	.83		1.24	
Paint	L.F.	.10	.32		.42	
Minimum Charge	Job		135		135	
14"						
Demolish	L.F.		.15		.15	Includes material and labor to install
Install	L.F.	.95	.68		1.63	flat galvanized steel flashing, 14"
Demolish and Install	L.F.	.95	.83		1.78	wide.
Paint	L.F.	.10	.32		.42	
Minimum Charge	Job		135		135	
20"						
Demolish	L.F.		.15		.15	Includes material and labor to install
Install	L.F.	1.34	.68		2.02	flat galvanized steel flashing, 20"
Demolish and Install	L.F.	1.34	.83		2.17	wide.
Paint	L.F.	.10	.32		.42	
Minimum Charge	Job		135		135	
Aluminum						
6"						
Demolish	L.F.		.15		.15	Includes material and labor to install
Install	L.F.	.25	.68		.93	flat aluminum flashing, 6" wide.
Demolish and Install	L.F.	.25	.83		1.08	
Paint	L.F.	.10	.32		.42	
Minimum Charge	Job		135		135	
14"						
Demolish	L.F.		.15		.15	Includes material and labor to install
Install	L.F.	.48	.68		1.16	flat aluminum flashing, 14" wide.
Demolish and Install	L.F.	.48	.83		1.31	
Paint	L.F.	.10	.32		.42	
Minimum Charge	Job		135		135	
20"						
Demolish	L.F.		.15		.15	Includes material and labor to install
Install	L.F.	.64	.68		1.32	flat aluminum flashing, 20" wide.
Demolish and Install	L.F.	.64	.83		1.47	
Paint	L.F.	.10	.32		.42	
Minimum Charge	Job		135		135	

Metal Flashing	Unit	Material	Labor	Equip.	Total	Specification
Copper						
6"						
Demolish	L.F.		.15		.15	Includes material and labor to install
Install	L.F.	1.72	.90		2.62	flat copper flashing, 6" wide.
Demolish and Install	L.F.	1.72	1.05		2.77	
Minimum Charge	Job		156		156	
14"						
Demolish	L.F.		.15		.15	Includes material and labor to install
Install	L.F.	3.98	.90		4.88	flat copper flashing, 14" wide.
Demolish and Install	L.F.	3.98	1.05		5.03	
Minimum Charge	Job		156		156	
18"						
Demolish	L.F.		.15		.15	Includes material and labor to install
Install	L.F.	5.70	.90		6.60	flat copper flashing, 18" wide.
Demolish and Install	L.F.	5.70	1.05		6.75	
Minimum Charge	Job		156		156	
Aluminum Valley						
Demolish	L.F.		.15		.15	Includes material and labor to install
Install	L.F.	2.29	1.68		3.97	aluminum valley flashing, .024" thick.
Demolish and Install	L.F.	2.29	1.83		4.12	
Paint	L.F.	.10	.32		.42	
Minimum Charge	Job		142		142	
Gravel Stop						
Demolish	L.F.		.14		.14	Includes material and labor to install
Install	L.F.	3.54	2.15		5.69	aluminum gravel stop, .050" thick, 4"
Demolish and Install	L.F.	3.54	2.29		5.83	high, mill finish.
Reinstall	L.F.		1.72		1.72	
Paint	L.F.	.15	.32		.47	
Minimum Charge	Job		142		142	
Drip Edge						
Demolish	L.F.		.14		.14	Includes material and labor to install
Install	L.F.	.22	.71		.93	aluminum drip edge, .016" thick, 5"
Demolish and Install	L.F.	.22	.85		1.07	wide, mill finish.
Reinstall	L.F.		.57		.57	
Paint	L.F.	.15	.32		.47	
Minimum Charge	Job		142		142	
End Wall						
Demolish	L.F.		.71		.71	Includes material and labor to install
Install	L.F.	1.42	1.68		3.10	aluminum end wall flashing, .024"
Demolish and Install	L.F.	1.42	2.39		3.81	thick.
Minimum Charge	Job		142		142	
Side Wall						
Demolish	L.F.		.14		.14	Includes material and labor to install
Install	L.F.	1.41	1.68		3.09	aluminum side wall flashing, .024"
Demolish and Install	L.F.	1.41	1.82		3.23	thick.
Minimum Charge	Job		142		142	
Coping and Wall Cap						
Demolish	L.F.		.96		.96	Includes material and labor to install
Install	L.F.	1.60	1.86		3.46	aluminum flashing, mill finish, 0.40
Demolish and Install	L.F.	1.60	2.82		4.42	thick, 12" wide.
Clean	L.F.	.07	.65		.72	
Minimum Charge	Job		135		135	

Roofing

Roof Shingles

	Unit	Material	Labor	Equip.	Total	Specification
Underlayment						
15#						
Demolish	Sq.		7.65		7.65	Includes material and labor to install
Install	Sq.	2.34	4.23		6.57	#15 felt underlayment.
Demolish and Install	Sq.	2.34	11.88		14.22	
Minimum Charge	Job		135		135	
30#						
Demolish	Sq.		7.65		7.65	Includes material and labor to install
Install	Sq.	5.40	4.66		10.06	#30 felt underlayment.
Demolish and Install	Sq.	5.40	12.31		17.71	
Minimum Charge	Job		135		135	
Self Adhering						
Demolish	Sq.		19.15		19.15	Includes material and labor to install
Install	Sq.	40.50	12.30		52.80	self adhering ice barrier roofing
Demolish and Install	Sq.	40.50	31.45		71.95	underlayment.
Minimum Charge	Job		135		135	

Rolled Roofing

	Unit	Material	Labor	Equip.	Total	Specification
90 lb						
Demolish	Sq.		19.15		19.15	Cost includes material and labor to
Install	Sq.	16.25	18.05		34.30	install 90 lb mineral surface rolled
Demolish and Install	Sq.	16.25	37.20		53.45	roofing.
Minimum Charge	Job		135		135	
110 lb						
Demolish	Sq.		19.15		19.15	Cost includes material and labor to
Install	Sq.	44.50	18.05		62.55	install 110 lb mineral surface rolled
Demolish and Install	Sq.	44.50	37.20		81.70	roofing.
Minimum Charge	Job		135		135	
140 lb						
Demolish	Sq.		19.15		19.15	Cost includes material and labor to
Install	Sq.	44.50	27		71.50	install 140 lb mineral surface rolled
Demolish and Install	Sq.	44.50	46.15		90.65	roofing.
Minimum Charge	Job		135		135	

Composition Shingles

	Unit	Material	Labor	Equip.	Total	Specification
Fiberglass (3-tab)						
225 lb, 20 Year						
Demolish	Sq.		21		21	Cost includes material and labor to
Install	Sq.	26	52.50		78.50	install 225 lb, 20 year fiberglass
Demolish and Install	Sq.	26	73.50		99.50	shingles.
Minimum Charge	Job		135		135	
300 lb, 25 Year						
Demolish	Sq.		21		21	Cost includes material and labor to
Install	Sq.	33.50	52.50		86	install 300 lb, 25 year fiberglass
Demolish and Install	Sq.	33.50	73.50		107	shingles.
Minimum Charge	Job		135		135	
Emergency Repairs						
Install	Ea.	72	135		207	Includes labor and material for
Minimum Charge	Job		135		135	emergency repairs.

Roofing

Composition Shingles	Unit	Material	Labor	Equip.	Total	Specification
Architectural						
Laminated, 25 Year						
Demolish	Sq.		21		21	Cost includes material and labor to
Install	Sq.	51	52.50		103.50	install 25 year fiberglass roof shingles.
Demolish and Install	Sq.	51	73.50		124.50	
Minimum Charge	Job		135		135	
Laminated, 30 Year						
Demolish	Sq.		21		21	Cost includes material and labor to
Install	Sq.	33.50	52.50		86	install 30 year fiberglass roof shingles.
Demolish and Install	Sq.	33.50	73.50		107	
Minimum Charge	Job		135		135	
Laminated, 40 Year						
Demolish	Sq.		21		21	Cost includes material and labor to
Install	Sq.	69	52.50		121.50	install 40 year fiberglass roof shingles.
Demolish and Install	Sq.	69	73.50		142.50	
Minimum Charge	Job		135		135	
Laminated Shake, 40 Year						
Demolish	Sq.		21		21	Cost includes material and labor to
Install	Sq.	98.50	70.50		169	install 40 year fiberglass roof shakes.
Demolish and Install	Sq.	98.50	91.50		190	
Minimum Charge	Job		135		135	
Emergency Repairs						
Install	Ea.	72	135		207	Includes labor and material for
Minimum Charge	Job		135		135	emergency repairs.
Roof Jack						
Demolish	Ea.		4.18		4.18	Includes material and labor to install
Install	Ea.	14.05	28.50		42.55	residential roof jack, w/bird screen,
Demolish and Install	Ea.	14.05	32.68		46.73	backdraft damper, 3" & 4" dia. round
Paint	Ea.	.06	3.19		3.25	duct.
Minimum Charge	Job		155		155	
Ridge Vent						
Demolish	L.F.		.74		.74	Includes material and labor to install a
Install	L.F.	2.35	2.01		4.36	mill finish aluminum ridge vent strip.
Demolish and Install	L.F.	2.35	2.75		5.10	
Minimum Charge	Job		142		142	
Shingle Molding						
1" x 2"						
Demolish	L.F.		.14		.14	Cost includes material and labor to
Install	L.F.	.28	.86		1.14	install 1" x 2" pine trim.
Demolish and Install	L.F.	.28	1		1.28	
Paint	L.F.	.02	.40		.42	
Minimum Charge	Job		142		142	
1" x 3"						
Demolish	L.F.		.14		.14	Cost includes material and labor to
Install	L.F.	.39	.98		1.37	install 1" x 3" pine trim.
Demolish and Install	L.F.	.39	1.12		1.51	
Paint	L.F.	.02	.40		.42	
Minimum Charge	Job		142		142	
1" x 4"						
Demolish	L.F.		.14		.14	Cost includes material and labor to
Install	L.F.	.64	1.14		1.78	install 1" x 4" pine trim.
Demolish and Install	L.F.	.64	1.28		1.92	
Paint	L.F.	.02	.40		.42	
Minimum Charge	Job		142		142	
Add for Steep Pitch						
Install	Sq.		16.90		16.90	Includes labor and material added for
						2nd story or steep roofs.

Roofing

Composition Shingles

Composition Shingles		Unit	Material	Labor	Equip.	Total	Specification
Add for Additional Story	Install	Sq.		16.90		16.90	Includes labor and material added for 2nd story or steep roofs.

Wood Shingles

Wood Shingles		Unit	Material	Labor	Equip.	Total	Specification
Cedar Wood Shingles							
16" Red Label (#2)							
	Demolish	Sq.		51		51	Includes material and labor to install
	Install	Sq.	127	114		241	wood shingles/shakes.
	Demolish and Install	Sq.	127	165		292	
	Minimum Charge	Job		142		142	
16" Blue Label (#1)							
	Demolish	Sq.		51		51	Includes material and labor to install
	Install	Sq.	166	87.50		253.50	wood shingles/shakes.
	Demolish and Install	Sq.	166	138.50		304.50	
	Minimum Charge	Job		142		142	
18" Red Label (#2)							
	Demolish	Sq.		51		51	Includes material and labor to install
	Install	Sq.	219	73		292	wood shingles/shakes.
	Demolish and Install	Sq.	219	124		343	
	Minimum Charge	Job		142		142	
18" Blue Label (#1)							
	Demolish	Sq.		51		51	Includes material and labor to install
	Install	Sq.	176	80		256	wood shingles/shakes.
	Demolish and Install	Sq.	176	131		307	
	Minimum Charge	Job		142		142	
Replace Shingle							
	Install	Ea.	13.20	7.10		20.30	Includes labor and material to replace
	Minimum Charge	Job		142		142	individual wood shingle/shake. Cost is per shingle.
Cedar Shake							
18" Medium Handsplit							
	Demolish	Sq.		51		51	Includes material and labor to install
	Install	Sq.	107	110		217	wood shingles/shakes.
	Demolish and Install	Sq.	107	161		268	
	Minimum Charge	Job		142		142	
18" Heavy Handsplit							
	Demolish	Sq.		51		51	Includes material and labor to install
	Install	Sq.	107	122		229	wood shingles/shakes.
	Demolish and Install	Sq.	107	173		280	
	Minimum Charge	Job		142		142	
24" Heavy Handsplit							
	Demolish	Sq.		51		51	Includes material and labor to install
	Install	Sq.	152	97.50		249.50	wood shingles/shakes.
	Demolish and Install	Sq.	152	148.50		300.50	
	Minimum Charge	Job		142		142	
24" Medium Handsplit							
	Demolish	Sq.		51		51	Includes material and labor to install
	Install	Sq.	152	87.50		239.50	wood shingles/shakes.
	Demolish and Install	Sq.	152	138.50		290.50	
	Minimum Charge	Job		142		142	

Roofing

Wood Shingles

Wood Shingles	Unit	Material	Labor	Equip.	Total	Specification
24" Straight Split						
Demolish	Sq.		51		51	Includes material and labor to install
Install	Sq.	163	129		292	wood shingles/shakes.
Demolish and Install	Sq.	163	180		343	
Minimum Charge	Job		142		142	
24" Tapersplit						
Demolish	Sq.		51		51	Includes material and labor to install
Install	Sq.	163	129		292	wood shingles/shakes.
Demolish and Install	Sq.	163	180		343	
Minimum Charge	Job		142		142	
18" Straight Split						
Demolish	Sq.		51		51	Includes material and labor to install
Install	Sq.	121	129		250	wood shingles/shakes.
Demolish and Install	Sq.	121	180		301	
Minimum Charge	Job		142		142	
Replace Shingle						
Install	Ea.	13.20	7.10		20.30	Includes labor and material to replace
Minimum Charge	Job		142		142	individual wood shingle/shake. Cost is per shingle.

Slate Tile Roofing

Slate Tile Roofing	Unit	Material	Labor	Equip.	Total	Specification
Unfading Green						
Demolish	Sq.		46		46	Includes material and labor to install
Install	Sq.	490	155		645	clear Vermont slate tile.
Demolish and Install	Sq.	490	201		691	
Reinstall	Sq.		124.16		124.16	
Minimum Charge	Job		136		136	
Unfading Purple						
Demolish	Sq.		46		46	Includes material and labor to install
Install	Sq.	430	155		585	clear Vermont slate tile.
Demolish and Install	Sq.	430	201		631	
Reinstall	Sq.		124.16		124.16	
Minimum Charge	Job		136		136	
Replace Slate Tiles						
Install	Ea.	5.95	14.30		20.25	Includes labor and material to replace
Minimum Charge	Job		136		136	individual slate tiles. Cost is per tile.
Variegated Purple						
Demolish	Sq.		46		46	Includes material and labor to install
Install	Sq.	415	155		570	clear Vermont slate tile.
Demolish and Install	Sq.	415	201		616	
Reinstall	Sq.		124.16		124.16	
Minimum Charge	Job		136		136	
Unfading Grey / Black						
Demolish	Sq.		46		46	Includes material and labor to install
Install	Sq.	380	155		535	clear Vermont slate tile.
Demolish and Install	Sq.	380	201		581	
Reinstall	Sq.		124.16		124.16	
Minimum Charge	Job		136		136	
Unfading Red						
Demolish	Sq.		46		46	Includes material and labor to install
Install	Sq.	1250	155		1405	clear Vermont slate tile.
Demolish and Install	Sq.	1250	201		1451	
Reinstall	Sq.		124.16		124.16	
Minimum Charge	Job		136		136	

Roofing

Slate Tile Roofing

Slate Tile Roofing	Unit	Material	Labor	Equip.	Total	Specification
Weathering Black						
Demolish	Sq.		46		46	Includes material and labor to install
Install	Sq.	480	155		635	clear Pennsylvania slate tile.
Demolish and Install	Sq.	480	201		681	
Reinstall	Sq.		124.16		124.16	
Minimum Charge	Job		136		136	
Weathering Green						
Demolish	Sq.		46		46	Includes material and labor to install
Install	Sq.	325	155		480	clear Vermont slate tile.
Demolish and Install	Sq.	325	201		526	
Reinstall	Sq.		124.16		124.16	
Minimum Charge	Job		136		136	

Flat Clay Tile Roofing

Flat Clay Tile Roofing	Unit	Material	Labor	Equip.	Total	Specification
Glazed						
Demolish	Sq.		51		51	Includes material and labor to install
Install	Sq.	495	109		604	tile roofing. Cost based on terra cotta
Demolish and Install	Sq.	495	160		655	red flat clay tile and includes ridge
Reinstall	Sq.		86.91		86.91	and rake tiles.
Minimum Charge	Job		136		136	
Terra Cotta Red						
Demolish	Sq.		51		51	Includes material and labor to install
Install	Sq.	495	109		604	tile roofing. Cost based on terra cotta
Demolish and Install	Sq.	495	160		655	red flat clay tile and includes ridge
Reinstall	Sq.		86.91		86.91	and rake tiles.
Minimum Charge	Job		136		136	

Mission Tile Roofing

Mission Tile Roofing	Unit	Material	Labor	Equip.	Total	Specification
Glazed Red						
Demolish	Sq.		51		51	Includes material and labor to install
Install	Sq.	715	181		896	tile roofing. Cost based on glazed red
Demolish and Install	Sq.	715	232		947	tile and includes birdstop, ridge and
Reinstall	Sq.		144.85		144.85	rake tiles.
Minimum Charge	Job		136		136	
Unglazed Red						
Demolish	Sq.		51		51	Includes material and labor to install
Install	Sq.	715	181		896	tile roofing. Cost based on unglazed
Demolish and Install	Sq.	715	232		947	red tile and includes birdstop, ridge
Reinstall	Sq.		144.85		144.85	and rake tiles.
Minimum Charge	Job		136		136	
Glazed Blue						
Demolish	Sq.		51		51	Includes material and labor to install
Install	Sq.	715	181		896	tile roofing. Cost based on glazed blue
Demolish and Install	Sq.	715	232		947	tile and includes birdstop, ridge and
Reinstall	Sq.		144.85		144.85	rake tiles.
Minimum Charge	Job		136		136	
Glazed White						
Demolish	Sq.		51		51	Includes material and labor to install
Install	Sq.	715	181		896	tile roofing. Cost based on glazed
Demolish and Install	Sq.	715	232		947	white tile and includes birdstop, ridge
Reinstall	Sq.		144.85		144.85	and rake tiles.
Minimum Charge	Job		136		136	

Mission Tile Roofing		Unit	Material	Labor	Equip.	Total	Specification
Unglazed White							
	Demolish	Sq.		51		51	Includes material and labor to install
	Install	Sq.	715	181		896	tile roofing. Cost based on unglazed
	Demolish and Install	Sq.	715	232		947	white tile and includes birdstop, ridge
	Reinstall	Sq.		144.85		144.85	and rake tiles.
	Minimum Charge	Job		136		136	
Color Blend							
	Demolish	Sq.		51		51	Includes material and labor to install
	Install	Sq.	715	181		896	tile roofing. Cost based on color blend
	Demolish and Install	Sq.	715	232		947	tile and includes birdstop, ridge and
	Reinstall	Sq.		144.85		144.85	rake tiles.
	Minimum Charge	Job		136		136	
Accessories / Extras							
Add for Cap Furring Strips							
	Install	Sq.	78	170		248	Includes labor and material to install vertically placed wood furring strips under cap tiles.
Add for Tile Adhesive							
	Install	Sq.	13.35	9.90		23.25	Includes material and labor for adhesive material placed between tiles.
Add for Wire Attachment							
	Install	Sq.	13.20	118		131.20	Includes labor and material to install single wire anchors for attaching tile.
Add for Braided Runners							
	Install	Sq.	23.50	113		136.50	Includes labor and material to install braided wire runners for secure attachment in high wind areas.
Add for Stainless Steel Nails							
	Install	Sq.	18.20			18.20	Includes material only for stainless steel nails.
Add for Brass Nails							
	Install	Sq.	24			24	Includes material only for brass nails.
Add for Hurricane Clips							
	Install	Sq.	15.95	160		175.95	Includes material and labor for Hurricane or wind clips for high wind areas.
Add for Copper Nails							
	Install	Sq.	24			24	Includes material only for copper nails.
Add for Vertical Furring Strips							
	Install	Sq.	15.40	31.50		46.90	Includes labor and material to install vertically placed wood furring strips under tiles.
Add for Horizontal Furring Strips							
	Install	Sq.	9.90	14.15		24.05	Includes labor and material to install horizontally placed wood furring strips under tiles.

Roofing

Spanish Tile Roofing	Unit	Material	Labor	Equip.	Total	Specification
Glazed Red						
Demolish	Sq.		51		51	Includes material and labor to install
Install	Sq.	495	113		608	tile roofing. Cost based on glazed red
Demolish and Install	Sq.	495	164		659	tile and includes birdstop, ridge and
Reinstall	Sq.		90.53		90.53	rake tiles.
Minimum Charge	Job		136		136	
Glazed White						
Demolish	Sq.		51		51	Includes material and labor to install
Install	Sq.	495	113		608	tile roofing. Cost based on glazed
Demolish and Install	Sq.	495	164		659	white tile and includes birdstop, ridge
Reinstall	Sq.		90.53		90.53	and rake tiles.
Minimum Charge	Job		136		136	
Glazed Blue						
Demolish	Sq.		51		51	Includes material and labor to install
Install	Sq.	495	113		608	tile roofing. Cost based on glazed blue
Demolish and Install	Sq.	495	164		659	tile and includes birdstop, ridge and
Reinstall	Sq.		90.53		90.53	rake tiles.
Minimum Charge	Job		136		136	
Unglazed Red						
Demolish	Sq.		51		51	Includes material and labor to install
Install	Sq.	495	113		608	tile roofing. Cost based on unglazed
Demolish and Install	Sq.	495	164		659	red tile and includes birdstop, ridge
Reinstall	Sq.		90.53		90.53	and rake tiles.
Minimum Charge	Job		136		136	
Unglazed White						
Demolish	Sq.		51		51	Includes material and labor to install
Install	Sq.	495	113		608	tile roofing. Cost based on unglazed
Demolish and Install	Sq.	495	164		659	white tile and includes birdstop, ridge
Reinstall	Sq.		90.53		90.53	and rake tiles.
Minimum Charge	Job		136		136	
Color Blend						
Demolish	Sq.		51		51	Includes material and labor to install
Install	Sq.	495	113		608	tile roofing. Cost based on color blend
Demolish and Install	Sq.	495	164		659	tile and includes birdstop, ridge and
Reinstall	Sq.		90.53		90.53	rake tiles.
Minimum Charge	Job		136		136	
Accessories / Extras						
Add for Vertical Furring Strips						
Install	Sq.	15.40	31.50		46.90	Includes labor and material to install vertically placed wood furring strips under tiles.
Add for Wire Attachment						
Install	Sq.	11	90.50		101.50	Includes labor and material to install single wire ties.
Add for Braided Runners						
Install	Sq.	19.45	77.50		96.95	Includes labor and material to install braided wire runners for secure attachment in high wind areas.
Add for Stainless Steel Nails						
Install	Sq.	15.40			15.40	Includes material only for stainless steel nails.
Add for Copper Nails						
Install	Sq.	20.50			20.50	Includes material only for copper nails.

Spanish Tile Roofing

Spanish Tile Roofing		Unit	Material	Labor	Equip.	Total	Specification
Add for Brass Nails	Install	Sq.	20.50			20.50	Includes material only for brass nails.
Add for Hurricane Clips	Install	Sq.	12.20	93.50		105.70	Includes material and labor to install hurricane or wind clips for high wind areas.
Add for Mortar Set Tiles	Install	Sq.	38	136		174	Includes material and labor to install setting tiles by using mortar material placed between tiles.
Add for Tile Adhesive	Install	Sq.	12.40	8.80		21.20	Includes material and labor for adhesive placed between tiles.
Add for Cap Furring Strips	Install	Sq.	78	170		248	Includes labor and material to install vertically placed wood furring strips under cap tiles.
Add for Horizontal Furring Strips	Install	Sq.	9.90	14.15		24.05	Includes labor and material to install horizontally placed wood furring strips under tiles.

Concrete Tile Roofing

Concrete Tile Roofing		Unit	Material	Labor	Equip.	Total	Specification
Corrugated Red / Brown							
	Demolish	Sq.		51		51	Includes material and labor to install
	Install	Sq.	121	201		322	tile roofing. Cost includes birdstop,
	Demolish and Install	Sq.	121	252		373	booster, ridge and rake tiles.
	Reinstall	Sq.		160.95		160.95	
	Minimum Charge	Job		136		136	
Corrugated Gray							
	Demolish	Sq.		51		51	Includes material and labor to install
	Install	Sq.	121	201		322	tile roofing. Cost includes birdstop,
	Demolish and Install	Sq.	121	252		373	booster, ridge and rake tiles.
	Reinstall	Sq.		160.95		160.95	
	Minimum Charge	Job		136		136	
Corrugated Bright Red							
	Demolish	Sq.		51		51	Includes material and labor to install
	Install	Sq.	121	201		322	tile roofing. Cost includes birdstop,
	Demolish and Install	Sq.	121	252		373	booster, ridge and rake tiles.
	Reinstall	Sq.		160.95		160.95	
	Minimum Charge	Job		136		136	
Corrugated Black							
	Demolish	Sq.		51		51	Includes material and labor to install
	Install	Sq.	121	201		322	tile roofing. Cost includes birdstop,
	Demolish and Install	Sq.	121	252		373	booster, ridge and rake tiles.
	Reinstall	Sq.		160.95		160.95	
	Minimum Charge	Job		136		136	
Corrugated Green							
	Demolish	Sq.		51		51	Includes material and labor to install
	Install	Sq.	121	201		322	tile roofing. Cost includes birdstop,
	Demolish and Install	Sq.	121	252		373	booster, ridge and rake tiles.
	Reinstall	Sq.		160.95		160.95	
	Minimum Charge	Job		136		136	

Concrete Tile Roofing

Concrete Tile Roofing	Unit	Material	Labor	Equip.	Total	Specification
Corrugated Blue						
Demolish	Sq.		51		51	Includes material and labor to install
Install	Sq.	121	201		322	tile roofing. Cost includes birdstop,
Demolish and Install	Sq.	121	252		373	booster, ridge and rake tiles.
Reinstall	Sq.		160.95		160.95	
Minimum Charge	Job		136		136	
Flat Natural Gray						
Demolish	Sq.		51		51	Includes material and labor to install
Install	Sq.	105	201		306	tile roofing. Cost includes birdstop,
Demolish and Install	Sq.	105	252		357	booster, ridge and rake tiles.
Reinstall	Sq.		160.95		160.95	
Minimum Charge	Job		136		136	
Flat Red / Brown						
Demolish	Sq.		51		51	Includes material and labor to install
Install	Sq.	105	201		306	tile roofing. Cost includes birdstop,
Demolish and Install	Sq.	105	252		357	booster, ridge and rake tiles.
Reinstall	Sq.		160.95		160.95	
Minimum Charge	Job		136		136	
Flat Bright Red						
Demolish	Sq.		51		51	Includes material and labor to install
Install	Sq.	105	201		306	tile roofing. Cost includes birdstop,
Demolish and Install	Sq.	105	252		357	booster, ridge and rake tiles.
Reinstall	Sq.		160.95		160.95	
Minimum Charge	Job		136		136	
Flat Green						
Demolish	Sq.		51		51	Includes material and labor to install
Install	Sq.	105	201		306	tile roofing. Cost includes birdstop,
Demolish and Install	Sq.	105	252		357	booster, ridge and rake tiles.
Minimum Charge	Job		136		136	
Flat Blue						
Demolish	Sq.		51		51	Includes material and labor to install
Install	Sq.	105	201		306	tile roofing. Cost includes birdstop,
Demolish and Install	Sq.	105	252		357	booster, ridge and rake tiles.
Reinstall	Sq.		160.95		160.95	
Minimum Charge	Job		136		136	
Flat Black						
Demolish	Sq.		51		51	Includes material and labor to install
Install	Sq.	105	201		306	tile roofing. Cost includes birdstop,
Demolish and Install	Sq.	105	252		357	booster, ridge and rake tiles.
Reinstall	Sq.		160.95		160.95	
Minimum Charge	Job		136		136	

Aluminum Sheet

Aluminum Sheet	Unit	Material	Labor	Equip.	Total	Specification
Corrugated						
.019" Thick Natural						
Demolish	S.F.		.55		.55	Includes material and labor to install
Install	S.F.	.88	1.30		2.18	aluminum sheet metal roofing.
Demolish and Install	S.F.	.88	1.85		2.73	
Reinstall	S.F.		1.04		1.04	
Minimum Charge	Job		310		310	
.016" Thick Natural						
Demolish	S.F.		.55		.55	Includes material and labor to install
Install	S.F.	.68	1.30		1.98	aluminum sheet metal roofing.
Demolish and Install	S.F.	.68	1.85		2.53	
Reinstall	S.F.		1.04		1.04	
Minimum Charge	Job		310		310	

Roofing

Aluminum Sheet	Unit	Material	Labor	Equip.	Total	Specification
.016" Colored Finish						
Demolish	S.F.		.55		.55	Includes material and labor to install
Install	S.F.	.98	1.30		2.28	aluminum sheet metal roofing.
Demolish and Install	S.F.	.98	1.85		2.83	
Reinstall	S.F.		1.04		1.04	
Minimum Charge	Job		310		310	
.019" Colored Finish						
Demolish	S.F.		.55		.55	Includes material and labor to install
Install	S.F.	1.09	1.30		2.39	aluminum sheet metal roofing.
Demolish and Install	S.F.	1.09	1.85		2.94	
Reinstall	S.F.		1.04		1.04	
Minimum Charge	Job		310		310	
Ribbed						
.019" Thick Natural						
Demolish	S.F.		.55		.55	Includes material and labor to install
Install	S.F.	.88	1.30		2.18	aluminum sheet metal roofing.
Demolish and Install	S.F.	.88	1.85		2.73	
Reinstall	S.F.		1.04		1.04	
Minimum Charge	Job		310		310	
.016" Thick Natural						
Demolish	S.F.		.55		.55	Includes material and labor to install
Install	S.F.	.68	1.30		1.98	aluminum sheet metal roofing.
Demolish and Install	S.F.	.68	1.85		2.53	
Reinstall	S.F.		1.04		1.04	
Minimum Charge	Job		310		310	
.050" Colored Finish						
Demolish	S.F.		.55		.55	Includes material and labor to install
Install	S.F.	2.89	1.30		4.19	aluminum sheet metal roofing.
Demolish and Install	S.F.	2.89	1.85		4.74	
Reinstall	S.F.		1.04		1.04	
Minimum Charge	Job		310		310	
.032" Thick Natural						
Demolish	S.F.		.55		.55	Includes material and labor to install
Install	S.F.	1.54	1.30		2.84	aluminum sheet metal roofing.
Demolish and Install	S.F.	1.54	1.85		3.39	
Reinstall	S.F.		1.04		1.04	
Minimum Charge	Job		310		310	
.040" Thick Natural						
Demolish	S.F.		.55		.55	Includes material and labor to install
Install	S.F.	1.87	1.30		3.17	aluminum sheet metal roofing.
Demolish and Install	S.F.	1.87	1.85		3.72	
Reinstall	S.F.		1.04		1.04	
Minimum Charge	Job		310		310	
.050" Thick Natural						
Demolish	S.F.		.55		.55	Includes material and labor to install
Install	S.F.	2.39	1.30		3.69	aluminum sheet metal roofing.
Demolish and Install	S.F.	2.39	1.85		4.24	
Reinstall	S.F.		1.04		1.04	
Minimum Charge	Job		310		310	
.016" Colored Finish						
Demolish	S.F.		.55		.55	Includes material and labor to install
Install	S.F.	.98	1.30		2.28	aluminum sheet metal roofing.
Demolish and Install	S.F.	.98	1.85		2.83	
Reinstall	S.F.		1.04		1.04	
Minimum Charge	Job		310		310	

Roofing

Aluminum Sheet

Aluminum Sheet		Unit	Material	Labor	Equip.	Total	Specification
.019″ Colored Finish							
	Demolish	S.F.		.55		.55	Includes material and labor to install
	Install	S.F.	1.09	1.30		2.39	aluminum sheet metal roofing.
	Demolish and Install	S.F.	1.09	1.85		2.94	
	Reinstall	S.F.		1.04		1.04	
	Minimum Charge	Job		310		310	
.032″ Colored Finish							
	Demolish	S.F.		.55		.55	Includes material and labor to install
	Install	S.F.	2.01	1.30		3.31	aluminum sheet metal roofing.
	Demolish and Install	S.F.	2.01	1.85		3.86	
	Reinstall	S.F.		1.04		1.04	
	Minimum Charge	Job		310		310	
.040″ Colored Finish							
	Demolish	S.F.		.55		.55	Includes material and labor to install
	Install	S.F.	2.41	1.30		3.71	aluminum sheet metal roofing.
	Demolish and Install	S.F.	2.41	1.85		4.26	
	Reinstall	S.F.		1.04		1.04	
	Minimum Charge	Job		310		310	

Fiberglass Sheet

Fiberglass Sheet		Unit	Material	Labor	Equip.	Total	Specification
12 Ounce Corrugated							
	Demolish	S.F.		.98		.98	Cost includes material and labor to
	Install	S.F.	5.70	1.04		6.74	install 12 ounce corrugated fiberglass
	Demolish and Install	S.F.	5.70	2.02		7.72	sheet roofing.
	Reinstall	S.F.		.83		.83	
	Minimum Charge	Job		135		135	
8 Ounce Corrugated							
	Demolish	S.F.		.98		.98	Cost includes material and labor to
	Install	S.F.	2.46	1.04		3.50	install 8 ounce corrugated fiberglass
	Demolish and Install	S.F.	2.46	2.02		4.48	roofing.
	Reinstall	S.F.		.83		.83	
	Minimum Charge	Job		135		135	

Galvanized Steel

Galvanized Steel		Unit	Material	Labor	Equip.	Total	Specification
Corrugated							
24 Gauge							
	Demolish	S.F.		.55		.55	Includes material and labor to install
	Install	S.F.	1.16	1.09		2.25	galvanized steel sheet metal roofing.
	Demolish and Install	S.F.	1.16	1.64		2.80	Cost based on 24 gauge corrugated
	Reinstall	S.F.		.87		.87	or ribbed steel roofing.
	Minimum Charge	Job		135		135	
26 Gauge							
	Demolish	S.F.		.55		.55	Includes material and labor to install
	Install	S.F.	.99	1.04		2.03	galvanized steel sheet metal roofing.
	Demolish and Install	S.F.	.99	1.59		2.58	Cost based on 26 gauge corrugated
	Reinstall	S.F.		.83		.83	or ribbed steel roofing.
	Minimum Charge	Job		135		135	
28 Gauge							
	Demolish	S.F.		.55		.55	Includes material and labor to install
	Install	S.F.	.89	.99		1.88	galvanized steel sheet metal roofing.
	Demolish and Install	S.F.	.89	1.54		2.43	Cost based on 28 gauge corrugated
	Reinstall	S.F.		.79		.79	or ribbed steel roofing.
	Minimum Charge	Job		135		135	

Roofing

Galvanized Steel

Galvanized Steel	Unit	Material	Labor	Equip.	Total	Specification
30 Gauge						
Demolish	S.F.		.55		.55	Includes material and labor to install
Install	S.F.	.85	.94		1.79	galvanized steel sheet metal roofing.
Demolish and Install	S.F.	.85	1.49		2.34	Cost based on 30 gauge corrugated
Reinstall	S.F.		.75		.75	or ribbed steel roofing.
Minimum Charge	Job		135		135	
Ribbed						
24 Gauge						
Demolish	S.F.		.55		.55	Includes material and labor to install
Install	S.F.	1.16	1.09		2.25	galvanized steel sheet metal roofing.
Demolish and Install	S.F.	1.16	1.64		2.80	Cost based on 24 gauge corrugated
Reinstall	S.F.		.87		.87	or ribbed steel roofing.
Minimum Charge	Job		135		135	
26 Gauge						
Demolish	S.F.		.55		.55	Includes material and labor to install
Install	S.F.	.99	1.04		2.03	galvanized steel sheet metal roofing.
Demolish and Install	S.F.	.99	1.59		2.58	Cost based on 26 gauge corrugated
Reinstall	S.F.		.83		.83	or ribbed steel roofing.
Minimum Charge	Job		135		135	
28 Gauge						
Demolish	S.F.		.55		.55	Includes material and labor to install
Install	S.F.	.89	.99		1.88	galvanized steel sheet metal roofing.
Demolish and Install	S.F.	.89	1.54		2.43	Cost based on 28 gauge corrugated
Reinstall	S.F.		.79		.79	or ribbed steel roofing.
Minimum Charge	Job		135		135	
30 Gauge						
Demolish	S.F.		.55		.55	Includes material and labor to install
Install	S.F.	.85	.94		1.79	galvanized steel sheet metal roofing.
Demolish and Install	S.F.	.85	1.49		2.34	Cost based on 30 gauge corrugated
Reinstall	S.F.		.75		.75	or ribbed steel roofing.
Minimum Charge	Job		135		135	

Standing Seam

Standing Seam	Unit	Material	Labor	Equip.	Total	Specification
Copper						
16 Ounce						
Demolish	Sq.		55		55	Includes material and labor to install
Install	Sq.	430	240		670	copper standing seam metal roofing.
Demolish and Install	Sq.	430	295		725	Cost based on 16 ounce copper
Reinstall	Sq.		191.75		191.75	roofing.
Minimum Charge	Job		156		156	
18 Ounce						
Demolish	Sq.		55		55	Includes material and labor to install
Install	Sq.	480	260		740	copper standing seam metal roofing.
Demolish and Install	Sq.	480	315		795	Cost based on 18 ounce copper
Reinstall	Sq.		207.73		207.73	roofing.
Minimum Charge	Job		156		156	
20 Ounce						
Demolish	Sq.		55		55	Includes material and labor to install
Install	Sq.	510	283		793	copper standing seam metal roofing.
Demolish and Install	Sq.	510	338		848	Cost based on 20 ounce copper
Reinstall	Sq.		226.62		226.62	roofing.

Roofing

Standing Seam

Standing Seam		Unit	Material	Labor	Equip.	Total	Specification
Stainless Steel							
26 Gauge							Cost includes material and labor to
	Demolish	Sq.		55		55	install 26 gauge stainless steel
	Install	Sq.	420	271		691	standing seam metal roofing.
	Demolish and Install	Sq.	420	326		746	
	Reinstall	Sq.		216.77		216.77	
	Minimum Charge	Job		156		156	
28 Gauge							Includes material and labor to install
	Demolish	Sq.		55		55	standing seam metal roofing. Cost
	Install	Sq.	335	260		595	based on 28 gauge stainless steel
	Demolish and Install	Sq.	335	315		650	roofing.
	Reinstall	Sq.		207.73		207.73	
	Minimum Charge	Job		156		156	

Elastomeric Roofing

Elastomeric Roofing		Unit	Material	Labor	Equip.	Total	Specification
Neoprene							
1/16"							Includes material and labor to install
	Demolish	Sq.		19		19	neoprene membrane, fully adhered,
	Install	Sq.	190	130	24	344	1/16" thick.
	Demolish and Install	Sq.	190	149	24	363	
	Minimum Charge	Job		620	88	708	
GRM Membrane							
	Demolish	Sq.		19		19	Includes material and labor to install
	Install	Sq.	239	207	29.50	475.50	coal tar based elastomeric roofing
	Demolish and Install	Sq.	239	226	29.50	494.50	membrane, polyester fiber reinforced.
	Minimum Charge	Job		620	88	708	
Cant Strips							
3"							Includes material and labor to install
	Demolish	L.F.		.59		.59	cants 3" x 3", treated timber, cut
	Install	L.F.	.44	.83		1.27	diagonally.
	Demolish and Install	L.F.	.44	1.42		1.86	
	Minimum Charge	Job		135		135	
4"							Includes material and labor to install
	Demolish	L.F.		.59		.59	cants 4" x 4", treated timber, cut
	Install	L.F.	1.36	.83		2.19	diagonally.
	Demolish and Install	L.F.	1.36	1.42		2.78	
	Minimum Charge	Job		135		135	
Polyvinyl Chloride (PVC)							
45 mil (loose laid)							Cost includes material and labor to
	Demolish	Sq.		19		19	install 45 mil PVC elastomeric roofing,
	Install	Sq.	89	24.50	3.44	116.94	loose-laid with stone.
	Demolish and Install	Sq.	89	43.50	3.44	135.94	
	Minimum Charge	Job		620	88	708	
48 mil (loose laid)							Cost includes material and labor to
	Demolish	Sq.		19		19	install 48 mil PVC elastomeric roofing,
	Install	Sq.	103	24.50	3.44	130.94	loose-laid with stone.
	Demolish and Install	Sq.	103	43.50	3.44	149.94	
	Minimum Charge	Job		620	88	708	
60 mil (loose laid)							Cost includes material and labor to
	Demolish	Sq.		19		19	install 60 mil PVC elastomeric roofing,
	Install	Sq.	101	24.50	3.44	128.94	loose-laid with stone.
	Demolish and Install	Sq.	101	43.50	3.44	147.94	
	Minimum Charge	Job		620	88	708	

Roofing

Elastomeric Roofing		Unit	Material	Labor	Equip.	Total	Specification
45 mil (attached)							
	Demolish	Sq.		28		28	Cost includes material and labor to
	Install	Sq.	77.50	48	6.75	132.25	install 45 mil PVC elastomeric roofing
	Demolish and Install	Sq.	77.50	76	6.75	160.25	fully attached to roof deck.
	Minimum Charge	Job		620	88	708	
48 mil (attached)							
	Demolish	Sq.		28		28	Cost includes material and labor to
	Install	Sq.	129	48	6.75	183.75	install 48 mil PVC elastomeric roofing
	Demolish and Install	Sq.	129	76	6.75	211.75	fully attached to roof deck.
	Minimum Charge	Job		620	88	708	
60 mil (attached)							
	Demolish	Sq.		28		28	Cost includes material and labor to
	Install	Sq.	127	48	6.75	181.75	install 60 mil PVC elastomeric roofing
	Demolish and Install	Sq.	127	76	6.75	209.75	fully attached to roof deck.
	Minimum Charge	Job		620	88	708	

CSPE Type

		Unit	Material	Labor	Equip.	Total	Specification
45 mil (loose laid w / stone)							
	Demolish	Sq.		19		19	Cost includes material and labor to
	Install	Sq.	143	24.50	3.44	170.94	install 45 mil CSPE (chlorosulfonated
	Demolish and Install	Sq.	143	43.50	3.44	189.94	polyethylene-hypalon) roofing material
	Minimum Charge	Job		620	88	708	loose laid on deck and ballasted with
							stone.
45 mil (attached at seams)							
	Demolish	Sq.		45.50		45.50	Cost includes material and labor to
	Install	Sq.	138	35.50	5	178.50	install 45 mil CSPE (chlorosulfonated
	Demolish and Install	Sq.	138	81	5	224	polyethylene-hypalon) roofing material
	Minimum Charge	Job		620	88	708	attached to deck at seams with batten
							strips.
45 mil (fully attached)							
	Demolish	Sq.		28		28	Cost includes material and labor to
	Install	Sq.	135	48	6.75	189.75	install 45 mil CSPE (chlorosulfonated
	Demolish and Install	Sq.	135	76	6.75	217.75	polyethylene-hypalon) roofing material
	Minimum Charge	Job		620	88	708	fully attached to deck.

EPDM Type

		Unit	Material	Labor	Equip.	Total	Specification
45 mil (attached at seams)							
	Demolish	Sq.		45.50		45.50	Cost includes material and labor to
	Install	Sq.	61	35.50	5	101.50	install 45 mil EPDM (ethylene
	Demolish and Install	Sq.	61	81	5	147	propylene diene monomer) roofing
	Minimum Charge	Job		620	88	708	material attached to deck at seams.
45 mil (fully attached)							
	Demolish	Sq.		28		28	Cost includes material and labor to
	Install	Sq.	88.50	48	6.75	143.25	install 45 mil EPDM (ethylene
	Demolish and Install	Sq.	88.50	76	6.75	171.25	propylene diene monomer) roofing
	Minimum Charge	Job		620	88	708	material fully attached to deck.
45 mil (loose laid w / stone)							
	Demolish	Sq.		19		19	Cost includes material and labor to
	Install	Sq.	70	24.50	3.44	97.94	install 45 mil EPDM (ethylene
	Demolish and Install	Sq.	70	43.50	3.44	116.94	propylene diene monomer) roofing
	Minimum Charge	Job		620	88	708	material loose laid on deck and
							ballasted with stones (approx. 1/2 ton
							of stone per square).
60 mil (attached at seams)							
	Demolish	Sq.		45.50		45.50	Cost includes material and labor to
	Install	Sq.	73.50	35.50	5	114	install 60 mil EPDM (ethylene
	Demolish and Install	Sq.	73.50	81	5	159.50	propylene diene monomer) roofing
	Minimum Charge	Job		620	88	708	material attached to deck at seams.

Roofing

Elastomeric Roofing

Elastomeric Roofing	Unit	Material	Labor	Equip.	Total	Specification
60 mil (fully attached)						Cost includes material and labor to
Demolish	Sq.		28		28	install 60 mil EPDM (ethylene
Install	Sq.	101	48	6.75	155.75	propylene diene monomer) roofing
Demolish and Install	Sq.	101	76	6.75	183.75	material fully attached to deck.
Minimum Charge	Job		620	88	708	
60 mil (loose laid w / stone)						Cost includes material and labor to
Demolish	Sq.		19		19	install 60 mil EPDM (ethylene
Install	Sq.	83.50	24.50	3.44	111.44	propylene diene monomer) roofing
Demolish and Install	Sq.	83.50	43.50	3.44	130.44	material loose laid on deck and
Minimum Charge	Job		620	88	708	ballasted with stones (approx. 1/2 ton
						of stone per square).
Silicone-urethane Foam						
Prep Roof for Foam System						Includes labor and material to removal
Install	Sq.	5.25	108		113.25	of any gravel and prepare existing
Minimum Charge	Job		620	88	708	built-up roof for application of
						silicone-urethane foam system.

Modified Bitumen Roofing

Modified Bitumen Roofing	Unit	Material	Labor	Equip.	Total	Specification
Fully Attached						
120 mil						
Demolish	Sq.		45.50		45.50	Cost includes material and labor to
Install	Sq.	77	6.05	1.13	84.18	install 120 mil modified bitumen
Demolish and Install	Sq.	77	51.55	1.13	129.68	roofing, fully attached to deck by
Minimum Charge	Job		135		135	torch.
150 mil						
Demolish	Sq.		45.50		45.50	Cost includes material and labor to
Install	Sq.	111	14.85	2.78	128.63	install 150 mil modified bitumen
Demolish and Install	Sq.	111	60.35	2.78	174.13	roofing, fully attached to deck by
Minimum Charge	Job		890	167	1057	torch.
160 mil						
Demolish	Sq.		45.50		45.50	Cost includes material and labor to
Install	Sq.	89	15.50	2.90	107.40	install 160 mil modified bitumen
Demolish and Install	Sq.	89	61	2.90	152.90	roofing, fully attached to deck by
Minimum Charge	Job		890	167	1057	torch.

Built-up Roofing

Built-up Roofing	Unit	Material	Labor	Equip.	Total	Specification
Emergency Repairs						
Install	Ea.	142	1275	238	1655	Minimum charge for work requiring
Minimum Charge	Job		890	167	1057	hot asphalt.
Asphalt						
3-ply Asphalt						
Demolish	Sq.		47		47	Cost includes material and labor to
Install	Sq.	31.50	74.50	13.90	119.90	install 3-ply asphalt built-up roof
Demolish and Install	Sq.	31.50	121.50	13.90	166.90	including one 30 lb and two 15 lb
Minimum Charge	Job		890	167	1057	layers of felt.

Roofing

Built-up Roofing

	Unit	Material	Labor	Equip.	Total	Specification
4-ply Asphalt						Cost includes material and labor to
Demolish	Sq.		56		56	install 4-ply asphalt built-up roof
Install	Sq.	45	81	15.15	141.15	including one 30 lb and three 15 lb
Demolish and Install	Sq.	45	137	15.15	197.15	layers of felt.
Minimum Charge	Job		890	167	1057	
5-ply Asphalt						Cost includes material and labor to
Demolish	Sq.		73.50		73.50	install 5-ply asphalt built-up roof
Install	Sq.	63.50	89	16.65	169.15	including one 30 lb and four 15 lb
Demolish and Install	Sq.	63.50	162.50	16.65	242.65	layers of felt.
Minimum Charge	Job		890	167	1057	
Components / Accessories						
Flood Coat						
Install	Sq.	11.35	41.50		52.85	Includes labor and material to install flood coat.
R / R Gravel and Flood Coat						
Install	Sq.	17	135		152	Includes labor and material to install flood coat and gravel.
Aluminum UV Coat						
Install	Sq.	14.15	155	22	191.15	Includes labor and material to install aluminum-based UV coating.
Gravel Coat						
Demolish	Sq.		23.50		23.50	Includes labor and material to install
Install	Sq.	5.65	22.50		28.15	gravel coat.
Demolish & Install	Sq.	5.65	46		51.65	
Mineral Surface Cap Sheet						
Install	Sq.	18.15	4.66		22.81	Cost includes labor and material to install 50 # mineral surfaced cap sheet.
Fibrated Aluminum UV Coating						
Install	Sq.	16.10	41.50		57.60	Includes labor and material to install fibered aluminum-based UV coating.
Impregnated Walk						
1"						
Install	S.F.	2.37	1.44		3.81	Cost includes labor and material to install 1" layer of asphalt coating.
1/2"						
Install	S.F.	1.60	1.14		2.74	Cost includes labor and material to install 1/2" layer of asphalt coating.
3/4"						
Install	S.F.	1.98	1.20		3.18	Cost includes labor and material to install 3/4" layer of asphalt coating.

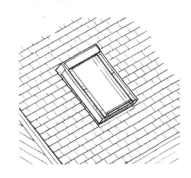

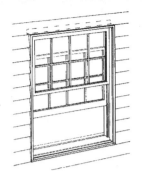

Doors	Roof Window	Double Hung Window

Exterior Type Door		Unit	Material	Labor	Equip.	Total	Specification
Entry							
Flush (1-3/4″)							
	Demolish	Ea.		26.50		26.50	Cost includes material and labor to
	Install	Ea.	187	15		202	install 3′ x 6′ 8″ pre-hung 1-3/4″ door,
	Demolish and Install	Ea.	187	41.50		228.50	including casing and stop, hinges,
	Reinstall	Ea.		14.99		14.99	jamb, aluminum sill, weatherstripped.
	Clean	Ea.	2.81	8.60		11.41	
	Paint	Ea.	7.50	36.50		44	
	Minimum Charge	Job		142		142	
Raised Panel							
	Demolish	Ea.		26.50		26.50	Cost includes material and labor to
	Install	Ea.	365	15.80		380.80	install 3′ x 6′ 8″ pre-hung 1-3/4″ door,
	Demolish and Install	Ea.	365	42.30		407.30	jamb, including casing and stop,
	Reinstall	Ea.		15.82		15.82	hinges, aluminum sill,
	Clean	Ea.	2.81	8.60		11.41	weatherstripping.
	Paint	Ea.	7.50	36.50		44	
	Minimum Charge	Job		142		142	
Entry w / Lights							
Good Quality							
	Demolish	Ea.		26.50		26.50	Cost includes material and labor to
	Install	Ea.	330	16.75		346.75	install 3′ x 6′ 8″ pre-hung 1-3/4″ door,
	Demolish and Install	Ea.	330	43.25		373.25	solid wood lower panel, with up to
	Reinstall	Ea.		16.75		16.75	9-light glass panels, casing, sill,
	Clean	Ea.	2.81	8.60		11.41	weatherstripped.
	Paint	Ea.	5.50	17		22.50	
	Minimum Charge	Job		142		142	
Better Quality							
	Demolish	Ea.		26.50		26.50	Cost includes material and labor to
	Install	Ea.	375	16.75		391.75	install 3′ x 6′ 8″ pre-hung 1-3/4″ Ash
	Demolish and Install	Ea.	375	43.25		418.25	door, solid wood, raised panel door
	Reinstall	Ea.		16.75		16.75	without glass panels.
	Clean	Ea.	2.81	8.60		11.41	
	Paint	Ea.	7.50	36.50		44	
	Minimum Charge	Job		142		142	
Premium Quality							
	Demolish	Ea.		26.50		26.50	Cost includes material and labor to
	Install	Ea.	510	16.75		526.75	install 3′ x 6′ 8″ pre-hung 1-3/4″ Oak
	Demolish and Install	Ea.	510	43.25		553.25	door, solid wood, raised panel door
	Reinstall	Ea.		16.75		16.75	without glass panels.
	Clean	Ea.	2.81	8.60		11.41	
	Paint	Ea.	7.50	36.50		44	
	Minimum Charge	Job		142		142	

Exterior Type Door		Unit	Material	Labor	Equip.	Total	Specification
Custom Quality							
	Demolish	Ea.		26.50		26.50	Cost includes material and labor to
	Install	Ea.	1200	16.75		1216.75	install 3' x 6' 8" pre-hung 1-3/4"
	Demolish and Install	Ea.	1200	43.25		1243.25	hand-made, solid wood, raised panel
	Reinstall	Ea.		16.75		16.75	door with custom stained glass.
	Clean	Ea.	.20	8.60		8.80	
	Paint	Ea.	2.07	85		87.07	
	Minimum Charge	Job		142		142	
Miami Style							
	Demolish	Ea.		26.50		26.50	Cost includes material and labor to
	Install	Ea.	175	14.25		189.25	install 3' x 6' 8" pre-hung 1-3/4"
	Demolish and Install	Ea.	175	40.75		215.75	lauan door of solid wood.
	Reinstall	Ea.		14.24		14.24	
	Clean	Ea.	.20	8.60		8.80	
	Paint	Ea.	7.50	36.50		44	
	Minimum Charge	Job		142		142	
French Style							
1-Light							
	Demolish	Ea.		26.50		26.50	Cost includes material and labor to
	Install	Ea.	320	20.50		340.50	install 3' x 6' 8" pre-hung 1-3/4"
	Demolish and Install	Ea.	320	47		367	french style door with 1 light.
	Reinstall	Ea.		20.34		20.34	
	Clean	Ea.	1.75	12.95		14.70	
	Paint	Ea.	8.80	64		72.80	
	Minimum Charge	Job		142		142	
5-Light							
	Demolish	Ea.		26.50		26.50	Cost includes material and labor to
	Install	Ea.	320	20.50		340.50	install 3' x 6' 8" pre-hung 1-3/4"
	Demolish and Install	Ea.	320	47		367	french style door with 5 lights.
	Reinstall	Ea.		20.34		20.34	
	Clean	Ea.	.39	17.25		17.64	
	Paint	Ea.	8.80	64		72.80	
	Minimum Charge	Job		142		142	
9-Light							
	Demolish	Ea.		26.50		26.50	Cost includes material and labor to
	Install	Ea.	325	20.50		345.50	install 3' x 6' 8" pre-hung 1-3/4"
	Demolish and Install	Ea.	325	47		372	french style door with 9 lights.
	Reinstall	Ea.		20.34		20.34	
	Clean	Ea.	.39	17.25		17.64	
	Paint	Ea.	8.80	64		72.80	
	Minimum Charge	Job		142		142	
10-Light							
	Demolish	Ea.		28.50		28.50	Cost includes material and labor to
	Install	Ea.	430	35.50		465.50	install 3' x 6' 8" pre-hung 1-3/4"
	Demolish and Install	Ea.	430	64		494	french style door with 10 lights.
	Reinstall	Ea.		35.60		35.60	
	Clean	Ea.	.39	17.25		17.64	
	Paint	Ea.	8.80	64		72.80	
	Minimum Charge	Job		142		142	
15-Light							
	Demolish	Ea.		28.50		28.50	Cost includes material and labor to
	Install	Ea.	635	40.50		675.50	install 3' x 6' 8" pre-hung 1-3/4"
	Demolish and Install	Ea.	635	69		704	french style door with 15 lights.
	Reinstall	Ea.		40.69		40.69	
	Clean	Ea.	.39	17.25		17.64	
	Paint	Ea.	8.80	64		72.80	
	Minimum Charge	Job		142		142	

Exterior Doors and Windows

Exterior Type Door		Unit	Material	Labor	Equip.	Total	Specification
Jamb							
Wood							
	Demolish	Ea.		15.80		15.80	Includes material and labor to install
	Install	Ea.	65	7.70		72.70	flat pine jamb with square cut heads
	Demolish and Install	Ea.	65	23.50		88.50	and rabbeted sides for 6' 8" high and
	Clean	Ea.	.09	5.15		5.24	3-9/16" door including trim sets for
	Paint	Ea.	5.50	17		22.50	both sides.
	Minimum Charge	Job		142		142	
Metal 6' 8" High							
	Demolish	Ea.		15.80		15.80	Cost includes material and labor to
	Install	Ea.	73.50	17.80		91.30	install 18 gauge hollow metal door
	Demolish and Install	Ea.	73.50	33.60		107.10	frame to fit a 4-1/2" jamb 6' 8" high
	Reinstall	Ea.		17.80		17.80	and up to 3' 6" opening.
	Clean	Ea.	.58	4.31		4.89	
	Paint	Ea.	1.03	5.10		6.13	
	Minimum Charge	Job		142		142	
Metal 7' High							
	Demolish	Ea.		15.80		15.80	Cost includes material and labor to
	Install	Ea.	76	19		95	install 18 gauge hollow metal door
	Demolish and Install	Ea.	76	34.80		110.80	frame to fit a 4-1/2" jamb 7' high and
	Reinstall	Ea.		18.99		18.99	up to 3' 6" opening.
	Clean	Ea.	.58	4.31		4.89	
	Paint	Ea.	1.03	5.10		6.13	
	Minimum Charge	Job		142		142	
Metal 8' High							
	Demolish	Ea.		15.80		15.80	Cost includes material and labor to
	Install	Ea.	92	23.50		115.50	install 18 gauge hollow metal door
	Demolish and Install	Ea.	92	39.30		131.30	frame to fit a 4-1/2" jamb 8' high and
	Reinstall	Ea.		23.73		23.73	up to 3' 6" opening.
	Clean	Ea.	.83	5.15		5.98	
	Paint	Ea.	1.16	5.65		6.81	
	Minimum Charge	Job		142		142	
Metal 9' High							
	Demolish	Ea.		15.80		15.80	Cost includes material and labor to
	Install	Ea.	109	28.50		137.50	install 18 gauge hollow metal door
	Demolish and Install	Ea.	109	44.30		153.30	frame to fit a 4-1/2" jamb 9' high and
	Reinstall	Ea.		28.48		28.48	up to 3' 6" opening.
	Clean	Ea.	.83	5.15		5.98	
	Paint	Ea.	1.16	5.65		6.81	
	Minimum Charge	Job		142		142	
Casing Trim							
Single Width							
	Demolish	Ea.		5		5	Cost includes material and labor to
	Install	Opng.	13.95	48.50		62.45	install 11/16" x 2-1/2" pine ranch
	Demolish and Install	Opng.	13.95	53.50		67.45	style casing for one side of a standard
	Reinstall	Opng.		38.62		38.62	door opening.
	Clean	Opng.	.40	2.07		2.47	
	Paint	Ea.	3.04	5.10		8.14	
	Minimum Charge	Job		142		142	
Double Width							
	Demolish	Ea.		5.95		5.95	Cost includes material and labor to
	Install	Opng.	17.15	57		74.15	install 11/16" x 2-1/2" pine ranch
	Demolish and Install	Opng.	17.15	62.95		80.10	style door casing for one side of a
	Reinstall	Opng.		45.57		45.57	double door opening.
	Clean	Opng.	.46	4.14		4.60	
	Paint	Ea.	3.04	5.80		8.84	
	Minimum Charge	Job		142		142	

Exterior Doors and Windows

Residential Metal Door	Unit	Material	Labor	Equip.	Total	Specification
Pre-hung, Steel-clad						
2' 8" x 6' 8"						
Demolish	Ea.		26.50		26.50	Cost includes material and labor to
Install	Ea.	220	35.50		255.50	install 2' 6" x 6' 8" pre-hung 1-3/4"
Demolish and Install	Ea.	220	62		282	24 gauge steel clad door with 4-1/2"
Reinstall	Ea.		35.60		35.60	wood frame, trims, hinges, aluminum
Clean	Ea.	2.81	8.60		11.41	sill, weatherstripped.
Paint	Ea.	8.80	36.50		45.30	
Minimum Charge	Job		142		142	
3' x 6' 8"						
Demolish	Ea.		26.50		26.50	Cost includes material and labor to
Install	Ea.	222	38		260	install 3' x 6' 8" pre-hung 1-3/4" 24
Demolish and Install	Ea.	222	64.50		286.50	gauge steel clad door with 4-1/2"
Reinstall	Ea.		37.97		37.97	wood frame, trims, hinges, aluminum
Clean	Ea.	2.81	8.60		11.41	sill, weatherstripped.
Paint	Ea.	8.80	36.50		45.30	
Minimum Charge	Job		142		142	

Metal Door	Unit	Material	Labor	Equip.	Total	Specification
2' 8" x 6' 8", 18 Gauge						
Demolish	Ea.		5.65		5.65	Cost includes material and labor to
Install	Ea.	216	17.80		233.80	install 18 gauge 2' 8" x 6' 8" steel
Demolish and Install	Ea.	216	23.45		239.45	door only, 1-3/4" thick, hinges.
Reinstall	Ea.		17.80		17.80	
Clean	Ea.	1.17	6.45		7.62	
Paint	Ea.	3.73	21.50		25.23	
Minimum Charge	Job		142		142	
3' x 6' 8", 18 Gauge						
Demolish	Ea.		5.65		5.65	Cost includes material and labor to
Install	Ea.	210	19		229	install 18 gauge 3' x 6' 8" steel door
Demolish and Install	Ea.	210	24.65		234.65	only, 1-3/4" thick, hinges.
Reinstall	Ea.		18.99		18.99	
Clean	Ea.	1.17	6.45		7.62	
Paint	Ea.	3.73	21.50		25.23	
Minimum Charge	Job		142		142	
2' 8" x 7', 18 Gauge						
Demolish	Ea.		5.65		5.65	Cost includes material and labor to
Install	Ea.	224	19		243	install 18 gauge 2' 8" x 7' steel door
Demolish and Install	Ea.	224	24.65		248.65	only, 1-3/4" thick, hinges.
Reinstall	Ea.		18.99		18.99	
Clean	Ea.	1.17	6.45		7.62	
Paint	Ea.	3.73	21.50		25.23	
Minimum Charge	Job		142		142	
3' x 7', 18 Gauge						
Demolish	Ea.		5.65		5.65	Cost includes material and labor to
Install	Ea.	218	20.50		238.50	install 18 gauge 3' x 7' steel door
Demolish and Install	Ea.	218	26.15		244.15	only, 1-3/4" thick, hinges.
Reinstall	Ea.		20.34		20.34	
Clean	Ea.	1.17	6.45		7.62	
Paint	Ea.	3.73	21.50		25.23	
Minimum Charge	Job		142		142	
3' 6" x 7', 18 Gauge						
Demolish	Ea.		5.65		5.65	Cost includes material and labor to
Install	Ea.	260	22		282	install 18 gauge 3' 6" x 7' steel door
Demolish and Install	Ea.	260	27.65		287.65	only, 1-3/4" thick, hinges.
Reinstall	Ea.		21.91		21.91	
Clean	Ea.	1.17	6.45		7.62	
Paint	Ea.	3.73	21.50		25.23	
Minimum Charge	Job		142		142	

Exterior Doors and Windows

Metal Door		Unit	Material	Labor	Equip.	Total	Specification
Casing Trim							
Single Width							
	Demolish	Ea.		5		5	Cost includes material and labor to
	Install	Opng.	13.95	48.50		62.45	install 11/16" x 2-1/2" pine ranch
	Demolish and Install	Opng.	13.95	53.50		67.45	style casing for one side of a standard
	Reinstall	Opng.		38.62		38.62	door opening.
	Clean	Opng.	.40	2.07		2.47	
	Paint	Ea.	3.04	5.10		8.14	
	Minimum Charge	Job		142		142	
Double Width							
	Demolish	Ea.		5.95		5.95	Cost includes material and labor to
	Install	Opng.	17.15	57		74.15	install 11/16" x 2-1/2" pine ranch
	Demolish and Install	Opng.	17.15	62.95		80.10	style door casing for one side of a
	Reinstall	Opng.		45.57		45.57	double door opening.
	Clean	Opng.	.46	4.14		4.60	
	Paint	Ea.	3.04	5.80		8.84	
	Minimum Charge	Job		142		142	

Solid Core Door		Unit	Material	Labor	Equip.	Total	Specification
Exterior Type							
Flush (1-3/4")							
	Demolish	Ea.		26.50		26.50	Cost includes material and labor to
	Install	Ea.	227	35.50		262.50	install 3' x 6' 8" pre-hung 1-3/4" door,
	Demolish and Install	Ea.	227	62		289	including casing and stop, hinges,
	Reinstall	Ea.		35.60		35.60	jamb, aluminum sill, weatherstripped.
	Clean	Ea.	2.81	8.60		11.41	
	Paint	Ea.	8.80	36.50		45.30	
	Minimum Charge	Job		142		142	
Raised Panel							
	Demolish	Ea.		26.50		26.50	Cost includes material and labor to
	Install	Ea.	365	15.80		380.80	install 3' x 6' 8" pre-hung 1-3/4" door,
	Demolish and Install	Ea.	365	42.30		407.30	jamb, including casing and stop,
	Reinstall	Ea.		15.82		15.82	hinges, aluminum sill,
	Clean	Ea.	2.81	8.60		11.41	weatherstripping.
	Paint	Ea.	8.80	85		93.80	
	Minimum Charge	Job		142		142	
Entry w / Lights							
	Demolish	Ea.		26.50		26.50	Cost includes material and labor to
	Install	Ea.	330	16.75		346.75	install 3' x 6' 8" pre-hung 1-3/4" door,
	Demolish and Install	Ea.	330	43.25		373.25	solid wood lower panel, with up to
	Reinstall	Ea.		16.75		16.75	9-light glass panels, casing, sill,
	Clean	Ea.	2.81	8.60		11.41	weatherstripped.
	Paint	Ea.	2.07	85		87.07	
	Minimum Charge	Job		142		142	
Custom Entry							
	Demolish	Ea.		26.50		26.50	Includes material and labor to install
	Install	Ea.	830	16.75		846.75	prehung, fir, single glazed with lead
	Demolish and Install	Ea.	830	43.25		873.25	caming, 1-3/4" x 6' 8" x 3'.
	Reinstall	Ea.		16.75		16.75	
	Clean	Ea.	2.81	8.60		11.41	
	Paint	Ea.	3.73	21.50		25.23	
	Minimum Charge	Job		142		142	

Solid Core Door		Unit	Material	Labor	Equip.	Total	Specification
Dutch Style							
	Demolish	Ea.		26.50		26.50	Includes material and labor to install
	Install	Ea.	655	47.50		702.50	dutch door, pine, 1-3/4" x 6' 8" x 2'
	Demolish and Install	Ea.	655	74		729	8" wide.
	Reinstall	Ea.		47.47		47.47	
	Clean	Ea.	2.81	8.60		11.41	
	Paint	Ea.	2.07	85		87.07	
	Minimum Charge	Job		142		142	
Miami Style							
	Demolish	Ea.		26.50		26.50	Cost includes material and labor to
	Install	Ea.	175	14.25		189.25	install 3' x 6' 8" pre-hung 1-3/4"
	Demolish and Install	Ea.	175	40.75		215.75	lauan door of solid wood.
	Reinstall	Ea.		14.24		14.24	
	Clean	Ea.	2.81	8.60		11.41	
	Paint	Ea.	7.50	36.50		44	
	Minimum Charge	Job		142		142	
French Style							
	Demolish	Ea.		28.50		28.50	Cost includes material and labor to
	Install	Ea.	635	40.50		675.50	install 3' x 6' 8" pre-hung 1-3/4"
	Demolish and Install	Ea.	635	69		704	french style door with 15 lights.
	Reinstall	Ea.		40.69		40.69	
	Clean	Ea.	.20	8.60		8.80	
	Paint	Ea.	5.55	128		133.55	
	Minimum Charge	Job		142		142	
Double							
	Demolish	Ea.		19.15		19.15	Includes material and labor to install a
	Install	Ea.	1075	71		1146	pre-hung double entry door including
	Demolish and Install	Ea.	1075	90.15		1165.15	frame and exterior trim.
	Clean	Ea.	.11	30		30.11	
	Paint	Ea.	17.65	128		145.65	
	Minimum Charge	Job		71		71	
Commercial Grade							
3' x 6' 8"							
	Demolish	Ea.		26.50		26.50	Includes material and labor to install
	Install	Ea.	261	16.75		277.75	flush solid core 1-3/4" hardwood
	Demolish and Install	Ea.	261	43.25		304.25	veneer 3' x 6' 8' door only.
	Reinstall	Ea.		16.75		16.75	
	Clean	Ea.	2.81	8.60		11.41	
	Paint	Ea.	6.20	21.50		27.70	
	Minimum Charge	Job		142		142	
3' 6" x 6' 8"							
	Demolish	Ea.		26.50		26.50	Includes material and labor to install
	Install	Ea.	350	16.75		366.75	flush solid core 1-3/4" hardwood
	Demolish and Install	Ea.	350	43.25		393.25	veneer 3' 6" x 6' 8' door only.
	Reinstall	Ea.		16.75		16.75	
	Clean	Ea.	2.81	8.60		11.41	
	Paint	Ea.	6.20	21.50		27.70	
	Minimum Charge	Job		142		142	
3' x 7'							
	Demolish	Ea.		26.50		26.50	Includes material and labor to install
	Install	Ea.	279	40.50		319.50	flush solid core 1-3/4" hardwood
	Demolish and Install	Ea.	279	67		346	veneer 3' x 7' door only.
	Reinstall	Ea.		40.69		40.69	
	Clean	Ea.	2.81	8.60		11.41	
	Paint	Ea.	6.20	21.50		27.70	
	Minimum Charge	Job		142		142	

Solid Core Door		Unit	Material	Labor	Equip.	Total	Specification
3' 6" x 7'							
	Demolish	Ea.		26.50		26.50	Includes material and labor to install
	Install	Ea.	380	20.50		400.50	flush solid core 1-3/4" hardwood
	Demolish and Install	Ea.	380	47		427	veneer 3' 6" x 7' door only.
	Reinstall	Ea.		20.34		20.34	
	Clean	Ea.	2.81	8.60		11.41	
	Paint	Ea.	6.20	21.50		27.70	
	Minimum Charge	Job		142		142	
3' x 8'							
	Demolish	Ea.		26.50		26.50	Includes material and labor to install
	Install	Ea.	325	35.50		360.50	flush solid core 1-3/4" hardwood
	Demolish and Install	Ea.	325	62		387	veneer 3' x 8' door only.
	Reinstall	Ea.		35.60		35.60	
	Clean	Ea.	3.37	12.95		16.32	
	Paint	Ea.	6.20	21.50		27.70	
	Minimum Charge	Job		142		142	
3' 6" x 8'							
	Demolish	Ea.		26.50		26.50	Includes material and labor to install
	Install	Ea.	400	35.50		435.50	flush solid core 1-3/4" hardwood
	Demolish and Install	Ea.	400	62		462	veneer 3' 6" x 8' door only.
	Reinstall	Ea.		35.60		35.60	
	Clean	Ea.	3.37	12.95		16.32	
	Paint	Ea.	6.20	21.50		27.70	
	Minimum Charge	Job		142		142	
3' x 9'							
	Demolish	Ea.		26.50		26.50	Includes material and labor to install
	Install	Ea.	425	40.50		465.50	flush solid core 1-3/4" hardwood
	Demolish and Install	Ea.	425	67		492	veneer 3' x 9' door only.
	Reinstall	Ea.		40.69		40.69	
	Clean	Ea.	3.37	12.95		16.32	
	Paint	Ea.	6.20	21.50		27.70	
	Minimum Charge	Job		142		142	
Stain							
	Install	Ea.	5.65	28.50		34.15	Includes labor and material to stain
	Minimum Charge	Job		128		128	exterior type door and trim on both sides.
Door Only (SC)							
2' 4" x 6' 8"							
	Demolish	Ea.		5.65		5.65	Cost includes material and labor to
	Install	Ea.	172	15.80		187.80	install 2' 4" x 6' 8" lauan solid core
	Demolish and Install	Ea.	172	21.45		193.45	door slab.
	Reinstall	Ea.		15.82		15.82	
	Clean	Ea.	1.17	6.45		7.62	
	Paint	Ea.	2.32	32		34.32	
	Minimum Charge	Job		142		142	
2' 8" x 6' 8"							
	Demolish	Ea.		5.65		5.65	Cost includes material and labor to
	Install	Ea.	176	15.80		191.80	install 2' 8" x 6' 8" lauan solid core
	Demolish and Install	Ea.	176	21.45		197.45	door slab.
	Reinstall	Ea.		15.82		15.82	
	Clean	Ea.	1.17	6.45		7.62	
	Paint	Ea.	2.32	32		34.32	
	Minimum Charge	Job		142		142	

Exterior Doors and Windows

Solid Core Door		Unit	Material	Labor	Equip.	Total	Specification
3' x 6' 8"							
	Demolish	Ea.		5.65		5.65	Cost includes material and labor to
	Install	Ea.	183	16.75		199.75	install 3' x 6' 8" lauan solid core door
	Demolish and Install	Ea.	183	22.40		205.40	slab.
	Reinstall	Ea.		16.75		16.75	
	Clean	Ea.	1.17	6.45		7.62	
	Paint	Ea.	2.32	32		34.32	
	Minimum Charge	Job		142		142	
3' 6" x 6' 8"							
	Demolish	Ea.		5.65		5.65	Cost includes material and labor to
	Install	Ea.	207	17.80		224.80	install 3' 6" x 6' 8" lauan solid core
	Demolish and Install	Ea.	207	23.45		230.45	door slab.
	Reinstall	Ea.		17.80		17.80	
	Clean	Ea.	1.17	6.45		7.62	
	Paint	Ea.	2.32	32		34.32	
	Minimum Charge	Job		142		142	
Panel							
	Demolish	Ea.		5.65		5.65	Cost includes material and labor to
	Install	Ea.	167	33.50		200.50	install 3' x 6' 8" six (6) panel interior
	Demolish and Install	Ea.	167	39.15		206.15	door.
	Reinstall	Ea.		33.51		33.51	
	Clean	Ea.	1.40	6.45		7.85	
	Paint	Ea.	2.32	32		34.32	
	Minimum Charge	Job		142		142	
Casing Trim							
Single Width							
	Demolish	Ea.		5		5	Cost includes material and labor to
	Install	Opng.	13.95	48.50		62.45	install 11/16" x 2-1/2" pine ranch
	Demolish and Install	Opng.	13.95	53.50		67.45	style casing for one side of a standard
	Reinstall	Opng.		38.62		38.62	door opening.
	Clean	Opng.	.40	2.07		2.47	
	Paint	Ea.	3.04	5.10		8.14	
	Minimum Charge	Job		142		142	
Double Width							
	Demolish	Ea.		5.95		5.95	Cost includes material and labor to
	Install	Opng.	17.15	57		74.15	install 11/16" x 2-1/2" pine ranch
	Demolish and Install	Opng.	17.15	62.95		80.10	style door casing for one side of a
	Reinstall	Opng.		45.57		45.57	double door opening.
	Clean	Opng.	.46	4.14		4.60	
	Paint	Ea.	3.04	5.80		8.84	
	Minimum Charge	Job		142		142	

Components		Unit	Material	Labor	Equip.	Total	Specification
Hardware							
Doorknob							
	Demolish	Ea.		10.55		10.55	Includes material and labor to install
	Install	Ea.	16.65	17.80		34.45	residential passage lockset, keyless
	Demolish and Install	Ea.	16.65	28.35		45	bored type.
	Reinstall	Ea.		14.24		14.24	
	Clean	Ea.	.28	6.45		6.73	
	Minimum Charge	Job		142		142	

Components		Unit	Material	Labor	Equip.	Total	Specification
Doorknob w / Lock							Includes material and labor to install
	Demolish	Ea.		10.55		10.55	privacy lockset.
	Install	Ea.	19.05	17.80		36.85	
	Demolish and Install	Ea.	19.05	28.35		47.40	
	Reinstall	Ea.		14.24		14.24	
	Clean	Ea.	.28	6.45		6.73	
	Minimum Charge	Job		142		142	
Lever Handle							Includes material and labor to install
	Demolish	Ea.		10.55		10.55	residential passage lockset, keyless
	Install	Ea.	26.50	28.50		55	bored type with lever handle.
	Demolish and Install	Ea.	26.50	39.05		65.55	
	Reinstall	Ea.		22.78		22.78	
	Clean	Ea.	.28	6.45		6.73	
	Minimum Charge	Job		142		142	
Deadbolt							Includes material and labor to install a
	Demolish	Ea.		9.90		9.90	deadbolt.
	Install	Ea.	36.50	20.50		57	
	Demolish and Install	Ea.	36.50	30.40		66.90	
	Reinstall	Ea.		16.27		16.27	
	Clean	Ea.	.28	6.45		6.73	
	Minimum Charge	Job		142		142	
Grip Handle Entry							Includes material and labor to install
	Demolish	Ea.		9.05		9.05	residential keyed entry lock set with
	Install	Ea.	114	31.50		145.50	grip type handle.
	Demolish and Install	Ea.	114	40.55		154.55	
	Reinstall	Ea.		25.32		25.32	
	Clean	Ea.	.28	6.45		6.73	
	Minimum Charge	Job		142		142	
Panic Device							Includes material and labor to install
	Demolish	Ea.		23		23	touch bar, low profile, exit only.
	Install	Ea.	320	47.50		367.50	
	Demolish and Install	Ea.	320	70.50		390.50	
	Reinstall	Ea.		37.97		37.97	
	Clean	Ea.	.14	11.50		11.64	
	Minimum Charge	Job		142		142	
Closer							Includes material and labor to install
	Demolish	Ea.		5.95		5.95	pneumatic heavy duty closer for
	Install	Ea.	141	47.50		188.50	exterior type doors.
	Demolish and Install	Ea.	141	53.45		194.45	
	Reinstall	Ea.		37.97		37.97	
	Clean	Ea.	.14	8.60		8.74	
	Minimum Charge	Job		142		142	
Peep-hole							Includes material and labor to install
	Demolish	Ea.		5.10		5.10	peep-hole for door.
	Install	Ea.	8.25	8.90		17.15	
	Demolish and Install	Ea.	8.25	14		22.25	
	Reinstall	Ea.		7.12		7.12	
	Clean	Ea.	.02	2.30		2.32	
	Minimum Charge	Job		142		142	
Exit Sign							Includes material and labor to install a
	Demolish	Ea.		15.65		15.65	wall mounted interior electric exit sign.
	Install	Ea.	53.50	39		92.50	
	Demolish and Install	Ea.	53.50	54.65		108.15	
	Reinstall	Ea.		31		31	
	Clean	Ea.	.02	4.66		4.68	
	Minimum Charge	Job		142		142	

Exterior Doors and Windows

Components		Unit	Material	Labor	Equip.	Total	Specification
Kickplate							
	Demolish	Ea.		8.80		8.80	Includes material and labor to install
	Install	Ea.	16.45	19		35.45	aluminum kickplate, 10" x 28".
	Demolish and Install	Ea.	16.45	27.80		44.25	
	Reinstall	Ea.		15.19		15.19	
	Clean	Ea.	.28	6.45		6.73	
	Minimum Charge	Job		142		142	
Threshold							
	Install	L.F.	3.41	2.85		6.26	Includes labor and material to install
	Minimum Charge	Job		71		71	oak threshold.
Weatherstripping							
	Install	L.F.	.26	.71		.97	Includes labor and material to install
	Minimum Charge	Job		71		71	rubber weatherstripping for door.
Metal Jamb							
6' 8" High							
	Demolish	Ea.		15.80		15.80	Cost includes material and labor to
	Install	Ea.	73.50	17.80		91.30	install 18 gauge hollow metal door
	Demolish and Install	Ea.	73.50	33.60		107.10	frame to fit a 4-1/2" jamb 6' 8" high
	Reinstall	Ea.		17.80		17.80	and up to 3' 6" opening.
	Clean	Ea.	.58	4.31		4.89	
	Paint	Ea.	1.03	5.10		6.13	
	Minimum Charge	Job		142		142	
7' High							
	Demolish	Ea.		15.80		15.80	Cost includes material and labor to
	Install	Ea.	76	19		95	install 18 gauge hollow metal door
	Demolish and Install	Ea.	76	34.80		110.80	frame to fit a 4-1/2" jamb 7' high and
	Reinstall	Ea.		18.99		18.99	up to 3' 6" opening.
	Clean	Ea.	.58	4.31		4.89	
	Paint	Ea.	1.03	5.10		6.13	
	Minimum Charge	Job		142		142	
8' High							
	Demolish	Ea.		15.80		15.80	Cost includes material and labor to
	Install	Ea.	92	23.50		115.50	install 18 gauge hollow metal door
	Demolish and Install	Ea.	92	39.30		131.30	frame to fit a 4-1/2" jamb 8' high and
	Reinstall	Ea.		23.73		23.73	up to 3' 6" opening.
	Clean	Ea.	.83	5.15		5.98	
	Paint	Ea.	1.16	5.65		6.81	
	Minimum Charge	Job		142		142	
9' High							
	Demolish	Ea.		15.80		15.80	Cost includes material and labor to
	Install	Ea.	109	28.50		137.50	install 18 gauge hollow metal door
	Demolish and Install	Ea.	109	44.30		153.30	frame to fit a 4-1/2" jamb 9' high and
	Reinstall	Ea.		28.48		28.48	up to 3' 6" opening.
	Clean	Ea.	.83	5.15		5.98	
	Paint	Ea.	1.16	5.65		6.81	
	Minimum Charge	Job		142		142	
Wood Jamb							
	Demolish	Ea.		19.80		19.80	Includes material and labor to install
	Install	Ea.	65	7.70		72.70	flat pine jamb with square cut heads
	Demolish and Install	Ea.	65	27.50		92.50	and rabbeted sides for 6' 8" high and
	Clean	Ea.	.09	5.15		5.24	3-9/16" door including trim sets for
	Paint	Ea.	5.50	17		22.50	both sides.
	Minimum Charge	Job		71		71	
Stain							
	Install	Ea.	3.91	21.50		25.41	Includes labor and material to stain
	Minimum Charge	Job		128		128	single door and trim on both sides.

Exterior Doors and Windows

Components		Unit	Material	Labor	Equip.	Total	Specification
Shave & Refit							Includes labor to shave and rework door to fit opening at the job site.
	Install	Ea.		23.50		23.50	
	Minimum Charge	Job		71		71	

Sliding Patio Door		Unit	Material	Labor	Equip.	Total	Specification
Aluminum							
6' Single Pane							Cost includes material and labor to install 6' x 6' 8" sliding anodized aluminum patio door with single pane tempered safety glass, anodized frame, screen, weatherstripped.
	Demolish	Ea.		39.50		39.50	
	Install	Ea.	400	142		542	
	Demolish and Install	Ea.	400	181.50		581.50	
	Reinstall	Ea.		113.92		113.92	
	Clean	Ea.	1.75	12.95		14.70	
	Minimum Charge	Job		142		142	
8' Single Pane							Cost includes material and labor to install 8' x 6' 8" sliding aluminum patio door with single pane tempered safety glass, anodized frame, screen, weatherstripped.
	Demolish	Ea.		39.50		39.50	
	Install	Ea.	455	190		645	
	Demolish and Install	Ea.	455	229.50		684.50	
	Reinstall	Ea.		151.89		151.89	
	Clean	Ea.	1.75	12.95		14.70	
	Minimum Charge	Job		142		142	
10' Single Pane							Cost includes material and labor to install 10' x 6' 8" sliding aluminum patio door with single pane tempered safety glass, anodized frame, screen, weatherstripped.
	Demolish	Ea.		39.50		39.50	
	Install	Ea.	595	285		880	
	Demolish and Install	Ea.	595	324.50		919.50	
	Reinstall	Ea.		227.84		227.84	
	Clean	Ea.	1.75	12.95		14.70	
	Minimum Charge	Job		142		142	
6' Insulated							Cost includes material and labor to install 6' x 6' 8" sliding aluminum patio door with double insulated tempered glass, baked-on enamel finish, screen, weatherstripped.
	Demolish	Ea.		39.50		39.50	
	Install	Ea.	525	142		667	
	Demolish and Install	Ea.	525	181.50		706.50	
	Reinstall	Ea.		113.92		113.92	
	Clean	Ea.	1.75	12.95		14.70	
	Minimum Charge	Job		142		142	
8' Insulated							Cost includes material and labor to install 8' x 6' 8" sliding aluminum patio door with insulated tempered glass, baked-on enamel finish, screen, weatherstripped.
	Demolish	Ea.		39.50		39.50	
	Install	Ea.	620	190		810	
	Demolish and Install	Ea.	620	229.50		849.50	
	Reinstall	Ea.		151.89		151.89	
	Clean	Ea.	1.75	12.95		14.70	
	Minimum Charge	Job		142		142	
10' Insulated							Cost includes material and labor to install 10' x 6' 8" sliding aluminum patio door with double insulated tempered glass, baked-on enamel finish, screen, weatherstripped.
	Demolish	Ea.		39.50		39.50	
	Install	Ea.	695	285		980	
	Demolish and Install	Ea.	695	324.50		1019.50	
	Reinstall	Ea.		227.84		227.84	
	Clean	Ea.	1.75	12.95		14.70	
	Minimum Charge	Job		142		142	

Exterior Doors and Windows

Sliding Patio Door	Unit	Material	Labor	Equip.	Total	Specification
Vinyl						
6' Single Pane						
Demolish	Ea.		39.50		39.50	Cost includes material and labor to
Install	Ea.	380	142		522	install 6' x 6' 8" sliding vinyl patio
Demolish and Install	Ea.	380	181.50		561.50	door with single pane tempered safety
Reinstall	Ea.		113.92		113.92	glass, anodized frame, screen,
Clean	Ea.	1.75	12.95		14.70	weatherstripped.
Minimum Charge	Job		142		142	
8' Single Pane						
Demolish	Ea.		39.50		39.50	Cost includes material and labor to
Install	Ea.	435	190		625	install 8' x 6' 8" sliding vinyl patio
Demolish and Install	Ea.	435	229.50		664.50	door with single pane tempered safety
Reinstall	Ea.		151.89		151.89	glass, anodized frame, screen,
Clean	Ea.	1.75	12.95		14.70	weatherstripped.
Minimum Charge	Job		142		142	
10' Single Pane						
Demolish	Ea.		39.50		39.50	Cost includes material and labor to
Install	Ea.	565	285		850	install 10' x 6' 8" sliding vinyl patio
Demolish and Install	Ea.	565	324.50		889.50	door with single pane tempered safety
Reinstall	Ea.		227.84		227.84	glass, anodized frame, screen,
Clean	Ea.	1.75	12.95		14.70	weatherstripped.
Minimum Charge	Job		142		142	
6' Insulated						
Demolish	Ea.		39.50		39.50	Cost includes material and labor to
Install	Ea.	595	142		737	install 6' x 6' 8" sliding vinyl patio
Demolish and Install	Ea.	595	181.50		776.50	door with double insulated tempered
Reinstall	Ea.		113.92		113.92	glass, anodized frame, screen,
Clean	Ea.	1.75	12.95		14.70	weatherstripped.
Minimum Charge	Job		142		142	
8' Insulated						
Demolish	Ea.		39.50		39.50	Cost includes material and labor to
Install	Ea.	755	190		945	install 8' x 6' 8" sliding vinyl patio
Demolish and Install	Ea.	755	229.50		984.50	door with double insulated tempered
Reinstall	Ea.		151.89		151.89	glass, anodized frame, screen,
Clean	Ea.	1.75	12.95		14.70	weatherstripped.
Minimum Charge	Job		142		142	
10' Insulated						
Demolish	Ea.		39.50		39.50	Cost includes material and labor to
Install	Ea.	855	285		1140	install 10' x 6' 8" sliding vinyl patio
Demolish and Install	Ea.	855	324.50		1179.50	door with double insulated tempered
Reinstall	Ea.		227.84		227.84	glass, anodized frame, screen,
Clean	Ea.	1.75	12.95		14.70	weatherstripped.
Minimum Charge	Job		142		142	
Wood Framed						
6' Premium Insulated						
Demolish	Ea.		39.50		39.50	Cost includes material and labor to
Install	Ea.	1050	142		1192	install 6' x 6' 8" sliding wood patio
Demolish and Install	Ea.	1050	181.50		1231.50	door with pine frame, double insulated
Reinstall	Ea.		113.92		113.92	glass, screen, lock and dead bolt,
Clean	Ea.	1.75	12.95		14.70	weatherstripped. Add for casing and
Minimum Charge	Job		142		142	finishing.

Exterior Doors and Windows

Sliding Patio Door		Unit	Material	Labor	Equip.	Total	Specification
8' Premium Insulated							Cost includes material and labor to
	Demolish	Ea.		39.50		39.50	install 8' x 6' 8" sliding wood patio
	Install	Ea.	1200	190		1390	door with pine frame, double insulated
	Demolish and Install	Ea.	1200	229.50		1429.50	glass, screen, lock and dead bolt,
	Reinstall	Ea.		151.89		151.89	weatherstripped. Add for casing and
	Clean	Ea.	1.75	12.95		14.70	finishing.
	Minimum Charge	Job		142		142	
9' Premium Insulated							Cost includes material and labor to
	Demolish	Ea.		39.50		39.50	install 9' x 6' 8" sliding wood patio
	Install	Ea.	1200	190		1390	door with pine frame, double insulated
	Demolish and Install	Ea.	1200	229.50		1429.50	glass, screen, lock and dead bolt,
	Reinstall	Ea.		151.89		151.89	weatherstripped. Add for casing and
	Clean	Ea.	1.75	12.95		14.70	finishing.
	Minimum Charge	Job		142		142	
Stain							Includes labor and material to stain
	Install	Ea.	5.65	28.50		34.15	exterior type door and trim on both
	Minimum Charge	Job		128		128	sides.
Casing Trim							Cost includes material and labor to
	Demolish	Ea.		5.95		5.95	install 11/16" x 2-1/2" pine ranch
	Install	Opng.	17.15	57		74.15	style door casing for one side of a
	Demolish and Install	Opng.	17.15	62.95		80.10	double door opening.
	Reinstall	Opng.		45.57		45.57	
	Clean	Opng.	.46	4.14		4.60	
	Paint	Ea.	3.04	5.80		8.84	
	Minimum Charge	Job		142		142	
Sliding Screen							Includes material and labor to install
	Demolish	Ea.		5.65		5.65	sliding screen door, 6' 8" x 3'.
	Install	Ea.	97.50	14.25		111.75	
	Demolish and Install	Ea.	97.50	19.90		117.40	
	Reinstall	Ea.		11.39		11.39	
	Clean	Ea.	.58	4.31		4.89	
	Minimum Charge	Job		142		142	

Screen Door		Unit	Material	Labor	Equip.	Total	Specification
Aluminum							Includes material and labor to install
	Demolish	Ea.		26.50		26.50	aluminum frame screen door with
	Install	Ea.	103	40.50		143.50	fiberglass screen cloth, closer, hinges,
	Demolish and Install	Ea.	103	67		170	latch.
	Reinstall	Ea.		32.55		32.55	
	Clean	Ea.	2.81	8.60		11.41	
	Paint	Ea.	2.92	10.20		13.12	
	Minimum Charge	Job		142		142	
Wood							Includes material and labor to install
	Demolish	Ea.		26.50		26.50	wood screen door with aluminum cloth
	Install	Ea.	131	47.50		178.50	screen. Frame and hardware not
	Demolish and Install	Ea.	131	74		205	included.
	Reinstall	Ea.		37.97		37.97	
	Clean	Ea.	2.81	8.60		11.41	
	Paint	Ea.	2.92	10.20		13.12	
	Minimum Charge	Job		142		142	
Shave & Refit							Includes labor to shave and rework
	Install	Ea.		23.50		23.50	door to fit opening at the job site.
	Minimum Charge	Job		142		142	

Exterior Doors and Windows

Storm Door

Storm Door	Unit	Material	Labor	Equip.	Total	Specification
Good Grade						
Demolish	Ea.		26.50		26.50	Includes material and labor to install
Install	Ea.	153	40.50		193.50	aluminum frame storm door with
Demolish and Install	Ea.	153	67		220	fiberglass screen cloth, upper glass
Reinstall	Ea.		32.55		32.55	panel, closer, hinges, latch.
Clean	Ea.	2.81	8.60		11.41	
Paint	Ea.	2.92	10.20		13.12	
Minimum Charge	Job		142		142	
Better Grade						
Demolish	Ea.		26.50		26.50	Includes material and labor to install
Install	Ea.	195	40.50		235.50	aluminum frame storm door with
Demolish and Install	Ea.	195	67		262	fiberglass screen cloth, upper and
Reinstall	Ea.		32.55		32.55	lower glass panel, closer, latch.
Clean	Ea.	2.81	8.60		11.41	
Paint	Ea.	2.92	10.20		13.12	
Minimum Charge	Job		142		142	
Premium Grade						
Demolish	Ea.		26.50		26.50	Includes material and labor to install
Install	Ea.	235	40.50		275.50	aluminum frame storm door with
Demolish and Install	Ea.	235	67		302	fiberglass screen cloth, upper and
Reinstall	Ea.		32.55		32.55	lower glass panel, closer, latch.
Clean	Ea.	2.81	8.60		11.41	
Paint	Ea.	2.92	10.20		13.12	
Minimum Charge	Job		142		142	
Insulated						
Demolish	Ea.		26.50		26.50	Includes material and labor to install
Install	Ea.	218	20.50		238.50	aluminum frame storm door with
Demolish and Install	Ea.	218	47		265	fiberglass screen cloth, upper and
Reinstall	Ea.		16.27		16.27	lower glass panel, closer, latch.
Clean	Ea.	2.81	8.60		11.41	
Paint	Ea.	2.92	10.20		13.12	
Minimum Charge	Job		142		142	

Garage Door

Garage Door	Unit	Material	Labor	Equip.	Total	Specification
9' One Piece Metal						
Demolish	Ea.		66.50		66.50	Includes material and labor to install
Install	Ea.	325	71		396	one piece steel garage door 9' x 7'
Demolish and Install	Ea.	325	137.50		462.50	primed including hardware.
Reinstall	Ea.		56.96		56.96	
Clean	Ea.	3.51	26		29.51	
Paint	Ea.	6	64		70	
Minimum Charge	Job		142		142	
16' One Piece Metal						
Demolish	Ea.		79		79	Includes material and labor to install
Install	Ea.	505	95		600	one piece steel garage door 16' x 7'
Demolish and Install	Ea.	505	174		679	primed including hardware.
Reinstall	Ea.		75.95		75.95	
Clean	Ea.	7	34.50		41.50	
Paint	Ea.	12	73		85	
Minimum Charge	Job		142		142	

Exterior Doors and Windows

Garage Door		Unit	Material	Labor	Equip.	Total	Specification
9' Metal Sectional							
	Demolish	Ea.		66.50		66.50	Includes material and labor to install
	Install	Ea.	294	108		402	sectional metal garage door 9' x 7'
	Demolish and Install	Ea.	294	174.50		468.50	primed including hardware.
	Reinstall	Ea.		86.30		86.30	
	Clean	Ea.	3.59	29.50		33.09	
	Paint	Ea.	12	73		85	
	Minimum Charge	Job		142		142	
16' Metal Sectional							
	Demolish	Ea.		79		79	Includes material and labor to install
	Install	Ea.	580	190		770	sectional metal garage door 16' x 7'
	Demolish and Install	Ea.	580	269		849	primed including hardware.
	Reinstall	Ea.		151.89		151.89	
	Clean	Ea.	7	34.50		41.50	
	Paint	Ea.	12	73		85	
	Minimum Charge	Job		142		142	
Metal / Steel Roll Up							
8' x 8' Steel							
	Demolish	Ea.		90.50		90.50	Cost includes material and labor to
	Install	Ea.	790	445		1235	install 8' x 8' steel overhead roll-up,
	Demolish and Install	Ea.	790	535.50		1325.50	chain hoist operated service door.
	Reinstall	Ea.		356.80		356.80	
	Clean	Ea.	3.59	29.50		33.09	
	Paint	Ea.	12.80	85		97.80	
	Minimum Charge	Job		715		715	
10' x 10' Steel							
	Demolish	Ea.		105		105	Cost includes material and labor to
	Install	Ea.	1050	510		1560	install 10' x 10' steel overhead roll-up,
	Demolish and Install	Ea.	1050	615		1665	chain hoist operated service door.
	Reinstall	Ea.		407.77		407.77	
	Clean	Ea.	5.60	41.50		47.10	
	Paint	Ea.	19.95	85		104.95	
	Minimum Charge	Job		715		715	
12' x 12' Steel							
	Demolish	Ea.		127		127	Cost includes material and labor to
	Install	Ea.	1350	595		1945	install 12' x 12' steel overhead roll-up,
	Demolish and Install	Ea.	1350	722		2072	chain hoist operated service door.
	Reinstall	Ea.		475.73		475.73	
	Clean	Ea.	8.10	46		54.10	
	Paint	Ea.	28.50	102		130.50	
	Minimum Charge	Job		715		715	
14' x 14' Steel							
	Demolish	Ea.		158		158	Cost includes material and labor to
	Install	Ea.	1800	890		2690	install 14' x 14' steel overhead roll-up,
	Demolish and Install	Ea.	1800	1048		2848	chain hoist operated service door.
	Reinstall	Ea.		713.60		713.60	
	Clean	Ea.	11	59		70	
	Paint	Ea.	33.50	128		161.50	
	Minimum Charge	Job		715		715	
18' x 18' Steel							
	Demolish	Ea.		176		176	Cost includes material and labor to
	Install	Opng.	2350	1200		3550	install 18' x 18' steel overhead roll-up,
	Demolish and Install	Opng.	2350	1376		3726	chain hoist operated service door.
	Reinstall	Opng.		951.47		951.47	
	Clean	Ea.	11	34.50		45.50	
	Paint	Ea.	65	255		320	
	Minimum Charge	Job		715		715	
Automatic Motor							
	Install	Ea.	200	28.50		228.50	Includes labor and material to install
	Minimum Charge	Job		142		142	electric opener motor, 1/3 HP.

Exterior Doors and Windows

Garage Door

	Unit	Material	Labor	Equip.	Total	Specification
9' One Piece Wood						
Demolish	Ea.		66.50		66.50	Includes material and labor to install
Install	Ea.	350	71		421	one piece wood garage door 9' x 7'
Demolish and Install	Ea.	350	137.50		487.50	primed including hardware.
Reinstall	Ea.		56.96		56.96	
Clean	Ea.	3.51	26		29.51	
Paint	Ea.	6	64		70	
Minimum Charge	Job		142		142	
9' Wood Sectional						
Demolish	Ea.		66.50		66.50	Includes material and labor to install
Install	Ea.	415	71		486	sectional wood garage door 9' x 7'
Demolish and Install	Ea.	415	137.50		552.50	unfinished including hardware.
Reinstall	Ea.		56.96		56.96	
Clean	Ea.	3.51	26		29.51	
Paint	Ea.	6	64		70	
Minimum Charge	Job		142		142	
16' Wood Sectional						
Demolish	Ea.		79		79	Includes material and labor to install
Install	Ea.	900	95		995	sectional fiberglass garage door 16' x
Demolish and Install	Ea.	900	174		1074	7' unfinished including hardware.
Reinstall	Ea.		75.95		75.95	
Clean	Ea.	7	34.50		41.50	
Paint	Ea.	12	73		85	
Minimum Charge	Job		142		142	
Electric Opener						
Demolish	Ea.		46		46	Includes material and labor to install
Install	Ea.	240	53.50		293.50	electric opener, 1/3 HP economy.
Demolish and Install	Ea.	240	99.50		339.50	
Reinstall	Ea.		42.75		42.75	
Clean	Ea.	.14	11.50		11.64	
Minimum Charge	Job		142		142	
Springs						
Install	Pr.	34	71		105	Includes labor and material to replace
Minimum Charge	Job		142		142	springs for garage door.

Commercial Metal Door

	Unit	Material	Labor	Equip.	Total	Specification
Pre-hung Steel Door						
2' 8" x 6' 8"						
Demolish	Ea.		39.50		39.50	Cost includes material and labor to
Install	Ea.	299	17.80		316.80	install 2' 8" x 6' 8" pre-hung 1-3/4"
Demolish and Install	Ea.	299	57.30		356.30	18 gauge steel door with steel frame,
Reinstall	Ea.		17.80		17.80	hinges, aluminum sill, weather-stripped.
Clean	Ea.	2.81	8.60		11.41	
Paint	Ea.	3.73	21.50		25.23	
Minimum Charge	Job		142		142	
3' x 6' 8"						
Demolish	Ea.		39.50		39.50	Cost includes material and labor to
Install	Ea.	294	19		313	install 3' x 6' 8" pre-hung 1-3/4" 18
Demolish and Install	Ea.	294	58.50		352.50	gauge steel door with steel frame,
Reinstall	Ea.		18.99		18.99	hinges, aluminum sill, weather-stripped.
Clean	Ea.	2.81	8.60		11.41	
Paint	Ea.	3.73	21.50		25.23	
Minimum Charge	Job		142		142	

Exterior Doors and Windows

Commercial Metal Door		Unit	Material	Labor	Equip.	Total	Specification
3' 6" x 6' 8"							
	Demolish	Ea.		39.50		39.50	Cost includes material and labor to
	Install	Ea.	340	22		362	install 3' 6" x 6' 8" pre-hung 1-3/4"
	Demolish and Install	Ea.	340	61.50		401.50	18 gauge steel door with steel frame,
	Reinstall	Ea.		21.91		21.91	hinges, aluminum sill, weather-stripped.
	Clean	Ea.	2.81	8.60		11.41	
	Paint	Ea.	3.73	21.50		25.23	
	Minimum Charge	Job		142		142	
4' x 6' 8"							
	Demolish	Ea.		39.50		39.50	Cost includes material and labor to
	Install	Ea.	370	28.50		398.50	install 4' x 6' 8" pre-hung 1-3/4" 18
	Demolish and Install	Ea.	370	68		438	gauge steel door with steel frame,
	Reinstall	Ea.		28.48		28.48	hinges, aluminum sill, weather-stripped.
	Clean	Ea.	2.81	8.60		11.41	
	Paint	Ea.	3.73	21.50		25.23	
	Minimum Charge	Job		142		142	
Metal Jamb							
6' 8" High							
	Demolish	Ea.		15.80		15.80	Cost includes material and labor to
	Install	Ea.	73.50	17.80		91.30	install 18 gauge hollow metal door
	Demolish and Install	Ea.	73.50	33.60		107.10	frame to fit a 4-1/2" jamb 6' 8" high
	Reinstall	Ea.		17.80		17.80	and up to 3' 6" opening.
	Clean	Ea.	.58	4.31		4.89	
	Paint	Ea.	1.03	5.10		6.13	
	Minimum Charge	Job		142		142	
7' High							
	Demolish	Ea.		15.80		15.80	Cost includes material and labor to
	Install	Ea.	76	19		95	install 18 gauge hollow metal door
	Demolish and Install	Ea.	76	34.80		110.80	frame to fit a 4-1/2" jamb 7' high and
	Reinstall	Ea.		18.99		18.99	up to 3' 6" opening.
	Clean	Ea.	.58	4.31		4.89	
	Paint	Ea.	1.03	5.10		6.13	
	Minimum Charge	Job		142		142	
8' High							
	Demolish	Ea.		15.80		15.80	Cost includes material and labor to
	Install	Ea.	92	23.50		115.50	install 18 gauge hollow metal door
	Demolish and Install	Ea.	92	39.30		131.30	frame to fit a 4-1/2" jamb 8' high and
	Reinstall	Ea.		23.73		23.73	up to 3' 6" opening.
	Clean	Ea.	.83	5.15		5.98	
	Paint	Ea.	1.16	5.65		6.81	
	Minimum Charge	Job		142		142	
9' High							
	Demolish	Ea.		15.80		15.80	Cost includes material and labor to
	Install	Ea.	109	28.50		137.50	install 18 gauge hollow metal door
	Demolish and Install	Ea.	109	44.30		153.30	frame to fit a 4-1/2" jamb 9' high and
	Reinstall	Ea.		28.48		28.48	up to 3' 6" opening.
	Clean	Ea.	.83	5.15		5.98	
	Paint	Ea.	1.16	5.65		6.81	
	Minimum Charge	Job		142		142	
Hardware							
Doorknob w / Lock							
	Demolish	Ea.		10.55		10.55	Includes material and labor to install
	Install	Ea.	97.50	23.50		121	keyed entry lock set, bored type
	Demolish and Install	Ea.	97.50	34.05		131.55	including knob trim, strike and strike
	Reinstall	Ea.		18.99		18.99	box for standard commercial
	Clean	Ea.	.28	6.45		6.73	application.
	Minimum Charge	Job		142		142	

Exterior Doors and Windows

Commercial Metal Door		Unit	Material	Labor	Equip.	Total	Specification
Lever Handle							Includes material and labor to install passage lockset, keyless bored type with lever handle, non-locking standard commercial latchset.
	Demolish	Ea.		10.55		10.55	
	Install	Ea.	53.50	28.50		82	
	Demolish and Install	Ea.	53.50	39.05		92.55	
	Reinstall	Ea.		22.78		22.78	
	Clean	Ea.	.28	6.45		6.73	
	Minimum Charge	Job		142		142	
Deadbolt							Includes material and labor to install a deadbolt.
	Demolish	Ea.		9.90		9.90	
	Install	Ea.	36.50	20.50		57	
	Demolish and Install	Ea.	36.50	30.40		66.90	
	Reinstall	Ea.		16.27		16.27	
	Clean	Ea.	.28	6.45		6.73	
	Minimum Charge	Job		142		142	
Panic Device							Includes material and labor to install touch bar, low profile, exit only.
	Demolish	Ea.		23		23	
	Install	Ea.	320	47.50		367.50	
	Demolish and Install	Ea.	320	70.50		390.50	
	Reinstall	Ea.		37.97		37.97	
	Clean	Ea.	.14	11.50		11.64	
	Minimum Charge	Job		142		142	
Closer							Includes material and labor to install pneumatic heavy duty model for exterior type doors.
	Demolish	Ea.		5.95		5.95	
	Install	Ea.	150	47.50		197.50	
	Demolish and Install	Ea.	150	53.45		203.45	
	Reinstall	Ea.		37.97		37.97	
	Clean	Ea.	.14	8.60		8.74	
	Minimum Charge	Job		142		142	
Peep-Hole							Includes material and labor to install peep-hole for door.
	Demolish	Ea.		5.10		5.10	
	Install	Ea.	8.25	8.90		17.15	
	Demolish and Install	Ea.	8.25	14		22.25	
	Reinstall	Ea.		7.12		7.12	
	Clean	Ea.	.02	2.30		2.32	
	Minimum Charge	Job		142		142	
Exit Sign							Includes material and labor to install a wall mounted interior electric exit sign.
	Demolish	Ea.		15.65		15.65	
	Install	Ea.	53.50	39		92.50	
	Demolish and Install	Ea.	53.50	54.65		108.15	
	Reinstall	Ea.		31		31	
	Clean	Ea.	.02	4.66		4.68	
	Minimum Charge	Job		142		142	
Kickplate							Includes material and labor to install stainless steel kickplate, 10" x 36".
	Demolish	Ea.		8.80		8.80	
	Install	Ea.	43	19		62	
	Demolish and Install	Ea.	43	27.80		70.80	
	Reinstall	Ea.		15.19		15.19	
	Clean	Ea.	.28	6.45		6.73	
	Minimum Charge	Job		142		142	

Aluminum Window		Unit	Material	Labor	Equip.	Total	Specification
Single Hung Two Light **2' x 2'**							Cost includes material and labor to install 2' x 2' single hung, two light, double glazed aluminum window including screen.
	Demolish	Ea.		14.35		14.35	
	Install	Ea.	58	65		123	
	Demolish and Install	Ea.	58	79.35		137.35	
	Reinstall	Ea.		51.90		51.90	
	Clean	Ea.	.03	5.35		5.38	
	Minimum Charge	Job		178		178	

Aluminum Window		Unit	Material	Labor	Equip.	Total	Specification
2' x 2' 6"							
	Demolish	Ea.		14.35		14.35	Cost includes material and labor to
	Install	Ea.	62.50	65		127.50	install 2' x 2' 6" single hung, two light,
	Demolish and Install	Ea.	62.50	79.35		141.85	double glazed aluminum window
	Reinstall	Ea.		51.90		51.90	including screen.
	Clean	Ea.	.03	5.35		5.38	
	Minimum Charge	Job		178		178	
3' x 1' 6"							
	Demolish	Ea.		14.35		14.35	Cost includes material and labor to
	Install	Ea.	59	71.50		130.50	install 3' x 1' 6" single hung, two light,
	Demolish and Install	Ea.	59	85.85		144.85	double glazed aluminum window
	Reinstall	Ea.		57.09		57.09	including screen.
	Clean	Ea.	.02	4.66		4.68	
	Minimum Charge	Job		178		178	
3' x 2'							
	Demolish	Ea.		14.35		14.35	Cost includes material and labor to
	Install	Ea.	71	71.50		142.50	install 3' x 2' single hung, two light,
	Demolish and Install	Ea.	71	85.85		156.85	double glazed aluminum window
	Reinstall	Ea.		57.09		57.09	including screen.
	Clean	Ea.	.02	4.66		4.68	
	Minimum Charge	Job		178		178	
3' x 2' 6"							
	Demolish	Ea.		14.35		14.35	Cost includes material and labor to
	Install	Ea.	74.50	71.50		146	install 3' x 2' 6" single hung, two light,
	Demolish and Install	Ea.	74.50	85.85		160.35	double glazed aluminum window
	Reinstall	Ea.		57.09		57.09	including screen.
	Clean	Ea.	.03	5.35		5.38	
	Minimum Charge	Job		178		178	
3' x 3'							
	Demolish	Ea.		14.35		14.35	Cost includes material and labor to
	Install	Ea.	83	71.50		154.50	install 3' x 3' single hung, two light,
	Demolish and Install	Ea.	83	85.85		168.85	double glazed aluminum window
	Reinstall	Ea.		57.09		57.09	including screen.
	Clean	Ea.	.03	5.35		5.38	
	Minimum Charge	Job		178		178	
3' x 3' 6"							
	Demolish	Ea.		14.35		14.35	Cost includes material and labor to
	Install	Ea.	87.50	71.50		159	install 3' x 3' 6" single hung, two light,
	Demolish and Install	Ea.	87.50	85.85		173.35	double glazed aluminum window
	Reinstall	Ea.		57.09		57.09	including screen.
	Clean	Ea.	.04	6.20		6.24	
	Minimum Charge	Job		178		178	
3' x 4'							
	Demolish	Ea.		14.35		14.35	Cost includes material and labor to
	Install	Ea.	95.50	71.50		167	install 3' x 4' single hung, two light,
	Demolish and Install	Ea.	95.50	85.85		181.35	double glazed aluminum window
	Reinstall	Ea.		57.09		57.09	including screen.
	Clean	Ea.	.04	6.20		6.24	
	Minimum Charge	Job		178		178	
3' x 5'							
	Demolish	Ea.		21		21	Cost includes material and labor to
	Install	Ea.	106	71.50		177.50	install 3' x 5' single hung, two light,
	Demolish and Install	Ea.	106	92.50		198.50	double glazed aluminum window
	Reinstall	Ea.		57.09		57.09	including screen.
	Clean	Ea.	.06	7.45		7.51	
	Minimum Charge	Job		178		178	

Aluminum Window	Unit	Material	Labor	Equip.	Total	Specification
3' x 6'						
Demolish	Ea.		21		21	Cost includes material and labor to
Install	Ea.	114	79.50		193.50	install 3' x 6' single hung, two light,
Demolish and Install	Ea.	114	100.50		214.50	double glazed aluminum window
Reinstall	Ea.		63.43		63.43	including screen.
Clean	Ea.	.07	8.80		8.87	
Minimum Charge	Job		178		178	
Double Hung Two Light						
2' x 2'						
Demolish	Ea.		14.35		14.35	Cost includes material and labor to
Install	Ea.	99.50	65		164.50	install 2' x 2' double hung, two light,
Demolish and Install	Ea.	99.50	79.35		178.85	double glazed aluminum window
Reinstall	Ea.		51.90		51.90	including screen.
Clean	Ea.	.02	4.66		4.68	
Minimum Charge	Job		178		178	
2' x 2' 6"						
Demolish	Ea.		14.35		14.35	Cost includes material and labor to
Install	Ea.	108	65		173	install 2' x 2' 6" double hung, two
Demolish and Install	Ea.	108	79.35		187.35	light, double glazed aluminum window
Reinstall	Ea.		51.90		51.90	including screen.
Clean	Ea.	.02	4.66		4.68	
Minimum Charge	Job		178		178	
3' x 1' 6"						
Demolish	Ea.		14.35		14.35	Cost includes material and labor to
Install	Ea.	256	71.50		327.50	install 3' x 1' 6" double hung, two
Demolish and Install	Ea.	256	85.85		341.85	light, double glazed aluminum window
Reinstall	Ea.		57.09		57.09	including screen.
Clean	Ea.	.02	4.66		4.68	
Minimum Charge	Job		178		178	
3' x 2'						
Demolish	Ea.		14.35		14.35	Cost includes material and labor to
Install	Ea.	271	71.50		342.50	install 3' x 2' double hung, two light,
Demolish and Install	Ea.	271	85.85		356.85	double glazed aluminum window
Reinstall	Ea.		57.09		57.09	including screen.
Clean	Ea.	.02	4.66		4.68	
Minimum Charge	Job		178		178	
3' x 2' 6"						
Demolish	Ea.		14.35		14.35	Cost includes material and labor to
Install	Ea.	264	71.50		335.50	install 3' x 2' 6" double hung, two
Demolish and Install	Ea.	264	85.85		349.85	light, double glazed aluminum window
Reinstall	Ea.		57.09		57.09	including screen.
Clean	Ea.	.03	5.35		5.38	
Minimum Charge	Job		178		178	
3' x 3'						
Demolish	Ea.		14.35		14.35	Cost includes material and labor to
Install	Ea.	286	71.50		357.50	install 3' x 3' double hung, two light,
Demolish and Install	Ea.	286	85.85		371.85	double glazed aluminum window
Reinstall	Ea.		57.09		57.09	including screen.
Clean	Ea.	.03	5.35		5.38	
Minimum Charge	Job		178		178	
3' x 3' 6"						
Demolish	Ea.		14.35		14.35	Cost includes material and labor to
Install	Ea.	315	71.50		386.50	install 3' x 3' 6" double hung, two
Demolish and Install	Ea.	315	85.85		400.85	light, double glazed aluminum window
Reinstall	Ea.		57.09		57.09	including screen.
Clean	Ea.	.04	6.20		6.24	
Minimum Charge	Job		178		178	

Exterior Doors and Windows

Aluminum Window		Unit	Material	Labor	Equip.	Total	Specification
3' x 4'							
	Demolish	Ea.		14.35		14.35	Cost includes material and labor to
	Install	Ea.	325	71.50		396.50	install 3' x 4' double hung, two light,
	Demolish and Install	Ea.	325	85.85		410.85	double glazed aluminum window
	Reinstall	Ea.		57.09		57.09	including screen.
	Clean	Ea.	.04	6.20		6.24	
	Minimum Charge	Job		178		178	
3' x 5'							
	Demolish	Ea.		21		21	Cost includes material and labor to
	Install	Ea.	365	71.50		436.50	install 3' x 5' double hung, two light,
	Demolish and Install	Ea.	365	92.50		457.50	double glazed aluminum window
	Reinstall	Ea.		57.09		57.09	including screen.
	Clean	Ea.	.06	7.45		7.51	
	Minimum Charge	Job		178		178	
3' x 6'							
	Demolish	Ea.		21		21	Cost includes material and labor to
	Install	Ea.	480	79.50		559.50	install 3' x 6' double hung, two light,
	Demolish and Install	Ea.	480	100.50		580.50	double glazed aluminum window
	Reinstall	Ea.		63.43		63.43	including screen.
	Clean	Ea.	.07	8.80		8.87	
	Minimum Charge	Job		178		178	
Sliding Sash							
1' 6" x 3'							
	Demolish	Ea.		14.35		14.35	Cost includes material and labor to
	Install	Ea.	55.50	65		120.50	install 1' 6" x 3' sliding sash, two light,
	Demolish and Install	Ea.	55.50	79.35		134.85	double glazed aluminum window
	Reinstall	Ea.		51.90		51.90	including screen.
	Clean	Ea.	.02	4.66		4.68	
	Minimum Charge	Job		178		178	
2' x 2'							
	Demolish	Ea.		14.35		14.35	Cost includes material and labor to
	Install	Ea.	50.50	71.50		122	install 2' x 2' sliding sash, two light,
	Demolish and Install	Ea.	50.50	85.85		136.35	double glazed aluminum window
	Reinstall	Ea.		57.09		57.09	including screen.
	Clean	Ea.	.02	4.66		4.68	
	Minimum Charge	Job		178		178	
3' x 2'							
	Demolish	Ea.		14.35		14.35	Cost includes material and labor to
	Install	Ea.	64.50	71.50		136	install 3' x 2' sliding sash, two light,
	Demolish and Install	Ea.	64.50	85.85		150.35	double glazed aluminum window
	Reinstall	Ea.		57.09		57.09	including screen.
	Clean	Ea.	.02	4.66		4.68	
	Minimum Charge	Job		178		178	
3' x 2' 6"							
	Demolish	Ea.		14.35		14.35	Cost includes material and labor to
	Install	Ea.	68	71.50		139.50	install 3' x 2' 6" sliding sash, two light,
	Demolish and Install	Ea.	68	85.85		153.85	double glazed aluminum window
	Reinstall	Ea.		57.09		57.09	including screen.
	Clean	Ea.	.03	5.35		5.38	
	Minimum Charge	Job		178		178	
3' x 3'							
	Demolish	Ea.		14.35		14.35	Cost includes material and labor to
	Install	Ea.	69	71.50		140.50	install 3' x 3' sliding sash, two light,
	Demolish and Install	Ea.	69	85.85		154.85	double glazed aluminum window
	Reinstall	Ea.		57.09		57.09	including screen.
	Clean	Ea.	.03	5.35		5.38	
	Minimum Charge	Job		178		178	

Exterior Doors and Windows

Aluminum Window	Unit	Material	Labor	Equip.	Total	Specification
3' x 3' 6"						
Demolish	Ea.		14.35		14.35	Cost includes material and labor to
Install	Ea.	81.50	71.50		153	install 3' x 3' 6" sliding sash, two light,
Demolish and Install	Ea.	81.50	85.85		167.35	double glazed aluminum window
Reinstall	Ea.		57.09		57.09	including screen.
Clean	Ea.	.04	6.20		6.24	
Minimum Charge	Job		178		178	
3' x 4'						
Demolish	Ea.		14.35		14.35	Cost includes material and labor to
Install	Ea.	89	79.50		168.50	install 3' x 4' sliding sash, two light,
Demolish and Install	Ea.	89	93.85		182.85	double glazed aluminum window
Reinstall	Ea.		63.43		63.43	including screen.
Clean	Ea.	.04	6.20		6.24	
Minimum Charge	Job		178		178	
3' x 5'						
Demolish	Ea.		21		21	Cost includes material and labor to
Install	Ea.	113	79.50		192.50	install 3' x 5' sliding sash, two light,
Demolish and Install	Ea.	113	100.50		213.50	double glazed aluminum window
Reinstall	Ea.		63.43		63.43	including screen.
Clean	Ea.	.06	7.45		7.51	
Minimum Charge	Job		178		178	
4' x 5'						
Demolish	Ea.		21		21	Cost includes material and labor to
Install	Ea.	114	102		216	install 4' x 5' sliding sash, two light,
Demolish and Install	Ea.	114	123		237	double glazed aluminum window
Reinstall	Ea.		81.55		81.55	including screen.
Clean	Ea.	.09	10.65		10.74	
Minimum Charge	Job		178		178	
5' x 5'						
Demolish	Ea.		21		21	Cost includes material and labor to
Install	Ea.	156	102		258	install 5' x 5' sliding sash, two light,
Demolish and Install	Ea.	156	123		279	double glazed aluminum window
Reinstall	Ea.		81.55		81.55	including screen.
Clean	Ea.	.09	10.65		10.74	
Minimum Charge	Job		178		178	
Awning Sash						
26" x 26", 2 Light						
Demolish	Ea.		14.35		14.35	Cost includes material and labor to
Install	Ea.	244	79.50		323.50	install 26" x 26" two light awning,
Demolish and Install	Ea.	244	93.85		337.85	double glazed aluminum window
Reinstall	Ea.		63.43		63.43	including screen.
Clean	Ea.	.03	5.35		5.38	
Minimum Charge	Job		178		178	
26" x 37", 2 Light						
Demolish	Ea.		14.35		14.35	Cost includes material and labor to
Install	Ea.	277	79.50		356.50	install 26" x 37" two light awning,
Demolish and Install	Ea.	277	93.85		370.85	double glazed aluminum window
Reinstall	Ea.		63.43		63.43	including screen.
Clean	Ea.	.03	5.35		5.38	
Minimum Charge	Job		178		178	
38" x 26", 3 Light						
Demolish	Ea.		14.35		14.35	Cost includes material and labor to
Install	Ea.	310	79.50		389.50	install 38" x 26" three light awning,
Demolish and Install	Ea.	310	93.85		403.85	double glazed aluminum window
Reinstall	Ea.		63.43		63.43	including screen.
Clean	Ea.	.04	6.20		6.24	
Minimum Charge	Job		178		178	

Exterior Doors and Windows

Aluminum Window		Unit	Material	Labor	Equip.	Total	Specification
38" x 37", 3 Light							
	Demolish	Ea.		14.35		14.35	Cost includes material and labor to
	Install	Ea.	320	89		409	install 38" x 37" three light awning,
	Demolish and Install	Ea.	320	103.35		423.35	double glazed aluminum window
	Reinstall	Ea.		71.36		71.36	including screen.
	Clean	Ea.	.04	6.20		6.24	
	Minimum Charge	Job		178		178	
38" x 53", 3 Light							
	Demolish	Ea.		21		21	Cost includes material and labor to
	Install	Ea.	515	89		604	install 38" x 53" three light awning,
	Demolish and Install	Ea.	515	110		625	double glazed aluminum window
	Reinstall	Ea.		71.36		71.36	including screen.
	Clean	Ea.	.06	7.45		7.51	
	Minimum Charge	Job		178		178	
50" x 37", 4 Light							
	Demolish	Ea.		21		21	Cost includes material and labor to
	Install	Ea.	525	89		614	install 50" x 37" four light awning,
	Demolish and Install	Ea.	525	110		635	double glazed aluminum window
	Reinstall	Ea.		71.36		71.36	including screen.
	Clean	Ea.	.06	7.45		7.51	
	Minimum Charge	Job		178		178	
50" x 53", 4 Light							
	Demolish	Ea.		21		21	Cost includes material and labor to
	Install	Ea.	865	102		967	install 50" x 53" four light awning,
	Demolish and Install	Ea.	865	123		988	double glazed aluminum window
	Reinstall	Ea.		81.55		81.55	including screen.
	Clean	Ea.	.07	8.80		8.87	
	Minimum Charge	Job		178		178	
63" x 37", 5 Light							
	Demolish	Ea.		21		21	Cost includes material and labor to
	Install	Ea.	675	102		777	install 63" x 37" five light awning,
	Demolish and Install	Ea.	675	123		798	double glazed aluminum window
	Reinstall	Ea.		81.55		81.55	including screen.
	Clean	Ea.	.07	8.80		8.87	
	Minimum Charge	Job		178		178	
63" x 53", 5 Light							
	Demolish	Ea.		21		21	Cost includes material and labor to
	Install	Ea.	930	102		1032	install 63" x 53" five light awning,
	Demolish and Install	Ea.	930	123		1053	double glazed aluminum window
	Reinstall	Ea.		81.55		81.55	including screen.
	Clean	Ea.	.09	10.65		10.74	
	Minimum Charge	Job		178		178	
Mullion Bars							
	Install	Ea.	8.90	28.50		37.40	Includes labor and material to install
	Minimum Charge	Job		178		178	mullions for sliding aluminum window.
Glass Louvered							
2' x 2'							
	Demolish	Ea.		14.35		14.35	Cost includes material and labor to
	Install	Ea.	45.50	65		110.50	install 2' x 2' aluminum window
	Demolish and Install	Ea.	45.50	79.35		124.85	including 4" glass louvers, hardware,
	Reinstall	Ea.		51.90		51.90	screen.
	Clean	Ea.	.02	4.66		4.68	
	Minimum Charge	Job		178		178	

Exterior Doors and Windows

Aluminum Window		Unit	Material	Labor	Equip.	Total	Specification
2' x 2' 6"							
	Demolish	Ea.		14.35		14.35	Cost includes material and labor to
	Install	Ea.	55.50	65		120.50	install 2' x 2' 6" aluminum window
	Demolish and Install	Ea.	55.50	79.35		134.85	including 4" glass louvers, hardware,
	Reinstall	Ea.		51.90		51.90	screen.
	Clean	Ea.	.02	4.66		4.68	
	Minimum Charge	Job		178		178	
3' x 1' 6"							
	Demolish	Ea.		14.35		14.35	Cost includes material and labor to
	Install	Ea.	58.50	71.50		130	install 3' x 1' 6" aluminum window
	Demolish and Install	Ea.	58.50	85.85		144.35	including 4" glass louvers, hardware,
	Reinstall	Ea.		57.09		57.09	screen.
	Clean	Ea.	.02	4.66		4.68	
	Minimum Charge	Job		178		178	
3' x 2'							
	Demolish	Ea.		14.35		14.35	Cost includes material and labor to
	Install	Ea.	67	71.50		138.50	install 3' x 2' aluminum window
	Demolish and Install	Ea.	67	85.85		152.85	including 4" glass louvers, hardware,
	Reinstall	Ea.		57.09		57.09	screen.
	Clean	Ea.	.02	4.66		4.68	
	Minimum Charge	Job		178		178	
3' x 2' 6"							
	Demolish	Ea.		14.35		14.35	Cost includes material and labor to
	Install	Ea.	75	71.50		146.50	install 3' x 2' 6" aluminum window
	Demolish and Install	Ea.	75	85.85		160.85	including 4" glass louvers, hardware,
	Reinstall	Ea.		57.09		57.09	screen.
	Clean	Ea.	.03	5.35		5.38	
	Minimum Charge	Job		178		178	
3' x 3'							
	Demolish	Ea.		14.35		14.35	Cost includes material and labor to
	Install	Ea.	85.50	79.50		165	install 3' x 3' aluminum window
	Demolish and Install	Ea.	85.50	93.85		179.35	including 4" glass louvers, hardware,
	Reinstall	Ea.		63.43		63.43	screen.
	Clean	Ea.	.03	5.35		5.38	
	Minimum Charge	Job		178		178	
3' x 3' 6"							
	Demolish	Ea.		14.35		14.35	Cost includes material and labor to
	Install	Ea.	97	79.50		176.50	install 3' x 3' 6" aluminum window
	Demolish and Install	Ea.	97	93.85		190.85	including 4" glass louvers, hardware,
	Reinstall	Ea.		63.43		63.43	screen.
	Clean	Ea.	.04	6.20		6.24	
	Minimum Charge	Job		178		178	
3' x 4'							
	Demolish	Ea.		14.35		14.35	Cost includes material and labor to
	Install	Ea.	108	79.50		187.50	install 3' x 4' aluminum window
	Demolish and Install	Ea.	108	93.85		201.85	including 4" glass louvers, hardware,
	Reinstall	Ea.		63.43		63.43	screen.
	Clean	Ea.	.04	6.20		6.24	
	Minimum Charge	Job		178		178	
3' x 5'							
	Demolish	Ea.		21		21	Cost includes material and labor to
	Install	Ea.	138	89		227	install 3' x 5' aluminum window with
	Demolish and Install	Ea.	138	110		248	4" glass louvers, hardware, screen.
	Reinstall	Ea.		71.36		71.36	
	Clean	Ea.	.06	7.45		7.51	
	Minimum Charge	Job		178		178	

Exterior Doors and Windows

Aluminum Window

		Unit	Material	Labor	Equip.	Total	Specification
3' x 6'							
	Demolish	Ea.		21		21	Cost includes material and labor to
	Install	Ea.	160	89		249	install 3' x 6' aluminum window with
	Demolish and Install	Ea.	160	110		270	4" glass louvers, hardware, screen.
	Reinstall	Ea.		71.36		71.36	
	Clean	Ea.	.07	8.80		8.87	
	Minimum Charge	Job		178		178	
Bay							
4' 8" x 6' 4"							
	Demolish	Ea.		15.30		15.30	Cost includes material and labor to
	Install	Ea.	1025	71		1096	install 4' 8" x 6' 4" angle bay double
	Demolish and Install	Ea.	1025	86.30		1111.30	hung unit, pine frame with aluminum
	Reinstall	Ea.		56.96		56.96	cladding, picture center sash,
	Clean	Ea.	.12	12.45		12.57	hardware, screens.
	Minimum Charge	Job		178		178	
4' 8" x 7' 2"							
	Demolish	Ea.		15.30		15.30	Cost includes material and labor to
	Install	Ea.	1050	71		1121	install 4' 8" x 7' 2" angle bay double
	Demolish and Install	Ea.	1050	86.30		1136.30	hung unit, pine frame with aluminum
	Reinstall	Ea.		56.96		56.96	cladding, picture center sash,
	Clean	Ea.	.12	12.45		12.57	hardware, screens.
	Minimum Charge	Job		178		178	
4' 8" x 7' 10"							
	Demolish	Ea.		15.30		15.30	Cost includes material and labor to
	Install	Ea.	1050	71		1121	install 4' 8" x 7' 10" angle bay double
	Demolish and Install	Ea.	1050	86.30		1136.30	hung unit, pine frame with aluminum
	Reinstall	Ea.		56.96		56.96	cladding, picture center sash,
	Clean	Ea.	.12	12.45		12.57	hardware, screens.
	Minimum Charge	Job		178		178	
4' 8" x 8' 6"							
	Demolish	Ea.		17.70		17.70	Cost includes material and labor to
	Install	Ea.	1200	81.50		1281.50	install 4' 8" x 8' 6" angle bay double
	Demolish and Install	Ea.	1200	99.20		1299.20	hung unit, pine frame with aluminum
	Reinstall	Ea.		65.10		65.10	cladding, picture center sash,
	Clean	Ea.	.02	16.60		16.62	hardware, screens.
	Minimum Charge	Job		178		178	
4' 8" x 8' 10"							
	Demolish	Ea.		17.70		17.70	Cost includes material and labor to
	Install	Ea.	1275	81.50		1356.50	install 4' 8" x 8' 10" angle bay double
	Demolish and Install	Ea.	1275	99.20		1374.20	hung unit, pine frame with aluminum
	Reinstall	Ea.		65.10		65.10	cladding, picture center sash,
	Clean	Ea.	.02	16.60		16.62	hardware, screens.
	Minimum Charge	Job		178		178	
4' 8" x 9' 2"							
	Demolish	Ea.		17.70		17.70	Cost includes material and labor to
	Install	Ea.	1325	142		1467	install 4' 8" x 9' 2" angle bay double
	Demolish and Install	Ea.	1325	159.70		1484.70	hung unit, pine frame with aluminum
	Reinstall	Ea.		113.92		113.92	cladding, picture center sash,
	Clean	Ea.	.02	16.60		16.62	hardware, screens.
	Minimum Charge	Job		178		178	
4' 8" x 9' 10"							
	Demolish	Ea.		17.70		17.70	Cost includes material and labor to
	Install	Ea.	1375	142		1517	install 4' 8" x 9' 10" angle bay double
	Demolish and Install	Ea.	1375	159.70		1534.70	hung unit, pine frame with aluminum
	Reinstall	Ea.		113.92		113.92	cladding, picture center sash,
	Clean	Ea.	.02	16.60		16.62	hardware, screens.
	Minimum Charge	Job		178		178	

Exterior Doors and Windows

Aluminum Window		Unit	Material	Labor	Equip.	Total	Specification
Casing							
	Demolish	Ea.		6.60		6.60	Cost includes material and labor to
	Install	Opng.	16.35	22		38.35	install 11/16" x 2-1/2" pine ranch
	Demolish and Install	Opng.	16.35	28.60		44.95	style window casing.
	Reinstall	Opng.		17.53		17.53	
	Clean	Opng.	.40	2.07		2.47	
	Paint	Ea.	3.04	5.10		8.14	
	Minimum Charge	Job		178		178	
Storm Window							
2' x 3' 6"							
	Demolish	Ea.		8.50		8.50	Includes material and labor to install
	Install	Ea.	67.50	19		86.50	residential aluminum storm window
	Demolish and Install	Ea.	67.50	27.50		95	with mill finish, 2' x 3' 5" high.
	Reinstall	Ea.		15.19		15.19	
	Clean	Ea.	.02	4.66		4.68	
	Minimum Charge	Job		178		178	
2' 6" x 5'							
	Demolish	Ea.		8.50		8.50	Includes material and labor to install
	Install	Ea.	75.50	20.50		96	residential aluminum storm window
	Demolish and Install	Ea.	75.50	29		104.50	with mill finish, 2' 6" x 5' high.
	Reinstall	Ea.		16.27		16.27	
	Clean	Ea.	.04	6.20		6.24	
	Minimum Charge	Job		178		178	
4' x 6'							
	Demolish	Ea.		16.40		16.40	Includes material and labor to install
	Install	Ea.	89.50	23		112.50	residential aluminum storm window, 4'
	Demolish and Install	Ea.	89.50	39.40		128.90	x 6' high.
	Reinstall	Ea.		18.23		18.23	
	Clean	Ea.	.09	9.35		9.44	
	Minimum Charge	Job		178		178	
Hardware							
Weatherstripping							
	Install	L.F.	.25	2.37		2.62	Includes labor and material to install
	Minimum Charge	Job		95		95	vinyl V strip weatherstripping for
							double-hung window.
Trim Set							
	Demolish	Ea.		6.60		6.60	Cost includes material and labor to
	Install	Opng.	16.35	22		38.35	install 11/16" x 2-1/2" pine ranch
	Demolish and Install	Opng.	16.35	28.60		44.95	style window casing.
	Reinstall	Opng.		17.53		17.53	
	Clean	Opng.	.40	2.07		2.47	
	Paint	Ea.	3.04	5.10		8.14	
	Minimum Charge	Job		142		142	

Vinyl Window		Unit	Material	Labor	Equip.	Total	Specification
Double Hung							
2' x 2' 6"							
	Demolish	Ea.		10.45		10.45	Cost includes material and labor to
	Install	Ea.	163	38		201	install 2' x 2' 6" double hung, two
	Demolish and Install	Ea.	163	48.45		211.45	light, vinyl window with screen.
	Reinstall	Ea.		30.38		30.38	
	Clean	Ea.	.02	4.66		4.68	
	Minimum Charge	Job		285		285	

Exterior Doors and Windows

Vinyl Window		Unit	Material	Labor	Equip.	Total	Specification
2' x 3' 6"							
	Demolish	Ea.		10.45		10.45	Cost includes material and labor to
	Install	Ea.	167	40.50		207.50	install 2' x 3' 6" double hung, two
	Demolish and Install	Ea.	167	50.95		217.95	light, vinyl window with screen.
	Reinstall	Ea.		32.55		32.55	
	Clean	Ea.	.03	5.35		5.38	
	Minimum Charge	Job		285		285	
2' 6" x 4' 6"							
	Demolish	Ea.		10.45		10.45	Cost includes material and labor to
	Install	Ea.	202	44		246	install 2' 6" x 4' 6" double hung, two
	Demolish and Install	Ea.	202	54.45		256.45	light, vinyl window with screen.
	Reinstall	Ea.		35.05		35.05	
	Clean	Ea.	.04	6.20		6.24	
	Minimum Charge	Job		285		285	
3' x 4'							
	Demolish	Ea.		10.45		10.45	Includes material and labor to install
	Install	Ea.	213	57		270	medium size double hung, 3' x 4', two
	Demolish and Install	Ea.	213	67.45		280.45	light, vinyl window with screen.
	Reinstall	Ea.		45.57		45.57	
	Clean	Ea.	.04	6.20		6.24	
	Minimum Charge	Job		285		285	
3' x 4' 6"							
	Demolish	Ea.		12.75		12.75	Cost includes material and labor to
	Install	Ea.	231	63.50		294.50	install 3' x 4' 6" double hung, two
	Demolish and Install	Ea.	231	76.25		307.25	light, vinyl window with screen.
	Reinstall	Ea.		50.63		50.63	
	Clean	Ea.	.06	7.45		7.51	
	Minimum Charge	Job		285		285	
4' x 4' 6"							
	Demolish	Ea.		12.75		12.75	Cost includes material and labor to
	Install	Ea.	250	71		321	install 4' x 4' 6" double hung, two
	Demolish and Install	Ea.	250	83.75		333.75	light, vinyl window with screen.
	Reinstall	Ea.		56.96		56.96	
	Clean	Ea.	.07	8.80		8.87	
	Minimum Charge	Job		285		285	
4' x 6'							
	Demolish	Ea.		12.75		12.75	Includes material and labor to install
	Install	Ea.	294	81.50		375.50	large double hung, 4' x 6', two light,
	Demolish and Install	Ea.	294	94.25		388.25	vinyl window with screen.
	Reinstall	Ea.		65.10		65.10	
	Clean	Ea.	.09	10.65		10.74	
	Minimum Charge	Job		285		285	
Trim Set							
	Demolish	Ea.		6.60		6.60	Cost includes material and labor to
	Install	Opng.	16.35	22		38.35	install 11/16" x 2-1/2" pine ranch
	Demolish and Install	Opng.	16.35	28.60		44.95	style window casing.
	Reinstall	Opng.		17.53		17.53	
	Clean	Opng.	.40	2.07		2.47	
	Paint	Ea.	3.04	5.10		8.14	
	Minimum Charge	Job		178		178	

Wood Window		Unit	Material	Labor	Equip.	Total	Specification
2' 2" x 3' 4"							
	Demolish	Ea.		10.45		10.45	Cost includes material and labor to
	Install	Ea.	176	38		214	install 2' 2" x 3' 4" double hung, two
	Demolish and Install	Ea.	176	48.45		224.45	light, double glazed wood window
	Reinstall	Ea.		30.38		30.38	with screen.
	Clean	Ea.	.03	5.35		5.38	
	Paint	Ea.	1.89	10.65		12.54	
	Minimum Charge	Job		142		142	

Exterior Doors and Windows

Wood Window		Unit	Material	Labor	Equip.	Total	Specification
2' 2" x 4' 4"							
	Demolish	Ea.		10.45		10.45	Cost includes material and labor to
	Install	Ea.	198	40.50		238.50	install 2' 2" x 4' 4" double hung, two
	Demolish and Install	Ea.	198	50.95		248.95	light, double glazed wood window
	Reinstall	Ea.		32.55		32.55	with screen.
	Clean	Ea.	.03	5.35		5.38	
	Paint	Ea.	1.89	10.65		12.54	
	Minimum Charge	Job		142		142	
2' 6" x 3' 4"							
	Demolish	Ea.		10.45		10.45	Cost includes material and labor to
	Install	Ea.	185	44		229	install 2' 6" x 3' 4" double hung, two
	Demolish and Install	Ea.	185	54.45		239.45	light, double glazed wood window
	Reinstall	Ea.		35.05		35.05	with screen.
	Clean	Ea.	.04	6.20		6.24	
	Paint	Ea.	2.43	12.75		15.18	
	Minimum Charge	Job		142		142	
2' 6" x 4'							
	Demolish	Ea.		10.45		10.45	Cost includes material and labor to
	Install	Ea.	200	47.50		247.50	install 2' 6" x 4' double hung, two
	Demolish and Install	Ea.	200	57.95		257.95	light, double glazed wood window
	Reinstall	Ea.		37.97		37.97	with screen.
	Clean	Ea.	.04	6.20		6.24	
	Paint	Ea.	2.43	12.75		15.18	
	Minimum Charge	Job		142		142	
2' 6" x 4' 8"							
	Demolish	Ea.		10.45		10.45	Cost includes material and labor to
	Install	Ea.	220	47.50		267.50	install 2' 6" x 4' 8" double hung, two
	Demolish and Install	Ea.	220	57.95		277.95	light, double glazed wood window
	Reinstall	Ea.		37.97		37.97	with screen.
	Clean	Ea.	.04	6.20		6.24	
	Paint	Ea.	2.43	12.75		15.18	
	Minimum Charge	Job		142		142	
2' 10" x 3' 4"							
	Demolish	Ea.		10.45		10.45	Cost includes material and labor to
	Install	Ea.	195	57		252	install 2' 10" x 3' 4" double hung, two
	Demolish and Install	Ea.	195	67.45		262.45	light, double glazed wood window
	Reinstall	Ea.		45.57		45.57	with screen.
	Clean	Ea.	.04	6.20		6.24	
	Paint	Ea.	2.43	12.75		15.18	
	Minimum Charge	Job		142		142	
2' 10" x 4'							
	Demolish	Ea.		10.45		10.45	Cost includes material and labor to
	Install	Ea.	215	57		272	install 2' 10" x 4' double hung, two
	Demolish and Install	Ea.	215	67.45		282.45	light, double glazed wood window
	Reinstall	Ea.		45.57		45.57	with screen.
	Clean	Ea.	.04	6.20		6.24	
	Paint	Ea.	2.43	12.75		15.18	
	Minimum Charge	Job		142		142	
3' 7" x 3' 4"							
	Demolish	Ea.		10.45		10.45	Cost includes material and labor to
	Install	Ea.	220	63.50		283.50	install 3' 7" x 3' 4" double hung, two
	Demolish and Install	Ea.	220	73.95		293.95	light, double glazed wood window
	Reinstall	Ea.		50.63		50.63	with screen.
	Clean	Ea.	.04	6.20		6.24	
	Paint	Ea.	2.43	12.75		15.18	
	Minimum Charge	Job		142		142	

Exterior Doors and Windows

Wood Window		Unit	Material	Labor	Equip.	Total	Specification
3' 7" x 5' 4"							
	Demolish	Ea.		12.75		12.75	Cost includes material and labor to
	Install	Ea.	283	63.50		346.50	install 3' 7" x 5' 4" double hung, two
	Demolish and Install	Ea.	283	76.25		359.25	light, double glazed wood window
	Reinstall	Ea.		50.63		50.63	with screen.
	Clean	Ea.	.09	10.65		10.74	
	Paint	Ea.	4.05	21.50		25.55	
	Minimum Charge	Job		142		142	
4' 3" x 5' 4"							
	Demolish	Ea.		12.75		12.75	Cost includes material and labor to
	Install	Ea.	445	71		516	install 4' 3" x 5' 4" double hung, two
	Demolish and Install	Ea.	445	83.75		528.75	light, double glazed wood window
	Reinstall	Ea.		56.96		56.96	with screen.
	Clean	Ea.	.09	10.65		10.74	
	Paint	Ea.	2.61	25.50		28.11	
	Minimum Charge	Job		142		142	
Casement							
2' x 3' 4"							
	Demolish	Ea.		10.45		10.45	Cost includes material and labor to
	Install	Ea.	185	28.50		213.50	install 2' x 3' 4" casement window
	Demolish and Install	Ea.	185	38.95		223.95	with 3/4" insulated glass, screens,
	Reinstall	Ea.		22.78		22.78	weatherstripping, hardware.
	Clean	Ea.	.03	5.35		5.38	
	Paint	Ea.	1.89	10.65		12.54	
	Minimum Charge	Job		285		285	
2' x 4'							
	Demolish	Ea.		10.45		10.45	Cost includes material and labor to
	Install	Ea.	207	31.50		238.50	install 2' x 4' casement window with
	Demolish and Install	Ea.	207	41.95		248.95	3/4" insulated glass, screens,
	Reinstall	Ea.		25.32		25.32	weatherstripping, hardware.
	Clean	Ea.	.03	5.35		5.38	
	Paint	Ea.	1.89	10.65		12.54	
	Minimum Charge	Job		285		285	
2' x 5'							
	Demolish	Ea.		10.45		10.45	Cost includes material and labor to
	Install	Ea.	232	33.50		265.50	install 2' x 5' casement window with
	Demolish and Install	Ea.	232	43.95		275.95	3/4" insulated glass, screens,
	Reinstall	Ea.		26.80		26.80	weatherstripping, hardware.
	Clean	Ea.	.04	6.20		6.24	
	Paint	Ea.	2.43	12.75		15.18	
	Minimum Charge	Job		285		285	
2' x 6'							
	Demolish	Ea.		10.45		10.45	Cost includes material and labor to
	Install	Ea.	262	35.50		297.50	install 2' x 6' casement window with
	Demolish and Install	Ea.	262	45.95		307.95	3/4" insulated glass, screens,
	Reinstall	Ea.		28.48		28.48	weatherstripping, hardware.
	Clean	Ea.	.04	6.20		6.24	
	Paint	Ea.	2.43	12.75		15.18	
	Minimum Charge	Job		285		285	
4' x 3' 4"							
	Demolish	Ea.		12.75		12.75	Cost includes material and labor to
	Install	Ea.	535	38		573	install 4' x 3' 4" casement windows
	Demolish and Install	Ea.	535	50.75		585.75	with 3/4" insulated glass, screens,
	Reinstall	Ea.		30.38		30.38	weatherstripping, hardware.
	Clean	Ea.	.04	6.20		6.24	
	Paint	Ea.	1.30	12.75		14.05	
	Minimum Charge	Job		285		285	

Exterior Doors and Windows

Wood Window		Unit	Material	Labor	Equip.	Total	Specification
4' x 4'							
	Demolish	Ea.		12.75		12.75	Cost includes material and labor to
	Install	Ea.	590	38		628	install 4' x 4' casement windows with
	Demolish and Install	Ea.	590	50.75		640.75	3/4" insulated glass, screens,
	Reinstall	Ea.		30.38		30.38	weatherstripping, hardware.
	Clean	Ea.	.07	8.80		8.87	
	Paint	Ea.	1.54	15.95		17.49	
	Minimum Charge	Job		285		285	
4' x 5'							
	Demolish	Ea.		12.75		12.75	Cost includes material and labor to
	Install	Ea.	660	40.50		700.50	install 4' x 5' casement windows with
	Demolish and Install	Ea.	660	53.25		713.25	3/4" insulated glass, screens,
	Reinstall	Ea.		32.55		32.55	weatherstripping, hardware.
	Clean	Ea.	.09	10.65		10.74	
	Paint	Ea.	2.01	21.50		23.51	
	Minimum Charge	Job		285		285	
4' x 6'							
	Demolish	Ea.		12.75		12.75	Cost includes material and labor to
	Install	Ea.	750	47.50		797.50	install 4' x 6' casement windows with
	Demolish and Install	Ea.	750	60.25		810.25	3/4" insulated glass, screens,
	Reinstall	Ea.		37.97		37.97	weatherstripping, hardware.
	Clean	Ea.	.09	10.65		10.74	
	Paint	Ea.	2.37	25.50		27.87	
	Minimum Charge	Job		285		285	
Casement Bow							
4' 8" x 8' 1"							
	Demolish	Ea.		17.70		17.70	Includes material and labor to install
	Install	Ea.	1400	107		1507	casement bow window unit with 4
	Demolish and Install	Ea.	1400	124.70		1524.70	lights, pine frame, 1/2" insulated
	Reinstall	Ea.		85.44		85.44	glass, weatherstripping, hardware,
	Clean	Ea.	.12	12.45		12.57	screens.
	Paint	Ea.	4.38	51		55.38	
	Minimum Charge	Job		285		285	
4' 8" x 10'							
	Demolish	Ea.		17.70		17.70	Includes material and labor to install
	Install	Ea.	1525	142		1667	casement bow window unit with 5
	Demolish and Install	Ea.	1525	159.70		1684.70	lights, pine frame, 1/2" insulated
	Reinstall	Ea.		113.92		113.92	glass, weatherstripping, hardware,
	Clean	Ea.	.02	16.60		16.62	screens.
	Paint	Ea.	5.45	64		69.45	
	Minimum Charge	Job		285		285	
5' 4" x 8' 1"							
	Demolish	Ea.		17.70		17.70	Includes material and labor to install
	Install	Ea.	1575	107		1682	casement bow window unit with 4
	Demolish and Install	Ea.	1575	124.70		1699.70	lights, pine frame, 1/2" insulated
	Reinstall	Ea.		85.44		85.44	glass, weatherstripping, hardware,
	Clean	Ea.	.02	16.60		16.62	screens.
	Paint	Ea.	4.97	51		55.97	
	Minimum Charge	Job		285		285	
5' 4" x 10'							
	Demolish	Ea.		17.70		17.70	Includes material and labor to install
	Install	Ea.	1725	142		1867	casement bow window unit with 5
	Demolish and Install	Ea.	1725	159.70		1884.70	lights, pine frame, 1/2" insulated
	Reinstall	Ea.		113.92		113.92	glass, weatherstripping, hardware,
	Clean	Ea.	.02	16.60		16.62	screens.
	Paint	Ea.	6.25	64		70.25	
	Minimum Charge	Job		285		285	

Exterior Doors and Windows

Wood Window		Unit	Material	Labor	Equip.	Total	Specification
6' x 8' 1"							
	Demolish	Ea.		17.70		17.70	Includes material and labor to install
	Install	Ea.	1525	142		1667	casement bow window unit with 5
	Demolish and Install	Ea.	1525	159.70		1684.70	lights, pine frame, 1/2" insulated
	Reinstall	Ea.		113.92		113.92	glass, weatherstripping, hardware,
	Clean	Ea.	.02	16.60		16.62	screens.
	Paint	Ea.	5.65	64		69.65	
	Minimum Charge	Job		285		285	
6' x 10'							
	Demolish	Ea.		17.70		17.70	Includes material and labor to install
	Install	Ea.	1800	142		1942	casement bow window unit with 5
	Demolish and Install	Ea.	1800	159.70		1959.70	lights, pine frame, 1/2" insulated
	Reinstall	Ea.		113.92		113.92	glass, weatherstripping, hardware,
	Clean	Ea.	.02	16.60		16.62	screens.
	Paint	Ea.	7.10	85		92.10	
	Minimum Charge	Job		285		285	
Casing							
	Demolish	Ea.		6.60		6.60	Cost includes material and labor to
	Install	Opng.	16.35	22		38.35	install 11/16" x 2-1/2" pine ranch
	Demolish and Install	Opng.	16.35	28.60		44.95	style window casing.
	Reinstall	Opng.		17.53		17.53	
	Clean	Opng.	.40	2.07		2.47	
	Paint	Ea.	3.04	5.10		8.14	
	Minimum Charge	Job		178		178	
Trim Set							
	Demolish	Ea.		5		5	Cost includes material and labor to
	Install	Opng.	16.35	22		38.35	install 11/16" x 2-1/2" pine ranch
	Demolish and Install	Opng.	16.35	27		43.35	style window casing.
	Reinstall	Opng.		17.53		17.53	
	Clean	Opng.	.40	2.07		2.47	
	Paint	Ea.	3.04	5.10		8.14	
	Minimum Charge	Job		142		142	
Wood Picture Window							
3' 6" x 4'							
	Demolish	Ea.		12.75		12.75	Includes material and labor to install a
	Install	Ea.	300	47.50		347.50	wood framed picture window
	Demolish and Install	Ea.	300	60.25		360.25	including exterior trim.
	Clean	Ea.	.09	10.65		10.74	
	Paint	Ea.	1.66	19.65		21.31	
	Minimum Charge	Job		285		285	
4' x 4' 6"							
	Demolish	Ea.		12.75		12.75	Includes material and labor to install a
	Install	Ea.	325	52		377	wood framed picture window
	Demolish and Install	Ea.	325	64.75		389.75	including exterior trim.
	Clean	Ea.	.09	10.65		10.74	
	Paint	Ea.	1.66	19.65		21.31	
	Minimum Charge	Job		285		285	
5' x 4'							
	Demolish	Ea.		12.75		12.75	Includes material and labor to install a
	Install	Ea.	405	52		457	wood framed picture window
	Demolish and Install	Ea.	405	64.75		469.75	including exterior trim.
	Clean	Ea.	.09	10.65		10.74	
	Paint	Ea.	3.54	32		35.54	
	Minimum Charge	Job		285		285	

Exterior Doors and Windows

Wood Window

	Unit	Material	Labor	Equip.	Total	Specification
6' x 4' 6"						
Demolish	Ea.		12.75		12.75	Includes material and labor to install a
Install	Ea.	525	57		582	wood framed picture window
Demolish and Install	Ea.	525	69.75		594.75	including exterior trim.
Clean	Ea.	.09	10.65		10.74	
Paint	Ea.	3.54	32		35.54	
Minimum Charge	Job		285		285	

Window Screens

	Unit	Material	Labor	Equip.	Total	Specification
Small						
Demolish	Ea.		2.39		2.39	Includes material and labor to install
Install	Ea.	12.45	8.65		21.10	small window screen, 4 S.F.
Demolish and Install	Ea.	12.45	11.04		23.49	
Reinstall	Ea.		6.90		6.90	
Clean	Ea.	.28	4.31		4.59	
Minimum Charge	Job		71		71	
Standard Size						
Demolish	Ea.		2.39		2.39	Includes material and labor to install
Install	Ea.	25.50	8.65		34.15	medium window screen, 12 S.F.
Demolish and Install	Ea.	25.50	11.04		36.54	
Reinstall	Ea.		6.90		6.90	
Clean	Ea.	.28	4.31		4.59	
Minimum Charge	Job		71		71	
Large						
Demolish	Ea.		2.39		2.39	Includes material and labor to install
Install	Ea.	33.50	8.65		42.15	large window screen, 16 S.F.
Demolish and Install	Ea.	33.50	11.04		44.54	
Reinstall	Ea.		6.90		6.90	
Clean	Ea.	.28	4.31		4.59	
Minimum Charge	Job		71		71	

Window Glass

	Unit	Material	Labor	Equip.	Total	Specification
Plate, Clear, 1/4"						
Demolish	S.F.		1.15		1.15	Includes material and labor to install
Install	S.F.	6.10	4.69		10.79	clear glass.
Demolish and Install	S.F.	6.10	5.84		11.94	
Reinstall	S.F.		3.75		3.75	
Clean	S.F.	.02	.12		.14	
Minimum Charge	Job		141		141	
Insulated						
Demolish	S.F.		1.15		1.15	Includes material and labor to install
Install	S.F.	9.95	8.05		18	insulated glass.
Demolish and Install	S.F.	9.95	9.20		19.15	
Reinstall	S.F.		6.44		6.44	
Clean	S.F.	.02	.12		.14	
Minimum Charge	Job		141		141	
Tinted						
Demolish	S.F.		1.15		1.15	Includes material and labor to install
Install	S.F.	6.15	4.33		10.48	tinted glass.
Demolish and Install	S.F.	6.15	5.48		11.63	
Reinstall	S.F.		3.47		3.47	
Clean	S.F.	.02	.12		.14	
Minimum Charge	Job		141		141	

Exterior Doors and Windows

Window Glass		Unit	Material	Labor	Equip.	Total	Specification
Obscure / Florentine							
	Demolish	S.F.		1.15		1.15	Includes material and labor to install
	Install	S.F.	7	4.02		11.02	obscure glass.
	Demolish and Install	S.F.	7	5.17		12.17	
	Reinstall	S.F.		3.22		3.22	
	Clean	S.F.	.02	.12		.14	
	Minimum Charge	Job		141		141	
Laminated Safety							
	Demolish	S.F.		1.15		1.15	Includes material and labor to install
	Install	S.F.	8.30	6.25		14.55	clear laminated glass.
	Demolish and Install	S.F.	8.30	7.40		15.70	
	Reinstall	S.F.		5.01		5.01	
	Clean	S.F.	.02	.12		.14	
	Minimum Charge	Job		141		141	
Wired							
	Demolish	S.F.		1.15		1.15	Includes material and labor to install
	Install	S.F.	11.55	4.17		15.72	rough obscure wire glass.
	Demolish and Install	S.F.	11.55	5.32		16.87	
	Reinstall	S.F.		3.34		3.34	
	Clean	S.F.	.02	.12		.14	
	Minimum Charge	Job		141		141	
Tempered							
	Demolish	S.F.		1.15		1.15	Includes material and labor to install
	Install	S.F.	6.10	4.69		10.79	clear glass.
	Demolish and Install	S.F.	6.10	5.84		11.94	
	Reinstall	S.F.		3.75		3.75	
	Clean	S.F.	.02	.12		.14	
	Minimum Charge	Job		141		141	
Stained							
	Demolish	S.F.		1.15		1.15	Includes material and labor to install
	Install	S.F.	47	4.69		51.69	stained glass.
	Demolish and Install	S.F.	47	5.84		52.84	
	Reinstall	S.F.		3.75		3.75	
	Clean	S.F.	.02	.12		.14	
	Minimum Charge	Job		141		141	
Etched							
	Demolish	S.F.		1.15		1.15	Includes material and labor to install
	Install	S.F.	38.50	4.69		43.19	etched glass.
	Demolish and Install	S.F.	38.50	5.84		44.34	
	Reinstall	S.F.		3.75		3.75	
	Clean	S.F.	.02	.12		.14	
	Minimum Charge	Job		141		141	
Wall Mirror							
	Demolish	S.F.		1.15		1.15	Includes material and labor to install
	Install	S.F.	6.75	4.51		11.26	distortion-free float glass mirror, 1/4"
	Demolish and Install	S.F.	6.75	5.66		12.41	thick, cut and polished edges.
	Reinstall	S.F.		3.60		3.60	
	Clean	S.F.	.02	.12		.14	
	Minimum Charge	Job		141		141	
Bullet Resistant							
	Demolish	S.F.		1.15		1.15	Includes material and labor to install
	Install	S.F.	80.50	56.50		137	bullet resistant clear laminated glass.
	Demolish and Install	S.F.	80.50	57.65		138.15	
	Reinstall	S.F.		45.06		45.06	
	Clean	S.F.	.02	.12		.14	
	Minimum Charge	Job		141		141	

Exterior Doors and Windows

Storefront System	Unit	Material	Labor	Equip.	Total	Specification
Clear Glass						
Stub Wall to 8'						
Demolish	S.F.		1.80		1.80	Includes material and labor to install
Install	S.F.	16.15	7.70		23.85	commercial grade 4-1/2" section,
Demolish and Install	S.F.	16.15	9.50		25.65	anodized aluminum with clear glass in
Reinstall	S.F.		6.16		6.16	upper section and safety glass in lower
Clean	S.F.		.25		.25	section.
Minimum Charge	Job		178		178	
Floor to 10'						
Demolish	S.F.		1.80		1.80	Includes material and labor to install
Install	S.F.	17.70	7.70		25.40	commercial grade 4-1/2" section,
Demolish and Install	S.F.	17.70	9.50		27.20	anodized aluminum with clear glass in
Reinstall	S.F.		6.16		6.16	upper section and safety glass in lower
Clean	S.F.		.25		.25	section.
Minimum Charge	Job		178		178	
Polished Plate Glass						
Stub Wall to 9'						
Demolish	S.F.		1.80		1.80	Cost includes material and labor to
Install	S.F.	12.25	7.70		19.95	install 4' x 9' polished plate glass
Demolish and Install	S.F.	12.25	9.50		21.75	window built on 8" stub wall.
Reinstall	S.F.		6.16		6.16	
Clean	S.F.		.25		.25	
Minimum Charge	Job		178		178	
Stub Wall to 13'						
Demolish	S.F.		1.80		1.80	Cost includes material and labor to
Install	S.F.	12.80	7.70		20.50	install 4' x 13' polished plate glass
Demolish and Install	S.F.	12.80	9.50		22.30	window built on 8" stub wall.
Reinstall	S.F.		6.16		6.16	
Clean	S.F.		.25		.25	
Minimum Charge	Job		178		178	
Floor to 9'						
Demolish	S.F.		1.80		1.80	Cost includes material and labor to
Install	S.F.	13.30	7.70		21	install 4' x 9' polished plate glass
Demolish and Install	S.F.	13.30	9.50		22.80	window built on floor.
Reinstall	S.F.		6.16		6.16	
Clean	S.F.		.25		.25	
Minimum Charge	Job		178		178	
Floor to 13'						
Demolish	S.F.		1.80		1.80	Cost includes material and labor to
Install	S.F.	14.30	7.70		22	install 4' x 13' polished plate glass
Demolish and Install	S.F.	14.30	9.50		23.80	window built on floor.
Reinstall	S.F.		6.16		6.16	
Clean	S.F.		.25		.25	
Minimum Charge	Job		178		178	
Clear Plate Glass						
Floor to 9'						
Demolish	S.F.		1.80		1.80	Cost includes material and labor to
Install	S.F.	19.20	7.70		26.90	install 4' x 9' clear plate glass window
Demolish and Install	S.F.	19.20	9.50		28.70	built on floor.
Reinstall	S.F.		6.16		6.16	
Clean	S.F.		.25		.25	
Minimum Charge	Job		178		178	

Exterior Doors and Windows

Storefront System		Unit	Material	Labor	Equip.	Total	Specification
Floor to 11'							
	Demolish	S.F.		1.80		1.80	Cost includes material and labor to
	Install	S.F.	18.65	7.70		26.35	install 4' x 11' clear plate glass
	Demolish and Install	S.F.	18.65	9.50		28.15	window built on floor.
	Reinstall	S.F.		6.16		6.16	
	Clean	S.F.		.25		.25	
	Minimum Charge	Job		178		178	
Floor to 13'							
	Demolish	S.F.		1.80		1.80	Cost includes material and labor to
	Install	S.F.	18.80	7.70		26.50	install 4' x 13' clear plate glass
	Demolish and Install	S.F.	18.80	9.50		28.30	window built on floor.
	Reinstall	S.F.		6.16		6.16	
	Clean	S.F.		.25		.25	
	Minimum Charge	Job		178		178	
Decorative Type							
	Demolish	S.F.		1.80		1.80	Includes material and labor to install
	Install	S.F.	14.65	5.65		20.30	decorative storefront system.
	Demolish and Install	S.F.	14.65	7.45		22.10	
	Reinstall	S.F.		4.51		4.51	
	Clean	S.F.		.25		.25	
	Minimum Charge	Job		141		141	
Decorative Curved							
	Demolish	S.F.		1.80		1.80	Includes material and labor to install
	Install	S.F.	27.50	11.25		38.75	decorative curved storefront system.
	Demolish and Install	S.F.	27.50	13.05		40.55	
	Reinstall	S.F.		9.01		9.01	
	Clean	S.F.		.25		.25	
	Minimum Charge	Job		141		141	
Entrance							
Narrow Stile 3' x 7"							
	Demolish	Ea.		15.80		15.80	Cost includes material and labor to
	Install	Ea.	650	190		840	install 3' x 7' narrow stile door, center
	Demolish and Install	Ea.	650	205.80		855.80	pivot concealed closer.
	Reinstall	Ea.		151.89		151.89	
	Clean	Ea.	3.51	26		29.51	
	Minimum Charge	Job		178		178	
Tempered Glass							
	Demolish	Ea.		15.80		15.80	Cost includes material and labor to
	Install	Ea.	2550	385		2935	install 3' x 7' tempered glass door,
	Demolish and Install	Ea.	2550	400.80		2950.80	center pivot concealed closer,.
	Reinstall	Ea.		308.58		308.58	
	Clean	Ea.	3.51	26		29.51	
	Minimum Charge	Job		178		178	
Heavy Section							
	Demolish	Ea.		15.80		15.80	Includes material and labor to install
	Install	Ea.	755	355		1110	wide stile door with 3' 6" x 7'
	Demolish and Install	Ea.	755	370.80		1125.80	opening.
	Reinstall	Ea.		285.44		285.44	
	Clean	Ea.	.70	8.60		9.30	
	Minimum Charge	Job		565		565	

Exterior Doors and Windows

Curtain Wall System		Unit	Material	Labor	Equip.	Total	Specification
Regular Weight							
Bronze Anodized							
	Demolish	S.F.		1.80		1.80	Includes material and labor to install
	Install	S.F.	30.50	7.70		38.20	structural curtain wall system with
	Demolish and Install	S.F.	30.50	9.50		40	bronze anodized frame of heavy
	Clean	S.F.		.25		.25	weight, float glass.
	Minimum Charge	Job		142		142	
Black Anodized							
	Demolish	S.F.		1.80		1.80	Includes material and labor to install
	Install	S.F.	32.50	7.70		40.20	structural curtain wall system with black
	Demolish and Install	S.F.	32.50	9.50		42	anodized frame of regular weight,
	Clean	S.F.		.25		.25	float glass.
	Minimum Charge	Job		142		142	
Heavy Weight							
Bronze Anodized							
	Demolish	S.F.		1.80		1.80	Includes material and labor to install
	Install	S.F.	30.50	7.70		38.20	structural curtain wall system with
	Demolish and Install	S.F.	30.50	9.50		40	bronze anodized frame of heavy
	Clean	S.F.		.25		.25	weight, float glass.
	Minimum Charge	Job		142		142	
Black Anodized							
	Demolish	S.F.		1.80		1.80	Includes material and labor to install
	Install	S.F.	31	7.70		38.70	structural curtain wall system with black
	Demolish and Install	S.F.	31	9.50		40.50	anodized frame of heavy weight, float
	Clean	S.F.		.25		.25	glass.
	Minimum Charge	Job		142		142	
Glass							
1" Insulated							
	Install	S.F.	12.25	7.50		19.75	Cost includes labor and material to
	Minimum Charge	Job		141		141	install 1" insulated glass.
Heat Absorbing							
	Install	S.F.	7.15	7.50		14.65	Includes labor an material to install
	Minimum Charge	Job		141		141	heat absorbing glass.
Low Transmission							
	Install	S.F.	4.68	7.50		12.18	Includes labor an material to install low
	Minimum Charge	Job		141		141	transmission glass.

Skylight		Unit	Material	Labor	Equip.	Total	Specification
Dome							
22" x 22"							
	Demolish	Ea.		56.50		56.50	Cost includes material and labor to
	Install	Ea.	46	86.50		132.50	install 22" x 22" fixed dome skylight.
	Demolish and Install	Ea.	46	143		189	
	Reinstall	Ea.		69.12		69.12	
	Clean	Ea.	.32	7.40		7.72	
	Minimum Charge	Job		520		520	
22" x 46"							
	Demolish	Ea.		56.50		56.50	Cost includes material and labor to
	Install	Ea.	104	104		208	install 22" x 46" fixed dome skylight.
	Demolish and Install	Ea.	104	160.50		264.50	
	Reinstall	Ea.		82.94		82.94	
	Clean	Ea.		11.50		11.50	
	Minimum Charge	Job		520		520	

Exterior Doors and Windows

Skylight		Unit	Material	Labor	Equip.	Total	Specification
30" x 30"							
	Demolish	Ea.		56.50		56.50	Cost includes material and labor to
	Install	Ea.	87	86.50		173.50	install 30" x 30" fixed dome skylight.
	Demolish and Install	Ea.	87	143		230	
	Reinstall	Ea.		69.12		69.12	
	Clean	Ea.		11.50		11.50	
	Minimum Charge	Job		520		520	
30" x 46"							
	Demolish	Ea.		56.50		56.50	Cost includes material and labor to
	Install	Ea.	151	104		255	install 30" x 46" fixed dome skylight.
	Demolish and Install	Ea.	151	160.50		311.50	
	Reinstall	Ea.		82.94		82.94	
	Clean	Ea.		11.50		11.50	
	Minimum Charge	Job		520		520	
Fixed							
22" x 27"							
	Demolish	Ea.		56.50		56.50	Includes material and labor to install
	Install	Ea.	221	86.50		307.50	double glazed skylight, 22" x 27",
	Demolish and Install	Ea.	221	143		364	fixed.
	Reinstall	Ea.		69.12		69.12	
	Clean	Ea.	.32	7.40		7.72	
	Minimum Charge	Job		520		520	
22" x 46"							
	Demolish	Ea.		56.50		56.50	Includes material and labor to install
	Install	Ea.	277	104		381	double glazed skylight, 22" x 46",
	Demolish and Install	Ea.	277	160.50		437.50	fixed.
	Reinstall	Ea.		82.94		82.94	
	Clean	Ea.		11.50		11.50	
	Minimum Charge	Job		520		520	
44" x 46"							
	Demolish	Ea.		56.50		56.50	Includes material and labor to install
	Install	Ea.	395	104		499	double glazed skylight, 44" x 46",
	Demolish and Install	Ea.	395	160.50		555.50	fixed.
	Reinstall	Ea.		82.94		82.94	
	Clean	Ea.		12.95		12.95	
	Minimum Charge	Job		520		520	
Operable							
22" x 27"							
	Demolish	Ea.		56.50		56.50	Includes material and labor to install
	Install	Ea.	330	86.50		416.50	double glazed skylight, 22" x 27",
	Demolish and Install	Ea.	330	143		473	operable.
	Reinstall	Ea.		69.12		69.12	
	Clean	Ea.	.32	7.40		7.72	
	Minimum Charge	Job		520		520	
22" x 46"							
	Demolish	Ea.		56.50		56.50	Includes material and labor to install
	Install	Ea.	385	104		489	double glazed skylight, 22" x 46",
	Demolish and Install	Ea.	385	160.50		545.50	operable.
	Reinstall	Ea.		82.94		82.94	
	Clean	Ea.		11.50		11.50	
	Minimum Charge	Job		520		520	
44" x 46"							
	Demolish	Ea.		56.50		56.50	Includes material and labor to install
	Install	Ea.	510	104		614	double glazed skylight, 44" x 46",
	Demolish and Install	Ea.	510	160.50		670.50	operable.
	Reinstall	Ea.		82.94		82.94	
	Clean	Ea.		12.95		12.95	
	Minimum Charge	Job		520		520	

Exterior Doors and Windows

Industrial Steel Window		Unit	Material	Labor	Equip.	Total	Specification
100% Fixed							
	Demolish	S.F.		1.47		1.47	Includes material and labor to install
	Install	S.F.	26	3.57		29.57	commercial grade steel windows,
	Demolish and Install	S.F.	26	5.04		31.04	including glazing.
	Reinstall	S.F.		2.85		2.85	
	Clean	Ea.	.12	.78		.90	
	Paint	S.F.	.11	.57		.68	
	Minimum Charge	Job		178		178	
50% Vented							
	Demolish	S.F.		1.47		1.47	Includes material and labor to install
	Install	S.F.	37.50	3.57		41.07	commercial grade steel windows,
	Demolish and Install	S.F.	37.50	5.04		42.54	including glazing.
	Reinstall	S.F.		2.85		2.85	
	Clean	Ea.	.12	.78		.90	
	Paint	S.F.	.11	.57		.68	
	Minimum Charge	Job		178		178	

Brick Veneer

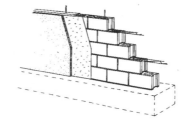

Concrete Masonry Units

Masonry Wall		Unit	Material	Labor	Equip.	Total	Specification
Unreinforced CMU							
4″ x 8″ x 16″							
	Demolish	S.F.		1.28		1.28	Includes material and labor to install
	Install	S.F.	1.02	2.02		3.04	normal weight 4″ x 8″ x 16″ block.
	Demolish and Install	S.F.	1.02	4.10		5.12	
	Clean	S.F.	.03	.32		.35	
	Paint	S.F.	.12	.58		.70	
	Minimum Charge	Job		143		143	
6″ x 8″ x 16″							
	Demolish	S.F.		1.35		1.35	Includes material and labor to install
	Install	S.F.	1.51	2.95		4.46	normal weight 6″ x 8″ x 16″ block.
	Demolish and Install	S.F.	1.51	4.30		5.81	
	Clean	S.F.	.03	.32		.35	
	Paint	S.F.	.12	.58		.70	
	Minimum Charge	Job		143		143	
8″ x 8″ x 16″							
	Demolish	S.F.		1.53		1.53	Includes material and labor to install
	Install	S.F.	1.63	3.25		4.88	normal weight 8″ x 8″ x 16″ block.
	Demolish and Install	S.F.	1.63	4.78		6.41	
	Clean	S.F.	.03	.32		.35	
	Paint	S.F.	.12	.58		.70	
	Minimum Charge	Job		143		143	
12″ x 8″ x 16″							
	Demolish	S.F.		1.53		1.53	Includes material and labor to install
	Install	S.F.	2.37	4.90		7.27	normal weight 12″ x 8″ x 16″ block.
	Demolish and Install	S.F.	2.37	6.43		8.80	
	Clean	S.F.	.03	.32		.35	
	Paint	S.F.	.12	.58		.70	
	Minimum Charge	Job		143		143	
Reinforced CMU							
4″ x 8″ x 16″							
	Demolish	S.F.		1.28	.41	1.69	Includes material and labor to install
	Install	S.F.	1.11	2.89		4	normal weight 4″ x 8″ x 16″ block,
	Demolish and Install	S.F.	1.11	4.17	.41	5.69	mortar and 1/2″ re-bar installed
	Clean	S.F.	.03	.32		.35	vertically every 24″ O.C.
	Paint	S.F.	.12	.58		.70	
	Minimum Charge	Job		253		253	
6″ x 8″ x 16″							
	Demolish	S.F.		1.34	.43	1.77	Includes material and labor to install
	Install	S.F.	1.58	3.02		4.60	normal weight 6″ x 8″ x 16″ block,
	Demolish and Install	S.F.	1.58	4.36	.43	6.37	mortar and 1/2″ re-bar installed
	Clean	S.F.	.03	.32		.35	vertically every 24″ O.C.
	Paint	S.F.	.12	.58		.70	
	Minimum Charge	Job		253		253	

Masonry

Masonry Wall		Unit	Material	Labor	Equip.	Total	Specification
8" x 8" x 16"							
	Demolish	S.F.		1.42	.46	1.88	Includes material and labor to install
	Install	S.F.	1.72	3.29		5.01	normal weight 8" x 8" x 16" block,
	Demolish and Install	S.F.	1.72	4.71	.46	6.89	mortar and 1/2" re-bar installed
	Clean	S.F.	.03	.32		.35	vertically every 24" O.C.
	Paint	S.F.	.12	.58		.70	
	Minimum Charge	Job		253		253	
12" x 8" x 16"							
	Demolish	S.F.		1.46	.47	1.93	Includes material and labor to install
	Install	S.F.	2.45	5.05		7.50	normal weight 12" x 8" x 16" block,
	Demolish and Install	S.F.	2.45	6.51	.47	9.43	mortar and 1/2" re-bar installed
	Clean	S.F.	.03	.32		.35	vertically every 24" O.C.
	Paint	S.F.	.12	.58		.70	
	Minimum Charge	Job		253		253	
Structural Brick							
4" Single Row							
	Demolish	S.F.		1.84	.59	2.43	Cost includes material and labor to
	Install	S.F.	2.92	6.05		8.97	install 4" red brick wall, running bond
	Demolish and Install	S.F.	2.92	7.89	.59	11.40	with 3/8" concave joints, mortar and
	Clean	S.F.	.03	.27		.30	ties.
	Paint	S.F.	.12	.58		.70	
	Minimum Charge	Job		253		253	
8" Double Row							
	Demolish	S.F.		1.84	.59	2.43	Cost includes material and labor to
	Install	S.F.	4.72	9.60		14.32	install 8" red brick wall, running bond,
	Demolish and Install	S.F.	4.72	11.44	.59	16.75	with 3/8" concave joints, mortar and
	Clean	S.F.	.03	.27		.30	wall ties.
	Paint	S.F.	.12	.58		.70	
	Minimum Charge	Job		253		253	
12" Triple Row							
	Demolish	S.F.		2.55	.82	3.37	Cost includes material and labor to
	Install	S.F.	7.10	13.65		20.75	install 12" red brick wall, running
	Demolish and Install	S.F.	7.10	16.20	.82	24.12	bond, with 3/8" concave joints, mortar
	Clean	S.F.	.03	.27		.30	and wall ties.
	Paint	S.F.	.12	.58		.70	
	Minimum Charge	Job		253		253	
Brick Veneer							
4" Red Common							
	Demolish	S.F.		1.84	.59	2.43	Cost includes material and labor to
	Install	S.F.	2.24	5.65		7.89	install 4" common red face brick,
	Demolish and Install	S.F.	2.24	7.49	.59	10.32	running bond with 3/8" concave
	Clean	S.F.	.03	.27		.30	joints, mortar and wall ties.
	Paint	S.F.	.12	.58		.70	
	Minimum Charge	Job		143		143	
4" Used							
	Demolish	S.F.		1.84	.59	2.43	Cost includes material and labor to
	Install	S.F.	2.92	6.05		8.97	install 4" red brick wall, running bond
	Demolish and Install	S.F.	2.92	7.89	.59	11.40	with 3/8" concave joints, mortar and
	Clean	S.F.	.03	.27		.30	ties.
	Paint	S.F.	.12	.58		.70	
	Minimum Charge	Job		143		143	

Masonry

Masonry Wall		Unit	Material	Labor	Equip.	Total	Specification
6" Jumbo							
	Demolish	S.F.		1.84	.59	2.43	Cost includes material and labor to
	Install	S.F.	3.88	2.99		6.87	install 6" red jumbo brick veneer,
	Demolish and Install	S.F.	3.88	4.83	.59	9.30	running bond with 3/8" concave
	Clean	S.F.	.03	.27		.30	joints, mortar and ties.
	Paint	S.F.	.12	.58		.70	
	Minimum Charge	Job		143		143	
Norman (11-1/2")							
	Demolish	S.F.		1.84	.59	2.43	Cost includes material and labor to
	Install	S.F.	3.85	4.06		7.91	install 4" norman red brick wall,
	Demolish and Install	S.F.	3.85	5.90	.59	10.34	running bond with 3/8" concave
	Clean	S.F.	.03	.27		.30	joints, mortar and ties.
	Paint	S.F.	.12	.58		.70	
	Minimum Charge	Job		143		143	
Glazed							
	Demolish	S.F.		1.84	.59	2.43	Includes material, labor and equipment
	Install	S.F.	7.50	6.20		13.70	to install glazed brick.
	Demolish and Install	S.F.	7.50	8.04	.59	16.13	
	Clean	S.F.	.03	.27		.30	
	Paint	S.F.	.12	.58		.70	
	Minimum Charge	Job		143		143	
Slumpstone							
6" x 4"							
	Demolish	S.F.		1.28		1.28	Cost includes material and labor to
	Install	S.F.	5.30	3.17		8.47	install 6" x 4" x 16" concrete slump
	Demolish and Install	S.F.	5.30	4.45		9.75	block.
	Clean	S.F.	.03	.32		.35	
	Paint	S.F.	.12	.58		.70	
	Minimum Charge	Job		143		143	
6" x 6"							
	Demolish	S.F.		1.35		1.35	Cost includes material and labor to
	Install	S.F.	4.33	3.27		7.60	install 6" x 6" x 16" concrete slump
	Demolish and Install	S.F.	4.33	4.62		8.95	block.
	Clean	S.F.	.03	.32		.35	
	Paint	S.F.	.12	.58		.70	
	Minimum Charge	Job		143		143	
8" x 6"							
	Demolish	S.F.		1.35		1.35	Cost includes material and labor to
	Install	S.F.	5.60	3.38		8.98	install 8" x 6" x 16" concrete slump
	Demolish and Install	S.F.	5.60	4.73		10.33	block.
	Clean	S.F.	.03	.32		.35	
	Paint	S.F.	.12	.58		.70	
	Minimum Charge	Job		143		143	
12" x 4"							
	Demolish	S.F.		1.28		1.28	Cost includes material and labor to
	Install	S.F.	11.35	3.90		15.25	install 12" x 4" x 16" concrete slump
	Demolish and Install	S.F.	11.35	5.18		16.53	block.
	Clean	S.F.	.03	.32		.35	
	Paint	S.F.	.12	.58		.70	
	Minimum Charge	Job		143		143	
12" x 6"							
	Demolish	S.F.		1.35		1.35	Cost includes material and labor to
	Install	S.F.	8.90	4.22		13.12	install 12" x 6" x 16" concrete slump
	Demolish and Install	S.F.	8.90	5.57		14.47	block.
	Clean	S.F.	.03	.32		.35	
	Paint	S.F.	.12	.58		.70	
	Minimum Charge	Job		143		143	

Masonry

Masonry Wall	Unit	Material	Labor	Equip.	Total	Specification
Stucco						
Three Coat						
Demolish	S.Y.		1.58		1.58	Includes material and labor to install
Install	S.Y.	3.58	6.15	.39	10.12	stucco on exterior masonry walls.
Demolish and Install	S.Y.	3.58	7.73	.39	11.70	
Clean	S.Y.		2.87		2.87	
Paint	S.F.	.12	.42		.54	
Minimum Charge	Job		131		131	
Three Coat w / Wire Mesh						
Demolish	S.Y.		2.87		2.87	Includes material and labor to install
Install	S.Y.	4.02	23.50	1.25	28.77	stucco on wire mesh over wood
Demolish and Install	S.Y.	4.02	26.37	1.25	31.64	framing.
Clean	S.Y.		2.87		2.87	
Paint	S.F.	.12	.42		.54	
Minimum Charge	Job		131		131	
Fill Cracks						
Install	S.F.	.40	2.10		2.50	Includes labor and material to fill-in
Minimum Charge	Job		131		131	hairline cracks up to 1/8" with filler, including sand and fill per S.F.
Furring						
1" x 2"						
Demolish	L.F.		.09		.09	Cost includes material and labor to
Install	L.F.	.23	.58		.81	install 1" x 2" furring on masonry wall.
Demolish and Install	L.F.	.23	.67		.90	
Minimum Charge	Job		142		142	
2" x 2"						
Demolish	L.F.		.10		.10	Cost includes material and labor to
Install	L.F.	.20	.63		.83	install 2" x 2" furring on masonry wall.
Demolish and Install	L.F.	.20	.73		.93	
Minimum Charge	Job		142		142	
2" x 4"						
Demolish	L.F.		.11		.11	Cost includes material and labor to
Install	L.F.	.40	.72		1.12	install 2" x 4" furring on masonry wall.
Demolish and Install	L.F.	.40	.83		1.23	
Reinstall	L.F.		.58		.58	
Minimum Charge	Job		142		142	
Maintenance / Cleaning						
Repoint						
Install	S.F.	.28	3.58		3.86	Includes labor and material to cut and
Minimum Charge	Hr.		36		36	repoint brick, hard mortar, running bond.
Acid Etch						
Install	S.F.	.02	.51		.53	Includes labor and material to acid
Minimum Charge	Job		530	97.50	627.50	wash smooth brick.
Pressure Wash						
Clean	S.F.		.71	.13	.84	Includes labor and material to high
Minimum Charge	Job		530	97.50	627.50	pressure water wash masonry, average.
Waterproof						
Install	S.F.	.17	.54		.71	Includes labor and material to install
Minimum Charge	Job		135		135	masory waterproofing.

Masonry

Chimney

Chimney		Unit	Material	Labor	Equip.	Total	Specification
Demo & Haul Exterior	Demolish	V.L.F.		20.50	6.65	27.15	Includes minimum labor and
	Minimum Charge	Job		115	37	152	equipment to remove masonry and haul debris to truck or dumpster.
Demo & Haul Interior	Demolish	V.L.F.		26	8.35	34.35	Includes minimum labor and
	Minimum Charge	Job		115	37	152	equipment to remove masonry and haul debris to truck or dumpster.
Install New (w / flue)							
Brick	Install	V.L.F.	25	31.50		56.50	Includes material and labor to install
	Minimum Charge	Job		143		143	brick chimney with flue from ground level up. Foundation not included.
Natural Stone	Install	L.F.	57	50.50		107.50	Includes labor and material to install
	Minimum Charge	Job		143		143	natural stone chimney.
Install From Roof Up							
Brick	Install	V.L.F.	25	31.50		56.50	Includes material and labor to install
	Minimum Charge	Job		143		143	brick chimney with flue from ground level up. Foundation not included.
Natural Stone	Install	L.F.	57	42		99	Includes labor and material to install
	Minimum Charge	Job		143		143	natural stone chimney.
Install Base Pad	Install	Ea.	93.50	158	1.63	253.13	Includes labor and material to replace
	Minimum Charge	Job		660	39	699	spread footing, 5' square x 16" deep.
Metal Cap	Install	Ea.	39.50	17.90		57.40	Includes labor and materials to install
	Minimum Charge	Job		142		142	bird and squirrel screens in a chimney flue.

Fireplace

Fireplace		Unit	Material	Labor	Equip.	Total	Specification
Common Brick							
30"	Demolish	Ea.		820	264	1084	Includes material and labor to install a
	Install	Ea.	1325	2525		3850	complete unit which includes common
	Demolish and Install	Ea.	1325	3345	264	4934	brick, foundation, damper, flue lining
	Minimum Charge	Job		143		143	stack to 15' high and a 30" fire box.
36"	Demolish	Ea.		820	264	1084	Includes material and labor to install a
	Install	Ea.	1400	2825		4225	complete unit which includes common
	Demolish and Install	Ea.	1400	3645	264	5309	brick, foundation, damper, flue lining
	Minimum Charge	Job		143		143	stack to 15' high and a 36" fire box.
42"	Demolish	Ea.		820	264	1084	Includes material and labor to install a
	Install	Ea.	1525	3175		4700	complete unit which includes common
	Demolish and Install	Ea.	1525	3995	264	5784	brick, foundation, damper, flue lining
	Minimum Charge	Job		143		143	stack to 15' high and a 42" fire box.

Masonry

Fireplace

	Unit	Material	Labor	Equip.	Total	Specification
48"						
Demolish	Ea.		820	264	1084	Includes material and labor to install a
Install	Ea.	1625	3600		5225	complete unit which includes common
Demolish and Install	Ea.	1625	4420	264	6309	brick, foundation, damper, flue lining
Minimum Charge	Job		143		143	stack to 15' high and a 48" fire box.
Raised Hearth						
Brick Hearth						
Demolish	S.F.		3.59	1.16	4.75	Includes material and labor to install a
Install	S.F.	12.80	21		33.80	brick fireplace hearth based on 30" x
Demolish and Install	S.F.	12.80	24.59	1.16	38.55	29" opening.
Clean	S.F.	.03	.27		.30	
Minimum Charge	Job		143		143	
Marble Hearth / Facing						
Demolish	Ea.		23	7.40	30.40	Includes material and labor to install
Install	Ea.	585	85.50		670.50	marble fireplace hearth.
Demolish and Install	Ea.	585	108.50	7.40	700.90	
Reinstall	Ea.		68.50		68.50	
Clean	Ea.	19.15	4.14		23.29	
Minimum Charge	Job		143		143	
Breast (face) Brick						
Demolish	S.F.		3.59	1.16	4.75	Includes material and labor to install
Install	S.F.	2.96	5.90		8.86	standard red brick, running bond.
Demolish and Install	S.F.	2.96	9.49	1.16	13.61	
Clean	S.F.		.71	.13	.84	
Minimum Charge	Hr.		36		36	
Fire Box						
Demolish	Ea.		184	59	243	Includes material and labor to install
Install	Ea.	138	253		391	fireplace box only (110 brick).
Demolish and Install	Ea.	138	437	59	634	
Clean	Ea.	.11	9.35		9.46	
Minimum Charge	Hr.		36		36	
Natural Stone						
Demolish	S.F.		3.59	1.16	4.75	Includes material and labor to install
Install	S.F.	12.30	10.80		23.10	high priced stone, split or rock face.
Demolish and Install	S.F.	12.30	14.39	1.16	27.85	
Clean	S.F.	.07	1.27		1.34	
Minimum Charge	Job		253		253	
Slumpstone Veneer						
Demolish	S.F.		1.35		1.35	Cost includes material and labor to
Install	S.F.	5.60	3.38		8.98	install 8" x 6" x 16" concrete slump
Demolish and Install	S.F.	5.60	4.73		10.33	block.
Clean	S.F.	.03	.32		.35	
Paint	S.F.	.12	.58		.70	
Minimum Charge	Job		143		143	
Prefabricated						
Firebox						
Demolish	Ea.		33		33	Includes material and labor to install
Install	Ea.	1325	259		1584	up to 43" radiant heat, zero
Demolish and Install	S.F.	1325	292		1617	clearance, prefabricated fireplace.
Reinstall	Ea.		207.13		207.13	Flues, doors or blowers not included.
Clean	Ea.	1.40	12.95		14.35	
Minimum Charge	Job		142		142	

Masonry

Fireplace

	Unit	Material	Labor	Equip.	Total	Specification
Flue						
Demolish	V.L.F.		3.83		3.83	Includes material and labor to install
Install	V.L.F.	10.60	10.80		21.40	prefabricated chimney vent, 8"
Demolish and Install	V.L.F.	10.60	14.63		25.23	exposed metal flue.
Reinstall	V.L.F.		8.62		8.62	
Clean	L.F.	.56	2.59		3.15	
Minimum Charge	Job		280		280	
Blower						
Demolish	Ea.		3.06		3.06	Includes material and labor to install
Install	Ea.	97	19.50		116.50	blower for metal fireplace flue.
Demolish and Install	Ea.	97	22.56		119.56	
Reinstall	Ea.		15.58		15.58	
Clean	Ea.	2.81	26		28.81	
Minimum Charge	Job		280		280	

Accessories
Wood Mantle

	Unit	Material	Labor	Equip.	Total	Specification
Demolish	L.F.		3.83		3.83	Includes material and labor to install
Install	L.F.	5.85	8.15		14	wood fireplace mantel.
Demolish and Install	L.F.	5.85	11.98		17.83	
Reinstall	L.F.		8.14		8.14	
Clean	Ea.	.02	.57		.59	
Paint	L.F.	.07	6.95		7.02	
Minimum Charge	Job		142		142	

Colonial Style

	Unit	Material	Labor	Equip.	Total	Specification
Demolish	Ea.		35		35	Includes material and labor to install
Install	Opng.	835	142		977	wood fireplace mantel.
Demolish and Install	Opng.	835	177		1012	
Reinstall	Opng.		142.40		142.40	
Clean	Ea.		.41		.41	
Paint	Ea.	11.20	95.50		106.70	
Minimum Charge	Job		142		142	

Modern Design

	Unit	Material	Labor	Equip.	Total	Specification
Demolish	Ea.		35		35	Includes material and labor to install
Install	Opng.	173	57		230	wood fireplace mantel.
Demolish and Install	Opng.	173	92		265	
Reinstall	Opng.		56.96		56.96	
Clean	Ea.		.41		.41	
Paint	Ea.	11.20	95.50		106.70	
Minimum Charge	Job		142		142	

Glass Door Unit

	Unit	Material	Labor	Equip.	Total	Specification
Demolish	Ea.		4.79		4.79	Includes material and labor to install a
Install	Ea.	120	5.95		125.95	fireplace glass door unit.
Demolish and Install	Ea.	120	10.74		130.74	
Reinstall	Ea.		5.96		5.96	
Clean	Ea.	.34	7.95		8.29	
Minimum Charge	Job		142		142	

Fire Screen

	Unit	Material	Labor	Equip.	Total	Specification
Demolish	Ea.		2.39		2.39	Includes material and labor to install a
Install	Ea.	53	2.98		55.98	fireplace fire screen.
Demolish and Install	Ea.	53	5.37		58.37	
Reinstall	Ea.		2.98		2.98	
Clean	Ea.	.17	6.90		7.07	
Minimum Charge	Job		142		142	

Siding

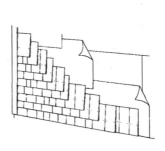

Shingles

Board & Batten

Texture 1-11

Exterior Siding		Unit	Material	Labor	Equip.	Total	Specification
Trim							
1″ x 2″							
	Demolish	L.F.		.19		.19	Cost includes material and labor to
	Install	L.F.	.28	.86		1.14	install 1″ x 2″ pine trim.
	Demolish and Install	L.F.	.28	1.05		1.33	
	Clean	L.F.	.01	.14		.15	
	Paint	L.F.	.02	.40		.42	
	Minimum Charge	Job		142		142	
1″ x 3″							
	Demolish	L.F.		.19		.19	Cost includes material and labor to
	Install	L.F.	.21	.95		1.16	install 1″ x 3″ pine trim.
	Demolish and Install	L.F.	.21	1.14		1.35	
	Clean	L.F.	.01	.14		.15	
	Paint	L.F.	.02	.40		.42	
	Minimum Charge	Job		142		142	
1″ x 4″							
	Demolish	L.F.		.19		.19	Cost includes material and labor to
	Install	L.F.	.64	1.14		1.78	install 1″ x 4″ pine trim.
	Demolish and Install	L.F.	.64	1.33		1.97	
	Clean	L.F.	.01	.14		.15	
	Paint	L.F.	.02	.40		.42	
	Minimum Charge	Job		142		142	
1″ x 6″							
	Demolish	L.F.		.19		.19	Cost includes material and labor to
	Install	L.F.	1.22	1.14		2.36	install 1″ x 6″ pine trim.
	Demolish and Install	L.F.	1.22	1.33		2.55	
	Clean	L.F.	.01	.14		.15	
	Paint	L.F.	.07	.40		.47	
	Minimum Charge	Job		142		142	
1″ x 8″							
	Demolish	L.F.		.21		.21	Cost includes material and labor to
	Install	L.F.	1.41	1.42		2.83	install 1″ x 8″ pine trim.
	Demolish and Install	L.F.	1.41	1.63		3.04	
	Clean	L.F.	.02	.15		.17	
	Paint	L.F.	.07	.40		.47	
	Minimum Charge	Job		142		142	
Aluminum							
8″ Non-Insulated							
	Demolish	S.F.		.52		.52	Includes material and labor to install
	Install	S.F.	1.35	1.14		2.49	horizontal, colored clapboard, 8″ to
	Demolish and Install	S.F.	1.35	1.66		3.01	10″ wide, plain.
	Reinstall	S.F.		1.14		1.14	
	Clean	S.F.		.21		.21	
	Minimum Charge	Job		142		142	

Siding

Exterior Siding		Unit	Material	Labor	Equip.	Total	Specification
8" Insulated							
	Demolish	S.F.		.52		.52	Includes material and labor to install
	Install	S.F.	1.53	1.14		2.67	horizontal, colored insulated
	Demolish and Install	S.F.	1.53	1.66		3.19	clapboard, 8" wide, plain.
	Reinstall	S.F.		1.14		1.14	
	Clean	S.F.		.21		.21	
	Minimum Charge	Job		142		142	
12" Non-Insulated							
	Demolish	S.F.		.52		.52	Includes material and labor to install
	Install	S.F.	1.42	.98		2.40	horizontal, colored clapboard, plain.
	Demolish and Install	S.F.	1.42	1.50		2.92	
	Reinstall	S.F.		.98		.98	
	Clean	S.F.		.21		.21	
	Minimum Charge	Job		142		142	
12" Insulated							
	Demolish	S.F.		.52		.52	Includes material and labor to install
	Install	S.F.	1.67	.98		2.65	horizontal, colored insulated
	Demolish and Install	S.F.	1.67	1.50		3.17	clapboard, plain.
	Reinstall	S.F.		.98		.98	
	Clean	S.F.		.21		.21	
	Minimum Charge	Job		142		142	
Clapboard 8" to 10"							
	Demolish	S.F.		.52		.52	Includes material and labor to install
	Install	S.F.	1.35	1.14		2.49	horizontal, colored clapboard, 8" to
	Demolish and Install	S.F.	1.35	1.66		3.01	10" wide, plain.
	Reinstall	S.F.		1.14		1.14	
	Clean	S.F.		.21		.21	
	Minimum Charge	Job		142		142	
Corner Strips							
	Demolish	L.F.		.27		.27	Includes material and labor to install
	Install	V.L.F.	1.87	1.14		3.01	corners for horizontal lapped
	Demolish and Install	V.L.F.	1.87	1.41		3.28	aluminum siding.
	Reinstall	V.L.F.		1.14		1.14	
	Clean	L.F.		.14		.14	
	Minimum Charge	Job		142		142	
Vinyl							
Non-Insulated							
	Demolish	S.F.		.41		.41	Cost includes material and labor to
	Install	S.F.	.76	1.12		1.88	install 10" non-insulated solid vinyl
	Demolish and Install	S.F.	.76	1.53		2.29	siding.
	Reinstall	S.F.		.89		.89	
	Clean	S.F.		.21		.21	
	Minimum Charge	Job		142		142	
Insulated							
	Demolish	S.F.		.41		.41	Includes material and labor to install
	Install	S.F.	.84	1.12		1.96	insulated solid vinyl siding panels.
	Demolish and Install	S.F.	.84	1.53		2.37	
	Reinstall	S.F.		.89		.89	
	Clean	S.F.		.21		.21	
	Minimum Charge	Job		142		142	
Corner Strips							
	Demolish	L.F.		.26		.26	Includes material and labor to install
	Install	L.F.	1.27	1.39		2.66	corner posts for vinyl siding panels.
	Demolish and Install	L.F.	1.27	1.65		2.92	
	Reinstall	L.F.		1.11		1.11	
	Clean	L.F.		.14		.14	
	Minimum Charge	Job		142		142	

Siding

Exterior Siding		Unit	Material	Labor	Equip.	Total	Specification
Hardboard							
4' x 8' Panel							
	Demolish	S.F.		.43		.43	Cost includes material and labor to
	Install	S.F.	1.02	.71		1.73	install 4' x 8' masonite siding 7/16"
	Demolish and Install	S.F.	1.02	1.14		2.16	thick.
	Clean	S.F.		.21		.21	
	Paint	S.F.	.23	.86		1.09	
	Minimum Charge	Job		142		142	
Lap							
	Demolish	S.F.		.42		.42	Cost includes material and labor to
	Install	S.F.	.93	.74		1.67	install 8" or 12" masonite lap siding
	Demolish and Install	S.F.	.93	1.16		2.09	7/16" thick with wood grain finish.
	Clean	S.F.		.21		.21	
	Paint	S.F.	.23	.86		1.09	
	Minimum Charge	Job		142		142	
Plywood Panel							
Douglas Fir (T-1-11)							
	Demolish	S.F.		.32		.32	Includes material and labor to install
	Install	S.F.	.95	.87		1.82	Douglas fir 4' x 8' plywood exterior
	Demolish and Install	S.F.	.95	1.19		2.14	siding plain or patterns.
	Reinstall	S.F.		.87		.87	
	Clean	S.F.		.21		.21	
	Paint	S.F.	.23	.86		1.09	
	Minimum Charge	Job		142		142	
Redwood							
	Demolish	S.F.		.32		.32	Includes material and labor to install
	Install	S.F.	1.98	.87		2.85	redwood 4' x 8' plywood exterior
	Demolish and Install	S.F.	1.98	1.19		3.17	siding plain or patterns.
	Reinstall	S.F.		.87		.87	
	Clean	S.F.		.21		.21	
	Paint	S.F.	.23	.86		1.09	
	Minimum Charge	Job		142		142	
Cedar							
	Demolish	S.F.		.32		.32	Cost includes material and labor to
	Install	S.F.	2.35	.87		3.22	install 4' x 8' cedar plywood exterior
	Demolish and Install	S.F.	2.35	1.19		3.54	siding plain or patterns.
	Reinstall	S.F.		.87		.87	
	Clean	S.F.		.21		.21	
	Paint	S.F.	.23	.86		1.09	
	Minimum Charge	Job		142		142	
Tongue and Groove							
Fir							
	Demolish	S.F.		.57		.57	Includes material and labor to install fir
	Install	S.F.	1.39	.76		2.15	tongue and groove exterior siding 1" x
	Demolish and Install	S.F.	1.39	1.33		2.72	8".
	Reinstall	S.F.		.61		.61	
	Clean	S.F.		.21		.21	
	Paint	S.F.	.23	.86		1.09	
	Minimum Charge	Job		142		142	
Pine							
	Demolish	S.F.		.57		.57	Includes material and labor to install
	Install	S.F.	.67	1.56		2.23	pine tongue and groove exterior siding
	Demolish and Install	S.F.	.67	2.13		2.80	1" x 8".
	Reinstall	S.F.		1.56		1.56	
	Clean	S.F.		.21		.21	
	Paint	S.F.	.23	.86		1.09	
	Minimum Charge	Job		142		142	

Siding

Exterior Siding

Exterior Siding	Unit	Material	Labor	Equip.	Total	Specification
Cedar						
Demolish	S.F.		.57		.57	Includes material and labor to install
Install	S.F.	3.04	.76		3.80	cedar tongue and groove exterior
Demolish and Install	S.F.	3.04	1.33		4.37	siding 1" x 8".
Reinstall	S.F.		.61		.61	
Clean	S.F.		.21		.21	
Paint	S.F.	.23	.86		1.09	
Minimum Charge	Job		142		142	
Redwood						
Demolish	S.F.		.57		.57	Includes material and labor to install
Install	S.F.	2.93	1.95		4.88	redwood tongue and groove exterior
Demolish and Install	S.F.	2.93	2.52		5.45	siding.
Reinstall	S.F.		1.95		1.95	
Clean	S.F.		.21		.21	
Paint	S.F.	.23	.86		1.09	
Minimum Charge	Job		142		142	
Board and Batten						
Fir						
Demolish	S.F.		.57		.57	Cost includes material and labor to
Install	S.F.	1.49	.71		2.20	install 1" x 8" fir boards with 1" x 3"
Demolish and Install	S.F.	1.49	1.28		2.77	battens.
Reinstall	S.F.		.57		.57	
Clean	S.F.		.21		.21	
Paint	S.F.	.23	.86		1.09	
Minimum Charge	Job		142		142	
Pine						
Demolish	S.F.		.57		.57	Cost includes material and labor to
Install	S.F.	.77	.71		1.48	install 1" x 10" pine boards with 1" x
Demolish and Install	S.F.	.77	1.28		2.05	3" battens.
Reinstall	S.F.		.57		.57	
Clean	S.F.		.21		.21	
Paint	S.F.	.23	.86		1.09	
Minimum Charge	Job		142		142	
Cedar						
Demolish	S.F.		.57		.57	Cost includes material and labor to
Install	S.F.	2.18	.71		2.89	install 1" x 10" cedar boards with 1" x
Demolish and Install	S.F.	2.18	1.28		3.46	3" battens.
Reinstall	S.F.		.57		.57	
Clean	S.F.		.21		.21	
Paint	S.F.	.23	.86		1.09	
Minimum Charge	Job		142		142	
Redwood						
Demolish	S.F.		.57		.57	Cost includes material and labor to
Install	S.F.	3.95	.71		4.66	install 1" x 10" redwood boards with
Demolish and Install	S.F.	3.95	1.28		5.23	1" x 3" battens.
Reinstall	S.F.		.57		.57	
Clean	S.F.		.21		.21	
Paint	S.F.	.23	.86		1.09	
Minimum Charge	Job		142		142	
Wood Shingle						
Demolish	Sq.		53.50		53.50	Includes material and labor to install
Install	Sq.	130	127		257	wood shingles/shakes.
Demolish and Install	Sq.	130	180.50		310.50	
Clean	Sq.		22		22	
Paint	Sq.	.14	76.50		76.64	
Minimum Charge	Job		142		142	

Siding

Exterior Siding	Unit	Material	Labor	Equip.	Total	Specification
Synthetic Stucco System						
Demolish	S.F.		1.91		1.91	Cost includes material and labor to
Install	S.F.	2.86	5.60	.36	8.82	install 2 coats of adhesive mixture,
Demolish and Install	S.F.	2.86	7.51	.36	10.73	glass fiber mesh, 1″ insulation board,
Clean	S.F.		.19		.19	and textured finish coat.
Paint	S.F.	.12	.42		.54	
Minimum Charge	Job		615	39	654	

Front-end Loader   **Bulldozer**

Grading

Grading		Unit	Material	Labor	Equip.	Total	Specification
Hand (fine)							
	Install	S.F.		.41		.41	Includes labor and material to install fine grade for slab on grade, hand grade.
	Minimum Charge	Job		103		103	
Machine (fine)							
	Install	S.Y.		.36	.35	.71	Includes labor and material to install fine grade for roadway, base or leveling course.
	Minimum Charge	Job		246	237	483	

Asphalt Paving

Asphalt Paving		Unit	Material	Labor	Equip.	Total	Specification
Seal Coat							
	Install	S.F.	.06	.08		.14	Includes labor and material to install sealcoat for a small area.
	Minimum Charge	Job		103		103	
Wearing Course							
	Install	S.F.	.07	.22	.17	.46	Cost includes labor and material to install 1" thick wearing course.
	Minimum Charge	Job		103		103	

Masonry Pavers

Masonry Pavers		Unit	Material	Labor	Equip.	Total	Specification
Natural Concrete							
Sand Base							
	Demolish	S.F.		2.30		2.30	Includes material and labor to install concrete pavers on sand base.
	Install	S.F.	1.98	4.77		6.75	
	Demolish and Install	S.F.	1.98	7.07		9.05	
	Reinstall	S.F.		3.81		3.81	
	Clean	S.F.		.83		.83	
	Minimum Charge	Job		143		143	
Mortar Base							
	Demolish	S.F.		3.81	1.09	4.90	Includes material and labor to install concrete pavers on mortar base.
	Install	S.F.	2.57	3.97		6.54	
	Demolish and Install	S.F.	2.57	7.78	1.09	11.44	
	Reinstall	S.F.		3.18		3.18	
	Clean	S.F.		.75		.75	
	Minimum Charge	Job		143		143	

Site Work

Masonry Pavers		Unit	Material	Labor	Equip.	Total	Specification
Adobe							
Sand Base							
	Demolish	S.F.		2.30		2.30	Includes material and labor to install
	Install	S.F.	1.44	3.18		4.62	adobe pavers on sand base.
	Demolish and Install	S.F.	1.44	5.48		6.92	
	Reinstall	S.F.		2.54		2.54	
	Clean	S.F.		.83		.83	
	Minimum Charge	Job		143		143	
Mortar Base							
	Demolish	S.F.		3.81	1.09	4.90	Includes material and labor to install
	Install	S.F.	1.99	3.97		5.96	adobe pavers on mortar base.
	Demolish and Install	S.F.	1.99	7.78	1.09	10.86	
	Reinstall	S.F.		3.18		3.18	
	Clean	S.F.		.75		.75	
	Minimum Charge	Job		143		143	
Standard Brick							
Sand Base							
	Demolish	S.F.		2.30		2.30	Includes material and labor to install
	Install	S.F.	2.37	5.05		7.42	standard brick pavers on sand base.
	Demolish and Install	S.F.	2.37	7.35		9.72	
	Reinstall	S.F.		4.05		4.05	
	Clean	S.F.		.83		.83	
	Minimum Charge	Job		143		143	
Mortar Base							
	Demolish	S.F.		3.81	1.09	4.90	Includes material and labor to install
	Install	S.F.	4.62	7.15		11.77	standard brick pavers on mortar base.
	Demolish and Install	S.F.	4.62	10.96	1.09	16.67	
	Reinstall	S.F.		5.72		5.72	
	Clean	S.F.		.75		.75	
	Minimum Charge	Job		143		143	
Deluxe Brick							
Sand Base							
	Demolish	S.F.		2.30		2.30	Includes material and labor to install
	Install	S.F.	4.57	3.97		8.54	deluxe brick pavers on sand base.
	Demolish and Install	S.F.	4.57	6.27		10.84	
	Reinstall	S.F.		3.18		3.18	
	Clean	S.F.		.83		.83	
	Minimum Charge	Job		143		143	
Mortar Base							
	Demolish	S.F.		3.81	1.09	4.90	Includes material and labor to install
	Install	S.F.	4.90	7.15		12.05	deluxe brick pavers on mortar base.
	Demolish and Install	S.F.	4.90	10.96	1.09	16.95	
	Reinstall	S.F.		5.72		5.72	
	Clean	S.F.		.75		.75	
	Minimum Charge	Job		143		143	

Fencing		Unit	Material	Labor	Equip.	Total	Specification
Block w / Footing							
4″							
	Demolish	S.F.		1.28		1.28	Cost includes material and labor to
	Install	S.F.	.99	3.02		4.01	install 4″ non-reinforced concrete
	Demolish and Install	S.F.	.99	4.30		5.29	block.
	Clean	S.F.	.11	.88	.16	1.15	
	Paint	S.F.	.15	.34		.49	
	Minimum Charge	Job		143		143	

Fencing	Unit	Material	Labor	Equip.	Total	Specification
4" Reinforced						
Demolish	S.F.		1.28	.41	1.69	Cost includes material and labor to
Install	S.F.	1.07	3.06		4.13	install 4" reinforced concrete block.
Demolish and Install	S.F.	1.07	4.34	.41	5.82	
Clean	S.F.	.11	.88	.16	1.15	
Paint	S.F.	.15	.34		.49	
Minimum Charge	Job		143		143	
6"						
Demolish	S.F.		1.35		1.35	Cost includes material and labor to
Install	S.F.	1.46	3.25		4.71	install 6" non-reinforced concrete
Demolish and Install	S.F.	1.46	4.60		6.06	block.
Clean	S.F.	.11	.88	.16	1.15	
Paint	S.F.	.15	.34		.49	
Minimum Charge	Job		143		143	
6" Reinforced						
Demolish	S.F.		1.34	.43	1.77	Cost includes material and labor to
Install	S.F.	1.55	3.29		4.84	install 6" reinforced concrete block.
Demolish and Install	S.F.	1.55	4.63	.43	6.61	
Clean	S.F.	.11	.88	.16	1.15	
Paint	S.F.	.15	.34		.49	
Minimum Charge	Job		143		143	
Cap for Block Wall						
Demolish	L.F.		1.44	.46	1.90	Includes labor and equipment to install
Install	L.F.	18.70	6.75		25.45	precast concrete coping.
Demolish and Install	L.F.	18.70	8.19	.46	27.35	
Clean	L.F.	.01	2.15		2.16	
Paint	S.F.	.15	.34		.49	
Minimum Charge	Job		143		143	
Block Pilaster						
Demolish	Ea.		98.50	32	130.50	Includes material and labor to install
Install	Ea.	56	101		157	block pilaster for fence.
Demolish and Install	Ea.	56	199.50	32	287.50	
Reinstall	Ea.		101.28		101.28	
Paint	Ea.	3.74	11.35		15.09	
Minimum Charge	Job		143		143	
Block w / o Footing						
4"						
Demolish	S.F.		1.28		1.28	Cost includes material and labor to
Install	S.F.	1.18	2.30		3.48	install 4" non-reinforced hollow
Demolish and Install	S.F.	1.18	3.58		4.76	lightweight block.
Clean	S.F.	.11	.88	.16	1.15	
Paint	S.F.	.15	.34		.49	
Minimum Charge	Job		143		143	
4" Reinforced						
Demolish	S.F.		1.28	.41	1.69	Cost includes material and labor to
Install	S.F.	1.34	2.99		4.33	install 4" reinforced hollow lightweight
Demolish and Install	S.F.	1.34	4.27	.41	6.02	block.
Clean	S.F.	.11	.88	.16	1.15	
Paint	S.F.	.15	.34		.49	
Minimum Charge	Job		143		143	
6"						
Demolish	S.F.		1.35		1.35	Cost includes material and labor to
Install	S.F.	1.61	2.53		4.14	install 6" non-reinforced hollow
Demolish and Install	S.F.	1.61	3.88		5.49	lightweight block.
Clean	S.F.	.11	.88	.16	1.15	
Paint	S.F.	.15	.34		.49	
Minimum Charge	Job		143		143	

Fencing	Unit	Material	Labor	Equip.	Total	Specification
6" Reinforced						
Demolish	S.F.		1.34	.43	1.77	Cost includes material and labor to
Install	S.F.	1.66	3.21		4.87	install 6" reinforced hollow lightweight
Demolish and Install	S.F.	1.66	4.55	.43	6.64	block.
Clean	S.F.	.11	.88	.16	1.15	
Paint	S.F.	.15	.34		.49	
Minimum Charge	Job		143		143	
Cap for Block Wall						
Demolish	L.F.		1.44	.46	1.90	Includes labor and equipment to install
Install	L.F.	18.70	6.75		25.45	precast concrete coping.
Demolish and Install	L.F.	18.70	8.19	.46	27.35	
Clean	L.F.	.01	2.15		2.16	
Paint	S.F.	.15	.34		.49	
Minimum Charge	Job		143		143	
Block Pilaster						
Demolish	Ea.		98.50	32	130.50	Includes material and labor to install
Install	Ea.	56	101		157	block pilaster for fence.
Demolish and Install	Ea.	56	199.50	32	287.50	
Reinstall	Ea.		101.28		101.28	
Paint	Ea.	3.74	11.35		15.09	
Minimum Charge	Job		143		143	
Chain Link						
3' High w / o Top Rail						
Demolish	L.F.		1.79	.51	2.30	Includes material and labor to install
Install	L.F.	2.32	1.23		3.55	residential galvanized fence 3' high
Demolish and Install	L.F.	2.32	3.02	.51	5.85	with 1-3/8" steel post 10' O.C. set
Reinstall	L.F.		.99		.99	without concrete.
Clean	L.F.	.09	.75		.84	
Minimum Charge	Job		325		325	
4' High w / o Top Rail						
Demolish	L.F.		1.79	.51	2.30	Includes material and labor to install
Install	L.F.	2.46	1.52		3.98	residential galvanized fence 4' high
Demolish and Install	L.F.	2.46	3.31	.51	6.28	with 1-3/8" steel post 10' O.C. set
Reinstall	L.F.		1.22		1.22	without concrete.
Clean	L.F.	.11	.83		.94	
Minimum Charge	Job		325		325	
5' High w / o Top Rail						
Demolish	L.F.		1.79	.51	2.30	Includes material and labor to install
Install	L.F.	2.89	1.99		4.88	residential galvanized fence 5' high
Demolish and Install	L.F.	2.89	3.78	.51	7.18	with 1-3/8" steel post 10' O.C. set
Reinstall	L.F.		1.59		1.59	without concrete.
Clean	L.F.	.14	.92		1.06	
Minimum Charge	Job		325		325	
3' High w / Top Rail						
Demolish	L.F.		1.90	.55	2.45	Includes material and labor to install
Install	L.F.	2.86	1.30		4.16	residential galvanized fence 3' high
Demolish and Install	L.F.	2.86	3.20	.55	6.61	with 1-3/8" steel post 10' O.C. set
Reinstall	L.F.		1.04		1.04	without concrete.
Clean	L.F.	.09	.77		.86	
Minimum Charge	Job		325		325	
4' High w / Top Rail						
Demolish	L.F.		1.90	.55	2.45	Includes material and labor to install
Install	L.F.	3.25	1.62		4.87	residential galvanized fence 4' high
Demolish and Install	L.F.	3.25	3.52	.55	7.32	with 1-5/8" steel post 10' O.C. set
Reinstall	L.F.		1.30		1.30	without concrete and 1-5/8" top rail
Clean	L.F.	.11	.84		.95	with sleeves.
Minimum Charge	Job		325		325	

Fencing	Unit	Material	Labor	Equip.	Total	Specification
5' High w / Top Rail						Includes material and labor to install
Demolish	L.F.		1.90	.55	2.45	residential galvanized fence 5' high
Install	L.F.	3.69	2.16		5.85	with 1-5/8" steel post 10' O.C. set
Demolish and Install	L.F.	3.69	4.06	.55	8.30	without concrete and 1-5/8" top rail
Reinstall	L.F.		1.73		1.73	with sleeves.
Clean	L.F.	.14	.94		1.08	
Minimum Charge	Job		325		325	
6' High w / Top Rail						Includes material and labor to install
Demolish	L.F.		1.90	.55	2.45	residential galvanized fence 6' high
Install	L.F.	3.94	3.24		7.18	with 2" steel post 10' O.C. set without
Demolish and Install	L.F.	3.94	5.14	.55	9.63	concrete and 1-3/8" top rail with
Reinstall	L.F.		2.59		2.59	sleeves.
Clean	L.F.	.17	1.06		1.23	
Minimum Charge	Job		325		325	
Barbed Wire						Cost includes material and labor to
Demolish	L.F.		1.07		1.07	install 3 strand galvanized barbed
Install	L.F.	.26	.41	.13	.80	wire fence.
Demolish and Install	L.F.	.26	1.48	.13	1.87	
Reinstall	L.F.		.33	.11	.44	
Minimum Charge	Job		325	310	635	
6' Redwood						Cost includes material and labor to
Demolish	L.F.		7.20		7.20	install 6' high redwood fencing.
Install	L.F.	9.45	5.20		14.65	
Demolish and Install	L.F.	9.45	12.40		21.85	
Reinstall	L.F.		4.14		4.14	
Clean	L.F.	.17	.96		1.13	
Paint	L.F.	.61	2.69		3.30	
Minimum Charge	Job		325		325	
6' Red Cedar						Cost includes material and labor to
Demolish	L.F.		7.20		7.20	install 6' cedar fence.
Install	L.F.	14.45	5.20		19.65	
Demolish and Install	L.F.	14.45	12.40		26.85	
Reinstall	L.F.		4.14		4.14	
Clean	L.F.	.17	.96		1.13	
Paint	L.F.	.61	2.69		3.30	
Minimum Charge	Job		325		325	
6' Shadowbox						Cost includes material and labor to
Demolish	L.F.		7.20		7.20	install 6' pressure treated pine fence.
Install	L.F.	11.05	4.32		15.37	
Demolish and Install	L.F.	11.05	11.52		22.57	
Reinstall	L.F.		3.45		3.45	
Clean	L.F.	.17	.96		1.13	
Paint	L.F.	.61	2.69		3.30	
Minimum Charge	Job		325		325	
3' Picket						Includes material, labor and equipment
Demolish	L.F.		7.20		7.20	to install pressure treated pine picket
Install	L.F.	4.18	4.63		8.81	fence.
Demolish and Install	L.F.	4.18	11.83		16.01	
Reinstall	L.F.		3.70		3.70	
Clean	L.F.	.09	.83		.92	
Paint	L.F.	.31	1.46		1.77	
Minimum Charge	Job		325		325	

Fencing

Fencing	Unit	Material	Labor	Equip.	Total	Specification
Wrought Iron						
Demolish	L.F.		15.30		15.30	Cost includes material and labor to
Install	L.F.	16.50	8.65		25.15	install 5' high wrought iron fence with
Demolish and Install	L.F.	16.50	23.95		40.45	pickets at 4-1/2" O.C.
Reinstall	L.F.		6.91		6.91	
Clean	L.F.		.83		.83	
Paint	L.F.	.55	3		3.55	
Minimum Charge	Job		325		325	
Post						
Dirt Based Wood						
Demolish	Ea.		18		18	Includes material and labor to install
Install	Ea.	10.20	81		91.20	wood post set in earth.
Demolish and Install	Ea.	10.20	99		109.20	
Reinstall	Ea.		64.75		64.75	
Clean	Ea.		2.59		2.59	
Paint	Ea.	.67	1.02		1.69	
Minimum Charge	Job		325		325	
Concrete Based Wood						
Demolish	Ea.		25.50	7.30	32.80	Includes material and labor to install
Install	Ea.	10.20	108		118.20	wood post set in concrete.
Demolish and Install	Ea.	10.20	133.50	7.30	151	
Clean	Ea.		2.59		2.59	
Paint	Ea.	.67	1.02		1.69	
Minimum Charge	Job		325		325	
Block Pilaster						
Demolish	Ea.		98.50	32	130.50	Includes material and labor to install
Install	Ea.	56	101		157	block pilaster for fence.
Demolish and Install	Ea.	56	199.50	32	287.50	
Reinstall	Ea.		101.28		101.28	
Paint	Ea.	3.74	11.35		15.09	
Minimum Charge	Job		143		143	
Gate						
Chain Link						
Demolish	Ea.		24		24	Cost includes material and labor to
Install	Ea.	98	36		134	install 3' wide chain link pass gate
Demolish and Install	Ea.	98	60		158	and hardware.
Reinstall	Ea.		28.78		28.78	
Clean	Ea.		2.87		2.87	
Minimum Charge	Job		325		325	
Redwood						
Demolish	Ea.		20.50		20.50	Includes material, labor and equipment
Install	Ea.	114	108		222	to install redwood pass gate and
Demolish and Install	Ea.	114	128.50		242.50	hardware.
Reinstall	Ea.		86.34		86.34	
Clean	Ea.		2.87		2.87	
Paint	Ea.	1	5.10		6.10	
Minimum Charge	Job		325		325	
Red Cedar						
Demolish	Ea.		20.50		20.50	Cost includes material and labor to
Install	Ea.	67	36		103	install 3' wide red cedar pass gate
Demolish and Install	Ea.	67	56.50		123.50	and hardware.
Reinstall	Ea.		28.78		28.78	
Clean	Ea.		2.87		2.87	
Paint	Ea.	1	5.10		6.10	
Minimum Charge	Job		325		325	

Site Work

Fencing

	Unit	Material	Labor	Equip.	Total	Specification
Wrought Iron						
Demolish	Ea.		15.30		15.30	Includes material, labor and equipment
Install	Ea.	87.50	81		168.50	to install wrought iron gate with
Demolish and Install	Ea.	87.50	96.30		183.80	hardware.
Reinstall	Ea.		64.75		64.75	
Clean	Ea.		2.87		2.87	
Paint	Ea.	1.10	5.10		6.20	
Minimum Charge	Job		325		325	

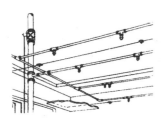

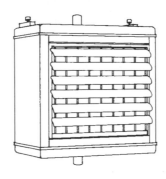

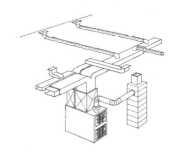

| Fire-extinguishing System | Space Heater | Hot-air Furnace |

Plumbing	Unit	Material	Labor	Equip.	Total	Specification
Components						
3/4" Supply						
Demolish	L.F.		1.74		1.74	Includes material and labor to install
Install	L.F.	2.28	4.12		6.40	type L copper tubing including
Demolish and Install	L.F.	2.28	5.86		8.14	couplings and hangers at 10' O.C.
Reinstall	L.F.		4.12		4.12	
Minimum Charge	Job		157		157	
1/2" Fixture Supply						
Install	Ea.	22.50	104		126.50	Includes labor and materials to install supply pipe only to a plumbing fixture.
2" Single Vent Stack						
Demolish	Ea.		29		29	Includes material and labor to install
Install	Ea.	11.95	157		168.95	PVC vent stack pipe with couplings at
Demolish and Install	Ea.	11.95	186		197.95	10' O.C.
Reinstall	Ea.		156.60		156.60	
Minimum Charge	Job		157		157	
4" Drain						
Demolish	L.F.		2.32		2.32	Includes material and labor to install
Install	L.F.	6.35	5.10		11.45	DVW type PVC pipe with couplings at
Demolish and Install	L.F.	6.35	7.42		13.77	10' O.C. and 3 strap hangers per 10'
Reinstall	L.F.		5.12		5.12	run.
Minimum Charge	Job		157		157	
1-1/2" Drain						
Demolish	L.F.		1.74		1.74	Includes material and labor to install
Install	L.F.	1.66	3.33		4.99	DVW type PVC pipe with couplings at
Demolish and Install	L.F.	1.66	5.07		6.73	10' O.C. and 3 strap hangers per 10'
Reinstall	L.F.		3.33		3.33	run.
Minimum Charge	Job		157		157	
Sewer / Septic						
Install	L.F.	2.43	2.92	.84	6.19	Includes labor and material to install sewerage and drainage piping, 6" diameter.
Maintenance						
Flush Out / Unclog						
Clean	Job		157		157	Includes 4 hour minimum labor charge
Minimum Charge	Job		157		157	for a plumber.

Rough Mechanical

Plumbing		Unit	Material	Labor	Equip.	Total	Specification
Vent Cap							
Large							
	Demolish	Ea.		7.90		7.90	Includes labor and material to install a
	Install	Ea.	33	15.65		48.65	PVC plumbing pipe vent cap.
	Demolish and Install	Ea.	33	23.55		56.55	
	Clean	Ea.	.39	4.70		5.09	
	Paint	Ea.	.15	5.80		5.95	
	Minimum Charge	Job		78.50		78.50	
Medium							
	Demolish	Ea.		7.90		7.90	Includes material and labor to install a
	Install	Ea.	27.50	14.25		41.75	PVC plumbing pipe vent cap.
	Demolish and Install	Ea.	27.50	22.15		49.65	
	Clean	Ea.	.39	4.70		5.09	
	Paint	Ea.	.15	5.80		5.95	
	Minimum Charge	Job		78.50		78.50	
Small							
	Demolish	Ea.		7.90		7.90	Includes material and labor to install a
	Install	Ea.	20.50	13.05		33.55	PVC plumbing pipe vent cap.
	Demolish and Install	Ea.	20.50	20.95		41.45	
	Clean	Ea.	.39	4.70		5.09	
	Paint	Ea.	.15	5.80		5.95	
	Minimum Charge	Job		78.50		78.50	

Plumbing		Unit	Material	Labor	Equip.	Total	Specification
Sump Pump							
1/4 HP							
	Demolish	Ea.		31.50		31.50	Includes material and labor to install a
	Install	Ea.	116	52		168	submersible sump pump.
	Demolish and Install	Ea.	116	83.50		199.50	
	Reinstall	Ea.		41.76		41.76	
	Clean	Ea.	.98	12.95		13.93	
	Minimum Charge	Job		157		157	
1/3 HP							
	Demolish	Ea.		31.50		31.50	Includes material and labor to install a
	Install	Ea.	140	62.50		202.50	submersible sump pump.
	Demolish and Install	Ea.	140	94		234	
	Reinstall	Ea.		50.11		50.11	
	Clean	Ea.	.98	12.95		13.93	
	Minimum Charge	Job		157		157	
1/2 HP							
	Demolish	Ea.		31.50		31.50	Includes material and labor to install a
	Install	Ea.	168	62.50		230.50	submersible sump pump.
	Demolish and Install	Ea.	168	94		262	
	Reinstall	Ea.		50.11		50.11	
	Clean	Ea.	.98	12.95		13.93	
	Minimum Charge	Job		157		157	
Clean and Service							
	Clean	Ea.		19.60		19.60	Includes labor to clean and service a
	Minimum Charge	Job		157		157	sump pump.

Water Heater	Unit	Material	Labor	Equip.	Total	Specification
30 Gallon						
Demolish	Ea.		98		98	Includes material and labor to install a
Install	Ea.	277	142		419	30 gallon electric water heater.
Demolish and Install	Ea.	277	240		517	
Reinstall	Ea.		113.89		113.89	
Clean	Ea.	.98	12.95		13.93	
Minimum Charge	Job		157		157	
40 Gallon						
Demolish	Ea.		98		98	Includes material and labor to install a
Install	Ea.	305	157		462	40 gallon electric water heater.
Demolish and Install	Ea.	305	255		560	
Reinstall	Ea.		125.28		125.28	
Clean	Ea.	.98	12.95		13.93	
Minimum Charge	Job		157		157	
52 Gallon						
Demolish	Ea.		98		98	Includes material and labor to install a
Install	Ea.	350	157		507	52 gallon electric water heater.
Demolish and Install	Ea.	350	255		605	
Reinstall	Ea.		125.28		125.28	
Clean	Ea.	.98	12.95		13.93	
Minimum Charge	Job		157		157	
82 Gallon						
Demolish	Ea.		98		98	Includes material and labor to install
Install	Ea.	540	196		736	an 82 gallon electric water heater.
Demolish and Install	Ea.	540	294		834	
Reinstall	Ea.		156.60		156.60	
Clean	Ea.	.98	12.95		13.93	
Minimum Charge	Job		157		157	
Gas-fired						
30 Gallon Gas-fired						
Demolish	Ea.		120		120	Includes material and labor to install a
Install	Ea.	365	157		522	30 gallon gas water heater.
Demolish and Install	Ea.	365	277		642	
Reinstall	Ea.		125.28		125.28	
Clean	Ea.	.98	12.95		13.93	
Minimum Charge	Job		157		157	
30 Gallon Gas-fired, Flue						
Install	Ea.	31.50	44.50		76	Includes labor and materials to install a
Minimum Charge	Job		157		157	flue for a water heater (up to 50 gallon size).
40 Gallon Gas-fired						
Demolish	Ea.		120		120	Includes material and labor to install a
Install	Ea.	385	165		550	40 gallon gas water heater.
Demolish and Install	Ea.	385	285		670	
Reinstall	Ea.		131.87		131.87	
Clean	Ea.	.98	12.95		13.93	
Minimum Charge	Job		157		157	
40 Gallon Gas-fired, Flue						
Install	Ea.	31.50	44.50		76	Includes labor and materials to install a
Minimum Charge	Job		157		157	flue for a water heater (up to 50 gallon size).
50 Gallon Gas-fired						
Demolish	Ea.		120		120	Includes material and labor to install a
Install	Ea.	485	174		659	50 gallon gas water heater.
Demolish and Install	Ea.	485	294		779	
Reinstall	Ea.		139.20		139.20	
Clean	Ea.	.98	12.95		13.93	
Minimum Charge	Job		157		157	

Rough Mechanical

Water Heater

Water Heater	Unit	Material	Labor	Equip.	Total	Specification
50 Gallon Gas-fired, Flue						
Install	Ea.	31.50	44.50		76	Includes labor and materials to install a
Minimum Charge	Job		157		157	flue for a water heater (up to 50 gallon size).
Solar Hot Water System						
Water Heater						
Demolish	Ea.		78.50		78.50	Includes material and labor to install a
Install	Ea.	770	209		979	solar hot water heat exchanger storage
Demolish and Install	Ea.	770	287.50		1057.50	tank, 100 gallon.
Reinstall	Ea.		167.04		167.04	
Minimum Charge	Job		158		158	
Solar Panel						
Demolish	S.F.		1.14		1.14	Includes material and labor to install
Install	S.F.	18.75	2.06		20.81	solar panel.
Demolish and Install	S.F.	18.75	3.20		21.95	
Reinstall	S.F.		1.65		1.65	
Minimum Charge	Job		158		158	
Repair Plumbing						
Install	Job		158		158	Includes 4 hour minimum labor charge
Minimum Charge	Job		158		158	for a steamfitter or pipefitter.
Insulating Wrap						
Demolish	Ea.		3.62		3.62	Includes material and labor to install
Install	Ea.	20.50	9.80		30.30	insulating wrap around a 100 gallon
Demolish and Install	Ea.	20.50	13.42		33.92	solar hot water heat exchanger storage
Reinstall	Ea.		7.83		7.83	tank.
Minimum Charge	Job		157		157	
Water Softener						
Demolish	Ea.		58		58	Includes material and labor to install a
Install	Ea.	1200	141		1341	14 GPM water softener.
Demolish and Install	Ea.	1200	199		1399	
Reinstall	Ea.		112.74		112.74	
Clean	Ea.	.98	12.95		13.93	
Minimum Charge	Ea.		157		157	

Ductwork

Ductwork	Unit	Material	Labor	Equip.	Total	Specification
Galvanized, Square or Rectangular						
6"						
Demolish	L.F.		1.44		1.44	Includes material and labor to install
Install	L.F.	1.94	13		14.94	rectangular ductwork with a greatest
Demolish and Install	L.F.	1.94	14.44		16.38	dimension of 6".
Reinstall	L.F.		10.39		10.39	
Clean	L.F.		1.66		1.66	
Minimum Charge	Job		156		156	
8"						
Demolish	L.F.		1.44		1.44	Includes material and labor to install
Install	L.F.	2.57	13		15.57	rectangular ductwork with a greatest
Demolish and Install	L.F.	2.57	14.44		17.01	dimension of 8".
Reinstall	L.F.		10.39		10.39	
Clean	L.F.		2.22		2.22	
Minimum Charge	Job		156		156	

Rough Mechanical

Ductwork

	Unit	Material	Labor	Equip.	Total	Specification
10"						
Demolish	L.F.		1.44		1.44	Includes material and labor to install
Install	L.F.	3.22	13		16.22	rectangular ductwork with a greatest
Demolish and Install	L.F.	3.22	14.44		17.66	dimension of 10".
Reinstall	L.F.		10.39		10.39	
Clean	L.F.		2.77		2.77	
Minimum Charge	Job		156		156	
Galvanized, Spiral						
4"						
Demolish	L.F.		1.73		1.73	Cost includes material and labor to
Install	L.F.	.94	1.56		2.50	install 4" diameter spiral pre-formed
Demolish and Install	L.F.	.94	3.29		4.23	steel galvanized ductwork.
Reinstall	L.F.		1.25		1.25	
Clean	L.F.		.87		.87	
Minimum Charge	Job		156		156	
6"						
Demolish	L.F.		1.73		1.73	Cost includes material and labor to
Install	L.F.	1.35	2		3.35	install 6" diameter spiral pre-formed
Demolish and Install	L.F.	1.35	3.73		5.08	steel galvanized ductwork.
Reinstall	L.F.		1.60		1.60	
Clean	L.F.		1.31		1.31	
Minimum Charge	Job		156		156	
8"						
Demolish	L.F.		1.73		1.73	Cost includes material and labor to
Install	L.F.	1.78	2.80		4.58	install 8" diameter spiral pre-formed
Demolish and Install	L.F.	1.78	4.53		6.31	steel galvanized ductwork.
Reinstall	L.F.		2.24		2.24	
Clean	L.F.		1.74		1.74	
Minimum Charge	Job		156		156	
10"						
Demolish	L.F.		2.16		2.16	Cost includes material and labor to
Install	L.F.	2.20	3.50		5.70	install 10" diameter spiral pre-formed
Demolish and Install	L.F.	2.20	5.66		7.86	steel galvanized ductwork.
Reinstall	L.F.		2.80		2.80	
Clean	L.F.		2.18		2.18	
Minimum Charge	Job		156		156	
12"						
Demolish	L.F.		2.89		2.89	Cost includes material and labor to
Install	L.F.	2.71	4.67		7.38	install 12" diameter spiral pre-formed
Demolish and Install	L.F.	2.71	7.56		10.27	steel galvanized ductwork.
Reinstall	L.F.		3.74		3.74	
Clean	L.F.		2.61		2.61	
Minimum Charge	Job		156		156	
16"						
Demolish	L.F.		5.75		5.75	Cost includes material and labor to
Install	L.F.	4.66	9.35		14.01	install 16" diameter spiral pre-formed
Demolish and Install	L.F.	4.66	15.10		19.76	steel galvanized ductwork.
Reinstall	L.F.		7.47		7.47	
Clean	L.F.		3.48		3.48	
Minimum Charge	Job		156		156	
Flexible Fiberglass						
6" Non-insulated						
Demolish	L.F.		1.33		1.33	Cost includes material and labor to
Install	L.F.	1.43	2		3.43	install 6" diameter non-insulated
Demolish and Install	L.F.	1.43	3.33		4.76	flexible fiberglass fabric on corrosion
Reinstall	L.F.		1.60		1.60	resistant metal ductwork.
Clean	L.F.		1.31		1.31	
Minimum Charge	Job		156		156	

Ductwork	Unit	Material	Labor	Equip.	Total	Specification
8" Non-insulated						
Demolish	L.F.		1.92		1.92	Cost includes material and labor to
Install	L.F.	1.94	2.80		4.74	install 8" diameter non-insulated
Demolish and Install	L.F.	1.94	4.72		6.66	flexible fiberglass fabric on corrosion
Reinstall	L.F.		2.24		2.24	resistant metal ductwork.
Clean	L.F.		1.74		1.74	
Minimum Charge	Job		156		156	
10" Non-insulated						
Demolish	L.F.		2.47		2.47	Cost includes material and labor to
Install	L.F.	2.48	3.50		5.98	install 10" diameter non-insulated
Demolish and Install	L.F.	2.48	5.97		8.45	flexible fiberglass fabric on corrosion
Reinstall	L.F.		2.80		2.80	resistant metal ductwork.
Clean	L.F.		2.18		2.18	
Minimum Charge	Job		156		156	
12" Non-insulated						
Demolish	L.F.		3.46		3.46	Cost includes material and labor to
Install	L.F.	2.94	4.67		7.61	install 12" diameter non-insulated
Demolish and Install	L.F.	2.94	8.13		11.07	flexible fiberglass fabric on corrosion
Reinstall	L.F.		3.74		3.74	resistant metal ductwork.
Clean	L.F.		2.61		2.61	
Minimum Charge	Job		156		156	
4" Insulated						
Demolish	L.F.		1.02		1.02	Cost includes material and labor to
Install	L.F.	1.28	1.65		2.93	install 4" diameter insulated flexible
Demolish and Install	L.F.	1.28	2.67		3.95	fiberglass fabric on corrosion resistant
Reinstall	L.F.		1.32		1.32	metal ductwork.
Clean	L.F.		.87		.87	
Minimum Charge	Job		156		156	
6" Insulated						
Demolish	L.F.		1.33		1.33	Cost includes material and labor to
Install	L.F.	1.62	2.16		3.78	install 6" diameter insulated flexible
Demolish and Install	L.F.	1.62	3.49		5.11	fiberglass fabric on corrosion resistant
Reinstall	L.F.		1.72		1.72	metal ductwork.
Clean	L.F.		1.31		1.31	
Minimum Charge	Job		156		156	
8" Insulated						
Demolish	L.F.		1.92		1.92	Cost includes material and labor to
Install	L.F.	2.02	3.11		5.13	install 8" diameter insulated flexible
Demolish and Install	L.F.	2.02	5.03		7.05	fiberglass fabric on corrosion resistant
Reinstall	L.F.		2.49		2.49	metal ductwork.
Clean	L.F.		1.74		1.74	
Minimum Charge	Job		156		156	
10" Insulated						
Demolish	L.F.		2.47		2.47	Cost includes material and labor to
Install	L.F.	2.49	4		6.49	install 10" diameter insulated flexible
Demolish and Install	L.F.	2.49	6.47		8.96	fiberglass fabric on corrosion resistant
Reinstall	L.F.		3.20		3.20	metal ductwork.
Clean	L.F.		2.18		2.18	
Minimum Charge	Job		156		156	
12" Insulated						
Demolish	L.F.		3.46		3.46	Cost includes material and labor to
Install	L.F.	3.06	5.60		8.66	install 12" diameter insulated flexible
Demolish and Install	L.F.	3.06	9.06		12.12	fiberglass fabric on corrosion resistant
Reinstall	L.F.		4.48		4.48	metal ductwork.
Clean	L.F.		2.61		2.61	
Minimum Charge	Job		156		156	

Rough Mechanical

Heating		Unit	Material	Labor	Equip.	Total	Specification
Hot Water Baseboard							
	Demolish	L.F.		5.40		5.40	Includes material and labor to install
	Install	L.F.	5.90	9.45		15.35	baseboard radiation.
	Demolish and Install	L.F.	5.90	14.85		20.75	
	Reinstall	L.F.		7.56		7.56	
	Clean	L.F.	.98	3.23		4.21	
	Minimum Charge	Job		157		157	
3'							
	Demolish	Ea.		17.40		17.40	Includes material and labor to install
	Install	Ea.	18.60	31.50		50.10	fin tube baseboard radiation in 3'
	Demolish and Install	Ea.	18.60	48.90		67.50	sections.
	Reinstall	Ea.		25.21		25.21	
	Clean	Ea.	.28	9.85		10.13	
	Minimum Charge	Job		157		157	
4'							
	Demolish	Ea.		23		23	Includes material and labor to install
	Install	Ea.	25	35.50		60.50	fin tube baseboard radiation in 4'
	Demolish and Install	Ea.	25	58.50		83.50	sections.
	Reinstall	Ea.		28.36		28.36	
	Clean	Ea.	.56	12.95		13.51	
	Minimum Charge	Job		157		157	
5'							
	Demolish	Ea.		29		29	Includes material and labor to install
	Install	Ea.	31	40.50		71.50	fin tube baseboard radiation in 5'
	Demolish and Install	Ea.	31	69.50		100.50	sections.
	Reinstall	Ea.		32.41		32.41	
	Clean	Ea.	.56	15.90		16.46	
	Minimum Charge	Job		157		157	
6'							
	Demolish	Ea.		35		35	Includes material and labor to install
	Install	Ea.	37.50	47.50		85	fin tube baseboard radiation in 6'
	Demolish and Install	Ea.	37.50	82.50		120	sections.
	Reinstall	Ea.		37.81		37.81	
	Clean	Ea.	.56	18.80		19.36	
	Minimum Charge	Job		157		157	
7'							
	Demolish	Ea.		38.50		38.50	Includes material and labor to install
	Install	Ea.	43.50	62.50		106	fin tube baseboard radiation in 7'
	Demolish and Install	Ea.	43.50	101		144.50	sections.
	Reinstall	Ea.		50.11		50.11	
	Clean	Ea.	.70	23		23.70	
	Minimum Charge	Job		157		157	
9'							
	Demolish	Ea.		58		58	Includes material and labor to install
	Install	Ea.	56	89.50		145.50	fin tube baseboard radiation in 9'
	Demolish and Install	Ea.	56	147.50		203.50	sections.
	Reinstall	Ea.		71.59		71.59	
	Clean	Ea.	1.12	29.50		30.62	
	Minimum Charge	Job		157		157	

Heating		Unit	Material	Labor	Equip.	Total	Specification
50 MBH							
	Demolish	Ea.		28.50		28.50	Includes material and labor to install a
	Install	Ea.	565	81		646	cabinet space heater with an output of
	Demolish and Install	Ea.	565	109.50		674.50	50 MBH.
	Reinstall	Ea.		64.82		64.82	
	Clean	Ea.	.70	26		26.70	
	Minimum Charge	Job		158		158	

Heating	Unit	Material	Labor	Equip.	Total	Specification
75 MBH						
Demolish	Ea.		28.50		28.50	Includes material and labor to install a
Install	Ea.	635	94.50		729.50	cabinet space heater with an output of
Demolish and Install	Ea.	635	123		758	75 MBH.
Reinstall	Ea.		75.63		75.63	
Clean	Ea.	.70	26		26.70	
Minimum Charge	Job		158		158	
125 MBH						
Demolish	Ea.		34		34	Includes material and labor to install a
Install	Ea.	840	113		953	cabinet space heater with an output of
Demolish and Install	Ea.	840	147		987	125 MBH.
Reinstall	Ea.		90.75		90.75	
Clean	Ea.	.70	26		26.70	
Minimum Charge	Job		158		158	
175 MBH						
Demolish	Ea.		42.50		42.50	Includes material and labor to install a
Install	Ea.	1025	162		1187	cabinet space heater with an output of
Demolish and Install	Ea.	1025	204.50		1229.50	175 MBH.
Reinstall	Ea.		129.65		129.65	
Clean	Ea.	.70	26		26.70	
Minimum Charge	Job		158		158	

Furnace Unit	Unit	Material	Labor	Equip.	Total	Specification
Wall (gas fired)						
25 MBH w / Thermostat						
Demolish	Ea.		70		70	Includes material and labor to install a
Install	Ea.	395	112		507	gas fired hot air furnace rated at 25
Demolish and Install	Ea.	395	182		577	MBH.
Reinstall	Ea.		89.68		89.68	
Clean	Ea.	1.40	57.50		58.90	
Minimum Charge	Job		158		158	
35 MBH w / Thermostat						
Demolish	Ea.		70		70	Includes material and labor to install a
Install	Ea.	475	125		600	gas fired hot air furnace rated at 35
Demolish and Install	Ea.	475	195		670	MBH.
Reinstall	Ea.		99.64		99.64	
Clean	Ea.	1.40	57.50		58.90	
Minimum Charge	Job		158		158	
50 MBH w / Thermostat						
Demolish	Ea.		70		70	Includes material and labor to install a
Install	Ea.	775	140		915	gas fired hot air furnace rated at 50
Demolish and Install	Ea.	775	210		985	MBH.
Reinstall	Ea.		112.10		112.10	
Clean	Ea.	1.40	57.50		58.90	
Minimum Charge	Job		158		158	
60 MBH w / Thermostat						
Demolish	Ea.		70		70	Includes material and labor to install a
Install	Ea.	805	156		961	gas fired hot air furnace rated at 60
Demolish and Install	Ea.	805	226		1031	MBH.
Reinstall	Ea.		124.55		124.55	
Clean	Ea.	1.40	57.50		58.90	
Minimum Charge	Job		158		158	

Furnace Unit

Furnace Unit		Unit	Material	Labor	Equip.	Total	Specification
Floor (gas fired)							
30 MBH w / Thermostat							Includes material and labor to install a gas fired hot air floor furnace rated at 30 MBH.
	Demolish	Ea.		70		70	
	Install	Ea.	845	112		957	
	Demolish and Install	Ea.	845	182		1027	
	Reinstall	Ea.		89.68		89.68	
	Clean	Ea.	1.40	57.50		58.90	
	Minimum Charge	Job		158		158	
50 MBH w / Thermostat							Includes material and labor to install a gas fired hot air floor furnace rated at 50 MBH.
	Demolish	Ea.		70		70	
	Install	Ea.	1075	140		1215	
	Demolish and Install	Ea.	1075	210		1285	
	Reinstall	Ea.		112.10		112.10	
	Clean	Ea.	1.40	57.50		58.90	
	Minimum Charge	Job		158		158	
Gas Forced Air							
50 MBH							Includes material and labor to install an up flow gas fired hot air furnace rated at 50 MBH.
	Demolish	Ea.		70		70	
	Install	Ea.	755	140		895	
	Demolish and Install	Ea.	755	210		965	
	Reinstall	Ea.		112.10		112.10	
	Clean	Ea.	1.40	57.50		58.90	
	Minimum Charge	Job		158		158	
80 MBH							Includes material and labor to install an up flow gas fired hot air furnace rated at 80 MBH.
	Demolish	Ea.		70		70	
	Install	Ea.	830	156		986	
	Demolish and Install	Ea.	830	226		1056	
	Reinstall	Ea.		124.55		124.55	
	Clean	Ea.	1.40	57.50		58.90	
	Minimum Charge	Job		158		158	
100 MBH							Includes material and labor to install an up flow gas fired hot air furnace rated at 100 MBH.
	Demolish	Ea.		70		70	
	Install	Ea.	950	175		1125	
	Demolish and Install	Ea.	950	245		1195	
	Reinstall	Ea.		140.12		140.12	
	Clean	Ea.	1.40	57.50		58.90	
	Minimum Charge	Job		158		158	
120 MBH							Includes material and labor to install an up flow gas fired hot air furnace rated at 120 MBH.
	Demolish	Ea.		70		70	
	Install	Ea.	1100	187		1287	
	Demolish and Install	Ea.	1100	257		1357	
	Reinstall	Ea.		149.46		149.46	
	Clean	Ea.	1.40	57.50		58.90	
	Minimum Charge	Job		158		158	
Electric Forced Air							
31.4 MBH							Includes material and labor to install an electric hot air furnace rated at 31.4 MBH.
	Demolish	Ea.		70		70	
	Install	Ea.	775	159		934	
	Demolish and Install	Ea.	775	229		1004	
	Reinstall	Ea.		127.18		127.18	
	Clean	Ea.	1.40	57.50		58.90	
	Minimum Charge	Job		158		158	

Rough Mechanical

Furnace Unit

Furnace Unit		Unit	Material	Labor	Equip.	Total	Specification
47.1 MBH							
	Demolish	Ea.		70		70	Includes material and labor to install
	Install	Ea.	820	166		986	an electric hot air furnace rated at
	Demolish and Install	Ea.	820	236		1056	47.1 MBH.
	Reinstall	Ea.		133.10		133.10	
	Clean	Ea.	1.40	57.50		58.90	
	Minimum Charge	Job		158		158	
62.9 MBH							
	Demolish	Ea.		70		70	Includes material and labor to install
	Install	Ea.	965	179		1144	an electric hot air furnace rated at
	Demolish and Install	Ea.	965	249		1214	62.9 MBH.
	Reinstall	Ea.		143.08		143.08	
	Clean	Ea.	1.40	57.50		58.90	
	Minimum Charge	Job		158		158	
78.5 MBH							
	Demolish	Ea.		70		70	Includes material and labor to install
	Install	Ea.	965	183		1148	an electric hot air furnace rated at
	Demolish and Install	Ea.	965	253		1218	78.5 MBH.
	Reinstall	Ea.		146.75		146.75	
	Clean	Ea.	1.40	57.50		58.90	
	Minimum Charge	Job		158		158	
110 MBH							
	Demolish	Ea.		70		70	Includes material and labor to install
	Install	Ea.	1550	193		1743	an electric hot air furnace rated at 110
	Demolish and Install	Ea.	1550	263		1813	MBH.
	Reinstall	Ea.		154.68		154.68	
	Clean	Ea.	1.40	57.50		58.90	
	Minimum Charge	Job		158		158	
A/C Junction Box							
	Install	Ea.	47	77.50		124.50	Includes labor and materials install a
	Minimum Charge	Job		158		158	heating system emergency shut-off switch. Cost includes up to 40 feet of non-metallic cable.

Boiler

Boiler		Unit	Material	Labor	Equip.	Total	Specification
Gas Fired							
60 MBH							
	Demolish	Ea.		305		305	Includes material and labor to install a
	Install	Ea.	1425	1025		2450	gas fired cast iron boiler rated at 60
	Demolish and Install	Ea.	1425	1330		2755	MBH.
	Reinstall	Ea.		825.02		825.02	
	Clean	Ea.	2.81	34.50		37.31	
	Minimum Charge	Job		158		158	
Gas Fired							
125 MBH							
	Demolish	Ea.		455		455	Includes material and labor to install a
	Install	Ea.	2500	1250		3750	gas fired cast iron boiler rated at 125
	Demolish and Install	Ea.	2500	1705		4205	MBH.
	Reinstall	Ea.		1008.36		1008.36	
	Clean	Ea.	2.81	34.50		37.31	
	Minimum Charge	Job		158		158	

Rough Mechanical

Boiler

Boiler		Unit	Material	Labor	Equip.	Total	Specification
Gas Fired							
400 MBH							
	Demolish	Ea.		455		455	Includes material and labor to install a
	Install	Ea.	3325	1775		5100	gas fired cast iron boiler rated at 400
	Demolish and Install	Ea.	3325	2230		5555	MBH.
	Reinstall	Ea.		1772.50		1772.50	
	Clean	Ea.	2.81	34.50		37.31	
	Minimum Charge	Job		158		158	

Heat Pump

Heat Pump		Unit	Material	Labor	Equip.	Total	Specification
2 Ton							
	Demolish	Ea.		74.50		74.50	Includes material and labor to install a
	Install	Ea.	1400	475		1875	2 ton heat pump.
	Demolish and Install	Ea.	1400	549.50		1949.50	
	Reinstall	Ea.		378.13		378.13	
	Clean	Ea.	2.81	26		28.81	
	Minimum Charge	Job		158		158	
3 Ton							
	Demolish	Ea.		141		141	Includes material and labor to install a
	Install	Ea.	1800	710		2510	3 ton heat pump.
	Demolish and Install	Ea.	1800	851		2651	
	Reinstall	Ea.		567.20		567.20	
	Clean	Ea.	2.81	26		28.81	
	Minimum Charge	Job		158		158	
4 Ton							
	Demolish	Ea.		256		256	Includes material and labor to install a
	Install	Ea.	2250	945		3195	4 ton heat pump.
	Demolish and Install	Ea.	2250	1201		3451	
	Reinstall	Ea.		756.27		756.27	
	Clean	Ea.	2.81	26		28.81	
	Minimum Charge	Job		158		158	
5 Ton							
	Demolish	Ea.		375		375	Includes material and labor to install a
	Install	Ea.	2575	1125		3700	5 ton heat pump.
	Demolish and Install	Ea.	2575	1500		4075	
	Reinstall	Ea.		907.52		907.52	
	Clean	Ea.	2.81	26		28.81	
	Minimum Charge	Job		158		158	
Thermostat							
	Demolish	Ea.		8.75		8.75	Includes material and labor to install
	Install	Ea.	122	39		161	an electric thermostat, 2 set back.
	Demolish and Install	Ea.	122	47.75		169.75	
	Reinstall	Ea.		31.16		31.16	
	Clean	Ea.	.06	6.45		6.51	
	Minimum Charge	Job		158		158	
A/C Junction Box							
	Install	Ea.	360	238		598	Includes labor and materials to install a
	Minimum Charge	Job		155		155	heat pump circuit including up to 40 feet of non-metallic cable.

Heating

Heating	Unit	Material	Labor	Equip.	Total	Specification
Electric Baseboard						
Demolish	L.F.		4.31		4.31	Includes material and labor to install
Install	L.F.	12.80	10.35		23.15	electric baseboard heating elements.
Demolish and Install	L.F.	12.80	14.66		27.46	
Reinstall	L.F.		8.27		8.27	
Clean	L.F.	.98	3.23		4.21	
Minimum Charge	Job		155		155	
2' 6"						
Demolish	Ea.		14.35		14.35	Includes material and labor to install a
Install	Ea.	38	39		77	2' 6" long section of electric
Demolish and Install	Ea.	38	53.35		91.35	baseboard heating elements.
Reinstall	Ea.		31		31	
Clean	Ea.	.28	7.95		8.23	
Minimum Charge	Job		155		155	
3'						
Demolish	Ea.		15.65		15.65	Includes material and labor to install a
Install	Ea.	46	39		85	3' long section of electric baseboard
Demolish and Install	Ea.	46	54.65		100.65	heating elements.
Reinstall	Ea.		31		31	
Clean	Ea.	.28	9.85		10.13	
Minimum Charge	Job		155		155	
4'						
Demolish	Ea.		17.20		17.20	Includes material and labor to install a
Install	Ea.	54	46.50		100.50	4' long section of electric baseboard
Demolish and Install	Ea.	54	63.70		117.70	heating elements.
Reinstall	Ea.		37.01		37.01	
Clean	Ea.	.11	2.15		2.26	
Minimum Charge	Job		155		155	
5'						
Demolish	Ea.		19.15		19.15	Includes material and labor to install a
Install	Ea.	64	54.50		118.50	5' long section of electric baseboard
Demolish and Install	Ea.	64	73.65		137.65	heating elements.
Reinstall	Ea.		43.51		43.51	
Clean	Ea.	.56	15.90		16.46	
Minimum Charge	Job		155		155	
6'						
Demolish	Ea.		21.50		21.50	Includes material and labor to install a
Install	Ea.	73	62		135	6' long section of electric baseboard
Demolish and Install	Ea.	73	83.50		156.50	heating elements.
Reinstall	Ea.		49.60		49.60	
Clean	Ea.	.11	2.59		2.70	
Minimum Charge	Job		155		155	
8'						
Demolish	Ea.		28.50		28.50	Includes material and labor to install
Install	Ea.	91	77.50		168.50	an 8' long section of electric
Demolish and Install	Ea.	91	106		197	baseboard heating elements.
Reinstall	Ea.		62		62	
Clean	Ea.	.11	3.23		3.34	
Minimum Charge	Job		155		155	
10'						
Demolish	Ea.		34.50		34.50	Includes material and labor to install a
Install	Ea.	151	94		245	10' long section of electric baseboard
Demolish and Install	Ea.	151	128.50		279.50	heating elements.
Reinstall	Ea.		75.15		75.15	
Clean	Ea.	1.12	32.50		33.62	
Minimum Charge	Job		155		155	

Rough Mechanical

Heating

Heating	Unit	Material	Labor	Equip.	Total	Specification
Electric Radiant Wall Panel						Includes material and labor to install an 18" x 23" electric radiant heat wall panel.
Demolish	Ea.		23		23	
Install	Ea.	390	62		452	
Demolish and Install	Ea.	390	85		475	
Reinstall	Ea.		49.60		49.60	
Clean	Ea.	.14	6.45		6.59	
Minimum Charge	Job		155		155	

Heating Control

Heating Control	Unit	Material	Labor	Equip.	Total	Specification
Thermostat						Includes material and labor to install an electric thermostat, 2 set back.
Demolish	Ea.		8.75		8.75	
Install	Ea.	122	39		161	
Demolish and Install	Ea.	122	47.75		169.75	
Reinstall	Ea.		31.16		31.16	
Clean	Ea.	.06	6.45		6.51	
Minimum Charge	Job		158		158	

Air Conditioning

Air Conditioning	Unit	Material	Labor	Equip.	Total	Specification
2 Ton						Includes material and labor to install a rooftop air conditioning unit, 2 ton. No hoisting is included.
Demolish	Ea.		290		290	
Install	Ea.	1250	490		1740	
Demolish and Install	Ea.	1250	780		2030	
Reinstall	Ea.		489.39		489.39	
Clean	Ea.	2.81	26		28.81	
Minimum Charge	Job		158		158	
3 Ton						Includes material and labor to install a rooftop air conditioning unit, 3 ton. No hoisting is included.
Demolish	Ea.		290		290	
Install	Ea.	1350	645		1995	
Demolish and Install	Ea.	1350	935		2285	
Reinstall	Ea.		645.28		645.28	
Clean	Ea.	2.81	26		28.81	
Minimum Charge	Job		158		158	
4 Ton						Includes material and labor to install a rooftop air conditioning unit, 4 ton. No hoisting is included.
Demolish	Ea.		290		290	
Install	Ea.	1700	750		2450	
Demolish and Install	Ea.	1700	1040		2740	
Reinstall	Ea.		748.28		748.28	
Clean	Ea.	2.81	26		28.81	
Minimum Charge	Job		158		158	
5 Ton						Includes material and labor to install a rooftop air conditioning unit, 5 ton. No hoisting is included.
Demolish	Ea.		290		290	
Install	Ea.	1900	810		2710	
Demolish and Install	Ea.	1900	1100		3000	
Reinstall	Ea.		807.98		807.98	
Clean	Ea.	2.81	26		28.81	
Minimum Charge	Job		158		158	
Compressor						
2 Ton						Includes material and labor to install a refrigeration compressor.
Demolish	Ea.		263		263	
Install	Ea.	555	158		713	
Demolish and Install	Ea.	555	421		976	
Reinstall	Ea.		126.08		126.08	
Clean	Ea.	2.81	26		28.81	
Minimum Charge	Job		158		158	

Rough Mechanical

Air Conditioning

Air Conditioning	Unit	Material	Labor	Equip.	Total	Specification
2.5 Ton						
Demolish	Ea.		263		263	Includes material and labor to install a
Install	Ea.	400	171		571	refrigeration compressor.
Demolish and Install	Ea.	400	434		834	
Reinstall	Ea.		136.60		136.60	
Clean	Ea.	2.81	26		28.81	
Minimum Charge	Job		158		158	
3 Ton						
Demolish	Ea.		263		263	Includes material and labor to install a
Install	Ea.	505	178		683	refrigeration compressor.
Demolish and Install	Ea.	505	441		946	
Reinstall	Ea.		142.54		142.54	
Clean	Ea.	2.81	26		28.81	
Minimum Charge	Job		158		158	
4 Ton						
Demolish	Ea.		263		263	Includes material and labor to install a
Install	Ea.	730	143		873	refrigeration compressor.
Demolish and Install	Ea.	730	406		1136	
Reinstall	Ea.		114.62		114.62	
Clean	Ea.	2.81	26		28.81	
Minimum Charge	Job		158		158	
5 Ton						
Demolish	Ea.		263		263	Includes material and labor to install a
Install	Ea.	870	195		1065	refrigeration compressor.
Demolish and Install	Ea.	870	458		1328	
Reinstall	Ea.		156.14		156.14	
Clean	Ea.	2.81	26		28.81	
Minimum Charge	Job		158		158	
Condensing Unit						
2 Ton Air-cooled						
Demolish	Ea.		75		75	Includes material and labor to install a
Install	Ea.	920	270		1190	2 ton condensing unit.
Demolish and Install	Ea.	920	345		1265	
Reinstall	Ea.		216.08		216.08	
Clean	Ea.	2.81	26		28.81	
Minimum Charge	Job		158		158	
2.5 Ton Air-cooled						
Demolish	Ea.		87.50		87.50	Includes material and labor to install a
Install	Ea.	1150	335		1485	2.5 ton condensing unit.
Demolish and Install	Ea.	1150	422.50		1572.50	
Reinstall	Ea.		266.92		266.92	
Clean	Ea.	2.81	26		28.81	
Minimum Charge	Job		158		158	
3 Ton Air-cooled						
Demolish	Ea.		105		105	Includes material and labor to install a
Install	Ea.	1325	435		1760	3 ton condensing unit.
Demolish and Install	Ea.	1325	540		1865	
Reinstall	Ea.		349.05		349.05	
Clean	Ea.	2.81	26		28.81	
Minimum Charge	Job		158		158	
4 Ton Air-cooled						
Demolish	Ea.		158		158	Includes material and labor to install a
Install	Ea.	1650	630		2280	4 ton condensing unit.
Demolish and Install	Ea.	1650	788		2438	
Reinstall	Ea.		504.18		504.18	
Clean	Ea.	2.81	26		28.81	
Minimum Charge	Job		158		158	

Rough Mechanical

Air Conditioning

	Unit	Material	Labor	Equip.	Total	Specification
5 Ton Air-cooled						
Demolish	Ea.		236		236	Includes material and labor to install a
Install	Ea.	1925	945		2870	5 ton condensing unit.
Demolish and Install	Ea.	1925	1181		3106	
Reinstall	Ea.		756.27		756.27	
Clean	Ea.	2.81	26		28.81	
Minimum Charge	Job		158		158	
Air Handler						
1200 CFM						
Demolish	Ea.		189		189	Includes material and labor to install a
Install	Ea.	620	435		1055	1200 CFM capacity air handling unit.
Demolish and Install	Ea.	620	624		1244	
Reinstall	Ea.		349.05		349.05	
Clean	Ea.	2.81	26		28.81	
Minimum Charge	Job		158		158	
2000 CFM						
Demolish	Ea.		189		189	Includes material and labor to install a
Install	Ea.	1025	515		1540	2000 CFM capacity air handling unit.
Demolish and Install	Ea.	1025	704		1729	
Reinstall	Ea.		412.51		412.51	
Clean	Ea.	2.81	26		28.81	
Minimum Charge	Job		158		158	
3000 CFM						
Demolish	Ea.		210		210	Includes material and labor to install a
Install	Ea.	1550	565		2115	3000 CFM capacity air handling unit.
Demolish and Install	Ea.	1550	775		2325	
Reinstall	Ea.		453.76		453.76	
Clean	Ea.	2.81	26		28.81	
Minimum Charge	Job		158		158	
Evaporative Cooler						
4,300 CFM, 1/3 HP						
Demolish	Ea.		77.50		77.50	Includes material and labor to install
Install	Ea.	605	175		780	an evaporative cooler.
Demolish and Install	Ea.	605	252.50		857.50	
Reinstall	Ea.		140.12		140.12	
Clean	Ea.	1.12	26		27.12	
Minimum Charge	Job		158		158	
4,700 CFM, 1/2 HP						
Demolish	Ea.		77.50		77.50	Includes material and labor to install
Install	Ea.	580	181		761	an evaporative cooler.
Demolish and Install	Ea.	580	258.50		838.50	
Reinstall	Ea.		144.64		144.64	
Clean	Ea.	1.12	26		27.12	
Minimum Charge	Job		158		158	
5,600 CFM, 3/4 HP						
Demolish	Ea.		77.50		77.50	Includes material and labor to install
Install	Ea.	995	187		1182	an evaporative cooler.
Demolish and Install	Ea.	995	264.50		1259.50	
Reinstall	Ea.		149.46		149.46	
Clean	Ea.	1.12	26		27.12	
Minimum Charge	Job		158		158	
Master Cool Brand						
Demolish	Ea.		77.50		77.50	Includes material and labor to install
Install	Ea.	605	193		798	an evaporative cooler.
Demolish and Install	Ea.	605	270.50		875.50	
Reinstall	Ea.		154.62		154.62	
Clean	Ea.	1.12	26		27.12	
Minimum Charge	Job		158		158	

Rough Mechanical

Air Conditioning

	Unit	Material	Labor	Equip.	Total	Specification
Motor						
Demolish	Ea.		43.50		43.50	Includes material and labor to install
Install	Ea.	206	136		342	an evaporative cooler motor.
Demolish and Install	Ea.	206	179.50		385.50	
Reinstall	Ea.		109.05		109.05	
Clean	Ea.	1.12	26		27.12	
Minimum Charge	Job		158		158	
Water Pump						
Demolish	Ea.		43.50		43.50	Includes material and labor to install
Install	Ea.	38.50	78		116.50	an evaporative cooler water pump.
Demolish and Install	Ea.	38.50	121.50		160	
Reinstall	Ea.		62.32		62.32	
Clean	Ea.	1.12	26		27.12	
Minimum Charge	Job		158		158	
Fan Belt						
Demolish	Ea.		8.70		8.70	Includes material and labor to install
Install	Ea.	25.50	15.60		41.10	an evaporative cooler fan belt.
Demolish and Install	Ea.	25.50	24.30		49.80	
Reinstall	Ea.		12.46		12.46	
Minimum Charge	Job		158		158	
Pads (4 ea.)						
Demolish	Ea.		8.70		8.70	Includes material and labor to install
Install	Ea.	29.50	39		68.50	pre-fabricated roof pads for an
Demolish and Install	Ea.	29.50	47.70		77.20	evaporative cooler.
Reinstall	Ea.		31.16		31.16	
Clean	Ea.	1.12	26		27.12	
Minimum Charge	Job		158		158	
Service call						
Install	Job		156		156	Includes 4 hour minimum labor charge for an sheetmetal worker.
Window Mounted						
Low Output BTU						
Install	Ea.	405	35.50		440.50	Includes material and labor to install a
Reinstall	Ea.		28.48		28.48	window air conditioning unit.
Clean	Ea.	.42	6.45		6.87	
Minimum Charge	Job		820		820	
Mid-range Output BTU						
Demolish	Ea.		25		25	Includes material and labor to install a
Install	Ea.	460	47.50		507.50	window air conditioning unit.
Demolish and Install	Ea.	460	72.50		532.50	
Reinstall	Ea.		37.97		37.97	
Clean	Ea.	.42	6.45		6.87	
Minimum Charge	Job		820		820	
High Output BTU						
Demolish	Ea.		31.50		31.50	Includes material and labor to install a
Install	Ea.	550	47.50		597.50	window air conditioning unit.
Demolish and Install	Ea.	550	79		629	
Reinstall	Ea.		37.97		37.97	
Clean	Ea.	.42	6.45		6.87	
Minimum Charge	Job		820		820	
Hotel-type Hot / Cold						
Demolish	Ea.		52.50		52.50	Includes material and labor to install
Install	Ea.	1300	189		1489	packaged air conditioning unit,
Demolish and Install	Ea.	1300	241.50		1541.50	15000 BTU cooling, 13900 BTU
Reinstall	Ea.		151.25		151.25	heating.
Clean	Ea.	.56	12.95		13.51	
Minimum Charge	Job		820		820	

Rough Mechanical

Air Conditioning

		Unit	Material	Labor	Equip.	Total	Specification
Thermostat							Includes material and labor to install
	Demolish	Ea.		8.75		8.75	an electric thermostat, 2 set back.
	Install	Ea.	122	39		161	
	Demolish and Install	Ea.	122	47.75		169.75	
	Reinstall	Ea.		31.16		31.16	
	Clean	Ea.	.06	6.45		6.51	
	Minimum Charge	Job		158		158	
Concrete Pad							Includes material and labor to install
	Demolish	S.F.		1.44		1.44	air conditioner pad.
	Install	S.F.	.94	3.26		4.20	
	Demolish and Install	S.F.	.94	4.70		5.64	
	Reinstall	S.F.		2.61		2.61	
	Clean	S.F.	.06	.41		.47	
	Paint	S.F.	.12	.26		.38	
	Minimum Charge	Job		820		820	
A/C Junction Box							Includes labor and materials to install
	Install	Ea.	151	88.50		239.50	an air conditioning circuit including up
	Minimum Charge	Job		155		155	to 40 feet of non-metallic cable.

Sprinkler System

		Unit	Material	Labor	Equip.	Total	Specification
Exposed							
Wet Type							Includes material and labor to install
	Demolish	SF Flr.		.14		.14	an exposed wet pipe fire sprinkler
	Install	SF Flr.	.84	1.39		2.23	system.
	Demolish and Install	SF Flr.	.84	1.53		2.37	
	Reinstall	SF Flr.		1.39		1.39	
	Minimum Charge	Job		157		157	
Dry Type							Includes material and labor to install
	Demolish	SF Flr.		.14		.14	an exposed dry pipe fire sprinkler
	Install	SF Flr.	.96	1.39		2.35	system.
	Demolish and Install	SF Flr.	.96	1.53		2.49	
	Reinstall	SF Flr.		1.39		1.39	
	Minimum Charge	Job		157		157	
Concealed							
Wet Type							Includes material and labor to install a
	Demolish	SF Flr.		.28		.28	concealed wet pipe fire sprinkler
	Install	SF Flr.	.84	1.89		2.73	system.
	Demolish and Install	SF Flr.	.84	2.17		3.01	
	Reinstall	SF Flr.		1.89		1.89	
	Minimum Charge	Job		157		157	
Dry Type							Includes material and labor to install a
	Demolish	SF Flr.		.28		.28	concealed dry pipe fire sprinkler
	Install	SF Flr.	.96	1.89		2.85	system.
	Demolish and Install	SF Flr.	.96	2.17		3.13	
	Reinstall	SF Flr.		1.89		1.89	
	Minimum Charge	Job		157		157	

Rough Electrical

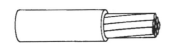

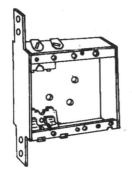

Junction Boxes	Cable	Switch Box

Electrical Per S.F.		Unit	Material	Labor	Equip.	Total	Specification
Residential							
Wiring, Lighting and Fixtures							Includes labor and material to replace house wiring, lighting fixtures, and built-in appliances. Apply S.F. cost to floor area including garages but not basements.
	Install	S.F.	1.18	1.29		2.47	
	Minimum Charge	Job		155		155	
Wiring Only							Includes labor and material to replace house wiring only. Apply S.F. cost to floor area including garages but not basements.
	Install	S.F.	.11	.51		.62	

Main Service		Unit	Material	Labor	Equip.	Total	Specification
100 Amp.							Cost includes material and labor to install 100 Amp. residential service panel including 12 breaker interior panel, 10 single pole breakers and hook-up. Wiring is not included.
	Demolish	Ea.		128		128	
	Install	Ea.	470	261		731	
	Demolish and Install	Ea.	470	389		859	
	Reinstall	Ea.		208.40		208.40	
	Clean	Ea.	.28	51.50		51.78	
	Minimum Charge	Job		155		155	
150 Amp.							Cost includes material and labor to install 150 Amp. residential service, incl. 20 breaker exterior panel, main switch, 1 GFI and 14 single pole breakers, meter socket including hookup. Wiring is not included.
	Demolish	Ea.		128		128	
	Install	Ea.	715	300		1015	
	Demolish and Install	Ea.	715	428		1143	
	Reinstall	Ea.		240.78		240.78	
	Clean	Ea.	.28	51.50		51.78	
	Minimum Charge	Job		155		155	
200 Amp.							Cost includes material and labor to install 200 Amp. residential service, incl. 20 breaker exterior panel, main switch, 1 GFI and 18 single pole breakers, meter socket including hookup. Wiring is not included.
	Demolish	Ea.		128		128	
	Install	Ea.	940	345		1285	
	Demolish and Install	Ea.	940	473		1413	
	Reinstall	Ea.		275.56		275.56	
	Clean	Ea.	.28	51.50		51.78	
	Minimum Charge	Job		155		155	

Rough Electrical

Main Service		Unit	Material	Labor	Equip.	Total	Specification
Masthead							
	Demolish	Ea.		21.50		21.50	Includes material and labor to install
	Install	Ea.	62.50	129		191.50	galvanized steel conduit including
	Demolish and Install	Ea.	62.50	150.50		213	masthead.
	Reinstall	Ea.		103.33		103.33	
	Minimum Charge	Job		155		155	
Allowance to Repair							
	Install	Job		155		155	Includes minimum cost for an
	Minimum Charge	Job		155		155	electrician.

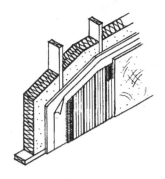

Wall Insulation

Floor Insulation		Unit	Material	Labor	Equip.	Total	Specification
Kraft Faced Batt							
3-1/2" (R-11)							
	Demolish	S.F.		.10		.10	Cost includes material and labor to
	Install	S.F.	.31	.41		.72	install 3-1/2" (R-11) kraft paper or foil
	Demolish and Install	S.F.	.31	.51		.82	faced roll and batt fiberglass
	Minimum Charge	Job		142		142	insulation, joists 16" O.C.
6" (R-19)							
	Demolish	S.F.		.10		.10	Cost includes material and labor to
	Install	S.F.	.42	.47		.89	install 6" (R-19) kraft paper or foil
	Demolish and Install	S.F.	.42	.57		.99	faced roll and batt fiberglass
	Minimum Charge	Job		142		142	insulation, joists 16" O.C.
10" (R-30)							
	Demolish	S.F.		.10		.10	Cost includes material and labor to
	Install	S.F.	.75	.57		1.32	install 10" (R-30) kraft paper-faced roll
	Demolish and Install	S.F.	.75	.67		1.42	and batt fiberglass insulation, joists 16"
	Minimum Charge	Job		142		142	O.C.
12" (R-38)							
	Demolish	S.F.		.10		.10	Cost includes material and labor to
	Install	S.F.	.80	.60		1.40	install 12" (R-38) kraft paper-faced roll
	Demolish and Install	S.F.	.80	.70		1.50	and batt fiberglass insulation, joists 16"
	Minimum Charge	Job		142		142	O.C.
Foil Faced Batt							
3-1/2" (R-11)							
	Demolish	S.F.		.10		.10	Cost includes material and labor to
	Install	S.F.	.31	.41		.72	install 3-1/2" (R-11) kraft paper or foil
	Demolish and Install	S.F.	.31	.51		.82	faced roll and batt fiberglass
	Minimum Charge	Job		142		142	insulation, joists 16" O.C.
6" (R-19)							
	Demolish	S.F.		.10		.10	Cost includes material and labor to
	Install	S.F.	.42	.47		.89	install 6" (R-19) kraft paper or foil
	Demolish and Install	S.F.	.42	.57		.99	faced roll and batt fiberglass
	Minimum Charge	Job		142		142	insulation, joists 16" O.C.
Unfaced Batt							
3-1/2" (R-11)							
	Demolish	S.F.		.10		.10	Cost includes material and labor to
	Install	S.F.	.23	.47		.70	install 3-1/2" (R-11) unfaced roll and
	Demolish and Install	S.F.	.23	.57		.80	batt fiberglass insulation, joists 16"
	Minimum Charge	Job		142		142	O.C.

Insulation

Floor Insulation

		Unit	Material	Labor	Equip.	Total	Specification
6" (R-19)							
	Demolish	S.F.		.10		.10	Cost includes material and labor to
	Install	S.F.	.37	.57		.94	install 6" (R-19) unfaced roll and batt
	Demolish and Install	S.F.	.37	.67		1.04	fiberglass insulation, joists 16" O.C.
	Minimum Charge	Job		142		142	
10" (R-30)							
	Demolish	S.F.		.10		.10	Cost includes material and labor to
	Install	S.F.	.75	.63		1.38	install 10" (R-30) unfaced roll and batt
	Demolish and Install	S.F.	.75	.73		1.48	fiberglass insulation, joists 16" O.C.
	Minimum Charge	Job		142		142	
12" (R-38)							
	Demolish	S.F.		.10		.10	Cost includes material and labor to
	Install	S.F.	.84	.67		1.51	install 12" (R-38) unfaced roll and batt
	Demolish and Install	S.F.	.84	.77		1.61	fiberglass insulation, joists 16" O.C.
	Minimum Charge	Job		142		142	
Rigid Board							
1/2"							
	Demolish	S.F.		.10		.10	Includes material and labor to install
	Install	S.F.	.32	.36		.68	rigid foam insulation board foil faced
	Demolish and Install	S.F.	.32	.46		.78	two sides.
	Minimum Charge	Job		142		142	
3/4"							
	Demolish	S.F.		.10		.10	Includes material and labor to install
	Install	S.F.	.34	.36		.70	rigid foam insulation board foil faced
	Demolish and Install	S.F.	.34	.46		.80	two sides.
	Minimum Charge	Job		142		142	
1-1/2"							
	Demolish	S.F.		.10		.10	Includes material and labor to install
	Install	S.F.	.42	.38		.80	rigid foam insulation board foil faced
	Demolish and Install	S.F.	.42	.48		.90	two sides.
	Minimum Charge	Job		142		142	
Support Wire							
	Demolish	S.F.		.04		.04	Includes material and labor to install
	Install	S.F.	.01	.08		.09	friction fit support wire.
	Demolish and Install	S.F.	.01	.12		.13	
	Minimum Charge	Job		142		142	
Vapor Barrier							
	Demolish	S.F.		.05		.05	Cost includes material and labor to
	Install	S.F.	.02	.08		.10	install 4 mil polyethylene vapor barrier
	Demolish and Install	S.F.	.02	.13		.15	10' wide sheets with 6" overlaps.
	Minimum Charge	Job		142		142	

Wall Insulation

		Unit	Material	Labor	Equip.	Total	Specification
Kraft Faced Batt							
3-1/2" (R-11)							
	Demolish	S.F.		.09		.09	Cost includes material and labor to
	Install	S.F.	.25	.18		.43	install 3-1/2" (R-11) kraft paper-faced
	Demolish and Install	S.F.	.25	.27		.52	roll and batt fiberglass insulation, joist
	Minimum Charge	Job		142		142	or studs 16" O.C.
6" (R-19)							
	Demolish	S.F.		.09		.09	Cost includes material and labor to
	Install	S.F.	.36	.21		.57	install 6" (R-19) kraft paper-faced roll
	Demolish and Install	S.F.	.36	.30		.66	and batt fiberglass insulation, joist or
	Minimum Charge	Job		142		142	studs 16" O.C.

Insulation

Wall Insulation

		Unit	Material	Labor	Equip.	Total	Specification
10" (R-30)							
	Demolish	S.F.		.09		.09	Cost includes material and labor to
	Install	S.F.	.66	.25		.91	install 10" (R-30) kraft paper-faced roll
	Demolish and Install	S.F.	.66	.34		1	and batt fiberglass insulation, joist or
	Minimum Charge	Job		142		142	studs 16" O.C.
12" (R-38)							
	Demolish	S.F.		.09		.09	Cost includes material and labor to
	Install	S.F.	.84	.28		1.12	install 12" (R-38) kraft paper-faced roll
	Demolish and Install	S.F.	.84	.37		1.21	and batt fiberglass insulation, joist or
	Minimum Charge	Job		142		142	studs 16" O.C.
Foil Faced Batt							
3-1/2" (R-11)							
	Demolish	S.F.		.09		.09	Cost includes material and labor to
	Install	S.F.	.37	.18		.55	install 3-1/2" (R-11) foil faced roll and
	Demolish and Install	S.F.	.37	.27		.64	batt fiberglass insulation, joist or studs
	Minimum Charge	Job		142		142	16" O.C.
6" (R-19)							
	Demolish	S.F.		.09		.09	Cost includes material and labor to
	Install	S.F.	.45	.21		.66	install 6" (R-19) foil faced roll and batt
	Demolish and Install	S.F.	.45	.30		.75	fiberglass insulation, joist or studs 16"
	Minimum Charge	Job		142		142	O.C.
Unfaced Batt							
3-1/2" (R-11)							
	Demolish	S.F.		.09		.09	Cost includes material and labor to
	Install	S.F.	.23	.21		.44	install 3-1/2" (R-11) unfaced roll and
	Demolish and Install	S.F.	.23	.30		.53	batt fiberglass insulation, joist or studs
	Minimum Charge	Job		142		142	16" O.C.
6" (R-19)							
	Demolish	S.F.		.09		.09	Cost includes material and labor to
	Install	S.F.	.37	.25		.62	install 6" (R-19) unfaced roll and batt
	Demolish and Install	S.F.	.37	.34		.71	fiberglass insulation, joist or studs 16"
	Minimum Charge	Job		142		142	O.C.
10" (R-30)							
	Demolish	S.F.		.09		.09	Cost includes material and labor to
	Install	S.F.	.66	.28		.94	install 10" (R-30) unfaced roll and batt
	Demolish and Install	S.F.	.66	.37		1.03	fiberglass insulation, joist or studs 16"
	Minimum Charge	Job		142		142	O.C.
12" (R-38)							
	Demolish	S.F.		.09		.09	Cost includes material and labor to
	Install	S.F.	.84	.28		1.12	install 12" (R-38) unfaced roll and batt
	Demolish and Install	S.F.	.84	.37		1.21	fiberglass insulation, joist or studs 16"
	Minimum Charge	Job		142		142	O.C.
Blown							
R-11							
	Demolish	S.F.		.09		.09	Includes material and labor to install
	Install	S.F.	.24	.94	.40	1.58	fiberglass blown-in insulation in wall
	Demolish and Install	S.F.	.24	1.03	.40	1.67	with wood siding.
	Minimum Charge	Job		325	139	464	
R-19							
	Demolish	S.F.		.09		.09	Includes material and labor to install
	Install	S.F.	.36	1.08	.46	1.90	fiberglass blown-in insulation in wall
	Demolish and Install	S.F.	.36	1.17	.46	1.99	with wood siding.
	Minimum Charge	Job		325	139	464	

Insulation

Wall Insulation

Wall Insulation		Unit	Material	Labor	Equip.	Total	Specification
Rigid Board							
1/2"							
	Demolish	S.F.		.11		.11	Includes material and labor to install
	Install	S.F.	.32	.36		.68	rigid foam insulation board, foil faced,
	Demolish and Install	S.F.	.32	.47		.79	two sides.
	Minimum Charge	Job		142		142	
3/4"							
	Demolish	S.F.		.11		.11	Includes material and labor to install
	Install	S.F.	.34	.36		.70	rigid foam insulation board, foil faced,
	Demolish and Install	S.F.	.34	.47		.81	two sides.
	Minimum Charge	Job		142		142	
1-1/2"							
	Demolish	S.F.		.11		.11	Includes material and labor to install
	Install	S.F.	.42	.39		.81	rigid foam insulation board, foil faced,
	Demolish and Install	S.F.	.42	.50		.92	two sides.
	Minimum Charge	Job		142		142	
Vapor Barrier							
	Demolish	S.F.		.03		.03	Cost includes material and labor to
	Install	S.F.	.02	.08		.10	install 4 mil polyethylene vapor barrier
	Demolish and Install	S.F.	.02	.11		.13	10' wide sheets with 6" overlaps.
	Minimum Charge	Job		142		142	

Ceiling Insulation

Ceiling Insulation		Unit	Material	Labor	Equip.	Total	Specification
Kraft Faced Batt							
3-1/2" (R-11)							
	Demolish	S.F.		.10		.10	Cost includes material and labor to
	Install	S.F.	.25	.18		.43	install 3-1/2" (R-11) kraft paper-faced
	Demolish and Install	S.F.	.25	.28		.53	roll and batt fiberglass insulation, joist
	Minimum Charge	Job		142		142	or studs 16" O.C.
6" (R-19)							
	Demolish	S.F.		.10		.10	Cost includes material and labor to
	Install	S.F.	.36	.21		.57	install 6" (R-19) kraft paper-faced roll
	Demolish and Install	S.F.	.36	.31		.67	and batt fiberglass insulation, joist or
	Minimum Charge	Job		142		142	studs 16" O.C.
10" (R-30)							
	Demolish	S.F.		.10		.10	Cost includes material and labor to
	Install	S.F.	.66	.25		.91	install 10" (R-30) kraft paper-faced roll
	Demolish and Install	S.F.	.66	.35		1.01	and batt fiberglass insulation, joist or
	Minimum Charge	Job		142		142	studs 16" O.C.
12" (R-38)							
	Demolish	S.F.		.10		.10	Cost includes material and labor to
	Install	S.F.	.84	.28		1.12	install 12" (R-38) kraft paper-faced roll
	Demolish and Install	S.F.	.84	.38		1.22	and batt fiberglass insulation, joist or
	Minimum Charge	Job		142		142	studs 16" O.C.
Foil Faced Batt							
3-1/2" (R-11)							
	Demolish	S.F.		.10		.10	Cost includes material and labor to
	Install	S.F.	.37	.18		.55	install 3-1/2" (R-11) foil faced roll and
	Demolish and Install	S.F.	.37	.28		.65	batt fiberglass insulation, joist or studs
	Minimum Charge	Job		142		142	16" O.C.

Insulation

Ceiling Insulation

Ceiling Insulation		Unit	Material	Labor	Equip.	Total	Specification
6" (R-19)							
	Demolish	S.F.		.10		.10	Cost includes material and labor to
	Install	S.F.	.45	.21		.66	install 6" (R-19) foil faced roll and batt
	Demolish and Install	S.F.	.45	.31		.76	fiberglass insulation, joist or studs 16"
	Minimum Charge	Job		142		142	O.C.
Unfaced Batt							
3-1/2" (R-11)							
	Demolish	S.F.		.10		.10	Cost includes material and labor to
	Install	S.F.	.23	.21		.44	install 3-1/2" (R-11) unfaced roll and
	Demolish and Install	S.F.	.23	.31		.54	batt fiberglass insulation, joist or studs
	Minimum Charge	Job		142		142	16" O.C.
6" (R-19)							
	Demolish	S.F.		.10		.10	Cost includes material and labor to
	Install	S.F.	.37	.25		.62	install 6" (R-19) unfaced roll and batt
	Demolish and Install	S.F.	.37	.35		.72	fiberglass insulation, joist or studs 16"
	Minimum Charge	Job		142		142	O.C.
10" (R-30)							
	Demolish	S.F.		.10		.10	Cost includes material and labor to
	Install	S.F.	.66	.28		.94	install 10" (R-30) unfaced roll and batt
	Demolish and Install	S.F.	.66	.38		1.04	fiberglass insulation, joist or studs 16"
	Minimum Charge	Job		142		142	O.C.
12" (R-38)							
	Demolish	S.F.		.10		.10	Cost includes material and labor to
	Install	S.F.	.84	.28		1.12	install 12" (R-38) unfaced roll and batt
	Demolish and Install	S.F.	.84	.38		1.22	fiberglass insulation, joist or studs 16"
	Minimum Charge	Job		142		142	O.C.
Blown							
5"							
	Demolish	S.F.		.29		.29	Includes material and labor to install
	Install	S.F.	.18	.17	.07	.42	fiberglass blown-in insulation.
	Demolish and Install	S.F.	.18	.46	.07	.71	
	Minimum Charge	Job		325	139	464	
6"							
	Demolish	S.F.		.29		.29	Includes material and labor to install
	Install	S.F.	.22	.22	.09	.53	fiberglass blown-in insulation.
	Demolish and Install	S.F.	.22	.51	.09	.82	
	Minimum Charge	Job		325	139	464	
9"							
	Demolish	S.F.		.29		.29	Includes material and labor to install
	Install	S.F.	.30	.29	.13	.72	fiberglass blown-in insulation.
	Demolish and Install	S.F.	.30	.58	.13	1.01	
	Minimum Charge	Job		325	139	464	
12"							
	Demolish	S.F.		.29		.29	Includes material and labor to install
	Install	S.F.	.43	.43	.19	1.05	fiberglass blown-in insulation.
	Demolish and Install	S.F.	.43	.72	.19	1.34	
	Minimum Charge	Job		325	139	464	
Rigid Board							
1/2"							
	Demolish	S.F.		.16		.16	Includes material and labor to install
	Install	S.F.	.32	.36		.68	rigid foam insulation board, foil faced,
	Demolish and Install	S.F.	.32	.52		.84	two sides.
	Minimum Charge	Job		142		142	

Insulation

Ceiling Insulation

	Unit	Material	Labor	Equip.	Total	Specification
3/4"						
Demolish	S.F.		.16		.16	Includes material and labor to install
Install	S.F.	.34	.36		.70	rigid foam insulation board, foil faced,
Demolish and Install	S.F.	.34	.52		.86	two sides.
Minimum Charge	Job		142		142	
1-1/2"						
Demolish	S.F.		.16		.16	Includes material and labor to install
Install	S.F.	.42	.39		.81	rigid foam insulation board, foil faced,
Demolish and Install	S.F.	.42	.55		.97	two sides.
Minimum Charge	Job		142		142	

Exterior Insulation

	Unit	Material	Labor	Equip.	Total	Specification
Rigid Board						
1/2"						
Demolish	S.F.		.09		.09	Includes material and labor to install
Install	S.F.	.32	.36		.68	rigid foam insulation board foil faced
Demolish and Install	S.F.	.32	.45		.77	two sides.
Minimum Charge	Job		142		142	
3/4"						
Demolish	S.F.		.09		.09	Includes material and labor to install
Install	S.F.	.34	.36		.70	rigid foam insulation board foil faced
Demolish and Install	S.F.	.34	.45		.79	two sides.
Minimum Charge	Job		142		142	
1-1/2"						
Demolish	S.F.		.09		.09	Includes material and labor to install
Install	S.F.	.42	.38		.80	rigid foam insulation board foil faced
Demolish and Install	S.F.	.42	.47		.89	two sides.
Minimum Charge	Job		142		142	
Vapor Barrier						
Demolish	S.F.		.05		.05	Cost includes material and labor to
Install	S.F.	.02	.08		.10	install 4 mil polyethylene vapor barrier
Demolish and Install	S.F.	.02	.13		.15	10' wide sheets with 6" overlaps.
Minimum Charge	Job		142		142	

Roof Insulation Board

	Unit	Material	Labor	Equip.	Total	Specification
Fiberglass						
3/4" Fiberglass						
Demolish	Sq.		30		30	Includes material and labor to install
Install	Sq.	50.50	21		71.50	fiberglass board insulation 3/4" thick,
Demolish and Install	Sq.	50.50	51		101.50	R-2.80 and C-0.36 values.
Minimum Charge	Job		142		142	
1" Fiberglass						
Demolish	Sq.		30		30	Includes material and labor to install
Install	Sq.	72	23.50		95.50	fiberglass board insulation 1" thick,
Demolish and Install	Sq.	72	53.50		125.50	R-4.20 and C-0.24 values.
Minimum Charge	Job		142		142	
1-3/8" Fiberglass						
Demolish	Sq.		30		30	Includes material and labor to install
Install	Sq.	116	26		142	fiberglass board insulation 1-3/8"
Demolish and Install	Sq.	116	56		172	thick, R-5.30 and C-0.19 values.
Minimum Charge	Job		142		142	

Insulation

Roof Insulation Board		Unit	Material	Labor	Equip.	Total	Specification
1-5/8" Fiberglass							
	Demolish	Sq.		30		30	Includes material and labor to install
	Install	Sq.	118	27		145	fiberglass board insulation 1-5/8"
	Demolish and Install	Sq.	118	57		175	thick, R-6.70 and C-0.15 values.
	Minimum Charge	Job		142		142	
2-1/4" Fiberglass							
	Demolish	Sq.		30		30	Includes material and labor to install
	Install	Sq.	141	30		171	fiberglass board insulation 2-1/4"
	Demolish and Install	Sq.	141	60		201	thick, R-8.30 and C-0.12 values.
	Minimum Charge	Job		142		142	
Perlite							
1" Perlite							
	Demolish	Sq.		30		30	Includes material and labor to install
	Install	Sq.	32	23.50		55.50	perlite board insulation 1" thick, R-2.80
	Demolish and Install	Sq.	32	53.50		85.50	and C-0.36 values.
	Minimum Charge	Job		142		142	
4" Perlite							
	Demolish	Sq.		30		30	Includes material and labor to install
	Install	Sq.	128	45.50		173.50	perlite board insulation 4" thick, R-10.0
	Demolish and Install	Sq.	128	75.50		203.50	and C-0.10 values.
	Minimum Charge	Job		142		142	
1-1/2" Perlite							
	Demolish	Sq.		30		30	Includes material and labor to install
	Install	Sq.	43	26		69	perlite board insulation 1-1/2" thick,
	Demolish and Install	Sq.	43	56		99	R-4.20 and C-0.24 values.
	Minimum Charge	Job		142		142	
2" Perlite							
	Demolish	Sq.		30		30	Includes material and labor to install
	Install	Sq.	62.50	31.50		94	perlite board insulation 2" thick, R-5.30
	Demolish and Install	Sq.	62.50	61.50		124	and C-0.19 values.
	Minimum Charge	Job		142		142	
2-1/2" Perlite							
	Demolish	Sq.		30		30	Includes material and labor to install
	Install	Sq.	85	35.50		120.50	perlite board insulation 2-1/2" thick,
	Demolish and Install	Sq.	85	65.50		150.50	R-6.70 and C-0.15 values.
	Minimum Charge	Job		142		142	
3" Perlite							
	Demolish	Sq.		30		30	Includes material and labor to install
	Install	Sq.	95.50	38		133.50	perlite board insulation 3" thick, R-8.30
	Demolish and Install	Sq.	95.50	68		163.50	and C-0.12 values.
	Minimum Charge	Job		142		142	
Polystyrene							
2" Polystyrene							
	Demolish	Sq.		30		30	Includes material and labor to install
	Install	Sq.	29.50	30		59.50	extruded polystyrene board, R5.0/ 2"
	Demolish and Install	Sq.	29.50	60		89.50	in thickness @25PSI compressive
	Minimum Charge	Job		142		142	strength.
1" Polystyrene							
	Demolish	Sq.		30		30	Includes material and labor to install
	Install	Sq.	28.50	20.50		49	extruded polystyrene board, R5.0/ 1"
	Demolish and Install	Sq.	28.50	50.50		79	in thickness @25PSI compressive
	Minimum Charge	Job		142		142	strength.
1-1/2" Polystyrene							
	Demolish	Sq.		30		30	Includes material and labor to install
	Install	Sq.	29	23.50		52.50	extruded polystyrene board, R5.0/
	Demolish and Install	Sq.	29	53.50		82.50	1-1/2" in thickness @25PSI
	Minimum Charge	Job		142		142	compressive strength.

Insulation

Roof Insulation Board	Unit	Material	Labor	Equip.	Total	Specification
Urethane						
3/4" Urethane						
Demolish	Sq.		30		30	Includes material and labor to install
Install	Sq.	35	17.80		52.80	urethane board insulation 3/4" thick,
Demolish and Install	Sq.	35	47.80		82.80	R-5.30 and C-0.19 values.
Minimum Charge	Job		142		142	
1" Urethane						
Demolish	Sq.		30		30	Includes material and labor to install
Install	Sq.	38.50	19		57.50	urethane board insulation 1" thick,
Demolish and Install	Sq.	38.50	49		87.50	R-6.70 and C-0.15 values.
Minimum Charge	Job		142		142	
1-1/2" Urethane						
Demolish	Sq.		30		30	Includes material and labor to install
Install	Sq.	40.50	22		62.50	urethane board insulation 1-1/2" thick,
Demolish and Install	Sq.	40.50	52		92.50	R-10.1 and C-0.09 values.
Minimum Charge	Job		142		142	
2" Urethane						
Demolish	Sq.		30		30	Includes material and labor to install
Install	Sq.	51	26		77	urethane board insulation 2" thick,
Demolish and Install	Sq.	51	56		107	R-13.4 and C-0.06 values.
Minimum Charge	Job		142		142	

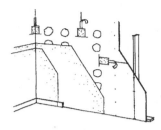

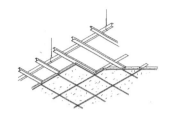

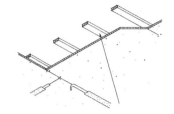

Gypsum Wallboard   **Tile Ceiling**   **Gypsum Wallboard Ceiling**

Wall Plaster	Unit	Material	Labor	Equip.	Total	Specification
Interior						
Cement						
Demolish	S.Y.		3.83		3.83	Includes material and labor to install
Install	S.Y.	13.65	16.65	1.06	31.36	cement plaster on interior wood
Demolish and Install	S.Y.	13.65	20.48	1.06	35.19	framing with metal lath.
Clean	S.Y.		1.88		1.88	
Paint	S.Y.	1.60	3.40		5	
Minimum Charge	Job		131		131	
Acoustic						
Demolish	S.Y.		3.83		3.83	Includes material and labor to install
Install	S.Y.	7.60	20	1.06	28.66	acoustical cement plaster on interior
Demolish and Install	S.Y.	7.60	23.83	1.06	32.49	wood framing with metal lath.
Clean	S.Y.		1.88		1.88	
Paint	S.Y.	1.60	3.40		5	
Minimum Charge	Job		131		131	
Gypsum						
Demolish	S.Y.		3.83		3.83	Includes material and labor to install
Install	S.Y.	6.50	17.20	.90	24.60	gypsum wall or ceiling plaster on
Demolish and Install	S.Y.	6.50	21.03	.90	28.43	interior wood framing with metal lath.
Clean	S.Y.		1.88		1.88	
Paint	S.Y.	1.60	3.40		5	
Minimum Charge	Job		131		131	
Stucco						
Demolish	S.Y.		9.20		9.20	Includes material and labor to install
Install	S.Y.	4.02	23.50	1.25	28.77	stucco on wire mesh over wood
Demolish and Install	S.Y.	4.02	32.70	1.25	37.97	framing.
Clean	S.Y.		1.88		1.88	
Paint	S.Y.	1.60	3.40		5	
Minimum Charge	Job		131		131	
Thin Coat						
Veneer						
Demolish	S.Y.		3.83		3.83	Includes materials and labor to install
Install	S.Y.	.69	3.08	.20	3.97	thin coat veneer plaster.
Demolish and Install	S.Y.	.69	6.91	.20	7.80	
Clean	S.Y.		1.88		1.88	
Paint	S.Y.	1.60	3.40		5	
Minimum Charge	Job		615	39	654	

Walls / Ceilings

Wall Plaster

Wall Plaster	Unit	Material	Labor	Equip.	Total	Specification
Lath						
Metal						
Demolish	S.Y.		.90		.90	Includes material and labor to install
Install	S.Y.	2.49	3.49		5.98	wire lath on steel framed walls.
Demolish and Install	S.Y.	2.49	4.39		6.88	
Clean	S.Y.		1.88		1.88	
Minimum Charge	Job		61.50		61.50	
Gypsum						
Demolish	S.Y.		.90		.90	Includes material and labor to install
Install	S.Y.	3.86	3.28		7.14	gypsum lath on walls.
Demolish and Install	S.Y.	3.86	4.18		8.04	
Clean	S.Y.		1.88		1.88	
Minimum Charge	Job		131		131	
Repairs						
Fill in Small Cracks						
Install	L.F.	.04	2.10		2.14	Includes labor and material to fill-in
Minimum Charge	Job		131		131	hairline cracks up to 1/8" with filler, sand and prep for paint.
Repair up to 1" Crack						
Install	L.F.	.19	2.63		2.82	Includes labor and material to fill-in
Minimum Charge	Job		131		131	hairline cracks up to 1" with filler, sand and prep for paint.
Patch Small Hole (2")						
Install	Ea.	.04	2.77		2.81	Includes labor and material to patch
Minimum Charge	Job		131		131	up to a 2" diameter hole in plaster.
Patch Large Hole						
Install	Ea.	5.80	44		49.80	Includes labor and material to patch
Minimum Charge	Job		131		131	up to a 20" diameter hole in plaster.
Patch Plaster Section						
Install	Ea.	1.99	2.63		4.62	Includes labor and material to repair
Minimum Charge	Job		131		131	section of plaster wall, area less than 20 S.F.
Repair Inside Corner						
Install	L.F.	2.30	6.55		8.85	Includes material and labor to patch
Minimum Charge	Job		131		131	plaster corners.

Ceiling Plaster

Ceiling Plaster	Unit	Material	Labor	Equip.	Total	Specification
Interior						
Cement						
Demolish	S.Y.		3.83		3.83	Includes material and labor to install
Install	S.Y.	13.65	16.65	1.06	31.36	cement plaster on interior wood
Demolish and Install	S.Y.	13.65	20.48	1.06	35.19	framing with metal lath.
Clean	S.Y.		1.97		1.97	
Paint	S.Y.	1.60	3.40		5	
Minimum Charge	Job		131		131	
Acoustic						
Demolish	S.Y.		3.83		3.83	Includes material and labor to install
Install	S.Y.	7.60	20	1.06	28.66	acoustical cement plaster on interior
Demolish and Install	S.Y.	7.60	23.83	1.06	32.49	wood framing with metal lath.
Clean	S.Y.		1.97		1.97	
Paint	S.Y.	1.60	3.40		5	
Minimum Charge	Job		131		131	

Walls / Ceilings

Ceiling Plaster		Unit	Material	Labor	Equip.	Total	Specification
Gypsum							
	Demolish	S.Y.		3.83		3.83	Includes material and labor to install
	Install	S.Y.	6.50	17.20	.90	24.60	gypsum wall or ceiling plaster on
	Demolish and Install	S.Y.	6.50	21.03	.90	28.43	interior wood framing with metal lath.
	Clean	S.Y.		1.97		1.97	
	Paint	S.Y.	1.60	3.40		5	
	Minimum Charge	Job		131		131	
Stucco							
	Demolish	S.Y.		9.20		9.20	Includes material and labor to install
	Install	S.Y.	4.02	23.50	1.25	28.77	stucco on wire mesh over wood
	Demolish and Install	S.Y.	4.02	32.70	1.25	37.97	framing.
	Clean	S.Y.		1.97		1.97	
	Paint	S.Y.	1.60	3.40		5	
	Minimum Charge	Job		131		131	
Thin Coat							
Veneer							
	Demolish	S.Y.		3.83		3.83	Includes materials and labor to install
	Install	S.Y.	.69	3.08	.20	3.97	thin coat veneer plaster.
	Demolish and Install	S.Y.	.69	6.91	.20	7.80	
	Clean	S.Y.		1.97		1.97	
	Paint	S.Y.	1.60	3.40		5	
	Minimum Charge	Job		131		131	
Lath							
Metal							
	Demolish	S.Y.		.90		.90	Includes material and labor to install
	Install	S.Y.	2.49	4.37		6.86	wire lath on steel framed ceilings.
	Demolish and Install	S.Y.	2.49	5.27		7.76	
	Minimum Charge	Job		131		131	
Gypsum							
	Demolish	S.Y.		.90		.90	Includes material and labor to install
	Install	S.Y.	3.86	2.73		6.59	gypsum lath on ceilings.
	Demolish and Install	S.Y.	3.86	3.63		7.49	
	Minimum Charge	Job		131		131	
Repairs							
Fill in Small Cracks							
	Install	S.F.	.04	.48		.52	Includes labor and material to fill in
	Minimum Charge	Job		263		263	hairline cracks up to 1/8" with filler, sand and prep for paint.

Gypsum Wallboard		Unit	Material	Labor	Equip.	Total	Specification
Finished							
1/4"							
	Demolish	S.F.		.23		.23	Cost includes material and labor to
	Install	S.F.	.25	.86		1.11	install 1/4" drywall, including joint
	Demolish and Install	S.F.	.25	1.09		1.34	taping, premixed compound and
	Clean	S.F.		.19		.19	screws.
	Paint	S.F.	.18	.22		.40	
	Minimum Charge	Job		142		142	
3/8"							
	Demolish	S.F.		.23		.23	Cost includes material and labor to
	Install	S.F.	.19	.87		1.06	install 3/8" drywall including joint
	Demolish and Install	S.F.	.19	1.10		1.29	tape, premixed compound and screws.
	Clean	S.F.		.19		.19	
	Paint	S.F.	.18	.22		.40	
	Minimum Charge	Job		142		142	

Gypsum Wallboard		Unit	Material	Labor	Equip.	Total	Specification
1/2″							
	Demolish	S.F.		.23		.23	Cost includes material and labor to
	Install	S.F.	.21	.88		1.09	install 1/2″ drywall including joint
	Demolish and Install	S.F.	.21	1.11		1.32	tape, premixed compound and screws.
	Clean	S.F.		.19		.19	
	Paint	S.F.	.18	.22		.40	
	Minimum Charge	Job		142		142	
1/2″ Water Resistant							
	Demolish	S.F.		.23		.23	Cost includes material and labor to
	Install	S.F.	.18	.88		1.06	install 1/2″ WR drywall including joint
	Demolish and Install	S.F.	.18	1.11		1.29	tape, premixed compound and screws.
	Clean	S.F.		.19		.19	
	Paint	S.F.	.18	.22		.40	
	Minimum Charge	Job		142		142	
1/2″ Fire-rated							
	Demolish	S.F.		.23		.23	Cost includes material and labor to
	Install	S.F.	.21	.88		1.09	install 1/2″ FR drywall including
	Demolish and Install	S.F.	.21	1.11		1.32	screws. Taping and finishing not
	Clean	S.F.		.19		.19	included.
	Paint	S.F.	.18	.22		.40	
	Minimum Charge	Job		142		142	
5/8″							
	Demolish	S.F.		.23		.23	Cost includes material and labor to
	Install	S.F.	.24	1		1.24	install 5/8″ drywall including joint
	Demolish and Install	S.F.	.24	1.23		1.47	tape, premixed compound and screws.
	Clean	S.F.		.19		.19	
	Paint	S.F.	.18	.22		.40	
	Minimum Charge	Job		142		142	
5/8″ Fire-rated							
	Demolish	S.F.		.23		.23	Cost includes material and labor to
	Install	S.F.	.24	1		1.24	install 5/8″ FR drywall, including joint
	Demolish and Install	S.F.	.24	1.23		1.47	taping, premixed compound and
	Clean	S.F.		.19		.19	screws.
	Paint	S.F.	.18	.22		.40	
	Minimum Charge	Job		142		142	
2-hour Fire-rated							
	Demolish	S.F.		.57		.57	Cost includes material and labor to
	Install	S.F.	.77	1.99		2.76	install 2 layers of 5/8″ type X drywall
	Demolish and Install	S.F.	.77	2.56		3.33	including joint taping, premixed
	Clean	S.F.		.19		.19	compound and screws.
	Paint	S.F.	.18	.22		.40	
	Minimum Charge	Job		142		142	
Unfinished							
1/4″							
	Demolish	S.F.		.23		.23	Cost includes material and labor to
	Install	S.F.	.18	.83		1.01	install 1/4″ drywall including screws.
	Demolish and Install	S.F.	.18	1.06		1.24	Taping and finishing not included.
	Clean	S.F.		.19		.19	
	Minimum Charge	Job		142		142	
3/8″							
	Demolish	S.F.		.23		.23	Cost includes material and labor to
	Install	S.F.	.16	.85		1.01	install 3/8″ drywall including screws.
	Demolish and Install	S.F.	.16	1.08		1.24	Tape, finish or texture is not included.
	Clean	S.F.		.19		.19	
	Minimum Charge	Job		142		142	
1/2″							
	Demolish	S.F.		.23		.23	Cost includes material and labor to
	Install	S.F.	.17	.86		1.03	install 1/2″ drywall including screws.
	Demolish and Install	S.F.	.17	1.09		1.26	Taping and finishing not included.
	Clean	S.F.		.19		.19	
	Minimum Charge	Job		142		142	

Gypsum Wallboard		Unit	Material	Labor	Equip.	Total	Specification
1/2" Water Resistant							
	Demolish	S.F.		.23		.23	Cost includes material and labor to
	Install	S.F.	.15	.86		1.01	install 1/2" WR drywall including
	Demolish and Install	S.F.	.15	1.09		1.24	screws. Taping and finishing is not
	Clean	S.F.		.19		.19	included.
	Minimum Charge	Job		142		142	
1/2" Fire-rated							
	Demolish	S.F.		.23		.23	Cost includes labor and material to
	Install	S.F.	.17	.21		.38	install 1/2" FR drywall including
	Demolish and Install	S.F.	.17	.44		.61	screws. Tape, finish or texture is not
	Clean	S.F.		.19		.19	included.
	Minimum Charge	Job		142		142	
5/8"							
	Demolish	S.F.		.23		.23	Cost includes material and labor to
	Install	S.F.	.20	.96		1.16	install 5/8" drywall including screws.
	Demolish and Install	S.F.	.20	1.19		1.39	Taping and finishing not included.
	Clean	S.F.		.19		.19	
	Minimum Charge	Job		142		142	
5/8" Fire-rated							
	Demolish	S.F.		.23		.23	Cost includes material and labor to
	Install	S.F.	.20	.96		1.16	install 5/8" FR drywall including
	Demolish and Install	S.F.	.20	1.19		1.39	screws. Taping and finishing not
	Clean	S.F.		.19		.19	included.
	Minimum Charge	Job		142		142	
2-hour Fire-rated							
	Demolish	S.F.		.57		.57	Cost includes material and labor to
	Install	S.F.	.77	1.99		2.76	install 2 layers of 5/8" type X drywall
	Demolish and Install	S.F.	.77	2.56		3.33	including joint taping, premixed
	Clean	S.F.		.19		.19	compound and screws.
	Minimum Charge	Job		142		142	
Accessories							
Tape & Finish							
	Install	S.F.	.04	.28		.32	Includes labor and material for taping,
	Minimum Charge	Job		142		142	sanding and finish.
Texture							
Sprayed							
	Install	S.F.	.06	.33		.39	Includes labor and material to install
	Minimum Charge	Job		142		142	by spray, texture finish.
Trowel							
	Install	S.F.	.01	.17		.18	Includes labor and material to apply
	Minimum Charge	Job		142		142	hand troweled texture.
Patch Hole in Gypsum Wallboard							
	Install	S.F.	.37	38.50		38.87	Includes labor and material to patch a
	Minimum Charge	Job		142		142	one square foot area of damaged
							drywall.
Furring Strips							
	Demolish	S.F.		.06		.06	Cost includes material and labor to
	Install	S.F.	.17	.63		.80	install 1" x 2" furring strips, 16" O.C.
	Demolish and Install	S.F.	.17	.69		.86	per S.F. of surface area to be covered.
	Minimum Charge	Job		71		71	

Walls / Ceilings

Ceramic Wall Tile

	Unit	Material	Labor	Equip.	Total	Specification
Thin Set						
2" x 2"						
Demolish	S.F.		.77		.77	Cost includes material and labor to
Install	S.F.	6.05	4.39		10.44	install 2" x 2" ceramic tile in organic
Demolish and Install	S.F.	6.05	5.16		11.21	adhesive including cutting and grout.
Clean	S.F.		.39		.39	
Minimum Charge	Job		132		132	
4-1/4" x 4-1/4"						
Demolish	S.F.		.77		.77	Cost includes material and labor to
Install	S.F.	2.30	2.50		4.80	install 4-1/4" x 4-1/4" ceramic tile in
Demolish and Install	S.F.	2.30	3.27		5.57	organic adhesive including grout.
Clean	S.F.		.39		.39	
Minimum Charge	Job		132		132	
6" x 6"						
Demolish	S.F.		.77		.77	Cost includes material and labor to
Install	S.F.	2.83	2.37		5.20	install 6" x 6" ceramic tile in organic
Demolish and Install	S.F.	2.83	3.14		5.97	adhesive including and grout.
Clean	S.F.		.39		.39	
Minimum Charge	Job		132		132	
8" x 8"						
Demolish	S.F.		.77		.77	Cost includes material and labor to
Install	S.F.	3.41	2.11		5.52	install 8" x 8" ceramic tile in organic
Demolish and Install	S.F.	3.41	2.88		6.29	adhesive including cutting and grout.
Clean	S.F.		.39		.39	
Minimum Charge	Job		132		132	
Thick Set						
2" x 2"						
Demolish	S.F.		.92		.92	Cost includes material and labor to
Install	S.F.	4.92	5.25		10.17	install 2" x 2" ceramic tile in mortar
Demolish and Install	S.F.	4.92	6.17		11.09	bed including cutting and grout.
Clean	S.F.		.39		.39	
Minimum Charge	Job		132		132	
4-1/4" x 4-1/4"						
Demolish	S.F.		.92		.92	Cost includes material and labor to
Install	S.F.	6.65	5.25		11.90	install 4-1/4" x 4-1/4" ceramic tile in
Demolish and Install	S.F.	6.65	6.17		12.82	mortar bed including cutting and grout.
Clean	S.F.		.39		.39	
Minimum Charge	Job		132		132	
6" x 6"						
Demolish	S.F.		.92		.92	Cost includes material and labor to
Install	S.F.	7.45	4.79		12.24	install 6" x 6" ceramic tile in mortar
Demolish and Install	S.F.	7.45	5.71		13.16	bed including cutting and grout.
Clean	S.F.		.39		.39	
Minimum Charge	Job		132		132	
8" x 8"						
Demolish	S.F.		.92		.92	Cost includes material and labor to
Install	S.F.	9.75	4.39		14.14	install 8" x 8" ceramic tile in mortar
Demolish and Install	S.F.	9.75	5.31		15.06	bed including cutting and grout.
Clean	S.F.		.39		.39	
Minimum Charge	Job		132		132	
Re-grout						
Install	S.F.	.14	2.63		2.77	Includes material and labor to regrout
Minimum Charge	Job		132		132	ceramic tile walls.

Walls / Ceilings

Wall Tile

Wall Tile		Unit	Material	Labor	Equip.	Total	Specification
Mirror							
Custom Cut Wall							
	Demolish	S.F.		.44		.44	Includes material and labor to install
	Install	S.F.	1.75	2.89		4.64	distortion-free float glass mirror, 1/8"
	Demolish and Install	S.F.	1.75	3.33		5.08	to 3/16" thick with cut and polished
	Clean	S.F.	.02	.12		.14	edges.
	Minimum Charge	Job		141		141	
Beveled Wall							
	Demolish	S.F.		.44		.44	Includes material and labor to install
	Install	S.F.	4.24	5.10		9.34	distortion-free float glass mirror, 1/8"
	Demolish and Install	S.F.	4.24	5.54		9.78	to 3/16" thick with beveled edges.
	Clean	S.F.	.02	.12		.14	
	Minimum Charge	Job		141		141	
Smoked Wall							
	Demolish	S.F.		.44		.44	Includes material and labor to install
	Install	S.F.	6.70	5.10		11.80	distortion-free smoked float glass
	Demolish and Install	S.F.	6.70	5.54		12.24	mirror, 1/8" to 3/16" thick with cut
	Clean	S.F.	.02	.12		.14	and polished edges.
	Minimum Charge	Job		141		141	
Marble							
Good Grade							
	Demolish	S.F.		1.44		1.44	Cost includes material and labor to
	Install	S.F.	7.60	11.45		19.05	install 3/8" x 12" x 12" marble tile in
	Demolish and Install	S.F.	7.60	12.89		20.49	mortar bed with grout.
	Clean	S.F.		.39		.39	
	Minimum Charge	Job		132		132	
Better Grade							
	Demolish	S.F.		1.44		1.44	Cost includes material and labor to
	Install	S.F.	9.80	11.45		21.25	install 3/8" x 12" x 12" marble, in
	Demolish and Install	S.F.	9.80	12.89		22.69	mortar bed with grout.
	Clean	S.F.		.39		.39	
	Minimum Charge	Job		132		132	
Premium Grade							
	Demolish	S.F.		1.44		1.44	Cost includes material and labor to
	Install	S.F.	18.90	11.45		30.35	install 3/8" x 12" x 12" marble, in
	Demolish and Install	S.F.	18.90	12.89		31.79	mortar bed with grout.
	Clean	S.F.		.39		.39	
	Minimum Charge	Job		132		132	
Glass Block							
	Demolish	S.F.		1.15		1.15	Cost includes material and labor to
	Install	S.F.	15.50	11.30		26.80	install 3-7/8" thick, 6" x 6" smooth
	Demolish and Install	S.F.	15.50	12.45		27.95	face glass block including mortar and
	Clean	S.F.		.39		.39	cleaning.
	Minimum Charge	Job		253		253	
Plastic							
	Demolish	S.F.		.35		.35	Cost includes material and labor to
	Install	S.F.	.92	1.50		2.42	install 4" plastic tile.
	Demolish and Install	S.F.	.92	1.85		2.77	
	Clean	S.F.		.39		.39	
	Minimum Charge	Job		132		132	
Cork							
	Demolish	S.F.		.18		.18	Cost includes material and labor to
	Install	S.F.	2.75	1.06		3.81	install 3/16" thick cork tile and
	Demolish and Install	S.F.	2.75	1.24		3.99	installation.
	Clean	S.F.		.39		.39	
	Minimum Charge	Job		127		127	

Walls / Ceilings

Wall Tile

	Unit	Material	Labor	Equip.	Total	Specification
Re-grout						
Install	S.F.	.14	2.63		2.77	Includes material and labor to regrout
Minimum Charge	Job		132		132	ceramic tile walls.

Wall Paneling

	Unit	Material	Labor	Equip.	Total	Specification
Plywood						
Good Grade						
Demolish	S.F.		.23		.23	Cost includes material and labor to
Install	S.F.	.81	1.14		1.95	install 4' x 8' x 1/4" paneling,
Demolish and Install	S.F.	.81	1.37		2.18	including nails and adhesive.
Clean	S.F.		.19		.19	
Paint	S.F.	.15	.34		.49	
Minimum Charge	Job		142		142	
Better Grade						
Demolish	S.F.		.23		.23	Cost includes material and labor to
Install	S.F.	1.23	1.36		2.59	install 4' x 8' x 1/4" plywood wall
Demolish and Install	S.F.	1.23	1.59		2.82	panel, including nails and adhesive.
Clean	S.F.		.19		.19	
Paint	S.F.	.15	.34		.49	
Minimum Charge	Job		142		142	
Premium Grade						
Demolish	S.F.		.23		.23	Cost includes material and labor to
Install	S.F.	1.80	1.63		3.43	install 4' x 8' x 1/4" plywood wall
Demolish and Install	S.F.	1.80	1.86		3.66	panel, including nails and adhesive.
Clean	S.F.		.19		.19	
Paint	S.F.	.15	.34		.49	
Minimum Charge	Job		142		142	
Hardboard						
Embossed Paneling						
Demolish	S.F.		.23		.23	Includes material and labor to install
Install	S.F.	.59	1.14		1.73	hardboard embossed paneling
Demolish and Install	S.F.	.59	1.37		1.96	including adhesives.
Clean	S.F.		.19		.19	
Minimum Charge	Job		142		142	
Plastic Molding						
Demolish	L.F.		.23		.23	Includes material and labor to install
Install	L.F.	.54	.71		1.25	plastic trim for paneling.
Demolish and Install	L.F.	.54	.94		1.48	
Clean	L.F.	.02	.12		.14	
Minimum Charge	Job		142		142	
Hardboard						
Embossed Brick						
Demolish	S.F.		.23		.23	Cost includes material and labor to
Install	S.F.	1.97	1.27		3.24	install 4' x 8' non-ceramic mineral
Demolish and Install	S.F.	1.97	1.50		3.47	brick-like veneer wall panels including
Clean	S.F.		.19		.19	adhesive.
Paint	S.F.	.18	.38		.56	
Minimum Charge	Job		142		142	
Embossed Ceramic Tile						
Demolish	S.F.		.23		.23	Includes material and labor to install
Install	S.F.	.59	1.14		1.73	hardboard embossed paneling
Demolish and Install	S.F.	.59	1.37		1.96	including adhesives.
Clean	S.F.		.19		.19	
Paint	S.F.	.18	.38		.56	
Minimum Charge	Job		142		142	

Walls / Ceilings

Wall Paneling	Unit	Material	Labor	Equip.	Total	Specification
Pegboard						
Demolish	S.F.		.23		.23	Cost includes material and labor to
Install	S.F.	.41	1.14		1.55	install 4' x 8' x 1/4" pegboard panel,
Demolish and Install	S.F.	.41	1.37		1.78	including adhesive.
Clean	S.F.		.19		.19	
Paint	S.F.	.18	.38		.56	
Minimum Charge	Job		142		142	
Furring Strips						
Demolish	S.F.		.06		.06	Cost includes material and labor to
Install	S.F.	.17	.63		.80	install 1" x 2" furring strips, 16" O.C.
Demolish and Install	S.F.	.17	.69		.86	per S.F. of surface area to be covered.
Minimum Charge	Job		142		142	
Molding						
Unfinished Base						
Demolish	L.F.		.38		.38	Cost includes material and labor to
Install	L.F.	.37	.88		1.25	install 1/2" x 2-1/2" pine or birch
Demolish and Install	L.F.	.37	1.26		1.63	base molding.
Reinstall	L.F.		.70		.70	
Clean	L.F.	.02	.12		.14	
Paint	L.F.	.03	.28		.31	
Minimum Charge	Job		142		142	
Unfinished Corner						
Demolish	L.F.		.38		.38	Includes material and labor to install
Install	L.F.	1.19	1.19		2.38	unfinished pine corner molding.
Demolish and Install	L.F.	1.19	1.57		2.76	
Reinstall	L.F.		.95		.95	
Clean	Ea.	.70	18.65		19.35	
Paint	L.F.	.12	.41		.53	
Minimum Charge	Job		142		142	
Unfinished Cove						
Demolish	L.F.		.38		.38	Cost includes material and labor to
Install	L.F.	1.56	1.05		2.61	install 3/4" x 3-1/2" unfinished pine
Demolish and Install	L.F.	1.56	1.43		2.99	cove molding.
Reinstall	L.F.		.84		.84	
Clean	Ea.	.70	18.65		19.35	
Paint	L.F.	.12	.41		.53	
Minimum Charge	Job		142		142	
Unfinished Crown						
Demolish	L.F.		.46		.46	Includes material and labor to install
Install	L.F.	1.67	1.14		2.81	unfinished pine crown molding.
Demolish and Install	L.F.	1.67	1.60		3.27	
Reinstall	L.F.		.91		.91	
Clean	L.F.	.03	.16		.19	
Paint	L.F.	.04	.28		.32	
Minimum Charge	Job		142		142	
Prefinished Base						
Demolish	L.F.		.38		.38	Cost includes material and labor to
Install	L.F.	1.69	.91		2.60	install 9/16" x 3-5/16" prefinished
Demolish and Install	L.F.	1.69	1.29		2.98	base molding.
Reinstall	L.F.		.73		.73	
Clean	L.F.	.02	.12		.14	
Paint	L.F.	.03	.28		.31	
Minimum Charge	Job		142		142	

Walls / Ceilings

Wall Paneling

	Unit	Material	Labor	Equip.	Total	Specification
Prefinished Corner						
Demolish	L.F.		.38		.38	Includes material and labor to install
Install	L.F.	2.08	1.19		3.27	inside or outside prefinished corner
Demolish and Install	L.F.	2.08	1.57		3.65	molding.
Reinstall	L.F.		.95		.95	
Clean	L.F.		.08		.08	
Paint	L.F.	.12	.41		.53	
Minimum Charge	Job		142		142	
Prefinished Crown						
Demolish	L.F.		.46		.46	Cost includes material and labor to
Install	L.F.	2.24	1.14		3.38	install 3/4" x 3-13/16" prefinished
Demolish and Install	L.F.	2.24	1.60		3.84	crown molding.
Reinstall	L.F.		.91		.91	
Clean	L.F.	.03	.16		.19	
Paint	L.F.	.04	.28		.32	
Minimum Charge	Job		142		142	

Wallcovering

	Unit	Material	Labor	Equip.	Total	Specification
Surface Prep						
Patch Walls						
Install	S.F.	.10	2.63		2.73	Includes labor and material to repair
Minimum Charge	Job		127		127	section of plaster wall, area less than
						20 S.F.
Sizing						
Install	S.F.	.07	.13		.20	Includes labor and materials to apply
Minimum Charge	Job		127		127	wall sizing.
Good Grade						
Walls						
Demolish	S.F.		.47		.47	Includes material and labor to install
Install	S.F.	.77	.53		1.30	pre-pasted, vinyl-coated wallcovering.
Demolish and Install	S.F.	.77	1		1.77	
Clean	S.F.	.01	.05		.06	
Minimum Charge	Job		127		127	
Ceiling						
Demolish	S.F.		.47		.47	Includes material and labor to install
Install	S.F.	.77	.53		1.30	pre-pasted, vinyl-coated wallcovering.
Demolish and Install	S.F.	.77	1		1.77	
Clean	S.F.	.02	.12		.14	
Minimum Charge	Job		127		127	
Better Grade						
Walls						
Demolish	S.F.		.47		.47	Includes material and labor to install
Install	S.F.	.87	.53		1.40	pre-pasted, vinyl-coated wallcovering.
Demolish and Install	S.F.	.87	1		1.87	
Clean	S.F.	.01	.05		.06	
Minimum Charge	Job		127		127	
Ceiling						
Demolish	S.F.		.47		.47	Includes material and labor to install
Install	S.F.	.87	.53		1.40	pre-pasted, vinyl-coated wallcovering.
Demolish and Install	S.F.	.87	1		1.87	
Clean	S.F.	.02	.12		.14	
Minimum Charge	Job		127		127	

Walls / Ceilings

Wallcovering

	Unit	Material	Labor	Equip.	Total	Specification
Premium Grade						
Walls						
Demolish	S.F.		.59		.59	Includes material and labor to install
Install	S.F.	1.10	.53		1.63	pre-pasted, vinyl-coated wallcovering.
Demolish and Install	S.F.	1.10	1.12		2.22	
Clean	S.F.	.01	.05		.06	
Minimum Charge	Job		127		127	
Ceiling						
Demolish	S.F.		.59		.59	Includes material and labor to install
Install	S.F.	1.10	.53		1.63	pre-pasted, vinyl-coated wallcovering.
Demolish and Install	S.F.	1.10	1.12		2.22	
Clean	S.F.	.02	.12		.14	
Minimum Charge	Job		127		127	
Mural						
Pre-printed						
Demolish	Ea.		72		72	Includes material and labor to install
Install	Ea.	206	191		397	wallcovering with a pre-printed mural.
Demolish and Install	Ea.	206	263		469	
Clean	Ea.		5.15		5.15	
Minimum Charge	Job		127		127	
Hand-painted						
Demolish	Ea.		72		72	Includes material and labor to install
Install	Ea.	415	385		800	wallcovering with a hand-painted
Demolish and Install	Ea.	415	457		872	mural.
Clean	Ea.		5.15		5.15	
Minimum Charge	Job		127		127	
Vinyl-coated						
Good Grade						
Demolish	Ea.		12.75		12.75	Includes material and labor to install
Install	Ea.	17.10	17.80		34.90	pre-pasted, vinyl-coated wallcovering.
Demolish and Install	Ea.	17.10	30.55		47.65	Based upon 30 S.F. rolls.
Clean	Ea.		5.15		5.15	
Minimum Charge	Job		127		127	
Better Grade						
Demolish	Ea.		12.75		12.75	Includes material and labor to install
Install	Ea.	22.50	17.80		40.30	pre-pasted, vinyl-coated wallcovering.
Demolish and Install	Ea.	22.50	30.55		53.05	Based upon 30 S.F. rolls.
Clean	Ea.		5.15		5.15	
Minimum Charge	Job		127		127	
Premium Grade						
Demolish	Ea.		12.75		12.75	Includes material and labor to install
Install	Ea.	39.50	17.80		57.30	pre-pasted, vinyl-coated wallcovering.
Demolish and Install	Ea.	39.50	30.55		70.05	Based upon 30 S.F. rolls.
Clean	Ea.		5.15		5.15	
Minimum Charge	Job		127		127	
Blank Underliner						
Demolish	Ea.		12.75		12.75	Includes material and labor to install
Install	Ea.	10.05	18.15		28.20	blank stock liner paper or bridging
Demolish and Install	Ea.	10.05	30.90		40.95	paper. Based upon 30 S.F. rolls.
Clean	Ea.		5.15		5.15	
Minimum Charge	Job		127		127	
Solid Vinyl						
Good Grade						
Demolish	Roll		15.70		15.70	Includes material and labor to install
Install	Ea.	23	17.80		40.80	pre-pasted, vinyl wallcovering. Based
Demolish and Install	Ea.	23	33.50		56.50	upon 30 S.F. rolls.
Clean	Ea.		5.15		5.15	
Minimum Charge	Job		127		127	

Walls / Ceilings

Wallcovering		Unit	Material	Labor	Equip.	Total	Specification
Better Grade							
	Demolish	Roll		15.70		15.70	Includes material and labor to install
	Install	Ea.	32	17.80		49.80	pre-pasted, vinyl wallcovering. Based
	Demolish and Install	Ea.	32	33.50		65.50	upon 30 S.F. rolls.
	Clean	Ea.		5.15		5.15	
	Minimum Charge	Job		127		127	
Premium Grade							
	Demolish	Roll		15.70		15.70	Includes material and labor to install
	Install	Ea.	40.50	17.80		58.30	pre-pasted, vinyl wallcovering. Based
	Demolish and Install	Ea.	40.50	33.50		74	upon 30 S.F. rolls.
	Clean	Ea.		5.15		5.15	
	Minimum Charge	Job		127		127	
Blank Underliner							
	Demolish	Ea.		12.75		12.75	Includes material and labor to install
	Install	Ea.	10.05	18.15		28.20	blank stock liner paper or bridging
	Demolish and Install	Ea.	10.05	30.90		40.95	paper. Based upon 30 S.F. rolls.
	Clean	Ea.		5.15		5.15	
	Minimum Charge	Job		127		127	
Grasscloth / String							
Good Grade							
	Demolish	Ea.		12.75		12.75	Includes material and labor to install
	Install	Ea.	32.50	23		55.50	grasscloth or string wallcovering.
	Demolish and Install	Ea.	32.50	35.75		68.25	Based upon 30 S.F. rolls.
	Clean	Ea.		6.90		6.90	
	Minimum Charge	Job		127		127	
Better Grade							
	Demolish	Ea.		12.75		12.75	Includes material and labor to install
	Install	Ea.	42	23		65	grasscloth or string wallcovering.
	Demolish and Install	Ea.	42	35.75		77.75	Based upon 30 S.F. rolls.
	Clean	Ea.		6.90		6.90	
	Minimum Charge	Job		127		127	
Premium Grade							
	Demolish	Ea.		12.75		12.75	Includes material and labor to install
	Install	Ea.	53.50	23		76.50	grasscloth or string wallcovering.
	Demolish and Install	Ea.	53.50	35.75		89.25	Based upon 30 S.F. rolls.
	Clean	Ea.		6.90		6.90	
	Minimum Charge	Job		127		127	
Blank Underliner							
	Demolish	Ea.		12.75		12.75	Includes material and labor to install
	Install	Ea.	10.05	18.15		28.20	blank stock liner paper or bridging
	Demolish and Install	Ea.	10.05	30.90		40.95	paper. Based upon 30 S.F. rolls.
	Clean	Ea.		5.15		5.15	
	Minimum Charge	Job		127		127	
Designer							
Premium Grade							
	Demolish	S.F.		.59		.59	Includes material and labor to install
	Install	Ea.	99.50	27		126.50	paperback vinyl, untrimmed and
	Demolish and Install	Ea.	99.50	27.59		127.09	hand-painted. Based upon 30 S.F.
	Clean	Ea.		5.15		5.15	rolls.
	Minimum Charge	Job		127		127	
Blank Underliner							
	Demolish	Ea.		12.75		12.75	Includes material and labor to install
	Install	Ea.	10.05	18.15		28.20	blank stock liner paper or bridging
	Demolish and Install	Ea.	10.05	30.90		40.95	paper. Based upon 30 S.F. rolls.
	Clean	Ea.		5.15		5.15	
	Minimum Charge	Job		127		127	

Walls / Ceilings

Wallcovering

Wallcovering		Unit	Material	Labor	Equip.	Total	Specification
Foil							
	Demolish	Ea.		12.75		12.75	Includes material and labor to install
	Install	Ea.	34	23		57	foil coated wallcovering. Based upon
	Demolish and Install	Ea.	34	35.75		69.75	30 S.F. rolls.
	Clean	Ea.		5.15		5.15	
	Minimum Charge	Job		127		127	
Wallcovering Border							
Good Grade							
	Demolish	L.F.		.84		.84	Includes material and labor install
	Install	L.F.	1.71	.98		2.69	vinyl-coated border 4" to 6" wide.
	Demolish and Install	L.F.	1.71	1.82		3.53	
	Clean	L.F.		.08		.08	
	Minimum Charge	Job		127		127	
Better Grade							
	Demolish	L.F.		.84		.84	Includes material and labor install
	Install	L.F.	2.28	.98		3.26	vinyl-coated border 4" to 6" wide.
	Demolish and Install	L.F.	2.28	1.82		4.10	
	Clean	L.F.		.08		.08	
	Minimum Charge	Job		127		127	
Premium Grade							
	Demolish	L.F.		.84		.84	Includes material and labor install
	Install	L.F.	2.85	.98		3.83	vinyl-coated border 4" to 6" wide.
	Demolish and Install	L.F.	2.85	1.82		4.67	
	Clean	L.F.		.08		.08	
	Minimum Charge	Job		127		127	

Acoustical Ceiling

Acoustical Ceiling		Unit	Material	Labor	Equip.	Total	Specification
Complete System							
2' x 2' Square Edge							
	Demolish	S.F.		.38		.38	Includes material and labor to install
	Install	S.F.	1.42	.88		2.30	T-bar grid acoustical ceiling system,
	Demolish and Install	S.F.	1.42	1.26		2.68	random pinhole 5/8" thick square
	Reinstall	S.F.		.70		.70	edge tile.
	Clean	S.F.	.03	.16		.19	
	Minimum Charge	Job		142		142	
2' x 2' Reveal Edge							
	Demolish	S.F.		.38		.38	Includes material and labor to install
	Install	S.F.	2.09	1.14		3.23	T-bar grid acoustical ceiling system,
	Demolish and Install	S.F.	2.09	1.52		3.61	random pinhole 5/8" thick reveal
	Reinstall	S.F.		.91		.91	edge tile.
	Clean	S.F.	.03	.16		.19	
	Minimum Charge	Job		142		142	
2' x 2' Fire-rated							
	Demolish	S.F.		.38		.38	Includes material and labor to install
	Install	S.F.	2.48	.88		3.36	T-bar grid FR acoustical ceiling system,
	Demolish and Install	S.F.	2.48	1.26		3.74	random pinhole 5/8" thick square
	Reinstall	S.F.		.70		.70	edge tile.
	Clean	S.F.	.03	.16		.19	
	Minimum Charge	Job		142		142	
2' x 4' Square Edge							
	Demolish	S.F.		.38		.38	Cost includes material and labor to
	Install	S.F.	1.18	.75		1.93	install 2' x 4' T-bar grid acoustical
	Demolish and Install	S.F.	1.18	1.13		2.31	ceiling system, random pinhole 5/8"
	Reinstall	S.F.		.60		.60	thick square edge tile.
	Clean	S.F.	.03	.16		.19	
	Minimum Charge	Job		142		142	

Walls / Ceilings

Acoustical Ceiling		Unit	Material	Labor	Equip.	Total	Specification
2' x 4' Reveal Edge							
	Demolish	S.F.		.38		.38	Includes material and labor to install
	Install	S.F.	2.09	1.04		3.13	T-bar grid acoustical ceiling system,
	Demolish and Install	S.F.	2.09	1.42		3.51	random pinhole 5/8" thick reveal
	Reinstall	S.F.		.83		.83	edge tile.
	Clean	S.F.	.03	.16		.19	
	Minimum Charge	Job		142		142	
2' x 4' Fire-rated							
	Demolish	S.F.		.38		.38	Includes material and labor to install
	Install	S.F.	2.48	.88		3.36	T-bar grid FR acoustical ceiling system,
	Demolish and Install	S.F.	2.48	1.26		3.74	random pinhole 5/8" thick square
	Reinstall	S.F.		.70		.70	edge tile.
	Clean	S.F.	.03	.16		.19	
	Minimum Charge	Job		142		142	
T-bar Grid							
2' x 2'							
	Demolish	S.F.		.45		.45	Includes material and labor to install
	Install	S.F.	.81	.44		1.25	T-bar grid acoustical ceiling suspension
	Demolish and Install	S.F.	.81	.89		1.70	system.
	Reinstall	S.F.		.35		.35	
	Clean	S.F.	.03	.16		.19	
	Minimum Charge	Job		131		131	
2' x 4'							
	Demolish	S.F.		.45		.45	Includes material and labor to install
	Install	S.F.	.70	.36		1.06	T-bar grid acoustical ceiling suspension
	Demolish and Install	S.F.	.70	.81		1.51	system.
	Reinstall	S.F.		.28		.28	
	Clean	S.F.	.03	.16		.19	
	Minimum Charge	Job		131		131	
Tile Panels							
2' x 2' Square Edge							
	Demolish	S.F.		.13		.13	Includes material and labor to install
	Install	S.F.	.47	.46		.93	square edge panels 5/8" thick with
	Demolish and Install	S.F.	.47	.59		1.06	pinhole pattern. T-bar grid not
	Reinstall	S.F.		.36		.36	included.
	Clean	S.F.	.03	.16		.19	
	Minimum Charge	Job		142		142	
2' x 2' Reveal Edge							
	Demolish	S.F.		.13		.13	Includes material and labor to install
	Install	S.F.	1.13	.61		1.74	reveal edge panels 5/8" thick with
	Demolish and Install	S.F.	1.13	.74		1.87	pinhole pattern. T-bar grid not
	Reinstall	S.F.		.48		.48	included.
	Clean	S.F.	.03	.16		.19	
	Minimum Charge	Job		142		142	
2' x 2' Fire-rated							
	Demolish	S.F.		.13		.13	Includes material and labor to install FR
	Install	S.F.	.91	.42		1.33	square edge panels 5/8" thick with
	Demolish and Install	S.F.	.91	.55		1.46	pinhole pattern. T-bar grid not
	Reinstall	S.F.		.34		.34	included.
	Clean	S.F.	.03	.16		.19	
	Minimum Charge	Job		142		142	
2' x 4' Square Edge							
	Demolish	S.F.		.13		.13	Includes material and labor to install
	Install	S.F.	.47	.46		.93	square edge panels 5/8" thick with
	Demolish and Install	S.F.	.47	.59		1.06	pinhole pattern. T-bar grid not
	Reinstall	S.F.		.36		.36	included.
	Clean	S.F.	.03	.16		.19	
	Minimum Charge	Job		142		142	

Walls / Ceilings

Acoustical Ceiling

	Unit	Material	Labor	Equip.	Total	Specification
2' x 4' Reveal Edge						Includes material and labor to install
Demolish	S.F.		.13		.13	reveal edge panels 5/8" thick with
Install	S.F.	1.13	.61		1.74	pinhole pattern. T-bar grid not
Demolish and Install	S.F.	1.13	.74		1.87	included.
Reinstall	S.F.		.48		.48	
Clean	S.F.	.03	.16		.19	
Minimum Charge	Job		142		142	
2' x 4' Fire-rated						Includes material and labor to install FR
Demolish	S.F.		.13		.13	square edge panels 5/8" thick with
Install	S.F.	.91	.42		1.33	pinhole pattern. T-bar grid not
Demolish and Install	S.F.	.91	.55		1.46	included.
Reinstall	S.F.		.34		.34	
Clean	S.F.	.03	.16		.19	
Minimum Charge	Job		142		142	
Bleach Out Stains						Includes labor and material to apply
Install	S.F.	.08	.21		.29	laundry type chlorine bleach to remove
Minimum Charge	Job		142		142	light staining of acoustic tile material.

Adhesive Tile
Good Grade

	Unit	Material	Labor	Equip.	Total	Specification
Demolish	S.F.		.51		.51	Cost includes material and labor to
Install	S.F.	.84	.95		1.79	install 12" x 12" tile with embossed
Demolish and Install	S.F.	.84	1.46		2.30	texture pattern. Furring strips not
Clean	S.F.	.02	.12		.14	included.
Minimum Charge	Job		142		142	

Better Grade

	Unit	Material	Labor	Equip.	Total	Specification
Demolish	S.F.		.51		.51	Cost includes material and labor to
Install	S.F.	1.12	.95		2.07	install 12" x 12" tile with embossed
Demolish and Install	S.F.	1.12	1.46		2.58	texture pattern. Furring strips not
Clean	S.F.	.02	.12		.14	included.
Minimum Charge	Job		142		142	

Premium Grade

	Unit	Material	Labor	Equip.	Total	Specification
Demolish	S.F.		.51		.51	Cost includes material and labor to
Install	S.F.	1.73	.95		2.68	install 12" x 12" tile with embossed
Demolish and Install	S.F.	1.73	1.46		3.19	texture pattern. Furring strips not
Clean	S.F.	.02	.12		.14	included.
Minimum Charge	Job		142		142	

Bleach Out Stains

	Unit	Material	Labor	Equip.	Total	Specification
Install	S.F.	.08	.21		.29	Includes labor and material to apply
Minimum Charge	Job		142		142	laundry type chlorine bleach to remove
						light staining of acoustic tile material.

Stapled Tile
Good Grade

	Unit	Material	Labor	Equip.	Total	Specification
Demolish	S.F.		.31		.31	Cost includes material and labor to
Install	S.F.	.84	.95		1.79	install 12" x 12" tile with embossed
Demolish and Install	S.F.	.84	1.26		2.10	texture pattern. Furring strips not
Clean	S.F.	.02	.12		.14	included.
Minimum Charge	Job		142		142	

Better Grade

	Unit	Material	Labor	Equip.	Total	Specification
Demolish	S.F.		.31		.31	Cost includes material and labor to
Install	S.F.	1.12	.95		2.07	install 12" x 12" tile with embossed
Demolish and Install	S.F.	1.12	1.26		2.38	texture pattern. Furring strips not
Clean	S.F.	.02	.12		.14	included.
Minimum Charge	Job		142		142	

Walls / Ceilings

Acoustical Ceiling

		Unit	Material	Labor	Equip.	Total	Specification
Premium Grade							Cost includes material and labor to install 12" x 12" tile with embossed texture pattern. Furring strips not included.
	Demolish	S.F.		.31		.31	
	Install	S.F.	1.73	.95		2.68	
	Demolish and Install	S.F.	1.73	1.26		2.99	
	Clean	S.F.	.02	.12		.14	
	Minimum Charge	Job		142		142	
Bleach Out Stains							Includes labor and material to apply laundry type chlorine bleach to remove light staining of acoustic tile material.
	Install	S.F.	.08	.21		.29	
	Minimum Charge	Job		142		142	
Blown							
Scrape Off Existing							Includes labor and material to remove existing blown acoustical ceiling material.
	Install	S.F.		.43		.43	
	Minimum Charge	Job		142		142	
Seal Ceiling Gypsum Wallboard							Includes labor and material to seal existing drywall with shellac-based material.
	Install	S.F.	.04	.22		.26	
	Minimum Charge	Job		128		128	
Reblow Existing							Includes labor and material to install by spray, texture finish.
	Install	S.F.	.06	.33		.39	
	Minimum Charge	Job		345	57.50	402.50	
Bleach Out Stains							Includes labor and material to apply laundry type chlorine bleach to remove light staining of acoustic tile material.
	Install	S.F.	.08	.21		.29	
	Minimum Charge	Job		142		142	
New Blown							Includes labor and material to install by spray, texture finish.
	Install	S.F.	.06	.33		.39	
	Minimum Charge	Job		128		128	
Apply Glitter To							Includes labor and material to apply glitter material to existing or new drywall.
	Install	S.F.	.09	.11		.20	
	Minimum Charge	Job		128		128	
Furring Strips							Cost includes material and labor to install 1" x 2" furring strips, 16" O.C. per S.F. of surface area to be covered.
	Demolish	S.F.		.06		.06	
	Install	S.F.	.17	.63		.80	
	Demolish and Install	S.F.	.17	.69		.86	
	Minimum Charge	Job		71		71	

Finished Stair

Bi-Fold Door

Raised Panel Door

Hollow Core Door	Unit	Material	Labor	Equip.	Total	Specification
Pre-hung Wood						
1' 6" x 6' 8"						
Demolish	Ea.		26.50		26.50	Cost includes material and labor to
Install	Ea.	153	13.55		166.55	install 1' 6" x 6' 8" pre-hung 1-3/8"
Demolish and Install	Ea.	153	40.05		193.05	lauan door with split pine jamb
Reinstall	Ea.		13.56		13.56	including casing, stops, and hinges.
Clean	Ea.	2.81	8.60		11.41	
Paint	Ea.	7.50	36.50		44	
Minimum Charge	Job		142		142	
2' x 6' 8"						
Demolish	Ea.		26.50		26.50	Cost includes material and labor to
Install	Ea.	157	14.25		171.25	install 2' x 6' 8" pre-hung 1-3/8"
Demolish and Install	Ea.	157	40.75		197.75	lauan door with split pine jamb
Reinstall	Ea.		14.24		14.24	including casing, stops, and hinges.
Clean	Ea.	2.81	8.60		11.41	
Paint	Ea.	7.50	36.50		44	
Minimum Charge	Job		142		142	
2' 4" x 6' 8"						
Demolish	Ea.		26.50		26.50	Cost includes material and labor to
Install	Ea.	165	14.25		179.25	install 2' 4" x 6' 8" pre-hung 1-3/8"
Demolish and Install	Ea.	165	40.75		205.75	lauan door with split pine jamb
Reinstall	Ea.		14.24		14.24	including casing, stops, and hinges.
Clean	Ea.	2.81	8.60		11.41	
Paint	Ea.	7.50	36.50		44	
Minimum Charge	Job		142		142	
2' 6" x 6' 8"						
Demolish	Ea.		26.50		26.50	Cost includes material and labor to
Install	Ea.	165	14.25		179.25	install 2' 6" x 6' 8" pre-hung 1-3/8"
Demolish and Install	Ea.	165	40.75		205.75	lauan door with split pine jamb
Reinstall	Ea.		14.24		14.24	including casing, stops, and hinges.
Clean	Ea.	2.81	8.60		11.41	
Paint	Ea.	7.50	36.50		44	
Minimum Charge	Job		142		142	
2' 8" x 6' 8"						
Demolish	Ea.		26.50		26.50	Cost includes material and labor to
Install	Ea.	168	14.25		182.25	install 2' 8" x 6' 8" pre-hung 1-3/8"
Demolish and Install	Ea.	168	40.75		208.75	lauan door with split pine jamb,
Reinstall	Ea.		14.24		14.24	including casing, stop and hinges.
Clean	Ea.	2.81	8.60		11.41	
Paint	Ea.	7.50	36.50		44	
Minimum Charge	Job		142		142	

Finish Carpentry

Hollow Core Door	Unit	Material	Labor	Equip.	Total	Specification
3' x 6' 8"						
Demolish	Ea.		26.50		26.50	Cost includes material and labor to
Install	Ea.	175	15		190	install 3' x 6' 8" pre-hung 1-3/8"
Demolish and Install	Ea.	175	41.50		216.50	lauan door with split pine jamb
Reinstall	Ea.		14.99		14.99	including casing, stops, and hinges.
Clean	Ea.	2.81	8.60		11.41	
Paint	Ea.	7.50	36.50		44	
Minimum Charge	Job		142		142	
Pocket Type						
Demolish	Ea.		39.50		39.50	Cost includes material and labor to
Install	Ea.	32.50	31.50		64	install 2' 8" x 6' 8" lauan door.
Demolish and Install	Ea.	32.50	71		103.50	
Reinstall	Ea.		31.64		31.64	
Clean	Ea.	2.81	8.60		11.41	
Paint	Ea.	7.50	36.50		44	
Minimum Charge	Job		142		142	
Stain						
Install	Ea.	3.91	21.50		25.41	Includes labor and material to stain
Minimum Charge	Job		128		128	single door and trim on both sides.
Pre-hung Masonite						
1' 6" x 6' 8"						
Demolish	Ea.		26.50		26.50	Cost includes material and labor to
Install	Ea.	188	13.55		201.55	install 1' 6" x 6' 8" pre-hung 1-3/8"
Demolish and Install	Ea.	188	40.05		228.05	masonite door with split pine jamb
Reinstall	Ea.		13.56		13.56	including casing, stops, and hinges.
Clean	Ea.	2.81	8.60		11.41	
Paint	Ea.	7.50	36.50		44	
Minimum Charge	Job		142		142	
2' x 6' 8"						
Demolish	Ea.		26.50		26.50	Cost includes material and labor to
Install	Ea.	189	14.25		203.25	install 2' x 6' 8" pre-hung 1-3/8"
Demolish and Install	Ea.	189	40.75		229.75	masonite door with split pine jamb
Reinstall	Ea.		14.24		14.24	including casing, stops, and hinges.
Clean	Ea.	2.81	8.60		11.41	
Paint	Ea.	7.50	36.50		44	
Minimum Charge	Job		142		142	
2' 4" x 6' 8"						
Demolish	Ea.		26.50		26.50	Cost includes material and labor to
Install	Ea.	191	14.25		205.25	install 2' 4" x 6' 8" pre-hung 1-3/8"
Demolish and Install	Ea.	191	40.75		231.75	masonite door with split pine jamb
Reinstall	Ea.		14.24		14.24	including casing, stops, and hinges.
Clean	Ea.	2.81	8.60		11.41	
Paint	Ea.	7.50	36.50		44	
Minimum Charge	Job		142		142	
2' 8" x 6' 8"						
Demolish	Ea.		26.50		26.50	Cost includes material and labor to
Install	Ea.	194	14.25		208.25	install 2' 8" x 6' 8" pre-hung 1-3/8"
Demolish and Install	Ea.	194	40.75		234.75	masonite door with split pine jamb
Reinstall	Ea.		14.24		14.24	including casing, stops, and hinges.
Clean	Ea.	2.81	8.60		11.41	
Paint	Ea.	7.50	36.50		44	
Minimum Charge	Job		142		142	
3' x 6' 8"						
Demolish	Ea.		26.50		26.50	Cost includes material and labor to
Install	Ea.	198	15		213	install 3' x 6' 8" pre-hung 1-3/8"
Demolish and Install	Ea.	198	41.50		239.50	masonite door with split pine jamb
Reinstall	Ea.		14.99		14.99	including casing, stops, and hinges.
Clean	Ea.	2.81	8.60		11.41	
Paint	Ea.	7.50	36.50		44	
Minimum Charge	Job		142		142	

Finish Carpentry

Hollow Core Door		Unit	Material	Labor	Equip.	Total	Specification
Pocket Type							
	Demolish	Ea.		39.50		39.50	Cost includes material and labor to
	Install	Ea.	32.50	31.50		64	install 2' 8" x 6' 8" lauan door.
	Demolish and Install	Ea.	32.50	71		103.50	
	Reinstall	Ea.		31.64		31.64	
	Clean	Ea.	2.81	8.60		11.41	
	Paint	Ea.	7.50	36.50		44	
	Minimum Charge	Job		142		142	
Stain							
	Install	Ea.	3.91	21.50		25.41	Includes labor and material to stain
	Minimum Charge	Job		128		128	single door and trim on both sides.

Hollow Core Door Only

		Unit	Material	Labor	Equip.	Total	Specification
1' 6" x 6' 8'							
	Demolish	Ea.		5.65		5.65	Cost includes material and labor to
	Install	Ea.	36	15		51	install 1' 6" x 6' 8" lauan hollow core
	Demolish and Install	Ea.	36	20.65		56.65	door slab.
	Reinstall	Ea.		14.99		14.99	
	Clean	Ea.	1.17	6.45		7.62	
	Paint	Ea.	2.32	32		34.32	
	Minimum Charge	Job		142		142	
2' x 6' 8'							
	Demolish	Ea.		5.65		5.65	Cost includes material and labor to
	Install	Ea.	38	15.80		53.80	install 2' x 6' 8" lauan hollow core
	Demolish and Install	Ea.	38	21.45		59.45	door slab.
	Reinstall	Ea.		15.82		15.82	
	Clean	Ea.	1.17	6.45		7.62	
	Paint	Ea.	2.32	32		34.32	
	Minimum Charge	Job		142		142	
2' 4" x 6' 8'							
	Demolish	Ea.		5.65		5.65	Cost includes material and labor to
	Install	Ea.	41.50	15.80		57.30	install 2' 4" x 6' 8" lauan hollow core
	Demolish and Install	Ea.	41.50	21.45		62.95	door slab.
	Reinstall	Ea.		15.82		15.82	
	Clean	Ea.	1.17	6.45		7.62	
	Paint	Ea.	2.32	32		34.32	
	Minimum Charge	Job		142		142	
2' 8" x 6' 8'							
	Demolish	Ea.		5.65		5.65	Cost includes material and labor to
	Install	Ea.	42.50	15.80		58.30	install 2' 8" x 6' 8" lauan hollow core
	Demolish and Install	Ea.	42.50	21.45		63.95	door slab.
	Reinstall	Ea.		15.82		15.82	
	Clean	Ea.	1.17	6.45		7.62	
	Paint	Ea.	2.32	32		34.32	
	Minimum Charge	Job		142		142	
3' x 6' 8'							
	Demolish	Ea.		5.65		5.65	Cost includes material and labor to
	Install	Ea.	44.50	16.75		61.25	install 3' x 6' 8" lauan hollow core
	Demolish and Install	Ea.	44.50	22.40		66.90	door slab.
	Reinstall	Ea.		16.75		16.75	
	Clean	Ea.	1.17	6.45		7.62	
	Paint	Ea.	2.32	32		34.32	
	Minimum Charge	Job		142		142	
Pocket Type							
	Demolish	Ea.		5.65		5.65	Cost includes material and labor to
	Install	Ea.	32.50	31.50		64	install 2' 8" x 6' 8" lauan door.
	Demolish and Install	Ea.	32.50	37.15		69.65	
	Reinstall	Ea.		31.64		31.64	
	Clean	Ea.	1.17	6.45		7.62	
	Paint	Ea.	2.32	32		34.32	
	Minimum Charge	Job		142		142	

Finish Carpentry

	Unit	Material	Labor	Equip.	Total	Specification
Stain						
Install	Ea.	2.16	28.50		30.66	Includes labor and materials to stain a
Minimum Charge	Job		128		128	flush style door on both sides by brush.
Casing Trim						
Single Width						
Demolish	Ea.		5		5	Cost includes material and labor to
Install	Opng.	13.95	48.50		62.45	install 11/16" x 2-1/2" pine ranch
Demolish and Install	Opng.	13.95	53.50		67.45	style casing for one side of a standard
Reinstall	Opng.		38.62		38.62	door opening.
Clean	Opng.	.40	2.07		2.47	
Paint	Ea.	3.04	5.10		8.14	
Minimum Charge	Job		142		142	
Double Width						
Demolish	Ea.		5.95		5.95	Cost includes material and labor to
Install	Opng.	17.15	57		74.15	install 11/16" x 2-1/2" pine ranch
Demolish and Install	Opng.	17.15	62.95		80.10	style door casing for one side of a
Reinstall	Opng.		45.57		45.57	double door opening.
Clean	Opng.	.46	4.14		4.60	
Paint	Ea.	3.04	5.80		8.84	
Minimum Charge	Job		142		142	
Hardware						
Doorknob w / Lock						
Demolish	Ea.		10.55		10.55	Includes material and labor to install
Install	Ea.	19.05	17.80		36.85	privacy lockset.
Demolish and Install	Ea.	19.05	28.35		47.40	
Reinstall	Ea.		14.24		14.24	
Clean	Ea.	.28	6.45		6.73	
Minimum Charge	Job		142		142	
Doorknob						
Demolish	Ea.		10.55		10.55	Includes material and labor to install
Install	Ea.	16.65	17.80		34.45	residential passage lockset, keyless
Demolish and Install	Ea.	16.65	28.35		45	bored type.
Reinstall	Ea.		14.24		14.24	
Clean	Ea.	.28	6.45		6.73	
Minimum Charge	Job		142		142	
Deadbolt						
Demolish	Ea.		9.90		9.90	Includes material and labor to install a
Install	Ea.	36.50	20.50		57	deadbolt.
Demolish and Install	Ea.	36.50	30.40		66.90	
Reinstall	Ea.		16.27		16.27	
Clean	Ea.	.28	6.45		6.73	
Minimum Charge	Job		142		142	
Lever Handle						
Demolish	Ea.		10.55		10.55	Includes material and labor to install
Install	Ea.	26.50	28.50		55	residential passage lockset, keyless
Demolish and Install	Ea.	26.50	39.05		65.55	bored type with lever handle.
Reinstall	Ea.		22.78		22.78	
Clean	Ea.	.28	6.45		6.73	
Minimum Charge	Job		142		142	
Closer						
Demolish	Ea.		5.95		5.95	Includes material and labor to install
Install	Ea.	80.50	44		124.50	pneumatic light duty closer for interior
Demolish and Install	Ea.	80.50	49.95		130.45	type doors.
Reinstall	Ea.		35.05		35.05	
Clean	Ea.	.14	8.60		8.74	
Minimum Charge	Job		142		142	

Hollow Core Door

Hollow Core Door		Unit	Material	Labor	Equip.	Total	Specification
Push Plate							Includes material and labor to install
	Demolish	Ea.		8.80		8.80	bronze push-pull plate.
	Install	Ea.	12.55	23.50		36.05	
	Demolish and Install	Ea.	12.55	32.30		44.85	
	Reinstall	Ea.		18.99		18.99	
	Clean	Ea.	.28	6.45		6.73	
	Minimum Charge	Job		142		142	
Kickplate							Includes material and labor to install
	Demolish	Ea.		8.80		8.80	aluminum kickplate, 10" x 28".
	Install	Ea.	16.45	19		35.45	
	Demolish and Install	Ea.	16.45	27.80		44.25	
	Reinstall	Ea.		15.19		15.19	
	Clean	Ea.	.28	6.45		6.73	
	Minimum Charge	Job		142		142	
Exit Sign							Includes material and labor to install a
	Demolish	Ea.		15.65		15.65	wall mounted interior electric exit sign.
	Install	Ea.	53.50	39		92.50	
	Demolish and Install	Ea.	53.50	54.65		108.15	
	Reinstall	Ea.		31		31	
	Clean	Ea.	.02	4.66		4.68	
	Minimum Charge	Job		142		142	
Jamb							Includes material and labor to install
	Demolish	Ea.		19.80		19.80	flat pine jamb with square cut heads
	Install	Ea.	65	7.70		72.70	and rabbeted sides for 6' 8" high and
	Demolish and Install	Ea.	65	27.50		92.50	3-9/16" door including trim sets for
	Clean	Ea.	.09	5.15		5.24	both sides.
	Paint	Ea.	5.50	17		22.50	
	Minimum Charge	Job		142		142	
Shave & Refit							Includes labor to shave and rework
	Install	Ea.		23.50		23.50	door to fit opening at the job site.
	Minimum Charge	Job		142		142	

Solid Core Door

Solid Core Door		Unit	Material	Labor	Equip.	Total	Specification
Pre-hung Wood							
2' 4" x 6' 8"							Cost includes material and labor to
	Demolish	Ea.		26.50		26.50	install 2' 4" x 6' 8" pre-hung 1-3/4"
	Install	Ea.	178	14.25		192.25	door, 4-1/2" split jamb, including
	Demolish and Install	Ea.	178	40.75		218.75	casing and stop, hinges, aluminum sill,
	Reinstall	Ea.		14.24		14.24	weatherstripping.
	Clean	Ea.	2.81	8.60		11.41	
	Paint	Ea.	8.80	36.50		45.30	
	Minimum Charge	Job		142		142	
2' 6" x 6' 8"							Cost includes material and labor to
	Demolish	Ea.		26.50		26.50	install 2' 6" x 6' 8" pre-hung 1-3/4"
	Install	Ea.	175	14.25		189.25	door, 4-1/2" split jamb, including
	Demolish and Install	Ea.	175	40.75		215.75	casing and stop, hinges, aluminum sill,
	Reinstall	Ea.		14.24		14.24	weatherstripping.
	Clean	Ea.	2.81	8.60		11.41	
	Paint	Ea.	8.80	36.50		45.30	
	Minimum Charge	Job		142		142	

Finish Carpentry

Solid Core Door

	Unit	Material	Labor	Equip.	Total	Specification
2' 8" x 6' 8"						
Demolish	Ea.		26.50		26.50	Cost includes material and labor to
Install	Ea.	179	14.25		193.25	install 2' 8" x 6' 8" pre-hung 1-3/4"
Demolish and Install	Ea.	179	40.75		219.75	door, 4-1/2" split jamb, including
Reinstall	Ea.		14.24		14.24	casing and stop, hinges, aluminum sill,
Clean	Ea.	2.81	8.60		11.41	weatherstripping.
Paint	Ea.	8.80	36.50		45.30	
Minimum Charge	Job		142		142	
3' x 6' 8"						
Demolish	Ea.		26.50		26.50	Cost includes material and labor to
Install	Ea.	187	15		202	install 3' x 6' 8" pre-hung 1-3/4" door,
Demolish and Install	Ea.	187	41.50		228.50	including casing and stop, hinges,
Reinstall	Ea.		14.99		14.99	jamb, aluminum sill, weatherstripped.
Clean	Ea.	2.81	8.60		11.41	
Paint	Ea.	8.80	36.50		45.30	
Minimum Charge	Job		142		142	
3' 6" x 6' 8"						
Demolish	Ea.		26.50		26.50	Cost includes material and labor to
Install	Ea.	231	15.80		246.80	install 3' 6" x 6' 8" pre-hung 1-3/4"
Demolish and Install	Ea.	231	42.30		273.30	door, 4-1/2" split jamb, including
Reinstall	Ea.		15.82		15.82	casing and stop, hinges, aluminum sill,
Clean	Ea.	2.81	8.60		11.41	weatherstripping.
Paint	Ea.	8.80	36.50		45.30	
Minimum Charge	Job		142		142	
Raised Panel						
Demolish	Ea.		26.50		26.50	Cost includes material and labor to
Install	Ea.	365	15.80		380.80	install 3' x 6' 8" pre-hung 1-3/4" door,
Demolish and Install	Ea.	365	42.30		407.30	jamb, including casing and stop,
Reinstall	Ea.		15.82		15.82	hinges, aluminum sill,
Clean	Ea.	2.81	8.60		11.41	weatherstripping.
Paint	Ea.	8.80	85		93.80	
Minimum Charge	Job		142		142	
Stain						
Install	Ea.	3.91	21.50		25.41	Includes labor and material to stain
Minimum Charge	Job		128		128	single door and trim on both sides.

Bifold Door

	Unit	Material	Labor	Equip.	Total	Specification
Wood, Single						
3'						
Demolish	Ea.		19.80		19.80	Cost includes material and labor to
Install	Ea.	49.50	44		93.50	install 3' wide solid wood bi-fold door
Demolish and Install	Ea.	49.50	63.80		113.30	not including jamb, trim, track, and
Reinstall	Ea.		43.82		43.82	hardware.
Clean	Ea.	2.81	8.60		11.41	
Paint	Ea.	7.50	36.50		44	
Minimum Charge	Job		142		142	
5'						
Demolish	Ea.		19.80		19.80	Includes material and labor to install
Install	Ea.	98.50	52		150.50	pair of 2' 6" wide solid wood bi-fold
Demolish and Install	Ea.	98.50	71.80		170.30	doors not including jamb, trim, track,
Reinstall	Ea.		51.78		51.78	and hardware.
Clean	Ea.	1.22	14.75		15.97	
Paint	Ea.	16.15	64		80.15	
Minimum Charge	Job		142		142	

Finish Carpentry

Bifold Door		Unit	Material	Labor	Equip.	Total	Specification
6'							
	Demolish	Ea.		19.80		19.80	Includes material and labor to install
	Install	Ea.	108	57		165	pair of 3' wide solid wood bi-fold
	Demolish and Install	Ea.	108	76.80		184.80	doors not including jamb, trim, track,
	Reinstall	Ea.		56.96		56.96	and hardware.
	Clean	Ea.	1.40	17.25		18.65	
	Paint	Ea.	16.15	64		80.15	
	Minimum Charge	Job		142		142	
8'							
	Demolish	Ea.		19.80		19.80	Includes material and labor to install
	Install	Ea.	206	31.50		237.50	pair of 4' wide solid wood bi-fold
	Demolish and Install	Ea.	206	51.30		257.30	doors not including jamb, trim, track,
	Reinstall	Ea.		31.64		31.64	and hardware.
	Clean	Ea.	1.93	20.50		22.43	
	Paint	Ea.	8.40	64		72.40	
	Minimum Charge	Job		142		142	
Mirrored							
5'							
	Demolish	Ea.		19.80		19.80	Includes material and labor to install
	Install	Ea.	375	26		401	pair of 2' 6" wide mirrored bi-fold
	Demolish and Install	Ea.	375	45.80		420.80	doors including jamb, trim, track, and
	Reinstall	Ea.		25.89		25.89	hardware.
	Clean	Ea.	1.22	7.40		8.62	
	Minimum Charge	Job		142		142	
6'							
	Demolish	Ea.		19.80		19.80	Includes material and labor to install
	Install	Ea.	415	31.50		446.50	pair of 3' wide mirrored bi-fold doors
	Demolish and Install	Ea.	415	51.30		466.30	including jamb, trim, track, and
	Reinstall	Ea.		31.64		31.64	hardware.
	Clean	Ea.	1.40	8.60		10	
	Minimum Charge	Job		142		142	
8'							
	Demolish	Ea.		19.80		19.80	Includes material and labor to install
	Install	Ea.	665	47.50		712.50	pair of 4' wide mirrored bi-fold doors
	Demolish and Install	Ea.	665	67.30		732.30	including jamb, trim, track, and
	Reinstall	Ea.		47.47		47.47	hardware.
	Clean	Ea.	1.93	10.35		12.28	
	Minimum Charge	Job		142		142	
Louvered							
3'							
	Demolish	Ea.		19.80		19.80	Cost includes material and labor to
	Install	Ea.	125	44		169	install 3' wide louvered bi-fold door
	Demolish and Install	Ea.	125	63.80		188.80	not including jamb, trim, track, and
	Reinstall	Ea.		43.82		43.82	hardware.
	Clean	Ea.	2.81	8.60		11.41	
	Paint	Ea.	7.50	36.50		44	
	Minimum Charge	Job		142		142	
5'							
	Demolish	Ea.		19.80		19.80	Includes material and labor to install
	Install	Ea.	223	52		275	pair of 2' 6" wide louvered wood
	Demolish and Install	Ea.	223	71.80		294.80	bi-fold doors not including jamb, trim,
	Reinstall	Ea.		51.78		51.78	track, and hardware.
	Clean	Ea.	1.22	14.75		15.97	
	Paint	Ea.	16.15	64		80.15	
	Minimum Charge	Job		142		142	

Finish Carpentry

Bifold Door

	Unit	Material	Labor	Equip.	Total	Specification
6'						
Demolish	Ea.		19.80		19.80	Includes material and labor to install
Install	Ea.	248	57		305	pair of 3' wide louvered wood bi-fold
Demolish and Install	Ea.	248	76.80		324.80	doors not including jamb, trim, track,
Reinstall	Ea.		56.96		56.96	and hardware.
Clean	Ea.	1.40	17.25		18.65	
Paint	Ea.	16.15	64		80.15	
Minimum Charge	Job		142		142	
8'						
Demolish	Ea.		19.80		19.80	Includes material and labor to install
Install	Ea.	485	28.50		513.50	pair of 4' wide solid wood bi-fold
Demolish and Install	Ea.	485	48.30		533.30	doors not including jamb, trim, track,
Reinstall	Ea.		28.48		28.48	and hardware.
Clean	Ea.	6.65	14.75		21.40	
Paint	Ea.	8.40	64		72.40	
Minimum Charge	Job		142		142	

Accordion Type

	Unit	Material	Labor	Equip.	Total	Specification
Demolish	S.F.		.68		.68	Includes material and labor to install
Install	S.F.	1.76	1.42		3.18	vinyl folding accordion closet doors,
Demolish and Install	S.F.	1.76	2.10		3.86	including track and frame.
Reinstall	S.F.		1.42		1.42	
Clean	S.F.		.25		.25	
Minimum Charge	Job		142		142	

Casing Trim
Single Width

	Unit	Material	Labor	Equip.	Total	Specification
Demolish	Ea.		5		5	Cost includes material and labor to
Install	Opng.	13.95	48.50		62.45	install 11/16" x 2-1/2" pine ranch
Demolish and Install	Opng.	13.95	53.50		67.45	style casing for one side of a standard
Reinstall	Opng.		38.62		38.62	door opening.
Clean	Opng.	.40	2.07		2.47	
Paint	Ea.	3.04	5.10		8.14	
Minimum Charge	Job		142		142	

Double Width

	Unit	Material	Labor	Equip.	Total	Specification
Demolish	Ea.		5.95		5.95	Cost includes material and labor to
Install	Opng.	17.15	57		74.15	install 11/16" x 2-1/2" pine ranch
Demolish and Install	Opng.	17.15	62.95		80.10	style door casing for one side of a
Reinstall	Opng.		45.57		45.57	double door opening.
Clean	Opng.	.46	4.14		4.60	
Paint	Ea.	3.04	5.80		8.84	
Minimum Charge	Job		142		142	

Jamb

	Unit	Material	Labor	Equip.	Total	Specification
Demolish	Ea.		19.80		19.80	Includes material and labor to install
Install	Ea.	65	7.70		72.70	flat pine jamb with square cut heads
Demolish and Install	Ea.	65	27.50		92.50	and rabbeted sides for 6' 8" high and
Clean	Ea.	.09	5.15		5.24	3-9/16" door including trim sets for
Paint	Ea.	5.50	17		22.50	both sides.
Minimum Charge	Job		71		71	

Stain

	Unit	Material	Labor	Equip.	Total	Specification
Install	Ea.	3.91	21.50		25.41	Includes labor and material to stain
Minimum Charge	Job		128		128	single door and trim on both sides.

Shave & Refit

	Unit	Material	Labor	Equip.	Total	Specification
Install	Ea.		23.50		23.50	Includes labor to shave and rework
Minimum Charge	Job		71		71	door to fit opening at the job site.

Finish Carpentry

Louver Door		Unit	Material	Labor	Equip.	Total	Specification
Full							
2′ x 6′ 8″							
	Demolish	Ea.		5.65		5.65	Cost includes material and labor to
	Install	Ea.	177	28.50		205.50	install 2′ x 6′ 8″ pine full louver door,
	Demolish and Install	Ea.	177	34.15		211.15	jamb, hinges.
	Reinstall	Ea.		28.48		28.48	
	Clean	Ea.	5.20	26		31.20	
	Paint	Ea.	7.50	36.50		44	
	Minimum Charge	Job		142		142	
2′ 8″ x 6′ 8″							
	Demolish	Ea.		5.65		5.65	Cost includes material and labor to
	Install	Ea.	196	28.50		224.50	install 2′ 8″ x 6′ 8″ pine full louver
	Demolish and Install	Ea.	196	34.15		230.15	door, jamb, hinges.
	Reinstall	Ea.		28.48		28.48	
	Clean	Ea.	5.20	26		31.20	
	Paint	Ea.	7.50	36.50		44	
	Minimum Charge	Job		142		142	
3′ x 6′ 8″							
	Demolish	Ea.		5.65		5.65	Cost includes material and labor to
	Install	Ea.	207	30		237	install 3′ x 6′ 8″ pine full louver door,
	Demolish and Install	Ea.	207	35.65		242.65	jamb, hinges.
	Reinstall	Ea.		29.98		29.98	
	Clean	Ea.	5.20	26		31.20	
	Paint	Ea.	7.50	36.50		44	
	Minimum Charge	Job		142		142	
Half							
2′ x 6′ 8″							
	Demolish	Ea.		5.65		5.65	Cost includes material and labor to
	Install	Ea.	281	28.50		309.50	install 2′ x 6′ 8″ pine half louver door,
	Demolish and Install	Ea.	281	34.15		315.15	jamb, hinges.
	Reinstall	Ea.		28.48		28.48	
	Clean	Ea.	5.20	26		31.20	
	Paint	Ea.	7.50	36.50		44	
	Minimum Charge	Job		142		142	
2′ 8″ x 6′ 8″							
	Demolish	Ea.		5.65		5.65	Cost includes material and labor to
	Install	Ea.	305	28.50		333.50	install 2′ 8″ x 6′ 8″ pine half louver
	Demolish and Install	Ea.	305	34.15		339.15	door, jamb, hinges.
	Reinstall	Ea.		28.48		28.48	
	Clean	Ea.	5.20	26		31.20	
	Paint	Ea.	7.50	36.50		44	
	Minimum Charge	Job		142		142	
3′ x 6′ 8″							
	Demolish	Ea.		5.65		5.65	Cost includes material and labor to
	Install	Ea.	315	30		345	install 3′ x 6′ 8″ pine half louver door,
	Demolish and Install	Ea.	315	35.65		350.65	jamb, hinges.
	Reinstall	Ea.		29.98		29.98	
	Clean	Ea.	5.20	26		31.20	
	Paint	Ea.	7.50	36.50		44	
	Minimum Charge	Job		142		142	
Jamb							
	Demolish	Ea.		19.80		19.80	Includes material and labor to install
	Install	Ea.	65	7.70		72.70	flat pine jamb with square cut heads
	Demolish and Install	Ea.	65	27.50		92.50	and rabbeted sides for 6′ 8″ high and
	Clean	Ea.	.09	5.15		5.24	3-9/16″ door including trim sets for
	Paint	Ea.	5.50	17		22.50	both sides.
	Minimum Charge	Job		71		71	

Finish Carpentry

Louver Door

Louver Door		Unit	Material	Labor	Equip.	Total	Specification
Stain							
	Install	Ea.	3.91	21.50		25.41	Includes labor and material to stain
	Minimum Charge	Job		128		128	single door and trim on both sides.
Shave & Refit							
	Install	Ea.		23.50		23.50	Includes labor to shave and rework
	Minimum Charge	Job		128		128	door to fit opening at the job site.

Bypass Sliding Door

Bypass Sliding Door		Unit	Material	Labor	Equip.	Total	Specification
Wood							
5'							
	Demolish	Ea.		26.50		26.50	Includes material and labor to install
	Install	Opng.	188	52		240	pair of 2' 6" wide lauan hollow core
	Demolish and Install	Opng.	188	78.50		266.50	wood bi-pass doors with jamb, track
	Reinstall	Opng.		51.78		51.78	hardware.
	Clean	Ea.	1.22	14.75		15.97	
	Paint	Ea.	16.15	64		80.15	
	Minimum Charge	Job		142		142	
6'							
	Demolish	Ea.		26.50		26.50	Includes material and labor to install
	Install	Opng.	201	57		258	pair of 3' wide lauan hollow core
	Demolish and Install	Opng.	201	83.50		284.50	wood bi-pass doors with jamb, track
	Reinstall	Opng.		56.96		56.96	and hardware.
	Clean	Ea.	1.40	17.25		18.65	
	Paint	Ea.	16.15	64		80.15	
	Minimum Charge	Job		142		142	
8'							
	Demolish	Ea.		26.50		26.50	Includes material and labor to install
	Install	Opng.	276	71		347	pair of 4' wide lauan hollow core
	Demolish and Install	Opng.	276	97.50		373.50	wood bi-pass doors with jamb, track
	Reinstall	Opng.		71.20		71.20	and hardware.
	Clean	Ea.	1.93	20.50		22.43	
	Paint	Ea.	8.40	64		72.40	
	Minimum Charge	Job		142		142	
Mirrored							
5'							
	Demolish	Ea.		26.50		26.50	Includes material and labor to install
	Install	Opng.	325	57		382	pair of 2' 6" wide mirrored bi-pass
	Demolish and Install	Opng.	325	83.50		408.50	doors with jamb, trim, track hardware.
	Reinstall	Opng.		56.96		56.96	
	Clean	Ea.	1.22	7.40		8.62	
	Minimum Charge	Job		142		142	
6'							
	Demolish	Ea.		26.50		26.50	Includes material and labor to install
	Install	Opng.	360	57		417	pair of 3' wide mirrored bi-pass doors
	Demolish and Install	Opng.	360	83.50		443.50	with jamb, trim, track hardware.
	Reinstall	Opng.		56.96		56.96	
	Clean	Ea.	1.40	8.60		10	
	Minimum Charge	Job		142		142	
8'							
	Demolish	Ea.		26.50		26.50	Includes material and labor to install
	Install	Opng.	455	63.50		518.50	pair of 4' wide mirrored bi-pass doors
	Demolish and Install	Opng.	455	90		545	with jamb, trim, track hardware.
	Reinstall	Opng.		63.29		63.29	
	Clean	Ea.	1.93	10.35		12.28	
	Minimum Charge	Job		142		142	

Finish Carpentry

Bypass Sliding Door

	Unit	Material	Labor	Equip.	Total	Specification
Casing Trim						
Single Width						
Demolish	Ea.		5		5	Cost includes material and labor to
Install	Opng.	13.95	48.50		62.45	install 11/16" x 2-1/2" pine ranch
Demolish and Install	Opng.	13.95	53.50		67.45	style casing for one side of a standard
Reinstall	Opng.		38.62		38.62	door opening.
Clean	Opng.	.40	2.07		2.47	
Paint	Ea.	3.04	5.10		8.14	
Minimum Charge	Job		142		142	
Double Width						
Demolish	Ea.		5.95		5.95	Cost includes material and labor to
Install	Opng.	17.15	57		74.15	install 11/16" x 2-1/2" pine ranch
Demolish and Install	Opng.	17.15	62.95		80.10	style door casing for one side of a
Reinstall	Opng.		45.57		45.57	double door opening.
Clean	Opng.	.46	4.14		4.60	
Paint	Ea.	3.04	5.80		8.84	
Minimum Charge	Job		142		142	
Jamb						
Demolish	Ea.		19.80		19.80	Includes material and labor to install
Install	Ea.	65	7.70		72.70	flat pine jamb with square cut heads
Demolish and Install	Ea.	65	27.50		92.50	and rabbeted sides for 6' 8" high and
Clean	Ea.	.09	5.15		5.24	3-9/16" door including trim sets for
Paint	Ea.	5.50	17		22.50	both sides.
Minimum Charge	Job		71		71	
Stain						
Install	Ea.	3.91	21.50		25.41	Includes labor and material to stain
Minimum Charge	Job		128		128	single door and trim on both sides.
Shave & Refit						
Install	Ea.		23.50		23.50	Includes labor to shave and rework
Minimum Charge	Job		71		71	door to fit opening at the job site.

Base Molding

	Unit	Material	Labor	Equip.	Total	Specification
One Piece						
1-5/8"						
Demolish	L.F.		.38		.38	Includes material and labor to install
Install	L.F.	.22	.84		1.06	pine or birch base molding.
Demolish and Install	L.F.	.22	1.22		1.44	
Reinstall	L.F.		.67		.67	
Clean	L.F.	.02	.12		.14	
Paint	L.F.	.03	.28		.31	
Minimum Charge	Job		142		142	
2-1/2"						
Demolish	L.F.		.38		.38	Cost includes material and labor to
Install	L.F.	.37	.88		1.25	install 1/2" x 2-1/2" pine or birch
Demolish and Install	L.F.	.37	1.26		1.63	base molding.
Reinstall	L.F.		.70		.70	
Clean	L.F.	.02	.12		.14	
Paint	L.F.	.03	.28		.31	
Minimum Charge	Job		142		142	

Finish Carpentry

Base Molding		Unit	Material	Labor	Equip.	Total	Specification
3-1/2"							
	Demolish	L.F.		.38		.38	Cost includes material and labor to
	Install	L.F.	.88	.91		1.79	install 9/16" x 3-1/2" pine or birch
	Demolish and Install	L.F.	.88	1.29		2.17	base molding.
	Reinstall	L.F.		.73		.73	
	Clean	L.F.	.02	.12		.14	
	Paint	L.F.	.03	.30		.33	
	Minimum Charge	Job		142		142	
6"							
	Demolish	L.F.		.38		.38	Cost includes material and labor to
	Install	L.F.	.67	1		1.67	install 1" x 6" pine or birch base
	Demolish and Install	L.F.	.67	1.38		2.05	molding.
	Reinstall	L.F.		.80		.80	
	Clean	L.F.	.02	.17		.19	
	Paint	L.F.	.04	.38		.42	
	Minimum Charge	Job		142		142	
8"							
	Demolish	L.F.		.46		.46	Cost includes material and labor to
	Install	L.F.	1.05	1.10		2.15	install 1" x 8" pine or birch base
	Demolish and Install	L.F.	1.05	1.56		2.61	molding.
	Reinstall	L.F.		.88		.88	
	Clean	L.F.	.03	.21		.24	
	Paint	L.F.	.06	.43		.49	
	Minimum Charge	Job		142		142	
Premium / Custom Grade							
	Demolish	L.F.		.46		.46	Includes material and labor to install
	Install	L.F.	2.66	2.74		5.40	custom 2 or 3 piece oak or other
	Demolish and Install	L.F.	2.66	3.20		5.86	hardwood, stain grade trim.
	Reinstall	L.F.		2.19		2.19	
	Clean	L.F.	.03	.21		.24	
	Paint	L.F.	.06	.43		.49	
	Minimum Charge	Job		142		142	
One Piece Oak							
1-5/8"							
	Demolish	L.F.		.38		.38	Cost includes material and labor to
	Install	L.F.	.69	.84		1.53	install 1/2" x 1-5/8" oak base
	Demolish and Install	L.F.	.69	1.22		1.91	molding.
	Reinstall	L.F.		.67		.67	
	Clean	L.F.	.02	.12		.14	
	Paint	L.F.	.07	.38		.45	
	Minimum Charge	Job		142		142	
2-1/2"							
	Demolish	L.F.		.38		.38	Cost includes material and labor to
	Install	L.F.	1.06	.86		1.92	install 1/2" x 2-1/2" oak base
	Demolish and Install	L.F.	1.06	1.24		2.30	molding.
	Reinstall	L.F.		.69		.69	
	Clean	L.F.	.02	.12		.14	
	Paint	L.F.	.08	.39		.47	
	Minimum Charge	Job		142		142	
3-1/2"							
	Demolish	L.F.		.38		.38	Cost includes material and labor to
	Install	L.F.	2.09	.88		2.97	install 1/2" x 3-1/2" oak base
	Demolish and Install	L.F.	2.09	1.26		3.35	molding.
	Reinstall	L.F.		.70		.70	
	Clean	L.F.	.02	.12		.14	
	Paint	L.F.	.08	.39		.47	
	Minimum Charge	Job		142		142	

Base Molding		Unit	Material	Labor	Equip.	Total	Specification
6"							
	Demolish	L.F.		.38		.38	Cost includes material and labor to
	Install	L.F.	2.26	1		3.26	install 1" x 6" oak base molding.
	Demolish and Install	L.F.	2.26	1.38		3.64	
	Reinstall	L.F.		.80		.80	
	Clean	L.F.	.03	.21		.24	
	Paint	L.F.	.08	.41		.49	
	Minimum Charge	Job		142		142	
8"							
	Demolish	L.F.		.46		.46	Cost includes material and labor to
	Install	L.F.	2.76	1.10		3.86	install 1" x 8" oak base molding.
	Demolish and Install	L.F.	2.76	1.56		4.32	
	Reinstall	L.F.		.88		.88	
	Clean	L.F.	.03	.21		.24	
	Paint	L.F.	.08	.43		.51	
	Minimum Charge	Job		142		142	

Vinyl Base Molding

		Unit	Material	Labor	Equip.	Total	Specification
2-1/2"							
	Demolish	L.F.		.38		.38	Cost includes material and labor to
	Install	L.F.	.45	.84		1.29	install 2-1/2" vinyl or rubber cove
	Demolish and Install	L.F.	.45	1.22		1.67	base including adhesive.
	Reinstall	L.F.		.84		.84	
	Clean	L.F.		.19		.19	
	Minimum Charge	Job		133		133	
4"							
	Demolish	L.F.		.38		.38	Cost includes material and labor to
	Install	L.F.	.52	.84		1.36	install 4" vinyl or rubber cove base
	Demolish and Install	L.F.	.52	1.22		1.74	including adhesive.
	Reinstall	L.F.		.84		.84	
	Clean	L.F.		.19		.19	
	Minimum Charge	Job		133		133	
6"							
	Demolish	L.F.		.38		.38	Cost includes material and labor to
	Install	L.F.	.83	.84		1.67	install 6" vinyl or rubber cove base
	Demolish and Install	L.F.	.83	1.22		2.05	including adhesive.
	Reinstall	L.F.		.84		.84	
	Clean	L.F.		.19		.19	
	Minimum Charge	Job		133		133	

Prefinished

		Unit	Material	Labor	Equip.	Total	Specification
	Demolish	L.F.		.38		.38	Cost includes material and labor to
	Install	L.F.	1.69	.91		2.60	install 9/16" x 3-5/16" prefinished
	Demolish and Install	L.F.	1.69	1.29		2.98	base molding.
	Reinstall	L.F.		.73		.73	
	Clean	L.F.	.02	.12		.14	
	Paint	L.F.	.03	.30		.33	
	Minimum Charge	Job		142		142	

Shoe

		Unit	Material	Labor	Equip.	Total	Specification
	Demolish	L.F.		.38		.38	Includes material and labor to install
	Install	L.F.	.22	.84		1.06	pine or birch base molding.
	Demolish and Install	L.F.	.22	1.22		1.44	
	Reinstall	L.F.		.67		.67	
	Clean	L.F.	.02	.12		.14	
	Paint	L.F.	.12	.41		.53	
	Minimum Charge	Job		142		142	

Finish Carpentry

Base Molding

Base Molding	Unit	Material	Labor	Equip.	Total	Specification
Carpeted						
Demolish	L.F.		.15		.15	Includes material and labor to install
Install	L.F.	1.13	1.60		2.73	carpet baseboard with adhesive.
Demolish and Install	L.F.	1.13	1.75		2.88	
Reinstall	L.F.		1.28		1.28	
Clean	L.F.		.08		.08	
Minimum Charge	Job		132		132	
Ceramic Tile						
Demolish	L.F.		.84		.84	Includes material and labor to install
Install	L.F.	3.32	3.70		7.02	thin set ceramic tile cove base
Demolish and Install	L.F.	3.32	4.54		7.86	including grout.
Clean	L.F.		.39		.39	
Minimum Charge	Job		132		132	
Quarry Tile						
Demolish	L.F.		.84		.84	Includes material and labor to install
Install	L.F.	4.18	4.31		8.49	quarry tile base including grout.
Demolish and Install	L.F.	4.18	5.15		9.33	
Clean	L.F.		.39		.39	
Minimum Charge	Job		132		132	
Caulk and Renail						
Install	L.F.	.01	.45		.46	Includes labor and material to renail
Minimum Charge	Job		142		142	base and caulk where necessary.

Molding

Molding	Unit	Material	Labor	Equip.	Total	Specification
Oak Base						
Demolish	L.F.		.38		.38	Cost includes material and labor to
Install	L.F.	1.06	.86		1.92	install 1/2" x 2-1/2" oak base
Demolish and Install	L.F.	1.06	1.24		2.30	molding.
Reinstall	L.F.		.69		.69	
Clean	L.F.	.02	.12		.14	
Paint	L.F.	.08	.39		.47	
Minimum Charge	Job		142		142	
Shoe						
Demolish	L.F.		.38		.38	Includes material and labor to install
Install	L.F.	.22	.84		1.06	pine or birch base molding.
Demolish and Install	L.F.	.22	1.22		1.44	
Reinstall	L.F.		.67		.67	
Clean	L.F.	.02	.12		.14	
Paint	L.F.	.12	.41		.53	
Minimum Charge	Job		142		142	
Quarter Round						
Demolish	L.F.		.38		.38	Includes material and labor to install
Install	L.F.	.46	1.12		1.58	pine base quarter round molding.
Demolish and Install	L.F.	.46	1.50		1.96	
Reinstall	L.F.		.89		.89	
Clean	L.F.	.02	.12		.14	
Paint	L.F.	.06	.64		.70	
Minimum Charge	Job		142		142	
Chair Rail						
Demolish	L.F.		.38		.38	Cost includes material and labor to
Install	L.F.	.94	1.05		1.99	install 5/8" x 2-1/2" oak chair rail
Demolish and Install	L.F.	.94	1.43		2.37	molding.
Reinstall	L.F.		.84		.84	
Clean	L.F.	.02	.12		.14	
Paint	L.F.	.06	.64		.70	
Minimum Charge	Job		142		142	

Finish Carpentry

Molding		Unit	Material	Labor	Equip.	Total	Specification
Crown							
	Demolish	L.F.		.38		.38	Includes material and labor to install
	Install	L.F.	1.67	1.14		2.81	unfinished pine crown molding.
	Demolish and Install	L.F.	1.67	1.52		3.19	
	Reinstall	L.F.		.91		.91	
	Clean	L.F.	.03	.16		.19	
	Paint	L.F.	.06	.64		.70	
	Minimum Charge	Job		142		142	
Cove							
	Demolish	L.F.		.38		.38	Cost includes material and labor to
	Install	L.F.	1.28	1.12		2.40	install 1/2" x 2-3/4" pine cove
	Demolish and Install	L.F.	1.28	1.50		2.78	molding.
	Reinstall	L.F.		.89		.89	
	Clean	L.F.	.02	.12		.14	
	Paint	L.F.	.06	.64		.70	
	Minimum Charge	Job		142		142	
Corner							
	Demolish	L.F.		.38		.38	Includes material and labor to install
	Install	L.F.	.56	.45		1.01	inside or outside pine corner molding.
	Demolish and Install	L.F.	.56	.83		1.39	
	Reinstall	L.F.		.36		.36	
	Clean	L.F.	.02	.12		.14	
	Paint	L.F.	.06	.64		.70	
	Minimum Charge	Job		142		142	
Picture							
	Demolish	L.F.		.38		.38	Cost includes material and labor to
	Install	L.F.	.75	1.19		1.94	install 9/16" x 2-1/2" pine casing.
	Demolish and Install	L.F.	.75	1.57		2.32	
	Reinstall	L.F.		.95		.95	
	Clean	L.F.	.02	.12		.14	
	Paint	L.F.	.06	.64		.70	
	Minimum Charge	Job		142		142	
Single Cased Opening							
	Demolish	Ea.		19.80		19.80	Includes material and labor to install
	Install	Ea.	13.35	17.80		31.15	flat pine jamb with square cut heads
	Demolish and Install	Ea.	13.35	37.60		50.95	and rabbeted sides for 6' 8" high
	Clean	Ea.	.20	4.31		4.51	opening including trim sets for both
	Paint	Ea.	.99	6.40		7.39	sides.
	Minimum Charge	Job		142		142	
Double Cased Opening							
	Demolish	Ea.		19.80		19.80	Includes material and labor to install
	Install	Ea.	27	20.50		47.50	flat pine jamb with square cut heads
	Demolish and Install	Ea.	27	40.30		67.30	and rabbeted sides for 6' 8" high
	Clean	Ea.	.23	5.05		5.28	opening including trim sets for both
	Paint	Ea.	1.14	7.50		8.64	sides.
	Minimum Charge	Job		142		142	

Window Trim Set		Unit	Material	Labor	Equip.	Total	Specification
Single							
	Demolish	Ea.		5.10		5.10	Cost includes material and labor to
	Install	Opng.	28	28.50		56.50	install 11/16" x 2-1/2" pine ranch
	Demolish and Install	Opng.	28	33.60		61.60	style window casing.
	Reinstall	Opng.		22.78		22.78	
	Clean	Ea.	.28	2.95		3.23	
	Paint	Ea.	.92	6.10		7.02	
	Minimum Charge	Job		142		142	

Finish Carpentry

Window Trim Set

	Unit	Material	Labor	Equip.	Total	Specification
Double						
Demolish	Ea.		5.75		5.75	Cost includes material and labor to
Install	Ea.	32	35.50		67.50	install 11/16" x 2-1/2" pine ranch
Demolish and Install	Ea.	32	41.25		73.25	style trim for casing one side of a
Reinstall	Ea.		28.48		28.48	double window opening.
Clean	Ea.	.51	3.45		3.96	
Paint	Ea.	1.55	10.20		11.75	
Minimum Charge	Job		142		142	
Triple						
Demolish	Ea.		6.55		6.55	Cost includes material and labor to
Install	Opng.	42	47.50		89.50	install 11/16" x 2-1/2" pine ranch
Demolish and Install	Opng.	42	54.05		96.05	style trim for casing one side of a triple
Reinstall	Opng.		37.97		37.97	window opening.
Clean	Ea.	.70	4.14		4.84	
Paint	Ea.	2.17	14.20		16.37	
Minimum Charge	Job		142		142	
Window Casing Per L.F.						
Demolish	L.F.		.38		.38	Cost includes material and labor to
Install	L.F.	.86	1.19		2.05	install 11/16" x 2-1/2" pine ranch
Demolish and Install	L.F.	.86	1.57		2.43	style trim for casing.
Reinstall	L.F.		.95		.95	
Clean	L.F.	.02	.12		.14	
Paint	L.F.	.06	.64		.70	
Minimum Charge	Job		142		142	

Window Sill

	Unit	Material	Labor	Equip.	Total	Specification
Wood						
Demolish	L.F.		.38		.38	Includes material and labor to install
Install	L.F.	1.44	1.42		2.86	flat, wood window stool.
Demolish and Install	L.F.	1.44	1.80		3.24	
Reinstall	L.F.		1.14		1.14	
Clean	L.F.	.02	.12		.14	
Paint	L.F.	.06	.64		.70	
Minimum Charge	Job		142		142	
Marble						
Demolish	L.F.		.57		.57	Includes material and labor to install
Install	L.F.	7.80	5.95		13.75	marble window sills, 6" x 3/4" thick.
Demolish and Install	L.F.	7.80	6.52		14.32	
Reinstall	L.F.		4.77		4.77	
Clean	L.F.	.02	.12		.14	
Minimum Charge	Job		132		132	

Shelving

	Unit	Material	Labor	Equip.	Total	Specification
Pine						
18"						
Demolish	L.F.		.66		.66	Cost includes material and labor to
Install	L.F.	6.90	3		9.90	install 1" thick custom shelving board
Demolish and Install	L.F.	6.90	3.66		10.56	18" wide.
Reinstall	L.F.		2.40		2.40	
Clean	L.F.	.04	.34		.38	
Paint	L.F.	.72	.40		1.12	
Minimum Charge	Job		142		142	

Finish Carpentry

Shelving		Unit	Material	Labor	Equip.	Total	Specification
24"							
	Demolish	L.F.		.66		.66	Cost includes material and labor to
	Install	L.F.	9.20	3.35		12.55	install 1" thick custom shelving board.
	Demolish and Install	L.F.	9.20	4.01		13.21	
	Reinstall	L.F.		2.68		2.68	
	Clean	L.F.	.06	.52		.58	
	Paint	L.F.	.97	.54		1.51	
	Minimum Charge	Job		142		142	
Particle Board							
	Demolish	L.F.		.60		.60	Cost includes material and labor to
	Install	L.F.	1.17	1.50		2.67	install 3/4" thick particle shelving
	Demolish and Install	L.F.	1.17	2.10		3.27	board 18" wide.
	Reinstall	L.F.		1.20		1.20	
	Clean	L.F.	.04	.34		.38	
	Paint	S.F.	.10	.59		.69	
	Minimum Charge	Job		142		142	
Plywood							
	Demolish	L.F.		.60		.60	Cost includes material and labor to
	Install	L.F.	2.04	4.38		6.42	install 3/4" thick plywood shelving
	Demolish and Install	L.F.	2.04	4.98		7.02	board.
	Reinstall	L.F.		3.51		3.51	
	Clean	L.F.	.04	.34		.38	
	Paint	S.F.	.10	.59		.69	
	Minimum Charge	Job		142		142	
Hardwood (oak)							
	Demolish	L.F.		.60		.60	Includes material and labor to install
	Install	L.F.	7.85	1.96		9.81	oak shelving, 1" x 12", incl. cleats and
	Demolish and Install	L.F.	7.85	2.56		10.41	bracing.
	Reinstall	L.F.		1.57		1.57	
	Clean	L.F.	.04	.34		.38	
	Paint	S.F.	.10	.59		.69	
	Minimum Charge	Job		142		142	
Custom Bookcase							
	Demolish	L.F.		7.65		7.65	Includes material and labor to install
	Install	L.F.	26	28.50		54.50	custom modular bookcase unit with
	Demolish and Install	L.F.	26	36.15		62.15	clear pine faced frames, shelves 12"
	Reinstall	L.F.		22.78		22.78	O.C., 7' high, 8" deep.
	Clean	L.F.	1.12	7.40		8.52	
	Paint	L.F.	.92	19.65		20.57	
	Minimum Charge	Job		142		142	
Glass							
	Demolish	L.F.		.60		.60	Includes material and labor to install
	Install	L.F.	22	1.96		23.96	glass shelving, 1" x 12", incl. cleats
	Demolish and Install	L.F.	22	2.56		24.56	and bracing.
	Reinstall	L.F.		1.57		1.57	
	Clean	L.F.	.06	.32		.38	
	Minimum Charge	Job		141		141	

Closet Shelving		Unit	Material	Labor	Equip.	Total	Specification
Closet Shelf and Rod							
	Demolish	L.F.		.60		.60	Cost includes material and labor to
	Install	L.F.	2.98	4.75		7.73	install 1" thick custom shelving board
	Demolish and Install	L.F.	2.98	5.35		8.33	18" wide and 1" diameter clothes pole
	Reinstall	L.F.		3.80		3.80	with brackets 3' O.C.
	Clean	L.F.	.03	.26		.29	
	Paint	L.F.	.11	.64		.75	
	Minimum Charge	Job		142		142	

Finish Carpentry

Closet Shelving

	Unit	Material	Labor	Equip.	Total	Specification
Clothing Rod						
Demolish	L.F.		.40		.40	Includes material and labor to install fir
Install	L.F.	1.32	1.42		2.74	closet pole, 1-5/8″ diameter.
Demolish and Install	L.F.	1.32	1.82		3.14	
Reinstall	L.F.		1.14		1.14	
Clean	L.F.	.03	.36		.39	
Paint	L.F.	.12	.70		.82	
Minimum Charge	Job		142		142	

Stair Assemblies

	Unit	Material	Labor	Equip.	Total	Specification
Straight Hardwood						
Demolish	Ea.		276		276	Includes material and labor to install
Install	Flight	855	190		1045	factory cut and assembled straight
Demolish and Install	Flight	855	466		1321	closed box stairs with oak treads and
Clean	Flight	2.81	18.10		20.91	prefinished stair rail with balusters.
Paint	Flight	9.95	34		43.95	
Minimum Charge	Job		142		142	
Clear Oak Tread						
Demolish	Ea.		7.20		7.20	Includes material and labor to install
Install	Ea.	25.50	15.80		41.30	clear oak treads per riser.
Demolish and Install	Ea.	25.50	23		48.50	
Clean	Ea.	.09	1.81		1.90	
Paint	Ea.	.33	1.89		2.22	
Minimum Charge	Job		142		142	
Landing						
Demolish	S.F.		2.39		2.39	Includes material and labor to install
Install	S.F.	8.60	15.80		24.40	clear oak landing.
Demolish and Install	S.F.	8.60	18.19		26.79	
Clean	S.F.		.26		.26	
Paint	S.F.	.25	.63		.88	
Minimum Charge	Job		142		142	
Refinish / Stain						
Install	S.F.	1.08	1.59		2.67	Includes labor and material to sand
Minimum Charge	Job		128		128	and finish (3 passes) with two coats of
						urethane on a new floor.
Spiral Hardwood						
Demolish	Ea.		276		276	Cost includes material and labor to
Install	Flight	4400	380		4780	install 4′ - 6′ diameter spiral stairs with
Demolish and Install	Flight	4400	656		5056	oak treads, factory cut and assembled
Clean	Flight	2.81	18.10		20.91	with double handrails.
Paint	Flight	9.95	34		43.95	
Minimum Charge	Job		142		142	
Curved Hardwood						
Demolish	Ea.		276		276	Includes material and labor to install
Install	Flight	7025	815		7840	curved stairs open on one side with
Demolish and Install	Flight	7025	1091		8116	clear oak treads and handrail.
Clean	Flight	2.81	18.10		20.91	
Paint	Flight	9.95	34		43.95	
Minimum Charge	Job		142		142	

Finish Carpentry

Stairs

	Unit	Material	Labor	Equip.	Total	Specification
Disappearing						
Demolish	Ea.		14.35		14.35	Includes material and labor to install a
Install	Ea.	108	81.50		189.50	folding staircase.
Demolish and Install	Ea.	108	95.85		203.85	
Reinstall	Ea.		65.10		65.10	
Clean	Ea.	.42	12.95		13.37	
Minimum Charge	Job		142		142	

Stair Components

	Unit	Material	Labor	Equip.	Total	Specification
Handrail w / Balusters						
Demolish	L.F.		1.91		1.91	Includes material and labor to install
Install	L.F.	29.50	5.95		35.45	prefinished assembled stair rail with
Demolish and Install	L.F.	29.50	7.86		37.36	brackets, turned balusters and newel.
Clean	L.F.	.56	1.43		1.99	
Paint	L.F.	1.32	3		4.32	
Minimum Charge	Job		142		142	
Bannister						
Demolish	L.F.		1.15		1.15	Includes material and labor to install
Install	L.F.	7.15	4.75		11.90	built-up oak railings.
Demolish and Install	L.F.	7.15	5.90		13.05	
Clean	L.F.	.56	1.29		1.85	
Paint	L.F.	1.32	2.32		3.64	
Minimum Charge	Job		142		142	

Wall and Base Cabinets

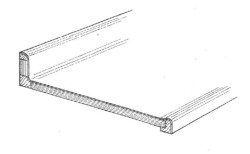

Countertop

Wall Cabinets	Unit	Material	Labor	Equip.	Total	Specification
Good Grade Laminated						
12" Wide, 1 Door						
Demolish	Ea.		5.75		5.75	Includes material and labor to install
Install	Ea.	98.50	26		124.50	good modular unit with melamine
Demolish and Install	Ea.	98.50	31.75		130.25	laminated to particle board, in textured
Reinstall	Ea.		20.71		20.71	colors or wood grain print finish,
Clean	Ea.	.42	3.98		4.40	hinges and pulls.
Paint	Ea.	.40	9.10		9.50	
Minimum Charge	Job		142		142	
15" Wide, 1 Door						
Demolish	Ea.		7.20		7.20	Includes material and labor to install
Install	Ea.	111	26.50		137.50	good modular unit with melamine
Demolish and Install	Ea.	111	33.70		144.70	laminated to particle board, in textured
Reinstall	Ea.		21.29		21.29	colors or wood grain print finish,
Clean	Ea.	.53	4.92		5.45	hinges and pulls.
Paint	Ea.	.50	11.60		12.10	
Minimum Charge	Job		142		142	
18" Wide, 1 Door						
Demolish	Ea.		8.65		8.65	Includes material and labor to install
Install	Ea.	123	27.50		150.50	good modular unit with melamine
Demolish and Install	Ea.	123	36.15		159.15	laminated to particle board, in textured
Reinstall	Ea.		21.80		21.80	colors or wood grain print finish,
Clean	Ea.	.63	5.90		6.53	hinges and pulls.
Paint	Ea.	.59	13.45		14.04	
Minimum Charge	Job		142		142	
21" Wide, 1 Door						
Demolish	Ea.		10		10	Includes material and labor to install
Install	Ea.	151	27.50		178.50	good modular unit with melamine
Demolish and Install	Ea.	151	37.50		188.50	laminated to particle board, in textured
Reinstall	Ea.		22.12		22.12	colors or wood grain print finish,
Clean	Ea.	.74	6.90		7.64	hinges and pulls.
Paint	Ea.	.69	15.95		16.64	
Minimum Charge	Job		142		142	
24" w / Blind Corner						
Demolish	Ea.		11.50		11.50	Includes material and labor to install
Install	Ea.	136	28		164	good modular unit with melamine
Demolish and Install	Ea.	136	39.50		175.50	laminated to particle board, in textured
Reinstall	Ea.		22.45		22.45	colors or wood grain print finish,
Clean	Ea.	.84	7.95		8.79	hinges and pulls.
Paint	Ea.	.79	18.25		19.04	
Minimum Charge	Job		142		142	

Cabinets and Countertops

Wall Cabinets		Unit	Material	Labor	Equip.	Total	Specification
27" Wide, 2 Door							
	Demolish	Ea.		12.75		12.75	Includes material and labor to install
	Install	Ea.	175	29		204	good modular unit with melamine
	Demolish and Install	Ea.	175	41.75		216.75	laminated to particle board, in textured
	Reinstall	Ea.		23.01		23.01	colors or wood grain print finish,
	Clean	Ea.	.95	9		9.95	hinges and pulls.
	Paint	Ea.	.90	21.50		22.40	
	Minimum Charge	Job		142		142	
30" Wide, 2 Door							
	Demolish	Ea.		14.35		14.35	Includes material and labor to install
	Install	Ea.	166	29.50		195.50	good modular unit with melamine
	Demolish and Install	Ea.	166	43.85		209.85	laminated to particle board, in textured
	Reinstall	Ea.		23.61		23.61	colors or wood grain print finish,
	Clean	Ea.	1.06	9.85		10.91	hinges and pulls.
	Paint	Ea.	.99	23		23.99	
	Minimum Charge	Job		142		142	
36" Wide, 2 Door							
	Demolish	Ea.		17		17	Includes material and labor to install
	Install	Ea.	190	30.50		220.50	good modular unit with melamine
	Demolish and Install	Ea.	190	47.50		237.50	laminated to particle board, in textured
	Reinstall	Ea.		24.24		24.24	colors or wood grain print finish,
	Clean	Ea.	1.27	12.15		13.42	hinges and pulls.
	Paint	Ea.	1.20	28.50		29.70	
	Minimum Charge	Job		142		142	
48" Wide, 2 Door							
	Demolish	Ea.		23		23	Includes material and labor to install
	Install	Ea.	233	31		264	good modular unit with melamine
	Demolish and Install	Ea.	233	54		287	laminated to particle board, in textured
	Reinstall	Ea.		24.77		24.77	colors or wood grain print finish,
	Clean	Ea.	1.68	15.90		17.58	hinges and pulls.
	Paint	Ea.	1.60	36.50		38.10	
	Minimum Charge	Job		142		142	
Above-Appliance							
	Demolish	Ea.		14.35		14.35	Includes material and labor to install
	Install	Ea.	117	23		140	good modular unit with melamine
	Demolish and Install	Ea.	117	37.35		154.35	laminated to particle board, in textured
	Reinstall	Ea.		18.37		18.37	colors or wood grain print finish,
	Clean	Ea.	1.06	9.85		10.91	hinges and pulls.
	Paint	Ea.	.99	23		23.99	
	Minimum Charge	Job		142		142	
Better Grade Wood							
12" Wide, 1 Door							
	Demolish	Ea.		5.75		5.75	Includes material and labor to install
	Install	Ea.	132	26		158	custom modular unit with solid
	Demolish and Install	Ea.	132	31.75		163.75	hardwood faced frames, hardwood
	Reinstall	Ea.		20.71		20.71	door frames and drawer fronts,
	Clean	Ea.	.42	3.98		4.40	hardwood veneer on raised door
	Paint	Ea.	.40	9.80		10.20	panels, hinges and pulls.
	Minimum Charge	Job		142		142	
15" Wide, 1 Door							
	Demolish	Ea.		7.20		7.20	Includes material and labor to install
	Install	Ea.	149	26.50		175.50	custom modular unit with solid
	Demolish and Install	Ea.	149	33.70		182.70	hardwood faced frames, hardwood
	Reinstall	Ea.		21.29		21.29	door frames and drawer fronts,
	Clean	Ea.	.53	4.92		5.45	hardwood veneer on raised door
	Paint	Ea.	.50	12.15		12.65	panels, hinges and pulls.
	Minimum Charge	Job		142		142	

Cabinets and Countertops

Wall Cabinets	Unit	Material	Labor	Equip.	Total	Specification
18″ Wide, 1 Door						
Demolish	Ea.		8.65		8.65	Includes material and labor to install
Install	Ea.	164	27.50		191.50	custom modular unit with solid
Demolish and Install	Ea.	164	36.15		200.15	hardwood faced frames, hardwood
Reinstall	Ea.		21.80		21.80	door frames and drawer fronts,
Clean	Ea.	.63	5.90		6.53	hardwood veneer on raised door
Paint	Ea.	.59	15		15.59	panels, hinges and pulls.
Minimum Charge	Job		142		142	
21″ Wide, 1 Door						
Demolish	Ea.		10		10	Includes material and labor to install
Install	Ea.	202	27.50		229.50	custom modular unit with solid
Demolish and Install	Ea.	202	37.50		239.50	hardwood faced frames, hardwood
Reinstall	Ea.		22.12		22.12	door frames and drawer fronts,
Clean	Ea.	.74	6.90		7.64	hardwood veneer on raised door
Paint	Ea.	.69	17		17.69	panels, hinges and pulls.
Minimum Charge	Job		142		142	
24″ w / Blind Corner						
Demolish	Ea.		11.50		11.50	Includes material and labor to install
Install	Ea.	183	28		211	custom modular unit with solid
Demolish and Install	Ea.	183	39.50		222.50	hardwood faced frames, hardwood
Reinstall	Ea.		22.45		22.45	door frames and drawer fronts,
Clean	Ea.	.84	7.95		8.79	hardwood veneer on raised door
Paint	Ea.	.79	19.65		20.44	panels, hinges and pulls.
Minimum Charge	Job		142		142	
27″ Wide, 2 Door						
Demolish	Ea.		12.75		12.75	Includes material and labor to install
Install	Ea.	206	29		235	custom modular unit with solid
Demolish and Install	Ea.	206	41.75		247.75	hardwood faced frames, hardwood
Reinstall	Ea.		23.01		23.01	door frames and drawer fronts,
Clean	Ea.	.95	9		9.95	hardwood veneer on raised door
Paint	Ea.	.90	21.50		22.40	panels, hinges and pulls.
Minimum Charge	Job		142		142	
30″ Wide, 2 Door						
Demolish	Ea.		14.35		14.35	Includes material and labor to install
Install	Ea.	221	29.50		250.50	custom modular unit with solid
Demolish and Install	Ea.	221	43.85		264.85	hardwood faced frames, hardwood
Reinstall	Ea.		23.61		23.61	door frames and drawer fronts,
Clean	Ea.	1.06	9.85		10.91	hardwood veneer on raised door
Paint	Ea.	.99	25.50		26.49	panels, hinges and pulls.
Minimum Charge	Job		142		142	
36″ Wide, 2 Door						
Demolish	Ea.		17		17	Includes material and labor to install
Install	Ea.	254	30.50		284.50	custom modular unit with solid
Demolish and Install	Ea.	254	47.50		301.50	hardwood faced frames, hardwood
Reinstall	Ea.		24.24		24.24	door frames and drawer fronts,
Clean	Ea.	1.27	12.15		13.42	hardwood veneer on raised door
Paint	Ea.	1.20	28.50		29.70	panels, hinges and pulls.
Minimum Charge	Job		142		142	
48″ Wide, 2 Door						
Demolish	Ea.		23		23	Includes material and labor to install
Install	Ea.	310	31		341	custom modular unit with solid
Demolish and Install	Ea.	310	54		364	hardwood faced frames, hardwood
Reinstall	Ea.		24.77		24.77	door frames and drawer fronts,
Clean	Ea.	1.68	15.90		17.58	hardwood veneer on raised door
Paint	Ea.	1.60	36.50		38.10	panels, hinges and pulls.
Minimum Charge	Job		142		142	

Cabinets and Countertops

Wall Cabinets	Unit	Material	Labor	Equip.	Total	Specification
Above-appliance						
Demolish	Ea.		14.35		14.35	Includes material and labor to install
Install	Ea.	151	23		174	custom modular unit with solid
Demolish and Install	Ea.	151	37.35		188.35	hardwood faced frames, hardwood
Reinstall	Ea.		18.37		18.37	door frames and drawer fronts,
Clean	Ea.	1.06	9.85		10.91	hardwood veneer on raised door
Paint	Ea.	.99	25.50		26.49	panels, hinges and pulls.
Minimum Charge	Job		142		142	
Premium Grade Wood						
12″ Wide, 1 Door						
Demolish	Ea.		5.75		5.75	Includes material and labor to install
Install	Ea.	174	26		200	premium modular unit with solid
Demolish and Install	Ea.	174	31.75		205.75	hardwood faced frames, hardwood
Reinstall	Ea.		20.71		20.71	door frames and drawer fronts,
Clean	Ea.	.42	3.98		4.40	hardwood veneer on raised door
Paint	Ea.	.40	10.65		11.05	panels, hinges and pulls.
Minimum Charge	Job		142		142	
15″ Wide, 1 Door						
Demolish	Ea.		7.20		7.20	Includes material and labor to install
Install	Ea.	198	26.50		224.50	premium modular unit with solid
Demolish and Install	Ea.	198	33.70		231.70	hardwood faced frames, hardwood
Reinstall	Ea.		21.29		21.29	door frames and drawer fronts,
Clean	Ea.	.53	4.92		5.45	hardwood veneer on raised door
Paint	Ea.	.50	13.45		13.95	panels, hinges and pulls.
Minimum Charge	Job		142		142	
18″ Wide, 1 Door						
Demolish	Ea.		8.65		8.65	Includes material and labor to install
Install	Ea.	213	27.50		240.50	premium modular unit with solid
Demolish and Install	Ea.	213	36.15		249.15	hardwood faced frames, hardwood
Reinstall	Ea.		21.80		21.80	door frames and drawer fronts,
Clean	Ea.	.63	5.90		6.53	hardwood veneer on raised door
Paint	Ea.	.59	15.95		16.54	panels, hinges and pulls.
Minimum Charge	Job		142		142	
21″ Wide, 1 Door						
Demolish	Ea.		10		10	Includes material and labor to install
Install	Ea.	244	27.50		271.50	premium modular unit with solid
Demolish and Install	Ea.	244	37.50		281.50	hardwood faced frames, hardwood
Reinstall	Ea.		22.12		22.12	door frames and drawer fronts,
Clean	Ea.	.74	6.90		7.64	hardwood veneer on raised door
Paint	Ea.	.69	18.25		18.94	panels, hinges and pulls.
Minimum Charge	Job		142		142	
24″ w / Blind Corner						
Demolish	Ea.		11.50		11.50	Includes material and labor to install
Install	Ea.	249	28		277	premium modular unit with solid
Demolish and Install	Ea.	249	39.50		288.50	hardwood faced frames, hardwood
Reinstall	Ea.		22.45		22.45	door frames and drawer fronts,
Clean	Ea.	.84	7.95		8.79	hardwood veneer on raised door
Paint	Ea.	.79	21.50		22.29	panels, hinges and pulls.
Minimum Charge	Job		142		142	
27″ Wide, 2 Door						
Demolish	Ea.		12.75		12.75	Includes material and labor to install
Install	Ea.	229	29		258	premium modular unit with solid
Demolish and Install	Ea.	229	41.75		270.75	hardwood faced frames, hardwood
Reinstall	Ea.		23.01		23.01	door frames and drawer fronts,
Clean	Ea.	.95	9		9.95	hardwood veneer on raised door
Paint	Ea.	.90	23		23.90	panels, hinges and pulls.
Minimum Charge	Job		142		142	

Cabinets and Countertops

Wall Cabinets		Unit	Material	Labor	Equip.	Total	Specification
30" Wide, 2 Door							
	Demolish	Ea.		14.35		14.35	Includes material and labor to install
	Install	Ea.	283	29.50		312.50	premium modular unit with solid
	Demolish and Install	Ea.	283	43.85		326.85	hardwood faced frames, hardwood
	Reinstall	Ea.		23.61		23.61	door frames and drawer fronts,
	Clean	Ea.	1.06	9.85		10.91	hardwood veneer on raised door
	Paint	Ea.	.99	25.50		26.49	panels, hinges and pulls.
	Minimum Charge	Job		142		142	
36" Wide, 2 Door							
	Demolish	Ea.		17		17	Includes material and labor to install
	Install	Ea.	325	30.50		355.50	premium modular unit with solid
	Demolish and Install	Ea.	325	47.50		372.50	hardwood faced frames, hardwood
	Reinstall	Ea.		24.24		24.24	door frames and drawer fronts,
	Clean	Ea.	1.27	12.15		13.42	hardwood veneer on raised door
	Paint	Ea.	1.20	32		33.20	panels, hinges and pulls.
	Minimum Charge	Job		142		142	
48" Wide, 2 Door							
	Demolish	Ea.		23		23	Includes material and labor to install
	Install	Ea.	400	31		431	premium modular unit with solid
	Demolish and Install	Ea.	400	54		454	hardwood faced frames, hardwood
	Reinstall	Ea.		24.77		24.77	door frames and drawer fronts,
	Clean	Ea.	1.68	15.90		17.58	hardwood veneer on raised door
	Paint	Ea.	1.60	42.50		44.10	panels, hinges and pulls.
	Minimum Charge	Job		142		142	
Above-appliance							
	Demolish	Ea.		14.35		14.35	Includes material and labor to install
	Install	Ea.	189	23		212	premium modular unit with solid
	Demolish and Install	Ea.	189	37.35		226.35	hardwood faced frames, hardwood
	Reinstall	Ea.		18.37		18.37	door frames and drawer fronts,
	Clean	Ea.	1.06	9.85		10.91	hardwood veneer on raised door
	Paint	Ea.	.99	25.50		26.49	panels, hinges, pulls.
	Minimum Charge	Job		142		142	
Premium Hardwood							
12" Wide, 1 Door							
	Demolish	Ea.		5.75		5.75	Includes material and labor to install
	Install	Ea.	202	26		228	premium hardwood modular unit with
	Demolish and Install	Ea.	202	31.75		233.75	solid hardwood faced frames, drawer
	Reinstall	Ea.		20.71		20.71	fronts, and door panels, steel drawer
	Clean	Ea.	.42	3.98		4.40	guides, hinges, pulls, laminated
	Paint	Ea.	.40	11.60		12	interior.
	Minimum Charge	Job		142		142	
15" Wide, 1 Door							
	Demolish	Ea.		7.20		7.20	Includes material and labor to install
	Install	Ea.	260	26.50		286.50	premium hardwood modular unit with
	Demolish and Install	Ea.	260	33.70		293.70	solid hardwood faced frames, drawer
	Reinstall	Ea.		21.29		21.29	fronts, and door panels, steel drawer
	Clean	Ea.	.53	4.92		5.45	guides, hinges, pulls, laminated
	Paint	Ea.	.50	14.20		14.70	interior.
	Minimum Charge	Job		142		142	
18" Wide, 1 Door							
	Demolish	Ea.		8.65		8.65	Includes material and labor to install
	Install	Ea.	242	27.50		269.50	premium hardwood modular unit with
	Demolish and Install	Ea.	242	36.15		278.15	solid hardwood faced frames, drawer
	Reinstall	Ea.		21.80		21.80	fronts, and door panels, steel drawer
	Clean	Ea.	.63	5.90		6.53	guides, hinges, pulls, laminated
	Paint	Ea.	.59	17		17.59	interior.
	Minimum Charge	Job		142		142	

Cabinets and Countertops

Wall Cabinets	Unit	Material	Labor	Equip.	Total	Specification
21" Wide, 1 Door						
Demolish	Ea.		10		10	Includes material and labor to install
Install	Ea.	263	27.50		290.50	premium hardwood modular unit with
Demolish and Install	Ea.	263	37.50		300.50	solid hardwood faced frames, drawer
Reinstall	Ea.		22.12		22.12	fronts, and door panels, steel drawer
Clean	Ea.	.74	6.90		7.64	guides, hinges, pulls, laminated
Paint	Ea.	.69	19.65		20.34	interior.
Minimum Charge	Job		142		142	
24" w / Blind Corner						
Demolish	Ea.		11.50		11.50	Includes material and labor to install
Install	Ea.	277	28		305	premium hardwood modular unit with
Demolish and Install	Ea.	277	39.50		316.50	solid hardwood faced frames, drawer
Reinstall	Ea.		22.45		22.45	fronts, and door panels, steel drawer
Clean	Ea.	.84	7.95		8.79	guides, hinges, pulls, laminated
Paint	Ea.	.79	23		23.79	interior.
Minimum Charge	Job		142		142	
27" Wide, 2 Door						
Demolish	Ea.		12.75		12.75	Includes material and labor to install
Install	Ea.	470	29		499	premium hardwood modular unit with
Demolish and Install	Ea.	470	41.75		511.75	solid hardwood faced frames, drawer
Reinstall	Ea.		23.01		23.01	fronts, and door panels, steel drawer
Clean	Ea.	.95	9		9.95	guides, hinges, pulls, laminated
Paint	Ea.	.90	25.50		26.40	interior.
Minimum Charge	Job		142		142	
30" Wide, 2 Door						
Demolish	Ea.		14.35		14.35	Includes material and labor to install
Install	Ea.	310	29.50		339.50	premium hardwood modular unit with
Demolish and Install	Ea.	310	43.85		353.85	solid hardwood faced frames, drawer
Reinstall	Ea.		23.61		23.61	fronts, and door panels, steel drawer
Clean	Ea.	1.06	9.85		10.91	guides, hinges, pulls, laminated
Paint	Ea.	.99	28.50		29.49	interior.
Minimum Charge	Job		142		142	
36" Wide, 2 Door						
Demolish	Ea.		17		17	Includes material and labor to install
Install	Ea.	350	30.50		380.50	premium hardwood modular unit with
Demolish and Install	Ea.	350	47.50		397.50	solid hardwood faced frames, drawer
Reinstall	Ea.		24.24		24.24	fronts, and door panels, steel drawer
Clean	Ea.	1.27	12.15		13.42	guides, hinges, pulls, laminated
Paint	Ea.	1.20	36.50		37.70	interior.
Minimum Charge	Job		142		142	
48" Wide, 2 Door						
Demolish	Ea.		23		23	Includes material and labor to install
Install	Ea.	430	31		461	premium hardwood modular unit with
Demolish and Install	Ea.	430	54		484	solid hardwood faced frames, drawer
Reinstall	Ea.		24.77		24.77	fronts, and door panels, steel drawer
Clean	Ea.	1.68	15.90		17.58	guides, hinges, pulls, laminated
Paint	Ea.	1.60	42.50		44.10	interior.
Minimum Charge	Job		142		142	
Above-appliance						
Demolish	Ea.		14.35		14.35	Includes material and labor to install
Install	Ea.	218	23		241	premium hardwood modular unit with
Demolish and Install	Ea.	218	37.35		255.35	solid hardwood faced frames, drawer
Reinstall	Ea.		18.37		18.37	fronts, and door panels, steel drawer
Clean	Ea.	1.06	9.85		10.91	guides, hinges, pulls, laminated
Paint	Ea.	.99	28.50		29.49	interior.
Minimum Charge	Job		142		142	

Cabinets and Countertops

Wall Cabinets		Unit	Material	Labor	Equip.	Total	Specification
Medicine Cabinet							
Good Grade							
	Demolish	Ea.		9.55		9.55	Cost includes material and labor to
	Install	Ea.	73.50	20.50		94	install 14" x 18" recessed medicine
	Demolish and Install	Ea.	73.50	30.05		103.55	cabinet with stainless steel frame,
	Reinstall	Ea.		16.27		16.27	mirror. Light not included.
	Clean	Ea.	.02	9.35		9.37	
	Paint	Ea.	.97	15.95		16.92	
	Minimum Charge	Job		142		142	
Good Grade Lighted							
	Demolish	Ea.		9.55		9.55	Cost includes material and labor to
	Install	Ea.	231	23.50		254.50	install 14" x 18" recessed medicine
	Demolish and Install	Ea.	231	33.05		264.05	cabinet with stainless steel frame,
	Reinstall	Ea.		18.99		18.99	mirror and light.
	Clean	Ea.	.02	9.35		9.37	
	Paint	Ea.	.97	15.95		16.92	
	Minimum Charge	Job		142		142	
Better Grade							
	Demolish	Ea.		9.55		9.55	Includes material and labor to install
	Install	Ea.	102	20.50		122.50	recessed medicine cabinet with
	Demolish and Install	Ea.	102	30.05		132.05	polished chrome frame and mirror.
	Reinstall	Ea.		16.27		16.27	Light not included.
	Clean	Ea.	.02	9.35		9.37	
	Paint	Ea.	.97	15.95		16.92	
	Minimum Charge	Job		142		142	
Better Grade Lighted							
	Demolish	Ea.		9.55		9.55	Includes material and labor to install
	Install	Ea.	260	23.50		283.50	recessed medicine cabinet with
	Demolish and Install	Ea.	260	33.05		293.05	polished chrome frame, mirror and
	Reinstall	Ea.		18.99		18.99	light.
	Clean	Ea.	.02	9.35		9.37	
	Paint	Ea.	.97	15.95		16.92	
	Minimum Charge	Job		142		142	
Premium Grade							
	Demolish	Ea.		9.55		9.55	Cost includes material and labor to
	Install	Ea.	130	20.50		150.50	install 14" x 24" recessed medicine
	Demolish and Install	Ea.	130	30.05		160.05	cabinet with beveled mirror, frameless
	Reinstall	Ea.		16.27		16.27	swing door. Light not included.
	Clean	Ea.	.02	9.35		9.37	
	Paint	Ea.	.97	15.95		16.92	
	Minimum Charge	Job		142		142	
Premium Grade Light							
	Demolish	Ea.		9.55		9.55	Cost includes material and labor to
	Install	Ea.	287	23.50		310.50	install 36" x 30" surface mounted
	Demolish and Install	Ea.	287	33.05		320.05	medicine cabinet with beveled tri-view
	Reinstall	Ea.		18.99		18.99	mirror, frameless swing door and light.
	Clean	Ea.	.02	9.35		9.37	
	Paint	Ea.	.97	15.95		16.92	
	Minimum Charge	Job		142		142	
Bath Mirror							
	Demolish	Ea.		7.20		7.20	Cost includes material and labor to
	Install	Ea.	70	14.25		84.25	install 18" x 24" surface mount mirror
	Demolish and Install	Ea.	70	21.45		91.45	with stainless steel frame.
	Reinstall	Ea.		11.39		11.39	
	Clean	Ea.	.02	.62		.64	
	Minimum Charge	Job		142		142	

Cabinets and Countertops

Wall Cabinets

Wall Cabinets		Unit	Material	Labor	Equip.	Total	Specification
Garage							Includes material and labor to install
	Demolish	L.F.		5.75		5.75	good modular unit with melamine
	Install	L.F.	49	14.25		63.25	laminated to particle board, in textured
	Demolish and Install	L.F.	49	20		69	colors or wood grain print finish,
	Reinstall	L.F.		11.39		11.39	hinges and pulls.
	Clean	L.F.	.42	3.98		4.40	
	Paint	L.F.	.40	9.10		9.50	
	Minimum Charge	Job		142		142	
Strip and Refinish							Includes labor and material to strip,
	Install	L.F.	1.07	4.64		5.71	prep and refinish exterior of cabinets.
	Minimum Charge	Job		128		128	

Tall Cabinets

Tall Cabinets		Unit	Material	Labor	Equip.	Total	Specification
Good Grade Laminated							Includes material and labor to install
	Demolish	L.F.		10.20		10.20	custom modular unit with solid
	Install	L.F.	199	160		359	hardwood faced frames, hardwood
	Demolish and Install	L.F.	199	170.20		369.20	door frames and drawer fronts,
	Reinstall	L.F.		128.36		128.36	hardwood veneer on raised door
	Clean	L.F.	1.12	7.40		8.52	panels, hinges and pulls.
	Paint	L.F.	.92	18.25		19.17	
	Minimum Charge	Job		142		142	
Better Grade Wood							Includes material and labor to install
	Demolish	L.F.		10.20		10.20	custom modular unit with solid
	Install	L.F.	265	160		425	hardwood faced frames, hardwood
	Demolish and Install	L.F.	265	170.20		435.20	door frames and drawer fronts,
	Reinstall	L.F.		128.36		128.36	hardwood veneer on raised door
	Clean	L.F.	1.12	7.40		8.52	panels, hinges and pulls.
	Paint	L.F.	.92	19.65		20.57	
	Minimum Charge	Job		142		142	
Premium Grade Wood							Includes material and labor to install
	Demolish	L.F.		10.20		10.20	premium modular unit with solid
	Install	L.F.	350	160		510	hardwood faced frames, hardwood
	Demolish and Install	L.F.	350	170.20		520.20	door frames and drawer fronts,
	Reinstall	L.F.		128.36		128.36	hardwood veneer on raised door
	Clean	L.F.	1.12	7.40		8.52	panels, hinges and pulls.
	Paint	L.F.	.92	21.50		22.42	
	Minimum Charge	Job		142		142	
Premium Hardwood							Includes material and labor to install
	Demolish	L.F.		10.20		10.20	premium hardwood modular unit with
	Install	L.F.	460	160		620	solid hardwood faced frames, drawer
	Demolish and Install	L.F.	460	170.20		630.20	fronts, and door panels, steel drawer
	Reinstall	L.F.		128.36		128.36	guides, hinges and pulls, laminated
	Clean	L.F.	1.12	7.40		8.52	interior.
	Paint	L.F.	.92	23		23.92	
	Minimum Charge	Job		142		142	

Cabinets and Countertops

Tall Cabinets	Unit	Material	Labor	Equip.	Total	Specification
Single Oven, 27″ Wide						
Good Grade Laminated						
Demolish	Ea.		23		23	Includes material and labor to install
Install	Ea.	445	71		516	good modular unit with melamine
Demolish and Install	Ea.	445	94		539	laminated to particle board, in textured
Reinstall	Ea.		56.96		56.96	colors or wood grain print finish,
Clean	Ea.	3.51	12.95		16.46	hinges and pulls.
Paint	Ea.	1.56	41		42.56	
Minimum Charge	Job		142		142	
Better Grade Veneer						
Demolish	Ea.		23		23	Includes material and labor to install
Install	Ea.	790	71		861	custom modular unit with solid
Demolish and Install	Ea.	790	94		884	hardwood faced frames, hardwood
Reinstall	Ea.		56.96		56.96	door frames and drawer fronts,
Clean	Ea.	3.51	12.95		16.46	hardwood veneer on raised door
Paint	Ea.	1.56	44		45.56	panels, hinges and pulls.
Minimum Charge	Job		142		142	
Premium Grade Veneer						
Demolish	Ea.		23		23	Includes material and labor to install
Install	Ea.	705	71		776	premium modular unit with solid
Demolish and Install	Ea.	705	94		799	hardwood faced frames, hardwood
Reinstall	Ea.		56.96		56.96	door frames and drawer fronts,
Clean	Ea.	3.51	12.95		16.46	hardwood veneer on raised door
Paint	Ea.	1.56	48		49.56	panels, hinges and pulls.
Minimum Charge	Job		142		142	
Premium Hardwood						
Demolish	Ea.		23		23	Includes material and labor to install
Install	Ea.	900	71		971	premium hardwood modular unit with
Demolish and Install	Ea.	900	94		994	solid hardwood faced frames, drawer
Reinstall	Ea.		56.96		56.96	fronts, and door panels, steel drawer
Clean	Ea.	3.51	12.95		16.46	guides, hinges and pulls, laminated
Paint	Ea.	1.56	52		53.56	interior.
Minimum Charge	Job		142		142	
Single Oven, 30″ Wide						
Good Grade Laminated						
Demolish	Ea.		23		23	Includes material and labor to install
Install	Ea.	390	71		461	good modular unit with melamine
Demolish and Install	Ea.	390	94		484	laminated to particle board, in textured
Reinstall	Ea.		56.96		56.96	colors or wood grain print finish,
Clean	Ea.	3.51	12.95		16.46	hinges and pulls.
Paint	Ea.	1.56	41		42.56	
Minimum Charge	Job		142		142	
Better Grade Veneer						
Demolish	Ea.		23		23	Includes material and labor to install
Install	Ea.	595	71		666	custom modular unit with solid
Demolish and Install	Ea.	595	94		689	hardwood faced frames, hardwood
Reinstall	Ea.		56.96		56.96	door frames and drawer fronts,
Clean	Ea.	3.51	12.95		16.46	hardwood veneer on raised door
Paint	Ea.	1.56	41		42.56	panels, hinges and pulls.
Minimum Charge	Job		142		142	

Cabinets and Countertops

Tall Cabinets

	Unit	Material	Labor	Equip.	Total	Specification
Premium Grade Veneer						
Demolish	Ea.		23		23	Includes material and labor to install
Install	Ea.	695	71		766	premium modular unit with solid
Demolish and Install	Ea.	695	94		789	hardwood faced frames, hardwood
Reinstall	Ea.		56.96		56.96	door frames and drawer fronts,
Clean	Ea.	3.51	12.95		16.46	hardwood veneer on raised door
Paint	Ea.	1.56	41		42.56	panels, hinges and pulls.
Minimum Charge	Job		142		142	
Premium Hardwood						
Demolish	Ea.		23		23	Includes material and labor to install
Install	Ea.	840	71		911	premium hardwood modular unit with
Demolish and Install	Ea.	840	94		934	solid hardwood faced frames, drawer
Reinstall	Ea.		56.96		56.96	fronts, and door panels, steel drawer
Clean	Ea.	3.51	12.95		16.46	guides, hinges and pulls, laminated
Paint	Ea.	1.56	41		42.56	interior.
Minimum Charge	Job		142		142	

Utility 18" W x 12" D

	Unit	Material	Labor	Equip.	Total	Specification
Good Grade Laminated						
Demolish	Ea.		23		23	Includes material and labor to install
Install	Ea.	365	57		422	good modular unit with melamine
Demolish and Install	Ea.	365	80		445	laminated to particle board, in textured
Reinstall	Ea.		45.57		45.57	colors or wood grain print finish,
Clean	Ea.	.83	6.25		7.08	hinges and pulls.
Paint	Ea.	.59	15.95		16.54	
Minimum Charge	Job		142		142	
Better Grade Veneer						
Demolish	Ea.		23		23	Includes material and labor to install
Install	Ea.	395	57		452	custom modular unit with solid
Demolish and Install	Ea.	395	80		475	hardwood faced frames, hardwood
Reinstall	Ea.		45.57		45.57	door frames and drawer fronts,
Clean	Ea.	.83	6.25		7.08	hardwood veneer on raised door
Paint	Ea.	.59	17		17.59	panels, hinges and pulls.
Minimum Charge	Job		142		142	
Premium Grade Veneer						
Demolish	Ea.		23		23	Includes material and labor to install
Install	Ea.	505	57		562	premium modular unit with solid
Demolish and Install	Ea.	505	80		585	hardwood faced frames, hardwood
Reinstall	Ea.		45.57		45.57	door frames and drawer fronts,
Clean	Ea.	.83	6.25		7.08	hardwood veneer on raised door
Paint	Ea.	.59	19.65		20.24	panels, hinges and pulls.
Minimum Charge	Job		142		142	
Premium Hardwood						
Demolish	Ea.		23		23	Includes material and labor to install
Install	Ea.	645	57		702	premium hardwood modular unit with
Demolish and Install	Ea.	645	80		725	solid hardwood faced frames, drawer
Reinstall	Ea.		45.57		45.57	fronts, and door panels, steel drawer
Clean	Ea.	.83	6.25		7.08	guides, hinges and pulls, laminated
Paint	Ea.	.59	21.50		22.09	interior.
Minimum Charge	Job		142		142	

Cabinets and Countertops

Tall Cabinets	Unit	Material	Labor	Equip.	Total	Specification
Utility 24″ W x 24″ D						
Good Grade Laminated						
Demolish	Ea.		23		23	Includes material and labor to install
Install	Ea.	440	71		511	good modular unit with melamine
Demolish and Install	Ea.	440	94		534	laminated to particle board, in textured
Reinstall	Ea.		56.96		56.96	colors or wood grain print finish,
Clean	Ea.	1.08	8.25		9.33	hinges and pulls.
Paint	Ea.	.79	21.50		22.29	
Minimum Charge	Job		142		142	
Better Grade Veneer						
Demolish	Ea.		23		23	Includes material and labor to install
Install	Ea.	535	71		606	custom modular unit with solid
Demolish and Install	Ea.	535	94		629	hardwood faced frames, hardwood
Reinstall	Ea.		56.96		56.96	door frames and drawer fronts,
Clean	Ea.	1.08	8.25		9.33	hardwood veneer on raised door
Paint	Ea.	.79	23		23.79	panels, hinges and pulls.
Minimum Charge	Job		142		142	
Premium Grade Veneer						
Demolish	Ea.		23		23	Includes material and labor to install
Install	Ea.	675	71		746	premium modular unit with solid
Demolish and Install	Ea.	675	94		769	hardwood faced frames, hardwood
Reinstall	Ea.		56.96		56.96	door frames and drawer fronts,
Clean	Ea.	1.08	8.25		9.33	hardwood veneer on raised door
Paint	Ea.	.79	25.50		26.29	panels, hinges and pulls.
Minimum Charge	Job		142		142	
Premium Hardwood						
Demolish	Ea.		23		23	Includes material and labor to install
Install	Ea.	825	71		896	premium hardwood modular unit with
Demolish and Install	Ea.	825	94		919	solid hardwood faced frames, drawer
Reinstall	Ea.		56.96		56.96	fronts, and door panels, steel drawer
Clean	Ea.	1.08	8.25		9.33	guides, hinges and pulls, laminated
Paint	Ea.	.79	28.50		29.29	interior.
Minimum Charge	Job		142		142	
Plain Shelves						
Install	Ea.	22	17.80		39.80	Includes labor and material to install
						tall cabinet shelving, per set.
Rotating Shelves						
Install	Ea.	72.50	14.25		86.75	Includes labor and material to install
						lazy susan shelving for wall cabinet.
Strip and Refinish						
Install	L.F.	1.68	11.60		13.28	Includes labor and material to strip,
Minimum Charge	Job		128		128	prep and refinish exterior of cabinets.
Stain						
Install	L.F.	.15	2.32		2.47	Includes labor and material to replace
Minimum Charge	Job		128		128	normal prep and stain on doors and
						exterior cabinets.

Cabinets and Countertops

Base Cabinets		Unit	Material	Labor	Equip.	Total	Specification
Good Grade Laminated							
12" w, 1 Door, 1 Drawer							
	Demolish	Ea.		5.75		5.75	Includes material and labor to install
	Install	Ea.	105	23		128	good modular unit with melamine
	Demolish and Install	Ea.	105	28.75		133.75	laminate, textured colors or wood
	Reinstall	Ea.		18.37		18.37	grain print finish including hinges and
	Clean	Ea.	.56	4.14		4.70	pulls.
	Paint	Ea.	.40	10.65		11.05	
	Minimum Charge	Job		142		142	
15" w, 1 Door, 1 Drawer							
	Demolish	Ea.		7.20		7.20	Includes material and labor to install
	Install	Ea.	143	23.50		166.50	good modular unit with melamine
	Demolish and Install	Ea.	143	30.70		173.70	laminate, textured colors or wood
	Reinstall	Ea.		18.99		18.99	grain print finish including hinges and
	Clean	Ea.	.70	5.15		5.85	pulls.
	Paint	Ea.	.50	13.45		13.95	
	Minimum Charge	Job		142		142	
18" w, 1 Door, 1 Drawer							
	Demolish	Ea.		8.50		8.50	Includes material and labor to install
	Install	Ea.	167	24.50		191.50	good modular unit with melamine
	Demolish and Install	Ea.	167	33		200	laminate, textured colors or wood
	Reinstall	Ea.		19.56		19.56	grain print finish including hinges and
	Clean	Ea.	.83	6.25		7.08	pulls.
	Paint	Ea.	.59	15.95		16.54	
	Minimum Charge	Job		142		142	
21" w, 1 Door, 1 Drawer							
	Demolish	Ea.		10		10	Includes material and labor to install
	Install	Ea.	160	25		185	good modular unit with melamine
	Demolish and Install	Ea.	160	35		195	laminate, textured colors or wood
	Reinstall	Ea.		20.07		20.07	grain print finish including hinges and
	Clean	Ea.	1	7.40		8.40	pulls.
	Paint	Ea.	.69	18.25		18.94	
	Minimum Charge	Job		142		142	
24" w, 1 Door, 1 Drawer							
	Demolish	Ea.		11.50		11.50	Includes material and labor to install
	Install	Ea.	185	25.50		210.50	good modular unit with melamine
	Demolish and Install	Ea.	185	37		222	laminate, textured colors or wood
	Reinstall	Ea.		20.43		20.43	grain print finish including hinges and
	Clean	Ea.	1.08	8.25		9.33	pulls.
	Paint	Ea.	.79	21.50		22.29	
	Minimum Charge	Job		142		142	
30" Wide Sink Base							
	Demolish	Ea.		14.35		14.35	Includes material and labor to install
	Install	Ea.	179	26.50		205.50	good modular unit with melamine
	Demolish and Install	Ea.	179	40.85		219.85	laminate, textured colors or wood
	Reinstall	Ea.		21.29		21.29	grain print finish including hinges and
	Clean	Ea.	1.40	10.35		11.75	pulls.
	Paint	Ea.	.99	25.50		26.49	
	Minimum Charge	Job		142		142	
36" Wide Sink Base							
	Demolish	Ea.		17.70		17.70	Includes material and labor to install
	Install	Ea.	201	28		229	good modular unit with melamine
	Demolish and Install	Ea.	201	45.70		246.70	laminate, textured colors or wood
	Reinstall	Ea.		22.45		22.45	grain print finish including hinges and
	Clean	Ea.	1.56	12.15		13.71	pulls.
	Paint	Ea.	1.20	32		33.20	
	Minimum Charge	Job		142		142	

Cabinets and Countertops

Base Cabinets	Unit	Material	Labor	Equip.	Total	Specification
36″ Blind Corner						Includes material and labor to install
Demolish	Ea.		17.70		17.70	good modular unit with melamine
Install	Ea.	178	31.50		209.50	laminate, textured colors or wood
Demolish and Install	Ea.	178	49.20		227.20	grain print finish including hinges and
Reinstall	Ea.		25.32		25.32	pulls.
Clean	Ea.	1.56	12.15		13.71	
Paint	Ea.	1.20	32		33.20	
Minimum Charge	Job		142		142	
42″ w, 2 Door, 2 Drawer						Includes material and labor to install
Demolish	Ea.		21		21	good modular unit with melamine
Install	Ea.	250	29		279	laminate, textured colors or wood
Demolish and Install	Ea.	250	50		300	grain print finish including hinges and
Reinstall	Ea.		23.01		23.01	pulls.
Clean	Ea.	2	14.75		16.75	
Paint	Ea.	1.38	36.50		37.88	
Minimum Charge	Job		142		142	
Clean Interior						Includes labor and materials to clean
Clean	L.F.	.56	3.13		3.69	the interior of a 27″ cabinet.
Minimum Charge	Job		103		103	

Better Grade Wood

	Unit	Material	Labor	Equip.	Total	Specification
12″ w, 1 Door, 1 Drawer						Includes material and labor to install
Demolish	Ea.		5.75		5.75	custom modular unit including solid
Install	Ea.	140	23		163	hardwood faced frames, hardwood
Demolish and Install	Ea.	140	28.75		168.75	door frames and drawer fronts,
Reinstall	Ea.		18.37		18.37	hardwood veneer on raised door
Clean	Ea.	.56	4.14		4.70	panels, hinges and pulls.
Paint	Ea.	.40	11.60		12	
Minimum Charge	Job		142		142	
15″ w, 1 Door, 1 Drawer						Includes material and labor to install
Demolish	Ea.		7.20		7.20	custom modular unit including solid
Install	Ea.	190	23.50		213.50	hardwood faced frames, hardwood
Demolish and Install	Ea.	190	30.70		220.70	door frames and drawer fronts,
Reinstall	Ea.		18.99		18.99	hardwood veneer on raised door
Clean	Ea.	.70	5.15		5.85	panels, hinges and pulls.
Paint	Ea.	.50	15		15.50	
Minimum Charge	Job		142		142	
18″ w, 1 Door, 1 Drawer						Includes material and labor to install
Demolish	Ea.		8.50		8.50	custom modular unit including solid
Install	Ea.	223	24.50		247.50	hardwood faced frames, hardwood
Demolish and Install	Ea.	223	33		256	door frames and drawer fronts,
Reinstall	Ea.		19.56		19.56	hardwood veneer on raised door
Clean	Ea.	.83	6.25		7.08	panels, hinges and pulls.
Paint	Ea.	.59	17		17.59	
Minimum Charge	Job		142		142	
21″ w, 1 Door, 1 Drawer						Includes material and labor to install
Demolish	Ea.		10		10	custom modular unit including solid
Install	Ea.	212	25		237	hardwood faced frames, hardwood
Demolish and Install	Ea.	212	35		247	door frames and drawer fronts,
Reinstall	Ea.		20.07		20.07	hardwood veneer on raised door
Clean	Ea.	1	7.40		8.40	panels, hinges and pulls.
Paint	Ea.	.69	19.65		20.34	
Minimum Charge	Job		142		142	

Cabinets and Countertops

Base Cabinets	Unit	Material	Labor	Equip.	Total	Specification
24″ w, 1 Door, 1 Drawer						
Demolish	Ea.		11.50		11.50	Includes material and labor to install
Install	Ea.	246	25.50		271.50	custom modular unit including solid
Demolish and Install	Ea.	246	37		283	hardwood faced frames, hardwood
Reinstall	Ea.		20.43		20.43	door frames and drawer fronts,
Clean	Ea.	1.08	8.25		9.33	hardwood veneer on raised door
Paint	Ea.	.79	23		23.79	panels, hinges and pulls.
Minimum Charge	Job		142		142	
30″ Wide Sink Base						
Demolish	Ea.		14.35		14.35	Includes material and labor to install
Install	Ea.	239	26.50		265.50	custom modular unit including solid
Demolish and Install	Ea.	239	40.85		279.85	hardwood faced frames, hardwood
Reinstall	Ea.		21.29		21.29	door frames and drawer fronts,
Clean	Ea.	1.40	10.35		11.75	hardwood veneer on raised door
Paint	Ea.	.99	28.50		29.49	panels, hinges and pulls.
Minimum Charge	Job		142		142	
36″ Wide Sink Base						
Demolish	Ea.		17.70		17.70	Includes material and labor to install
Install	Ea.	268	28		296	custom modular unit including solid
Demolish and Install	Ea.	268	45.70		313.70	hardwood faced frames, hardwood
Reinstall	Ea.		22.45		22.45	door frames and drawer fronts,
Clean	Ea.	1.56	12.15		13.71	hardwood veneer on raised door
Paint	Ea.	1.20	36.50		37.70	panels, hinges and pulls.
Minimum Charge	Job		142		142	
36″ Blind Corner						
Demolish	Ea.		17.70		17.70	Includes material and labor to install
Install	Ea.	237	31.50		268.50	custom modular unit including solid
Demolish and Install	Ea.	237	49.20		286.20	hardwood faced frames, hardwood
Reinstall	Ea.		25.32		25.32	door frames and drawer fronts,
Clean	Ea.	1.56	12.15		13.71	hardwood veneer on raised door
Paint	Ea.	1.20	36.50		37.70	panels, hinges and pulls.
Minimum Charge	Job		142		142	
42″ w, 2 Door, 2 Drawer						
Demolish	Ea.		21		21	Includes material and labor to install
Install	Ea.	335	29		364	modular unit including solid hardwood
Demolish and Install	Ea.	335	50		385	faced frames, hardwood door frames
Reinstall	Ea.		23.01		23.01	and drawer fronts, hardwood veneer
Clean	Ea.	2	14.75		16.75	on raised door panels, hinges and
Paint	Ea.	1.38	42.50		43.88	pulls.
Minimum Charge	Job		142		142	
Clean Interior						
Clean	L.F.	.56	3.13		3.69	Includes labor and materials to clean
Minimum Charge	Job		103		103	the interior of a 27″ cabinet.
Premium Grade Wood						
12″ w, 1 Door, 1 Drawer						
Demolish	Ea.		5.75		5.75	Includes material and labor to install
Install	Ea.	240	11.50		251.50	premium hardwood modular unit with
Demolish and Install	Ea.	240	17.25		257.25	solid hardwood faced frames, drawer
Reinstall	Ea.		9.19		9.19	fronts, and door panels, steel drawer
Clean	Ea.	.56	4.14		4.70	guides, hinges, pulls and laminated
Paint	Ea.	.40	12.75		13.15	interior.
Minimum Charge	Job		142		142	

Cabinets and Countertops

Base Cabinets	Unit	Material	Labor	Equip.	Total	Specification
15″ w, 1 Door, 1 Drawer						
Demolish	Ea.		7.20		7.20	Includes material and labor to install
Install	Ea.	246	23.50		269.50	premium modular unit including solid
Demolish and Install	Ea.	246	30.70		276.70	hardwood faced frames, hardwood
Reinstall	Ea.		18.99		18.99	door frames and drawer fronts,
Clean	Ea.	.70	5.15		5.85	hardwood veneer on raised door
Paint	Ea.	.50	15.95		16.45	panels, hinges and pulls.
Minimum Charge	Job		142		142	
18″ w, 1 Door, 1 Drawer						
Demolish	Ea.		8.50		8.50	Includes material and labor to install
Install	Ea.	267	24.50		291.50	premium modular unit including solid
Demolish and Install	Ea.	267	33		300	hardwood faced frames, hardwood
Reinstall	Ea.		19.56		19.56	door frames and drawer fronts,
Clean	Ea.	.83	6.25		7.08	hardwood veneer on raised door
Paint	Ea.	.59	19.65		20.24	panels, hinges and pulls.
Minimum Charge	Job		142		142	
21″ w, 1 Door, 1 Drawer						
Demolish	Ea.		10		10	Includes material and labor to install
Install	Ea.	278	25		303	premium modular unit including solid
Demolish and Install	Ea.	278	35		313	hardwood faced frames, hardwood
Reinstall	Ea.		20.07		20.07	door frames and drawer fronts,
Clean	Ea.	1	7.40		8.40	hardwood veneer on raised door
Paint	Ea.	.69	21.50		22.19	panels, hinges and pulls.
Minimum Charge	Job		142		142	
24″ w, 1 Door, 1 Drawer						
Demolish	Ea.		11.50		11.50	Includes material and labor to install
Install	Ea.	320	25.50		345.50	premium modular unit including solid
Demolish and Install	Ea.	320	37		357	hardwood faced frames, hardwood
Reinstall	Ea.		20.43		20.43	door frames and drawer fronts,
Clean	Ea.	1.08	8.25		9.33	hardwood veneer on raised door
Paint	Ea.	.79	25.50		26.29	panels, hinges and pulls.
Minimum Charge	Job		142		142	
30″ Wide Sink Base						
Demolish	Ea.		14.35		14.35	Includes material and labor to install
Install	Ea.	283	26.50		309.50	premium modular unit including solid
Demolish and Install	Ea.	283	40.85		323.85	hardwood faced frames, hardwood
Reinstall	Ea.		21.29		21.29	door frames and drawer fronts,
Clean	Ea.	1.40	10.35		11.75	hardwood veneer on raised door
Paint	Ea.	.99	32		32.99	panels, hinges and pulls.
Minimum Charge	Job		142		142	
36″ Wide Sink Base						
Demolish	Ea.		17.70		17.70	Includes material and labor to install
Install	Ea.	320	28		348	premium modular unit including solid
Demolish and Install	Ea.	320	45.70		365.70	hardwood faced frames, hardwood
Reinstall	Ea.		22.45		22.45	door frames and drawer fronts,
Clean	Ea.	1.56	12.15		13.71	hardwood veneer on raised door
Paint	Ea.	1.20	36.50		37.70	panels, hinges and pulls.
Minimum Charge	Job		142		142	
36″ Blind Corner						
Demolish	Ea.		17.70		17.70	Includes material and labor to install
Install	Ea.	292	31.50		323.50	premium modular unit including solid
Demolish and Install	Ea.	292	49.20		341.20	hardwood faced frames, hardwood
Reinstall	Ea.		25.32		25.32	door frames and drawer fronts,
Clean	Ea.	1.56	12.15		13.71	hardwood veneer on raised door
Paint	Ea.	1.20	36.50		37.70	panels, hinges and pulls.
Minimum Charge	Job		142		142	

Cabinets and Countertops

Base Cabinets	Unit	Material	Labor	Equip.	Total	Specification
42" w, 2 Door, 2 Drawer						
Demolish	Ea.		21		21	Includes material and labor to install
Install	Ea.	445	29		474	premium modular unit including solid
Demolish and Install	Ea.	445	50		495	hardwood faced frames, hardwood
Reinstall	Ea.		23.01		23.01	door frames and drawer fronts,
Clean	Ea.	2	14.75		16.75	hardwood veneer on raised door
Paint	Ea.	1.38	42.50		43.88	panels, hinges and pulls.
Minimum Charge	Job		142		142	
Clean Interior						
Clean	L.F.	.56	3.13		3.69	Includes labor and materials to clean
Minimum Charge	Job		103		103	the interior of a 27" cabinet.

Premium Hardwood

	Unit	Material	Labor	Equip.	Total	Specification
12" w, 1 Door, 1 Drawer						
Demolish	Ea.		5.75		5.75	Includes material and labor to install
Install	Ea.	294	23		317	premium hardwood modular unit with
Demolish and Install	Ea.	294	28.75		322.75	solid hardwood faced frames, drawer
Reinstall	Ea.		18.37		18.37	fronts, and door panels, steel drawer
Clean	Ea.	.56	4.14		4.70	guides, hinges, pulls and laminated
Paint	Ea.	.40	14.20		14.60	interior.
Minimum Charge	Job		142		142	
15" w, 1 Door, 1 Drawer						
Demolish	Ea.		7.20		7.20	Includes material and labor to install
Install	Ea.	298	23.50		321.50	premium hardwood modular unit with
Demolish and Install	Ea.	298	30.70		328.70	solid hardwood faced frames, drawer
Reinstall	Ea.		18.99		18.99	fronts, and door panels, steel drawer
Clean	Ea.	.70	5.15		5.85	guides, hinges, pulls and laminated
Paint	Ea.	.50	18.25		18.75	interior.
Minimum Charge	Job		142		142	
18" w, 1 Door, 1 Drawer						
Demolish	Ea.		8.50		8.50	Includes material and labor to install
Install	Ea.	320	24.50		344.50	premium hardwood modular unit with
Demolish and Install	Ea.	320	33		353	solid hardwood faced frames, drawer
Reinstall	Ea.		19.56		19.56	fronts, and door panels, steel drawer
Clean	Ea.	.83	6.25		7.08	guides, hinges, pulls and laminated
Paint	Ea.	.59	21.50		22.09	interior.
Minimum Charge	Job		142		142	
21" w, 1 Door, 1 Drawer						
Demolish	Ea.		10		10	Includes material and labor to install
Install	Ea.	335	25		360	premium hardwood modular unit with
Demolish and Install	Ea.	335	35		370	solid hardwood faced frames, drawer
Reinstall	Ea.		20.07		20.07	fronts, and door panels, steel drawer
Clean	Ea.	1	7.40		8.40	guides, hinges, pulls and laminated
Paint	Ea.	.69	23		23.69	interior.
Minimum Charge	Job		142		142	
24" w, 1 Door, 1 Drawer						
Demolish	Ea.		11.50		11.50	Includes material and labor to install
Install	Ea.	375	25.50		400.50	premium hardwood modular unit with
Demolish and Install	Ea.	375	37		412	solid hardwood faced frames, drawer
Reinstall	Ea.		20.43		20.43	fronts, and door panels, steel drawer
Clean	Ea.	1.08	8.25		9.33	guides, hinges and pulls, laminated
Paint	Ea.	.79	28.50		29.29	interior.
Minimum Charge	Job		142		142	

Cabinets and Countertops

Base Cabinets		Unit	Material	Labor	Equip.	Total	Specification
30" Wide Sink Base							Includes material and labor to install
	Demolish	Ea.		14.35		14.35	premium hardwood modular unit with
	Install	Ea.	335	26.50		361.50	solid hardwood faced frames, drawer
	Demolish and Install	Ea.	335	40.85		375.85	fronts, and door panels, steel drawer
	Reinstall	Ea.		21.29		21.29	guides, hinges, pulls and laminated
	Clean	Ea.	1.40	10.35		11.75	interior.
	Paint	Ea.	.99	32		32.99	
	Minimum Charge	Job		142		142	
36" Wide Sink Base							Includes material and labor to install
	Demolish	Ea.		17.70		17.70	premium hardwood modular unit with
	Install	Ea.	375	28		403	solid hardwood faced frames, drawer
	Demolish and Install	Ea.	375	45.70		420.70	fronts, and door panels, steel drawer
	Reinstall	Ea.		22.45		22.45	guides, hinges, pulls and laminated
	Clean	Ea.	1.56	12.15		13.71	interior.
	Paint	Ea.	1.20	42.50		43.70	
	Minimum Charge	Job		142		142	
36" Blind Corner							Includes material and labor to install
	Demolish	Ea.		17.70		17.70	premium hardwood modular unit with
	Install	Ea.	345	31.50		376.50	solid hardwood faced frames, drawer
	Demolish and Install	Ea.	345	49.20		394.20	fronts, and door panels, steel drawer
	Reinstall	Ea.		25.32		25.32	guides, hinges, pulls and laminated
	Clean	Ea.	1.56	12.15		13.71	interior.
	Paint	Ea.	1.20	42.50		43.70	
	Minimum Charge	Job		142		142	
42" w, 2 Door, 2 Drawer							Includes material and labor to install
	Demolish	Ea.		21		21	premium hardwood modular unit with
	Install	Ea.	585	29		614	solid hardwood faced frames, drawer
	Demolish and Install	Ea.	585	50		635	fronts, and door panels, steel drawer
	Reinstall	Ea.		23.01		23.01	guides, hinges, pulls and laminated
	Clean	Ea.	2	14.75		16.75	interior.
	Paint	Ea.	1.38	51		52.38	
	Minimum Charge	Job		142		142	
Clean Interior							Includes labor and materials to clean
	Clean	L.F.	.56	3.13		3.69	the interior of a 27" cabinet.
	Minimum Charge	Job		103		103	
Island							
24" Wide							Includes material and labor to install
	Demolish	Ea.		11.50		11.50	custom modular unit with solid
	Install	Ea.	345	23.50		368.50	hardwood faced frames, hardwood
	Demolish and Install	Ea.	345	35		380	door frames and drawer fronts,
	Reinstall	Ea.		18.99		18.99	hardwood veneer on raised door
	Clean	Ea.	1.56	12.15		13.71	panels, hinges and pulls.
	Paint	Ea.	1.19	36.50		37.69	
	Minimum Charge	Job		142		142	
30" Wide							Includes material and labor to install
	Demolish	Ea.		14.35		14.35	custom modular unit with solid
	Install	Ea.	415	29.50		444.50	hardwood faced frames, hardwood
	Demolish and Install	Ea.	415	43.85		458.85	door frames and drawer fronts,
	Reinstall	Ea.		23.73		23.73	hardwood veneer on raised door
	Clean	Ea.	2	14.75		16.75	panels, hinges and pulls.
	Paint	Ea.	1.50	42.50		44	
	Minimum Charge	Job		142		142	

Cabinets and Countertops

Base Cabinets		Unit	Material	Labor	Equip.	Total	Specification
36" Wide							
	Demolish	Ea.		17.70		17.70	Includes material and labor to install
	Install	Ea.	475	35.50		510.50	custom modular unit with solid
	Demolish and Install	Ea.	475	53.20		528.20	hardwood faced frames, hardwood
	Reinstall	Ea.		28.48		28.48	door frames and drawer fronts,
	Clean	Ea.	2.33	18.80		21.13	hardwood veneer on raised door
	Paint	Ea.	1.80	51		52.80	panels, hinges and pulls.
	Minimum Charge	Job		142		142	
48" Wide							
	Demolish	Ea.		23		23	Includes material and labor to install
	Install	Ea.	695	47.50		742.50	custom modular unit with solid
	Demolish and Install	Ea.	695	70.50		765.50	hardwood faced frames, hardwood
	Reinstall	Ea.		37.97		37.97	door frames and drawer fronts,
	Clean	Ea.	2.81	23		25.81	hardwood veneer on raised door
	Paint	Ea.	2.07	64		66.07	panels, hinges and pulls.
	Minimum Charge	Job		142		142	
60" Wide							
	Demolish	Ea.		25.50		25.50	Includes material and labor to install
	Install	Ea.	830	59.50		889.50	custom modular unit with solid
	Demolish and Install	Ea.	830	85		915	hardwood faced frames, hardwood
	Reinstall	Ea.		47.47		47.47	door frames and drawer fronts,
	Clean	Ea.	3.51	29.50		33.01	hardwood veneer on raised door
	Paint	Ea.	2.07	85		87.07	panels, hinges and pulls.
	Minimum Charge	Job		142		142	
Clean Interior							
	Clean	L.F.	.56	3.13		3.69	Includes labor and materials to clean
	Minimum Charge	Job		103		103	the interior of a 27" cabinet.
Liquor Bar							
	Demolish	L.F.		5.75		5.75	Includes material and labor to install
	Install	L.F.	128	28.50		156.50	custom modular unit with solid
	Demolish and Install	L.F.	128	34.25		162.25	hardwood faced frames, hardwood
	Reinstall	L.F.		22.78		22.78	door frames and drawer fronts,
	Clean	L.F.	.56	4.31		4.87	hardwood veneer on raised door
	Paint	L.F.	.40	11.60		12	panels, hinges and pulls.
	Minimum Charge	Job		142		142	
Clean Interior							
	Clean	L.F.	.56	3.13		3.69	Includes labor and materials to clean
	Minimum Charge	Job		103		103	the interior of a 27" cabinet.
Seal Interior							
	Install	L.F.	.28	4.18		4.46	Includes labor and materials to seal a
	Minimum Charge	Job		128		128	cabinet interior.
Back Bar							
	Demolish	L.F.		5.75		5.75	Includes material and labor to install
	Install	L.F.	128	28.50		156.50	custom modular unit with solid
	Demolish and Install	L.F.	128	34.25		162.25	hardwood faced frames, hardwood
	Reinstall	L.F.		22.78		22.78	door frames and drawer fronts,
	Clean	L.F.	.56	4.31		4.87	hardwood veneer on raised door
	Paint	L.F.	.40	11.60		12	panels, hinges and pulls.
	Minimum Charge	Job		142		142	
Clean Interior							
	Clean	L.F.	.56	3.13		3.69	Includes labor and materials to clean
	Minimum Charge	Job		103		103	the interior of a 27" cabinet.

Cabinets and Countertops

Base Cabinets		Unit	Material	Labor	Equip.	Total	Specification
Seal Interior							
	Install	L.F.	.28	4.18		4.46	Includes labor and materials to seal a
	Minimum Charge	Job		128		128	cabinet interior.
Storage (garage)							
	Demolish	L.F.		5.75		5.75	Includes material and labor to install
	Install	L.F.	95	28.50		123.50	good modular unit with melamine
	Demolish and Install	L.F.	95	34.25		129.25	laminate, textured colors or wood
	Reinstall	L.F.		22.78		22.78	grain print finish including hinges and
	Clean	L.F.	.56	4.31		4.87	pulls.
	Paint	L.F.	.40	11.60		12	
	Minimum Charge	Job		142		142	
Clean Interior							
	Clean	L.F.	.56	3.13		3.69	Includes labor and materials to clean
	Minimum Charge	Job		103		103	the interior of a 27" cabinet.
Seal Interior							
	Install	L.F.	.28	4.18		4.46	Includes labor and materials to seal a
	Minimum Charge	Job		128		128	cabinet interior.
Built-in Desk							
	Demolish	L.F.		5.75		5.75	Includes material and labor to install
	Install	L.F.	128	28.50		156.50	custom modular unit with solid
	Demolish and Install	L.F.	128	34.25		162.25	hardwood faced frames, hardwood
	Reinstall	L.F.		22.78		22.78	door frames and drawer fronts,
	Clean	L.F.	.56	4.31		4.87	hardwood veneer on raised door
	Paint	L.F.	.40	11.60		12	panels, hinges and pulls.
	Minimum Charge	Job		142		142	
Built-in Bookcase							
	Demolish	L.F.		7.65		7.65	Includes material and labor to install
	Install	L.F.	26	28.50		54.50	custom modular bookcase unit with
	Demolish and Install	L.F.	26	36.15		62.15	clear pine faced frames, shelves 12"
	Reinstall	L.F.		22.78		22.78	O.C., 7' high, 8" deep.
	Clean	L.F.	1.12	7.40		8.52	
	Paint	L.F.	.92	19.65		20.57	
	Minimum Charge	Job		142		142	
Strip and Refinish							
	Install	L.F.	1.07	4.64		5.71	Includes labor and material to strip,
	Minimum Charge	Job		128		128	prep and refinish exterior of cabinets.
Stain							
	Install	L.F.	.34	1.19		1.53	Includes labor and material to stain
	Minimum Charge	Job		142		142	door and exterior of cabinets.

Countertop		Unit	Material	Labor	Equip.	Total	Specification
Laminated							
With Splash							
	Demolish	L.F.		3.83		3.83	Includes material and labor to install
	Install	L.F.	25.50	10.15		35.65	one piece laminated top with 4"
	Demolish and Install	L.F.	25.50	13.98		39.48	backsplash.
	Reinstall	L.F.		8.14		8.14	
	Clean	L.F.	.07	.52		.59	
	Minimum Charge	Job		142		142	

Cabinets and Countertops

Countertop		Unit	Material	Labor	Equip.	Total	Specification
Roll Top							
	Demolish	L.F.		3.83		3.83	Includes material and labor to install
	Install	L.F.	9.40	9.50		18.90	one piece laminated top with rolled
	Demolish and Install	L.F.	9.40	13.33		22.73	drip edge (post formed) and
	Reinstall	L.F.		7.59		7.59	backsplash.
	Clean	L.F.	.10	.78		.88	
	Minimum Charge	Job		142		142	
Ceramic Tile							
	Demolish	S.F.		1.91		1.91	Cost includes material and labor to
	Install	S.F.	13.60	5.70		19.30	install 4-1/4" x 4-1/4" to 6" x 6"
	Demolish and Install	S.F.	13.60	7.61		21.21	glazed tile set in mortar bed and grout
	Clean	S.F.	.06	.39		.45	on particle board substrate.
	Minimum Charge	Job		132		132	
Cultured Marble							
	Demolish	L.F.		3.83		3.83	Includes material and labor to install
	Install	L.F.	24	28.50		52.50	marble countertop, 24" wide, no
	Demolish and Install	L.F.	24	32.33		56.33	backsplash.
	Reinstall	L.F.		22.88		22.88	
	Clean	L.F.	.10	.78		.88	
	Minimum Charge	Job		132		132	
With Splash							
	Demolish	L.F.		3.83		3.83	Includes material and labor to install
	Install	L.F.	27.50	28.50		56	marble countertop, 24" wide, with
	Demolish and Install	L.F.	27.50	32.33		59.83	backsplash.
	Reinstall	L.F.		22.88		22.88	
	Clean	L.F.	.10	.78		.88	
	Minimum Charge	Job		132		132	
Quarry Tile							
	Demolish	S.F.		1.91		1.91	Includes material and labor to install
	Install	S.F.	7.85	5.70		13.55	quarry tile countertop with no
	Demolish and Install	S.F.	7.85	7.61		15.46	backsplash.
	Clean	S.F.	.06	.39		.45	
	Minimum Charge	Job		132		132	
With Splash							
	Demolish	S.F.		1.91		1.91	Includes material and labor to install
	Install	S.F.	9.95	6.35		16.30	quarry tile countertop with backsplash.
	Demolish and Install	S.F.	9.95	8.26		18.21	
	Clean	S.F.	.06	.39		.45	
	Minimum Charge	Job		132		132	
Butcher Block							
	Demolish	S.F.		1.91		1.91	Includes material and labor to install
	Install	S.F.	17	5.10		22.10	solid laminated maple countertop with
	Demolish and Install	S.F.	17	7.01		24.01	no backsplash.
	Reinstall	S.F.		4.07		4.07	
	Clean	S.F.	.02	.16		.18	
	Minimum Charge	Job		142		142	
Solid Surface							
	Demolish	L.F.		3.83		3.83	Includes material and labor to install
	Install	L.F.	48	20.50		68.50	solid surface counter top 22" deep.
	Demolish and Install	L.F.	48	24.33		72.33	
	Reinstall	L.F.		16.27		16.27	
	Clean	L.F.	.10	.78		.88	
	Minimum Charge	Job		142		142	

Vanity Cabinets	Unit	Material	Labor	Equip.	Total	Specification
Good Grade Laminated						
24" Wide, 2 Door						
Demolish	Ea.		11.50		11.50	Includes material and labor to install
Install	Ea.	133	28.50		161.50	modular unit with melamine laminated
Demolish and Install	Ea.	133	40		173	to particle board, textured colors or
Reinstall	Ea.		22.78		22.78	wood grain print finish, hinges and
Clean	Ea.	1.08	8.25		9.33	pulls.
Paint	Ea.	.79	21.50		22.29	
Minimum Charge	Job		142		142	
30" Wide, 2 Door						
Demolish	Ea.		14.35		14.35	Includes material and labor to install
Install	Ea.	153	35.50		188.50	modular unit with melamine laminated
Demolish and Install	Ea.	153	49.85		202.85	to particle board, textured colors or
Reinstall	Ea.		28.48		28.48	wood grain print finish, hinges and
Clean	Ea.	1.40	10.35		11.75	pulls.
Paint	Ea.	.99	25.50		26.49	
Minimum Charge	Job		142		142	
36" Wide, 2 Door						
Demolish	Ea.		17.70		17.70	Includes material and labor to install
Install	Ea.	204	42.50		246.50	modular unit with melamine laminated
Demolish and Install	Ea.	204	60.20		264.20	to particle board, textured colors or
Reinstall	Ea.		34.18		34.18	wood grain print finish, hinges and
Clean	Ea.	1.56	12.15		13.71	pulls.
Paint	Ea.	1.20	32		33.20	
Minimum Charge	Job		142		142	
42" w, 3 Doors / Drawer						
Demolish	Ea.		21		21	Includes material and labor to install
Install	Ea.	293	46		339	modular unit with melamine laminated
Demolish and Install	Ea.	293	67		360	to particle board, textured colors or
Reinstall	Ea.		36.81		36.81	wood grain print finish, hinges and
Clean	Ea.	2	14.75		16.75	pulls.
Paint	Ea.	1.38	36.50		37.88	
Minimum Charge	Job		142		142	
48" w, 3 Doors / Drawer						
Demolish	Ea.		23		23	Includes material and labor to install
Install	Ea.	243	50		293	modular unit with melamine laminated
Demolish and Install	Ea.	243	73		316	to particle board, textured colors or
Reinstall	Ea.		39.87		39.87	wood grain print finish, hinges and
Clean	Ea.	2.81	23		25.81	pulls.
Paint	Ea.	2.07	64		66.07	
Minimum Charge	Job		142		142	
Clean Interior						
Install	L.F.	.56	4.31		4.87	Includes labor and materials to clean
Minimum Charge	Job		103		103	base cabinetry.
Better Grade Wood						
24" Wide, 2 Door						
Demolish	Ea.		11.50		11.50	Includes material and labor to install
Install	Ea.	177	28.50		205.50	custom modular unit with solid
Demolish and Install	Ea.	177	40		217	hardwood faced frames, hardwood
Reinstall	Ea.		22.78		22.78	door frames and drawer fronts,
Clean	Ea.	1.08	8.25		9.33	hardwood veneer on raised door
Paint	Ea.	.79	23		23.79	panels, hinges and pulls.
Minimum Charge	Job		142		142	

Cabinets and Countertops

Vanity Cabinets

	Unit	Material	Labor	Equip.	Total	Specification
30" Wide, 2 Door						
Demolish	Ea.		14.35		14.35	Includes material and labor to install
Install	Ea.	204	35.50		239.50	custom modular unit with solid
Demolish and Install	Ea.	204	49.85		253.85	hardwood faced frames, hardwood
Reinstall	Ea.		28.48		28.48	door frames and drawer fronts,
Clean	Ea.	1.40	10.35		11.75	hardwood veneer on raised door
Paint	Ea.	.99	28.50		29.49	panels, hinges and pulls.
Minimum Charge	Job		142		142	
36" Wide, 2 Door						
Demolish	Ea.		17.70		17.70	Includes material and labor to install
Install	Ea.	272	42.50		314.50	custom modular unit with solid
Demolish and Install	Ea.	272	60.20		332.20	hardwood faced frames, hardwood
Reinstall	Ea.		34.18		34.18	door frames and drawer fronts,
Clean	Ea.	1.56	12.15		13.71	hardwood veneer on raised door
Paint	Ea.	1.20	36.50		37.70	panels, hinges and pulls.
Minimum Charge	Job		142		142	
42" w, 3 Doors / Drawer						
Demolish	Ea.		21		21	Includes material and labor to install
Install	Ea.	293	46		339	custom modular unit with solid
Demolish and Install	Ea.	293	67		360	hardwood faced frames, hardwood
Reinstall	Ea.		36.81		36.81	door frames and drawer fronts,
Clean	Ea.	2	14.75		16.75	hardwood veneer on raised door
Paint	Ea.	1.38	42.50		43.88	panels, hinges and pulls.
Minimum Charge	Job		142		142	
48" w, 3 Doors / Drawer						
Demolish	Ea.		23		23	Includes material and labor to install
Install	Ea.	325	50		375	custom modular unit with solid
Demolish and Install	Ea.	325	73		398	hardwood faced frames, hardwood
Reinstall	Ea.		39.87		39.87	door frames and drawer fronts,
Clean	Ea.	2.81	23		25.81	hardwood veneer on raised door
Paint	Ea.	2.07	64		66.07	panels, hinges and pulls.
Minimum Charge	Job		142		142	
Clean Interior						
Install	L.F.	.56	4.31		4.87	Includes labor and materials to clean
Minimum Charge	Job		103		103	base cabinetry.
Premium Grade Wood						
24" Wide, 2 Door						
Demolish	Ea.		11.50		11.50	Includes material and labor to install
Install	Ea.	210	28.50		238.50	premium modular unit with solid
Demolish and Install	Ea.	210	40		250	hardwood faced frames, hardwood
Reinstall	Ea.		22.78		22.78	door frames and drawer fronts,
Clean	Ea.	1.08	8.25		9.33	hardwood veneer on raised door
Paint	Ea.	.79	25.50		26.29	panels, hinges and pulls.
Minimum Charge	Job		142		142	
30" Wide, 2 Door						
Demolish	Ea.		14.35		14.35	Includes material and labor to install
Install	Ea.	242	35.50		277.50	premium modular unit with solid
Demolish and Install	Ea.	242	49.85		291.85	hardwood faced frames, hardwood
Reinstall	Ea.		28.48		28.48	door frames and drawer fronts,
Clean	Ea.	1.40	10.35		11.75	hardwood veneer on raised door
Paint	Ea.	.99	32		32.99	panels, hinges and pulls.
Minimum Charge	Job		142		142	

Cabinets and Countertops

Vanity Cabinets		Unit	Material	Labor	Equip.	Total	Specification
36″ Wide, 2 Door							
	Demolish	Ea.		17.70		17.70	Includes material and labor to install
	Install	Ea.	375	42.50		417.50	premium modular unit with solid
	Demolish and Install	Ea.	375	60.20		435.20	hardwood faced frames, hardwood
	Reinstall	Ea.		34.18		34.18	door frames and drawer fronts,
	Clean	Ea.	1.56	12.15		13.71	hardwood veneer on raised door
	Paint	Ea.	1.20	36.50		37.70	panels, hinges and pulls.
	Minimum Charge	Job		142		142	
42″ w, 3 Doors / Drawer							
	Demolish	Ea.		21		21	Includes material and labor to install
	Install	Ea.	365	46		411	premium modular unit with solid
	Demolish and Install	Ea.	365	67		432	hardwood faced frames, hardwood
	Reinstall	Ea.		36.81		36.81	door frames and drawer fronts,
	Clean	Ea.	2	14.75		16.75	hardwood veneer on raised door
	Paint	Ea.	1.38	42.50		43.88	panels, hinges and pulls.
	Minimum Charge	Job		142		142	
48″ w, 3 Doors / Drawer							
	Demolish	Ea.		23		23	Includes material and labor to install
	Install	Ea.	440	50		490	premium modular unit with solid
	Demolish and Install	Ea.	440	73		513	hardwood faced frames, hardwood
	Reinstall	Ea.		39.87		39.87	door frames and drawer fronts,
	Clean	Ea.	2.81	23		25.81	hardwood veneer on raised door
	Paint	Ea.	2.07	64		66.07	panels, hinges and pulls.
	Minimum Charge	Job		142		142	
Clean Interior							
	Install	L.F.	.56	4.31		4.87	Includes labor and materials to clean
	Minimum Charge	Job		103		103	base cabinetry.
Premium Hardwood							
24″ Wide, 2 Door							
	Demolish	Ea.		11.50		11.50	Includes material and labor to install
	Install	Ea.	264	28.50		292.50	premium modular unit with solid
	Demolish and Install	Ea.	264	40		304	hardwood faced frames, hardwood
	Reinstall	Ea.		22.78		22.78	door frames and drawer fronts,
	Clean	Ea.	1.08	8.25		9.33	hardwood veneer on raised door
	Paint	Ea.	.79	28.50		29.29	panels, hinges and pulls.
	Minimum Charge	Job		142		142	
30″ Wide, 2 Door							
	Demolish	Ea.		14.35		14.35	Includes material and labor to install
	Install	Ea.	296	35.50		331.50	premium modular unit with solid
	Demolish and Install	Ea.	296	49.85		345.85	hardwood faced frames, hardwood
	Reinstall	Ea.		28.48		28.48	door frames and drawer fronts,
	Clean	Ea.	1.40	10.35		11.75	hardwood veneer on raised door
	Paint	Ea.	.99	32		32.99	panels, hinges and pulls.
	Minimum Charge	Job		142		142	
36″ Wide, 2 Door							
	Demolish	Ea.		17.70		17.70	Includes material and labor to install
	Install	Ea.	435	42.50		477.50	premium modular unit with solid
	Demolish and Install	Ea.	435	60.20		495.20	hardwood faced frames, hardwood
	Reinstall	Ea.		34.18		34.18	door frames and drawer fronts,
	Clean	Ea.	1.56	12.15		13.71	hardwood veneer on raised door
	Paint	Ea.	1.20	42.50		43.70	panels, hinges and pulls.
	Minimum Charge	Job		142		142	

Cabinets and Countertops

Vanity Cabinets

	Unit	Material	Labor	Equip.	Total	Specification
42″ w, 3 Doors / Drawer						
Demolish	Ea.		21		21	Includes material and labor to install
Install	Ea.	400	46		446	premium modular unit with solid
Demolish and Install	Ea.	400	67		467	hardwood·faced frames, hardwood
Reinstall	Ea.		36.81		36.81	door frames and drawer fronts,
Clean	Ea.	2	14.75		16.75	hardwood veneer on raised door
Paint	Ea.	1.38	51		52.38	panels, hinges and pulls.
Minimum Charge	Job		142		142	
48″ w, 3 Doors / Drawer						
Demolish	Ea.		23		23	Includes material and labor to install
Install	Ea.	495	50		545	premium modular unit with solid
Demolish and Install	Ea.	495	73		568	hardwood faced frames, hardwood
Reinstall	Ea.		39.87		39.87	door frames and drawer fronts,
Clean	Ea.	2.81	23		25.81	hardwood veneer on raised door
Paint	Ea.	2.07	64		66.07	panels, hinges and pulls.
Minimum Charge	Job		142		142	
Clean Interior						
Install	L.F.	.56	4.31		4.87	Includes labor and materials to clean
Minimum Charge	Job		103		103	base cabinetry.
Strip and Refinish						
Install	L.F.	1.07	4.64		5.71	Includes labor and material to strip,
Minimum Charge	Job		128		128	prep and refinish exterior of cabinets.

Vanity Cabinet Tops

	Unit	Material	Labor	Equip.	Total	Specification
Cultured Marble Top						
Demolish	L.F.		3.83		3.83	Includes material and labor to install
Install	L.F.	33	16.80		49.80	cultured marble vanity top with integral
Demolish and Install	L.F.	33	20.63		53.63	sink, 22″ deep.
Reinstall	L.F.		13.46		13.46	
Clean	L.F.	.10	.78		.88	
Minimum Charge	Job		132		132	
Laminated Top						
Demolish	L.F.		2.30		2.30	Includes material and labor to install
Install	L.F.	25.50	10.15		35.65	one piece laminated top with 4″
Demolish and Install	L.F.	25.50	12.45		37.95	backsplash.
Reinstall	L.F.		8.14		8.14	
Clean	L.F.	.07	.52		.59	
Minimum Charge	Job		142		142	
Solid Surface						
Demolish	L.F.		3.83		3.83	Includes material and labor to install
Install	L.F.	67	21		88	solid surface vanity top with integral
Demolish and Install	L.F.	67	24.83		91.83	sink installed, 22″ deep.
Reinstall	L.F.		16.88		16.88	
Clean	L.F.	.10	.78		.88	
Minimum Charge	Job		142		142	

Painting

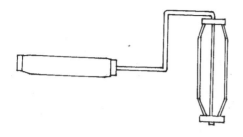

Roller Handle

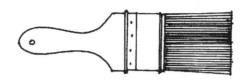

Paint Brush

Paint Preparation, Walls		Unit	Material	Labor	Equip.	Total	Specification
Cover / Protect Floors							
	Install	S.F.	.01	.10		.11	Includes material and labor to install
	Minimum Charge	Job		127		127	plastic masking sheet on large uninterrupted areas.
Cover / Protect Walls							
	Install	S.F.	.01	.10		.11	Includes material and labor to install
	Minimum Charge	Job		127		127	plastic masking sheet on walls.
Clean Walls							
Light							
	Clean	S.F.		.08		.08	Includes labor to wash gypsum drywall
	Minimum Charge	Job		127		127	or plaster wall surfaces.
Heavy							
	Clean	S.F.		.10		.10	Includes labor and material for heavy
	Minimum Charge	Job		127		127	cleaning (multiple applications) with detergent and solvent.
Prep Walls							
	Paint	S.F.	.03	.13		.16	Includes labor and material to prepare
	Minimum Charge	Job		127		127	for painting including scraping, patching and puttying.
Sand Walls							
	Paint	S.F.		.08		.08	Includes labor to sand gypsum drywall
	Minimum Charge	Job		127		127	wall surfaces.
Seal Walls							
Large Area							
	Paint	S.F.	.04	.13		.17	Includes labor and material to paint
	Minimum Charge	Job		127		127	with primer / sealer by roller.
Spot							
	Paint	S.F.	.04	.22		.26	Includes labor and material to seal
	Minimum Charge	Job		127		127	existing drywall with shellac-based material.

Painting

Paint Preparation, Ceilings		Unit	Material	Labor	Equip.	Total	Specification
Cover / Protect Floors							
	Install	S.F.	.01	.10		.11	Includes material and labor to install
	Minimum Charge	Job		127		127	plastic masking sheet on large uninterrupted areas.
Cover / Protect Walls							
	Install	S.F.	.01	.10		.11	Includes material and labor to install
	Minimum Charge	Job		127		127	plastic masking sheet on walls.
Prep Ceiling							
	Paint	S.F.	.04	.48		.52	Includes labor and material to fill in
	Minimum Charge	Job		127		127	hairline cracks up to 1/8" with filler, sand and prep for paint.
Sand Ceiling							
	Paint	S.F.		.12		.12	Includes labor to sand gypsum drywall
	Minimum Charge	Job		127		127	ceiling surfaces.
Seal Ceiling							
Large Area							
	Paint	S.F.	.06	.20		.26	Includes labor and material to paint
	Minimum Charge	Job		128		128	ceiling, one coat flat latex.
Spot							
	Paint	S.F.	.04	.22		.26	Includes labor and material to seal
	Minimum Charge	Job		128		128	existing drywall with shellac-based material.

Paint / Texture, Walls		Unit	Material	Labor	Equip.	Total	Specification
Texture Walls							
Spray							
	Install	S.F.	.06	.33		.39	Includes labor and material to install
	Minimum Charge	Job		128		128	by spray, texture finish.
Trowel							
	Install	S.F.	.01	.17		.18	Includes labor and material to apply
	Minimum Charge	Job		128		128	hand troweled texture.
Paint Walls 1 Coat							
	Paint	S.F.	.06	.20		.26	Includes labor and material to paint,
	Minimum Charge	Job		128		128	one coat flat latex.
Paint Walls 2 Coats							
	Paint	S.F.	.10	.32		.42	Includes labor and material to paint,
	Minimum Charge	Job		128		128	two coats flat latex.
Paint Walls 3 Coats							
	Paint	S.F.	.15	.39		.54	Includes labor and material to paint,
	Minimum Charge	Job		128		128	three coats flat latex.
Clean and Seal							
	Paint	S.F.	.21	.68		.89	Includes labor and material to do light
	Minimum Charge	Job		128		128	cleaning, sealing with 2 coats of latex paint.

Painting

Paint / Texture, Ceilings		Unit	Material	Labor	Equip.	Total	Specification
Texture Ceiling							
Spray							
	Install	S.F.	.06	.33		.39	Includes labor and material to install
	Minimum Charge	Job		128		128	by spray, texture finish.
Trowel							
	Install	S.F.	.01	.17		.18	Includes labor and material to apply
	Minimum Charge	Job		128		128	hand troweled texture.
Paint Ceiling, 1 Coat							
	Paint	S.F.	.06	.20		.26	Includes labor and material to paint
	Minimum Charge	Job		128		128	ceiling, one coat flat latex.
Paint Ceiling, 2 Coats							
	Paint	S.F.	.10	.32		.42	Includes labor and material to paint
	Minimum Charge	Job		128		128	two coats flat latex paint.
Paint Ceiling, 3 Coats							
	Paint	S.F.	.15	.38		.53	Includes labor and material to paint
	Minimum Charge	Job		128		128	ceiling, three coats flat latex.
Clean and Seal							
	Paint	S.F.	.15	.54		.69	Includes labor and material for light
	Minimum Charge	Job		128		128	cleaning, sealing and paint 3 coats of
							flat latex paint.

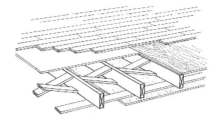

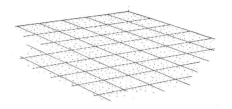

Plank Flooring		Wood Strip Flooring		Tile Flooring		

Wood Plank Flooring	Unit	Material	Labor	Equip.	Total	Specification
Maple						
2-1/4″						
Demolish	S.F.		.92		.92	Includes material and labor to install
Install	S.F.	3.44	1.42		4.86	unfinished T&G maple flooring,
Demolish and Install	S.F.	3.44	2.34		5.78	25/32″ thick, 2-1/4″ wide, random 3′
Reinstall	S.F.		1.14		1.14	to 16′ lengths including felt
Clean	S.F.		.26		.26	underlayment, nailed in place over
Paint	S.F.	1.08	1.59		2.67	prepared subfloor.
Minimum Charge	Job		142		142	
3-1/4″						
Demolish	S.F.		.92		.92	Includes material and labor to install
Install	S.F.	2.93	1.42		4.35	unfinished T&G maple flooring,
Demolish and Install	S.F.	2.93	2.34		5.27	33/32″ thick, 3-1/4″ wide, random 3′
Reinstall	S.F.		1.14		1.14	to 16′ lengths including felt
Clean	S.F.		.26		.26	underlayment, nailed in place over
Paint	S.F.	1.08	1.59		2.67	prepared subfloor.
Minimum Charge	Job		142		142	
Sand and Finish						
Install	S.F.	.72	.52		1.24	Includes labor and material to sand (3
Minimum Charge	Job		142		142	passes) and finish and two coats of
						urethane existing floor.
Oak						
2-1/4″						
Demolish	S.F.		.92		.92	Includes material and labor to install
Install	S.F.	3.61	1.42		5.03	unfinished T&G oak flooring, 25/32″
Demolish and Install	S.F.	3.61	2.34		5.95	thick, 2-1/4″ wide, random 3′ to 16′
Reinstall	S.F.		1.14		1.14	lengths including felt underlayment,
Clean	S.F.		.26		.26	nailed in place over prepared subfloor.
Paint	S.F.	1.08	1.59		2.67	
Minimum Charge	Job		142		142	
3-1/4″						
Demolish	S.F.		.92		.92	Includes material and labor to install
Install	S.F.	4.96	1.01		5.97	unfinished T&G oak flooring, 25/32″
Demolish and Install	S.F.	4.96	1.93		6.89	thick, 3-1/4″ wide, random 3′ to 16′
Reinstall	S.F.		.80		.80	lengths including felt underlayment,
Clean	S.F.		.26		.26	nailed in place over prepared subfloor.
Paint	S.F.	1.08	1.59		2.67	
Minimum Charge	Job		142		142	
Sand and Finish						
Install	S.F.	1.08	1.59		2.67	Includes labor and material to sand
Minimum Charge	Job		142		142	and finish (3 passes) with two coats of
						urethane on a new floor.

Flooring

Wood Plank Flooring	Unit	Material	Labor	Equip.	Total	Specification
Walnut						
3" to 7"						
Demolish	S.F.		.92		.92	Includes material and labor to install
Install	S.F.	8.55	1.01		9.56	unfinished T&G walnut flooring,
Demolish and Install	S.F.	8.55	1.93		10.48	25/32" thick, random 3' to 16'
Reinstall	S.F.		.80		.80	lengths including felt underlayment,
Clean	S.F.		.26		.26	nailed in place over prepared subfloor.
Paint	S.F.	1.08	1.59		2.67	
Minimum Charge	Job		142		142	
Sand and Finish						
Install	S.F.	1.08	1.59		2.67	Includes labor and material to sand
Minimum Charge	Job		142		142	and finish (3 passes) with two coats of
						urethane on a new floor.
Pine						
2-1/4"						
Demolish	S.F.		.92		.92	Includes material and labor to install
Install	S.F.	6.95	1.07		8.02	unfinished T&G pine flooring, 25/32"
Demolish and Install	S.F.	6.95	1.99		8.94	thick, 2-1/4" wide, random 3' to 16'
Reinstall	S.F.		.86		.86	lengths including felt underlayment,
Clean	S.F.		.26		.26	nailed in place over prepared subfloor.
Paint	S.F.	.72	.52		1.24	
Minimum Charge	Job		142		142	
Sand and Finish						
Install	S.F.	1.08	1.59		2.67	Includes labor and material to sand
Minimum Charge	Job		142		142	and finish (3 passes) with two coats of
						urethane on a new floor.
Prefinished Oak						
2-1/4"						
Demolish	S.F.		.92		.92	Includes material and labor to install
Install	S.F.	5.30	1.42		6.72	prefinished T&G oak flooring, 2-1/4"
Demolish and Install	S.F.	5.30	2.34		7.64	wide, random 3' to 16' lengths
Reinstall	S.F.		1.14		1.14	including felt underlayment, nailed in
Clean	S.F.		.26		.26	place over prepared subfloor.
Minimum Charge	Job		142		142	
3-1/4"						
Demolish	S.F.		.92		.92	Includes material and labor to install
Install	S.F.	6.75	1.30		8.05	prefinished T&G oak flooring, 25/32"
Demolish and Install	S.F.	6.75	2.22		8.97	thick, 3" to 7" wide, random 3' to 16'
Reinstall	S.F.		1.04		1.04	lengths including felt underlayment,
Clean	S.F.		.26		.26	nailed in place over prepared subfloor.
Minimum Charge	Job		142		142	
Sand and Finish New						
Install	S.F.	.72	.70		1.42	Includes labor and material to sand (3
Minimum Charge	Job		142		142	passes) and finish, two coats of
						urethane, new floor.
Refinish Existing						
Install	S.F.	.72	.52		1.24	Includes labor and material to sand (3
Minimum Charge	Job		142		142	passes) and finish and two coats of
						urethane existing floor.
Urethane Coat						
Install	S.F.	.13	.13		.26	Includes labor and material to install
Minimum Charge	Job		142		142	two coats of urethane, on existing
						floor.
Clean and Wax						
Clean	S.F.	.02	.16		.18	Includes labor and material to wash
Minimum Charge	Job		142		142	and wax a hardwood floor.

Flooring

Wood Plank Flooring

	Unit	Material	Labor	Equip.	Total	Specification
Underlayment Per S.F.						
Demolish	S.F.		.42		.42	Cost includes material and labor to
Install	S.F.	.53	.38		.91	install 1/4" lauan subfloor, standard
Demolish and Install	S.F.	.53	.80		1.33	interior grade, nailed every 6".
Clean	S.F.		.20		.20	
Minimum Charge	Job		142		142	

Wood Parquet Tile Floor

	Unit	Material	Labor	Equip.	Total	Specification
Oak						
9" x 9"						
Demolish	S.F.		.70		.70	Includes material and labor to install
Install	S.F.	4.62	2.28		6.90	prefinished oak 9" x 9" parquet block
Demolish and Install	S.F.	4.62	2.98		7.60	flooring, 5/16" thick, installed in
Reinstall	S.F.		1.82		1.82	mastic.
Clean	S.F.		.26		.26	
Paint	S.F.	1.08	1.59		2.67	
Minimum Charge	Job		142		142	
13" x 13"						
Demolish	S.F.		.70		.70	Includes material and labor to install
Install	S.F.	8.75	1.78		10.53	prefinished oak 13" x 13" parquet
Demolish and Install	S.F.	8.75	2.48		11.23	block flooring, 5/16" thick, installed in
Reinstall	S.F.		1.42		1.42	mastic.
Clean	S.F.		.26		.26	
Paint	S.F.	1.08	1.59		2.67	
Minimum Charge	Job		142		142	
Cherry						
9" x 9"						
Demolish	S.F.		.70		.70	Includes material and labor to install
Install	S.F.	7.65	2.28		9.93	prefinished cherry 9" x 9" parquet
Demolish and Install	S.F.	7.65	2.98		10.63	block flooring, 5/16" thick, installed in
Reinstall	S.F.		2.28		2.28	mastic.
Clean	S.F.		.26		.26	
Paint	S.F.	1.08	1.59		2.67	
Minimum Charge	Job		142		142	
13" x 13"						
Demolish	S.F.		.70		.70	Includes material and labor to install
Install	S.F.	8.75	1.78		10.53	prefinished cherry 13" x 13" parquet
Demolish and Install	S.F.	8.75	2.48		11.23	block flooring, 5/16" thick, installed in
Reinstall	S.F.		1.78		1.78	mastic.
Clean	S.F.		.26		.26	
Paint	S.F.	1.08	1.59		2.67	
Minimum Charge	Job		142		142	
Walnut						
9" x 9"						
Demolish	S.F.		.70		.70	Includes material and labor to install
Install	S.F.	4.73	2.28		7.01	prefinished walnut 9" x 9" parquet
Demolish and Install	S.F.	4.73	2.98		7.71	flooring in mastic.
Reinstall	S.F.		1.82		1.82	
Clean	S.F.		.26		.26	
Paint	S.F.	1.08	1.59		2.67	
Minimum Charge	Job		142		142	

Flooring

Wood Parquet Tile Floor		Unit	Material	Labor	Equip.	Total	Specification
13" x 13"							Includes material and labor to install
	Demolish	S.F.		.70		.70	prefinished walnut 13" x 13" parquet
	Install	S.F.	8.80	1.78		10.58	block flooring, 5/16" thick, installed in
	Demolish and Install	S.F.	8.80	2.48		11.28	mastic.
	Reinstall	S.F.		1.78		1.78	
	Clean	S.F.		.26		.26	
	Paint	S.F.	1.08	1.59		2.67	
	Minimum Charge	Job		142		142	
Acrylic Impregnated							
Oak 12" x 12"							Includes material and labor to install
	Demolish	S.F.		.70		.70	red oak 12" x 12" acrylic impregnated
	Install	S.F.	7.10	2.03		9.13	parquet block flooring, 5/16" thick,
	Demolish and Install	S.F.	7.10	2.73		9.83	installed in mastic.
	Reinstall	S.F.		2.03		2.03	
	Clean	S.F.		.26		.26	
	Minimum Charge	Job		142		142	
Cherry 12" x 12"							Includes material and labor to install
	Demolish	S.F.		.70		.70	prefinished cherry 12" x 12" acrylic
	Install	S.F.	10.75	2.03		12.78	impregnated parquet block flooring,
	Demolish and Install	S.F.	10.75	2.73		13.48	5/16" thick, installed in mastic.
	Reinstall	S.F.		2.03		2.03	
	Clean	S.F.		.26		.26	
	Minimum Charge	Job		142		142	
Ash 12" x 12"							Includes material and labor to install
	Demolish	S.F.		.70		.70	ash 12" x 12" acrylic impregnated
	Install	S.F.	9.65	2.03		11.68	parquet block flooring, 5/16" thick in
	Demolish and Install	S.F.	9.65	2.73		12.38	mastic.
	Reinstall	S.F.		2.03		2.03	
	Clean	S.F.		.26		.26	
	Minimum Charge	Job		142		142	
Teak							Includes material and labor to install
	Demolish	S.F.		.70		.70	prefinished teak parquet block
	Install	S.F.	7.20	1.78		8.98	flooring, 5/16" thick, and installed in
	Demolish and Install	S.F.	7.20	2.48		9.68	mastic.
	Reinstall	S.F.		1.78		1.78	
	Clean	S.F.		.26		.26	
	Paint	S.F.	1.08	1.59		2.67	
	Minimum Charge	Job		142		142	
Clean and Wax							Includes labor and material to wash
	Clean	S.F.	.02	.16		.18	and wax a hardwood floor.
	Minimum Charge	Job		142		142	

Ceramic Tile Flooring		Unit	Material	Labor	Equip.	Total	Specification
Economy Grade							Cost includes material and labor to
	Demolish	S.F.		.68		.68	install 4-1/4" x 4-1/4" ceramic tile in
	Install	S.F.	4.20	5.15		9.35	mortar bed including grout.
	Demolish and Install	S.F.	4.20	5.83		10.03	
	Clean	S.F.		.39		.39	
	Minimum Charge	Job		132		132	
Average Grade							Cost includes material and labor to
	Demolish	S.F.		.68		.68	install 4-1/4" x 4-1/4" ceramic tile in
	Install	S.F.	5.60	5.25		10.85	mortar bed including grout.
	Demolish and Install	S.F.	5.60	5.93		11.53	
	Clean	S.F.		.39		.39	
	Minimum Charge	Job		132		132	

Flooring

Ceramic Tile Flooring

	Unit	Material	Labor	Equip.	Total	Specification
Premium Grade						
Demolish	S.F.		.68		.68	Cost includes material and labor to
Install	S.F.	8.80	5.25		14.05	install 4-1/4" x 4-1/4" ceramic tile in
Demolish and Install	S.F.	8.80	5.93		14.73	mortar bed including grout.
Clean	S.F.		.39		.39	
Minimum Charge	Job		132		132	
Re-grout						
Install	S.F.	.14	2.11		2.25	Includes material and labor to regrout
Minimum Charge	Job		132		132	tile floors.

Hard Tile Flooring

	Unit	Material	Labor	Equip.	Total	Specification
Thick Set Paver						
Brick						
Demolish	S.F.		1.44		1.44	Cost includes material and labor to
Install	S.F.	.72	12.05		12.77	install 6" x 12" adobe brick paver with
Demolish and Install	S.F.	.72	13.49		14.21	1/2" mortar joints.
Clean	S.F.		.39		.39	
Minimum Charge	Job		132		132	
Mexican Red						
Demolish	S.F.		1.44		1.44	Cost includes material and labor to
Install	S.F.	1.43	5.50		6.93	install 12" x 12" red Mexican paver
Demolish and Install	S.F.	1.43	6.94		8.37	tile in mortar bed with grout.
Clean	S.F.		.39		.39	
Minimum Charge	Job		132		132	
Saltillo						
Demolish	S.F.		.68		.68	Cost includes material and labor to
Install	S.F.	2.24	5.50		7.74	install 12" x 12"saltillo tile in mortar
Demolish and Install	S.F.	2.24	6.18		8.42	bed with grout.
Clean	S.F.		.39		.39	
Minimum Charge	Job		132		132	
Marble						
Premium Grade						
Demolish	S.F.		.68		.68	Cost includes material and labor to
Install	S.F.	18.90	11.45		30.35	install 3/8" x 12" x 12" marble, in
Demolish and Install	S.F.	18.90	12.13		31.03	mortar bed with grout.
Clean	S.F.		.39		.39	
Minimum Charge	Job		132		132	
Terrazzo						
Gray Cement						
Demolish	S.F.		.91		.91	Cost includes material and labor to
Install	S.F.	2.68	3.69	1.33	7.70	install 1-3/4" terrazzo , #1 and #2
Demolish and Install	S.F.	2.68	4.60	1.33	8.61	chips in gray Portland cement.
Clean	S.F.		.39		.39	
Minimum Charge	Job		240	86	326	
White Cement						
Demolish	S.F.		.91		.91	Cost includes material and labor to
Install	S.F.	3.06	3.69	1.33	8.08	install 1-3/4" terrazzo, #1 and #2
Demolish and Install	S.F.	3.06	4.60	1.33	8.99	chips in white Portland cement.
Clean	S.F.		.39		.39	
Minimum Charge	Job		240	86	326	
Non-skid Gray						
Demolish	S.F.		.91		.91	Cost includes material and labor to
Install	S.F.	4.88	8	2.87	15.75	install 1-3/4" terrazzo, #1 and #2
Demolish and Install	S.F.	4.88	8.91	2.87	16.66	chips in gray Portland cement with
Clean	S.F.		.39		.39	light non-skid abrasive.
Minimum Charge	Job		240	86	326	

Flooring

Hard Tile Flooring		Unit	Material	Labor	Equip.	Total	Specification
Non-skid White							
	Demolish	S.F.		.91		.91	Cost includes material and labor to
	Install	S.F.	5.35	8	2.87	16.22	install 1-3/4" terrazzo, #1 and #2
	Demolish and Install	S.F.	5.35	8.91	2.87	17.13	chips in white Portland cement with
	Clean	S.F.		.39		.39	light non-skid abrasive.
	Minimum Charge	Job		240	86	326	
Gray w / Brass Divider							
	Demolish	S.F.		.92		.92	Cost includes material and labor to
	Install	S.F.	6.70	8.75	3.13	18.58	install 1-3/4" terrazzo, #1 and #2
	Demolish and Install	S.F.	6.70	9.67	3.13	19.50	chips in gray Portland cement with
	Clean	S.F.		.39		.39	brass strips 2' O.C. each way.
	Minimum Charge	Job		240	86	326	
Clean							
	Clean	S.F.	.12	.26		.38	Includes labor and material to clean
	Minimum Charge	Job		240	86	326	terrazzo flooring.
Slate							
	Demolish	S.F.		.82		.82	Includes material and labor to install
	Install	S.F.	4.55	2.63		7.18	slate tile flooring in thin set with grout.
	Demolish and Install	S.F.	4.55	3.45		8	
	Clean	S.F.		.39		.39	
	Minimum Charge	Job		132		132	
Granite							
	Demolish	S.F.		.68		.68	Includes material and labor to install
	Install	S.F.	18.55	22		40.55	granite tile flooring in thin set with
	Demolish and Install	S.F.	18.55	22.68		41.23	grout.
	Reinstall	S.F.		21.93		21.93	
	Clean	S.F.		.39		.39	
	Minimum Charge	Job		132		132	
Re-grout							
	Install	S.F.	.14	2.11		2.25	Includes material and labor to regrout
	Minimum Charge	Job		132		132	tile floors.

Sheet Vinyl Per S.F.		Unit	Material	Labor	Equip.	Total	Specification
Economy Grade							
	Demolish	S.F.		.33		.33	Includes material and labor to install
	Install	S.F.	1.36	.82		2.18	resilient sheet vinyl flooring.
	Demolish and Install	S.F.	1.36	1.15		2.51	
	Clean	S.F.		.26		.26	
	Minimum Charge	Job		132		132	
Average Grade							
	Demolish	S.F.		.33		.33	Includes material and labor to install
	Install	S.F.	2.19	.82		3.01	resilient sheet vinyl flooring.
	Demolish and Install	S.F.	2.19	1.15		3.34	
	Clean	S.F.		.26		.26	
	Minimum Charge	Job		132		132	
Premium Grade							
	Demolish	S.F.		.33		.33	Includes material and labor to install
	Install	S.F.	3.45	.82		4.27	resilient sheet vinyl flooring.
	Demolish and Install	S.F.	3.45	1.15		4.60	
	Clean	S.F.		.26		.26	
	Minimum Charge	Job		132		132	
Clean and Wax							
	Clean	S.F.	.02	.13		.15	Includes labor and material to wash
	Minimum Charge	Job		132		132	and wax a vinyl tile floor.

Flooring

Sheet Vinyl

Sheet Vinyl	Unit	Material	Labor	Equip.	Total	Specification
Economy Grade						
Demolish	S.Y.		2.96		2.96	Includes material and labor to install
Install	S.Y.	12.20	7.40		19.60	no wax sheet vinyl flooring.
Demolish and Install	S.Y.	12.20	10.36		22.56	
Clean	S.Y.		1.80		1.80	
Minimum Charge	Job		132		132	
Average Grade						
Demolish	S.Y.		2.96		2.96	Includes material and labor to install
Install	S.Y.	19.55	7.40		26.95	no wax sheet vinyl flooring.
Demolish and Install	S.Y.	19.55	10.36		29.91	
Clean	S.Y.		1.80		1.80	
Minimum Charge	Job		132		132	
Premium Grade						
Demolish	S.Y.		2.96		2.96	Includes material and labor to install
Install	S.Y.	31	7.40		38.40	no wax sheet vinyl flooring.
Demolish and Install	S.Y.	31	10.36		41.36	
Clean	S.Y.		1.80		1.80	
Minimum Charge	Job		132		132	
Clean and Wax						
Clean	S.F.	.02	.13		.15	Includes labor and material to wash
Minimum Charge	Job		132		132	and wax a vinyl tile floor.

Vinyl Tile

Vinyl Tile	Unit	Material	Labor	Equip.	Total	Specification
Economy Grade						
Demolish	S.F.		.46		.46	Includes material and labor to install
Install	S.F.	1.75	.53		2.28	no wax 12" x 12" vinyl tile.
Demolish and Install	S.F.	1.75	.99		2.74	
Clean	S.F.		.26		.26	
Minimum Charge	Job		132		132	
Average Grade						
Demolish	S.F.		.46		.46	Includes material and labor to install
Install	S.F.	4.93	.53		5.46	no wax 12" x 12" vinyl tile.
Demolish and Install	S.F.	4.93	.99		5.92	
Clean	S.F.		.26		.26	
Minimum Charge	Job		132		132	
Premium Grade						
Demolish	S.F.		.46		.46	Includes material and labor to install
Install	S.F.	8.30	.53		8.83	no wax 12" x 12" vinyl tile.
Demolish and Install	S.F.	8.30	.99		9.29	
Clean	S.F.		.26		.26	
Minimum Charge	Job		132		132	
Clean and Wax						
Clean	S.F.	.02	.13		.15	Includes labor and material to wash
Minimum Charge	Job		132		132	and wax a vinyl tile floor.

Carpeting Per S.F.

Carpeting Per S.F.	Unit	Material	Labor	Equip.	Total	Specification
Economy Grade						
Demolish	S.F.		.05		.05	Includes material and labor to install
Install	S.F.	1.01	.51		1.52	carpet including tack strips and hot
Demolish and Install	S.F.	1.01	.56		1.57	melt tape on seams.
Clean	S.F.		.36		.36	
Minimum Charge	Job		132		132	

Flooring

Carpeting Per S.F.	Unit	Material	Labor	Equip.	Total	Specification
Average Grade						
Demolish	S.F.		.05		.05	Includes material and labor to install
Install	S.F.	1.23	.51		1.74	carpet including tack strips and hot
Demolish and Install	S.F.	1.23	.56		1.79	melt tape on seams.
Clean	S.F.		.36		.36	
Minimum Charge	Job		132		132	
Premium Grade						
Demolish	S.F.		.05		.05	Includes material and labor to install
Install	S.F.	2.21	.51		2.72	carpet including tack strips and hot
Demolish and Install	S.F.	2.21	.56		2.77	melt tape on seams.
Clean	S.F.		.36		.36	
Minimum Charge	Job		132		132	
Indoor/Outdoor						
Demolish	S.F.		.05		.05	Includes material and labor to install
Install	S.F.	.95	.62		1.57	indoor-outdoor carpet.
Demolish and Install	S.F.	.95	.67		1.62	
Clean	S.F.		.36		.36	
Minimum Charge	Job		132		132	
100% Wool						
Average Grade						
Demolish	S.F.		.05		.05	Includes material and labor to install
Install	S.F.	5.45	.52		5.97	carpet including tack strips and hot
Demolish and Install	S.F.	5.45	.57		6.02	melt tape on seams.
Clean	S.F.		.36		.36	
Minimum Charge	Job		132		132	
Premium Grade						
Demolish	S.F.		.05		.05	Includes material and labor to install
Install	S.F.	6.05	.52		6.57	carpet including tack strips and hot
Demolish and Install	S.F.	6.05	.57		6.62	melt tape on seams.
Clean	S.F.		.36		.36	
Minimum Charge	Job		132		132	
Luxury Grade						
Demolish	S.F.		.05		.05	Includes material and labor to install
Install	S.F.	8.60	.52		9.12	carpet including tack strips and hot
Demolish and Install	S.F.	8.60	.57		9.17	melt tape on seams.
Clean	S.F.		.36		.36	
Minimum Charge	Job		132		132	
Berber						
Average Grade						
Demolish	S.F.		.05		.05	Includes material and labor to install
Install	S.F.	2.55	.62		3.17	carpet including tack strips and hot
Demolish and Install	S.F.	2.55	.67		3.22	melt tape on seams.
Clean	S.F.		.36		.36	
Minimum Charge	Job		132		132	
Premium Grade						
Demolish	S.F.		.05		.05	Includes material and labor to install
Install	S.F.	5.50	.62		6.12	carpet including tack strips and hot
Demolish and Install	S.F.	5.50	.67		6.17	melt tape on seams.
Clean	S.F.		.36		.36	
Minimum Charge	Job		132		132	

Flooring

Carpeting		Unit	Material	Labor	Equip.	Total	Specification
Indoor/Outdoor							
	Demolish	S.Y.		.77		.77	Includes material and labor to install
	Install	S.Y.	8.55	5.60		14.15	indoor-outdoor carpet.
	Demolish and Install	S.Y.	8.55	6.37		14.92	
	Reinstall	S.Y.		4.48		4.48	
	Clean	S.Y.		3.23		3.23	
	Minimum Charge	Job		132		132	
Economy Grade							
	Demolish	S.Y.		.77		.77	Includes material and labor to install
	Install	S.Y.	9.15	4.62		13.77	carpet including tack strips and hot
	Demolish and Install	S.Y.	9.15	5.39		14.54	melt tape on seams.
	Reinstall	S.Y.		3.69		3.69	
	Clean	S.Y.		3.23		3.23	
	Minimum Charge	Job		132		132	
Average Grade							
	Demolish	S.Y.		.77		.77	Includes material and labor to install
	Install	S.Y.	11.10	4.62		15.72	carpet including tack strips and hot
	Demolish and Install	S.Y.	11.10	5.39		16.49	melt tape on seams.
	Reinstall	S.Y.		3.69		3.69	
	Clean	S.Y.		3.23		3.23	
	Minimum Charge	Job		132		132	
Premium Grade							
	Demolish	S.Y.		.77		.77	Includes material and labor to install
	Install	S.Y.	19.85	4.62		24.47	carpet including tack strips and hot
	Demolish and Install	S.Y.	19.85	5.39		25.24	melt tape on seams.
	Reinstall	S.Y.		3.69		3.69	
	Clean	S.Y.		3.23		3.23	
	Minimum Charge	Job		132		132	
100% Wool							
Average Grade							
	Demolish	S.Y.		.77		.77	Includes material and labor to install
	Install	S.Y.	49	4.70		53.70	wool carpet including tack strips and
	Demolish and Install	S.Y.	49	5.47		54.47	hot melt tape on seams.
	Reinstall	S.Y.		3.76		3.76	
	Clean	S.Y.		3.23		3.23	
	Minimum Charge	Job		132		132	
Premium Grade							
	Demolish	S.Y.		.77		.77	Includes material and labor to install
	Install	S.Y.	54.50	4.70		59.20	carpet including tack strips and hot
	Demolish and Install	S.Y.	54.50	5.47		59.97	melt tape on seams.
	Reinstall	S.Y.		3.76		3.76	
	Clean	S.Y.		3.23		3.23	
	Minimum Charge	Job		132		132	
Luxury Grade							
	Demolish	S.Y.		.77		.77	Includes material and labor to install
	Install	S.Y.	77	4.70		81.70	carpet including tack strips and hot
	Demolish and Install	S.Y.	77	5.47		82.47	melt tape on seams.
	Reinstall	S.Y.		3.76		3.76	
	Clean	S.Y.		3.23		3.23	
	Minimum Charge	Job		132		132	
Berber							
Average Grade							
	Demolish	S.Y.		.77		.77	Includes material and labor to install
	Install	S.Y.	23	5.60		28.60	berber carpet including tack strips and
	Demolish and Install	S.Y.	23	6.37		29.37	hot melt tape on seams.
	Reinstall	S.Y.		4.48		4.48	
	Clean	S.Y.		3.23		3.23	
	Minimum Charge	Job		132		132	

Flooring

Carpeting

	Unit	Material	Labor	Equip.	Total	Specification
Premium Grade						
Demolish	S.Y.		.77		.77	Includes material and labor to install
Install	S.Y.	49.50	5.60		55.10	carpet including tack strips and hot
Demolish and Install	S.Y.	49.50	6.37		55.87	melt tape on seams.
Reinstall	S.Y.		4.48		4.48	
Clean	S.Y.		3.23		3.23	
Minimum Charge	Job		132		132	

Carpet Pad Per S.F.

	Unit	Material	Labor	Equip.	Total	Specification
Urethane						
Demolish	S.F.		.01		.01	Includes material and labor to install
Install	S.F.	.30	.20		.50	urethane carpet pad.
Demolish and Install	S.F.	.30	.21		.51	
Minimum Charge	Job		132		132	
Foam Rubber Slab						
Demolish	S.F.		.01		.01	Includes material and labor to install
Install	S.F.	.50	.20		.70	carpet pad, 3/8" thick foam rubber.
Demolish and Install	S.F.	.50	.21		.71	
Minimum Charge	Job		132		132	
Waffle						
Demolish	S.F.		.01		.01	Includes material and labor to install
Install	S.F.	.32	.02		.34	rubber waffle carpet pad.
Demolish and Install	S.F.	.32	.03		.35	
Minimum Charge	Job		132		132	
Jute						
Demolish	S.F.		.01		.01	Includes material and labor to install
Install	S.F.	.57	.17		.74	jute hair carpet pad.
Demolish and Install	S.F.	.57	.18		.75	
Minimum Charge	Job		132		132	
Rebound						
Demolish	S.F.		.01		.01	Includes material and labor to install
Install	S.F.	.27	.15		.42	rebound carpet pad.
Demolish and Install	S.F.	.27	.16		.43	
Minimum Charge	Job		132		132	

Carpet Pad

	Unit	Material	Labor	Equip.	Total	Specification
Urethane						
Demolish	S.Y.		.13		.13	Includes material and labor to install
Install	S.Y.	2.65	1.75		4.40	urethane carpet pad.
Demolish and Install	S.Y.	2.65	1.88		4.53	
Reinstall	S.Y.		1.40		1.40	
Minimum Charge	Job		132		132	
Foam Rubber Slab						
Demolish	S.Y.		.13		.13	Includes material and labor to install
Install	S.Y.	4.46	1.75		6.21	rubber slab carpet pad.
Demolish and Install	S.Y.	4.46	1.88		6.34	
Reinstall	S.Y.		1.40		1.40	
Minimum Charge	Job		132		132	
Waffle						
Demolish	S.Y.		.13		.13	Includes material and labor to install
Install	S.Y.	2.84	.20		3.04	rubber waffle carpet pad.
Demolish and Install	S.Y.	2.84	.33		3.17	
Reinstall	S.Y.		.16		.16	
Minimum Charge	Job		132		132	

Flooring

Carpet Pad

	Unit	Material	Labor	Equip.	Total	Specification
Jute						
Demolish	S.Y.		.13		.13	Includes material and labor to install
Install	S.Y.	5.15	1.55		6.70	jute hair carpet pad.
Demolish and Install	S.Y.	5.15	1.68		6.83	
Reinstall	S.Y.		1.24		1.24	
Minimum Charge	Job		132		132	
Rebound						
Demolish	S.Y.		.13		.13	Includes material and labor to install
Install	S.Y.	2.41	1.31		3.72	rebound carpet pad.
Demolish and Install	S.Y.	2.41	1.44		3.85	
Reinstall	S.Y.		1.05		1.05	
Minimum Charge	Job		132		132	

Stair Components

	Unit	Material	Labor	Equip.	Total	Specification
Carpeting						
Demolish	Ea.		1.39		1.39	Includes material and labor to install
Install	Riser	27.50	6.95		34.45	carpet and pad on stairs.
Demolish and Install	Riser	27.50	8.34		35.84	
Reinstall	Riser		5.54		5.54	
Clean	Ea.		3.23		3.23	
Minimum Charge	Job		132		132	

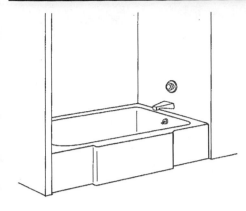

Tub/Shower

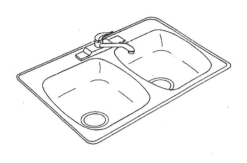

Stainless Steel Double Sink

Water Closet

Commode	Unit	Material	Labor	Equip.	Total	Specification
Floor Mounted w/Tank						
Demolish	Ea.		31.50		31.50	Includes material and labor to install a
Install	Ea.	154	106		260	toilet with valve, seat and cover.
Demolish and Install	Ea.	154	137.50		291.50	
Reinstall	Ea.		85.08		85.08	
Clean	Ea.	.28	10.35		10.63	
Minimum Charge	Job		157		157	
Wall w / Flush Valve						
Demolish	Ea.		31.50		31.50	Includes material and labor to install a
Install	Ea.	375	97		472	wall hung toilet with flush valve, seat
Demolish and Install	Ea.	375	128.50		503.50	and cover.
Reinstall	Ea.		77.75		77.75	
Clean	Ea.	.28	10.35		10.63	
Minimum Charge	Job		157		157	
Designer Floor Mount						
Demolish	Ea.		31.50		31.50	Includes material and labor to install a
Install	Ea.	545	106		651	toilet with valve, seat and cover.
Demolish and Install	Ea.	545	137.50		682.50	
Reinstall	Ea.		85.08		85.08	
Clean	Ea.	.28	10.35		10.63	
Minimum Charge	Job		157		157	
Urinal						
Demolish	Ea.		31.50		31.50	Includes material and labor to install a
Install	Ea.	310	188		498	wall hung urinal with flush valve.
Demolish and Install	Ea.	310	219.50		529.50	
Reinstall	Ea.		150.31		150.31	
Clean	Ea.	.28	10.35		10.63	
Minimum Charge	Job		157		157	
Bidet						
Vitreous China						
Demolish	Ea.		31.50		31.50	Includes material and labor to install a
Install	Ea.	600	113		713	vitreous china bidet complete with trim.
Demolish and Install	Ea.	600	144.50		744.50	
Reinstall	Ea.		90.19		90.19	
Clean	Ea.	.28	10.35		10.63	
Minimum Charge	Job		157		157	
Chrome Fittings						
Install	Ea.	145	39		184	Includes labor and materials to install chrome fittings for a bidet.
Brass Fittings						
Install	Ea.	160	39		199	Includes labor and materials to install brass fittings for a bidet.

Finish Mechanical

Commode

Commode	Unit	Material	Labor	Equip.	Total	Specification
Seat						
Demolish	Ea.		13.05		13.05	Includes material and labor to install a
Install	Ea.	29	13.05		42.05	toilet seat and cover.
Demolish and Install	Ea.	29	26.10		55.10	
Reinstall	Ea.		10.44		10.44	
Clean	Ea.	.14	4.31		4.45	
Minimum Charge	Job		157		157	
Rough-in						
Install	Ea.	152	198		350	Includes labor and materials to install water supply pipe with valves and drain, waste and vent pipe with all couplings, hangers and fasteners necessary.

Sink (assembly)

Sink (assembly)	Unit	Material	Labor	Equip.	Total	Specification
Single						
Porcelain						
Demolish	Ea.		19.60		19.60	Includes material and labor to install a
Install	Ea.	272	101		373	single bowl enamel finished cast iron
Demolish and Install	Ea.	272	120.60		392.60	kitchen sink with faucet and drain.
Reinstall	Ea.		80.53		80.53	
Clean	Ea.	.19	7.40		7.59	
Minimum Charge	Job		157		157	
Stainless Steel						
Demolish	Ea.		19.60		19.60	Includes material and labor to install a
Install	Ea.	340	101		441	single bowl stainless steel kitchen sink
Demolish and Install	Ea.	340	120.60		460.60	with faucet and drain.
Reinstall	Ea.		80.53		80.53	
Clean	Ea.	.19	7.40		7.59	
Minimum Charge	Job		157		157	
Double						
Porcelain						
Demolish	Ea.		22.50		22.50	Includes material and labor to install a
Install	Ea.	515	117		632	double bowl enamel finished cast iron
Demolish and Install	Ea.	515	139.50		654.50	kitchen sink with faucet and drain.
Reinstall	Ea.		93.95		93.95	
Clean	Ea.	.28	10.35		10.63	
Minimum Charge	Job		157		157	
Stainless Steel						
Demolish	Ea.		22.50		22.50	Includes material and labor to install a
Install	Ea.	490	117		607	double bowl stainless steel kitchen sink
Demolish and Install	Ea.	490	139.50		629.50	with faucet and drain.
Reinstall	Ea.		93.95		93.95	
Clean	Ea.	.28	10.35		10.63	
Minimum Charge	Job		157		157	
Bar						
Demolish	Ea.		19.60		19.60	Includes material and labor to install a
Install	Ea.	70	78.50		148.50	small single bowl stainless steel bar /
Demolish and Install	Ea.	70	98.10		168.10	vegetable / kitchen sink with faucet
Reinstall	Ea.		62.64		62.64	and drain.
Clean	Ea.	.19	7.40		7.59	
Minimum Charge	Job		157		157	

Finish Mechanical

Sink (assembly)

Sink (assembly)	Unit	Material	Labor	Equip.	Total	Specification
Floor						Includes material and labor to install
Demolish	Ea.		62.50		62.50	an enameled cast iron floor mounted
Install	Ea.	540	128		668	corner service sink with faucet and
Demolish and Install	Ea.	540	190.50		730.50	drain.
Reinstall	Ea.		102.49		102.49	
Clean	Ea.	.28	5.15		5.43	
Minimum Charge	Job		157		157	
Pedestal						Includes material and labor to install a
Demolish	Ea.		19.60		19.60	vitreous china pedestal lavatory with
Install	Ea.	400	88		488	faucet set and pop-up drain.
Demolish and Install	Ea.	400	107.60		507.60	
Reinstall	Ea.		70.46		70.46	
Clean	Ea.	.19	7.40		7.59	
Minimum Charge	Job		157		157	
Vanity Lavatory						Includes material and labor to install a
Demolish	Ea.		19.60		19.60	vitreous china lavatory with faucet set
Install	Ea.	252	104		356	and pop-up drain.
Demolish and Install	Ea.	252	123.60		375.60	
Reinstall	Ea.		83.51		83.51	
Clean	Ea.	.19	7.40		7.59	
Minimum Charge	Job		157		157	
Rough-in						Includes labor and materials to install
Install	Ea.	93.50	263		356.50	copper supply pipe with valves and
						drain, waste and vent pipe with all
						couplings, hangers and fasteners
						necessary.
Laundry						Includes material and labor to install a
Demolish	Ea.		20.50		20.50	laundry sink (wall mounted or with
Install	Ea.	93.50	86.50		180	legs) including faucet and pop up
Demolish and Install	Ea.	93.50	107		200.50	drain.
Clean	Ea.	.19	7.40		7.59	
Minimum Charge	Job		157		157	

Sink Only

Sink Only	Unit	Material	Labor	Equip.	Total	Specification
Single						
Porcelain						Includes material and labor to install a
Demolish	Ea.		19.60		19.60	single bowl enamel finished cast iron
Install	Ea.	204	112		316	kitchen sink.
Demolish and Install	Ea.	204	131.60		335.60	
Reinstall	Ea.		89.49		89.49	
Clean	Ea.	.19	7.40		7.59	
Minimum Charge	Job		157		157	
Stainless Steel						Includes material and labor to install a
Demolish	Ea.		19.60		19.60	single bowl stainless steel kitchen sink.
Install	Ea.	274	78.50		352.50	
Demolish and Install	Ea.	274	98.10		372.10	
Reinstall	Ea.		62.64		62.64	
Clean	Ea.	.19	7.40		7.59	
Minimum Charge	Job		157		157	

Finish Mechanical

Sink Only

	Unit	Material	Labor	Equip.	Total	Specification
Double						
Porcelain						
Demolish	Ea.		22.50		22.50	Includes material and labor to install a
Install	Ea.	234	131		365	double bowl enamel finished cast iron
Demolish and Install	Ea.	234	153.50		387.50	kitchen sink.
Reinstall	Ea.		104.40		104.40	
Clean	Ea.	.28	10.35		10.63	
Minimum Charge	Job		157		157	
Stainless Steel						
Demolish	Ea.		22.50		22.50	Includes material and labor to install a
Install	Ea.	405	101		506	double bowl stainless steel kitchen sink.
Demolish and Install	Ea.	405	123.50		528.50	
Reinstall	Ea.		80.83		80.83	
Clean	Ea.	.28	10.35		10.63	
Minimum Charge	Job		157		157	
Bar						
Demolish	Ea.		19.60		19.60	Includes material and labor to install a
Install	Ea.	36.50	78.50		115	small single bowl stainless steel bar /
Demolish and Install	Ea.	36.50	98.10		134.60	vegetable / kitchen sink.
Reinstall	Ea.		62.64		62.64	
Clean	Ea.	.19	7.40		7.59	
Minimum Charge	Job		157		157	
Floor						
Demolish	Ea.		62.50		62.50	Includes material and labor to install
Install	Ea.	445	142		587	an enameled cast iron floor mounted
Demolish and Install	Ea.	445	204.50		649.50	corner service sink.
Reinstall	Ea.		113.89		113.89	
Clean	Ea.	.28	5.15		5.43	
Minimum Charge	Job		157		157	
Pedestal						
Demolish	Ea.		19.60		19.60	Includes material and labor to install a
Install	Ea.	345	98		443	vitreous china pedestal lavatory.
Demolish and Install	Ea.	345	117.60		462.60	
Reinstall	Ea.		78.30		78.30	
Clean	Ea.	.19	7.40		7.59	
Minimum Charge	Job		157		157	
Vanity Lavatory						
Demolish	Ea.		19.60		19.60	Includes material and labor to install a
Install	Ea.	145	98		243	vitreous china lavatory.
Demolish and Install	Ea.	145	117.60		262.60	
Reinstall	Ea.		78.30		78.30	
Clean	Ea.	.19	7.40		7.59	
Minimum Charge	Job		157		157	
Rough-in						
Install	Ea.	81.50	245		326.50	Includes labor and materials to install copper supply pipe with valves and drain, waste and vent pipe with all couplings, hangers and fasteners necessary.

Finish Mechanical

Sink Only

	Unit	Material	Labor	Equip.	Total	Specification
Faucet Sink						
Good Grade						
Demolish	Ea.		15.65		15.65	Includes material and labor to install a
Install	Ea.	55	21.50		76.50	sink faucet and fittings.
Demolish and Install	Ea.	55	37.15		92.15	
Reinstall	Ea.		17.29		17.29	
Clean	Ea.	.11	6.45		6.56	
Minimum Charge	Job		157		157	
Better Grade						
Demolish	Ea.		15.65		15.65	Includes material and labor to install a
Install	Ea.	92.50	21.50		114	sink faucet and fittings.
Demolish and Install	Ea.	92.50	37.15		129.65	
Reinstall	Ea.		17.29		17.29	
Clean	Ea.	.11	6.45		6.56	
Minimum Charge	Job		157		157	
Premium Grade						
Demolish	Ea.		15.65		15.65	Includes material and labor to install a
Install	Ea.	180	27		207	sink faucet and fittings.
Demolish and Install	Ea.	180	42.65		222.65	
Reinstall	Ea.		21.56		21.56	
Clean	Ea.	.11	6.45		6.56	
Minimum Charge	Job		157		157	
Drain & Basket						
Demolish	Ea.		9.80		9.80	Includes material and labor to install a
Install	Ea.	13.35	19.60		32.95	sink drain and basket.
Demolish and Install	Ea.	13.35	29.40		42.75	
Reinstall	Ea.		15.66		15.66	
Clean	Ea.	.11	6.45		6.56	
Minimum Charge	Job		157		157	

Bathtub

	Unit	Material	Labor	Equip.	Total	Specification
Enameled						
Steel						
Demolish	Ea.		56.50		56.50	Includes material and labor to install a
Install	Ea.	310	102		412	formed steel bath tub with spout,
Demolish and Install	Ea.	310	158.50		468.50	mixing valve, shower head and pop-up
Reinstall	Ea.		81.99		81.99	drain.
Clean	Ea.	.56	17.25		17.81	
Minimum Charge	Job		157		157	
Cast Iron						
Demolish	Ea.		56.50		56.50	Includes material and labor to install a
Install	Ea.	405	128		533	cast iron bath tub with spout, mixing
Demolish and Install	Ea.	405	184.50		589.50	valve, shower head and pop-up drain.
Reinstall	Ea.		102.49		102.49	
Clean	Ea.	.56	17.25		17.81	
Minimum Charge	Job		157		157	
Fiberglass						
Demolish	Ea.		56.50		56.50	Includes material and labor to install
Install	Ea.	855	102		957	an acrylic soaking tub with spout,
Demolish and Install	Ea.	855	158.50		1013.50	mixing valve, shower head and pop-up
Reinstall	Ea.		81.99		81.99	drain.
Clean	Ea.	.56	17.25		17.81	
Minimum Charge	Job		157		157	

Finish Mechanical

Bathtub

	Unit	Material	Labor	Equip.	Total	Specification
Institutional						
Demolish	Ea.		56.50		56.50	Includes material and labor to install a
Install	Ea.	970	188		1158	hospital / institutional type bathtub
Demolish and Install	Ea.	970	244.50		1214.50	with spout, mixing valve, shower head
Reinstall	Ea.		150.31		150.31	and pop-up drain.
Clean	Ea.	.56	17.25		17.81	
Minimum Charge	Job		157		157	
Whirlpool (Acrylic)						
Demolish	Ea.		174		174	Includes material and labor to install a
Install	Ea.	1975	565		2540	molded fiberglass whirlpool tub.
Demolish and Install	Ea.	1975	739		2714	
Reinstall	Ea.		450.94		450.94	
Clean	Ea.	.56	17.25		17.81	
Minimum Charge	Job		157		157	
Pump / Motor						
Demolish	Ea.		43.50		43.50	Includes material and labor to install a
Install	Ea.	158	131		289	whirlpool tub pump / motor.
Demolish and Install	Ea.	158	174.50		332.50	
Reinstall	Ea.		104.40		104.40	
Clean	Ea.	.14	12.95		13.09	
Minimum Charge	Job		157		157	
Heater / Motor						
Demolish	Ea.		43.50		43.50	Includes material and labor to install a
Install	Ea.	211	139		350	whirlpool tub heater.
Demolish and Install	Ea.	211	182.50		393.50	
Reinstall	Ea.		111.36		111.36	
Clean	Ea.	.14	12.95		13.09	
Minimum Charge	Job		157		157	
Thermal Cover						
Demolish	Ea.		6.95		6.95	Includes material and labor to install a
Install	Ea.	142	19.60		161.60	whirlpool tub thermal cover.
Demolish and Install	Ea.	142	26.55		168.55	
Reinstall	Ea.		15.66		15.66	
Clean	Ea.	1.40	12.95		14.35	
Minimum Charge	Job		157		157	
Tub / Shower Combination						
Demolish	Ea.		35		35	Includes material and labor to install a
Install	Ea.	770	141		911	fiberglass module tub with shower
Demolish and Install	Ea.	770	176		946	surround with spout, mixing valve,
Reinstall	Ea.		112.74		112.74	shower head and pop-up drain.
Clean	Ea.	.70	26		26.70	
Minimum Charge	Job		157		157	

Accessories
Sliding Door

	Unit	Material	Labor	Equip.	Total	Specification
Demolish	Ea.		14.35		14.35	Includes material and labor to install a
Install	Ea.	360	65.50		425.50	48" aluminum framed tempered glass
Demolish and Install	Ea.	360	79.85		439.85	shower door.
Reinstall	Ea.		52.48		52.48	
Clean	Ea.	1.17	8.60		9.77	
Minimum Charge	Job		157		157	
Shower Head						
Demolish	Ea.		3.92		3.92	Includes material and labor to install a
Install	Ea.	69.50	13.05		82.55	water saving shower head.
Demolish and Install	Ea.	69.50	16.97		86.47	
Reinstall	Ea.		10.44		10.44	
Clean	Ea.	.01	2.59		2.60	
Minimum Charge	Job		157		157	

Finish Mechanical

Bathtub

		Unit	Material	Labor	Equip.	Total	Specification
Faucet Set							Includes material and labor to install a combination spout / diverter for a bathtub.
	Demolish	Ea.		19.60		19.60	
	Install	Ea.	74.50	39		113.50	
	Demolish and Install	Ea.	74.50	58.60		133.10	
	Reinstall	Ea.		31.32		31.32	
	Clean	Ea.	.11	6.45		6.56	
	Minimum Charge	Job		157		157	
Shower Rod							Includes material and labor to install a chrome plated shower rod.
	Demolish	Ea.		2.39		2.39	
	Install	Ea.	13.15	22		35.15	
	Demolish and Install	Ea.	13.15	24.39		37.54	
	Reinstall	Ea.		17.53		17.53	
	Clean	Ea.		2.59		2.59	
	Minimum Charge	Job		157		157	
Rough-in							Includes labor and materials to install copper supply pipe with valves and drain, waste and vent pipe with all couplings, hangers and fasteners necessary.
	Install	Ea.	135	272		407	

Shower

		Unit	Material	Labor	Equip.	Total	Specification
Fiberglass							
32" x 32"							Includes material and labor to install a fiberglass shower stall with door, mixing valve and shower head and drain fitting.
	Demolish	Ea.		117		117	
	Install	Ea.	370	235		605	
	Demolish and Install	Ea.	370	352		722	
	Reinstall	Ea.		187.89		187.89	
	Clean	Ea.	.56	17.25		17.81	
	Minimum Charge	Job		157		157	
36" x 36"							Includes material and labor to install a fiberglass shower stall with door, mixing valve and shower head and drain fitting.
	Demolish	Ea.		117		117	
	Install	Ea.	420	235		655	
	Demolish and Install	Ea.	420	352		772	
	Reinstall	Ea.		187.89		187.89	
	Clean	Ea.	.56	17.25		17.81	
	Minimum Charge	Job		157		157	
35" x 60"							Includes material and labor to install a handicap fiberglass shower stall with door & seat, mixing valve and shower head and drain fitting.
	Demolish	Ea.		117		117	
	Install	Ea.	700	282		982	
	Demolish and Install	Ea.	700	399		1099	
	Reinstall	Ea.		225.47		225.47	
	Clean	Ea.	.56	17.25		17.81	
	Minimum Charge	Job		157		157	
Accessories							
Single Door							Includes material and labor to install a shower door.
	Demolish	Ea.		14.35		14.35	
	Install	Ea.	106	34.50		140.50	
	Demolish and Install	Ea.	106	48.85		154.85	
	Reinstall	Ea.		27.70		27.70	
	Clean	Ea.	1.17	8.60		9.77	
	Minimum Charge	Job		157		157	

Finish Mechanical

Shower

	Unit	Material	Labor	Equip.	Total	Specification
Shower Head						
Demolish	Ea.		3.92		3.92	Includes material and labor to install a
Install	Ea.	69.50	13.05		82.55	water saving shower head.
Demolish and Install	Ea.	69.50	16.97		86.47	
Reinstall	Ea.		10.44		10.44	
Clean	Ea.	.01	2.59		2.60	
Minimum Charge	Job		157		157	
Faucet Set						
Demolish	Ea.		19.60		19.60	Includes material and labor to install a
Install	Ea.	74.50	39		113.50	combination spout / diverter for a
Demolish and Install	Ea.	74.50	58.60		133.10	bathtub.
Reinstall	Ea.		31.32		31.32	
Clean	Ea.	.11	6.45		6.56	
Minimum Charge	Job		157		157	
Shower Pan						
Demolish	Ea.		14.50		14.50	Includes material and labor to install
Install	Ea.	177	39		216	the base portion of a fiberglass shower
Demolish and Install	Ea.	177	53.50		230.50	unit.
Reinstall	Ea.		31.32		31.32	
Clean	Ea.	.56	17.25		17.81	
Minimum Charge	Job		157		157	
Rough-in						
Install	Ea.	88.50	275		363.50	Includes labor and materials to install copper supply pipe with valves and drain, waste and vent pipe with all couplings, hangers and fasteners necessary.

Ductwork

	Unit	Material	Labor	Equip.	Total	Specification
Return Grill						
Under 10" Wide						
Demolish	Ea.		6.90		6.90	Includes material and labor to install a
Install	Ea.	33	17.30		50.30	10" x 10" air return register.
Demolish and Install	Ea.	33	24.20		57.20	
Reinstall	Ea.		13.85		13.85	
Clean	Ea.	.14	5.75		5.89	
Minimum Charge	Job		156		156	
12" to 20" Wide						
Demolish	Ea.		6.90		6.90	Includes material and labor to install a
Install	Ea.	59	18.35		77.35	16" x 16" air return register.
Demolish and Install	Ea.	59	25.25		84.25	
Reinstall	Ea.		14.66		14.66	
Clean	Ea.	.14	5.75		5.89	
Minimum Charge	Job		156		156	
Over 20" Wide						
Demolish	Ea.		10.50		10.50	Includes material and labor to install a
Install	Ea.	117	28.50		145.50	24" x 24" air return register.
Demolish and Install	Ea.	117	39		156	
Reinstall	Ea.		22.66		22.66	
Clean	Ea.	.14	6.45		6.59	
Minimum Charge	Job		156		156	

Finish Mechanical

Ductwork	Unit	Material	Labor	Equip.	Total	Specification
Supply Grill						
Baseboard Type						
Demolish	Ea.		4.95		4.95	Includes material and labor to install a
Install	Ea.	12.65	15.60		28.25	14" x 6" baseboard air supply register.
Demolish and Install	Ea.	12.65	20.55		33.20	
Reinstall	Ea.		12.46		12.46	
Clean	Ea.	.14	5.75		5.89	
Minimum Charge	Job		156		156	
10" Wide						
Demolish	Ea.		5.75		5.75	Includes material and labor to install a
Install	Ea.	25	15.60		40.60	10" x 6" air supply register.
Demolish and Install	Ea.	25	21.35		46.35	
Reinstall	Ea.		12.46		12.46	
Clean	Ea.	.14	5.75		5.89	
Minimum Charge	Job		156		156	
12" to 15" Wide						
Demolish	Ea.		5.75		5.75	Includes material and labor to install a
Install	Ea.	34	18.35		52.35	14" x 8" air supply register.
Demolish and Install	Ea.	34	24.10		58.10	
Reinstall	Ea.		14.66		14.66	
Clean	Ea.	.14	5.75		5.89	
Minimum Charge	Job		156		156	
18" to 24" Wide						
Demolish	Ea.		6.90		6.90	Includes material and labor to install a
Install	Ea.	47.50	24		71.50	24" x 8" air supply register.
Demolish and Install	Ea.	47.50	30.90		78.40	
Reinstall	Ea.		19.18		19.18	
Clean	Ea.	.14	6.45		6.59	
Minimum Charge	Job		156		156	
30" to 36" Wide						
Demolish	Ea.		8.65		8.65	Includes material and labor to install a
Install	Ea.	62	22.50		84.50	30" x 8" air supply register.
Demolish and Install	Ea.	62	31.15		93.15	
Reinstall	Ea.		17.81		17.81	
Clean	Ea.	.14	12.95		13.09	
Minimum Charge	Job		156		156	
Diffuser						
12" Louver						
Demolish	Ea.		6.90		6.90	Includes material and labor to install a
Install	Ea.	25.50	22.50		48	12" aluminum louvered diffuser.
Demolish and Install	Ea.	25.50	29.40		54.90	
Reinstall	Ea.		17.81		17.81	
Clean	Ea.	.14	5.75		5.89	
Minimum Charge	Job		156		156	
14" to 20" Louver						
Demolish	Ea.		6.90		6.90	Includes material and labor to install a
Install	Ea.	36	31		67	14" to 20" aluminum louvered diffuser.
Demolish and Install	Ea.	36	37.90		73.90	
Reinstall	Ea.		24.93		24.93	
Clean	Ea.	.14	6.45		6.59	
Minimum Charge	Job		156		156	
25" to 32" Louver						
Demolish	Ea.		10.50		10.50	Includes material and labor to install a
Install	Ea.	40	44.50		84.50	25" to 32" aluminum louvered diffuser.
Demolish and Install	Ea.	40	55		95	
Reinstall	Ea.		35.61		35.61	
Clean	Ea.	.14	8.60		8.74	
Minimum Charge	Job		156		156	

Ductwork		Unit	Material	Labor	Equip.	Total	Specification
12" Round							
	Demolish	Ea.		9.60		9.60	Includes material and labor to install a
	Install	Ea.	29	26		55	12" diameter aluminum diffuser with a
	Demolish and Install	Ea.	29	35.60		64.60	butterfly damper.
	Reinstall	Ea.		20.77		20.77	
	Clean	Ea.	.14	5.75		5.89	
	Minimum Charge	Job		156		156	
14" to 20" Round							
	Demolish	Ea.		12.80		12.80	Includes material and labor to install a
	Install	Ea.	111	34.50		145.50	20" diameter aluminum diffuser with a
	Demolish and Install	Ea.	111	47.30		158.30	butterfly damper.
	Reinstall	Ea.		27.70		27.70	
	Clean	Ea.	.14	6.45		6.59	
	Minimum Charge	Job		156		156	
Flush-out / Sanitize							
	Install	L.F.	.56	2.59		3.15	Includes labor and material costs to
	Minimum Charge	Job		156		156	clean ductwork.

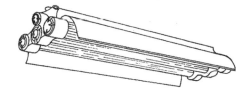

Lighting Fixture

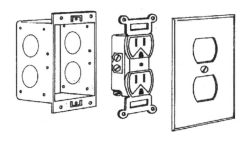

Duplex Receptical

Electrical Per S.F.	Unit	Material	Labor	Equip.	Total	Specification
Residential						
Light Fixtures						Includes labor and material to replace house light fixtures. Apply S.F. cost to floor area including garages but not basements.
Install	S.F.	.22	.16		.38	

Circuits	Unit	Material	Labor	Equip.	Total	Specification
Outlet with Wiring						Includes material and labor to install general purpose outlet with cover, up to 20 feet of #12/2 wire.
Demolish	Ea.		17.20		17.20	
Install	Ea.	5.55	21.50		27.05	
Demolish and Install	Ea.	5.55	38.70		44.25	
Reinstall	Ea.		17.04		17.04	
Clean	Ea.		1.29		1.29	
Minimum Charge	Job		155		155	
GFCI Outlet w / Wiring						Cost includes material and labor to install 120V GFCI receptacle and wall plate, with up to 20 feet of #12/2 wire.
Demolish	Ea.		17.20		17.20	
Install	Ea.	36	25		61	
Demolish and Install	Ea.	36	42.20		78.20	
Reinstall	Ea.		20.15		20.15	
Clean	Ea.		1.29		1.29	
Minimum Charge	Job		155		155	
Exterior Outlet w / Wiring						Cost includes material and labor to install 110V waterproof external receptacle and cover plate with up to 20' of #12/2 wire.
Demolish	Ea.		17.20		17.20	
Install	Ea.	23.50	26		49.50	
Demolish and Install	Ea.	23.50	43.20		66.70	
Reinstall	Ea.		20.67		20.67	
Clean	Ea.		1.29		1.29	
Minimum Charge	Job		155		155	
240V Outlet w / Wiring						Cost includes material and labor to install 240V receptacle and cover plate with up to 20' of #12/2 wire.
Demolish	Ea.		17.20		17.20	
Install	Ea.	52.50	48.50		101	
Demolish and Install	Ea.	52.50	65.70		118.20	
Reinstall	Ea.		38.69		38.69	
Clean	Ea.		1.29		1.29	
Minimum Charge	Job		155		155	

Finish Electrical

Circuits

	Unit	Material	Labor	Equip.	Total	Specification
TV / Cable Jack w / Wiring						Includes material and labor to install
Demolish	Ea.		17.20		17.20	TV/cable outlet box and cover plate
Install	Ea.	12.40	19.40		31.80	including 20' of wiring.
Demolish and Install	Ea.	12.40	36.60		49	
Reinstall	Ea.		15.50		15.50	
Clean	Ea.		1.29		1.29	
Minimum Charge	Job		155		155	
Phone Jack with Wiring						Includes material and labor to install
Demolish	Ea.		17.20		17.20	phone jack and cover plate including
Install	Ea.	7.50	11.90		19.40	up to 20' of telephone cable.
Demolish and Install	Ea.	7.50	29.10		36.60	
Reinstall	Ea.		9.54		9.54	
Clean	Ea.		.81		.81	
Minimum Charge	Job		155		155	

Light Switch

	Unit	Material	Labor	Equip.	Total	Specification
Single						
Switch						
Demolish	Ea.		3.44		3.44	Includes material and labor to install
Install	Ea.	4.42	14.75		19.17	single switch and wall plate. Wiring is
Demolish and Install	Ea.	4.42	18.19		22.61	not included.
Reinstall	Ea.		11.81		11.81	
Clean	Ea.		1.29		1.29	
Minimum Charge	Job		155		155	
Plate						
Demolish	Ea.		1.72		1.72	Includes material and labor to install a
Install	Ea.	.33	3.88		4.21	one gang brown wall switch plate.
Demolish and Install	Ea.	.33	5.60		5.93	
Reinstall	Ea.		3.10		3.10	
Clean	Ea.	.06	.26		.32	
Minimum Charge	Job		155		155	
Double						
Switch						
Demolish	Ea.		6.90		6.90	Includes material and labor to install
Install	Ea.	6.10	22		28.10	double switch and wall plate. Wiring
Demolish and Install	Ea.	6.10	28.90		35	is not included.
Reinstall	Ea.		17.71		17.71	
Clean	Ea.	.06	4.14		4.20	
Minimum Charge	Job		155		155	
Plate						
Demolish	Ea.		1.72		1.72	Includes material and labor to install a
Install	Ea.	.85	5.85		6.70	two gang brown wall switch plate.
Demolish and Install	Ea.	.85	7.57		8.42	
Reinstall	Ea.		4.68		4.68	
Clean	Ea.	.06	.26		.32	
Minimum Charge	Job		155		155	
Triple						
Switch						
Demolish	Ea.		10.45		10.45	Includes material and labor to install
Install	Ea.	20.50	26		46.50	triple switch and wall plate. Wiring is
Demolish and Install	Ea.	20.50	36.45		56.95	not included.
Reinstall	Ea.		20.67		20.67	
Clean	Ea.	.06	6.20		6.26	
Minimum Charge	Job		155		155	

Finish Electrical

Light Switch

	Unit	Material	Labor	Equip.	Total	Specification
Plate						
Demolish	Ea.		1.72		1.72	Includes material and labor to install a
Install	Ea.	1.25	9.70		10.95	three gang brown wall switch plate.
Demolish and Install	Ea.	1.25	11.42		12.67	
Reinstall	Ea.		7.75		7.75	
Clean	Ea.	.06	.26		.32	
Minimum Charge	Job		155		155	
Dimmer						
Switch						
Demolish	Ea.		3.44		3.44	Includes material and labor to install
Install	Ea.	17.35	18.25		35.60	dimmer switch. Wiring is not included.
Demolish and Install	Ea.	17.35	21.69		39.04	
Reinstall	Ea.		14.59		14.59	
Clean	Ea.		1.29		1.29	
Minimum Charge	Job		155		155	
Plate						
Demolish	Ea.		1.72		1.72	Includes material and labor to install a
Install	Ea.	.33	3.88		4.21	one gang brown wall switch plate.
Demolish and Install	Ea.	.33	5.60		5.93	
Reinstall	Ea.		3.10		3.10	
Clean	Ea.	.06	.26		.32	
Minimum Charge	Job		155		155	
With Wiring						
Single						
Demolish	Ea.		17.20		17.20	Includes material and labor to install
Install	Ea.	7.15	18.15		25.30	single switch and plate including up to
Demolish and Install	Ea.	7.15	35.35		42.50	20' of romex cable.
Reinstall	Ea.		14.50		14.50	
Clean	Ea.		1.29		1.29	
Minimum Charge	Job		155		155	
Double						
Demolish	Ea.		17.20		17.20	Includes material and labor to install
Install	Ea.	17.70	31		48.70	double switch and plate including up
Demolish and Install	Ea.	17.70	48.20		65.90	to 20' of romex cable.
Reinstall	Ea.		24.80		24.80	
Clean	Ea.	.06	4.14		4.20	
Minimum Charge	Job		155		155	
Triple						
Demolish	Ea.		26		26	Includes material and labor to install
Install	Ea.	25.50	35		60.50	triple switch and plate including up to
Demolish and Install	Ea.	25.50	61		86.50	20' of romex cable.
Reinstall	Ea.		27.90		27.90	
Clean	Ea.	.06	6.20		6.26	
Minimum Charge	Job		155		155	
Dimmer						
Demolish	Ea.		17.20		17.20	Includes material and labor to install
Install	Ea.	20	21.50		41.50	dimmer switch and cover plate
Demolish and Install	Ea.	20	38.70		58.70	including up to 20' of romex cable.
Reinstall	Ea.		17.04		17.04	
Clean	Ea.		1.29		1.29	
Minimum Charge	Job		155		155	

Finish Electrical

Cover for Outlet / Switch

	Unit	Material	Labor	Equip.	Total	Specification
High Grade						
Demolish	Ea.		1.72		1.72	Includes material and labor to install
Install	Ea.	1.98	3.88		5.86	wall plate, stainless steel, 1 gang.
Demolish and Install	Ea.	1.98	5.60		7.58	
Reinstall	Ea.		3.10		3.10	
Clean	Ea.	.06	.26		.32	
Minimum Charge	Job		155		155	
Deluxe Grade						
Demolish	Ea.		1.72		1.72	Includes material and labor to install
Install	Ea.	4.24	3.88		8.12	wall plate, brushed brass, 1 gang.
Demolish and Install	Ea.	4.24	5.60		9.84	
Reinstall	Ea.		3.10		3.10	
Clean	Ea.	.06	.26		.32	
Minimum Charge	Job		155		155	

Residential Light Fixture

	Unit	Material	Labor	Equip.	Total	Specification
Ceiling						
Good Quality						
Demolish	Ea.		7.20		7.20	Includes material and labor to install
Install	Ea.	28	7.75		35.75	standard quality incandescent ceiling
Demolish and Install	Ea.	28	14.95		42.95	light fixture. Wiring is not included.
Reinstall	Ea.		6.20		6.20	
Clean	Ea.	.14	8.60		8.74	
Minimum Charge	Job		155		155	
Better Quality						
Demolish	Ea.		7.20		7.20	Includes material and labor to install
Install	Ea.	83.50	16.30		99.80	custom quality incandescent ceiling
Demolish and Install	Ea.	83.50	23.50		107	light fixture. Wiring is not included.
Reinstall	Ea.		13.05		13.05	
Clean	Ea.	.14	8.60		8.74	
Minimum Charge	Job		155		155	
Premium Quality						
Demolish	Ea.		7.20		7.20	Includes material and labor to install
Install	Ea.	248	16.30		264.30	deluxe quality incandescent ceiling
Demolish and Install	Ea.	248	23.50		271.50	light fixture. Wiring is not included.
Reinstall	Ea.		13.05		13.05	
Clean	Ea.	.14	8.60		8.74	
Minimum Charge	Job		155		155	
Recessed Ceiling						
Demolish	Ea.		14.35		14.35	Includes material and labor to install
Install	Ea.	38.50	10.35		48.85	standard quality recessed eyeball
Demolish and Install	Ea.	38.50	24.70		63.20	spotlight with housing. Wiring is not
Reinstall	Ea.		8.27		8.27	included.
Clean	Ea.	.03	2.15		2.18	
Minimum Charge	Job		155		155	
Recessed Eyeball						
Demolish	Ea.		14.35		14.35	Includes material and labor to install
Install	Ea.	55	11.05		66.05	custom quality recessed eyeball
Demolish and Install	Ea.	55	25.40		80.40	spotlight with housing. Wiring is not
Reinstall	Ea.		8.86		8.86	included.
Clean	Ea.	.03	2.15		2.18	
Minimum Charge	Job		155		155	

Finish Electrical

Residential Light Fixture

	Unit	Material	Labor	Equip.	Total	Specification
Recessed Shower Type						Includes material and labor to install deluxe quality recessed eyeball spotlight with housing. Wiring is not included.
Demolish	Ea.		14.35		14.35	
Install	Ea.	47.50	10.35		57.85	
Demolish and Install	Ea.	47.50	24.70		72.20	
Reinstall	Ea.		8.27		8.27	
Clean	Ea.	.03	2.15		2.18	
Minimum Charge	Job		155		155	
Run Wiring						Includes labor and material to install a electric fixture utility box with non-metallic cable.
Install	Ea.	8.15	12.40		20.55	
Minimum Charge	Job		155		155	
Fluorescent						
Good Quality						Includes material and labor to install standard quality 12" wide by 48" long decorative surface mounted fluorescent fixture w/acrylic diffuser.
Demolish	Ea.		15.65		15.65	
Install	Ea.	47	44.50		91.50	
Demolish and Install	Ea.	47	60.15		107.15	
Reinstall	Ea.		35.43		35.43	
Clean	Ea.	.03	2.15		2.18	
Minimum Charge	Job		155		155	
Better Quality						Includes material and labor to install an interior fluorescent lighting fixture.
Demolish	Ea.		15.65		15.65	
Install	Ea.	87	50		137	
Demolish and Install	Ea.	87	65.65		152.65	
Reinstall	Ea.		40		40	
Clean	Ea.	.03	2.15		2.18	
Minimum Charge	Job		155		155	
Premium Quality						Includes material and labor to install deluxe quality 24" wide by 48" long decorative surface mounted fluorescent fixture w/acrylic diffuser.
Demolish	Ea.		15.65		15.65	
Install	Ea.	100	58.50		158.50	
Demolish and Install	Ea.	100	74.15		174.15	
Reinstall	Ea.		46.79		46.79	
Clean	Ea.	.03	2.15		2.18	
Minimum Charge	Job		155		155	
Run Wiring						Includes labor and material to install a electric fixture utility box with non-metallic cable.
Install	Ea.	8.15	12.40		20.55	
Minimum Charge	Job		155		155	
Exterior						
Good Quality						Includes material and labor to install standard quality incandescent outdoor light fixture. Wiring is not included.
Demolish	Ea.		13.80		13.80	
Install	Ea.	34	19.40		53.40	
Demolish and Install	Ea.	34	33.20		67.20	
Reinstall	Ea.		15.50		15.50	
Clean	Ea.	.14	8.60		8.74	
Minimum Charge	Job		155		155	
Better Quality						Includes material and labor to install custom quality incandescent outdoor light fixture. Wiring is not included.
Demolish	Ea.		13.80		13.80	
Install	Ea.	86	19.40		105.40	
Demolish and Install	Ea.	86	33.20		119.20	
Reinstall	Ea.		15.50		15.50	
Clean	Ea.	.14	8.60		8.74	
Minimum Charge	Job		155		155	
Premium Quality						Includes material and labor to install deluxe quality incandescent outdoor light fixture. Wiring is not included.
Demolish	Ea.		13.80		13.80	
Install	Ea.	164	77.50		241.50	
Demolish and Install	Ea.	164	91.30		255.30	
Reinstall	Ea.		62		62	
Clean	Ea.	.14	8.60		8.74	
Minimum Charge	Job		155		155	

Finish Electrical

Residential Light Fixture	Unit	Material	Labor	Equip.	Total	Specification
Outdoor w / Pole						Includes material and labor to install
Demolish	Ea.		13.80		13.80	post lantern type incandescent outdoor
Install	Ea.	121	77.50		198.50	light fixture. Wiring is not included.
Demolish and Install	Ea.	121	91.30		212.30	
Reinstall	Ea.		62		62	
Clean	Ea.	.14	8.60		8.74	
Minimum Charge	Job		155		155	
Run Wiring						Includes labor and material to install a
Install	Ea.	8.15	12.40		20.55	electric fixture utility box with
Minimum Charge	Job		155		155	non-metallic cable.
Track Lighting						Includes material and labor to install
Demolish	L.F.		4.78		4.78	track lighting.
Install	L.F.	12.20	12.90		25.10	
Demolish and Install	L.F.	12.20	17.68		29.88	
Reinstall	L.F.		10.33		10.33	
Clean	L.F.	.14	4.14		4.28	
Minimum Charge	Job		155		155	

Commercial Light Fixture	Unit	Material	Labor	Equip.	Total	Specification
Fluorescent						
2 Bulb, 2'						Includes material and labor to install a
Demolish	Ea.		13.80		13.80	2' long surface mounted fluorescent
Install	Ea.	31	39		70	light fixture with two 40 watt bulbs.
Demolish and Install	Ea.	31	52.80		83.80	
Reinstall	Ea.		31		31	
Clean	Ea.	.70	14.75		15.45	
Minimum Charge	Job		155		155	
2 Bulb, 4'						Includes material and labor to install a
Demolish	Ea.		13.80		13.80	4' long surface mounted fluorescent
Install	Ea.	58	44.50		102.50	light fixture with two 40 watt bulbs.
Demolish and Install	Ea.	58	58.30		116.30	
Reinstall	Ea.		35.43		35.43	
Clean	Ea.	.70	14.75		15.45	
Minimum Charge	Job		155		155	
3 Bulb, 4'						Includes material and labor to install a
Demolish	Ea.		13.80		13.80	4' long pendant mounted fluorescent
Install	Ea.	98	44.50		142.50	light fixture with three 34 watt bulbs.
Demolish and Install	Ea.	98	58.30		156.30	
Reinstall	Ea.		35.43		35.43	
Clean	Ea.	.70	14.75		15.45	
Minimum Charge	Job		155		155	
4 Bulb, 4'						Includes material and labor to install a
Demolish	Ea.		13.80		13.80	4' long pendant mounted fluorescent
Install	Ea.	89	47.50		136.50	light fixture with four 34 watt bulbs.
Demolish and Install	Ea.	89	61.30		150.30	
Reinstall	Ea.		38.15		38.15	
Clean	Ea.	.70	14.75		15.45	
Minimum Charge	Job		155		155	
2 Bulb, 8'						Includes material and labor to install a
Demolish	Ea.		17.20		17.20	8' long surface mounted fluorescent
Install	Ea.	89	58.50		147.50	light fixture with two 110 watt bulbs.
Demolish and Install	Ea.	89	75.70		164.70	
Reinstall	Ea.		46.79		46.79	
Clean	Ea.	.70	14.75		15.45	
Minimum Charge	Job		155		155	

Finish Electrical

Commercial Light Fixture		Unit	Material	Labor	Equip.	Total	Specification
Run Wiring							
	Install	Ea.	8.15	12.40		20.55	Includes labor and material to install a
	Minimum Charge	Job		155		155	electric fixture utility box with
							non-metallic cable.
Ceiling, Recessed							
Eyeball Type							
	Demolish	Ea.		14.35		14.35	Includes material and labor to install
	Install	Ea.	55	11.05		66.05	custom quality recessed eyeball
	Demolish and Install	Ea.	55	25.40		80.40	spotlight with housing. Wiring is not
	Reinstall	Ea.		8.86		8.86	included.
	Clean	Ea.	.03	2.15		2.18	
	Minimum Charge	Job		155		155	
Shower Type							
	Demolish	Ea.		14.35		14.35	Includes material and labor to install
	Install	Ea.	47.50	10.35		57.85	deluxe quality recessed eyeball
	Demolish and Install	Ea.	47.50	24.70		72.20	spotlight with housing. Wiring is not
	Reinstall	Ea.		8.27		8.27	included.
	Clean	Ea.	.03	2.15		2.18	
	Minimum Charge	Job		155		155	
Run Wiring							
	Install	Ea.	8.15	12.40		20.55	Includes labor and material to install a
	Minimum Charge	Job		155		155	electric fixture utility box with
							non-metallic cable.
Ceiling Grid Type							
2 Tube							
	Demolish	Ea.		20.50		20.50	Cost includes material and labor to
	Install	Ea.	55.50	58.50		114	install 2 lamp fluorescent light fixture in
	Demolish and Install	Ea.	55.50	79		134.50	2' x 4' ceiling grid system including
	Reinstall	Ea.		46.79		46.79	lens and tubes.
	Clean	Ea.	.70	14.75		15.45	
	Minimum Charge	Job		155		155	
4 Tube							
	Demolish	Ea.		23		23	Cost includes material and labor to
	Install	Ea.	62	66		128	install 4 lamp fluorescent light fixture in
	Demolish and Install	Ea.	62	89		151	2' x 4' ceiling grid system including
	Reinstall	Ea.		52.77		52.77	lens and tubes.
	Clean	Ea.	.70	14.75		15.45	
	Minimum Charge	Job		155		155	
Acrylic Diffuser							
	Demolish	Ea.		3.59		3.59	Includes material and labor to install
	Install	Ea.	38.50	9.40		47.90	fluorescent light fixture w/acrylic
	Demolish and Install	Ea.	38.50	12.99		51.49	diffuser.
	Reinstall	Ea.		7.52		7.52	
	Clean	Ea.	.45	2.59		3.04	
	Minimum Charge	Job		155		155	
Louver Diffuser							
	Demolish	Ea.		4.31		4.31	Includes material and labor to install
	Install	Ea.	42	9.40		51.40	fluorescent light fixture w/louver
	Demolish and Install	Ea.	42	13.71		55.71	diffuser.
	Reinstall	Ea.		7.52		7.52	
	Clean	Ea.	.45	2.59		3.04	
	Minimum Charge	Job		155		155	
Run Wiring							
	Install	Ea.	8.15	12.40		20.55	Includes labor and material to install a
	Minimum Charge	Job		155		155	electric fixture utility box with
							non-metallic cable.

Finish Electrical

Commercial Light Fixture

	Unit	Material	Labor	Equip.	Total	Specification
Track Lighting						
Demolish	L.F.		4.78		4.78	Includes material and labor to install
Install	L.F.	12.20	12.90		25.10	track lighting.
Demolish and Install	L.F.	12.20	17.68		29.88	
Reinstall	L.F.		10.33		10.33	
Clean	L.F.	.14	4.14		4.28	
Minimum Charge	Job		155		155	
Emergency						
Demolish	Ea.		24.50		24.50	Includes material and labor to install
Install	Ea.	121	77.50		198.50	battery-powered emergency lighting
Demolish and Install	Ea.	121	102		223	unit with two (2) lights, including
Reinstall	Ea.		62		62	wiring.
Clean	Ea.	.35	14.75		15.10	
Minimum Charge	Job		155		155	
Run Wiring						
Install	Ea.	8.15	12.40		20.55	Includes labor and material to install a
Minimum Charge	Job		155		155	electric fixture utility box with non-metallic cable.

Fan

	Unit	Material	Labor	Equip.	Total	Specification
Ceiling Paddle						
Good Quality						
Demolish	Ea.		19.15		19.15	Includes material and labor to install
Install	Ea.	82.50	31		113.50	standard ceiling fan.
Demolish and Install	Ea.	82.50	50.15		132.65	
Reinstall	Ea.		24.80		24.80	
Clean	Ea.	.28	12.95		13.23	
Minimum Charge	Job		155		155	
Better Quality						
Demolish	Ea.		19.15		19.15	Includes material and labor to install
Install	Ea.	137	31		168	better ceiling fan.
Demolish and Install	Ea.	137	50.15		187.15	
Reinstall	Ea.		24.80		24.80	
Clean	Ea.	.28	12.95		13.23	
Minimum Charge	Job		155		155	
Premium Quality						
Demolish	Ea.		19.15		19.15	Includes material and labor to install
Install	Ea.	320	39		359	deluxe ceiling fan.
Demolish and Install	Ea.	320	58.15		378.15	
Reinstall	Ea.		31		31	
Clean	Ea.	.28	12.95		13.23	
Minimum Charge	Job		155		155	
Light Kit						
Install	Ea.	32	39		71	Includes labor and material to install a
Minimum Charge	Job		155		155	ceiling fan light kit.
Bathroom Exhaust						
Ceiling Mounted						
Demolish	Ea.		15.80		15.80	Cost includes material and labor to
Install	Ea.	39.50	31		70.50	install 60 CFM ceiling mounted
Demolish and Install	Ea.	39.50	46.80		86.30	bathroom exhaust fan, up to 10' of
Reinstall	Ea.		24.73		24.73	wiring with one wall switch.
Clean	Ea.	.14	5.15		5.29	
Minimum Charge	Job		155		155	

Finish Electrical

Fan

Fan	Unit	Material	Labor	Equip.	Total	Specification
Wall Mounted						
Demolish	Ea.		15.80		15.80	Cost includes material and labor to
Install	Ea.	53.50	31		84.50	install 110 CFM wall mounted
Demolish and Install	Ea.	53.50	46.80		100.30	bathroom exhaust fan, up to 10' of
Reinstall	Ea.		24.73		24.73	wiring with one wall switch.
Clean	Ea.	.14	5.15		5.29	
Minimum Charge	Job		155		155	
Lighted						
Demolish	Ea.		15.80		15.80	Cost includes material and labor to
Install	Ea.	36.50	31		67.50	install 50 CFM ceiling mounted lighted
Demolish and Install	Ea.	36.50	46.80		83.30	exhaust fan, up to 10' of wiring with
Reinstall	Ea.		24.73		24.73	one wall switch..
Clean	Ea.	.14	5.15		5.29	
Minimum Charge	Job		155		155	
Blower Heater w / Light						
Demolish	Ea.		15.80		15.80	Includes material and labor to install
Install	Ea.	86.50	51.50		138	ceiling blower type ventilator with
Demolish and Install	Ea.	86.50	67.30		153.80	switch, light and snap-on grill. Includes
Reinstall	Ea.		41.21		41.21	1300 watt/120 volt heater.
Clean	Ea.	.14	5.15		5.29	
Minimum Charge	Job		155		155	
Fan Heater w / Light						
Demolish	Ea.		15.80		15.80	Includes material and labor to install
Install	Ea.	109	51.50		160.50	circular ceiling fan heater unit, 1500
Demolish and Install	Ea.	109	67.30		176.30	watt, surface mounted.
Reinstall	Ea.		41.21		41.21	
Clean	Ea.	.14	5.15		5.29	
Minimum Charge	Job		155		155	
Whole House Exhaust						
36" Ceiling Mounted						
Install	Ea.	475	77.50		552.50	Includes material and labor to install a
Clean	Ea.	.04	3.73		3.77	whole house exhaust fan.
Minimum Charge	Job		155		155	
Kitchen Exhaust						
Standard Model						
Install	Ea.	62.50	20.50		83	Includes labor and materials to install a
Clean	Ea.	.04	3.73		3.77	bathroom or kitchen vent fan.
Minimum Charge	Job		155		155	
Low Noise Model						
Install	Ea.	82.50	20.50		103	Includes labor and materials to install a
Clean	Ea.	.04	3.73		3.77	bathroom or kitchen vent fan, low
Minimum Charge	Job		155		155	noise model.

Low Voltage Systems	Unit	Material	Labor	Equip.	Total	Specification
Smoke Detector						
Pre-wired						
Demolish	Ea.		7.20		7.20	Includes material and labor to install
Install	Ea.	19.65	58		77.65	AC type smoke detector including
Demolish and Install	Ea.	19.65	65.20		84.85	wiring.
Reinstall	Ea.		46.53		46.53	
Clean	Ea.	.06	6.45		6.51	
Minimum Charge	Job		155		155	

Finish Electrical

Low Voltage Systems		Unit	Material	Labor	Equip.	Total	Specification
Battery-powered							
	Demolish	Ea.		7.20		7.20	Includes material and labor to install
	Install	Ea.	24	19.40		43.40	battery-powered type smoke detector.
	Demolish and Install	Ea.	24	26.60		50.60	
	Reinstall	Ea.		15.50		15.50	
	Clean	Ea.	.06	6.45		6.51	
	Minimum Charge	Job		155		155	
Run Wiring							
	Install	Ea.	8.15	12.40		20.55	Includes labor and material to install a
	Minimum Charge	Job		155		155	electric fixture utility box with
							non-metallic cable.
Door Bell / Chimes							
Good Quality							
	Demolish	Ea.		21.50		21.50	Includes material and labor to install
	Install	Ea.	41.50	77.50		119	surface mounted 2 note door bell.
	Demolish and Install	Ea.	41.50	99		140.50	Wiring is not included.
	Reinstall	Ea.		62		62	
	Clean	Ea.	.14	6.45		6.59	
	Minimum Charge	Job		155		155	
Better Quality							
	Demolish	Ea.		21.50		21.50	Includes material and labor to install
	Install	Ea.	50.50	77.50		128	standard quality surface mounted 2
	Demolish and Install	Ea.	50.50	99		149.50	note door bell. Wiring is not included.
	Reinstall	Ea.		62		62	
	Clean	Ea.	.14	6.45		6.59	
	Minimum Charge	Job		155		155	
Premium Quality							
	Demolish	Ea.		21.50		21.50	Includes material and labor to install
	Install	Ea.	69.50	77.50		147	deluxe quality surface mounted 2 note
	Demolish and Install	Ea.	69.50	99		168.50	door bell. Wiring is not included.
	Reinstall	Ea.		62		62	
	Clean	Ea.	.14	6.45		6.59	
	Minimum Charge	Job		155		155	
Run Wiring							
	Install	Ea.	8.15	12.40		20.55	Includes labor and material to install a
	Minimum Charge	Job		155		155	electric fixture utility box with
							non-metallic cable.
Intercom System							
Intercom (master)							
	Demolish	Ea.		57.50		57.50	Includes material and labor to install
	Install	Ea.	455	155		610	master intercom station with AM/FM
	Demolish and Install	Ea.	455	212.50		667.50	music and room monitoring. Wiring is
	Reinstall	Ea.		124		124	not included.
	Clean	Ea.	.14	17.25		17.39	
	Minimum Charge	Job		155		155	
Intercom (remote)							
	Demolish	Ea.		34.50		34.50	Includes material and labor to install
	Install	Ea.	41.50	39		80.50	remote station for master intercom
	Demolish and Install	Ea.	41.50	73.50		115	system. Wiring is not included.
	Reinstall	Ea.		31		31	
	Clean	Ea.	.14	6.45		6.59	
	Minimum Charge	Job		155		155	

Finish Electrical

Low Voltage Systems

	Unit	Material	Labor	Equip.	Total	Specification
Security System						
Alarm Panel						
Demolish	Ea.		69		69	Includes material and labor to install a
Install	Ea.	165	155		320	6 zone burglar alarm panel.
Demolish and Install	Ea.	165	224		389	
Reinstall	Ea.		124		124	
Clean	Ea.	.14	6.45		6.59	
Minimum Charge	Job		155		155	
Motion Detector						
Demolish	Ea.		49		49	Includes material and labor to install a
Install	Ea.	227	135		362	ultrasonic motion detector for a security
Demolish and Install	Ea.	227	184		411	system.
Reinstall	Ea.		107.83		107.83	
Clean	Ea.	.14	6.45		6.59	
Minimum Charge	Job		155		155	
Door Switch						
Demolish	Ea.		21.50		21.50	Includes material and labor to install a
Install	Ea.	34.50	58.50		93	door / window contact for a security
Demolish and Install	Ea.	34.50	80		114.50	system.
Reinstall	Ea.		46.79		46.79	
Clean	Ea.	.14	2.07		2.21	
Minimum Charge	Job		155		155	
Window Switch						
Demolish	Ea.		21.50		21.50	Includes material and labor to install a
Install	Ea.	34.50	58.50		93	door / window contact for a security
Demolish and Install	Ea.	34.50	80		114.50	system.
Reinstall	Ea.		46.79		46.79	
Clean	Ea.	.14	2.07		2.21	
Minimum Charge	Job		155		155	
Satellite System						
Dish						
Demolish	Ea.		95.50		95.50	Includes material, labor and equipment
Install	Ea.	605	258		863	to install 10' mesh dish.
Demolish and Install	Ea.	605	353.50		958.50	
Reinstall	Ea.		206.67		206.67	
Clean	Ea.	2.81	26		28.81	
Minimum Charge	Job		155		155	
Motor						
Demolish	Ea.		48		48	Includes material and labor to install a
Install	Ea.	305	129		434	television satellite dish motor unit.
Demolish and Install	Ea.	305	177		482	
Reinstall	Ea.		103.33		103.33	
Clean	Ea.	.14	6.45		6.59	
Minimum Charge	Job		155		155	
Television Antenna						
40' Pole						
Demolish	Ea.		54		54	Includes material and labor to install
Install	Ea.	22	97		119	stand-alone 1"-2" metal pole, 10' long.
Demolish and Install	Ea.	22	151		173	Cost does not include antenna.
Reinstall	Ea.		77.50		77.50	
Clean	Ea.	.56	26		26.56	
Paint	Ea.	6.55	32		38.55	
Minimum Charge	Job		155		155	
Rotor Unit						
Demolish	Ea.		43		43	Includes material and labor to install a
Install	Ea.	71.50	39		110.50	television antenna rotor.
Demolish and Install	Ea.	71.50	82		153.50	
Reinstall	Ea.		31		31	
Clean	Ea.	.56	26		26.56	
Minimum Charge	Job		155		155	

Finish Electrical

Low Voltage Systems

Low Voltage Systems	Unit	Material	Labor	Equip.	Total	Specification
Single Booster						Includes material and labor to install
Demolish	Ea.		43		43	standard grade VHF television signal
Install	Ea.	14.30	39		53.30	booster unit and all hardware required
Demolish and Install	Ea.	14.30	82		96.30	for connection to TV cable.
Reinstall	Ea.		31		31	
Clean	Ea.	.03	3.23		3.26	
Minimum Charge	Job		155		155	

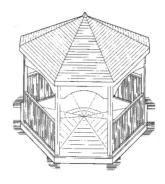

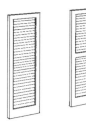

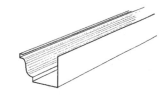

Gazebo	Gutter	Shutter

Window Treatment		Unit	Material	Labor	Equip.	Total	Specification
Drapery							
Good Grade							
	Install	L.F.	31.50	4.14		35.64	Includes material and labor to install
	Reinstall	L.F.		3.31		3.31	good quality drapery.
	Clean	L.F.	2.31	.10		2.41	
	Minimum Charge	Job		103		103	
Premium Grade							
	Install	L.F.	55	4.14		59.14	Includes material and labor to install
	Reinstall	L.F.		3.31		3.31	premium quality drapery.
	Clean	L.F.	2.31	.11		2.42	
	Minimum Charge	Job		103		103	
Lining							
	Install	L.F.	13.70	4.14		17.84	Includes material and labor to install
	Reinstall	L.F.		3.31		3.31	drapery lining.
	Clean	L.F.	1.16	.06		1.22	
	Minimum Charge	Job		103		103	
Valance Board							
	Demolish	L.F.		1.15		1.15	Includes material and labor to install a
	Install	L.F.	4.13	8.25		12.38	drapery valance board.
	Demolish and Install	L.F.	4.13	9.40		13.53	
	Reinstall	L.F.		6.62		6.62	
	Clean	L.F.	1.16	.21		1.37	
	Minimum Charge	Job		103		103	
Rod							
	Demolish	L.F.		2.87		2.87	Includes material and labor to install
	Install	L.F.	1.60	4.83		6.43	standard traverse drapery hardware.
	Demolish and Install	L.F.	1.60	7.70		9.30	
	Reinstall	L.F.		3.86		3.86	
	Clean	L.F.	.06	.19		.25	
	Paint	L.F.	.06	.49		.55	
	Minimum Charge	Job		103		103	
Blinds							
Mini-type							
	Demolish	S.F.		.62		.62	Includes material and labor to install
	Install	S.F.	2.13	.48		2.61	horizontal 1″ slat blinds.
	Demolish and Install	S.F.	2.13	1.10		3.23	
	Reinstall	S.F.		.39		.39	
	Clean	S.F.	.44	.02		.46	
	Minimum Charge	Job		103		103	

Improvements / Appliances / Treatments

Window Treatment		Unit	Material	Labor	Equip.	Total	Specification
Vertical Type							
	Demolish	S.F.		.62		.62	Includes material and labor to install
	Install	S.F.	7.35	.62		7.97	vertical 3" - 5" cloth or PVC blinds.
	Demolish and Install	S.F.	7.35	1.24		8.59	
	Reinstall	S.F.		.50		.50	
	Clean	S.F.	.23	.02		.25	
	Minimum Charge	Job		103		103	
Vertical Type per L.F.							
	Demolish	L.F.		.96		.96	Includes material and labor to install
	Install	L.F.	44.50	2.76		47.26	vertical 3" - 5" cloth or PVC blinds x
	Demolish and Install	L.F.	44.50	3.72		48.22	72" long.
	Reinstall	L.F.		2.21		2.21	
	Clean	L.F.	1.64	.14		1.78	
	Minimum Charge	Job		103		103	
Venetian Type							
	Demolish	S.F.		.62		.62	Includes material and labor to install
	Install	S.F.	3.17	.48		3.65	horizontal 2" slat blinds.
	Demolish and Install	S.F.	3.17	1.10		4.27	
	Reinstall	S.F.		.39		.39	
	Clean	S.F.	.23	.02		.25	
	Minimum Charge	Job		103		103	
Wood Shutter							
27" x 36", 4 Panel							
	Demolish	Ea.		19.80		19.80	Includes material and labor to install
	Install	Pr.	76.50	16.75		93.25	moveable louver, up to 33" x 36", 4
	Demolish and Install	Pr.	76.50	36.55		113.05	panel shutter.
	Reinstall	Pr.		13.40		13.40	
	Clean	Ea.	.06	6.20		6.26	
	Paint	Ea.	1.05	18.25		19.30	
	Minimum Charge	Job		142		142	
33" x 36", 4 Panel							
	Demolish	Ea.		19.80		19.80	Includes material and labor to install
	Install	Pr.	76.50	16.75		93.25	moveable louver, up to 33" x 36", 4
	Demolish and Install	Pr.	76.50	36.55		113.05	panel shutter.
	Reinstall	Pr.		13.40		13.40	
	Clean	Ea.	.06	6.20		6.26	
	Paint	Ea.	1.09	19.65		20.74	
	Minimum Charge	Job		142		142	
39" x 36", 4 Panel							
	Demolish	Ea.		19.80		19.80	Includes material and labor to install
	Install	Pr.	86.50	16.75		103.25	moveable louver, up to 47" x 36", 4
	Demolish and Install	Pr.	86.50	36.55		123.05	panel shutter.
	Reinstall	Pr.		13.40		13.40	
	Clean	Ea.	.06	6.20		6.26	
	Paint	Ea.	1.09	19.65		20.74	
	Minimum Charge	Job		142		142	
47" x 36", 4 Panel							
	Demolish	Ea.		19.80		19.80	Includes material and labor to install
	Install	Pr.	86.50	16.75		103.25	moveable louver, up to 47" x 36", 4
	Demolish and Install	Pr.	86.50	36.55		123.05	panel shutter.
	Reinstall	Pr.		13.40		13.40	
	Clean	Ea.	.06	6.20		6.26	
	Paint	Ea.	1.14	21.50		22.64	
	Minimum Charge	Job		142		142	

Improvements / Appliances / Treatments

Stairs		Unit	Material	Labor	Equip.	Total	Specification
Concrete Steps							
Precast							
	Demolish	Ea.		39.50	33	72.50	Includes material and labor to install
	Install	Flight	310	98	39.50	447.50	precast concrete front entrance stairs,
	Demolish and Install	Flight	310	137.50	72.50	520	4' wide, with 48" platform and 2
	Clean	Ea.		2.87		2.87	risers.
	Paint	Ea.	2.20	32		34.20	
	Minimum Charge	Job		253		253	
Metal							
Concrete Filled							
	Demolish	Ea.		11.50		11.50	Includes material and labor to install
	Install	Riser	197	48.50	3.25	248.75	steel, cement filled metal pan stairs
	Demolish and Install	Riser	197	60	3.25	260.25	with picket rail.
	Clean	Ea.	.09	1.81		1.90	
	Paint	Ea.	.33	1.89		2.22	
	Minimum Charge	Job		178		178	
Landing							
	Demolish	S.F.		2.87		2.87	Includes material and labor to install
	Install	S.F.	40.50	5.70	.38	46.58	pre-erected conventional steel pan
	Demolish and Install	S.F.	40.50	8.57	.38	49.45	landing.
	Clean	S.F.	.09	.37		.46	
	Paint	S.F.	.11	.54		.65	
	Minimum Charge	Job		178		178	
Railing							
	Demolish	L.F.		1.58		1.58	Includes material and labor to install
	Install	L.F.	6.75	8.30	.55	15.60	primed steel pipe.
	Demolish and Install	L.F.	6.75	9.88	.55	17.18	
	Clean	L.F.	.56	1.29		1.85	
	Paint	L.F.	.63	4.25		4.88	
	Minimum Charge	Job		178		178	

Elevator		Unit	Material	Labor	Equip.	Total	Specification
2 Stop Residential							
	Install	Ea.	8875	3275		12150	Includes labor, material and equipment
	Clean	Ea.	.64	12.95		13.59	to install 2 stop elevator for residential
	Minimum Charge	Job		325		325	use.
2 Stop Commercial							
	Install	Ea.	31100	6525		37625	Includes labor, material and equipment
	Clean	Ea.	.64	12.95		13.59	to install 2 stop elevator for apartment
	Minimum Charge	Job		325		325	or commercial building with 2,000
							lb/13 passenger capacity.
3 Stop Commercial							
	Install	Ea.	35800	10000		45800	Includes labor, material and equipment
	Clean	Ea.	.64	12.95		13.59	to install 3 stop elevator for apartment
	Minimum Charge	Job		325		325	or commercial building with 2,000
							lb/13 passenger capacity.
4 Stop Commercial							
	Install	Ea.	40500	13600		54100	Includes labor, material and equipment
	Clean	Ea.	.64	12.95		13.59	to install 4 stop elevator for apartment
	Minimum Charge	Job		325		325	or commercial building with 2,000
							lb/13 passenger capacity.

Improvements / Appliances / Treatments

Elevator

	Unit	Material	Labor	Equip.	Total	Specification
5 Stop Commercial						
Install	Ea.	45100	17200		62300	Includes labor, material and equipment
Clean	Ea.	.64	12.95		13.59	to install 5 stop elevator for apartment
Minimum Charge	Job		325		325	or commercial building with 2,000 lb/13 passenger capacity.

Rangetop

	Unit	Material	Labor	Equip.	Total	Specification
4-burner						
Demolish	Ea.		21		21	Cost includes material and labor to
Install	Ea.	210	51.50		261.50	install 4-burner electric surface unit.
Demolish and Install	Ea.	210	72.50		282.50	
Reinstall	Ea.		41.33		41.33	
Clean	Ea.	.04	18.65		18.69	
Minimum Charge	Job		51.50		51.50	
6-burner						
Demolish	Ea.		21		21	Includes material and labor to install a
Install	Ea.	435	62		497	6-burner cooktop unit.
Demolish and Install	Ea.	435	83		518	
Reinstall	Ea.		49.60		49.60	
Clean	Ea.	.04	18.65		18.69	
Minimum Charge	Job		51.50		51.50	
Premium Brand w / Grill						
Demolish	Ea.		21		21	Includes material and labor to install
Install	Ea.	565	62		627	electric downdraft cooktop with grill.
Demolish and Install	Ea.	565	83		648	
Reinstall	Ea.		49.60		49.60	
Clean	Ea.	.04	18.65		18.69	
Minimum Charge	Job		51.50		51.50	

Rangehood

	Unit	Material	Labor	Equip.	Total	Specification
Vented						
30"						
Demolish	Ea.		19.15		19.15	Includes material and labor to install a
Install	Ea.	39	62		101	vented range hood.
Demolish and Install	Ea.	39	81.15		120.15	
Reinstall	Ea.		49.60		49.60	
Clean	Ea.	.04	5.35		5.39	
Minimum Charge	Job		51.50		51.50	
36"						
Demolish	Ea.		19.15		19.15	Includes material and labor to install a
Install	Ea.	79	62		141	vented range hood.
Demolish and Install	Ea.	79	81.15		160.15	
Reinstall	Ea.		49.60		49.60	
Clean	Ea.	.04	5.35		5.39	
Minimum Charge	Job		51.50		51.50	
42"						
Demolish	Ea.		19.15		19.15	Includes material and labor to install a
Install	Ea.	189	72.50		261.50	vented range hood.
Demolish and Install	Ea.	189	91.65		280.65	
Reinstall	Ea.		57.97		57.97	
Clean	Ea.	.04	5.35		5.39	
Minimum Charge	Job		51.50		51.50	

Improvements / Appliances / Treatments

Rangehood		Unit	Material	Labor	Equip.	Total	Specification
Ventless							
30"							
	Demolish	Ea.		19.15		19.15	Includes material and labor to install a
	Install	Ea.	40	39		79	ventless range hood.
	Demolish and Install	Ea.	40	58.15		98.15	
	Reinstall	Ea.		31		31	
	Clean	Ea.	.04	5.35		5.39	
	Minimum Charge	Job		51.50		51.50	
36"							
	Demolish	Ea.		19.15		19.15	Includes material and labor to install a
	Install	Ea.	40.50	62		102.50	ventless range hood.
	Demolish and Install	Ea.	40.50	81.15		121.65	
	Reinstall	Ea.		49.60		49.60	
	Clean	Ea.	.04	5.35		5.39	
	Minimum Charge	Job		51.50		51.50	
42"							
	Demolish	Ea.		19.15		19.15	Includes material and labor to install a
	Install	Ea.	210	51.50		261.50	ventless range hood.
	Demolish and Install	Ea.	210	70.65		280.65	
	Reinstall	Ea.		41.33		41.33	
	Clean	Ea.	.04	5.35		5.39	
	Minimum Charge	Job		51.50		51.50	

Oven		Unit	Material	Labor	Equip.	Total	Specification
Free Standing							
	Demolish	Ea.		21		21	Cost includes material and labor to
	Install	Ea.	450	41.50		491.50	install 30" free standing electric range
	Demolish and Install	Ea.	450	62.50		512.50	with self-cleaning oven.
	Reinstall	Ea.		33.09		33.09	
	Clean	Ea.	.04	18.65		18.69	
	Minimum Charge	Job		51.50		51.50	
Single Wall Oven							
	Demolish	Ea.		21		21	Includes material and labor to install a
	Install	Ea.	405	77.50		482.50	built-in oven.
	Demolish and Install	Ea.	405	98.50		503.50	
	Reinstall	Ea.		62		62	
	Clean	Ea.	.04	18.65		18.69	
	Minimum Charge	Job		51.50		51.50	
Double Wall Oven							
	Demolish	Ea.		21		21	Includes material and labor to install a
	Install	Ea.	1050	142		1192	conventional double oven.
	Demolish and Install	Ea.	1050	163		1213	
	Reinstall	Ea.		113.92		113.92	
	Clean	Ea.	.04	18.65		18.69	
	Minimum Charge	Job		51.50		51.50	
Drop-in Type w / Range							
	Demolish	Ea.		21		21	Includes material and labor to install a
	Install	Ea.	350	51.50		401.50	built-in cooking range with oven.
	Demolish and Install	Ea.	350	72.50		422.50	
	Reinstall	Ea.		41.33		41.33	
	Clean	Ea.	.04	18.65		18.69	
	Minimum Charge	Job		51.50		51.50	

Improvements / Appliances / Treatments

Oven	Unit	Material	Labor	Equip.	Total	Specification
Hi/Lo w / Range, Microwave						
Demolish	Ea.		21		21	Includes material and labor to install a
Install	Ea.	1700	285		1985	double oven, one conventional, one
Demolish and Install	Ea.	1700	306		2006	microwave.
Reinstall	Ea.		227.84		227.84	
Clean	Ea.	.04	18.65		18.69	
Minimum Charge	Job		51.50		51.50	
Hi/Lo w/ Range / Double Oven						
Demolish	Ea.		21		21	Includes material and labor to install a
Install	Ea.	1050	142		1192	conventional double oven.
Demolish and Install	Ea.	1050	163		1213	
Reinstall	Ea.		113.92		113.92	
Clean	Ea.	.04	18.65		18.69	
Minimum Charge	Job		51.50		51.50	
Countertop Microwave						
Demolish	Ea.		7.20		7.20	Includes material and labor to install a
Install	Ea.	131	26		157	1.0 cubic foot microwave oven.
Demolish and Install	Ea.	131	33.20		164.20	
Reinstall	Ea.		20.68		20.68	
Clean	Ea.	.04	9.35		9.39	
Minimum Charge	Job		51.50		51.50	
Cabinet / Wall Mounted Microwave						
Demolish	Ea.		14.35		14.35	Includes material and labor to install a
Install	Ea.	605	77.50		682.50	space saver microwave oven.
Demolish and Install	Ea.	605	91.85		696.85	
Reinstall	Ea.		62		62	
Clean	Ea.	.04	9.35		9.39	
Minimum Charge	Job		51.50		51.50	

Dryer	Unit	Material	Labor	Equip.	Total	Specification
Basic Grade						
Demolish	Ea.		9.55		9.55	Includes material and labor to install
Install	Ea.	276	166		442	electric or gas dryer. Vent kit not
Demolish and Install	Ea.	276	175.55		451.55	included.
Reinstall	Ea.		132.69		132.69	
Clean	Ea.	.04	18.65		18.69	
Minimum Charge	Job		51.50		51.50	
Good Grade						
Demolish	Ea.		9.55		9.55	Includes material and labor to install
Install	Ea.	345	166		511	electric or gas dryer. Vent kit not
Demolish and Install	Ea.	345	175.55		520.55	included.
Reinstall	Ea.		132.69		132.69	
Clean	Ea.	.04	18.65		18.69	
Minimum Charge	Job		51.50		51.50	
Premium Grade						
Demolish	Ea.		9.55		9.55	Includes material and labor to install
Install	Ea.	615	249		864	electric or gas dryer. Vent kit not
Demolish and Install	Ea.	615	258.55		873.55	included.
Reinstall	Ea.		199.04		199.04	
Clean	Ea.	.04	18.65		18.69	
Minimum Charge	Job		51.50		51.50	

Improvements / Appliances / Treatments

Dryer

	Unit	Material	Labor	Equip.	Total	Specification
Washer / Dryer Combination Unit						
Demolish	Ea.		9.55		9.55	Includes material and labor to install
Install	Ea.	955	41.50		996.50	electric washer/dryer combination
Demolish and Install	Ea.	955	51.05		1006.05	unit, 27" wide, stackable or unitized.
Reinstall	Ea.		33.09		33.09	
Clean	Ea.	.04	18.65		18.69	
Minimum Charge	Job		51.50		51.50	

Washer

	Unit	Material	Labor	Equip.	Total	Specification
Basic Grade						
Demolish	Ea.		9.55		9.55	Includes material and labor to install
Install	Ea.	365	104		469	washing machine. New hoses not
Demolish and Install	Ea.	365	113.55		478.55	included.
Reinstall	Ea.		83.52		83.52	
Clean	Ea.	.04	18.65		18.69	
Minimum Charge	Job		51.50		51.50	
Good Grade						
Demolish	Ea.		9.55		9.55	Includes material and labor to install
Install	Ea.	600	157		757	washing machine. New hoses not
Demolish and Install	Ea.	600	166.55		766.55	included.
Reinstall	Ea.		125.28		125.28	
Clean	Ea.	.04	18.65		18.69	
Minimum Charge	Job		51.50		51.50	
Premium Grade						
Demolish	Ea.		9.55		9.55	Includes material and labor to install
Install	Ea.	715	315		1030	washing machine with digital computer
Demolish and Install	Ea.	715	324.55		1039.55	readouts and large capacity. New
Reinstall	Ea.		250.56		250.56	hoses not included.
Clean	Ea.	.04	18.65		18.69	
Minimum Charge	Job		51.50		51.50	
Washer / Dryer Combination Unit						
Demolish	Ea.		9.55		9.55	Includes material and labor to install
Install	Ea.	955	41.50		996.50	electric washer/dryer combination
Demolish and Install	Ea.	955	51.05		1006.05	unit, 27" wide, stackable or unitized.
Reinstall	Ea.		33.09		33.09	
Clean	Ea.	.04	18.65		18.69	
Minimum Charge	Job		51.50		51.50	

Refrigerator

	Unit	Material	Labor	Equip.	Total	Specification
12 Cubic Foot						
Demolish	Ea.		28.50		28.50	Includes material and labor to install a
Install	Ea.	495	41.50		536.50	refrigerator.
Demolish and Install	Ea.	495	70		565	
Reinstall	Ea.		33.09		33.09	
Clean	Ea.	.04	18.65		18.69	
Minimum Charge	Job		51.50		51.50	
16 Cubic Foot						
Demolish	Ea.		28.50		28.50	Includes material and labor to install a
Install	Ea.	505	46		551	refrigerator.
Demolish and Install	Ea.	505	74.50		579.50	
Reinstall	Ea.		36.76		36.76	
Clean	Ea.	.04	18.65		18.69	
Minimum Charge	Job		51.50		51.50	

Improvements / Appliances / Treatments

Refrigerator		Unit	Material	Labor	Equip.	Total	Specification
18 Cubic Foot							
	Demolish	Ea.		28.50		28.50	Includes material and labor to install a
	Install	Ea.	585	51.50		636.50	refrigerator.
	Demolish and Install	Ea.	585	80		665	
	Reinstall	Ea.		41.36		41.36	
	Clean	Ea.	.04	18.65		18.69	
	Minimum Charge	Job		51.50		51.50	
21 Cubic Foot							
	Demolish	Ea.		28.50		28.50	Includes material and labor to install a
	Install	Ea.	745	59		804	refrigerator.
	Demolish and Install	Ea.	745	87.50		832.50	
	Reinstall	Ea.		47.27		47.27	
	Clean	Ea.	.04	18.65		18.69	
	Minimum Charge	Job		51.50		51.50	
24 Cubic Foot							
	Demolish	Ea.		28.50		28.50	Includes material and labor to install a
	Install	Ea.	990	59		1049	refrigerator.
	Demolish and Install	Ea.	990	87.50		1077.50	
	Reinstall	Ea.		47.27		47.27	
	Clean	Ea.	.04	18.65		18.69	
	Minimum Charge	Job		51.50		51.50	
27 Cubic Foot							
	Demolish	Ea.		28.50		28.50	Includes material and labor to install a
	Install	Ea.	1400	41.50		1441.50	refrigerator.
	Demolish and Install	Ea.	1400	70		1470	
	Reinstall	Ea.		33.09		33.09	
	Clean	Ea.	.04	18.65		18.69	
	Minimum Charge	Job		51.50		51.50	
Ice Maker							
	Install	Ea.	67.50	39		106.50	Includes labor and material to install
	Minimum Charge	Job		51.50		51.50	an automatic ice maker in a refrigerator.

Freezer		Unit	Material	Labor	Equip.	Total	Specification
15 Cubic Foot							
	Demolish	Ea.		28.50		28.50	Cost includes material and labor to
	Install	Ea.	460	41.50		501.50	install 15 cubic foot freezer.
	Demolish and Install	Ea.	460	70		530	
	Reinstall	Ea.		33.09		33.09	
	Clean	Ea.	.04	18.65		18.69	
	Minimum Charge	Job		51.50		51.50	
18 Cubic Foot							
	Demolish	Ea.		28.50		28.50	Cost includes material and labor to
	Install	Ea.	615	41.50		656.50	install 18 cubic foot freezer.
	Demolish and Install	Ea.	615	70		685	
	Reinstall	Ea.		33.09		33.09	
	Clean	Ea.	.04	18.65		18.69	
	Minimum Charge	Job		51.50		51.50	
21 Cubic Foot							
	Demolish	Ea.		28.50		28.50	Includes material and labor to install a
	Install	Ea.	540	41.50		581.50	15 to 23 cubic foot deep freezer.
	Demolish and Install	Ea.	540	70		610	
	Reinstall	Ea.		33.09		33.09	
	Clean	Ea.	.04	18.65		18.69	
	Minimum Charge	Job		51.50		51.50	

Improvements / Appliances / Treatments

Freezer		Unit	Material	Labor	Equip.	Total	Specification
24 Cubic Foot							
	Demolish	Ea.		28.50		28.50	Includes material and labor to install a
	Install	Ea.	595	82.50		677.50	24 cubic foot deep freezer.
	Demolish and Install	Ea.	595	111		706	
	Reinstall	Ea.		66.18		66.18	
	Clean	Ea.	.04	18.65		18.69	
	Minimum Charge	Job		51.50		51.50	
Chest-type							
	Demolish	Ea.		28.50		28.50	Cost includes material and labor to
	Install	Ea.	460	41.50		501.50	install 15 cubic foot freezer.
	Demolish and Install	Ea.	460	70		530	
	Clean	Ea.	.04	18.65		18.69	
	Minimum Charge	Job		51.50		51.50	

Dishwasher		Unit	Material	Labor	Equip.	Total	Specification
4 Cycle							
	Demolish	Ea.		23		23	Includes material and labor to install
	Install	Ea.	315	97.50		412.50	good grade automatic dishwasher.
	Demolish and Install	Ea.	315	120.50		435.50	
	Reinstall	Ea.		78.14		78.14	
	Clean	Ea.	.04	18.65		18.69	
	Minimum Charge	Job		51.50		51.50	

Garbage Disposal		Unit	Material	Labor	Equip.	Total	Specification
In Sink Unit							
	Demolish	Ea.		22		22	Cost includes material and labor to
	Install	Ea.	114	39		153	install 1/2 HP custom disposal unit.
	Demolish and Install	Ea.	114	61		175	
	Reinstall	Ea.		31.26		31.26	
	Clean	Ea.	.02	5.35		5.37	
	Minimum Charge	Job		51.50		51.50	

Trash Compactor		Unit	Material	Labor	Equip.	Total	Specification
4 to 1 Compaction							
	Demolish	Ea.		21.50		21.50	Includes material and labor to install a
	Install	Ea.	525	57		582	trash compactor.
	Demolish and Install	Ea.	525	78.50		603.50	
	Reinstall	Ea.		45.57		45.57	
	Clean	Ea.	.04	12.95		12.99	
	Minimum Charge	Job		51.50		51.50	

Kitchenette Unit		Unit	Material	Labor	Equip.	Total	Specification
Range, Refrigerator and Sink							
	Demolish	Ea.		86		86	Includes material and labor to install
	Install	Ea.	3000	325		3325	range/refrigerator/sink unit, 72" wide,
	Demolish and Install	Ea.	3000	411		3411	base unit only.
	Reinstall	Ea.		260.47		260.47	
	Clean	Ea.	.70	9.35		10.05	
	Minimum Charge	Job		51.50		51.50	

Improvements / Appliances / Treatments

Bath Accessories	Unit	Material	Labor	Equip.	Total	Specification
Towel Bar						
Demolish	Ea.		4.79		4.79	Includes material and labor to install
Install	Ea.	29.50	11.85		41.35	towel bar up to 24" long.
Demolish and Install	Ea.	29.50	16.64		46.14	
Reinstall	Ea.		9.49		9.49	
Clean	Ea.		2.59		2.59	
Minimum Charge	Job		142		142	
Toothbrush Holder						
Demolish	Ea.		4.79		4.79	Includes material and labor to install a
Install	Ea.	26.50	14.25		40.75	surface mounted tumbler and
Demolish and Install	Ea.	26.50	19.04		45.54	toothbrush holder.
Reinstall	Ea.		11.39		11.39	
Clean	Ea.		2.59		2.59	
Minimum Charge	Job		142		142	
Grab Rail						
Demolish	Ea.		7.20		7.20	Includes material and labor to install a
Install	Ea.	53	12.40		65.40	24" long grab bar. Blocking is not
Demolish and Install	Ea.	53	19.60		72.60	included.
Reinstall	Ea.		9.91		9.91	
Clean	Ea.	.28	4.31		4.59	
Minimum Charge	Job		142		142	
Soap Dish						
Demolish	Ea.		4.79		4.79	Includes material and labor to install a
Install	Ea.	22	14.25		36.25	surface mounted soap dish.
Demolish and Install	Ea.	22	19.04		41.04	
Reinstall	Ea.		11.39		11.39	
Clean	Ea.		2.59		2.59	
Minimum Charge	Job		142		142	
Toilet Paper Roller						
Demolish	Ea.		4.79		4.79	Includes material and labor to install a
Install	Ea.	12.95	9.50		22.45	surface mounted toilet tissue dispenser.
Demolish and Install	Ea.	12.95	14.29		27.24	
Reinstall	Ea.		7.59		7.59	
Clean	Ea.	.28	6.45		6.73	
Minimum Charge	Job		142		142	
Dispenser						
Soap						
Demolish	Ea.		6.40		6.40	Includes material and labor to install a
Install	Ea.	47	14.25		61.25	surface mounted soap dispenser.
Demolish and Install	Ea.	47	20.65		67.65	
Reinstall	Ea.		11.39		11.39	
Clean	Ea.	.28	6.45		6.73	
Minimum Charge	Job		142		142	
Towel						
Demolish	Ea.		7.20		7.20	Includes material and labor to install a
Install	Ea.	42	17.80		59.80	surface mounted towel dispenser.
Demolish and Install	Ea.	42	25		67	
Reinstall	Ea.		14.24		14.24	
Clean	Ea.	.28	8.60		8.88	
Minimum Charge	Job		142		142	
Seat Cover						
Demolish	Ea.		4.79		4.79	Includes material and labor to install a
Install	Ea.	27	19		46	surface mounted toilet seat cover
Demolish and Install	Ea.	27	23.79		50.79	dispenser.
Reinstall	Ea.		15.19		15.19	
Clean	Ea.	.28	6.45		6.73	
Minimum Charge	Job		142		142	

Improvements / Appliances / Treatments

Bath Accessories		Unit	Material	Labor	Equip.	Total	Specification
Sanitary Napkin							Includes material and labor to install a
	Demolish	Ea.		12.10		12.10	surface mounted sanitary napkin
	Install	Ea.	26	30		56	dispenser.
	Demolish and Install	Ea.	26	42.10		68.10	
	Reinstall	Ea.		23.98		23.98	
	Clean	Ea.	.14	8.60		8.74	
	Minimum Charge	Job		142		142	
Partition							
Urinal							Includes material and labor to install a
	Demolish	Ea.		14.35		14.35	urinal screen.
	Install	Ea.	180	71		251	
	Demolish and Install	Ea.	180	85.35		265.35	
	Reinstall	Ea.		56.96		56.96	
	Clean	Ea.	.42	5.75		6.17	
	Minimum Charge	Job		142		142	
Toilet							Includes material and labor to install
	Demolish	Ea.		42.50		42.50	baked enamel standard size partition,
	Install	Ea.	400	114		514	floor or ceiling mounted with one wall
	Demolish and Install	Ea.	400	156.50		556.50	and one door.
	Reinstall	Ea.		91.14		91.14	
	Clean	Ea.	2.81	12.95		15.76	
	Minimum Charge	Job		142		142	
Handicap							Includes material and labor to install
	Demolish	Ea.		42.50		42.50	baked enamel handicap partition,
	Install	Ea.	690	114		804	floor or ceiling mounted with one wall
	Demolish and Install	Ea.	690	156.50		846.50	and one door.
	Reinstall	Ea.		91.14		91.14	
	Clean	Ea.	2.81	12.95		15.76	
	Minimum Charge	Job		142		142	

Fire Prevention / Protection		Unit	Material	Labor	Equip.	Total	Specification
Fire Extinguisher							
5# Carbon Dioxide							Includes labor and material to install
	Install	Ea.	111			111	one wall mounted 5 lb. carbon dioxide factory charged unit, complete with hose, horn and wall mounting bracket.
10# Carbon Dioxide							Includes labor and material to install
	Install	Ea.	165			165	one wall mounted 10 lb. carbon dioxide factory charged unit, complete with hose, horn and wall mounting bracket.
15# Carbon Dioxide							Includes labor and material to install
	Install	Ea.	189			189	one wall mounted 15 lb. carbon dioxide factory charged unit, complete with hose, horn and wall mounting bracket.
5# Dry Chemical							Includes labor and material to install
	Install	Ea.	44			44	one wall mounted 5 lb. dry chemical factory charged unit, complete with hose, horn and wall mounting bracket.

Improvements / Appliances / Treatments

Fire Prevention / Protection		Unit	Material	Labor	Equip.	Total	Specification
20# Dry Chemical							
	Install	Ea.	99			99	Includes labor and material to install one wall mounted 20 lb. dry chemical factory charged unit, complete with hose, horn and wall mounting bracket.

Gutters		Unit	Material	Labor	Equip.	Total	Specification
Galvanized							
	Demolish	L.F.		.96		.96	Cost includes material and labor to
	Install	L.F.	1.14	2.60		3.74	install 5" galvanized steel gutter with
	Demolish and Install	L.F.	1.14	3.56		4.70	enamel finish, fittings, hangers, and
	Reinstall	L.F.		2.08		2.08	corners.
	Clean	L.F.		.28		.28	
	Paint	L.F.	.18	.79		.97	
	Minimum Charge	Job		156		156	
Aluminum							
	Demolish	L.F.		.96		.96	Cost includes material and labor to
	Install	L.F.	1.33	2.60		3.93	install 5" aluminum gutter with enamel
	Demolish and Install	L.F.	1.33	3.56		4.89	finish, fittings, hangers, and corners.
	Reinstall	L.F.		2.08		2.08	
	Clean	L.F.		.28		.28	
	Paint	L.F.	.18	.79		.97	
	Minimum Charge	Job		156		156	
Copper							
	Demolish	L.F.		.96		.96	Cost includes material and labor to
	Install	L.F.	3.43	2.60		6.03	install 5" half-round copper gutter with
	Demolish and Install	L.F.	3.43	3.56		6.99	fittings, hangers, and corners.
	Reinstall	L.F.		2.08		2.08	
	Clean	L.F.		.28		.28	
	Minimum Charge	Job		156		156	
Plastic							
	Demolish	L.F.		.96		.96	Cost includes material and labor to
	Install	L.F.	.94	2.59		3.53	install 4" white vinyl gutter fittings,
	Demolish and Install	L.F.	.94	3.55		4.49	hangers, and corners.
	Reinstall	L.F.		2.07		2.07	
	Clean	L.F.		.28		.28	
	Paint	L.F.	.18	.79		.97	
	Minimum Charge	Job		156		156	

Downspouts		Unit	Material	Labor	Equip.	Total	Specification
Galvanized							
	Demolish	L.F.		.66		.66	Cost includes material and labor to
	Install	L.F.	1.18	2.15		3.33	install 4" diameter downspout with
	Demolish and Install	L.F.	1.18	2.81		3.99	enamel finish.
	Reinstall	L.F.		1.72		1.72	
	Clean	L.F.		.28		.28	
	Paint	L.F.	.18	.79		.97	
	Minimum Charge	Job		156		156	

Downspouts		Unit	Material	Labor	Equip.	Total	Specification
Aluminum							
	Demolish	L.F.		.66		.66	Includes material and labor to install
	Install	L.F.	1.75	2.23		3.98	aluminum enameled downspout.
	Demolish and Install	L.F.	1.75	2.89		4.64	
	Reinstall	L.F.		1.78		1.78	
	Clean	L.F.		.28		.28	
	Paint	L.F.	.18	.79		.97	
	Minimum Charge	Job		156		156	
Copper							
	Demolish	L.F.		.66		.66	Includes material and labor to install
	Install	L.F.	4.47	1.64		6.11	round copper downspout.
	Demolish and Install	L.F.	4.47	2.30		6.77	
	Reinstall	L.F.		1.31		1.31	
	Clean	L.F.		.28		.28	
	Paint	L.F.	.18	.79		.97	
	Minimum Charge	Job		156		156	
Plastic							
	Demolish	L.F.		.66		.66	Cost includes material and labor to
	Install	L.F.	.79	1.48		2.27	install 2" x 3" vinyl rectangular
	Demolish and Install	L.F.	.79	2.14		2.93	downspouts.
	Reinstall	L.F.		1.19		1.19	
	Clean	L.F.		.28		.28	
	Paint	L.F.	.18	.79		.97	
	Minimum Charge	Job		156		156	

Shutters		Unit	Material	Labor	Equip.	Total	Specification
Exterior							
25" High							
	Demolish	Ea.		7.20		7.20	Includes material and labor to install
	Install	Pr.	84	28.50		112.50	pair of exterior shutters 25" x 16",
	Demolish and Install	Pr.	84	35.70		119.70	unpainted, installed as fixed shutters on
	Reinstall	Pr.		28.48		28.48	concrete or wood frame.
	Clean	Ea.	.06	6.20		6.26	
	Paint	Ea.	1.39	13.70		15.09	
	Minimum Charge	Job		142		142	
39" High							
	Demolish	Ea.		7.20		7.20	Includes material and labor to install
	Install	Pr.	91	28.50		119.50	pair of shutters 39" x 16", unpainted,
	Demolish and Install	Pr.	91	35.70		126.70	installed as fixed shutters on concrete
	Reinstall	Pr.		28.48		28.48	or wood frame.
	Clean	Ea.	.06	6.20		6.26	
	Paint	Ea.	2.17	18.50		20.67	
	Minimum Charge	Job		142		142	
51" High							
	Demolish	Ea.		7.20		7.20	Includes material and labor to install
	Install	Pr.	101	28.50		129.50	pair of shutters 51" x 16", unpainted,
	Demolish and Install	Pr.	101	35.70		136.70	installed as fixed shutters on concrete
	Reinstall	Pr.		28.48		28.48	or wood frame.
	Clean	Ea.	.06	6.20		6.26	
	Paint	Ea.	2.82	19.20		22.02	
	Minimum Charge	Job		142		142	

Improvements / Appliances / Treatments

Shutters		Unit	Material	Labor	Equip.	Total	Specification
59" High							
	Demolish	Ea.		7.20		7.20	Includes material and labor to install
	Install	Pr.	142	28.50		170.50	pair of shutters 59" x 16", unpainted,
	Demolish and Install	Pr.	142	35.70		177.70	installed as fixed shutters on concrete
	Reinstall	Pr.		28.48		28.48	or wood frame.
	Clean	Ea.	.06	6.20		6.26	
	Paint	Ea.	3.25	21		24.25	
	Minimum Charge	Job		142		142	
67" High							
	Demolish	Ea.		7.20		7.20	Includes material and labor to install
	Install	Pr.	143	31.50		174.50	pair of shutters 67" x 16", unpainted,
	Demolish and Install	Pr.	143	38.70		181.70	installed as fixed shutters on concrete
	Reinstall	Pr.		31.64		31.64	or wood frame.
	Clean	Ea.	.06	6.20		6.26	
	Paint	Ea.	3.71	23.50		27.21	
	Minimum Charge	Job		142		142	
Interior Wood							
23" x 24", 2 Panel							
	Demolish	Ea.		7.20		7.20	Cost includes material and labor to
	Install	Ea.	78	16.75		94.75	install 23" x 24", 4 panel interior
	Demolish and Install	Ea.	78	23.95		101.95	moveable pine shutter, 1-1/4" louver,
	Reinstall	Ea.		13.40		13.40	knobs and hooks and hinges.
	Clean	Ea.	.06	6.20		6.26	
	Paint	Ea.	1.05	18.25		19.30	
	Minimum Charge	Job		142		142	
27" x 24", 4 Panel							
	Demolish	Ea.		7.20		7.20	Cost includes material and labor to
	Install	Ea.	90	16.75		106.75	install 27" x 24", 4 panel interior
	Demolish and Install	Ea.	90	23.95		113.95	moveable pine shutter, 1-1/4" louver,
	Reinstall	Ea.		13.40		13.40	knobs and hooks and hinges.
	Clean	Ea.	.06	6.20		6.26	
	Paint	Ea.	1.05	18.25		19.30	
	Minimum Charge	Job		142		142	
31" x 24", 4 Panel							
	Demolish	Ea.		7.20		7.20	Cost includes material and labor to
	Install	Ea.	104	16.75		120.75	install 31" x 24", 4 panel interior
	Demolish and Install	Ea.	104	23.95		127.95	moveable pine shutter, 1-1/4" louver,
	Reinstall	Ea.		13.40		13.40	knobs and hooks and hinges.
	Clean	Ea.	.06	6.20		6.26	
	Paint	Ea.	1.05	18.25		19.30	
	Minimum Charge	Job		142		142	
35" x 24", 4 Panel							
	Demolish	Ea.		7.20		7.20	Cost includes material and labor to
	Install	Ea.	104	16.75		120.75	install 35" x 24", 4 panel interior
	Demolish and Install	Ea.	104	23.95		127.95	moveable pine shutter, 1-1/4" louver,
	Reinstall	Ea.		13.40		13.40	knobs and hooks and hinges.
	Clean	Ea.	.06	6.20		6.26	
	Paint	Ea.	1.05	18.25		19.30	
	Minimum Charge	Job		142		142	
39" x 24", 4 Panel							
	Demolish	Ea.		7.20		7.20	Cost includes material and labor to
	Install	Ea.	120	16.75		136.75	install 39" x 24", 4 panel interior
	Demolish and Install	Ea.	120	23.95		143.95	moveable pine shutter, 1-1/4" louver,
	Reinstall	Ea.		13.40		13.40	knobs and hooks and hinges.
	Clean	Ea.	.06	6.20		6.26	
	Paint	Ea.	1.05	18.25		19.30	
	Minimum Charge	Job		142		142	

Improvements / Appliances / Treatments

Shutters

	Unit	Material	Labor	Equip.	Total	Specification
47" x 24", 4 Panel						
Demolish	Ea.		7.20		7.20	Cost includes material and labor to
Install	Ea.	132	16.75		148.75	install 47" x 24", 4 panel interior
Demolish and Install	Ea.	132	23.95		155.95	moveable pine shutter, 1-1/4" louver,
Reinstall	Ea.		13.40		13.40	knobs and hooks and hinges.
Clean	Ea.	.06	6.20		6.26	
Paint	Ea.	1.09	19.65		20.74	
Minimum Charge	Job		142		142	

Awning

	Unit	Material	Labor	Equip.	Total	Specification
Standard Aluminum						
36" Wide x 30" Deep						
Demolish	Ea.		7.20		7.20	Includes material and labor to install
Install	Ea.	155	23.50		178.50	one aluminum awning with
Demolish and Install	Ea.	155	30.70		185.70	weather-resistant finish.
Reinstall	Ea.		18.99		18.99	
Clean	Ea.		8.60		8.60	
Minimum Charge	Job		142		142	
48" Wide x 30" Deep						
Demolish	Ea.		7.20		7.20	Includes material and labor to install
Install	Ea.	190	28.50		218.50	one aluminum awning with
Demolish and Install	Ea.	190	35.70		225.70	weather-resistant finish.
Reinstall	Ea.		22.78		22.78	
Clean	Ea.		8.60		8.60	
Minimum Charge	Job		142		142	
60" Wide x 30" Deep						
Demolish	Ea.		14.35		14.35	Includes material and labor to install
Install	Ea.	208	31.50		239.50	one aluminum awning with
Demolish and Install	Ea.	208	45.85		253.85	weather-resistant finish.
Reinstall	Ea.		25.32		25.32	
Clean	Ea.		8.60		8.60	
Minimum Charge	Job		142		142	
72" Wide x 30" Deep						
Demolish	Ea.		14.35		14.35	Includes material and labor to install
Install	Ea.	228	35.50		263.50	one aluminum awning with
Demolish and Install	Ea.	228	49.85		277.85	weather-resistant finish.
Reinstall	Ea.		28.48		28.48	
Clean	Ea.		8.60		8.60	
Minimum Charge	Job		142		142	
Roll-up Type						
Demolish	S.F.		.52		.52	Includes material and labor to install
Install	S.F.	6.20	2.85		9.05	an aluminum roll-up awning.
Demolish and Install	S.F.	6.20	3.37		9.57	
Reinstall	S.F.		2.28		2.28	
Clean	S.F.	.03	.43		.46	
Minimum Charge	Job		142		142	
Canvas						
30" Wide						
Demolish	Ea.		4.31		4.31	Includes material and labor to install a
Install	Ea.	182	23.50		205.50	canvas window awning.
Demolish and Install	Ea.	182	27.81		209.81	
Reinstall	Ea.		18.99		18.99	
Clean	Ea.		2.59		2.59	
Minimum Charge	Job		142		142	

Improvements / Appliances / Treatments

Awning

	Unit	Material	Labor	Equip.	Total	Specification
36" Wide						
Demolish	Ea.		4.31		4.31	Includes material and labor to install a
Install	Ea.	219	28.50		247.50	canvas window awning.
Demolish and Install	Ea.	219	32.81		251.81	
Reinstall	Ea.		22.78		22.78	
Clean	Ea.		2.83		2.83	
Minimum Charge	Job		142		142	
42" Wide						
Demolish	Ea.		4.31		4.31	Includes material and labor to install a
Install	Ea.	237	35.50		272.50	canvas window awning.
Demolish and Install	Ea.	237	39.81		276.81	
Reinstall	Ea.		28.48		28.48	
Clean	Ea.		3.36		3.36	
Minimum Charge	Job		142		142	
48" Wide						
Demolish	Ea.		4.31		4.31	Includes material and labor to install a
Install	Ea.	261	40.50		301.50	canvas window awning.
Demolish and Install	Ea.	261	44.81		305.81	
Reinstall	Ea.		32.55		32.55	
Clean	Ea.		3.90		3.90	
Minimum Charge	Job		142		142	

Cloth Canopy Cover

	Unit	Material	Labor	Equip.	Total	Specification
8' x 10'						
Demolish	Ea.		241		241	Includes material and labor to install
Install	Ea.	294	142		436	one 8' x 10' cloth canopy patio cover
Demolish and Install	Ea.	294	383		677	with front bar and tension support
Reinstall	Ea.		113.92		113.92	rafters and 9" valance.
Clean	Ea.	2.24	34.50		36.74	
Minimum Charge	Job		285		285	
8' x 15'						
Demolish	Ea.		241		241	Includes material and labor to install
Install	Ea.	400	142		542	one 8' x 15' cloth canopy patio cover
Demolish and Install	Ea.	400	383		783	with front bar and tension support
Reinstall	Ea.		113.92		113.92	rafters and 9" valance.
Clean	Ea.	2.24	51.50		53.74	
Minimum Charge	Job		285		285	

Vent

	Unit	Material	Labor	Equip.	Total	Specification
Small Roof Turbine						
Demolish	Ea.		7.20		7.20	Includes material and labor to install
Install	Ea.	57	28		85	spinner ventilator, wind driven,
Demolish and Install	Ea.	57	35.20		92.20	galvanized, 4" neck diam, 180 CFM.
Reinstall	Ea.		22.42		22.42	
Clean	Ea.		4.60		4.60	
Minimum Charge	Job		157		157	
Large Roof Turbine						
Demolish	Ea.		5.75		5.75	Includes material and labor to install
Install	Ea.	66.50	40		106.50	spinner ventilator, wind driven,
Demolish and Install	Ea.	66.50	45.75		112.25	galvanized, 8" neck diam, 360 CFM.
Reinstall	Ea.		32.03		32.03	
Clean	Ea.		5.15		5.15	
Minimum Charge	Job		157		157	

Improvements / Appliances / Treatments

Vent		Unit	Material	Labor	Equip.	Total	Specification
Roof Ventilator							
	Demolish	Ea.		7.20		7.20	Includes material and labor to install a
	Install	Ea.	163	35		198	roof ventilator.
	Demolish and Install	Ea.	163	42.20		205.20	
	Reinstall	Ea.		28.02		28.02	
	Clean	Ea.	.56	5.15		5.71	
	Paint	Ea.	1.31	6.40		7.71	
	Minimum Charge	Job		157		157	
Gable Louvered							
	Demolish	Ea.		14.35		14.35	Includes material and labor to install a
	Install	Ea.	28.50	9.50		38	vinyl gable end vent.
	Demolish and Install	Ea.	28.50	23.85		52.35	
	Reinstall	Ea.		7.59		7.59	
	Clean	Ea.		2.76		2.76	
	Paint	Ea.	.88	3.93		4.81	
	Minimum Charge	Job		142		142	
Ridge Vent							
	Demolish	L.F.		.74		.74	Includes material and labor to install a
	Install	L.F.	2.35	2.01		4.36	mill finish aluminum ridge vent strip.
	Demolish and Install	L.F.	2.35	2.75		5.10	
	Minimum Charge	Job		142		142	
Foundation							
	Demolish	Ea.		5.10		5.10	Includes material and labor to install
	Install	Ea.	19.80	9.55		29.35	galvanized foundation block vent.
	Demolish and Install	Ea.	19.80	14.65		34.45	
	Reinstall	Ea.		7.63		7.63	
	Clean	Ea.	.14	5.15		5.29	
	Minimum Charge	Job		142		142	
Frieze							
	Demolish	L.F.		.51		.51	Includes material and labor to install
	Install	L.F.	.87	.65		1.52	pine frieze board.
	Demolish and Install	L.F.	.87	1.16		2.03	
	Reinstall	L.F.		.52		.52	
	Clean	L.F.	.03	.17		.20	
	Minimum Charge	Job		142		142	
Water Heater Cap							
	Demolish	Ea.		10.90		10.90	Includes material and labor to install a
	Install	Ea.	23	39		62	galvanized steel water heater cap.
	Demolish and Install	Ea.	23	49.90		72.90	
	Reinstall	Ea.		31.16		31.16	
	Clean	Ea.	.98	12.95		13.93	

Cupolas		Unit	Material	Labor	Equip.	Total	Specification
22″ x 22″							
	Demolish	Ea.		138		138	Includes material and labor to install a
	Install	Ea.	268	71		339	cedar cupola with aluminum roof
	Demolish and Install	Ea.	268	209		477	covering.
	Reinstall	Ea.		56.96		56.96	
	Minimum Charge	Job		142		142	
29″ x 29″							
	Demolish	Ea.		138		138	Includes material and labor to install a
	Install	Ea.	350	71		421	cedar cupola with aluminum roof
	Demolish and Install	Ea.	350	209		559	covering.
	Reinstall	Ea.		56.96		56.96	
	Minimum Charge	Job		142		142	

Improvements / Appliances / Treatments

Cupolas

Cupolas	Unit	Material	Labor	Equip.	Total	Specification
35" x 35"						
Demolish	Ea.		138		138	Includes material and labor to install a
Install	Ea.	640	95		735	cedar cupola with aluminum roof
Demolish and Install	Ea.	640	233		873	covering.
Reinstall	Ea.		75.95		75.95	
Minimum Charge	Job		142		142	
47" x 47"						
Demolish	Ea.		138		138	Includes material and labor to install a
Install	Ea.	1025	142		1167	cedar cupola with aluminum roof
Demolish and Install	Ea.	1025	280		1305	covering.
Reinstall	Ea.		113.92		113.92	
Minimum Charge	Job		142		142	
Weather Vane						
Install	Ea.	43	35.50		78.50	Includes minimum labor and
Minimum Charge	Job		142		142	equipment to install residential type weathervane.

Aluminum Carport

Aluminum Carport	Unit	Material	Labor	Equip.	Total	Specification
Natural Finish						
Demolish	S.F.		1.44		1.44	Includes material, labor and equipment
Install	S.F.	18.80	4.87	1	24.67	to install an aluminum carport.
Demolish and Install	S.F.	18.80	6.31	1	26.11	Foundations are not included.
Reinstall	S.F.		3.90	.80	4.70	
Clean	S.F.	.03	.16		.19	
Minimum Charge	Job		285		285	
Enamel Finish						
Demolish	S.F.		1.44		1.44	Includes material, labor and equipment
Install	S.F.	18.80	4.87	1	24.67	to install an aluminum carport.
Demolish and Install	S.F.	18.80	6.31	1	26.11	Foundations are not included.
Reinstall	S.F.		3.90	.80	4.70	
Clean	S.F.	.03	.16		.19	
Minimum Charge	Job		285		285	
20' x 20' Complete						
Demolish	Ea.		144		144	Includes material, labor and equipment
Install	Ea.	5875	485	100	6460	to install an aluminum carport.
Demolish and Install	Ea.	5875	629	100	6604	Foundations are not included.
Reinstall	Ea.		389.76	80.26	470.02	
Clean	Ea.	.14	51.50		51.64	
Minimum Charge	Job		285		285	
24' x 24' Complete						
Demolish	Ea.		144		144	Includes material, labor and equipment
Install	Ea.	8000	650	134	8784	to install an aluminum carport.
Demolish and Install	Ea.	8000	794	134	8928	Foundations are not included.
Reinstall	Ea.		519.68	107.01	626.69	
Clean	Ea.	.14	103		103.14	
Minimum Charge	Job		285		285	
Metal Support Posts						
Demolish	Ea.		1.91		1.91	Includes material and labor to install
Install	Ea.	13.10	35.50		48.60	metal support posts for a carport.
Demolish and Install	Ea.	13.10	37.41		50.51	
Reinstall	Ea.		28.48		28.48	
Clean	Ea.	.14	2.15		2.29	
Paint	Ea.	.12	5.10		5.22	
Minimum Charge	Job		285		285	

Storage Shed	Unit	Material	Labor	Equip.	Total	Specification
Aluminum						
Pre-fab (8' x 10')						
Demolish	Ea.		42		42	Includes material and labor to install
Install	Ea.	273	415		688	an aluminum storage shed.
Demolish and Install	Ea.	273	457		730	
Clean	Ea.	.94	26		26.94	
Minimum Charge	Ea.		355		355	
Pre-fab (10' x 12')						
Demolish	Ea.		80.50		80.50	Includes material and labor to install
Install	Ea.	460	415		875	an aluminum storage shed.
Demolish and Install	Ea.	460	495.50		955.50	
Clean	Ea.	.94	28.50		29.44	
Minimum Charge	Ea.		355		355	
Wood						
Pre-fab (8' x 10')						
Demolish	Ea.		42		42	Includes material and labor to install a
Install	Ea.	760	415		1175	pre-fabricated wood storage shed.
Demolish and Install	Ea.	760	457		1217	
Clean	Ea.	.94	26		26.94	
Minimum Charge	Ea.		355		355	
Pre-fab (10' x 12')						
Demolish	Ea.		80.50		80.50	Includes material and labor to install a
Install	Ea.	990	415		1405	pre-fabricated wood storage shed.
Demolish and Install	Ea.	990	495.50		1485.50	
Clean	Ea.	.94	28.50		29.44	
Minimum Charge	Ea.		355		355	

Gazebo	Unit	Material	Labor	Equip.	Total	Specification
Good Grade						
Demolish	S.F.		2.30		2.30	Includes material and labor to install a
Install	S.F.	18.90	21.50		40.40	gazebo.
Demolish and Install	S.F.	18.90	23.80		42.70	
Reinstall	S.F.		17.09		17.09	
Clean	S.F.	.11	1.38		1.49	
Minimum Charge	Job		142		142	
Custom Grade						
Demolish	S.F.		2.30		2.30	Includes material and labor to install a
Install	S.F.	30.50	21.50		52	gazebo.
Demolish and Install	S.F.	30.50	23.80		54.30	
Reinstall	S.F.		17.09		17.09	
Clean	S.F.	.11	1.38		1.49	
Minimum Charge	Job		142		142	
Bench Seating						
Demolish	L.F.		3.83		3.83	Includes material and labor to install
Install	L.F.	3.01	14.25		17.26	pressure treated bench seating.
Demolish and Install	L.F.	3.01	18.08		21.09	
Reinstall	L.F.		11.39		11.39	
Clean	L.F.	.11	1.03		1.14	
Paint	L.F.	.48	2.04		2.52	
Minimum Charge	Job		142		142	
Re-screen						
Install	S.F.	.51	1.14		1.65	Includes labor and material to
Minimum Charge	Job		142		142	re-screen wood frame.

Improvements / Appliances / Treatments

Pool		Unit	Material	Labor	Equip.	Total	Specification
Screen Enclosure							
Re-screen							
	Install	SF Wall		3.57		3.57	Includes material and labor to install a
	Minimum Charge	Job		142		142	screen enclosure for a pool.
Screen Door							
	Demolish	Ea.		5.65		5.65	Includes material and labor to install
	Install	Ea.	131	47.50		178.50	wood screen door with aluminum cloth
	Demolish and Install	Ea.	131	53.15		184.15	screen. Frame and hardware not
	Reinstall	Ea.		37.97		37.97	included.
	Clean	Ea.	.11	7.45		7.56	
	Paint	Ea.	2.92	10.20		13.12	
	Minimum Charge	Job		142		142	
Heater / Motor							
	Demolish	Ea.		27.50		27.50	Includes material and labor to install
	Install	Ea.	1850	350		2200	swimming pool heater, not incl. base
	Demolish and Install	Ea.	1850	377.50		2227.50	or pad, elec., 12 kW, 4,800 gal pool,
	Reinstall	Ea.		280.70		280.70	incl. pump.
	Clean	Ea.	2.81	26		28.81	
	Minimum Charge	Job		158		158	
Filter System							
	Demolish	Ea.		46		46	Includes material, labor and equipment
	Install	Total	545	251		796	to install sand filter system tank
	Demolish and Install	Total	545	297		842	including hook-up to existing
	Reinstall	Total		200.45		200.45	equipment. Pump and motor not
	Minimum Charge	Job		157		157	included.
Pump / Motor							
	Demolish	Ea.		27.50		27.50	Includes material and labor to install a
	Install	Ea.	565	62.50		627.50	22 GPM pump.
	Demolish and Install	Ea.	565	90		655	
	Reinstall	Ea.		50.11		50.11	
	Clean	Ea.	2.81	26		28.81	
	Minimum Charge	Job		158		158	
Pump Water							
	Install	Day		285	63	348	Includes labor and equipment to pump
	Minimum Charge	Job		130		130	water from a swimming pool.
Replaster							
	Install	SF Surf	.91	7		7.91	Includes labor and material to replaster
	Minimum Charge	Job		130		130	gunite pool with a surface area of 500
							to 600 S.F.
Solar Panels							
	Demolish	S.F.		1.16		1.16	Includes material and labor to install
	Install	S.F.	18.75	2.06		20.81	solar panel.
	Demolish and Install	S.F.	18.75	3.22		21.97	
	Reinstall	S.F.		1.65		1.65	
	Minimum Charge	Ea.		355		355	

Construction Clean-up	Unit	Material	Labor	Equip.	Total	Specification
Final						
Clean	S.F.		.18		.18	Includes labor for final site/job
Minimum Charge	Job		103		103	clean-up including detail cleaning.

Location Factors

Costs shown in *Means cost data publications* are based on National Averages for materials and installation. To adjust these costs to a specific location, simply multiply the base cost by the factor for that city. The data is arranged alphabetically by state and postal zip code numbers. For a city not listed, use the factor for a nearby city with similar economic characteristics.

STATE/ZIP	CITY	Residential	Commercial
ALABAMA			
350-352	Birmingham	.85	.86
354	Tuscaloosa	.80	.78
355	Jasper	.76	.77
356	Decatur	.79	.80
357-358	Huntsville	.81	.82
359	Gadsden	.80	.81
360-361	Montgomery	.82	.80
362	Anniston	.73	.74
363	Dothan	.79	.77
364	Evergreen	.79	.77
365-366	Mobile	.81	.82
367	Selma	.79	.77
368	Phenix City	.82	.80
369	Butler	.79	.77
ALASKA			
995-996	Anchorage	1.25	1.24
997	Fairbanks	1.25	1.24
998	Juneau	1.24	1.23
999	Ketchikan	1.30	1.29
ARIZONA			
850,853	Phoenix	.92	.89
852	Mesa/Tempe	.87	.84
855	Globe	.88	.85
856-857	Tucson	.90	.87
859	Show Low	.89	.85
860	Flagstaff	.92	.88
863	Prescott	.90	.86
864	Kingman	.89	.85
865	Chambers	.88	.84
ARKANSAS			
716	Pine Bluff	.80	.80
717	Camden	.70	.70
718	Texarkana	.74	.74
719	Hot Springs	.69	.69
720-722	Little Rock	.81	.81
723	West Memphis	.79	.79
724	Jonesboro	.79	.79
725	Batesville	.75	.75
726	Harrison	.76	.76
727	Fayetteville	.69	.66
728	Russellville	.77	.74
729	Fort Smith	.83	.80
CALIFORNIA			
900-902	Los Angeles	1.08	1.08
903-905	Inglewood	1.06	1.06
906-908	Long Beach	1.07	1.07
910-912	Pasadena	1.07	1.07
913-916	Van Nuys	1.09	1.09
917-918	Alhambra	1.08	1.08
919-921	San Diego	1.10	1.06
922	Palm Springs	1.09	1.05
923-924	San Bernardino	1.08	1.04
925	Riverside	1.11	1.07
926-927	Santa Ana	1.09	1.06
928	Anaheim	1.10	1.08
930	Oxnard	1.13	1.08
931	Santa Barbara	1.11	1.08
932-933	Bakersfield	1.11	1.06
934	San Luis Obispo	1.14	1.08
935	Mojave	1.09	1.05
936-938	Fresno	1.12	1.08
939	Salinas	1.12	1.12
940-941	San Francisco	1.21	1.24
942,956-958	Sacramento	1.11	1.10
943	Palo Alto	1.15	1.18
944	San Mateo	1.16	1.19
945	Vallejo	1.11	1.14
946	Oakland	1.16	1.19
947	Berkeley	1.16	1.18
948	Richmond	1.14	1.17
949	San Rafael	1.26	1.20
950	Santa Cruz	1.16	1.14
951	San Jose	1.22	1.20
952	Stockton	1.13	1.09
953	Modesto	1.13	1.09

STATE/ZIP	CITY	Residential	Commercial
CALIFORNIA (CONT'D)			
954	Santa Rosa	1.14	1.17
955	Eureka	1.10	1.09
959	Marysville	1.10	1.09
960	Redding	1.11	1.10
961	Susanville	1.11	1.10
COLORADO			
800-802	Denver	.99	.95
803	Boulder	.88	.84
804	Golden	.97	.93
805	Fort Collins	.98	.92
806	Greeley	.90	.84
807	Fort Morgan	.97	.91
808-809	Colorado Springs	.94	.92
810	Pueblo	.94	.92
811	Alamosa	.89	.87
812	Salida	.89	.87
813	Durango	.88	.86
814	Montrose	.86	.84
815	Grand Junction	.90	.85
816	Glenwood Springs	.95	.91
CONNECTICUT			
060	New Britain	1.04	1.05
061	Hartford	1.04	1.05
062	Willimantic	1.03	1.04
063	New London	1.05	1.04
064	Meriden	1.03	1.04
065	New Haven	1.04	1.05
066	Bridgeport	1.02	1.05
067	Waterbury	1.05	1.05
068	Norwalk	1.01	1.05
069	Stamford	1.04	1.08
D.C.			
200-205	Washington	.93	.95
DELAWARE			
197	Newark	1.00	1.01
198	Wilmington	1.00	1.01
199	Dover	1.00	1.01
FLORIDA			
320,322	Jacksonville	.83	.82
321	Daytona Beach	.87	.86
323	Tallahassee	.75	.77
324	Panama City	.70	.72
325	Pensacola	.84	.82
326,344	Gainesville	.84	.81
327-328,347	Orlando	.86	.84
329	Melbourne	.90	.89
330-332,340	Miami	.83	.85
333	Fort Lauderdale	.83	.85
334,349	West Palm Beach	.86	.83
335-336,346	Tampa	.80	.82
337	St. Petersburg	.81	.83
338	Lakeland	.79	.81
339,341	Fort Myers	.79	.79
342	Sarasota	.78	.80
GEORGIA			
300-303,399	Atlanta	.85	.90
304	Statesboro	.72	.74
305	Gainesville	.76	.80
306	Athens	.77	.82
307	Dalton	.68	.67
308-309	Augusta	.76	.78
310-312	Macon	.81	.81
313-314	Savannah	.80	.81
315	Waycross	.74	.74
316	Valdosta	.76	.76
317	Albany	.77	.79
318-319	Columbus	.78	.78
HAWAII			
967	Hilo	1.27	1.23
968	Honolulu	1.27	1.23

Location Factors

STATE/ZIP	CITY	Residential	Commercial
STATES & POSS.			
969	Guam	1.37	1.33
IDAHO			
832	Pocatello	.94	.93
833	Twin Falls	.79	.78
834	Idaho Falls	.83	.82
835	Lewiston	1.09	1.01
836-837	Boise	.94	.93
838	Coeur d'Alene	.95	.88
ILLINOIS			
600-603	North Suburban	1.11	1.09
604	Joliet	1.11	1.10
605	South Suburban	1.10	1.09
606	Chicago	1.13	1.12
609	Kankakee	1.00	1.00
610-611	Rockford	1.05	1.04
612	Rock Island	1.06	.97
613	La Salle	1.06	.98
614	Galesburg	1.09	1.01
615-616	Peoria	1.09	1.02
617	Bloomington	1.05	1.00
618-619	Champaign	1.04	1.01
620-622	East St. Louis	1.00	1.00
623	Quincy	.99	.97
624	Effingham	1.02	.99
625	Decatur	1.01	.98
626-627	Springfield	1.01	.98
628	Centralia	.99	.99
629	Carbondale	.97	.97
INDIANA			
460	Anderson	.95	.93
461-462	Indianapolis	.98	.96
463-464	Gary	1.04	1.02
465-466	South Bend	.94	.92
467-468	Fort Wayne	.92	.93
469	Kokomo	.93	.92
470	Lawrenceburg	.93	.90
471	New Albany	.93	.89
472	Columbus	.96	.93
473	Muncie	.94	.93
474	Bloomington	.96	.93
475	Washington	.93	.93
476-477	Evansville	.95	.95
478	Terre Haute	.96	.95
479	Lafayette	.92	.92
IOWA			
500-503,509	Des Moines	.97	.93
504	Mason City	.86	.81
505	Fort Dodge	.84	.78
506-507	Waterloo	.88	.82
508	Creston	.89	.84
510-511	Sioux City	.95	.88
512	Sibley	.80	.78
513	Spencer	.80	.78
514	Carroll	.84	.80
515	Council Bluffs	.96	.89
516	Shenandoah	.82	.77
520	Dubuque	.99	.88
521	Decorah	.88	.79
522-524	Cedar Rapids	1.01	.92
525	Ottumwa	.94	.86
526	Burlington	.92	.86
527-528	Davenport	.98	.96
KANSAS			
660-662	Kansas City	.96	.94
664-666	Topeka	.86	.85
667	Fort Scott	.85	.83
668	Emporia	.81	.81
669	Belleville	.87	.81
670-672	Wichita	.89	.86
673	Independence	.82	.79
674	Salina	.85	.81
675	Hutchinson	.79	.76
676	Hays	.84	.80
677	Colby	.85	.81
678	Dodge City	.84	.81
679	Liberal	.78	.75
KENTUCKY			
400-402	Louisville	.95	.92
403-405	Lexington	.87	.84

STATE/ZIP	CITY	Residential	Commercial
KENTUCKY (CONT'D)			
406	Frankfort	.92	.86
407-409	Corbin	.78	.73
410	Covington	.98	.95
411-412	Ashland	.96	.97
413-414	Campton	.77	.73
415-416	Pikeville	.82	.83
417-418	Hazard	.76	.73
420	Paducah	.97	.92
421-422	Bowling Green	.96	.91
423	Owensboro	.91	.89
424	Henderson	.94	.92
425-426	Somerset	.75	.72
427	Elizabethtown	.94	.90
LOUISIANA			
700-701	New Orleans	.86	.85
703	Thibodaux	.85	.85
704	Hammond	.84	.83
705	Lafayette	.84	.81
706	Lake Charles	.83	.83
707-708	Baton Rouge	.82	.81
710-711	Shreveport	.81	.81
712	Monroe	.79	.79
713-714	Alexandria	.78	.78
MAINE			
039	Kittery	.86	.88
040-041	Portland	.91	.93
042	Lewiston	.92	.93
043	Augusta	.88	.88
044	Bangor	.93	.93
045	Bath	.89	.89
046	Machias	.87	.87
047	Houlton	.89	.89
048	Rockland	.86	.86
049	Waterville	.86	.85
MARYLAND			
206	Waldorf	.87	.87
207-208	College Park	.90	.90
209	Silver Spring	.89	.89
210-212	Baltimore	.91	.91
214	Annapolis	.89	.90
215	Cumberland	.87	.88
216	Easton	.73	.73
217	Hagerstown	.90	.88
218	Salisbury	.76	.77
219	Elkton	.82	.83
MASSACHUSETTS			
010-011	Springfield	1.04	1.02
012	Pittsfield	.99	.99
013	Greenfield	1.02	1.00
014	Fitchburg	1.08	1.04
015-016	Worcester	1.10	1.06
017	Framingham	1.06	1.06
018	Lowell	1.08	1.08
019	Lawrence	1.09	1.09
020-022, 024	Boston	1.14	1.15
023	Brockton	1.06	1.08
025	Buzzards Bay	1.02	1.04
026	Hyannis	1.04	1.05
027	New Bedford	1.06	1.07
MICHIGAN			
480,483	Royal Oak	1.03	1.02
481	Ann Arbor	1.04	1.03
482	Detroit	1.07	1.06
484-485	Flint	.99	1.00
486	Saginaw	.97	.98
487	Bay City	.96	.97
488-489	Lansing	1.01	.98
490	Battle Creek	1.01	.95
491	Kalamazoo	1.00	.94
492	Jackson	.99	.96
493,495	Grand Rapids	.88	.85
494	Muskegon	.95	.92
496	Traverse City	.87	.84
497	Gaylord	.87	.88
498-499	Iron Mountain	.98	.95
MINNESOTA			
550-551	Saint Paul	1.09	1.07
553-555	Minneapolis	1.11	1.08

STATE/ZIP	CITY	Residential	Commercial
556-558	Duluth	1.04	1.05
559	Rochester	1.03	.99
560	Mankato	1.00	.99
561	Windom	.90	.89
562	Willmar	.93	.92
563	St. Cloud	1.11	1.03
564	Brainerd	1.06	.99
565	Detroit Lakes	.88	.95
566	Bemidji	.91	.98
567	Thief River Falls	.87	.94
MISSISSIPPI			
386	Clarksdale	.70	.66
387	Greenville	.80	.77
388	Tupelo	.71	.71
389	Greenwood	.72	.68
390-392	Jackson	.80	.76
393	Meridian	.76	.75
394	Laurel	.72	.69
395	Biloxi	.84	.80
396	McComb	.72	.70
397	Columbus	.70	.71
MISSOURI			
630-631	St. Louis	1.00	1.03
633	Bowling Green	.92	.94
634	Hannibal	.99	.93
635	Kirksville	.86	.90
636	Flat River	.94	.97
637	Cape Girardeau	.93	.96
638	Sikeston	.90	.92
639	Poplar Bluff	.90	.92
640-641	Kansas City	1.04	1.01
644-645	St. Joseph	.90	.94
646	Chillicothe	.82	.86
647	Harrisonville	.98	.96
648	Joplin	.84	.86
650-651	Jefferson City	.98	.92
652	Columbia	.99	.93
653	Sedalia	.99	.92
654-655	Rolla	.95	.89
656-658	Springfield	.86	.88
MONTANA			
590-591	Billings	.93	.91
592	Wolf Point	.92	.90
593	Miles City	.91	.89
594	Great Falls	.92	.91
595	Havre	.90	.89
596	Helena	.91	.90
597	Butte	.90	.89
598	Missoula	.89	.88
599	Kalispell	.88	.87
NEBRASKA			
680-681	Omaha	.92	.91
683-685	Lincoln	.88	.83
686	Columbus	.74	.73
687	Norfolk	.84	.83
688	Grand Island	.88	.83
689	Hastings	.82	.78
690	Mccook	.79	.75
691	North Platte	.86	.82
692	Valentine	.77	.74
693	Alliance	.75	.71
NEVADA			
889-891	Las Vegas	1.05	1.04
893	Ely	.93	.94
894-895	Reno	.95	1.00
897	Carson City	.96	.99
898	Elko	.90	.93
NEW HAMPSHIRE			
030	Nashua	.94	.95
031	Manchester	.94	.95
032-033	Concord	.93	.94
034	Keene	.78	.79
035	Littleton	.82	.83
036	Charleston	.77	.77
037	Claremont	.76	.77
038	Portsmouth	.93	.92

STATE/ZIP	CITY	Residential	Commercial
NEW JERSEY			
070-071	Newark	1.14	1.12
072	Elizabeth	1.09	1.08
073	Jersey City	1.11	1.10
074-075	Paterson	1.12	1.12
076	Hackensack	1.10	1.10
077	Long Branch	1.10	1.08
078	Dover	1.11	1.09
079	Summit	1.08	1.06
080,083	Vineland	1.11	1.08
081	Camden	1.11	1.08
082,084	Atlantic City	1.11	1.08
085-086	Trenton	1.12	1.10
087	Point Pleasant	1.10	1.08
088-089	New Brunswick	1.12	1.10
NEW MEXICO			
870-872	Albuquerque	.88	.90
873	Gallup	.88	.91
874	Farmington	.88	.91
875	Santa Fe	.88	.90
877	Las Vegas	.88	.90
878	Socorro	.87	.89
879	Truth/Consequences	.87	.87
880	Las Cruces	.84	.84
881	Clovis	.89	.89
882	Roswell	.90	.90
883	Carrizozo	.91	.91
884	Tucumcari	.90	.90
NEW YORK			
100-102	New York	1.35	1.35
103	Staten Island	1.31	1.31
104	Bronx	1.30	1.30
105	Mount Vernon	1.20	1.20
106	White Plains	1.19	1.19
107	Yonkers	1.22	1.22
108	New Rochelle	1.20	1.20
109	Suffern	1.14	1.14
110	Queens	1.30	1.30
111	Long Island City	1.31	1.31
112	Brooklyn	1.31	1.31
113	Flushing	1.32	1.32
114	Jamaica	1.30	1.30
115,117,118	Hicksville	1.26	1.26
116	Far Rockaway	1.32	1.32
119	Riverhead	1.27	1.27
120-122	Albany	.97	.97
123	Schenectady	.98	.98
124	Kingston	1.11	1.09
125-126	Poughkeepsie	1.13	1.11
127	Monticello	1.09	1.07
128	Glens Falls	.95	.93
129	Plattsburgh	.95	.93
130-132	Syracuse	.99	.97
133-135	Utica	.91	.94
136	Watertown	.92	.95
137-139	Binghamton	.94	.94
140-142	Buffalo	1.05	1.02
143	Niagara Falls	1.07	1.03
144-146	Rochester	.99	1.00
147	Jamestown	.98	.94
148-149	Elmira	.95	.93
NORTH CAROLINA			
270,272-274	Greensboro	.75	.76
271	Winston-Salem	.74	.75
275-276	Raleigh	.76	.76
277	Durham	.75	.76
278	Rocky Mount	.68	.68
279	Elizabeth City	.70	.70
280	Gastonia	.74	.75
281-282	Charlotte	.74	.75
283	Fayetteville	.75	.75
284	Wilmington	.73	.75
285	Kinston	.67	.67
286	Hickory	.66	.67
287-288	Asheville	.73	.75
289	Murphy	.66	.67
NORTH DAKOTA			
580-581	Fargo	.79	.84
582	Grand Forks	.77	.82
583	Devils Lake	.76	.81
584	Jamestown	.76	.81
585	Bismarck	.80	.84

STATE/ZIP	CITY	Residential	Commercial
NORTH DAKOTA (CONT'D)			
586	Dickinson	.81	.85
587	Minot	.82	.87
588	Williston	.76	.80
OHIO			
430-432	Columbus	.98	.96
433	Marion	.92	.93
434-436	Toledo	1.02	1.01
437-438	Zanesville	.93	.92
439	Steubenville	.97	.97
440	Lorain	1.05	.98
441	Cleveland	1.09	1.03
442-443	Akron	1.02	1.01
444-445	Youngstown	1.01	.98
446-447	Canton	.97	.96
448-449	Mansfield	.96	.94
450	Hamilton	1.00	.94
451-452	Cincinnati	1.00	.94
453-454	Dayton	.94	.93
455	Springfield	.95	.93
456	Chillicothe	1.02	.96
457	Athens	.92	.91
458	Lima	.96	.95
OKLAHOMA			
730-731	Oklahoma City	.82	.84
734	Ardmore	.83	.82
735	Lawton	.84	.83
736	Clinton	.80	.82
737	Enid	.83	.82
738	Woodward	.82	.81
739	Guymon	.69	.68
740-741	Tulsa	.84	.81
743	Miami	.86	.83
744	Muskogee	.75	.73
745	Mcalester	.76	.77
746	Ponca City	.82	.81
747	Durant	.79	.81
748	Shawnee	.79	.81
749	Poteau	.85	.81
OREGON			
970-972	Portland	1.08	1.06
973	Salem	1.06	1.05
974	Eugene	1.05	1.04
975	Medford	1.05	1.04
976	Klamath Falls	1.05	1.04
977	Bend	1.06	1.05
978	Pendleton	1.03	1.01
979	Vale	.98	.96
PENNSYLVANIA			
150-152	Pittsburgh	1.04	1.02
153	Washington	1.02	1.00
154	Uniontown	1.01	.99
155	Bedford	1.03	.96
156	Greensburg	1.02	1.00
157	Indiana	1.05	.98
158	Dubois	1.04	.97
159	Johnstown	1.04	.97
160	Butler	1.01	.98
161	New Castle	1.01	.98
162	Kittanning	1.02	.99
163	Oil City	.91	.95
164-165	Erie	.98	.97
166	Altoona	1.04	.96
167	Bradford	.99	.97
168	State College	.96	.96
169	Wellsboro	.93	.94
170-171	Harrisburg	.98	.97
172	Chambersburg	.96	.95
173-174	York	.97	.95
175-176	Lancaster	.95	.93
177	Williamsport	.91	.90
178	Sunbury	.95	.94
179	Pottsville	.95	.94
180	Lehigh Valley	1.04	1.03
181	Allentown	1.01	1.00
182	Hazleton	.97	.96
183	Stroudsburg	1.01	1.00
184-185	Scranton	.95	.98
186-187	Wilkes-Barre	.93	.96
188	Montrose	.93	.96
189	Doylestown	.94	1.06

STATE/ZIP	CITY	Residential	Commercial
PENNSYLVANIA (CONT'D)			
190-191	Philadelphia	1.13	1.11
193	Westchester	1.08	1.06
194	Norristown	1.09	1.07
195-196	Reading	.97	.98
PUERTO RICO			
009	San Juan	.86	.86
RHODE ISLAND			
028	Newport	1.02	1.04
029	Providence	1.02	1.04
SOUTH CAROLINA			
290-292	Columbia	.72	.75
293	Spartanburg	.71	.73
294	Charleston	.73	.75
295	Florence	.71	.73
296	Greenville	.70	.73
297	Rock Hill	.64	.67
298	Aiken	.80	.83
299	Beaufort	.68	.70
SOUTH DAKOTA			
570-571	Sioux Falls	.88	.81
572	Watertown	.84	.78
573	Mitchell	.83	.77
574	Aberdeen	.84	.78
575	Pierre	.84	.79
576	Mobridge	.84	.77
577	Rapid City	.85	.79
TENNESSEE			
370-372	Nashville	.86	.86
373-374	Chattanooga	.82	.81
375,380-381	Memphis	.84	.84
376	Johnson City	.80	.79
377-379	Knoxville	.80	.80
382	Mckenzie	.69	.69
383	Jackson	.68	.75
384	Columbia	.76	.76
385	Cookeville	.68	.68
TEXAS			
750	Mckinney	.88	.81
751	Waxahackie	.82	.82
752-753	Dallas	.89	.85
754	Greenville	.78	.72
755	Texarkana	.87	.77
756	Longview	.84	.74
757	Tyler	.91	.80
758	Palestine	.72	.72
759	Lufkin	.76	.76
760-761	Fort Worth	.83	.82
762	Denton	.87	.78
763	Wichita Falls	.80	.80
764	Eastland	.73	.72
765	Temple	.77	.76
766-767	Waco	.81	.80
768	Brownwood	.72	.71
769	San Angelo	.79	.76
770-772	Houston	.87	.88
773	Huntsville	.73	.73
774	Wharton	.75	.76
775	Galveston	.86	.87
776-777	Beaumont	.82	.83
778	Bryan	.81	.82
779	Victoria	.78	.78
780	Laredo	.76	.77
781-782	San Antonio	.82	.83
783-784	Corpus Christi	.80	.79
785	Mc Allen	.78	.76
786-787	Austin	.78	.81
788	Del Rio	.68	.68
789	Giddings	.72	.71
790-791	Amarillo	.81	.81
792	Childress	.75	.78
793-794	Lubbock	.78	.80
795-796	Abilene	.79	.79
797	Midland	.78	.79
798-799,885	El Paso	.79	.78
UTAH			
840-841	Salt Lake City	.90	.89
842,844	Ogden	.90	.88

STATE/ZIP	CITY	Residential	Commercial
UTAH(CONT'D)			
843	Logan	.91	.89
845	Price	.81	.80
846-847	Provo	.90	.89
VERMONT			
050	White River Jct.	.73	.72
051	Bellows Falls	.73	.73
052	Bennington	.72	.71
053	Brattleboro	.74	.73
054	Burlington	.85	.86
056	Montpelier	.84	.85
057	Rutland	.87	.86
058	St. Johnsbury	.74	.75
059	Guildhall	.73	.74
VIRGINIA			
220-221	Fairfax	.89	.90
222	Arlington	.89	.90
223	Alexandria	.89	.90
224-225	Fredericksburg	.83	.84
226	Winchester	.78	.79
227	Culpeper	.78	.79
228	Harrisonburg	.75	.75
229	Charlottesville	.83	.82
230-232	Richmond	.86	.84
233-235	Norfolk	.82	.82
236	Newport News	.82	.81
237	Portsmouth	.81	.81
238	Petersburg	.86	.84
239	Farmville	.74	.72
240-241	Roanoke	.76	.76
242	Bristol	.79	.74
243	Pulaski	.73	.72
244	Staunton	.76	.74
245	Lynchburg	.80	.76
246	Grundy	.72	.72
WASHINGTON			
980-981,987	Seattle	1.00	1.05
982	Everett	.97	1.03
983-984	Tacoma	1.05	1.03
985	Olympia	1.05	1.03
986	Vancouver	1.11	1.04
988	Wenatchee	.94	.97
989	Yakima	1.02	1.00
990-992	Spokane	.99	.98
993	Richland	1.00	.99
994	Clarkston	.99	.98
WEST VIRGINIA			
247-248	Bluefield	.89	.89
249	Lewisburg	.90	.90
250-253	Charleston	.93	.93
254	Martinsburg	.75	.76
255-257	Huntington	.93	.95
258-259	Beckley	.90	.90
260	Wheeling	.93	.95
261	Parkersburg	.92	.94
262	Buckhannon	.97	.94
263-264	Clarksburg	.97	.94
265	Morgantown	.97	.94
266	Gassaway	.93	.93
267	Romney	.90	.90
268	Petersburg	.95	.92
WISCONSIN			
530,532	Milwaukee	1.02	1.01
531	Kenosha	1.02	1.01
534	Racine	1.06	1.00
535	Beloit	1.00	.98
537	Madison	1.00	.98
538	Lancaster	.91	.89
539	Portage	.98	.96
540	New Richmond	1.03	.95
541-543	Green Bay	1.00	.97
544	Wausau	.98	.94
545	Rhinelander	.98	.94
546	La Crosse	.98	.95
547	Eau Claire	1.04	.96
548	Superior	1.03	.97
549	Oshkosh	.97	.94

STATE/ZIP	CITY	Residential	Commercial
WYOMING			
820	Cheyenne	.86	.81
821	Yellowstone Nat. Pk.	.80	.77
822	Wheatland	.83	.78
823	Rawlins	.81	.77
824	Worland	.78	.76
825	Riverton	.81	.78
826	Casper	.86	.82
827	Newcastle	.79	.75
828	Sheridan	.83	.80
829-831	Rock Springs	.83	.78
CANADIAN FACTORS (reflect Canadian currency)			
ALBERTA			
	Calgary	.99	.96
	Edmonton	.99	.96
	Fort McMurray	.98	.95
	Lethbridge	.98	.95
	Lloydminster	.98	.95
	Medicine Hat	.98	.95
	Red Deer	.98	.95
BRITISH COLUMBIA			
	Kamloops	1.02	1.03
	Prince George	1.04	1.05
	Vancouver	1.05	1.06
	Victoria	1.04	1.05
MANITOBA			
	Brandon	.97	.96
	Portage la Prairie	.97	.96
	Winnipeg	.97	.96
NEW BRUNSWICK			
	Bathurst	.93	.91
	Dalhousie	.93	.91
	Fredericton	.95	.93
	Moncton	.92	.90
	Newcastle	.93	.91
	Saint John	.96	.94
NEWFOUNDLAND			
	Corner Brook	.95	.94
	St. John's	.94	.93
NORTHWEST TERRITORIES			
	Yellowknife	.91	.90
NOVA SCOTIA			
	Dartmouth	.96	.95
	Halifax	.96	.95
	New Glasgow	.96	.95
	Sydney	.94	.93
	Yarmouth	.96	.95
ONTARIO			
	Barrie	1.08	1.07
	Brantford	1.10	1.08
	Cornwall	1.08	1.06
	Hamilton	1.12	1.08
	Kingston	1.08	1.07
	Kitchener	1.05	1.03
	London	1.08	1.06
	North Bay	1.07	1.05
	Oshawa	1.09	1.07
	Ottawa	1.09	1.07
	Owen Sound	1.08	1.07
	Peterborough	1.07	1.06
	Sarnia	1.10	1.08
	St. Catharines	1.04	1.02
	Sudbury	1.04	1.02
	Thunder Bay	1.05	1.03
	Toronto	1.12	1.11
	Windsor	1.06	1.04
PRINCE EDWARD ISLAND			
	Charlottetown	.92	.90
	Summerside	.92	.90

Location Factors

STATE/ZIP	CITY	Residential	Commercial
QUEBEC			
	Cap-de-la-Madeleine	1.03	1.02
	Charlesbourg	1.03	1.02
	Chicoutimi	1.02	1.01
	Gatineau	1.01	1.00
	Laval	1.02	1.01
	Montreal	1.08	1.01
	Quebec	1.10	1.02
	Sherbrooke	1.02	1.01
	Trois Rivieres	1.03	1.02
SASKATCHEWAN			
	Moose Jaw	.91	.91
	Prince Albert	.91	.91
	Regina	.92	.92
	Saskatoon	.91	.91
YUKON			
	Whitehorse	.91	.90

Abbreviations

A	Area
ASTM	American Society for Testing and Materials
B.F.	Board feet
Carp.	Carpenter
C.F.	Cubic feet
CWJ	Composite wood joist
C.Y.	Cubic yard
Ea.	Each
Equip.	Equipment
Exp.	Exposure
Ext.	Exterior
F	Fahrenheit
Ft.	Foot, feet
Gal.	Gallon
Hr.	Hour
in.	Inch, inches
Inst.	Installation
Int.	Interior
Lb.	Pound
L.F.	Linear feet
LVL	Laminated veneer lumber
Mat.	Material
Max.	Maximum
MBF	Thousand board feet
MBM	Thousand feet board measure
MSF	Thousand square feet
Min.	Minimum
O.C.	On center
O&P	Overhead and profit
OWJ	Open web wood joist
Oz.	Ounce
Pr.	Pair
Quan.	Quantity
S.F.	Square foot
Sq.	Square, 100 square feet
S.Y.	Square yard
V.L.F.	Vertical linear feet
'	Foot, feet
"	Inch, inches
°	Degrees

Index

Index

R.S. Means Company, Inc., a CMD company, is the leading provider of construction cost data in North America and supplies comprehensive construction cost guides, related technical publications and education services.

CMD, a leading worldwide provider of total construction information solutions, is comprised of three synergistic product groups designed specifically to help construction professionals advance their businesses with timely, accurate and actionable project, product and cost data. CMD is a division of Cahners Business Information, a member of the Reed Elsevier plc group of companies.

The *Project, Product, and Cost & Estimating* divisions offer a variety of innovative products designed for the full spectrum of design, construction and manufacturing professionals. Together with Cahners, CMD created *Buildingteam.com,* a valuable Internet portal of the construction community. Through it's *International* companies, CMD's reputation for quality construction market data is growing worldwide.

Project Data

CMD provides complete, accurate and relevant project information through all stages of construction. Customers are supplied industry data through leads, project reports, contact lists, plans and specifications surveys, market penetration analyses and sales evaluation reports. Any of these products can pinpoint a county, look at a state, or cover the country. Data is delivered via paper, e-mail, CD-ROM or the Internet.

Building Product Information

The First Source suite of products is the only integrated building product information system offered to the commercial construction industry for comparing and specifying building products. These print and online resources include *First Source for Products,* SPEC-DATA™, MANU-SPEC™, CADBlocks, First Source Exchange (www.firstsourceexchange.com), and Manufacturer Catalogs. Written by industry professionals and organized using CSI's MasterFormat™, construction professionals use this information to make better design decisions.

Cost Information

R.S. Means, the undisputed market leader and authority on construction costs, publishes current cost and estimating information in annual cost books and on the CostWorks CD-ROM. R.S. Means furnishes the construction industry with a rich library of complementary reference books and a series of professional seminars that are designed to sharpen professional skills and maximize the effective use of cost estimating and management tools. R.S. Means also provides construction cost consulting for Owners, Manufacturers Designers and Contractors.

Buildingteam.com

Combining CMD's project, product and cost data with news and information from Cahners' *Building Design & Construction* and *Consulting-Specifying Engineer,* this industry-focused site offers easy and unlimited access to vital information for all construction professionals.

International

BIMSA/Mexico provides construction project news, product information, cost-data, seminars and consulting services to construction professionals in Mexico. Its subsidiary, PRISMA, provides job costing software.

Byggfakta Scandinavia AB, founded in 1936, is the parent company for the leaders of customized construction market data for Denmark, Estonia, Finland, Norway and Sweden. Each company fully covers the local construction market and provides information across several platforms including subscription, ad-hoc basis, electronically and on paper.

CMD Canada serves the Canadian construction market with reliable and comprehensive project and product information services that cover all facets of construction. Core services include: Buildcore, product selection and specification tools available in print and on the Internet; CMD Building Reports, a national construction project lead service; CanaData, statistical and forecasting information; *Daily Commercial News,* a construction newspaper reporting on news and projects in Ontario; and *Journal of Commerce,* reporting news in British Columbia and Alberta.

Cordell Building Information Services, with its complete range of project and cost and estimating services, is Australia's specialist in the construction information industry. Cordell provides in-depth and historical information on all aspects of construction projects and estimation, including several customized reports, construction and sales leads, and detailed cost information among others.

For more information, please visit our website at www.cmdg.com.

CMD Corporate Office
30 Technology Parkway South
Norcross, GA 30092-2912
(800) 793-0304
(700) 417-4002 (fax)
info@cmdg.com
www.cmdg.com

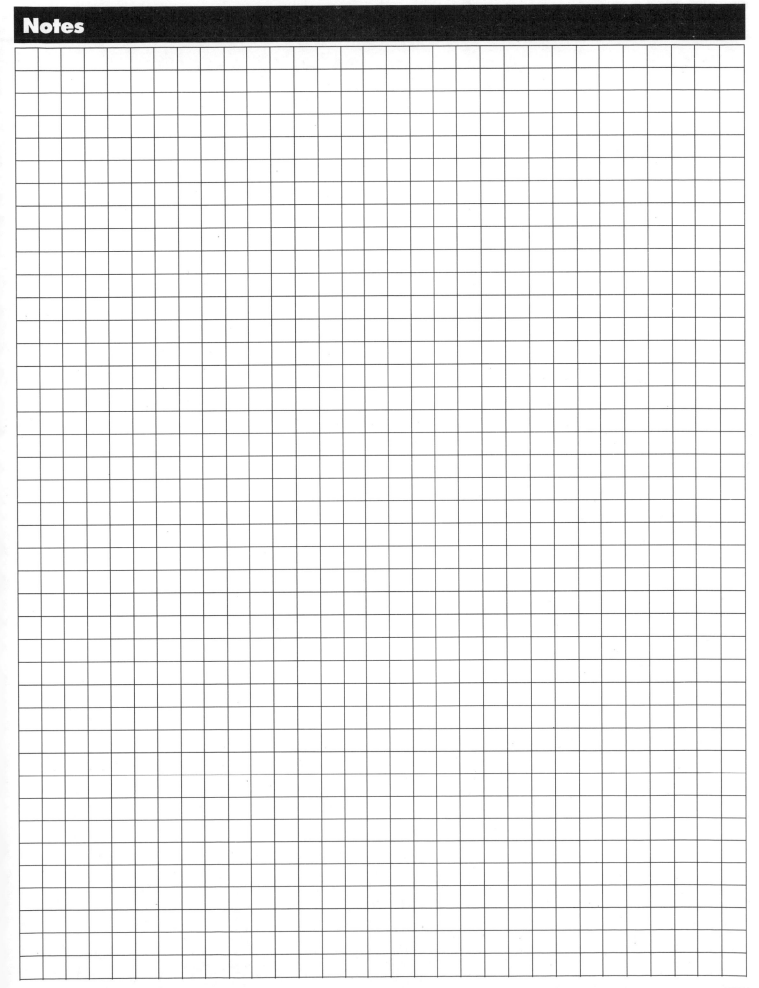

Contractor's Pricing Guides

Means ADA Compliance Pricing Guide

Accurately plan and budget for the ADA modifications you are most likely to need... with the first available cost guide for business owners, facility managers, and all who are involved in building modifications to comply with the Americans With Disabilities Act.

75 major projects—the most frequently needed modifications—include complete estimates with itemized materials and labor, plus contractor's total fees. Over 260 project variations fit almost any site conditions or budget constraints. Location Factors to adjust costs for 927 cities and towns.

A collaboration between Adaptive Environments Center, Inc. and R.S. Means Engineering Staff.

$59.98 per copy
Over 350 pages, illustrated, softcover
Catalog No. 67310   ISBN 0-87629-351-8

Contractor's Pricing Guide: Residential Square Foot Costs 2002

Now available in one concise volume, all you need to know to plan and budget the cost of new homes. If you are looking for a quick reference, the model home section contains costs for over 250 different sizes and types of residences, with hundreds of easily applied modifications. If you need even more detail, the Assemblies Section lets you build your own costs or modify the model costs further. Hundreds of graphics are provided, along with forms and procedures to help you get it right.

$39.95 per copy
Over 250 pages, illustrated, 8-1/2 x 11
Catalog No. 60322   ISBN 0-87629-647-9

Contractor's Pricing Guide: Residential Detailed Costs 2002

Every aspect of residential construction, from overhead costs to residential lighting and wiring, is in here. All the detail you need to accurately estimate the costs of your work with or without markups–labor-hours, typical crews and equipment are included as well. When you need a detailed estimate, this publication has all the costs to help you come up with a complete, on the money, price you can rely on to win profitable work.

$36.95 per copy
Over 300 pages, with charts and tables, 8-1/2 x 11
Catalog No. 60332   ISBN 0-87629-648-7

Contractor's Pricing Guide: Residential Repair & Remodeling Costs 2002

This book provides total unit price costs for every aspect of the most common repair & remodeling projects. Organized in the order of construction by component and activity, it includes demolition and installation, cleaning, painting, and more.

With simplified estimating methods; clear, concise descriptions; and technical specifications for each component, the book is a valuable tool for contractors who want to speed up their estimating time, while making sure their costs are on target.

$36.95 per copy
Over 250 pages, illustrated, 8-1/2 x 11
Catalog No. 60342   ISBN 0-87629-655-X

Means Repair & Remodeling Estimating Methods

3rd Edition

By Edward B. Wetherill and R.S. Means Engineering Staff

This updated edition focuses on the unique problems of estimating renovations in existing structures—using the latest cost resources and construction methods. The book helps you determine the true costs of remodeling, and includes:

   Part I–The Estimating Process
   Part II–Estimating by CSI Division
   Part III–Two Complete Sample
         Estimates–Unit Price & Assemblies
         New Section on Disaster Reconstruction

$69.95 per copy
Over 450 pages, illustrated, hardcover
Catalog No. 67265A   ISBN 0-87629-454-9

Means Landscape Estimating Methods New 3rd Edition

By Sylvia H. Fee

Professional Methods for Estimating and Bidding Landscaping Projects and Grounds Maintenance Contracts

• Easy-to-understand text. Clearly explains the estimating process and how to use *Means Site Work & Landscape Cost Data*.
• Sample forms and worksheets to save you time and avoid errors.
• Tips on best techniques for saving money and winning jobs.
• **Two new chapters** help you control your equipment costs and bid landscape maintenance projects.

$62.95 per copy
Over 300 pages, illustrated, hardcover
Catalog No. 67295A   ISBN 0-87629-534-0

For more information
visit Means Web Site
at www.rsmeans.com

Annual Cost Guides

Means Building Construction Cost Data 2002

Offers you unchallenged unit price reliability in an easy-to-use arrangement. Whether used for complete, finished estimates or for periodic checks, it supplies more cost facts better and faster than any comparable source. Over 23,000 unit prices for 2002. The City Cost Indexes now cover over 930 areas, for indexing to any project location in North America.

$99.95 per copy
Over 700 pages, softcover
Catalog No. 60012   ISBN 0-87629-620-7

Means Open Shop Building Construction Cost Data 2002

The open-shop version of the *Means Building Construction Cost Data*. More than 22,000 reliable unit cost entries based on open shop trade labor rates. Eliminates time-consuming searches for these prices. The first book with open shop labor rates and crews. Labor information is itemized by labor-hours, crew, hourly/daily output, equipment, overhead and profit. For contractors, owners and facility managers.

$99.95 per copy
Over 680 pages, softcover
Catalog No. 60152   ISBN 0-87629-628-2

Means Plumbing Cost Data 2002

Comprehensive unit prices and assemblies for plumbing, irrigation systems, commercial and residential fire protection, point-of-use water heaters, and the latest approved materials. This publication and its companion, *Means Mechanical Cost Data*, provide full-range cost estimating coverage for all the mechanical trades.

$99.95 per copy
Over 570 pages, softcover
Catalog No. 60212   ISBN 0-87629-629-0

Means Residential Cost Data 2002

Speeds you through residential construction pricing with more than 100 illustrated complete house square-foot costs. Alternate assemblies cost selections are located on adjoining pages, so that you can develop tailor-made estimates in minutes. Complete data for detailed unit cost estimates is also provided.

$87.95 per copy
Over 600 pages, softcover
Catalog No. 60172   ISBN 0-87629-623-1

Means Electrical Cost Data 2002

Pricing information for every part of electrical cost planning: unit and systems costs with design tables; engineering guides and illustrated estimating procedures; complete labor-hour, materials, and equipment costs for better scheduling and procurement. With the latest products and construction methods used in electrical work. More than 15,000 unit and systems costs, clear specifications and drawings.

$99.95 per copy
Over 480 pages, softcover
Catalog No. 60032   ISBN 0-87629-635-5

Means Repair & Remodeling Cost Data 2002

Commercial/Residential

You can use this valuable tool to estimate commercial and residential renovation and remodeling. By using the specialized costs in this manual, you'll find it's not necessary to force fit prices for new construction into remodeling cost planning. Provides comprehensive unit costs, building systems costs, extensive labor data and estimating assistance for every kind of building improvement.

$87.95 per copy
Over 660 pages, softcover
Catalog No. 60042   ISBN 0-87629-622-3

Means Site Work & Landscape Cost Data 2002

Hard-to-find costs are presented in an easy-to-use format for every type of site work and landscape construction. Costs are organized, described, and laid out for earthwork, utilities, roads and bridges, as well as grading, planting, lawns, trees, irrigation systems, and site improvements.

$99.95 per copy
Over 630 pages, softcover
Catalog No. 60282   ISBN 0-87629-624-X

Means Light Commercial Cost Data 2002

Specifically addresses the light commercial market, which is an increasingly specialized niche in the industry. Aids you, the owner/designer/contractor, in preparing all types of estimates, from budgets to detailed bids. Includes new advances in methods and materials. Assemblies section allows you to evaluate alternatives in early stages of design/planning.

$87.95 per copy
Over 672 pages, softcover
Catalog No. 60182   ISBN 0-87629-626-6

Books for Builders

For more information
visit Means Web Site
at www.rsmeans.com

Builder's Essentials:
Plan Reading & Material Takeoff

A complete course in reading and interpreting building plans—and performing quantity takeoffs to professional standards.

This book shows and explains, in clear language and with over 160 illustrations, typical working drawings encountered by contractors in residential and light commercial construction. The author describes not only how all common features are represented, but how to translate that information into a material list. Organized by CSI division, each chapter uses plans, details and tables, and a summary checklist.

$35.95 per copy
Over 420 pages, illustrated, softcover
Catalog No. 67307   ISBN 0-87629-348-8

Builder's Essentials:
Best Business Practices for Builders & Remodelers:
An Easy-to-Use Checklist System
By Thomas N. Frisby

A comprehensive guide covering all aspects of running a construction business, with more than 40 user–friendly checklists. This book provides expert guidance on: increasing your revenue and keeping more of your profit; planning for long-term growth; keeping good employees and managing subcontractors.

$29.95 per copy
Over 220 pages, softcover
Catalog No. 67329   ISBN 0-87629-619-3

Means Estimating Handbook

This comprehensive reference is for use in the field and the office. It covers a full spectrum of technical data required for estimating, with information on sizing, productivity, equipment requirements, codes, design standards and engineering factors. It will help you evaluate architectural plans and specifications; prepare accurate quantity takeoffs; perform value engineering; compare design alternatives; prepare estimates from conceptual to detail; evaluate change orders.

$99.95 per copy
Over 900 pages, hardcover
Catalog No. 67276   ISBN 0-87629-177-9

Builder's Essentials:
Framing & Rough Carpentry, 2nd Edition

A complete, illustrated do-it-yourself course on framing and rough carpentry. The book covers walls, floors, stairs, windows, doors, and roofs, as well as nailing patterns and procedures. Additional sections are devoted to equipment and material handling, standards, codes, and safety requirements.

The "framer-friendly" approach includes easy-to-follow, step-by-step instructions. This practical guide will benefit both the carpenter's apprentice and the experienced carpenter, and sets a uniform standard for framing crews.

$24.95 per copy
Over 125 pages, illustrated, softcover
Catalog No. 67298A   ISBN 0-87629-617-7

Interior Home Improvement Costs, New 7th Edition

Estimates for 66 interior projects, including:

- Attic/Basement Conversions
- Kitchen/Bath Remodeling
- Stairs, Doors, Walls/Ceilings
- Fireplaces
- Home Offices/In-law Apartments

$19.95 per copy
Over 230 pages, illustrated, softcover
Catalog No. 67308C   ISBN 0-87629-576-6

Exterior Home Improvement Costs, New 7th Edition

Quick estimates for 64 projects, including:

- Room Additions/Garages
- Roofing/Siding/Painting
- Windows/Doors
- Landscaping/Patios
- Porches/Decks

$19.95 per copy
Over 250 pages, illustrated, softcover
Catalog No. 67309C   ISBN 0-87629-575-8

Practical Pricing Guides for Homeowners and Contractors

These updated resources on the cost and complexity of the nation's most popular home improvement projects include estimates of materials quantities, total project costs, and labor hours. With costs localized to over 900 zip code locations.

Books for Builders

For more information
visit Means Web Site
at www.rsmeans.com

Means Illustrated Construction Dictionary (Condensed Edition)

Based on *Means Illustrated Construction Dictionary, New Unabridged Edition*, the condensed version features 9,000 construction terms. If your work overlaps the construction business—from insurance, banking and real estate to building inspectors, attorneys, owners, and students—you will surely appreciate this valuable reference source.

$59.95 per copy
Over 500 pages, softcover
Catalog No. 67282   ISBN 0-87629-219-8

Superintending for Contractors:
How to Bring Jobs in On-time, On-budget
by Paul J. Cook

Today's superintendent has become a field project manager, directing and coordinating a large number of subcontractors, and overseeing the administration of contracts, change orders, and purchase orders. This book examines the complex role of the superintendent/field project manager, and provides guidelines for the efficient organization of this job.

$35.95 per copy
Over 220 pages, illustrated, softcover
Catalog No. 67233   ISBN 0-87629-272-4

Means Forms for Contractors
The most-needed forms for contractors of various-size firms and specialties.

Includes a variety of forms for each project phase — from bidding to punch list. With sample project correspondence. Includes forms for project administration, safety and inspection, scheduling, estimating, change orders, and personnel evaluation. Blank forms are printed on heavy stock for easy photocopying. Each has a filled-in sample, with instructions and circumstances for use. 0 years of experience in construction project management, providing contractors with the tools they need to develop competitive bids.

49.98 per copy
ver 400 pages, three-ring binder
atalog No. 67288

Estimating for Contractors:
How to Make Estimates that Win Jobs
by Paul J. Cook

This widely used reference offers clear, step-by-step estimating instructions that lead to achieving the following goals: objectivity, thoroughness, and accuracy.

Estimating for Contractors is a reference that will be used over and over, whether to check a specific estimating procedure, or to take a complete course in estimating.

$35.95 per copy
Over 225 pages, illustrated, softcover
Catalog No. 67160   ISBN 0-87629-271-6

Business Management for Contractors:
How to Make Profits in Today's Market
by Paul J. Cook

Focuses on the manager's role in ensuring that the company fulfills contracts, realizes a profit, and grows steady growth. Offers guidance on planning company growth, financial controls, and industry lations.

ew reduced price
ow $17.98 per copy; limited quantity
er 230 pages, softcover
atalog No. 67250   ISBN 0-87629-269-4

Building Spec Homes Profitably
by Kenneth V. Johnson

The author offers a system to reduce risk and ensure profits in spec home building no matter what the economic climate. Includes:
- The 3 Keys to Success: location, floor plan and value
- Market Research: How to perform an effective analysis
- Site Selection: How to find and purchase the best properties
- Financing: How to select and arrange the best method
- Design Development: Combining value with market appeal
- Scheduling & Supervision: Expert guidance for improving your operation

$29.95 per copy
Over 200 pages, softcover
Catalog No. 67312   ISBN 0-87629-357-7

MeansData™

CONSTRUCTION COSTS FOR SOFTWARE APPLICATIONS
Your construction estimating software is only as good as your cost data.

Software Integration

A proven construction cost database is a mandatory part of any estimating package. We have linked MeansData™ directly into the industry's leading software applications. The following list of software providers can offer you MeansData™ as an added feature for their estimating systems. Visit them on-line at *www.rsmeans.com/demo/* for more information and free demos. Or call their numbers listed below.

3D International
713-871-7000 venegas@3di.com

4Clicks-Solutions, LLC
719-574-7721
mbrown@4clicks-solutions.com

ACT
Applied Computer Technologies
Facility Management Software
919-859-1335 info@srs.net

AEPCO, Inc.
301-670-4642 blueworks@aepco.com

**American Contractor/
Maxwell Systems**
800-333-8435 info@amercon.com

ArenaSoft Estimating
888-370-8806 info@arenasoft.com

Ares Corporation
650-401-7100
sales@arescorporation.com

**AssetWork
CSI-Maximus**
Facility Management Software
800-659-9001 info@assetworks.com

Benchmark, Inc.
800-393-9193 sales@benchmark-inc.com

BSD
Building Systems Design, Inc.
888-273-7638 bsd@bsdsoftlink.com

CProjects, Inc.
203-262-6248 sales@cprojects.com

cManagement
800-945-7093 sales@cmanagement.com

CDCI
Construction Data Controls, Inc.
800-285-3929 sales@cdci.com

CMS
Computerized Micro Solutions
800-255-7407 cms@proest.com

Conac Group
800-663-2338 sales@conac.com

Eagle Point Software
800-678-6565 sales@eaglepoint.com

Estimating Systems, Inc.
800-967-8572 pulsar@capecod.net

G2 Estimator
A Div. of Valli Info. Syst., Inc.
800-657-6312 info@g2estimator.com

G/C EMUNI, Inc.
514-953-5148 rpa@gcei.ca

Geac Commercial Systems, Inc.
800-554-9865 info@geac.com

Hard Dollar
800-637-7496 sales@harddollar.com

IQ Beneco
801-565-1122 mdover@beneco.com

Luqs International
888-682-5573 info@luqs.com

MC²
Management Computer Controls
800-225-5622 vkeys@mc2-ice.com

Prism Computer Corporation
Facility Management Software
800-774-7622 famis@prismcc.com

Quest Solutions, Inc.
800-452-2342 info@questsolutions.com

Sanders Software, Inc.
800-280-9760 hsander@vallnet.com

Sinisoft, Inc.
877-669-4949 info.usa@sinistre.com

Timberline Software Corp.
800-628-6583
product.info@timberline.com

TMA Systems, Inc.
Facility Management Software
800-862-1130 sales@tmasys.com

US Cost, Inc.
800-372-4003
sales@uscost.com

Vertigraph, Inc.
800-989-4243
info-request@vertigraph.com

Wendlware
714-895-7222 sales@corecon.com

Winestimator, Inc.
800-950-2374 sales@winest.com

DemoSource™

One-stop shopping for the latest cost estimating software for just $19.95. This evaluation tool includes product literature and demo diskettes for ten or more estimating systems, all of which link to MeansData™. **Call 1-800-334-3509 to order.**

FOR MORE INFORMATION ON ELECTRONIC PRODUCTS CALL
1-800-448-8182 OR FAX 1-800-632-6732.

MeansData™ is a registered trademark of R.S. Means Co., Inc., *CMD*.

For more information
visit Means Web Site
at www.rsmeans.com

New Titles

From Model Codes to the IBC: A Transitional Guide

By Rolf Jensen & Associates, Inc.

NEW!

A time–saving resource for Architects, Engineers, Building Officials and Authorities Having Jurisdiction (AHJs), Contractors, Manufacturers, Building Owners, and Facility Managers.

Provides comprehensive, user-friendly guidance on making the transition to the International Building Code® from the model codes you're familiar with. Includes side-by-side code comparison of the IBC to the UBC, NBC, SBC, and NFPA 101®. Also features professional code commentary, quick-find indexes, and a Web site with regular code updates.

Also contains illustrations, abbreviations key, and an extensive resource section.

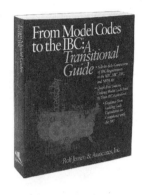

$14.95 per copy
30 pages, Softcover
Catalog No. 67328

Historic Preservation: Project Planning & Estimating

By Swanke Hayden Connell Architects

Managing Historic Restoration, Rehabilitation, and Preservation Building Projects and Determining and Controlling Their Costs

The authors explain:
- How to determine whether a structure qualifies as historic
- Where to obtain funding and other assistance
- How to evaluate and repair more than 75 historic building materials
- How to properly research, document, and manage the project to meet code, agency, and other special requirements
- How to approach the upgrade of major building systems

$9.95 per copy
Over 675 pages, Hardcover
Catalog No. 67323

Means Illustrated Construction Dictionary, 3rd Edition

New Updated Edition with interactive CD-ROM

Long regarded as the Industry's finest, the Means Illustrated Construction Dictionary is now even better. With the addition of over 1,000 new terms and hundreds of new illustrations, it is the clear choice for the most comprehensive and current information.

The companion CD-ROM that comes with this new edition adds many extra features: larger graphics, expanded definitions, and links to both CSI MasterFormat numbers and product information.

- 19,000 construction words, terms, phrases, symbols, weights, measures, and equivalents
- 1,000 new entries
- 1,200 helpful illustrations
- Easy-to-use format, with thumbtabs

$.95 per copy
Over 790 pages, illustrated Hardcover
Catalog No. 67292A

2002 Order Form

Qty.	Book No.	COST ESTIMATING BOOKS	Unit Price	Total
	60062	Assemblies Cost Data 2002	$164.95	
	60012	Building Construction Cost Data 2002	99.95	
	61012	Building Const. Cost Data–Looseleaf Ed. 2002	124.95	
	63012	Building Const. Cost Data–Metric Version 2002	99.95	
	60222	Building Const. Cost Data–Western Ed. 2002	99.95	
	60112	Concrete & Masonry Cost Data 2002	92.95	
	60142	Construction Cost Indexes 2002	218.00	
	60142A	Construction Cost Index–January 2002	54.50	
	60142B	Construction Cost Index–April 2002	54.50	
	60142C	Construction Cost Index–July 2002	54.50	
	60142D	Construction Cost Index–October 2002	54.50	
	60342	Contr. Pricing Guide: Resid. R & R Costs 2002	36.95	
	60332	Contr. Pricing Guide: Resid. Detailed 2002	36.95	
	60322	Contr. Pricing Guide: Resid. Sq. Ft. 2002	39.95	
	64022	ECHOS Assemblies Cost Book 2002	164.95	
	64012	ECHOS Unit Cost Book 2002	109.95	
	54002	ECHOS (Combo set of both books)	229.95	
	60232	Electrical Change Order Cost Data 2002	99.95	
	60032	Electrical Cost Data 2002	99.95	
	60202	Facilities Construction Cost Data 2002	241.95	
	60302	Facilities Maintenance & Repair Cost Data 2002	219.95	
	60162	Heavy Construction Cost Data 2002	99.95	
	63162	Heavy Const. Cost Data–Metric Version 2002	99.95	
	60092	Interior Cost Data 2002	99.95	
	60122	Labor Rates for the Const. Industry 2002	219.95	
	60182	Light Commercial Cost Data 2002	87.95	
	60022	Mechanical Cost Data 2002	99.95	
	60152	Open Shop Building Const. Cost Data 2002	99.95	
	60212	Plumbing Cost Data 2002	99.95	
	60042	Repair and Remodeling Cost Data 2002	87.95	
	60172	Residential Cost Data 2002	87.95	
	60282	Site Work & Landscape Cost Data 2002	99.95	
	60052	Square Foot Costs 2002	109.95	
		REFERENCE BOOKS		
	67147A	ADA in Practice	59.98	
	67310	ADA Pricing Guide	59.98	
	67273	Basics for Builders: How to Survive and Prosper	34.95	
	67330	Bldrs Essentials: Adv. Framing Techniques	24.95	
	67329	Bldrs Essentials: Best Bus. Practices for Bldrs	29.95	
	67298A	Bldrs Essentials: Framing/Carpentry 2nd Ed.	24.95	
	67298AS	Bldrs Essentials: Framing/Carpentry Spanish	24.95	
	67307	Bldrs Essentials: Plan Reading & Takeoff	35.95	
	67261A	Bldg. Prof. Guide to Contract Documents–3rd Ed.	64.95	
	67312	Building Spec Homes Profitably	29.95	
	67250	Business Management for Contractors	17.98	
	67146	Concrete Repair & Maintenance Illustrated	69.95	
	67278	Construction Delays	29.48	
	67255	Contractor's Business Handbook	21.48	
	67314	Cost Planning & Est. for Facil. Maint.	82.95	
	67317A	Cyberplaces: The Internet Guide–2nd Ed.	59.95	
	67230A	Electrical Estimating Methods–2nd Ed.	64.95	
	64777	Environmental Remediation Est. Methods	99.95	
	67160	Estimating for Contractors	35.95	
	67276	Estimating Handbook	99.95	

Qty.	Book No.	REFERENCE BOOKS (Cont.)	Unit Price	Total
	67249	Facilities Maintenance Management	$ 86.95	
	67246	Facilities Maintenance Standards	69.95	
	67318	Facilities Operations & Engineering Reference	99.95	
	67301	Facilities Planning & Relocation	89.95	
	67231	Forms for Building Const. Professional	47.48	
	67288	Forms for Contractors	49.98	
	67328	From Model Codes to IBC: Transitional Guide	114.95	
	67260	Fundamentals of the Construction Process	34.98	
	67148	Heavy Construction Handbook	74.95	
	67323	Historic Preservation: Proj. Planning & Est.	99.95	
	67308C	Home Improvement Costs–Int. Projects 7th Ed.	19.95	
	67309C	Home Improvement Costs–Ext. Projects 7th Ed.	19.95	
	67324	How to Estimate w/Means Data & CostWorks	59.95	
	67304	How to Estimate with Metric Units	9.98	
	67306	HVAC: Design Criteria, Options, Select.–2nd Ed.	84.95	
	67281	HVAC Systems Evaluation	84.95	
	67282	Illustrated Construction Dictionary, Condensed	59.95	
	67292A	Illustrated Construction Dictionary, w/CD-ROM	99.95	
	67295A	Landscape Estimating–3rd Ed.	62.95	
	67299	Maintenance Management Audit	32.48	
	67302	Managing Construction Purchasing	19.98	
	67294	Mechanical Estimating–2nd Ed.	64.95	
	67245A	Planning and Managing Interior Projects–2nd Ed.	69.95	
	67283A	Plumbing Estimating Methods–2nd Ed.	59.95	
	67326	Preventive Maint. Guidelines for School Facil.	149.95	
	67236A	Productivity Standards for Constr.–3rd Ed.	69.98	
	67247A	Project Scheduling & Management for Constr.	64.95	
	67262	Quantity Takeoff for Contractors	17.98	
	67265A	Repair & Remodeling Estimating–3rd Ed.	69.95	
	67322	Residential & Light Commercial Const. Stds.	59.95	
	67254	Risk Management for Building Professionals	15.98	
	67291	Scheduling Manual–3rd Ed.	32.48	
	67327	Spanish/English Construction Dictionary	22.95	
	67145B	Sq. Ft. & Assem. Estimating Methods–3rd Ed.	69.95	
	67287	Successful Estimating Methods	64.95	
	67313	Successful Interior Projects	24.98	
	67233	Superintending for Contractors	35.95	
	67321	Total Productive Facilities Management	39.98	
	67284	Understanding Building Automation Systems	29.98	
	67303	Unit Price Estimating Methods–2nd Ed.	59.95	
	67319	Value Engineering: Practical Applications	79.95	

MA residents add 5% state sales tax	
Shipping & Handling**	
Total (U.S. Funds)*	

Prices are subject to change and are for U.S. delivery only. *Canadian customers may call for current prices. **Shipping & handling charges: Add 7% of total order for check and credit card payments. Add 9% of total order for invoiced orders.

Send Order To: **ADDV-1001**

Name (Please Print) _____

Company _____

☐ **Company**

☐ **Home**   Address _____

City/State/Zip _____

Phone # _____ P.O. # _____